THE GERMAN HIGH
COMMAND AT WAR

THE GERMAN
HIGH COMMAND
AT WAR

———◆———

*Hindenburg and Ludendorff
Conduct World War I*

ROBERT B. ASPREY

QUILL
WILLIAM MORROW
New York

Grateful acknowledgment is made for permission to use the following maps:

Curtis Brown on behalf of the estate of Sir Winston Churchill. Copyright the estate of Sir Winston Churchill: pages 24, 32, 33, 71, 72, 82, 83, 107, 108, 117, 118, 158, 159, 176, 192, 211, 226, 227, 241, 264, 301, 344, 379, 390, 409, 425, 434, 457, 477

The Great War by Cyril Falls, courtesy Curtis Brown and Putnam Publishing. Copyright © 1959 by Cyril Falls: pages 174, 175, 228, 302, 456

The National Archives, Washington, D.C.: page 34

It is the policy of William Morrow and Company, Inc., and its imprints and affiliates, recognizing the importance of preserving what has been written, to print the books we publish on acid-free paper, and we exert our best efforts to that end.

Library of Congress Cataloging-in-Publication Data

Asprey, Robert B.
    The German high command at war: Hindenburg and Ludendorff conduct
World War I / by Robert B. Asprey.
        p. cm.
    Includes bibliographical references.
    ISBN 0-688-12842-4
    1. World War, 1914–1918—Campaigns—Western. 2. Hindenburg, Paul
von, 1847–1934. 3. Ludendorff, Erich, 1865–1937. 4. World War,
1914–1918—Germany. I. Title.
DC530.A77 1991
940.4′144—dc20   90-22733
                                                                              CIP

Printed in the United States of America

First Quill Edition

1 2 3 4 5 6 7 8 9 10

BOOK DESIGN BY LINDA DINGLER

This book is dedicated to

Ivy and Graham Rosser,
dear friends of still happy days

Acknowledgments

A great many people have helped me in researching this book. I would like to thank the staffs of the Vassar College Library, the New York Public Library, the Library of Congress, the Bodleian Library, the New College Library, the Codrington Library, the London Library, the British (Museum) Library, the Imperial War Museum and the University of Freiburg Library for their generous and valuable assistance. In particular I would like to thank Agnes Peterson of the Hoover Institute for War, Peace, and Revolution for her many kindnesses during my prolonged research at that august institution. I am equally indebted to Professor Doktor Wilhelm Deist and his staff of the *Militär Forschungsamt* Library and to Doktor Hans Heinrich Fleisher and Doktor Gerhard Granier for allowing me access to the files in the *Bundesarchiv (Militärarchiv)* and for their assistance during my research in Freiburg im Breisgau. I am further indebted to the staffs of the U.S. Naval War College and the U.S. Army War College. It was a great pleasure to work once again in the U.S. National Archives under the guiding hands of John Taylor and Richard Gould and their always helpful staffs. I must add my thanks to Professor Norman Stone of Oxford University for his always stimulating conversation and encouragement.

As usual I am indebted to a host of old friends for their generous hospitality and many other kindnesses: my sister, Winifred Asprey, Elle Gohl, the late Arthur Wittenstein, Aileen and Andrew Wittenstein, Belle Griffith, Kate and Ed Ahmann, Joan and Hayden Peake, Ivy and

Graham Rosser (to whom this book is dedicated), the late Allan McMartin, Nydia McMartin, Sheila and Gordon Seaver, Jacques W. Kleynhans, Jennifer and Ian Langlands-Pearse, Inge Kienzle, Mary and Fred Hall, Siri and Peter MacEwen, Joan and Hans Rosenthal, Margarethe Bernstrom, Marjory Sangster and Ana and José Polanco.

I cannot sufficiently thank three linguistic experts (and friends) whose helpful suggestions and corrections of my translations devoured many of their precious hours: Professor Margaret McKenzie, Doktor Dieter Poetzsch, and Doktor Oskar Kienzle. I am enormously indebted to my beatific editor, Maria Guarnaschelli, for her unstinting effort in turning typed manuscript to printed book.

Jibsail
Warwick
Bermuda

A Note to the Reader

U ntil I began writing about World War I a good many years ago, I was inclined to view this immense and tragic conflict from the Allied side in general, and because of America's partici-pation in the war during 1917–18, from the western front in particular. Further study widened my vista. It will probably surprise a good many readers to learn of the lengthy, complex, and extremely costly campaigns that were fought by the Germans and Austro-Hungarians against Russian arms on the eastern front—the front where Field Marshal Paul von Hindenburg and General Erich Ludendorff made such immense repu-tations—beginning with the German victory at Tannenberg in August 1914.

Tannenberg and subsequent German battles in the east, each ad-vertised as a great victory by Hindenburg and Ludendorff, polished their military reputations until they seemed virtually invincible. In mid-1916 German officers, government ministers, civil officials, and ordinary ci-vilians generally applauded when General Erich von Falkenhayn, chief of the Great German General Staff, was replaced by Hindenburg, with Ludendorff his all-powerful deputy. A magnificent public relations effort, aided by strict military censorship, caused this aura of invincibility to grow to godlike proportions during the next two turbulent years as Hin-denburg and Ludendorff—the Duo—established a military dictatorship that trampled on the Empire's constitution and dealt Germany's wavering democracy a fatal blow. Germany's final defeat should have returned

Hindenburg and Ludendorff to mere mortal status, but by their adroit transference of the blame to the civil government and population—the famous "stab-in-the-back" thesis—they largely retained their formidable military reputations. This thesis was developed in their hastily written, turgid, and often inaccurate memoirs: Defeat was not their fault, the homeland let them down despite their strategic and tactical brilliance. (That message was to be repeated by some senior American officers and civilian officials after the Vietnam War.) Hindenburg and Ludendorff's *cri de coeur* was taken up with a vengeance by German militarists who would preserve the honor of the army at all costs. During the twenties and thirties paeans of praise poured from the pens of nationalist biographers and historians. Their reputations survived World War II and are accepted by some even today, particularly in the new Germany where Hindenburg is being dusted off and again presented as a national hero.

Not everyone was a believer. In relating their personal accounts of the war, such principals as Crown Prince Rupprecht of Bavaria, General Max Hoffmann, the chief of the Austro-Hungarian general staff Conrad von Hötzendorf, Karl Helfferich, Prince Max of Baden, and Rudolf von Valentini openly criticized not only Hindenburg and Ludendorff's strategy and tactics but also the reprehensible methods they used in gaining power and then enlarging their personal empires—to Germany's irreparable cost. Emil Ludwig published a highly revealing biography of Hindenburg in 1935. This was followed a year later by John Wheeler-Bennett's scathing work, *Hindenburg, The Wooden Titan*. The impact of these books on German and Western readers was impressive but was soon absorbed by the turbulent events of these frenetic years, as was the case with the severe condemnation of Ludendorff's generalship published in 1939 in the memoirs of a highly decorated German general-staff officer, General Friedrich von Lossberg.

Studied appraisal of Hindenburg and Ludendorff's role in World War I was renewed after Germany's defeat in World War II. A distinguished historian, Erich Eyck, published a critical article on the German high command, "The Generals and the Downfall of the German Monarchy," in 1952. Lossberg's important book was picked up by a German scholar, S. A. Kaehler. Kaehler combined it with the unpublished memoirs of a disgruntled general-staff officer, Albrecht von Thaer, in an article that also drew on the writings of the German military archivist Wolfgang Foerster. In attempting to praise Ludendorff, Foerster had merely damned him. In 1957 the highly critical and immensely informative memoirs of General Wilhelm Groener, one of the principals of the German high command in World War I, were published. Another German scholar, Karl-Heinz Janssen, followed in 1959 with a thought-provoking article on Hindenburg and Ludendorff's takeover of the supreme military command in 1916, a work complemented by Walther Hubatsch's article of the same year on the German supreme headquarters. Hubatsch struck again in 1963 and 1966, publishing *Hindenburg und der Staat* in the latter year. This work was especially important because of his access to some of Hindenburg's wartime letters to his wife, scarcely flattering to the once national hero. Karl-Heinz Janssen reappeared in 1966 with a splendid study of the vapid chancellor Bethmann Hollweg and General von Falkenhayn that threw a great deal of light on the ruthless ambitions of Hindenburg and Ludendorff. A real literary bomb exploded in 1967 with publication of Fritz Fischer's *Germany's Aims in the First World War*, which blamed German industrialists and militarists for the war (a thesis that so enraged German establishment scholars that Fischer followed it two years later with a book defending his first). Peter von Kielmansegg published his learned work, *Deutschland und der erste Weltkrieg*, in 1968, the same year that Martin Kitchen's *The Silent Dictatorship* appeared. The first volume of Gerhard Ritter's splendid four-volume work, *The Sword and the Sceptre*, was published in 1969 (the final volume appearing in 1973). Wilhelm Deist added new perspectives the following year with his book, *Militär und Innenpolitik im Weltkrieg, 1914–1918*. Three years later Konrad Jarausch offered fresh insights into Chancellor Bethmann Hollweg's role in *The Enigmatic Chancellor Bethmann Hollweg and the Hubris of Imperial Germany*. Norman Stone added to informative historical rethinking in 1975 with *The Eastern Front 1914–1917*, a contribution made even more noteworthy by material gleaned from Russian archives. Roger Parkinson attempted, unsuccessfully in my opinion, to stem the tide of criticism in 1978 with *Tormented Warrior: Ludendorff and the Supreme Command*.

Neither those nor other interesting and informative books appeared to me to tie the parts into a whole that explains Germany's disastrous military defeat as a result of expanded military egos unchecked by civil authority. How did Hindenburg and Ludendorff achieve and maintain their exalted status? What exactly did they do and not do? What was the extent of their collaboration? What were their successes and failures? Their strengths and weaknesses? What does history owe to them—or they to history?

It is not easy to find the answers. German World War I archives were destroyed along with most of Potsdam by Allied bombers late in the war. Late in World War II remnants survive in the *Militärarchiv* in Freiburg im Breisgau, which also contain diaries and letters subsequently acquired. Any reader accustomed to normal military-security precautions would be surprised to read the diaries and letters of such principals as Wilhelm Groener, Max Hoffmann, Georg von Muller, Adolf Wild von Hohenborn, and others. They were often as catty as women at a bridge party. What's more, they telephoned their wives, often daily, to report the latest battle development or plan of forthcoming battle. One wonders when they had time to work. Field Marshal von Hindenburg wrote more than fifteen hundred letters to his wife during the war—more than seven letters a week—and his wife often lived for prolonged periods near his headquarters, during which he wrote no letters. We unfortunately have access to only a few of his letters because of the alleged intransigence of his heirs. It is also believed that Ludendorff's letters are still extant, so the full story is not yet told.

I hope, however, to have brought the story up to date. I hope also that the reader will find it as fascinating to read as I found it to write. Hindenburg told his court painter, Hugo Vogel, on one occasion during the war that "legends are necessary." Perhaps they are. But legends can also be fragile—as the reader will learn in the following pages.

Contents

BOOK ONE

CONTENTS

BOOK TWO

BOOK ONE

If the war which has hung over our heads like the sword of Damocles for more than ten years past ever breaks out, its duration and end cannot be foreseen. The greatest powers of Europe, armed as they never have been armed before, will then stand face to face. No one can be shattered in one or two campaigns so completely as to confess himself beaten, and conclude peace on hard terms. It may be a Seven Years' War, it may be a Thirty Years' War—woe to him who first sets fire to Europe, and is the first to apply the torch to the magazine.
—FIELD MARSHAL COUNT HELMUTH VON MOLTKE, 1890[1]

1

The Storm Breaks

The more I have meditated on past events, the more continually I have come to the point that the refusal of a Conference
in July last year was the fatal moment that decided the question
of peace or war. Austria had presented a tremendous ultimatum
to Serbia. Serbia had accepted nine tenths of that ultimatum.
Russia was prepared to leave the outstanding points to a Conference of Germany, Italy, France and ourselves. France, Italy
and ourselves were ready: Germany refused.
> —SIR EDWARD GREY TO COLONEL EDWARD HOUSE,
> JULY 14, 1915[1]

It had never been a more beautiful summer, Stefan Zweig wrote. The
Austrian poet was spending it at Baden, a romantic little town not
far from Vienna. "Throughout the days and nights the heavens were
a silky blue, the air soft yet not sultry, the meadows fragrant and warm,
the forests dark and profuse in their tender green."[2] A quiet summer,
that summer of 1914—until a Serbian student named Gavrilo Princip
fired two bullets into the corpulent body of Archduke Francis Ferdinand,
heir to the throne of the Austro-Hungarian Empire.

Now the war began to build like a July thunderstorm. You knew it
was coming: heavy, humid air; dust thick on caterpillar-covered leaves;
garden flowers wilting; green grass browning; a hot burning sun—altogether a lethargy of nature unnatural and unreal. But it was coming all
right, for far off on the horizon the clouds, which looked first like white
elephants, darkened to form rumbling thunderheads pushed by a cooling
breeze and splashed by savage streaks of lightning.

The war storm that broke in August of 1914 had been forming for many years. Since 1908 the Triple Alliance, composed of Germany, Austria-Hungary, and a dejected and wavering Italy, had faced the Entente of France, Russia, and England through crisis after crisis, each settled diplomatically but only with difficulty and to no one's real satisfaction.

Though formed from centuries-old antagonisms that stemmed from religious, economic, social, territorial, and trade conflicts, the violent political air of 1914 had its genesis in the aftermath of the Franco-Prussian War of 1870–1871, when the victors threw the glove of a new and ambitious German empire into the power ring of the world.

Germany's chief problem lay in consolidating her gains before further expanding her empire. While Field Marshal Count von Moltke, hero of the Franco-Prussian War, set about planning for Germany's new aggression, the brilliant if Machiavellian chancellor, Prince Otto von Bismarck, turned to the comprehensive political situation. Bismarck first concluded a defensive alliance in 1879 with her southeastern neighbor, Austria-Hungary. Bismarck adroitly expanded this to the Triple Alliance by signing a treaty with Italy in 1882.

Bismarck simultaneously wove a series of alliances designed to keep France politically isolated, particularly from Russia, and to keep Austria-Hungary quiet, particularly in the Balkans. The cornerstone of Bismarck's southern policy, the Three Emperors' Alliance signed in 1881, committed Russia, Austria-Hungary, and Germany to common action in all Balkan affairs. Such was the innate antagonism between Russia and Austria-Hungary that this alliance lasted only six years. Bismarck countered its lapse by renewing the Triple Alliance with Austria-Hungary and Italy and by signing the Reinsurance Treaty with Russia, a secret agreement by which each country was to remain neutral if the other went to war, but not if Germany attacked France, or if Russia attacked Austria-Hungary.

The reinsurance treaty was more than a stopgap measure. It could possibly have led to a better relationship with Russia had Bismarck retained his immense physical and mental powers. These were in decline by the late 1880s, at a time when Russia was growing closer to France and when Bismarck was losing his young kaiser's favor.

Bismarck's diplomatic subtlety far exceeded the comprehension of either Kaiser Wilhelm II or the chief of the general staff, Field Marshal Count Alfred von Waldersee, who both favored a preventive war against Russia. Wilhelm had become emperor of Germany and king of Prussia in 1888. He was twenty-nine years old, an egotistical dilettante who will be presented in detail later in this book. Shortly after ascending to the throne he fell under the pernicious influence of an anti-Bismarck (and anti-Russian) clique headed by the sinister éminence grise of the foreign ministry, Baron Friedrich von Holstein. To the world's surprise, Bismarck was dumped in 1890. The new chancellor, Count Leo von Caprivi, soon abandoned the Reinsurance Treaty, and Russia found herself standing alone. But not for long. In 1891 formal talks were begun with France, which a year later resulted in a military agreement and the dual alliance so dreaded by Bismarck.

With the powers of Europe thus divided, albeit loosely, Great Britain emerged as an isolated power, a position not to her liking. Her conflicts with Russia in Persia and with France in Egypt caused her to lean toward an alliance with Germany, and in 1902 she did align herself with Japan. But Germany's steady and determined transition from internal consolidation to overseas expansion, coupled with Kaiser Wilhelm and Admiral von Tirpitz's insistence on building a powerful surface navy, created increasingly serious incidents that finally drove England to rapprochement with France. Omnipresent fear of a rapacious German neighbor helped France to resolve the vexatious colonial conflict with England in favor of the 1904 Entente, strengthened two years later by Germany's bellicose behavior during the Algeciras Crisis.* This shift in the power struggle cost Germany more than the support of England, whose strong political ties with Italy automatically weakened the latter's allegiance to Germany and Austria-Hungary.

Kaiser Wilhelm's personal friendship with the czar of Russia, the famous Willy-Nicky relationship, partially offset Germany's loss. But willing as Nicholas was to connive against England, whom he loathed for her hostility in the Russo-Japanese War of 1904–1905, he could not be induced to abandon his agreement with France, particularly since French loans had allowed him to begin rebuilding his shattered army and to undertake major railway expansion. Germany's continued attempts at chest-thumping expansion, in this case toward Turkey and Palestine as exemplified by the Berlin–Baghdad railway, also cooled the Russian czar's ardor to the extent that he opened negotiations with England which in 1907 led to an understanding over Persia.

---

*This was a quarrel between Germany and France precipitated by the French desire to insert herself economically into Morocco. It was settled in favor of France because of the support of Britain and other powers.

The outlines of the European power picture were now so fully drawn that the Annexation Crisis of 1909 almost exactly anticipated the final political reaction of 1914. Late in 1908 Austria-Hungary summarily annexed the Balkan provinces of Bosnia and Herzegovina. Serbia protested and mobilized her army, Russia backed Serbia, and Germany backed Austria. The combined action of England and Germany finally averted war, but the political-military alignment of the 1909 crisis changed only in intensity during the Moroccan crisis of 1911, which was brought on by French expansionism in Morocco, and which ended in another German diplomatic defeat.

A year later the First Balkan War, fought by Greece, Serbia, Bulgaria, and Montenegro against Turkey, forced that power to yield the European portion of her vast but crumbling empire. Once again general war was averted thanks to the dexterous diplomacy of Britain's foreign minister, Sir Edward Grey, who arranged a conference of the Great Powers, which only with difficulty worked out a political solution. The victors subsequently quarreled over spoils, and in the end Serbia and Greece triumphed over Bulgaria, which lost most of her earlier gains. Victory in the Balkans left Serbia in a powerful and threatening position, her eyes on Bosnia and Herzegovina, her political hand clasped in that of her Russian ally.

The crisis strengthened the German general staff's belief that war was inevitable—as Moltke put it in a *Kriegsrat*, or war council, of December 1912, it should come sooner rather than later. Up to this point Kaiser Wilhelm had not wished to intervene in the Balkans, a stance that was slowly alienating his Austro-Hungarian ally. What Wilhelm regarded as England's pro-Entente attitude on the Balkan crisis changed his mind. The chief of the German Great General Staff, General Count Helmuth von Moltke, the elder Moltke's nephew, had been insisting all along that war was inevitable, as had a good many of Wilhelm's other generals and admirals. They were right, Wilhelm now decided. But Germany needed time for Admiral von Tirpitz to complete naval preparations.

By 1914 the pattern of conflict and crisis motivated by the two fountainheads of power—Germany and Austria-Hungary on the one hand, France, Russia, and Britain on the other—had exacerbated the political situation to a dangerous degree. Worse yet, the interim years had improved the military readiness of the key nations, a process that put too much power in military hands, far too much hope in military plans.

* * *

Shocked by the assassination of Archduke Francis Ferdinand and his wife on June 28, 1914, European diplomats hoped that Austria-Hungary would not convert it to a casus belli. Count Berchtold, Austria's foreign minister, whose own position was as shaky as his country's prestige, did exactly this. Backed by General Franz Conrad von Hötzendorf, chief of the general staff, who had wanted war against Serbia and Italy for years, Berchtold persuaded the old emperor Francis Joseph to seek German support for aggressive Austrian action.

A strong German government would have backed away while emotions calmed to let reason act. The German government was not strong. Its authority lay in the hands of a kaiser and his appointed chancellor, who could be dismissed at will. Kaiser Wilhelm had allowed his authority to erode as his chauvinist ambitions demanded the continued support of the military. Chancellor Bethmann Hollweg had also yielded to the siren song of armed force. Army and navy leaders were convinced that Germany would be attacked by Russia and France in 1917 at the latest; therefore, so their martial reasoning went, it was better to fight them before they were ready. "We are ready," Moltke declared on June 1, 1914, "and the sooner it comes the better for us."[3]

Francis Ferdinand's assassination had provided the perfect opportunity. Bethmann and his foreign secretary, Gottlieb von Jagow, agreed that the time had come to stand up to these hostile powers. It was not necessary to consult the Reichstag, which was not even in session. It was a simple matter to persuade the confused kaiser that nothing must jeopardize the security or strength of his Austrian ally. "The necessity for a powerful Austria . . . must be recognized as a firm basis of our foreign policy," said Bethmann, stating an inviolable principle established by Prince Bismarck.[4]

So it was that Bethmann was willing to fight what the general staff called a defensive war if this were necessary. Perhaps, though, it would not come to that. A strong stand might cause Russia or France to back down, particularly if England remained neutral, as Bethmann hoped would be the case. And what if Germany did not support her only major ally? Might not that ally withdraw from the alliance? Might not that ally even join the Entente to complete the encirclement and ensure the destruction of the German empire? No historian has satisfactorily unraveled Bethmann Hollweg's thought processes at this critical point, and they seemed to have remained a mystery to their owner, whose professional survival had depended and would depend on studied and at times not-so-studied ambivalence.

Whatever the case, Bethmann decided to gamble. On July 5 Kaiser Wilhelm's reply—the famous "blank check"—guaranteed Austria-Hungary the complete military and political support of Germany in whatever way she chose to act, an unusual act of diplomacy that reduced the German empire to the immediate political dictate of her impassioned and very weak southern ally.

European powers, particularly Germany and Austria-Hungary, now began quiet military preparations. On July 23 Count Berchtold, Austria's foreign minister, delivered an ultimatum to Serbia and demanded her reply within forty-eight hours. The extreme insult of the terms, which Serbia could not have accepted without forfeiting her sovereignty, shocked all of Europe, even Kaiser Wilhelm and Bethmann, who nonetheless recovered to reaffirm military support of their ally the next day. Russia simultaneously reiterated her support of Serbia, and France pledged her aid to Russia. Britain's foreign minister, Sir Edward Grey, hoping to repeat his diplomatic success of 1912, urged Germany to arrange an extension of time for Serbia to reply to the Austrian note. This request was ignored, as were Grey's determined attempts in the following days to settle the affair by convening a conference of European powers. Serbia, however, met the deadline and agreed to all but two of Austria's demands, a conciliatory effort immediately rejected by Berchtold. On July 28 Austria declared war on Serbia.

The next three days witnessed a frenzied scheme of formal ultimatums and informal propositions among the chancelleries of Berlin, Vienna, St. Petersburg, Rome, Paris, and London. Diplomacy at times seemed to hold hope of peace, but in the end came to naught. Neither Czar Nicholas nor his foreign secretary, Sergey Sazonov, wanted to go to war, but such was the hatred of Austria-Hungary and the strength of the war party in the aristocratic officer corps that a palace revolution probably would have broken out had they not supported Serbia.

Russia ordered general mobilization on July 31. Austria-Hungary followed a few hours later. Germany immediately declared partial mobilization, which despite actual mobilization measures and armed raids into France, kept from her the stigma of general mobilization while she carried out frantic attempts to gain England's neutrality, the more important since Italy had declared herself neutral.

Such was the inflexibility of war plans that, with general mobilization under way in Russia and Austria, nothing could have saved the peace of Europe. On August 1 the president of the United States, Wood-row Wilson, telegraphed an appeal for peace to the belligerents and offered his services as mediator. He was ignored. Germany declared war on Russia on the same day and ordered general mobilization. The following day she delivered an ultimatum to Belgium, demanding the right of German troops to cross Belgian territory, which was refused. On August 3 she declared war on France and on August 4 German troops crossed the Belgian border, an act that brought Great Britain's declaration of war.

World War One had begun.

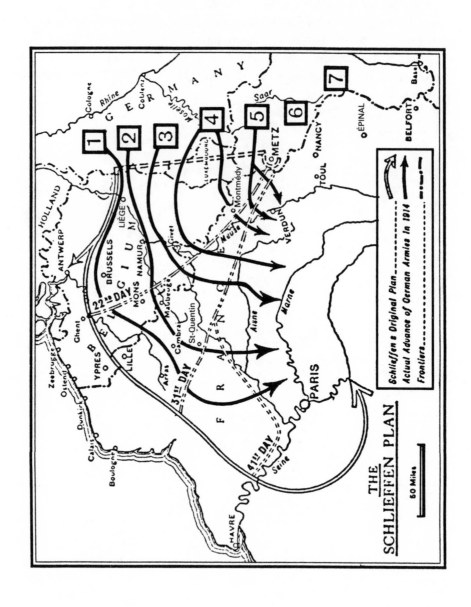

THE
SCHLIEFFEN PLAN

Schlieffen's Original Plan

Actual Advance of German Armies in 1914

Frontiers

50 Miles

2

War Plans I

The situation is extraordinary. It is militarism run stark mad.
Unless someone acting for you can bring about a different
understanding, there is some day to be an awful cataclysm.
—COLONEL EDWARD HOUSE TO PRESIDENT WOODROW
WILSON, BERLIN, MAY 29, 1914[1]

To create an empire is one thing, to defend it another. The challenge was particularly acute to Bismarck's creation. Although the German *Reich* that altered the map of Europe in 1871 was an impressive expansion of Frederick the Great's Brandenburg-Prussia, it did not alter Frederick's manifold problems of exposed borders. For forty-three years German military planners had been obsessed with the thought of a two-front war against Russia and France.

There were more twists in this strategical thinking than in a mountain road. The chief of the German general staff, Field Marshal Count von Moltke, who had led Germany to victory over France, initially envisaged an offensive action against France, a fast, sharp attack to defeat the French army and gain Germany a separate peace necessary to free her forces for the eastern front to defeat the Russian army and end the war in total victory (*Vernichtungsstrategie*). The French military renascence caused Moltke to change his priority eastward—that is, to attack Russia first. His planning finally resulted in a defensive-offensive strategy designed to achieve not total victory against either Russia or France but sufficient victory to win Germany a favorable peace (*Ermattungsstrategie*). His successor, Count von Waldersee, did little to alter this strategy.

The major legacy of the Moltke-Waldersee era was as much political as military. Bismarck's constitution placed the army under imperial rather than parliamentary control. This was exercised by the kaiser through the minister of war with the Reichstag's role limited to approving military budgets. The kaiser's military adviser was the chief of the general staff, who in theory remained subordinate to the minister of war.

The elder Moltke's imperishable fame threatened but did not topple this precarious balance of power. Prince Bismarck more than held his own against Moltke and what he derisively called the *Halbgötter* (demigods) of the general staff. But Bismarck's fear of the parliamentary process led to his being hoist with his own petard, and in the 1880's control of the army began to slip away from the war ministry. By the accession of Wilhelm II in 1888, the crown was firmly in control of the army with its virtually autonomous general staff. Because of the peculiar and weak nature of the new kaiser, the power of the general staff could only continue to grow.

Waldersee's successor, General Alfred Count von Schlieffen, scorned "safe" strategy. Instead he turned to Moltke's original concept of gaining a swift, decisive victory on one front before turning on the other opponent. Under the terms of the Schlieffen plan of 1905 the bulk of the German army would deploy in the west. Two smaller armies reinforced by Italian divisions would defend Alsace-Lorraine and the upper Rhine area. The extreme right of this force, two very strong armies, would smash through Holland and Belgium, debouch into northern France, sweep down west of Paris, and wheel on the enemy left, a gargantuan envelopment designed for swift total victory.

The plan held serious defects. It called for Italy's participation, which even in 1905 could not be guaranteed. It required additional forces, which would have to be funded by a reluctant, increasingly liberal German parliament. Schlieffen appraised the enemy's offensive intentions remarkably well, even counting on a British force 100,000 strong operating on the French left, but he seems to have ignored the French army's defensive capability and the advantage it would gain by operating on interior lines that included a superb railway complex behind Paris. Although he built an impressive railway system to serve military needs within Germany, he paid scant attention to supplying his right wing by rail, perhaps because he believed in a lightning victory in France. His most serious operational error, one shared by even his most critical colleagues, was failure to consider what Germany would do if the plan failed in execution. His greatest error, however, was political—failure to assess international moral opprobrium for violating the neutrality of

Holland and Belgium, since Germany had signed the treaty of 1839 that guaranteed Belgium's neutrality.

Schlieffen paid little attention to external criticism, of which there was ample, and refused to allow even healthy questioning by subordinates (who called him the Sphinx). He nonetheless recognized some of the weak spots in his plan and continued to try to strengthen them until his death in 1913. But, providing that he was given sufficient military muscle, he believed to the end in his essential strategy: crushing envelopment by successful exploitation of time-space factors to win total victory. Several generations of historians have repeated his alleged deathbed words: "It must come to a war. Keep the right wing strong." More to the point was his witty warning to a select group of generals a few weeks before his death. "Don't let the campaign stall. An attrition strategy is nonsense if it costs billions to support millions."[2]

Schlieffen's purely land strategy had meanwhile been challenged by a new twist in Germany's military development. Not content with commanding the most powerful army in the world, Kaiser Wilhelm wanted to build an equally powerful navy, in an attempt to challenge Great Britain's control of the high seas.

The question of a German navy was scarcely new. King Frederick William, Frederick the Great's father, felt "that he must absolutely have a foot on the sea in order to participate in world commerce," and he was immensely proud of wresting the Baltic port of Stettin from Sweden. A half century later his son sagely observed, in a secret "political testament" written for his successor, that Holland, England, France, and Spain had captured overseas commerce and there was little that Prussia could do about it. Prussia should not acquire overseas provinces "because they drain the state of people, they must be supported by a large fleet, and they constantly provide new reasons for war, as if we did not have enough already with our neighbors."[3]

Germany's present position vis-à-vis overseas possessions bore a marked similarity to that of 1768. Having joined the industrial revolution about a century too late, Germany had failed to participate in the great grab for colonies. England, France, Belgium, and Holland, yes—Germany, no, other than a few minimal holdings in Africa and China. This was particularly galling to the ambitious and chauvinistic German emperor who was determined to have a voice in *Weltpolitik*.

Wilhelm found his alter ego in Alfred von Tirpitz, a hulking, fork-bearded admiral who in 1900 called for construction of a battleship fleet to challenge British naval supremacy (and thus ensure enduring conflict). Tirpitz's *Risikoprinzip*—risk policy—was swallowed hook, line and sinker by his imperial master. The naval race that followed, perhaps more than any other factor, changed the power balance of Europe to Germany's disadvantage while costing billions of marks that could have been better used both to strengthen her army further and to expand her industrial base, thereby increasing already extensive and profitable trade with numerous European and world markets.

Unlike Schlieffen, who formulated a positive role for the army, Tirpitz never seemed to hit on an essential role for the navy, settling in 1912 for a somewhat innocuous "waiting strategy" that postulated a "close blockade" of the German coast by the British navy in case of war—an erroneous and costly assumption.[4] Aggressive intention could not overcome geographical restriction. Tirpitz's dreadnoughts turned out to be mere watchdogs chained to a few North Sea and Baltic ports. Apart from some roving cruiser squadrons that were blown out of the water within a few months of after the start of the war, the German High Seas Fleet functioned like the physical phenomenon that scientists call a neutrino—a whirling nothing.

Schlieffen's daring plan was bequeathed to his successor, General Helmuth Count von Moltke, the elder Moltke's nephew, in 1906. The fifty-eight-year-old Moltke possessed most of his predecessor's shortcomings and little of his imagination and boldness. Of splendid military appearance and aristocratic manners, he had long been a favorite of Kaiser Wilhelm, who was said to find a comfortable tradition of victory in the name. Erich Ludendorff, at the time a forty-one-year-old general staff officer in Berlin, wrote that the appointment "surprised everyone."[5] The Austro-Hungarian military attaché in Berlin reported sharp criticism of the appointment in the newspapers.[6] Moltke himself was said to have argued against it, but perhaps he was swayed when the kaiser fatuously told him, "You can look after what little work there is in peacetime, but in war I am my own chief of staff."[7]

Courteous to a marked degree, intellectually (and socially) superior to most of his colleagues, he was scarcely the Prussian ideal. He was soft almost to the point of feyness and he was frequently ill, eventually suffering from severe heart and kidney problems. He embraced mysticism instead of mistresses and generally spent staff "rides" reading Goethe's

Faust and writing rather pedestrian and sometimes melancholy letters to his wife, whose interest in the occult he was said to share.[8]

As his uncle had worried about the French military renascence, so did his nephew, who grew so apprehensive over a possible French offensive into Alsace-Lorraine that he advocated a preventive war and was upset, as he wrote to Conrad von Hötzendorf, chief of staff of the Austro-Hungarian army, in 1909, over the peaceful settlement of the Bosnian crisis.

Schlieffen's reasoning that a temporary sacrifice of territory in Alsace-Lorraine would not interfere with the right-wing offensive seemed specious to Moltke. He now made the momentous decision to reinforce his left at the expense of his right. Schlieffen's right wing was to have been eight times stronger than his left. Moltke's right wing was to be only three times stronger. It remains a mystery why his deputy, Hermann von Stein, or such subordinates as Erich Ludendorff, did not actively oppose these fundamental changes.[9]

Moltke's other major change was to make Holland a neutral "windpipe." Instead of violating her neutrality he would try to get her permission to cross, but if this failed, and Moltke seemed to think it would, then he would invade Belgium and seize Liège by a coup de main—a plan worked out by Major Erich Ludendorff.

These changes merely diluted the operational potential of the Schlieffen plan without solving any of its defects. More troops were needed to carry it off, but the German Reichstag, which had to approve military expenditures, had grown more liberal and less willing to spend money for a war that many Germans believed would never come. Italy's tenuous value as ally had diminished sharply. Austro-Hungarian participation—an offensive in Galicia to check the Russians—was nebulous. Moltke halfheartedly committed himself to support Conrad von Hötzendorf's operations, but only after France was defeated.

War in the west was to be a purely German affair. Once France was conquered, the easy conquest of Russia would follow. Moltke and his principal staff officers were displaying the arrogance of ignorance familiar to various commanders through the ages. There were no combined staff meetings with the Austro-Hungarian high command, no overall agreed-on plans, nor did the German general staff, so far as the record shows, make any attempt to evaluate the combat worth of the money-starved Austro-Hungarian army; at the same time it greatly undervalued the Russian army and state as "backwards and petrified."[10] Moltke's planners were as unconcerned as Schlieffen regarding the lack of railroads to supply the right wing, and little was done to increase motor transport capability (even though Schlieffen stressed its value in 1909).[11] The war would be over before resupply became a problem.

Violation of Belgian neutrality, guaranteed by Prussia, France, Britain, Austria, and Russia in a treaty signed in 1839, remained a political time bomb gently ticking away. The turbulent political situation in 1905, taken with Schlieffen's political naïveté, partially excused him for ignoring this factor. In view of the Great Power coalescence in ensuing years, there was no excuse for either the German government or the army to ignore it, except for the arrogant assumption that the war would be won before international protest could influence the situation.

No one in the German government or the military seemed to ask what Germany would do once this great victory was achieved. For thirty years the kaiser and his publicists had been bleating about Germany's God-given right to occupy a place in the sun and to achieve Great Power status commensurate with God's chosen people. Ironically she was on the verge of accomplishing these ambitions by peaceful means. By 1914 she was mining almost as much coal as Great Britain, she was milling more steel than Britain, France, and Russia combined, her electrical consortiums dominated Europe, her chemical consortiums produced most of the world's dyes and were leaders in many other manufactures, her mining consortiums owned large interests in France, Belgium, and other countries. Germany was nudging Great Britain as the leading world exporter, with the world's second-largest merchant marine to carry forth merchandise and bring raw materials home. By 1914 Germany "had become the economic powerhouse of Europe," Paul Kennedy writes, "and even its much-publicized lack of capital did not seem to be slowing it down."[12]

What was there to gain by waging aggressive warfare? In June 1914 Kaiser Wilhelm told President Woodrow Wilson's confidant, Edward House, that Germany did not want war, which was against her best interests, but that she was menaced from every side. The primary argument of the men around the kaiser—army generals and navy admirals, the Junker agrarian nobility, Pan-German industrialists, the Navy Leaguers, bankers, and conservative politicians—was to prevent an invasion of Germany. Ample evidence exists to show that neither Russia nor France intended such an invasion, which would not have been supported by either Great Britain or the United States, not in 1914, not in 1917. This was a specious and highly inflammatory argument intended to win over the German people to an aggressive military-industrial policy in which greed for new territories and markets and for vast new powers overrode common sense—and it succeeded beyond any doubt.

An even more serious question also remained unanswered. What was Germany to do if the Schlieffen plan failed in its magic, if France did not succumb? In December 1913 a respected German military historian, Hans Delbrück, publicly warned that in view of French military strength, war with France would not only be prolonged but would undoubtedly bring in Russia and probably Britain against Germany.[13] Germany was not in a good position to fight a long war. Her industrial combines demanded massive quantities of diverse imported raw materials to continue production, just as her peoples demanded massive amounts of imported food to continue life.[14] The navy that would have to protect the sea-lanes was untried in warfare and was inferior in strength to the Entente navies should Britain go to war. There had been no joint planning with the army: the Admiralty was a closed corporation, its war plans nebulous in the extreme, its command ranks split almost beyond repair.

Nor had Germany's political growth kept pace with industrial growth and the changing needs and desires of her bourgeois peoples. The kaiser was suffered, not enjoyed, by many Germans (who nonetheless remained intensely loyal to the royal ethos). The chancellor was weak, not the man to direct an all-powerful general staff, an arrogant navy, a confused and divided foreign office, and an increasingly divided Reichstag. Particularism reigned at all levels of command: generals, admirals, and diplomats "had no spirit of mutual trust, and seldom worked together in a common cause."[15] To Max Weber it seemed as if "we were ruled by a bunch of maniacs."[16]

Who then would say if it would be wise to fight on or wiser to accept a face-saving peace if the opening blow failed? The question does not appear to have been asked, much less answered, by August 1914.

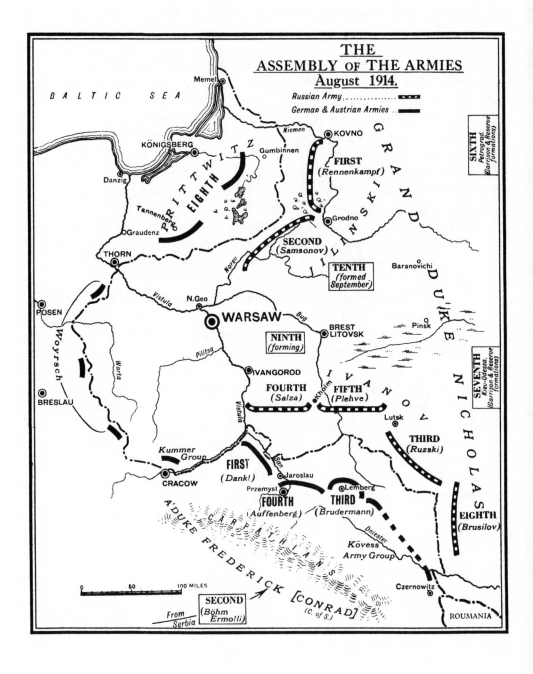

THE
ASSEMBLY OF THE ARMIES
August 1914.

Russian Army . . . .
German & Austrian Armies . .

BALTIC SEA

Memel

KÖNIGSBERG

Niemen

KOVNO

FIRST
(Rennenkampf)

Danzig

P R I T T W I T Z

EIGHTH

Gumbinnen

Tannenberg

Graudenz

Grodno

THORN

Narew

SECOND
(Samsonov)

Baranovichi

TENTH
(formed
September)

POSEN

Vistula

N.Geo

WARSAW

Bug

BREST
LITOVSK

Pinsk

Woyrsch

Warta

Pilitsa

NINTH
(forming)

IVANGOROD

Kholm

FOURTH
(Salza)

FIFTH
(Plehve)

BRESLAU

Lutsk

THIRD
(Ruzski)

Kummer
Group

Vistula

San

FIRST
(Dankl)

Jaroslau

CRACOW

Przemysl

Lemberg

FOURTH
(Auffenberg)

THIRD
(Brudermann)

EIGHTH
(Brusilov)

Kövess
Army Group

Dniester

Czernowitz

0   50   100 MILES

A'DUKE FREDERICK [CONRAD]
(C. of S.)

CARPATHIANS

SECOND
(Böhm
Ermolli)

From
Serbia

ROUMANIA

G R A N D   D U K E   N I C H O L A S

I L I N S K I

I V A N O V

SIXTH
Petrograd.
(Garrison & Reserve
formations)

SEVENTH
Kiev-Odessa.
(Garrison & Reserve
formations)

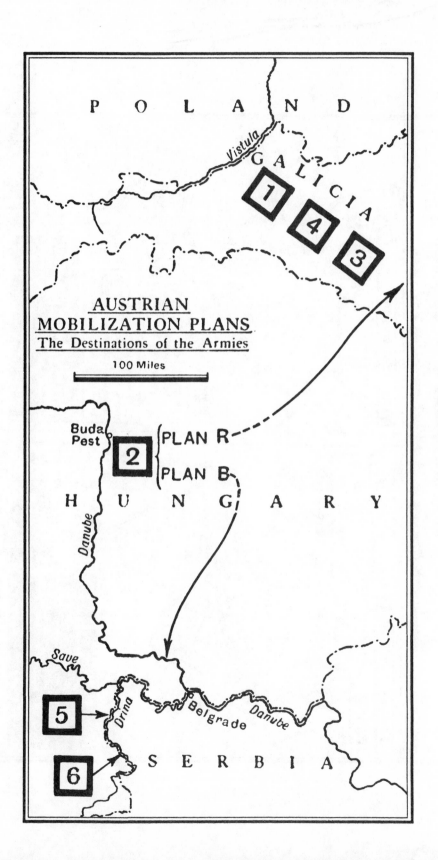

POLAND

Vistula

GALICIA

1
4
3

AUSTRIAN
MOBILIZATION PLANS
The Destinations of the Armies

100 Miles

Buda
Pest

2 { PLAN R

PLAN B

H U N G A R Y

Danube

Save

5

Drina

Belgrade

Danube

6

S E R B I A

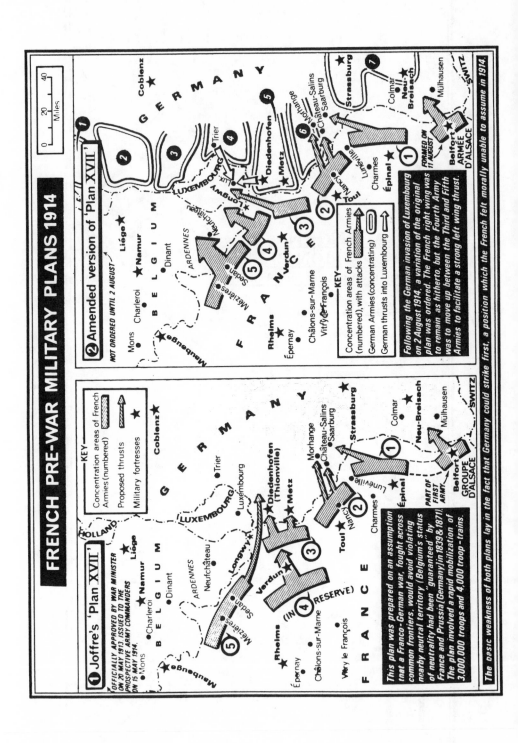

FRENCH PRE-WAR MILITARY PLANS 1914

① Joffre's 'Plan XVII'

KEY
- ▨ Concentration areas of French Armies (numbered)
- ⟿ Proposed thrusts
- ★ Military fortresses

OFFICIALLY APPROVED BY WAR MINISTER ON 20 MAY 1913. ISSUED TO THE PROSPECTIVE ARMY COMMANDERS ON 15 MAY 1914.

This plan was prepared on an assumption that a Franco-German war, fought across common frontiers, would avoid violating nearby neutral territory (Belgium's status of neutrality had been "guaranteed" by France and Prussia (Germany) in 1839 & 1871). The plan involved a rapid mobilization of 3,000,000 troops and 4,000 troop-trains.

② Amended version of 'Plan XVII'

NOT ORDERED UNTIL 2 AUGUST

KEY
- ▨ Concentration areas of French Armies (numbered), with attacks
- ⬭ German Armies (concentrating)
- ⟹ German thrusts into Luxembourg

Following the German invasion of Luxembourg on 2 August 1914, a variation of the original plan was ordered. The French right wing was to remain as hitherto, but the Fourth Army was to move up between the Third and Fifth Armies to facilitate a strong left wing thrust.

The basic weakness of both plans lay in the fact that Germany could strike first, a position which the French felt morally unable to assume in 1914.

0 20 40
Miles

3

War Plans II

Sole means to a solution: Overthrow Serbia by war undismayed by consequences. . . . Though the Entente Powers together with Serbia may be strong enough jointly to threaten the Monarchy, yet we are powerful enough to confront these states with the choice of a general war of which the most important of them is in fact afraid.

>—FIELD MARSHAL CONRAD VON HÖTZENDORF, CHIEF OF
>THE AUSTRO-HUNGARIAN GENERAL STAFF,
>DECEMBER 1912[1]

For the attack only two things are necessary: to know where the enemy is and to decide what to do. What the enemy intends to do is of no consequence.

>—LIEUTENANT COLONEL DE GRANDMAISON, CHIEF OF
>OPERATIONS, FRENCH MINISTRY OF WAR, 1911[2]

Russia's preparedness for war has made gigantic progress since the Russo-Japanese war, and is now much greater than ever in the past.

>—GENERAL HELMUTH VON MOLTKE, CHIEF OF
>THE GERMAN GENERAL STAFF, 1914[3]

The question of whether we went to war would depend upon how the war comes about. . . . Public opinion would not support any aggressive war for a *revanche*, or to hem Germany in, and we desired to see difficulties between Germany and other Powers, particularly France, smoothed over when they arose. If, however, Germany was led by her great, I might say, unprecedented strength, to attempt to crush France, I did not think we should stand by and look on.

>—SIR EDWARD GREY, BRITISH FOREIGN SECRETARY,
>SEPTEMBER 1912[4]

Complementing Germany's unhealthy military obsession was that of her Austro-Hungarian ally, whose military leaders looked to a war against Russia, Serbia, and possibly the third member of the Triple Alliance, Italy. General Franz Conrad von Hötzendorf inherited the problem when he became chief of the general staff in 1906. From a military family, Conrad was fifty-four years old, trim, polished, and urbane, well-known in the army as a ladies' man and as an inspiring lecturer and writer. He was also an inveterate nationalist who wished to wean the empire's southern Slavs from Serbian and Montenegrin influence, its Italians from Rome's influence. His solution was to wage preventive wars against Serbia and Italy, ambitious notions disallowed by his government.

His practical problem was to utilize the empire's relatively slim military forces in the best way. It was patently impossible for him to fight against Serbia, Russia, and possibly Italy without German aid. In 1909, as one result of the Bosnia-Herzegovina crisis, Conrad began an exchange of letters with the chief of the German general staff, Helmuth von Moltke on the strategy to be employed in case of war.

Conrad had already worked out an operational scenario. His major force, A-Staffel, of some thirty divisions would be committed to the defense of Galicia. A smaller force of about ten divisions, Minimal Gruppe Balkan, was earmarked for defending the southern border against a Serbian strike. A third force of twelve divisions, B-Staffel, could be used on either front as the situation demanded. Conrad's preference was to eliminate Serbia in the opening clash, and for this purpose he wanted to know whether Moltke was prepared to assist materially in the Austro-Hungarian effort in the east.[5]

Moltke was—but only after he had settled with France, a vital proviso that was neither sufficiently stressed nor fully accepted by either correspondent. The exchange of letters that continued on and off up to and even after war broke out has been presented in detail by Norman Stone and others, and it is a dismal record of false assumptions, half-truths, and undeclared secrets on either side. Conrad and Moltke assumed that Russia would require six weeks to mobilize her massive resources and armies. By that time Germany would have conquered France and would have been able to support Austria-Hungary in the east. Personal prejudices played a considerable role, as they invariably do in combined planning. Moltke was a convinced "westerner," who regarded France as

Germany's most important enemy. Conrad regarded Serbia as *his* major enemy and planned accordingly. Neither leader seems to have accepted the possibility of a more rapid Russian mobilization, much less the effect of such on their entirely too vague plans.[6]

Conrad's plans had more holes than a Swiss cheese, mainly because they depended on military forces that were lacking both quantitatively and qualitatively. His army, in reality three armies—the Imperial and Royal Army, the Austrian Landwehr, and the Hungarian Honvéd—was poorly equipped and poorly armed, particularly in artillery. From a population of fifty-two million, Austria-Hungary would field an army of only 1,400,000 in 1914 (compared to France, which with a population of thirty-seven million would put an army of 2,150,000 into the field). Austria-Hungary's military expenditure was a quarter of Russian or German expenditures, a third of British or French expenditures. The army was plagued by ammunition shortages and other problems. German was the language of command, but regiments were provincial in makeup. Troops of any one regiment might speak German, Czech, Polish, Ruthenian, Hungarian, Italian, Serbo-Croat, or a mixture of all with a dialect of any. In 1914 mobilization orders had to be published in fifteen different languages.

Land communication posed another problem. Austria and Hungary maintained separate railway networks with few connecting lines. Conrad could not easily move his divisions from one front to another. His reserve divisions, B-Staffel, once on their way, be it to Galicia or to the Serbian border, could not be suddenly shifted.[7]

These were serious weaknesses of which the Russian and Serb enemy were fully cognizant. An Austro-Hungarian general staff officer, Colonel Alfred Redl, had for years systematically betrayed his army's mobilization plans, fortress defenses, codes, and other such information, not only to Russia but to France and Italy. Caught in 1913, he was allowed to commit suicide, a bizarre story that I have told elsewhere.[8] The scandal sent army morale plunging and tore further great rents in the military-political fabric of empire.

Austria-Hungary was more political anachronism than empire. Emperor Francis Joseph was a man born to defeat. He had neither the talent nor the will to weld a host of strikingly different nationalities into a political whole, and perhaps no man could have. Austrians and Hungarians did not trust each other. An active group of dissidents known as the "young Czechs" wanted to liberate Bohemia and had turned that lovely country into a hotbed of sedition against the German-speaking overlords. The southern Slavs detested both Hungarians and Austrians and looked toward political union with Serbia and Montenegro under Russia's benevolent eye. Galician Poles and Galician-Bukovina Ruthenes, or "little Russians," looked also toward Petersburg to support them in their demands for autonomy, just as southern Italians looked toward Rome. There was more. Hungarian political leaders did not trust Germany and suspiciously eyed Field Marshal Conrad von Hözendorf's desired military alliance with the neighboring empire. Emperor Francis Joseph detested Germany for having humiliated him in battle at Königgrätz in 1866, which put him at odds with his heir presumptive, Francis Ferdinand, a proponent of the Greater German movement.

Some of these antagonisms might have been watered down had Austria-Hungary followed up earlier efforts to industrialize. She was richer in coal than either Russia or France. Late in the nineteenth century she seemed well on her way to becoming an industrialized country, but unlike Germany she let it slip away. By 1914 her steel production was almost at the bottom of the list, scarcely sufficient to feed the hungry furnaces of the Škoda armament complex as it tooled up for war. Agriculturally she was rich in some areas, poor in others, a semifeudal society that lacked efficient production and distribution methods.

Germany did not seem to pay much attention to the deficiencies of her southern neighbor. The Bismarckian alliance was traditional—after all, she did defend Germany's southern border. In German eyes Austria-Hungary's task was to hold the Russian bear at bay until German arms, having disposed of France, could finish the job in the east. Germany would thus be the ruler of all Europe. Austria-Hungary was a necessary convenience, her military tasks relatively light (in the opinion of the German general staff). German arms would surely win the war before serious problems could develop.

A defensive power always suffers tactically vis-á-vis an aggressor who retains the initiative. An objective assessment of the aggressor's capabilities is the basis of a good defense, and this was what France lacked in the years before the war. Not believing that Germany could mount sufficient strength for such a wide sweep as that called for in the Schlieffen plan, and hampered by domestic political dissension, Belgian neutrality, and British caution, the French general staff worked out a number of plans that culminated in the famous—or infamous—Plan XVII, the brainchild of a junior but aggressive general, Joseph Jacques Césaire

Joffre, who was appointed minister of war and chief of the general staff in 1911.

Joffre was a leading member of a small but influential group of officers who had challenged the traditional defensive-offensive strategy with a more dynamic concept based on the doctrine of the *offensive à outrance*—the all-out offensive—in case Germany declared war. Joffre at once began incorporating the new spirit into concrete directives and plans. While working these out he sent his deputy, General Dubail, to Russia to impress Czar Nicholas with the need for rapid offensive action on the eastern front in case of war against Germany. Nicholas agreed to act before completing mobilization and to send two armies across the Prussian frontier on the sixteenth day of war. "It is at the very heart of Germany that we must strike," he told Dubail. "The objective of both of us ought to be Berlin."[9]

Taken with England's quasi commitment to an expeditionary force 125,000 strong to commence military operations in France on the fifteenth day of mobilization, the czar's words fell warmly on Joffre's ears. The upshot was Plan XVII, completed in early 1913.

Plan XVII involved five strong field armies. Greatly strengthened covering forces would fight a defensive action along the northeastern frontier until the thirteenth day of mobilization. Then the two armies on the right would attack into Lorraine, the center army would strike east of fortress Metz, and the left army, positioned opposite the Ardennes, would move either into Belgium or straight ahead on Metz, depending on the route of the German invaders. The final army was to remain in reserve left of center. Reserve divisions would buttress either flank, and a cavalry corps would operate on the left as contact with the British force still farther to the left.

Unlike the Schlieffen plan as modified by Moltke, which dictated an entire operation, Plan XVII was essentially a plan of concentration so developed that the commander in chief could attack the German armies with the bulk of his forces. In essence it was a refined *compression* of earlier French plans. The nationalist revival caused by the Moroccan crisis in 1911, the increased strength of the Russian army, the czar's willingness to assume an early offensive in the east, the British quasi commitment to send a force to France, the near certainty of Italian neutrality—each lent itself to the resurgence of the French spirit of *revanche*, a pervasive attitude that offered Joffre the increased means to what all thought would be a swift and victorious military end to German aggression.

This seemed reasonable enough on the surface. Joffre could count on an army after mobilization of about 1,650,000 offensively trained soldiers with good morale. Their 1886 Lebel rifle was satisfactory, and if her armies were greatly inferior to the German army in machine-gun and heavy artillery strength, they possessed the 75-mm field gun, the best in the world. Forty percent of her population farmed rich fields, so she would not starve. By 1914 France possessed the second largest colonial empire in the world (after Britain's) and could count on troop reinforcements and essential raw materials, providing Entente navies kept open vital sea-lanes. Her alliance with Russia was firm, and if that ally lacked certain essentials, she could be counted on to hold at least some of the enemy forces in the east. France's tentative alliance with Great Britain had freed the French fleet for service in the Mediterranean, leaving the Channel shores to the protection of the Royal Navy. If Britain did come into the war, her military, material, and financial aid would be immeasurable.

There were drawbacks. Joffre received a nasty shock when he learned that if France violated Belgium's neutrality before Germany, she would lose Britain's support. He accordingly switched his offensive to Lorraine, but Belgium remained leery of French (and British) intentions. The French nation was riding a patriotic wave, but nation and army had been split over the infamous Dreyfus case,* the wounds were not entirely healed, and not all French commanders accepted the offensive doctrine, as for example Lieutenant Colonel A. Grouard, who publicly recommended a return to a defensive strategy.[10] The French high command contained a great deal of deadwood—aged, decrepit generals and colonels unfit to fight *any* war. The army was seriously deficient in noncommissioned officers, its St-Étienne machine guns were inferior and in short supply, and, due to the pervading optimism about the *offensive à outrance*, its heavy artillery sorely neglected.[11] The *poilu*'s uniform, red trousers topped by a long, clumsy combination jacket-coat of blue—the *capote* —made him an easy target for rifle and machine-gun fire.

Despite the popular president, Raymond Poincaré, French politics

*In 1894, Alfred Dreyfus, a Jewish general-staff captain in the French army, was convicted by a military court of spying for Germany and was sent to Devil's Island to serve his sentence in solitary confinement. Evidence of his innocence was eventually discovered but was not accepted by the army. The famous author Émile Zola took up the case. Aided by such as Georges Clemenceau, Jean Jaurès, and Anatole France, Zola finally succeeded in having him pardoned and restored to active duty in 1906. Army prestige never fully recovered from what many French civilians believed to be blatant persecution of a Jewish officer by the predominantly monarchist and Catholic officer corps.

would continue to suffer (or perhaps enjoy) a traditional instability (forty-two ministers of war in forty-three years) that boded no good for the civil-military cooperation necessary to prosecute a successful war. Her industrial plant could not compare with Germany's, and she would need new imports to make up for those provided by her eastern neighbors.

In 1914, however, none of these deficiencies seemed very important to the French general staff. The time had at last come to avenge the humiliation inflicted by her defeat in the Franco-Prussian War of 1870–1871. Almost everyone agreed that the war would result in a short and glorious victory of French and Russian arms.

Thirty-five years after France had been defeated by Prussia, Russia suffered a similar humiliation at the hands of the Japanese. Military defeat in 1905 followed by internal uprisings left army and navy in a confused and impotent state. Largely because of administrative incompetence and severe schisms in the high command, recovery was slow. The man largely responsible for the limited success it enjoyed was General Vladimir Aleksandrovich Sukhomlinov, who became chief of the general staff in 1908 and subsequently minister of war.

A military conservative, Sukhomlinov was made a whipping boy of history by the later attacks of his many enemies. Aleksey Brusilov, one of the most competent Russian generals, who had known him for a long time, later described him as "undoubtedly a man of intelligence . . . who could grasp a situation and decide upon his course very rapidly, but of a superficial and flippant mentality. His chief fault was that he would not probe things to the bottom and was content if his orders and arrangements made a show of success."[12] A modern historian, Norman Stone, offers a more balanced portrait in his groundbreaking book, *The Eastern Front—1914-1917*. Sukhomlinov and his deputy, General Jurij Danilov, able enough but "a man of narrow, stubborn temperament," according to Brusilov,[13] were largely responsible for important prewar reforms. In pushing these through, the Sukhomlinites collided with such ranking aristocrats as Grand Duke Sergey Mikhailovich, inspector general of artillery, and Grand Duke Nicholas, each of whom had followers in the officer corps, the government, the court, and the Duma, or parliament. Nothing was pleasant about this divisiveness, which would carry over into the war with often disastrous consequences.

Preparations for war continued as Germany flexed martial muscles. As with France, Russia originally planned to remain on the defensive, her armies grouped around what Sukhomlinov and Danilov believed to be obsolete fortresses. Convinced by the Bosnian crisis of 1909 that war with Germany was inevitable, Sukhomlinov and Danilov wrote a new and radical Plan 19, which called for a two-pronged attack against East Prussia from the south and east. Nineteen out of twenty-eight army corps would be committed, leaving nine corps to contain any attack by the Austro-Hungarians. The obsolete fortresses, expensive to maintain, would be razed.[14]

The opposition vigorously opposed such strategy. Important voices pointed to the danger of war with Austria-Hungary and to unsettling political events that seemed to justify their concern. In the spring of 1912 the plan was altered to deploy the bulk of strength against the expected invasion by Austria-Hungary. Only two armies would invade East Prussia. The remaining armies, the bulk of Russian military strength, would take up the offensive as soon as mobilization enabled it to do so, and the fortresses would not be razed. According to Brusilov, subordinate army and corps commanders knew of no plan for a major offensive in the south; indeed it was possible that one did not exist.[15] In late 1913 France agreed in case of war to proceed against Germany with all her forces on the eleventh day of mobilization. Russia in turn promised that two armies—800,000 men—would attack East Prussia on the fifteenth day of mobilization.[16]

Conflicting plans aside, the Russian military plant continued to grow. Between 1909 and 1913 one third of government revenue was spent on the army and navy. The "Great Program" that became law in June 1914 raised the annual recruit levy to 585,000 men, who would serve for three years. There would be more infantry divisions, more field artillery, better railways.

This was in the future. If her army was the world's largest in 1914, it was also one of the worst led and equipped. Other than a good rifle and good field guns, both of which were in short supply, it was sorely deficient in weapons and equipment, both in numbers and quality. It had virtually no air force and only a handful of motor vehicles. Favoritism ruled officer selection and promotion. Probably fifty percent of its conscripts were illiterate—and seventy-five percent of its noncommissioned officers were conscripts. Training was haphazard, with most commanders favoring unimaginative "steamroller" tactics.[17]

Russia's industrial plant, although scoring substantial gains in the previous decade, could not support an army of over a million men. In case of war her allies would have to provide arms and ammunition. These could arrive through Turkey, through her northern ports, or through Vladivostok. Turkish cooperation was largely discounted due to her pro-German leanings. Supply from her own ports depended on inadequate railways—one-half mile of railway to every hundred square miles (compared to twenty miles in England). Archangel, closed half the year, was served by a single narrow-gauge line and was some two thousand miles from the front, while freight from Vladivostok would have to travel eight thousand miles.[18] Mobilization would rely on the same inadequate system, which meant that, as in the case of Austria and Germany, once the units started out they could not easily be recalled until they reached their destinations. The same system had to supply the armies from rear-area depots. The few lines of track were not efficiently maintained and were certainly not up to what would be gigantic supply requirements, including daily fodder for one million horses![19]

There were other problems. The two years before the war were marked by spiraling protests and strikes put down by massive arrests, while the army crushed revolts in the ethnic-minority states. Many of these problems stemmed from an obsolete and corrupt political system. Czar Nicholas was surrounded by a host of favorites, whose intrigues were far too subtle for his minimal brain to comprehend. The advice of his most able ministers, even if received, generally went unheeded. He and his court treated the parliament as a bad joke. Under such a system, reforms could never be achieved, yet nothing short of all-out reforms could have repaired the greatest danger that could befall empire and army—schism of command.

Perched on the periphery of the European continent, master of vast portions of the world ("the sun never sets on the British empire"), torn between protecting India from the Russians and guaranteeing the security of her other dominions while maintaining the European balance of power, Great Britain had slowly emerged with a strategy fully compatible with its tradition of ambiguous, often isolationist foreign policies.

The watershed of British strategy was marked by the end of the Boer War in 1902. In a brave effort to rectify divergent military strategies the better to defend her vast empire, Britain established the Committee of Imperial Defence in 1902 and an army general staff in 1904. Up to this critical point Britain envisaged her enemies to be France and Russia. Balfour's government had desired to ally with Germany and, when this effort failed, did ally with Japan. Britain's major strategical worry in these early years of the century centered on Russian expansionism in the Far East and in Central Asia with the concomitant threat to India.

Britain traditionally was a sea power, with the navy dominant in strategical planning. The new general staff challenged this concept on the basis of European political antagonisms. In 1905 Prime Minister Balfour warned that undoubtedly "Germany would march through Belgium and that Britain must go to war with Germany because of the treaty of 1839." Sir Edward Grey, foreign secretary in the new Liberal government, authorized military talks with France. By early 1906 "members of the [General] Staff were meeting regularly with their French counterparts to plan war against Germany."[20]

Despite ensuing crises that brought Britain closer to France and Russia, these talks did not prosper. But in 1910 Brigadier General Henry Wilson became director of military operations in the war office. An ardent Francophile, Wilson at once started pushing for a military alliance with France. The Moroccan crisis of 1911 supported his cause, and combined staff talks were soon based on a British expeditionary force of "six infantry divisions, one cavalry division and two mounted brigades, a total of 125,000 men," which would be ready to start military operations in France on the fifteenth day of mobilization.[21]

The Royal Navy had not taken kindly to the army's intrusion into strategical planning. The scenario of a German invasion of France with a British land force coming to the latter's aid was not to the Admiralty's liking. On the other hand, a Continental war sorely restricted grandiose fleet operations. About the best that the first sea lord, the dynamic John Arbuthnot Fisher, could come up with was a series of naval "descents" on the German coast in which the army would serve as "a projectile to be fired by the navy."[22] One of Britain's more capable naval strategists, Julian Corbett, correctly foresaw that the major naval role in a European land war would be to maintain an open blockade, which in time would bring Germany to heel. But this was nebulous stuff compared to Henry Wilson's dynamic land strategy, although a "naval understanding" between France and England made in 1912 consigned the French navy to Mediterranean waters while the British navy undertook to protect the French Channel coast from enemy invasion.

These were more moral than material commitments. Belgium was the pivotal country. If France deliberately invaded Belgium, no matter the military justification, then France could expect to forfeit Britain's aid. Although Joffre abandoned his otherwise sensible plan, the lingering question of his sincerity remained in many minds.

This was the situation in 1914. Under certain conditions Britain was prepared to go to war but had made no formal commitment to do so. One should not hasten to criticize this wait-and-see policy. Sir Edward Grey had demonstrated the advantages of nonalliance in 1912 when he prevented the First Balkan War from turning into a general conflagration. He remained only too well aware that impartial arbitration would be necessary in the future if war were to be avoided. Great Britain was in no hurry to go to war, but was ready to do so should Germany invade Belgium and attack France.

She was far better prepared for a naval than for a land war. Her fleet more than doubled those of her next two rivals, Germany and the United States, and she possessed the world's largest merchant marine.[23] Due to her vast empire, however, her navy could not be everywhere, and her small voluntary army would have to be dramatically increased for it to play a major role in a land war.

In 1914 Britain held two major advantages over both her allies and potential enemies. She was very rich and she possessed a tried political system that could cope with the exigencies of war.

The Planned German Advance

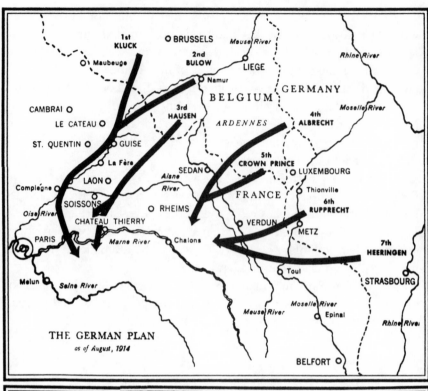

THE GERMAN PLAN
as of August, 1914

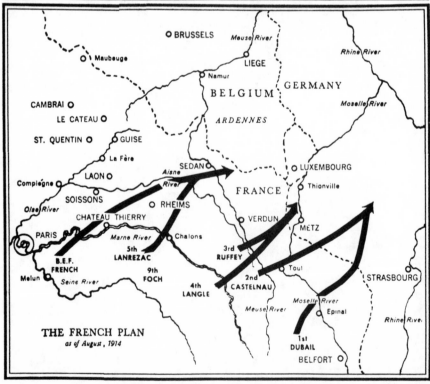

THE FRENCH PLAN
as of August, 1914

4

German Victory and Defeat

Whatever we have in store, we may well believe that August
4, 1914, will for all times remain one of Germany's greatest
days.

—IMPERIAL CHANCELLOR THEOBALD VON BETHMANN
HOLLWEG, ADDRESS TO THE REICHSTAG,
AUGUST 4, 1914[1]

The war began well for Germany.

Officers and men were quietly recalled from furlough, mobilization rosters appeared overnight in every newspaper and were
posted on public buildings in every hamlet, village, and city of the
German empire, while heralds went round the towns blowing trumpets
to summon reservists to the colors. "An amazing organization is revealed," an American naval officer, code-named "Z," reported from
Berlin. "The mobilization order puts six million men in the field under
arms and affects the daily occupation of some twelve millions, yet at the
War Department all was serene."[2]

While two million reservists were issued field-gray uniforms, spiked
leather helmets (*Pickelhauben*), and grease-covered Mauser magazine rifles, volunteers filled recruiting offices and training camps. In those hot
and long days seemingly endless columns of gray-clad infantry and
brightly uniformed cavalry marched to the disciplined cadences of military bands through city streets flanked with cheering civilians.

Kaiser Wilhelm greeted the war in an enthusiastic speech in Berlin
on the first day of August. "The streets of Berlin were thronged with
crowds, singing and cheering for war," the American ambassador, James

Gerard, reported. "An order was given that all communications including letters, telegrams and telephonic conversation must be in German, and that only German should be spoken on the street."[3] After explaining how war had been forced on Germany, the kaiser told his audience "to go to the church and pray," reported the American military attaché, Major George Langhorne. "In Berlin open air services were held, thousands and thousands attending."[4] The kaiser ended his speech with a peroration that swept through the empire: "For my part there are no more political parties, for me there are only Germans."[5] Three days later he hoisted the veil of Germany's aggression in a speech to the Reichstag. "We are not driven by the pleasure of conquest; an inflexible will inspires us to preserve what God has given us for ourselves and for all future generations. . . . With a clear conscience and with clean hands we take up arms in self-defense that has been forced upon us."[6] Aggressive neighbors must be defeated, he went on in "a strained and tired voice," one member noted, and for this national unity was necessary.[7]

Again his speech was well received. "The kaiser is the most adored man of the moment," Princess Blücher recorded.[8] Karl von Treutler, a soldier turned diplomat and a veteran member of the kaiser's intimate circle, was convinced that his master's trust in God and his will to fight a *defensive* war would bring "an unshakable position for our future."[9]

Wilhelm had started the ball rolling as intended by his chancellor, Bethmann Hollweg, a civilian who wore the uniform of his old dragoon regiment as he mounted the rostrum to address a formal session of the Reichstag, the first since Francis Ferdinand's assassination. Some four hundred members ranging in representation from far right to far left had neither been consulted about the decision to wage war nor even informed of the slipshod diplomacy that led to the decision. Now they listened attentively to the government's apologia for war:

Forty-four years we have lived in peace. We are drawing the sword only in defense of a righteous cause. Russia has set the torch to the house (wild applause). It would be a crime to wait until these powers, between which we are squeezed, break loose. France has already violated the peace. French flyers have crossed the frontier and have dropped bombs. French cavalry patrols and infantry companies have broken into Alsace. We are therefore acting in self-defense. Our troops have occupied Luxembourg and perhaps are already in Belgium [great commotion]. Our invasion of Belgium violates international law, but we will atone for the injustice which we have thus committed [great applause]. Whoever is as badly threatened as we are can think only of cutting his way through. We are standing shoulder to shoulder with Austria-Hungary. We have told England that we will attack neither Belgium's sovereignty nor her independence. Germany's great hour of trial has come. Our army is in the field. Our navy is ready for battle. Back of them stands a united people.[10]

So began the *Burgfriede*, a political truce intended to last as long as the war. A motion was put to the Reichstag for approval of a five-billion-mark war appropriation. The Social Democrats, who in late July had attacked the militant Austro-Hungarian government, now joined their fellows in a unanimous vote of approval. As frosting on the cake, the major trade unions voluntarily renounced "the right to strike for the duration of the war."[11] Neither the Reichstag nor the people objected when the government invoked the Siege Law of 1871 that placed Germany virtually under martial law administered by twenty-four army-corps districts, each commanded by a general usually called from retirement who "wielded an almost unlimited power in the case of civil administration and political rights generally, as well as in military matters." The generals and their staffs, as a rule untrained in civil administration, "were practically exempt from either ministerial or parliamentary control"—a dangerously independent authority overlooked in those euphoric days.[12]

Bethmann was still hoping to avoid war with Great Britain, a hope shattered when the British ambassador that evening delivered an ultimatum from his government. Germany, along with Britain, France, Austria, and Russia, had formally guaranteed Belgium's neutrality in the 1839 treaty. She must respect her pledge. Bethmann could not understand all the diplomatic fuss. The treaty was nothing more than "a scrap of paper," he told the British ambassador in refusing the ultimatum.[13] Kaiser Wilhelm accepted the break as a personal insult. "This was the thanks for Waterloo," was his bitter message to his cousin, King George, to whom he returned the honorary insignia of a British field marshal and admiral of the fleet.[14]

It was an emotional explosion. Germans everywhere went wild. For years they had been taught that Germany's neighbors had oppressed her in every respect, denying the natural right of territorial expansion, closing overseas colonies to her trade, humiliating her in the marketplace of diplomacy. They were falsely told that their neighbors had attacked Germany's borders, now they must be defeated. "The mood is splendid," Admiral Müller recorded in his diary. ". . . The government has shown a fortunate hand in making us appear innocent."[15] "Z," the American naval officer quoted earlier, reported that "officers and men with whom I have talked appear grave, but resolved. They are convinced of the righteousness of their cause and that the war was forced upon them."[16]

The legend of Allied attack, pompously announced by the chancellor in the Reichstag, was in part the work of three bright and ambitious general-staff officers at Moltke's headquarters, the Oberste Heeresleitung, or OHL: Majors Walther Nicolai, Hans von Haeften (who was Moltke's adjutant), and Max Bauer, each of whom we will meet again. Propaganda was their trade. The enemy had attacked defenseless Germany, the French were in Belgium, French planes had bombed Nürnberg, enemy spies were everywhere. Russians dressed as Prussian officers were carrying bottles of typhoid germs to poison lakes and reservoirs; similarly disguised French officers were racing across Germany in cars packed full of gold for Russia. Strange lights were the work of spies charged with guiding aircraft to German targets. A spy mania swept the country as rumors filled the air like notes from a military band. Russians in Berlin were rounded up in droves and imprisoned, and it was said that some were shot. French and British embassy personnel departed from Berlin only with difficulty. "The fury of the public against England is intense," Ambassador Gerard reported to Washington.[17] Innocent motorists in the countryside were arrested and sometimes shot. Plump militia officers who had outgrown their uniforms were shot at as potential spies. Irate citizens boycotted and even attacked foreign shops. It was a good time to be a German.

"The spirit of the people is splendid," reported the American naval officer "Z." "No sacrifice of life or money is too great to make. They are determined to win, and feel that defeat means the end of their national existence. . . . The women of Germany are doing their full share. Hospitals great and small, convalescent homes and establishments to care for families left in distress have sprung up everywhere and vast sums of money and donations of goods have been given. . . . All face the situation with the greatest courage and self-sacrifice."[18]

It was "the most popular war in history" for the middle-class youth. A few months earlier thousands of youngsters, members of the Wandervögel clubs, were hiking in the woods and mountains, strumming guitars around cozy campfires. Now they happily rushed to war to celebrate what one writer, Ernst Jünger, termed "the holy moment" of August 1914.[19] To Fritz von Unruh, a twenty-nine-year-old novelist from an aristocratic family, the war would soon prove to be a "spiritual purgative," the beginning of "a new zest for life."[20] A medical student in Freiburg im Breisgau, Stephen Westman, rushed to volunteer, as did his entire student fraternity. Wrote a twenty-year-old artillery reservist named Herbert Sulzbach: "Try as I may, I simply can't convey the splendid spirit and wild enthusiasm that has come over us all. We feel we've been attacked, and the idea that we have to defend ourselves gives us unbelievable strength."[21] The parents of Walter Limmer, a twenty-four-year-old law student, read that "our march to the station was a gripping and uplifting experience. . . . It seemed as if one had lived through as much in that hour as ordinarily in months and years. . . . The whole battalion with helmets and tunics decked with flowers—handkerchiefs waving untiringly—cheers on every side—and over and over again the ever-fresh and wonderful reassurance from the soldiers [singing]: '*fest steht und treu die Wacht am Rhein!*' "[22]

The army held center stage. Soldiers marching to their trains were buried in garlands of flowers, and flowers dangled from cavalry lances as the dragoons marched down Unter den Linden in the rain, their heavy voices singing "Die Wacht am Rhein." "I think I shall hear these words ringing in my ears to my dying day," Princess Blücher confided to her diary. "The whole life in the Germany of today seems to move to the rhythm of this tune. . . . It rings through the streets, almost like a solemn vow sung by these men on their way to death."[23] A traveler described a troop train with flowers sticking from the windows, the carriages chalk-marked "To Moscow," "To Paris," "To London." At every stop young ladies dressed in white offered "coffee, lemonade, milk, sandwiches and cigars." Other young ladies tended special yellow-and-black *Liebesgaben* cars to distribute donated "love gifts" to the passing troops.[24]

Meanwhile, the well-oiled machinery of mobilization whined to frenetic pace. Bridges, viaducts, rail terminals, and road junctions were immediately guarded by militiamen too old for front-line duty. Households were left without servants, stores without clerks, hotels without staffs, wives without husbands, children without fathers. While crowds cheered and brave men marched, mothers and wives wept and prayed, their single solace the well-known fact that the war would be over shortly—by Christmas at the latest.

While loved ones wept, troops packed haversacks, "folded our greatcoats with ground sheets on top of them, received iron rations—a tin of canned beef, a small box of coffee beans, and two tiny bags of biscuits hard as bricks"—sharpened bayonets on grindstones in the barracks square, received ninety rounds of rifle ammunition, a prayer book, and a song book, and were hustled aboard trains waiting like avenging chariots to haul human cargoes against the hosts of hell.[25] Every twenty-four hours 550 troop trains crossed Rhine bridges. In sixteen days, 2,150 trains transited the Hohenzollern Bridge at Cologne—an average of one train every ten minutes.[26]

The march west began on the same day that the chancellor assured Reichstag and empire that Germany was "acting in self-defense." Neutral Luxembourg was occupied without opposition. Not so little Belgium. Vital to German success was a coup de main against Liège, the Belgian city-fortress that stood in the way of the German right wing. It was to be captured within forty-eight hours by General Otto von Emmich's X Corps of General Karl von Bülow's Second Army. Spearheaded by cavalry, Emmich's special strike force of six reinforced infantry brigades crossed into Belgium early in the day. Lead units struck cursory but determined resistance from Belgian *franc-tireurs*, armed civilians who fought bravely and well and who were summarily shot when captured. The aggressors killed as many of the guerrillas as they could, seized hostages, and burned errant villages to the ground. Army publicists presented a picture greatly at odds with the truth. Captain Walter Bloem, a well-known novelist who was on a troop train heading west, bought the morning papers on August 8 to read "of priests, armed, at the heads of marauding bands of Belgian civilians, committing every kind of atrocity . . . of treacherous ambushes on patrols, and sentries found later with eyes pierced and tongues cut off, of poisoned wells and other horrors."[27]

By the following morning Emmich's forward troops finished an eighteen-mile march over torn-up, barricaded roads and demolished bridges to approach the vital target. No easy nut to crack, Liège rose from either side of the Meuse River, girdled at four to five miles' distance by a dozen reinforced concrete forts sprouting some 400 guns. A vigorous old veteran named General Gérard Leman commanded a garrison of about 40,000 soldiers, including those of a newly arrived division and brigade, and he intended to carry out personal orders from King Albert "to hold to the end."

Leman brusquely refused a demand to surrender early on August 5 and Emmich opened an artillery bombardment. Infantry assaults between the forts in the afternoon and evening failed despite casualties so severe that Emmich had to call on Bülow for reinforcements. Leman's mobile troops continued to hold their own on the following day. But now the weight of enemy attacks, coupled with cavalry penetrations from the north, brought home to the Belgian commander the ultimate hopelessness of his situation. To save what he could, he ordered his division and brigade to march to the main army that was defending the line of the Gete River.

This order helped to bring fame to Major General Erich Ludendorff, quartermaster general or deputy chief of staff to the Second Army, who had accompanied Emmich's force as observer. When a brigade commander was killed, Ludendorff took command to lead the troops personally between the outer fortresses to the inner citadel of Liège. This was now undefended by regular troops, but his was nonetheless a bold and brave action that resulted in occupation of the citadel and in capture of the city the next day.

Came now the first unpleasant surprise. On August 7 Bülow announced a "great victory," only to discover that Leman's ring forts remained unbroken. Another eight days passed before heavy siege artillery, immense 420-mm guns that blasted the first tactical surprise of the war, finally crumbled the last fort into surrender.

The delay had already unnerved both the sixty-six-year-old Moltke, chief of the German general staff, who was not a well man, and Kaiser Wilhelm, who spent hours huddled over maps in the general-staff building in Berlin. Wilhelm had been greatly perplexed by the suddenness of the war which he had not wanted and for which, along with his chancellor, he was primarily responsible. In the hope of persuading Britain to remain neutral, he had ingeniously ordered Moltke to halt the advance into Luxembourg, indeed to cancel mobilization in the west and march the army eastward *against Russia*. Moltke explained that this was technically impossible. "Your uncle would have given me a different answer," the kaiser replied. "With that I was dismissed," Moltke later wrote. "I cannot describe my feeling as I returned home. I was a broken man and wept tears of despair. . . . Something within me had been destroyed that could not be restored, my faith and confidence were shattered." Britain's entry into the war, along with the delay at Liège, brought another caustic outcry from the supreme warlord. "Yes, I thought so. This move against Belgium has burdened me with a war with England."[28] The combined effect of the two reprimands caused Moltke to suffer a mild stroke—or so his wife later informed Major Haeften.[29] The OHL's move to Coblenz, about one hundred miles from Liège, did little to repair Moltke's feelings or to calm the kaiser's fragile nerves. The kaiser had become increasingly military-oriented, perhaps the result of being served with Frederick the Great's field silver in his new abode. Rather grandly he startled his staff by announcing that henceforth all would eat as the soldiers in the field—a laudatory sacrifice quietly revoked when it appeared that the war would last longer than a month or two.[30] Working conditions were not the best. General-staff sections were jammed together in a hotel. Telephone communications with army groups were difficult, owing to a limited number of circuits, and wireless communication was often uncertain. The town was filled with private automobiles that belonged to wealthy civilians who had joined the Imperial Volunteer Automobile Corps and were used to carry staff officers and priority orders to forward commands.

Coblenz was a long way from war, yet war was never far removed. General Count von Stürgkh, the Austrian representative at the OHL, recalled watching the heavy barge traffic on the river from his hotel window. From the street came the booted cadence of troops marching to the strains of "Die Wacht am Rhein," while hordes of recruits were shepherded through the old streets to be outfitted and trained in camps across the river.

Delay at Liège increased the uncertain mood at the OHL. Reports from General von Prittwitz in East Prussia that the Eighth Army was retreating before the savage Russians filled the kaiser with grim foreboding. He had been assured that this would not happen, and the news made him impatient and ill-tempered as protests and complaints from land-owning East Prussian Junkers poured into the OHL. When walking in the garden of his palace with Admiral Müller and General Lyncker, the chiefs of his naval and army cabinets, he sat on a bench and directed them to join him. The bench being short, they brought up another. "Am I already such a figure of contempt," he asked, "that no one wants to sit next to me?"[31]

With the fall of Liège, Moltke ordered the advance of his great right wing (already weakened by the transfer of six reserve divisions to the Sixth Army in Lorraine). The offensive that was to end the war within a few weeks began on August 18: Max von Hausen's Third Army was to march west along the Meuse toward Namur, Karl von Bülow's Second Army and Alexander von Kluck's First Army to cross the Meuse, march on the Gete River, and cut the Belgian army's retreat to Antwerp.

But delay at Liège had told. The Belgian army had slowly fought its way back to fortress Antwerp to form a tactical thorn not in the least dulled by enemy occupation of Brussels and Kluck's continued advance westward. While General Sixt von Arnim's corps staged a massive victory parade through Brussels, Kluck grudgingly detached a corps to take up permanent shielding positions against the flanking threat of Antwerp—

a task that Schlieffen had allotted to the reserve divisions that Moltke had transferred to Alsace.

Hausen and Bülow meanwhile tied in before the fortified city of Namur, soon to be pounded to rubble by powerful Austrian 305-mm mortars that fired nine-hundred-pound shells from two and a half miles away. But now cavalry sniffed out French concentrations (General Charles Lanrezac's Fifth Army) west of Namur behind the Sambre River. Moltke placed Hausen and Kluck under the unpopular Bülow's command and ordered the latter to leave a siege force at Namur and move on the estimated seven or eight French corps on the Sambre. As for the British army, "It is the view here that no important debarkations [in France] have so far taken place."[32]

Bülow ordered Hausen to strike west across the Meuse while his own army marched south to the Sambre with Kluck tying in to his right flank. The order caught Kluck's First Army—more than 250,000 strong—moving southwest toward Lille-Tournai. This was Schlieffen strategy. It was well understood by Kluck and by his fiery chief of staff, Hermann von Kuhl, and each argued hotly with Bülow for its pursuance. But Bülow was commanding and Bülow refused to yield. With that, Kluck turned south and began heading for the British army that the Germans believed to be still in England. Here was a real mistake. It was Moltke and Bülow's fault, and it started a chain of events that three weeks later would end in German failure on the Marne.

The error was not immediately evident. Five days of victory had filled the OHL with an irrepressible optimism surpassed only by that of jubilant army commanders. First had come Crown Prince Rupprecht's report from Lorraine, where his Bavarians had captured twelve thousand prisoners and fifty guns, "a complete victory" with the enemy in "complete retreat . . . in complete dissolution." Similar messages arrived from Crown Prince Wilhelm and Duke Albrecht in the Ardennes and from Bülow, Hausen, and Kluck in Belgium. Together they formed an immense tidal wave of victory that smashed over the OHL in Coblenz to flow on to Germany and the world. By August 25 Moltke and his staff officers had persuaded themselves that not only had their armies fought a great battle in the west but that their feats had resulted in the "decisive victory" on which German strategy rested.[33]

The war also began well for Austria-Hungary. The fact that very few Austrian subjects wanted war could not suppress general elation that war had arrived. Notices of general mobilization immediately appeared in official buildings, post offices, train stations. In Vienna one parade of recruits followed another with flags flying, bands playing, women rushing to the young warriors to cover them with flowers and kisses. "I must acknowledge that there was a majestic, rapturous, and even seductive something in this first outbreak of the people," Stefan Zweig recalled. ". . . As never before, thousands and hundreds of thousands felt what they should have felt in peacetime, that they belonged together. A city of two million, a country of nearly fifty million, in that hour felt that they were participating in world history, in a moment which would never recur, and that each one was called upon to cast his infinitesimal self into the glowing mass, there to be purified of all selfishness."[34]

Fritz Kreisler, the famous violinist, commanded a platoon in a reserve Landsturm regiment which was called up at once. He was thirty-nine, a virtuoso who shortly before departing for the eastern front gave a performance in aid of the Red Cross. "Among the reserve officers of my battalion was a famous sculptor, a well-known philologist, two university professors . . . a prince and a civil engineer at the head of one of the largest Austrian steel corporations. The surgeon of our battalion was the head of a great medical institution and a man of international fame. Among my men in the platoon were a painter, two college professors, a singer of repute, and a post official of high rank. Nobody cared and in fact I myself did not know until much later what distinguished men were in my platoon. A great cloak of brotherhood seemed to have enveloped everybody and everything."[35]

The general euphoria was short-lived.

Despite pleas from his German ally to concentrate the bulk of Austro-Hungarian strength against the Russian threat in Galicia, as had somewhat informally been agreed, Conrad von Hötzendorf insisted on sending three armies to invade Serbia, which immensely complicated mobilization and deployment.

Two of the three armies commanded by General Oskar Potiorek crossed the Drina and Sava rivers on August 12. They marched in two columns to the sound of music, "as on a maneuver," one survivor recalled.[36] Little Serbia had mobilized an army of some half million (from a population of five million), which was backed by perhaps 50,000 Montenegrin militia. Ill-armed and ill-equipped, lacking ammunition and proper food, they nonetheless fought like wildcats. These were their mountains, and they defended them with tactics inspired by centuries-long hatred of their northern neighbors. For twelve days the invading enemy attempted to push them southward. In vain. The Austro-Hungarian Second Army might have tilted the tactical scales. But to everyone's surprise the Russians had mobilized more quickly than was believed possible, and Conrad was forced to redeploy this army to Galicia to meet his own timetable of attack. On August 24 the two invading armies began to slink back across the river to reorganize for another attempt. The enemy saw them to the riverbanks and said good-bye with vicious gunfire that shredded pontoon bridges to let water claim what metal had missed.

The opening failure cost Conrad about 50,000 casualties, and no amount of censorship could hide the failure. Frivolous young officers had taken to the field with the cynical observation that "[Emperor] Franz Joseph has lost all wars, he will also lose this one"—and it seemed they had a point.[37]

A second attempt two weeks later fared no better. By November Potiorek's troops had again retreated behind the Sava to bring the Serbian offensive to a standstill. Estimated casualties: 225,000.

True to her promise to her allies, Russia had immediately mobilized two armies to invade East Prussia, Pavel Rennenkampf's First Army to strike from the east, Aleksandr Samsonov's Second Army from the south, their mission "to assume a determined offensive" with the object of cutting the enemy "from Königsberg and seizing his line of retreat to the Vistula."[38] On paper the armies counted nearly thirty infantry and ten cavalry divisions; in reality they suffered from rapid mobilization and were at least twenty percent under strength and woefully deficient in artillery, communications, and supply—scarcely up to a concentric advance through channeled country of immense forests and lakes.

The defender of East Prussia, sixty-six-year-old General Maximilian von Prittwitz und Gaffron, whose chief of staff was General Count von Waldersee, commanded only thirteen divisions, of which half were second line. Prittwitz's chief of operations, forty-five-year-old Lieutenant Colonel Max Hoffmann, wrote in his diary on August 13: "If it ever becomes known how little we had to hold the Eastern Front [with], it will be called the greatest piece of impudence in history."[39] To make matters worse, Prittwitz was a fat, arrogant incompetent, while Waldersee was "somewhat weak," according to Hoffmann.

Russian intentions had been known to the German general staff since 1902, when a Russian general-staff colonel had been bribed to reveal the plan. In 1910 the general staff learned that Russia intended to attack simultaneously from north and south, on either side of the Masurian Lakes—in what strength was not known. The threat had been studied in numerous prewar scenarios written by the general staff and rehearsed in annual maneuvers. Prittwitz was to commit the bulk of his forces against Rennenkampf's First Army before meeting Samsonov's Second Army. Considering the supposed disparate strengths, this in effect meant that Prittwitz was to hold on as best he could, and when he no longer could hold he was to retreat to a line behind the Vistula River, there to await reinforcements. *

Rennenkampf's army reached East Prussia on August 17. Prittwitz duly ordered outposts to fall back while he shifted his forces for an attack. His orders were foolishly ignored by a feisty corps commander bravely contemptuous of the Russian army. This was General Hermann von François, who commanded I Corps, composed mostly of men from East Prussia who did not want to see their country overrun. Allowing emotion to overcome discipline, François attacked the Russian vanguard. A brief series of bloody engagements proved little more than the obvious fact that warfare kills men, in this instance men whom François would sorely miss in the trials ahead. Cured of his folly by higher command, François nevertheless persuaded Prittwitz to take up the offensive. Three days later Prittwitz attacked to begin the battle of Gumbinnen.

Negligent Russian cavalry failed to detect a night march by François, whose two divisions shattered the enemy around Gumbinnen. Otto von Below's I Reserve Corps on the right also made good progress, but in the center General August von Mackensen's XVII Corps attacked without having waited for adequate artillery preparation. Mackensen lost 8,000 men in a couple of hours and was saved from a Russian flank attack only with difficulty. But the Russians had suffered some 17,000 casualties, perhaps twenty percent of Rennenkampf's fighting strength. [40]

Prittwitz and his staff had decided to renew the attack when General von Scholtz, whose XX Army Corps was protecting the southern flank, reported that Samsonov's army had begun to cross the border.

The shock was the more considerable, since Prittwitz had been blind

---

* The genesis of this strategy went back to 1772, when King Frederick the Great acquired West Prussia to form a defensible buffer zone, the key to which was the Vistula. "Where earlier his army in East Prussia could fall back only on Königsberg and there perish, now, with the Niemen as the first line of defense, it could make a fighting withdrawal back to a second line, that of the Pregel, and finally to the Vistula." Robert B. Asprey, *Frederick the Great—The Magnificent Enigma.*

in the south. Early reports from Polish Jewish agents had dried up as Samsonov's vanguard occupied frontier districts. The Eighth Army possessed only one small aircraft unit, but reconnaissance in any event would have been difficult, since Samsonov's army marched mainly at night. The news caused Prittwitz and Waldersee to panic. Without discussing the matter with his staff, Prittwitz informed Moltke by telephone that he must retreat to the lower Vistula to avoid total defeat; indeed he must have immediate reinforcements if he were to hold there.

Moltke made it clear that he had no intention of abandoning East Prussia. Prittwitz was to hold at any cost. Waldersee meanwhile had become convinced by his staff that a retreat was unnecessary, even dangerous in view of Samsonov's army coming up from the south. Prittwitz instead should either continue with the present attack or back off from Rennenkampf's army, reinforce XX Corps, and attack Samsonov's left flank.

Having been suitably chastened by Moltke, Prittwitz accepted this plan but failed to notify the OHL of his decision. Two days later he learned by telegram that he had been replaced by his cousin, a sixty-seven-year-old retired general named Paul von Beneckendorff und von Hindenburg. Waldersee's replacement would be the recent hero of Liège and enfant terrible of the general staff, forty-nine-year-old General Erich Ludendorff.

5

Hindenburg and Ludendorff: The Meeting

> I am thirsting for a man's work to do, and it will be given me in full measure.
>   —General Erich Ludendorff, April 1914[1]

> At three o'clock in the afternoon of August 22 I received an inquiry from the Headquarters of His Majesty the Emperor as to whether I was prepared for immediate employment. My answer ran: "I am ready."
>   —General Paul von Hindenburg, August 1914[2]

Paul von Beneckendorff und von Hindenburg was the quintessential Prussian general from the Junker ruling classes. He claimed ancestors among the Teutonic knights who in 1410 were defeated at the battle of Tannenberg in East Prussia, and the family was supposed to have had a tenuous connection with Frederick the Great.

Born in Posen, West Prussia (today's Poland), in 1847, the son of an army lieutenant, he was the eldest of four children. His childhood was unpretentious but pleasant. The air he breathed was military: obedience to God and the German king, not necessarily in that order, a discipline enforced by a Prussian nurse whose favorite command to her wards was "Silence in the ranks."[3] School in Posen, where he had difficulty with arithmetic, was broken by long vacations at Neudeck, his grandparents' modest estate. Here he never tired of listening to stories told by a gardener who had served as a drummer boy in Frederick the Great's army.

True to Prussian tradition, he entered cadet school in Silesia at age eleven. Six years later he was commissioned a second lieutenant in the foot guards. His regiment had recently won a war against Denmark and was preparing for a new war against Austria. The eighteen-year-old lieutenant fought with distinction in the crucial battle of Königgrätz, was lightly wounded and suitably decorated. Four years later he fought in the Franco-Prussian War and was again decorated, this time with the Iron Cross. He was also chosen to represent his regiment at the coronation of Emperor Wilhelm I, a splendid event held in 1871 at the Palais de Versailles outside a besieged Paris.

Beneckendorff, as he was known in the army, spent a few years in mundane regimental duties before passing the necessary examinations to enter the Kriegsakademie for three years of advanced military studies. (He was carried on army lists as Beneckendorff and did not become famous as Hindenburg until the victory of Tannenberg. For convenience's sake, I shall henceforth call him Hindenburg.) Soon after graduation he was transferred to the Great General Staff. Promoted to captain and assigned to a corps at Stettin, he married Gertrude Wilhelmine von Sperling, a general's daughter who would bear him a son and two daughters. After several years of general-staff duties at corps and division level, including the famous annual "rides" during which various war plans were tested, he was transferred back to troop duty as a company commander in Posen.

Promoted to major and recalled to the Great General Staff, headed now by Field Marshal Count von Moltke, Hindenburg worked under Count von Schlieffen in writing the Field Service Regulations. He subsequently taught tactics at the Kriegsakademie while also serving as the senior general-staff officer of a corps. One of his numerous general-staff rides took place in East Prussia, where he and his fellow officers took the oath to the new emperor, Wilhelm II, in an inn at Gumbinnen.

Hindenburg by now was known in the general staff as a serious, hard-working professional soldier, moderate consumer of food and wine, articulate in speech and written word, a capable amateur painter, loyal to kaiser and God, not the brightest officer in the world but conscientious and, above all, cool, calm, and collected. Four years of duty in the war ministry were followed by assignment as chief of staff to an army corps, then to command of a division, and finally of a corps that, as a lieutenant general, he commanded at Magdeburg for over eight years.

Hindenburg later wrote that his decision to retire in 1911 at age sixty-four was made because there was no prospect of war and he believed that he should make way for younger officers. This is almost too noble. Hindenburg had never enjoyed royal favor. In 1905 Kaiser Wilhelm dismissed his candidacy for chief of the general staff on the grounds that he was a faultfinder. They subsequently clashed during an important maneuver. As commander in chief of the armed forces, the kaiser insisted on commanding an army corps in these annual exercises. Wilhelm knew very little about either strategy or tactics, but to the annoyance of the professionals he always insisted on winning "battles." Hindenburg, commanding an enemy corps, was said to have got the better of him, an insult never forgotten.

The Hindenburgs retired to the pleasant Guelph city of Hanover. The general led an active life, traveling to Italy with his wife, painting in watercolors, attending functions in nearby royal palaces, shooting birds, hunting deer and wild boar on private estates, enjoying numerous luncheon and dinner parties, the retired waistline comfortably expanding with each festive year.

Came August 1914. He saw son Oskar off to war. "As an old soldier let me tell you two things," he wrote to him, a latter-day Polonius. First, one must maintain "iron composure," which radiates downwards and prevents nervousness and panic among the troops. Second, one must exercise "untiring care for the troops. They sense that quickly and reward it with true devotion on the battlefield."[4] In Hanover trumpets sounded and horses neighed. Off went an importunate letter to General von Moltke. Nothing happened. Hindenburg had decided that nothing would happen when he received a telegram from the OHL asking if he would accept immediate service. He replied, "Am ready." From subsequent telegrams he learned that he had been promoted to full general and was to replace Maximilian von Prittwitz (his wife's cousin) in command of the Eighth Army in East Prussia. Frau von Hindenburg spent the afternoon in letting out his old-fashioned blue tunic and trousers.

At three in the morning of August 23 Paul von Hindenburg was waiting in the Hanover station for a special train from Coblenz. It consisted of two coaches holding one passenger, his newly appointed chief of staff, Erich Ludendorff.

Erich Friedrich Wilhelm Ludendorff, the quintessential general-staff technocrat from an impoverished family of tradesmen. He was born on a modest holding near Posen in 1865, the third of six children. The youngsters were educated by a maternal aunt. Erich entered cadet school in Holstein at age twelve. He was a good student who particularly liked military history, mathematics, and geography. Commissioned a lieutenant at seventeen, he served in a variety of peacetime garrisons before passing into the coveted Kriegsakademie. Appointment to the Great General Staff followed, where he served in the usual variety of staff and command posts before being promoted to major.

Ludendorff's considerable talents and unquestionable industry had soon brought him to Count von Schlieffen's attention. In 1904 he was assigned to the second section of the general staff, the "German Department," where he was involved with troop deployment plans. His work pleased both Schlieffen and his successor as chief of the German general staff, Helmuth von Moltke. After a two-year stint of teaching tactics and military history at the Kriegsakademie, Ludendorff was recalled to the second section, this time as its chief, a prestigious appointment, since it was presumed that in time of war he would become chief of operations, the most vital post in the German army.

Ludendorff was in habit a Schlieffen man. His first wife, Margarethe, whom he married in 1909, later wrote: "He was a man of iron principles. If work kept him up very late or we were at a ball or a party he still mounted his horse at seven the next morning, winter and summer." He was punctual to the minute: "Time was not reckoned in our house by hours, but by minutes." He could not have been easy to live or work with. He was generally tense, cold as a fish, a monocled humorless eye staring from a heavily jowled red face as he barked orders in a high, nasal voice, his second (and later third) chin quivering from the effort. He was rigid and inflexible in thought, given to sudden rages, a table banger, frequently rude to subordinates, often tactless to superiors. Margarethe wrote that "anyone who knows Ludendorff knows that he has not a spark of humor." The painter Hugo Vogel, who splashed out scores of heroic portraits of Hindenburg and Ludendorff during the war, told Margarethe that "your husband gives me cold shivers down my back."[5]

The serious-minded major was an advocate of what he called the "true form of war."[6] Contrary to Clausewitz's teachings, he subordinated politics to warfare and insisted that war must actively involve the entire nation. Convinced that war was inevitable against France and Russia, Ludendorff preached the necessity of a preventive war while doing what he could to prepare the army to fight it.

His friend and general-staff colleague, Wilhelm Groener, later described him as not unduly self-confident and ambitious in these early years, but also noted that he was uncompromising in belief. Groener wrote that at this time he won a considerable following of subordinates and students who were as eager for war as he was, but who were more impressed with his frankness and determination to prepare for this war than with his strategical thinking.[7]

Ludendorff waged an uphill battle in attempting to expand and strengthen the army. Although the imperial constitution drawn by Bismarck drastically limited the powers of the Reichstag, this body of elected representatives had to approve military budgets. Expenditures had long since grown to an awkward sum, thanks in large part to Admiral von Tirpitz's naval construction programs designed to attain warship parity with Great Britain, a fanciful desire ardently encouraged by Kaiser Wilhelm. The strong liberal contingent in the Reichstag, the Social Democrats, did not want increased military expenditures to prepare for a war that most believed would never come, a belief shared by a good many ordinary German subjects who would probably have agreed with Prince Bismarck that preventive war "represented an unwarranted interference with the ways of providence and was in any case as irrational as committing suicide because one was afraid to die."[8]

The Great General Staff preferred Frederick the Great's sophistry expressed on the eve of Prussian aggression that began the Seven Years' War:

Hostilities should not be confused with aggression. The one who makes the first plan to attack his neighbor breaks the engagements that he has undertaken for the peace—he plots, he conspires; this is in what true aggression consists. The one who has learned of it and who does not take the initiative is a coward; the one who foresees [the plan of] his enemy commits the first hostilities, but he is not the aggressor.[9]

Here was a perfect formula leapt on by the general staff. Having decided that France and Russia were planning *eventually* to *attack* Germany—a hypothetical assumption fed to the German people in massive daily doses over the years—the justifiable defense was to *attack* the enemy. To read general-staff correspondence with the war ministry in the four years prior to 1914 leaves little doubt that it was not only preparing for war, it was spoiling for war. "Our political and military situation makes it our duty to assemble all our available manpower for a struggle which will decide the existence or destruction of the German Empire"—this in the autumn of 1910.[10] The bellicose theme was hammered home in a best-selling book, *Germany and the Next War* by General

Friedrich von Bernhardi (whom Schlieffen had discharged from the general staff), that called for Germany to choose between "World Power or Decline."[11]

Ludendorff's proposed reforms were entirely in line with this pervasive and distorted military thinking, but they would have a cost a great deal of money. In 1908 he had begun pushing for a large increase in troop strength, arguing that the present annual increase of 10,000 recruits was insufficient. Germany, with a population of 65 million, supported an army of just over 600,000 men. France, with a population of less than 40 million, maintained an army of over 750,000. Germany called up 52 percent of its youth for training, France 82 percent. Russia boasted nearly twice as many soldiers and was about to increase the annual intake. Despite the figures, Moltke recognized that the Reichstag would not grant the necessary funds and declined to pursue the subject further.

But Ludendorff, the enfant terrible of the general staff, had already moved to greener pastures. Foreseeing immense battles upon the outbreak of war, he was arguing for more heavy artillery such as the heavy Krupp 420-mm "Big Bertha" howitzers, and for larger shell allowances for all artillery weapons, a campaign in which he was actively assisted by a clever if overly aggressive subordinate, Major Max Bauer. In 1912 Moltke, undoubtedly at Ludendorff's instigation, warned the minister of war that "after the first big battles the field artillery will have enough ammunition for a second battle . . . however, the supply for the heavy field howitzers cannot be fully replaced. We shall have to make do with these amounts of ammunition for seven to eight weeks and more. . . . That appears to me to be completely impossible. . . . I am virtually convinced that in a European war the last full [artillery] limber will have a vital influence on its outcome. Since we must reckon with two opponents who collectively are considerably superior to us, so must we provide considerably more ammunition than either of them."[12] The demand was again turned down, both on political and financial grounds.

A man with a cause is persistent. Ludendorff continued to argue, sometimes successfully, for other improvements, such as mobile field kitchens, better wireless equipment, more airships, or Zeppelins, and better antiaircraft defenses. When the airplane suggested tactical possibilities, he called for more planes and an air corps independent of the ground transport corps. He formed a number of reserve corps from mobile reserve divisions, but they were only half as strong in field artillery as a regular division, and they lacked adequate support troops. With great difficulty he converted the pool of replacement troops into six *ersatz* or replacement divisions, but failed to persuade the war ministry to fund the training of necessary reservists.

He continued to call for a large increase in troops. The Moroccan crisis of 1911 had caused the government to raise the annual increase in recruits to 40,000, but Ludendorff insisted on more. He found only lukewarm support from Moltke. "I have to make Moltke stand his ground by gripping him like a vise," he complained to Margarethe, "otherwise I think his weakness would bring him to utter ruin."[13] Ludendorff now vented his frustration by covertly (and illegally) turning to a retired general, August Keim, who was a bastion of the Pan-German League, an expansionist organization supported by powerful industrialists and conservative bankers, agrarians, and politicians. In 1912 Keim organized the Wehrverein, or Union of Defense, whose propagandistic appeals for a larger army were widely supported by middle-class industrialists, businessmen, and educators—even by Kaiser Wilhelm when Turkey's collapse in the Balkans exposed Germany's main ally, Austria-Hungary, to attack from the south. The ensuing campaign, which raised an impressive thousand million marks by voluntary contributions, resulted in another increase for the army of over 100,000 men.

Ludendorff continued to pound at what he believed to be serious deficiencies. In early November 1912 he was probably responsible for a letter from Moltke to the war minister warning against the concept of a one-battle war. "We must realize now that we are faced with a tedious campaign, with a series of severe and long drawn-out battles before we overthrow *even one* of our enemies; our efforts and wastage will increase if we are compelled to obtain successive victories in different theaters of war in the west and east, and have to fight against superior numbers from the outset. A large amount of ammunition for a very long period of time will become an inexorable necessity."[14] A letter later in the month called for Germany to utilize fully "our human assets. We must again become a nation in arms. . . . For Germany there can be no going backward, only forward."[15]

In late December 1912 the chancellor of Germany, Theobald von Bethmann Hollweg, the minister of war, General Josias von Heeringen, and the chief of the kaiser's military cabinet, General Moritz Baron von Lyncker, received a general-staff study almost certainly written by Ludendorff that called attention to Germany's precarious position vis-à-vis Russia and France. The army must have an additional 300,000 men in order to form three new corps. Arms and equipment had to be improved, and large-scale construction of land fortifications was vital, above all in the east. The demands drew a prescient observation from a general in the war ministry that "Ludendorff would end by driving Germany to revolution."[16] Ludendorff by now had made so many enemies in the kaiser's military cabinet and in the war ministry that Moltke was forced to put him out to pasture in the form of a regimental command in Düsseldorf.

This was scarcely more than a slap on the wrist. We shortly find Moltke writing to congratulate Ludendorff on being decorated by the kaiser "in recognition of your effort" on behalf of the army. Moltke thanked him "once again for his effort and support."[17]

A young lieutenant remembered Ludendorff as an aloof and uncommunicative commander with the ways of a petty-minded bureaucrat, yet he preferred subordinates who would speak up when necessary. Younger officers were often guests in his house, which was made particularly pleasant by his charming and warm-hearted wife and her four children, to whom Ludendorff seemed to be more father than stepfather. They also enjoyed his practice of taking them to his study after dinner to relate his experiences in the general staff and his bureaucratic battles to improve the strength of the army.

He was obviously an active and rigorous commander. Not long after joining the regiment, he characteristically wrote to General von Stein "that he did not entirely agree with the prevalent views of discipline," which he found surprisingly soft and indulgent: "Thus it became necessary for me to apply a firm hand." Nor did the tactical development of officers entirely please him. "There is much, very much to make up for. I've taken it in hand. But everything takes time and one can't accomplish one's goal by rashness. I therefore designed my own training style. I hope to bring them around more in the long summer training; I particularly look forward to the regimental and brigade exercises and maneuvers."

The maneuvers disappointed him tactically, as did the performance of his corps commander, General Karl von Einem. "We fought in too close formation," he wrote to von Stein. "For a corps maneuver against a specific enemy, the corps in the end had a breadth of only three kilometers. So we could not use our guns efficiently, but General von Einem will have it that way." His own regiment's performance pleased him. It "is now considered to be in good shape. After the maneuver I shall turn to the individual training of officers and men. To my delight I find that most of them conform and are grateful. A few will always prefer eternal sleep . . . anyway I've given the troops more to think about than was earlier the case here."[18]

Ludendorff may have had powerful enemies, but Moltke highly valued his professional ability. Transferred to a brigade command in April 1914, he was recalled to the general staff three months later. "I am thirsting for a man's work to do," he wrote to his wife, "and it will be given me in full measure."[19] The first pouring occurred at Liège shortly after the outbreak of war, when Ludendorff reaped sudden fame by his meritorious surprise of Liège. He was still in Belgium when Moltke appointed him chief of staff of the Eighth Army on the critical East Prussian front, writing to the forty-nine-year-old general: "You are being given a new and difficult task, perhaps even more difficult than the assault on Lüttich [Liège]. . . . I know no other man in whom I would have such absolute trust as yourself. Perhaps you can salvage the situation in the east. Naturally you cannot be held responsible for what has happened but with your energy you can still prevent the worst. Accept then this new call, which is the greatest honor a soldier can receive. I know that you will not belie the trust placed in you."[20] As an afterthought Moltke added that one Lieutenant General von Beneckendorff was probably going to be the new commander of the Eighth Army.

This was confirmed when Ludendorff arrived in Coblenz on August 22 to be greeted by Moltke and the kaiser, who decorated him with the coveted medal, the elegant blue, white, and gold cross called the Pour le mérite. There Ludendorff learned that the Eighth Army was slowly retreating westward. Ludendorff's orders, telegraphed directly to corps commanders (thus bypassing Prittwitz and his staff), called for François's I Corps to move south by rail to support Scholtz's XX Corps against Samsonov's advance. Mackensen's and Below's corps were to rest for a day and await further orders. Eighth Army headquarters was ordered to move to Marienburg.

Ludendorff departed from Coblenz that evening on a small private train that reached Hanover shortly after three A.M. Hindenburg was waiting on the platform, wearing his recently altered old blue uniform. Ludendorff, smartly dressed in a tailored gray uniform, monocle at the ready, "stepped briskly from the train" and saluted his superior. They resumed the journey to begin what Hindenburg later called a "happy marriage" (without mentioning that it ended in explosive divorce).[21]

Hindenburg had never met Ludendorff and, inexplicably, "had not yet heard of his feats at Liège." Ludendorff dutifully briefed him on the events in East Prussia, apparently in the broadest of terms, since the conference lasted "scarcely more than half an hour" before they retired.[22]

The train stopped in Berlin the next morning to pick up Ludendorff's wife, Margarethe. She found Hindenburg to be "calm and cheerful," but grumbling about his obsolete uniform and boots.[23] The little train passed several immense troop trains heading east, the carriages festooned with flowers, the soldiers laughing and singing. Margarethe left them at Cüstrin. Hindenburg and Ludendorff arrived in Marienburg that evening.

They were met by senior general-staff officers of the Eighth Army, only a few of whom recognized General von Hindenburg. All of them knew Ludendorff. The key staff officer was the chief of operations, forty-five-year-old Lieutenant Colonel Max Hoffmann. Carl Adolf Maximilian Hoffmann: *der Lange*—the tall one, as he was known to his colleagues —was scarcely the quintessential Prussian officer, despite close-cropped hair that covered a massive skull, pince-nez resting on a nose above thin lips and a determined chin. He was "almost the worst athlete, horseman, swordsman of them all," wrote his biographer. His gargantuan appetite for food, drink, and "creature comforts" was legendary. At times he lived on Moselle wine (two bottles before breakfast), strong Turkish coffee, and large snifters of brandy.

Ludendorff was no stranger to this eccentric behavior. They had served together at Posen and for four years had lived in the same house in Berlin. Hoffmann's grace was more than saving, it was vital. His was one of the keenest minds in the Great General Staff. Though their styles were different, Ludendorff and Hoffmann shared a common belief in the Frederician-Schlieffen tradition of desiring "decisive" battles.[24]

So began the saga of what the staff called *das Hünentrio*—the Three Giants.

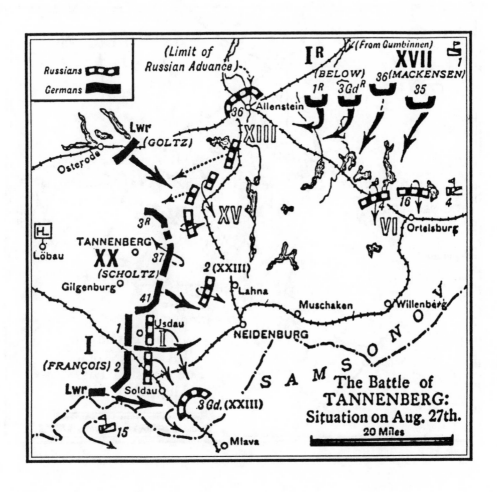

Russians ▭▭
Germans ▬

(Limit of
Russian Advance)

I R
(From Gumbinnen)
XVII
(BELOW)
36 (MACKENSEN)

1R 3Gd R   35

36 Allenstein

XIII

Lwr
(GOLTZ)

Osterode

XV

16   4
4

3R   VI   Ortelsburg
TANNENBERG   37
Löbau
XX
(SCHOLTZ)   2 (XXIII)
Gilgenburg   41   Lahna
Muschaken   Willenberg
1   Usdau
I   NEIDENBURG
(FRANÇOIS) 2
S A M S O N O V
Lwr   Soldau
3 Gd. (XXIII)   The Battle of
TANNENBERG:
Situation on Aug. 27th.
15   20 Miles
Mlava

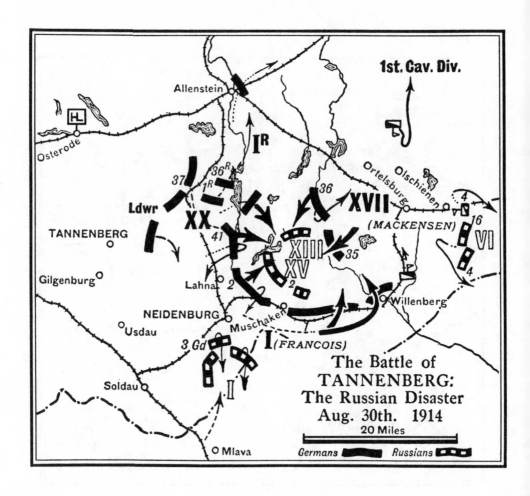

1st. Cav. Div.

Allenstein

Osterode

I^R

Ortelsburg

Olschienen

37 36^R

36

1^R

Ldwr

XX

XVII

(MACKENSEN)

16

TANNENBERG

41

XIII

35

VI

XV

Gilgenburg

Lahna

2

2

Willenberg

NEIDENBURG

Muschaken

Usdau

I (FRANCOIS)

3 Gd

The Battle of
TANNENBERG:
The Russian Disaster
Aug. 30th. 1914

Soldau

II

20 Miles

Mlava

Germans   Russians

6

The Battle of Tannenberg

There has never been and no doubt will never be again such
a war as this—fought with such bestial fury. The Russians are
burning everything down.
—LIEUTENANT COLONEL MAX HOFFMANN,
AUGUST 23, 1914[1]

L egends abound. It was Hindenburg who planned the entire battle
of the East Prussian frontiers years before while tramping through
the flat landscape of the Masurian Lakes; or it was Ludendorff who
planned the entire battle after a quick look at Eighth Army reports in
Coblenz; or it was Max Hoffmann who planned the entire battle on the
basis of personal belief that Rennenkampf and Samsonov hated each
other's guts and one would not come to the aid of the other.[2]

None of these gentlemen planned the entire battle. The possibility
of such a battle had been foreseen by Frederick the Great, who almost
a century and a half earlier had joined in the first rape of Poland in order
to create a buffer zone against the Russian menace. The battle had been
foreseen by General von Schlieffen over a decade earlier. The attacking
Russian armies would perforce be split by the fifty-mile-long chain of the
Masurian Lakes. The problem was first to check the attack that offered
the less serious threat, then use interior lines of communication to shift
forces to meet the main attack.

This scenario had become general-staff dogma. It had been worked
out over the years in numerous "rides" participated in by Hindenburg,
Ludendorff, Hoffmann, and many, many others. It was why General Max
von Prittwitz, commanding the Eighth Army, was prodded by his chief

of staff, Count von Waldersee, his quartermaster general, General Grü-
nert, and his operations officer, Max Hoffmann, to reverse his decision
to retreat in favor of screening General Rennenkampf's army, attacking
from the northeast while shifting his divisions to strike the left flank of
General Samsonov's army, which was driving into East Prussia from the
southeast. It was why Ludendorff had telegraphed similar orders from
Coblenz, though obfuscating matters by authorizing a day of rest to two
corps when they should have been on the march southward, a "rather
unfortunate" twist, as Hoffmann later noted.[3]

So in one important sense the little group gathered around the maps
in Marienburg headquarters on that Sunday evening in August had very
little to discuss. François's somewhat battered I Corps was being shuttled
by rail from Gumbinnen and the Insterburg gap southwest to tie in with
Scholtz's XX Corps, already in action, in order to attack Samsonov's left
wing. This was a move of well over one hundred miles. Impeded by an
inadequate rail system and by thousands of refugees jamming the few
narrow roads, it would not be completed for a day or two, although
advance elements had detrained and were marching on a village called
Tannenberg. The newly arrived German commanders learned that according to German cavalry reports, Rennenkampf, some thirty miles
distant, was still standing. Ludendorff nevertheless was not yet ready to
move the two remaining corps south to attack Samsonov's right wing.

Two days later, when cavalry reports and intercepted wireless messages confirmed that Rennenkampf showed no inclination to advance,
Ludendorff ordered Below's I Reserve Corps and Mackensen's XVII Corps
to march southwest and attack Samsonov's right. His decision was not
made lightly. It meant that only one cavalry division and a brigade of
Landwehr would stand between Rennenkampf and the widely deployed
Eighth Army to the south. One can readily sympathize with Ludendorff's
hesitation and subsequent worries. He would have been greatly relieved,
however, if he had known what was happening in the enemy camp.

Rennenkampf and Samsonov were operating virtually independently
of each other, largely the fault of General Zhilinski, commanding the
Russian northwestern front from headquarters in Volkovysk, about two
hundred miles from the two armies. Misinformed by Rennenkampf that
two German corps were retreating on fortress Königsberg, Zhilinski would
soon order the fortress to be invested, thus relieving Rennenkampf of
responsibility for offensive action southward.

Samsonov's advancing Second Army had fallen into such disarray that one is reminded of Frederick the Great's caustic description of his army after the disastrous campaign of 1759: Part of it "was fit only to be shown at a distance to the enemy . . . the other part was discouraged and dispirited."[4] This was the inevitable result of conflicting orders based on inaccurate intelligence, poor internal organization, and a general breakdown of communications and supply.

Aleksandr Samsonov had commanded a cavalry division in the Russo-Japanese War. A subsequent rather undistinguished career had scarcely fitted him for command of an army of thirteen divisions. Fifty-five years old, an asthmatic, "a man of simple and kindly nature," according to his British liaison officer, General Alfred Knox, he was doing his best to carry out his mission of outflanking the Eighth Army to prevent its retreat to the Vistula. He was assisted by his chief of staff, General Potovski, a nervous man known to the army as "the mad Mullah," who regarded the advance as an "adventure."[5]

It certainly was that. The army that began moving into East Prussia on August 19 was not ready for war. Its regiments were composed largely of peasants who had left the harvest for the recruiting depot "and thence to the church" to take communion.[6] Neither spirit nor trust was lacking. Maurice Paléologue, the French ambassador in Petrograd, wrote of the enormous crowd that gathered in front of the Winter Palace to hear Czar Nicholas's proclamation of war. When he appeared on the balcony "the entire crowd at once knelt and sang the Russian national anthem. To those thousands of men on their knees at that moment the Tsar was really the autocrat appointed of God, the military, political and religious leader of his people, the absolute power of their bodies and souls." Eight days later on August 10 he noted: "Everywhere . . . the same popular demonstrations, the same grave and religious enthusiasms, the same impulse to rally round the Tsar, the same faith in victory, the same exultation of the national conscience. No opposition, no dissentient voice. The bad days of 1905 seem to have gone from the memory of all. The collective soul of Holy Russia has never manifested itself so forcibly since 1812."[7]

Spirit and trust were unable to overcome poor planning and command ineptitude. Eager peasants, rushed into ill-fitting uniforms and given a rifle and pack, found themselves in units short of officers and NCOs. March orders were confusing and often contradictory. There were not enough horses to pull the heavy artillery and the thousands of supply wagons over narrow, sandy roads. Communications were totally inadequate, both within single corps and between corps commands and army. Telegrams from Zhilinski's headquarters piled up in Warsaw, and those that did reach Samsonov were not very helpful. *Hurry . . . hurry . . . hurry* was their gist. "The Army is advancing according to the timetable . . . without halting, covering marches of more than twelve miles [a day] over the sand. . . . I cannot go more quickly," Samsonov protested. "I must have immediate and decisive operations," Zhilinski demanded on August 22. Samsonov again replied that he could not move more rapidly. "It is essential to organize the rear services [of supply]. This has up to the present not been done. The country is devastated, the horses have long been without oats, and there is no bread."[8]

Samsonov's center first made contact with the Germans in heavily wooded country broken by marshes and a few unimproved roads. This was XV Corps commanded by General Martos, "a small man with a grey beard," Knox tells us, "and a great reputation as a disciplinarian."[9] Corps Martos pushed Scholtz back some ten miles while XIII Corps came up on Martos's right with VI Corps protecting the army's extreme flank. Zhilinski informed Samsonov on August 23 that the enemy was retreating, leaving only inconsiderable forces in front of him. "Therefore . . . you will advance energetically . . . to meet the enemy retreating in front of General Rennenkampf, and to cut off his retreat from the Vistula."[10]

Prompted in part by Zhilinski's peremptory order, in part by initial local successes, Samsonov ordered a general attack for the next day. Lacking sufficient wire to communicate with their corps, army headquarters had to rely on wireless. Proper codes were lacking. Samsonov's orders went out in clear, that is, without being coded, and were intercepted by German listening stations.

General Knox witnessed the enthusiastic attack by Corps Martos, which was supported by highly effective artillery fire. "The Russians used the spade freely. . . . I saw rifle trenches scooped out within 130 yards of the defenders' trenches. The German machine guns were deadly, running down rows of Russians immediately they raised themselves in the potato-fields to fire or to advance. . . . one Russian regiment had nine company commanders killed out of sixteen, and one company which went into action 190 strong lost all its officers and 120 men killed." After spending the night seven hundred yards from the German trenches, a dawn assault broke the German right. As the action petered out the battlefield was cleared only with difficulty. "We saw German and Russian wounded being carried from a field on which they must have lain at least thirty-six hours." The Russians estimated their losses at 4,000, enemy losses at 6,000.[11]

Aware of Samsonov's plans, Ludendorff had ordered Hermann von François's I Corps to attack the Russian left wing on August 25. François refused. His troops, tired from earlier fighting in which he had taken considerable casualties, were still detraining, neither his heavy artillery nor his ammunition trains had arrived, and he had been assured by General Scholtz that XX Corps could hold its ground. His insubordination infuriated Ludendorff, already upset by a report that Rennenkampf's "formidable host," which "hung like a threatening thunder-cloud to the northeast," showed signs of marching southwest. "He need only have closed with us and we should have been beaten," he later wrote.[12] Hoffmann sardonically noted that the hero of Liège "seems to have lost his nerve a little."[13] Hindenburg, who claimed not to have had the slightest hesitation in thinly screening Rennenkampf's army, later wrote of overcoming the "inward crisis" by adhering to "our original intention,"[14] a process considerably aided by additional intercepted wireless messages: Rennenkampf had been ordered to invest Königsberg fortress, which meant that he no longer offered an immediate threat to the battle in the south.

Accompanied by Hindenburg and Hoffmann, Ludendorff was driven to François's headquarters on August 26. Here he explained that Samsonov was attacking the German center. Even while they were talking, Below and Mackensen were moving on the Russian right wing. It was vital for François to attack. He did not agree with what he later called "a piece of tactical impudence that would have doubtless led to complete disaster."[15] With Ludendorff breathing down his neck, François responded with a deliberately cautious attack that picked up momentum only when his artillery was in position.[16]

Ludendorff was not the only general to be seized by a fit of nerves during these crucial days. Although Samsonov remained calm, a host of tactical doubts was feeding on his chief of staff's mind. The troops were tired and hungry, they had eaten their emergency rations, no food was coming forward, they were nearly out of ammunition, no provisions had been made for wounded men. A division staff officer reported that the men are "terribly exhausted, having very few rounds [of rifle ammunition] in their possession. They had been three days without bread or sugar." A regimental commander counted only "450 men. For two days they had received no rations."[17] Aware now that he was not attacking a retreating enemy, as Zhilinski, prompted by Rennenkampf, insisted was the case, Samsonov requested permission to shift his advance to the west, a request peremptorily refused by the army group commander, who insisted that he continue his present attack to the north.

Zhilinski himself was in a dangerous mental state, privately believing "that an offensive in East Prussia is doomed to certain defeat."[18] That he had lost control of the situation was obvious to the Stavka supreme command. On August 26 the commander in chief of the Russian army, Grand Duke Nicholas, who was the czar's uncle, visited Zhilinski's headquarters and apparently ordered his subordinate to support Samsonov. Zhilinksi instead ordered two corps of Rennenkampf's army to invest fortress Königsberg and the other two corps to pursue the retreating enemy. Nothing was urgent; Samsonov's plight was not mentioned. Only on August 27 did Zhilinski seem to realize that Samsonov was in serious trouble. He telegraphed this information to Rennenkampf and ordered him to move his left flank as far forward as possible. These and other orders were as usual sent by wireless in the clear and were intercepted by the Germans.

General Helmuth von Moltke at the OHL, Coblenz, was also a worried man. The Great General Staff had badly miscalculated. Russian mobilization was supposed to take a minimum of six weeks. Yet within two weeks two large armies had fallen on weakly defended East Prussia. Prittwitz's retreat could not totally be hidden from the German people. Thousands of refugees carried tales of horror to cities and towns throughout Germany. Junker landowners demanded that their estates, with thousands of hectares of rich grain, be saved from Cossack predators. Moltke knew that Ludendorff intended to attack, but he could not know that the attack would succeed. The situation on the western front, on the other hand, was very favorable. The battle of the Frontiers, which cost the French three hundred thousand casualties according to some estimates, had been irreversibly won. The German right wing was sweeping into France. The war would shortly be over, but it would avail nothing if meanwhile Russian armies arrived in Berlin.

So it was that on August 25 Moltke's chief of operations, Lieutenant Colonel Gerhard Tappen, telephoned Ludendorff to say that the OHL was sending him three infantry corps and one cavalry division. Ludendorff was surprised, but like most generals he was not inclined to look a gift horse in the mouth. According to his own account, he told Tappen that he did not really need the reinforcement, which in any event would arrive too late for the pending battle, but when Tappen said that the troops could be spared he obligingly agreed to take them. In any event, two infantry corps and one cavalry division were sent.[19]

François cut loose before dawn on August 27, a vicious artillery bombardment preceding an attack by two divisions against the right wing of General Artamonov's I Corps at Usdau. Ludendorff, with Hindenburg and Hoffmann in tow, was still on his way to the battlefield when he learned that the attack had broken through Artamonov's right. By late morning the defenders were in full flight to the border and beyond. By evening François's vanguard was in Soldau in the rear of the Russian left.

Samsonov's attack in the center had meanwhile been pushing back Scholtz's XX Corps. On August 28 Ludendorff conferred with Scholtz in corps headquarters at the village of Frögenau. Ludendorff, in a state of nerves and seemingly unaware of the tactical opportunity presented by François's brilliant advance, ordered François to send back a division to support the "greatly exhausted" XX Corps and to advance his remaining division northeast toward Lahna. François ignored the order to continue his push eastward toward Neidenburg.[20] Upon learning that his center was after all secure, Ludendorff awoke to splendid reality of the favorable tactical situation and ordered François to press on toward Willenberg while Mackensen attacked from the other wing.

None of these movements was easy on a confused battlefield that stretched across more than sixty miles of marshy woods and lakes intersected by primitive sandy roads. Reports from cavalry patrols were limited and often confused, as were those from pilots of the army's few aircraft. Communications were primitive. Motorcars carrying staff-officer messengers got lost or bogged down, orders were late in arriving. Despite these and other difficulties, François's cavalry linked up the next morning with forward elements of Mackensen's corps. By nightfall François held the road between Neidenburg and Willenberg. Samsonov's army was surrounded, its lines of retreat blocked to such an extent that Hindenburg had already reported the complete collapse of the Narev Army to Kaiser Wilhelm.

The game was up for Samsonov. There was no sign of help from Rennenkampf, whose closest corps were still miles away. Cut from his left and right, his center began to disintegrate. Panic-stricken men threw down rifles and ran, only to find that there was no escape. The hated Cossacks tore distinguishing broad stripes from their trousers to avoid being shot on sight by German captors. Companies, battalions, regiments, even entire brigades surrendered. In a last-ditch effort to restore order Samsonov, with a small staff, rode from his Neidenburg headquarters to take personal command of the battle. General Knox described him as worried but calmly philosophical. "The enemy has luck one day, we shall have luck another," he told Knox as he rode off.[21]

Samsonov soon accepted the inevitable and ordered a general retreat. The army now collapsed, many of its generals and senior officers killed or captured. Samsonov and his small party, in trying to reach Willenberg (already held by the Germans), got lost in a swampy wood. Samsonov was deep in melancholy, wheezing painfully, repeatedly telling his chief of staff, "The Emperor trusted me. How can I face him again after such a disaster?" Shortly after midnight he slipped away from his officers and was believed to have killed himself.[22]

Samsonov's Second Army had virtually ceased to exist by August 31. A jubilant Hindenburg informed the kaiser that "the XIII, XV and XVIII [Russian army corps] have been destroyed. We have already taken more than 60,000 prisoners. . . . The guns are still in the forests and are now being brought in. The booty is immense though it cannot yet be assessed in detail."[23] The final prisoner count was well over 90,000. Probably ninety percent of Samsonov's artillery was lost, along with thousands of horses killed or captured. Two corps were almost totally destroyed, three other corps were shattered, the remnants in retreat all the way to Warsaw. Perhaps 30,000 Russians were killed. The official German figures claim a total Russian loss of some 250,000 against 37,000 German casualties.[24]

It was a curious victory that does not easily lend itself to fruitful analysis. Hoffmann generously praised Ludendorff for planning the thrust through Usdau. François denied Ludendorff "any credit for the success," and years later wrote to Hoffmann that "Ludendorff's memoirs have no historical value."[25] Certainly the inept Russian performance contributed mightily to the outcome. Conflicting orders from the top, uncoordinated movements by ill-trained and ill-equipped soldiers, wireless messages sent in the clear—what enemy could have dreamed of it?

What Max Hoffmann called "one of the greatest victories in history" needed a name.[26] Frögenau, from where Hindenburg and Ludendorff directed the battle, seemed far too prosaic. The nearby village of Tannenberg had a better ring. Here the Teutonic Knights had been defeated by the Polish and Lithuanians just over five hundred years earlier, a defeat at long last avenged—or so went the somewhat odd reasoning. Hindenburg, Ludendorff, and Hoffmann each claimed credit for the inspiration. No matter the author. News of the victory had already swept through the empire. God was obviously on the side of Germany. The army was obviously invincible. No good German could now doubt that the war would soon end in total victory.

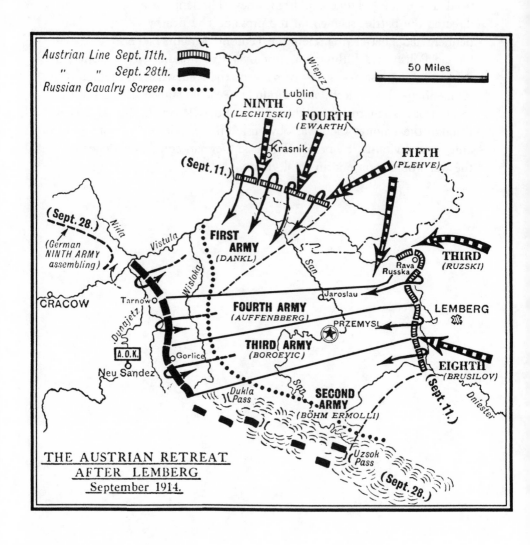

Austrian Line Sept. 11th. ⊞⊞⊞⊞
"   "   Sept. 28th. ■■
Russian Cavalry Screen ●●●●●●

50 Miles

Lublin

NINTH
(LECHITSKI)   FOURTH
(EWARTH)

FIFTH
(PLEHVE)

Krasnik

(Sept. 11.)

(Sept. 28.)

(German
NINTH ARMY
assembling)

FIRST
ARMY
(DANKL)

THIRD
(RUZSKI)

Rava
Russka

CRACOW

Tarnow

Vistula

Nitla

Wisloka

San

Jaroslau

LEMBERG

FOURTH ARMY
(AUFFENBBERG)

PRZEMYSL

Dunajetz

A.O.K.

Gorlice

THIRD ARMY
(BOROEVIC)

EIGHTH
(BRUSILOV)

Neu Sandez

Dukla
Pass

Sm

SECOND
ARMY
(BÖHM ERMOLLI)

(Sept. 11.)

Dniester

THE AUSTRIAN RETREAT
AFTER LEMBERG
September 1914.

Uzsok
Pass

(Sept. 28.)

Wiepiz

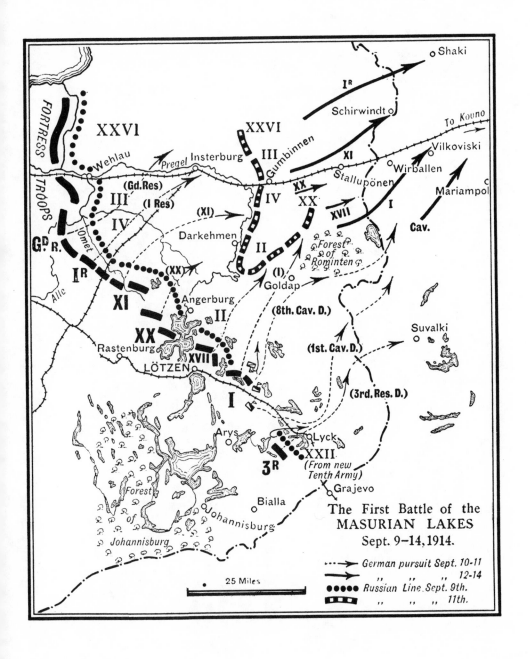

The First Battle of the
MASURIAN LAKES
Sept. 9–14, 1914.

German pursuit Sept. 10-11
,,   ,,   ,,   12-14
Russian Line Sept. 9th.
,,   ,,   ,,   11th.

25 Miles

7

The New Idols

Now we are preparing for something new. Ludendorff is a first-
class fellow to work with. He is the right man for this
business—ruthless and hard. We get on admirably.
—LIEUTENANT COLONEL MAX HOFFMANN,
SEPTEMBER 4, 1914[1]

Ludendorff later wrote that he could not rejoice over victory at
Tannenberg "because the strain on my nerves by the uncertainty
about Rennenkampf's army had been too great."[2] That concern
remained. German troops were singing a hymn of thanks composed over
a century and a half earlier to commemorate Frederick the Great's victory
at Leuthen when a new order from the OHL arrived: "The first task of
the Eighth Army is to clear East Prussia of Rennenkampf's army. . . .
When the situation in East Prussia has been restored, you are to contemplate employing the Eighth Army in the direction of Warsaw."[3]

Samsonov's Second Army may have been temporarily knocked out
of the war, but Rennenkampf's First Army remained a very dangerous
entity that stretched across East Prussia from the portals of fortress Königsberg southeast to the border of Russian Poland. Zhilinski had sent
reinforcements to bring Rennenkampf's strength to twelve divisions and
was also assembling a new Tenth Army to cover his weak left flank.[4]

Ludendorff's concern was compounded by the successful Russian
offensive against Conrad von Hötzendorf's Austro-Hungarian armies in
Galicia. Here General Nikolai Ivanov, whose chief of staff was General
Mikhail Alekseyev, commanded Army Group Southwest. Ivanov, according to Brusilov, was a devoted professional soldier but was "narrow-

minded, lacking in decision, a stickler for details, and in a general way deficient in intelligence, though not in self-esteem."[5] General Knox described him as the "most thoroughly Russian in appearance and character of all the Russian leaders," a kind and thoughtful man, simple and unpretentious, and very popular with his staff, "with whom he continually converses."[6] Brusilov judged Alekseyev to be "a very intelligent man, and a fine strategist. His chief fault was indecision and a want of moral courage."[7]

Ivanov's immense command consisted of four armies—from right to left the Fourth (Baron Salza, soon replaced by Evert), the Fifth (Paval Plehve), the Third (Nikolai Ruzski), and the Eighth (Aleksey Brusilov). Opposite this force of some 750,000 men, the sixty-four-year-old Conrad had assembled three armies—from left to right the First (Viktor Count Dankl), the Fourth (Moritz Baron Auffenberg), and the Third (Rudolf von Brudermann)—some 500,000 troops soon to be reinforced by General Eduard Baron von Böhm-Ermolli's Second Army which Conrad had sent to Serbia only to summon it hastily to Galicia.

On August 23, the day that Hindenburg and Ludendorff arrived in Marienburg, Conrad opened an offensive on a 175-mile front, his right flank on the Dniester River, his left flank south of Lublin where it was supported by General Remus von Woyrsch's weak corps of German Landwehr troops. Conrad's main threat came from his left, where Dankl's First Army and Auffenberg's Fourth Army attacked north from fortress Przemyśl while von Brudermann's Third Army disobeyed orders by attacking northeast from Lemberg. Dankl almost immediately struck Salza's Fourth Russian Army at Kraśnik, a surprise for the Russians, whose cavalry was rapidly proving useless in reconnaissance, but a surprise, too, for the Austrians, whose cavalry ran into Russian infantry and was shot from the field.

Somewhere along that vicious battle line a young Austrian named Friedrich Feuchtinger would never forget the terrible day of August 26. As he later described it, his regiment coming from reserve to the front was struck by an artillery barrage that sent the troops temporarily to ground. "We crept slowly forward, saw our comrades suddenly fall, heard them scream and bellow in pain, saw the white puffs of exploding shells overhead." Then came the bugle call to attack. The men moved out shrieking and howling against fear. "I glance briefly to the left at my friend; his eyes loom ghastly from their sockets, his face is distorted, I no longer recognize him. On the right the young drummer with his bloodshot feverish eyes, his quivering almost crying mouth and the pale lips, no longer is he that young lad whose vigorous drumrolls brought us once more to our tired feet. I look at him once again, see his eyes widen and his mouth open; blood runs from it and he calls a throaty 'Mother,' then he sinks down dead. We run on with gasping breath; dead and wounded lie all around and we look at them indifferently, like wild animals." The assault struck the first enemy trenches. The Russians ran. One of them stopped not far ahead of Feuchtinger, turned, held out his right hand while his left hand went to his tunic pocket. Feuchtinger bayonetted him. "I see his blood redden his uniform, hear him moan and groan as he twists with the bayonet in the young body. I am seized with terror. I throw myself down, crawl to him, wanting to help him. But he is dead. I pull my blood-stained bayonet from the dead body. Wanting to fold his hands, I see in the left hand a crumpled photo of his wife and child."[8]

The battle lasted for three days of attack and counterattack before Salza broke it off to retire on Lublin. He had suffered heavy casualties (including 6,000 men taken prisoner), and was replaced by Evert.

As the battle of Kraśnik ended, the action shifted to Auffenberg's Austrian Fourth Army, which attacked General Paval Plehve's Fifth Army to begin a week of vicious fighting. Auffenberg was winning when he was forced to help Baron von Brudermann's Third Army on his right. Brudermann's precipitate two-pronged attack to the north and northeast had run into General Ruzski's Third Army and Brusilov's Eighth Army. The ensuing battle was a serious Austrian defeat which forced Brudermann to retire on Lemberg within a few days and with extremely heavy losses. On Ivanov's command, Ruzski and Brusilov stayed where they were until Grand Duke Nicholas overruled the decision and ordered them to attack. Two days later Brudermann, under heavy attack, abandoned his new line to leave Lemberg under siege.[9]

The famous Austrian violinist Fritz Kreisler commanded a platoon in this furious action. In but a brief period of time he and his fifty-five men had forgotten "luxury, refinement, in fact all the gentler aspects of life. . . . Centuries drop from one, and one becomes a primeval man. . . . For twenty-one days I went without taking off my clothes, sleeping on wet grass or in mud, or in the swamps. . . . Many things considered necessities of civilization simply drop out of existence. A toothbrush was not imaginable. We ate instinctively, when we had food, with our hands. . . . We were all looking like shaggy, lean wolves, from the necessity of subsisting on next to nothing. I remember having gone for more than three days at a time without any food whatsoever, and many a time we had to lick the dew from the grass for want of water. A certain fierceness arises in you, an absolute indifference to anything the world holds except your duty of fighting." At one point in the retreat Kreisler's platoon held a trench for four days about five hundred yards from a Russian trench. One enemy began calling to another until a virtual truce resulted. It culminated in one unarmed Austrian soldier meeting one unarmed Russian soldier midway between trenches. The laughing Russian gave the laughing Austrian a packet of tobacco and received a cigar. Soldiers leaned from both trenches to join in the fun. The unofficial truce lasted about twenty minutes "and succeeded more in restoring good humor and joy of life among our soldiers than a trainload of provisions would have done." The two men returned to their trenches and the war began again, but when medics went to collect the wounded and dead, no one fired on them.[10]

Some historians have called Conrad the greatest strategist of the war, though this writer cannot imagine why. Conrad was a great dreamer, forever coming up with Tannenberg-like envelopment schemes while forgetting the pathetic inadequacy of the forces at his disposal. At this crucial point he ordered Brudermann and Böhm-Ermolli, who commanded the newly arrived Second Army, to remain on the defensive while Auffenberg's Fourth Army marched south to strike the flank of Ruzski's Third Army, at which moment Brudermann and Böhm-Ermolli would fall on the Russian left. This plan fell through when Brudermann's front again gave way to force another serious retreat, the prelude to a tactical disaster that would drastically change the fortunes of war.

Ludendorff's considerable assets partially countered these worries. He had been reinforced by two infantry corps and a cavalry division from the western front. The Eighth Army now counted eighteen-plus infantry divisions, two cavalry divisions, and over twelve hundred guns. It was slightly stronger than Rennenkampf's First Army and was far better organized and supplied. Influenced by victory at Tannenberg, Ludendorff's plans called for a strong force of two corps under von François to traverse the lake region, roll up the extended and weak Russian left, and work behind Rennenkampf's center, the anvil on which the enemy would be pounded by the hammer of Ludendorff's remaining corps. François's push would be followed by two divisions of cavalry to cut Russian rear communications.

The new offensive opened on September 4. It almost worked. Shrugging off suggestions that the Germans would try to snake around his weak left flank, Rennenkampf pointed to intercepted messages that suggested an attack from the Königsberg garrison. He did not know that these were false messages sent by German intelligence. He was unpleasantly surprised on September 7 when François, whose force had marched seventy-seven miles in four days while fighting several actions, fell on his left wing and in two days pushed north to Lötzen, capturing thousands of prisoners along with sixty cannon.[11]

This was the high point of what became known as the first battle of the Masurian Lakes. The cavalry following François failed to keep up with infantry. Ludendorff's four center corps, despite initial local successes along a thirty-mile front, could not break through what Ludendorff described as the "strong and cleverly constructed Russian defenses."[12] Nor did a successful counterattack against two of his corps make him more daring. With François threatening Rennenkampf's left, however, the Russian general had little choice but to retreat, welcome news to Max Hoffmann, who thought it "very doubtful" that Ludendorff's further frontal attacks would have succeeded.[13] One week after the initial German attack, Rennenkampf's First Army crossed the border to fall back fifty-five miles to a fortified line behind the Niemen River—he and his staff virtually deserted the army by striking off on their own to the comparative safety of Kovno.[14]

Ludendorff unwisely pursued the retreating army. His soldiers were tired, he was outrunning his supply lines, he had taken very heavy casualties, his transport was inadequate. A week after he had crossed the border his forward units were encountering resistance. This culminated a few days later in a Russian counteroffensive that soon pushed the Eighth Army back to a defensive position in East Prussia. Still, Hindenburg and Ludendorff—the Duo—had accomplished their mission. East Prussia was free of the Russian threat—at least for the time being.

Historical verdicts on this important campaign are as varied as the characters involved. No one could doubt that it was a tactical victory for the Germans. One Russian army cut to ribbons, the other pushed from East Prussia, over 300,000 enemy casualties (including 135,000 prisoners), thousands of dead and captured horses, hundreds of captured guns. But German losses were also heavy, particularly in the battle of the Masurian Lakes and the thrust into Russian Lithuania. The Eighth Army suffered about forty percent casualties—100,000 out of 250,000 men.[15] Thousands of artillery shells, daily growing more scarce, had been expended, as had large quantities of horses and guns.

The strategic verdict is not so favorable as it would appear at first sight. East Prussia was practically free of the enemy but that enemy was not far away. Prussian arms did not control the northern portion of the eastern front any more than did Russian arms. The campaign ended in stalemate. Ludendorff later wrote in an extraordinary display of linguistic gymnastics that the battle of the Masurian Lakes "was a decisive engagement" even while suggesting that Rennenkampf "does not seem to have ever intended a serious stand." Rennenkampf's army, he went on, "for the next few weeks . . . need not be regarded as first-class fighting material, unless the Russians should reinforce them [sic] with fresh troops."[16] But Stavka could and did make up the losses, which Russia, with vast reserves of manpower, could afford far more than Germany.

Yet the Duo's exaggerated claims seemed to vindicate a *Vernichtungsstrategie*, an annihilation strategy to be accomplished by waging "decisive battles." Henceforth they would try to pursue this strategy with the avidity of Frederick the Great, who nearly lost the Seven Years' War (1756–1763) before realizing his error and switching to more sensible strategy and far less costly tactics.

The decision by the OHL and the Duo to move north in pursuit of another "decisive victory" contravened Helmuth von Moltke's loose prewar agreement with the Austro-Hungarian general-staff chief. Conrad von Hötzendorf, who blamed Hindenburg for the decision, deeply resented what he regarded as a selfish move in view of his having held the enemy by his offensive in Galicia. His repeated protests echoed the lament of the cavalry general Maharbal after the Carthaginian victory at Cannae (216 B.C.): "You know how to gain a victory, Hannibal; you know not how to use one." The Duo resented these blunt reproaches, as did Kaiser Wilhelm, and this must mark the beginning of the rot in German-Austrian command relationships.[17]

Finally, and very important, the Russian invasion of East Prussia, no matter the cost, had given an enormous morale boost to France at a crucial time, not to mention a major tactical relief when Moltke summarily dispatched two corps of infantry and a cavalry division to East Prussia.

But tactical and strategical considerations pale in the light of human considerations. The victory made Hindenburg, an obscure retired general, into a household hero almost overnight. The Germans have always loved gods and suddenly they found themselves with a new Siegfried, who slew Russian dragons by the thousands. "Again news of German successes everywhere," Princess Blücher noted on September 4. ". . . The Russian hordes are being driven like cattle into the lakes and morasses of East Prussia. Hindenburg is marvelous, they say."[18]

Here he was, Unser Hindenburg—our Hindenburg—sixty-seven years old, still wearing his prewar blue uniform and old-fashioned boots, a big man, six feet tall, solid, cropped gray hair, enigmatic blue eyes ("never . . . have I seen such hard, cruel, nay, such utterly brutal eyes," one observer noted),[19] a large, impressively squared head, determined but cool, calm, collected, master of the scene, "a living symbol of embattled Germany" in one biographer's words.[20]

Hindenburg was comfortable and comforting, a true Christian who frequently invoked the deity's aid. One could rely on him, one could grasp his pronouncements, a big-picture man unconcerned with tiresome details, oblivious to threatening disaster, a military Pollyanna of bubbling optimism. "The war suits me like a visit to a health resort," he proclaimed, his words traveling with the speed of light to delighted peoples of the empire.[21]

He was also courtly, a gentleman of the old aristocratic school, devoted to kaiser and fatherland, an easy sense of humor, gemütlich, compassionate, a human being. When the Germans captured General Martos, Hindenburg treated him kindly, taking his hand between his own hands and telling him the German admiration of the bravery of his troops. "I wish you happier days," he told the luckless prisoner upon departing and promised to return his sword.[22] A raconteur of sorts, he loved company, loved to eat and drink, smoke expensive cigars, and he was also concerned with the welfare of his troops in the immediate vicinity.

As commanding general of the Eighth Army, he was little more than a figurehead. He generally remained silent during the daily command conference until the end, when he asked: "Have any of you gentlemen anything to add? No? Then, God willing, let us go ahead."[23] If Hindenburg won the battle of Tannenberg, Max Hoffmann sourly noted, then one could no longer believe in the existence of Caesar or Hannibal. Later in the war Hoffmann would show visitors the headquarters at Tannenberg, saying, "The field marshal [Hindenburg] slept here before and after the battle and, between us, also during the battle."[24]

The campaign did not make Ludendorff suddenly famous, although it enhanced his prestige within the general staff. That he made some important mistakes was evident to only a few, including Hoffmann, who counted them like a pedantic schoolmaster listening to a faulty declension of a Latin verb. Ludendorff's behavior was in marked contrast to Hindenburg's. He was impatient, impetuous, dictatorial, at times imperious, at times a nervous wreck. No one can fault his devotion to duty, his immense energy, his generally disciplined intelligence. Neither can it be doubted that he was opinionated and obstinate, rude to subordinates and often seniors, a bully. Unlike Hindenburg he threw defeat into the face of the broken General Martos, gloating over Russia's now defenseless borders. He refused to admit to his own errors. He never hesitated to place blame on others, on von François, for instance, when the attacks against Rennenkampf's army broke down.

Victory at Tannenberg only confirmed what Ludendorff had all along known: that he was a master strategist and tactician, in short the man who would have to command the entire army if Germany were to win the war. As a contemporary and one-time friend later wrote, in Ludendorff's mind another such victory as Tannenberg would make him immortal—"Glory took possession of his mind."[25]

Using Hindenburg as a front man, Ludendorff now set out to gain this exalted status, a campaign in which he would be aided and abetted by the ignorance of the German public as to the true state of the war, the divisive nature of the German government, and the appalling errors of the German and Austro-Hungarian high commands.

On August 30, 1914, the day that Hindenburg and Ludendorff were pulling tight the net at Tannenberg, a Russian attack far to the south in Galicia broke through the line of Brudermann's Third Army that fronted Lemberg.

This was the beginning of the end for the Austro-Hungarians. Brudermann and Böhm-Ermolli's newly arrived Second Army at once retreated. The Russian left wing, Brusilov's and Ruszki's armies, followed with orders to encircle the Austrian right. General Ivanov, commanding on this front, next pushed his center and right, Evert's Fourth Army and Plehve's hastily reconstituted Fifth Army (which Auffenberg had mauled a few days earlier and which the Austro-Hungarians believed was out of action), south against Conrad's left, Dankl's First Army, and Auffenberg's Fourth Army.

Conrad immediately counterattacked. Although Brusilov's right was pushed back, a gap opened between the two armies on the Austrian left. Russian cavalry pushed through, followed by Evert and Plehve's infantry.

Ivanov's orders to move in for the kill were sent by wireless in clear and were intercepted. Conrad in consequence broke off the battle and retired his armies over sixty miles to the sanctuary of the San River. Here he learned that Evert's Fourth Army was about to outflank his own left, thus causing another withdrawal. By early October the Austro-Hungarian army had retreated to the Gorlice–Tarnów line some 140 miles west of Lemberg, its left on the Vistula River, its right on the Carpathian Mountains. Conrad's force, about one million strong, had suffered 250,000 dead and wounded, not including the loss of 100,000 prisoners and incalculable quantities of weapons and materiel.

This major defeat irrevocably shattered the nebulous prewar plans as to how the Central Powers would fight the war. According to these plans, never fully agreed upon by either principal, Conrad with the bulk of the Austro-Hungarian army supported by a small German force was to have held the Russian juggernaut until Germany had defeated France. German armies would then be transferred to the east to join their ally in defeating the Russians.

Conrad's disastrous retreat canceled all this. It was no longer a question of defeating the Russians. The problem suddenly was to shore up an increasingly unreliable ally before the Russians poured into Silesia and Berlin from one side, into Hungary and Vienna from the other. The crisis could have been comfortably met had another prewar supposition worked out, namely the defeat of France within six weeks. Unfortunately for the Central Powers, this was not the case.

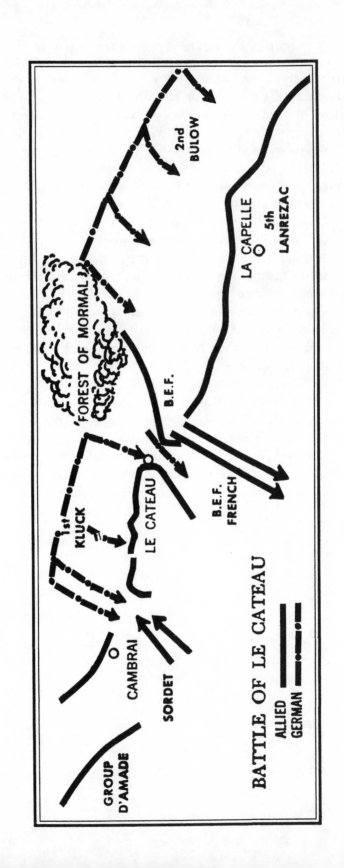

BATTLE OF LE CATEAU

ALLIED ▬▬▬▬
GERMAN ▬●▬●▬●

GROUP D'AMADE

CAMBRAI

SORDET

1st KLUCK

LE CATEAU

'FOREST OF MORMAL'

B.E.F.

B.E.F. FRENCH

2nd BULOW

LA CAPELLE

5th LANREZAC

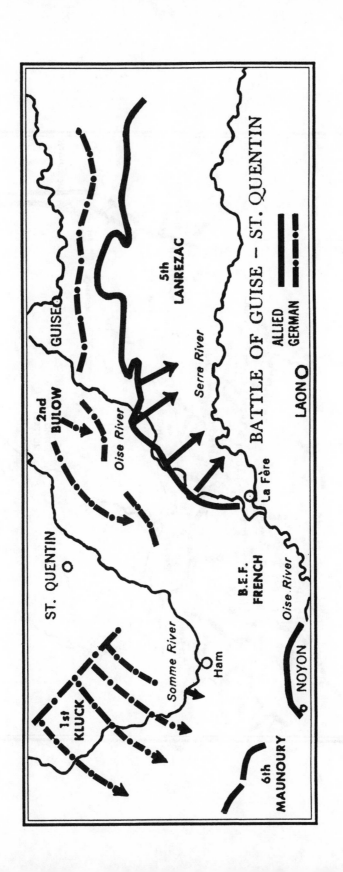

BATTLE OF GUISE – ST. QUENTIN

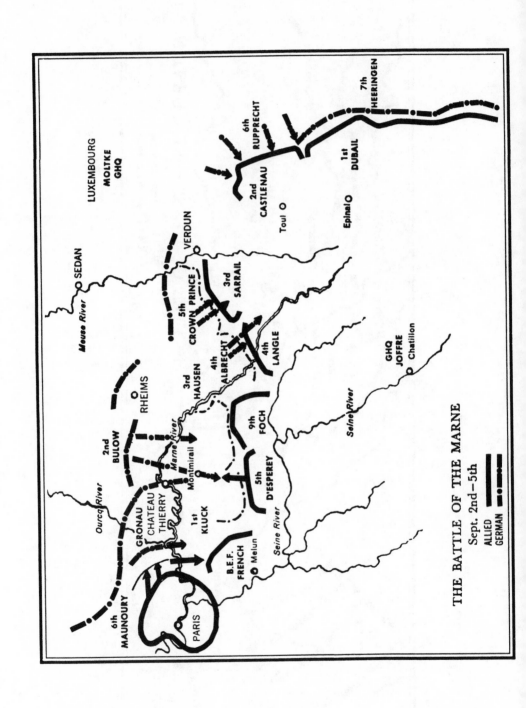

THE BATTLE OF THE MARNE
Sept. 2nd – 5th

ALLIED
GERMAN

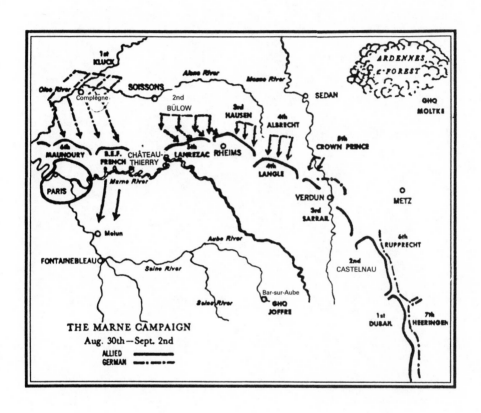

THE MARNE CAMPAIGN
Aug. 30th — Sept. 2nd

ALLIED ━━━━━━━
GERMAN ━ ▪ ━ ▪ ━

8

The First Battle of the Marne:
Defeat in the West

It is going badly. The battles to the east of Paris will go against
us. One of our armies must fall back and the others will have
to follow. The great hopes with which we began the war will
abruptly change.

—GENERAL HELMUTH VON MOLTKE TO HIS WIFE,
SEPTEMBER 9, 1914[1]

On August 25, when General von François chose to disobey
Ludendorff's order to attack Samsonov's left wing, Helmuth von
Moltke and his OHL staff at Coblenz were convinced that a
"decisive victory" had been won in the west.[2] Moltke's left and center
armies had smashed Joffre's vainglorious opening attacks. A dreadful
shroud covered the corpse of his Plan XVII. Four French armies had
been pushed into inglorious retreat, their combined strength reduced by
an estimated 800,000 casualties. On Moltke's right Bülow's Second Army
had fallen on Lanrezac's Fifth Army to force the French to another costly
retreat. On the extreme right Kluck's First Army struck the small British
Expeditionary Force, the BEF commanded by old Sir John French, one
corps of which made a valiant stand at Mons before following Lanrezac
in disordered and demoralized retreat.

A good many commanders would have given up. Joffre did not.
Unlike Moltke he came from peasant stock and was tough as nails. He
sensed that his armies were beaten, but not broken. He knew the terrain
and the staying power of artillery, particularly the French 75-mm field

gun, the most advanced field artillery piece of the day. On August 24 he revealed the secret of what would become the battle of the Marne to the minister of war: "We are therefore compelled to resort to the defensive, using our fortresses and our great topographical obstacles to enable us to yield as little ground as possible, trying to wear the enemy out, and to resume the offensive when the time comes."[3]

For nearly two weeks the French and British retreated, the British stopping to fight the bitter battle of Le Cateau, the French the vicious battle of Guise–Saint-Quentin. Time and again Joffre attempted to halt the retreat, to reorganize and strike back. Time and again the advancing gray columns upset his plans. Time and again he faced disaster from recalcitrant commanders such as Sir John French and General Lanrezac, who loathed each other more than they did the enemy. He could not persuade French to slow his retreat. He had to bludgeon Lanrezac into fighting at Guise. Yet with stolid calm he continued to face each crisis as it arose, patching here, plugging there, while desperately trying to form a new army of maneuver, Maunoury's Sixth Army outside of Paris. Evil days these, but patience, like virtue, can be its own reward, and Joffre was to find this true.

While Joffre roamed the battlefield like a frustrated Napoleon, his German counterpart was trying to control a battle from headquarters 170 miles from his right-wing army in a day of of primitive and uncertain communications. The burden of direction lay on Moltke's chief of operations, forty-eight-year-old Gerhard Tappen, an able and energetic if not brilliant tactician, a "school solution" man, calm so long as all went well but frequently imperious and sarcastic to subordinates, who, according to one of his colleagues, disliked him intensely.[4]

Reports of great victories along the line had lulled Moltke and Tappen into a false optimism that was soon to cost Moltke his job. This optimism was shared by the German government and public, which were feeding on exaggerated communiqués that streamed from the OHL's press section.

What neither government nor public knew was that during those August weeks Moltke had reduced the strong right wing called for by Schlieffen from seventeen to less than twelve corps. No longer could von Kluck wheel west of Paris. But the fantastic victories claimed by other army commanders seemed to render this unnecessary. In late August, with Kluck encountering only slight resistance and with the British (in Kluck's mind) obviously shattered, Moltke and his staff reasoned that the main French strength lay in front of their center armies. If Crown

Prince Rupprecht could break through on the left and Bülow and Kluck (again operating independently of Bülow's command) on the right, Moltke would win a classic envelopment battle.

To better control the climactic offensive, Moltke moved the OHL to Luxembourg, still about 170 miles from Kluck's First Army. This did not greatly improve communications—there were no telephone connections to army commands, partly because the Belgians and French had destroyed civil lines. Telegrams often arrived twenty-four hours late (and had to be decoded), aerial delivery was confused and uncertain, motorcycle and automobile service slow and sometimes dangerous, carrier pigeons limited in range and number. The OHL staff groused about being billeted in "the appalling Hotel Saar close to the station . . . very hot, dirty and noisy," nor were they pleased with their offices located in a girls' school.[5] The vision of stiff-necked, monocled staff officers running the greatest war in history from behind childrens' desks is thought-provoking.

Kluck meanwhile had been urged by Bülow to wheel eastward toward the line La Fère–Laon. This did not seem logical if the flank and rear of the retreating French were to be attacked. Instead, he decided to turn southeast toward the line Compiègne–Soissons and so informed the OHL.

Kluck's message found Moltke in two minds. Continuing operations along the battle line had rubbed the gloss off the "complete victories" earlier reported. On August 29 Moltke was complaining in a letter to his wife of the kaiser's chauvinism and ignorance "of the seriousness of the situation."[6] On August 30 he learned that the British had landed troops at Ostend, the vanguard, it was rumored, of an expeditionary force of 80,000 Russians. But now came Albrecht's message that the passages of the Meuse were forced, a "great victory," the French armies routed. Then Bülow's message announcing "complete victory" (at a cost of 6,000 German casualties) at Saint-Quentin, and finally Hindenburg's confirmation of the Tannenberg victory in Prussia. Once again fired by the thought of winning the greatest battle in history, Moltke approved Kluck's change of direction: Bülow to march toward Rheims, Kluck toward Compiègne–Noyon.[7]

Kluck now pushed his tired army recklessly to the south. It was a bold move. His battalions had been thinned by combat losses, illness, lines-of-communication duty, and sheer exhaustion. His railheads were anywhere from forty to eighty miles behind his front. Captain Bloem's company had outmarched its supply train already by August 23: "We had to live on the country, fortunately a very well-stocked one. . . . Of coffee, meat, potatoes and vegetables there was no lack—only bread, that failed us completely."[8] Only the rich autumn countryside and immense quantities of captured supplies had allowed Kluck to continue the pursuit, that and the superb will of the troops. Bloem's company had marched for three weeks without a rest day. Severe foot problems developed early and morale was scarcely raised by no mail delivery. By September 5 nails were sticking through boot soles "which were as thin as paper."[9]

Lack of fodder was seriously hampering cavalry operations, of little value in any event, but short rations and tired horses were already telling on the ability of both the big guns and vital ammunition wagons to keep up with the infantry. This shifted responsibility for ammunition supply to inefficient motor transport companies, which were soon suffering from massive vehicle breakdowns.[10]

Armed with his own misconceptions of enemy location and strength, but correctly believing that his troops would conquer fatigue and that ammunition would soon be on hand, Kluck was not to be stopped. When Moltke, worried by new reports of French troop movements from east to west, ordered him to "follow in echelon behind the Second Army," where he would be responsible for the flank protection of the force, Kluck refused the order. Demonstrating the arrogant independence that characterized most German generals, he continued to push his advance across the Marne River.[11]

Moltke's optimism had visibly dimmed by September 4. He held only a dim knowledge of the front but sensed the worst. "We must not deceive ourselves," he told a colleague. "We have had successes, but we have not yet had victory. . . . When armies of millions of men are opposed, the victor has prisoners. Where are ours? . . . Besides, the relatively small number of captured guns shows me that the French have withdrawn in good order and according to plan. The hardest work is yet to be done."[12]

Moltke's new directive of September 5 informed his army commanders of the growing threat to the German right wing. Since a decision could only be sought in the center and on the left, "the First and Second Armies [Kluck and Bülow] will remain facing the eastern front of Paris, to act offensively against any operations of the enemy from Paris." Even though Kluck had reported the previous day to the OHL that his units "were fast approaching the point of collapse,"[13] he regarded Moltke's directive as nonsense. He was convinced that "the strong forces suspected in Paris are only in the act of assembly," and that the beaten British force was a tactical cipher. He informed the OHL that he was continuing his march to south of the Marne River, leaving only Gronau's corps to shield against the remote chance of an attack from Paris.[14]

Kluck's reply further confused Moltke and his staff. Erich von Falkenhayn, the minister of war, noted on September 5: "Only one thing is certain: our general staff has completely lost its head. Schlieffen's notes end and therefore Moltke's wits also come to an end."[15]

Joffre learned of Kluck's change of direction on August 31. Joffre had been moving mountains to form two new forces, Maunoury's Sixth Army north of Paris and Foch's Ninth Army in the center of the line. A hurried visit from the British war minister, Lord Kitchener, brought an end to the British retreat. To win over Sir John French to his plans—the BEF was vital to the hoped-for counteroffensive—Joffre appeased the British commander by relieving the obstinate and defeatist Lanrezac, whom French detested, in favor of the dashing Franchet d'Esperey. In all, in these critical days Joffre relieved two army commanders, seven corps commanders, twenty infantry-division commanders, and four cavalry-division commanders by September 6, the opening day of his counteroffensive.

Joffre's plan was to hold in the center and on the right while Maunoury's Sixth Army attacked Kluck's right wing from the west, with the BEF striking from the south. It was risky but not foolish. If the Sixth Army were beaten, neither Joffre nor Gallieni, the old and ailing but indefatigable governor of Paris, cherished any illusions that Paris would hold out. If the counteroffensive failed, Joffre would fail with it and the government would undoubtedly fall, leaving matters ripe for a growing peace-at-any-price movement among frightened officials in Paris and Bordeaux.

The action soon took an important twist. The vanguard of Maunoury's Sixth Army, in moving to the jump-off line on September 5, struck Gronau's shielding corps. Gronau withdrew some six miles eastward to a better defensive position and called for reinforcements.

Kluck did not learn of this development until late evening. His optimism meanwhile had received a severe jolt from Moltke's emissary, Lieutenant Colonel Richard Hentsch, who was in charge of the intelligence section at the OHL. A colleague described the forty-five-year-old Hentsch as exceedingly clever, intelligent, and industrious, with an expert knowledge of the French army, but noted that a lack of decisiveness and an inability to sort out the true from the false in incoming reports made him increasingly a pessimist.[16] In precise terms Hentsch told the army commander and his chief of staff, von Kuhl, that the general picture looked dubious, that the "complete victories" reported by the left and center armies were no more than local gains. At the moment, Crown Prince Rupprecht was suffering heavy losses in Lorraine, and Crown Prince Wilhelm and Duke Albrecht were meeting strong resistance along the line. British troops had landed in Ostend, and it was rumored that an enormous Russian force would follow. The OHL knew for certain that the French had been transferring forces to Paris. Hentsch's words were confirmed by the uncomfortable exclamation point of Gronau's call for help. Kluck was still not convinced of a serious attack, but he began grudgingly to feed back a corps to Gronau with another to follow the next day. Kluck did not know it, but the battle of the Marne had begun.

The battle lasted for four furious days. The battle line curved from north of Paris down and across the Marne River and south to its tiny tributary, the Petit Morin, then east in a wavering line where it climbed to the fortress of Verdun. There it joined at a right angle the Lorraine battle line that ran south almost to the Alps. On either side of the line for twenty-five miles the impedimenta of fourteen great armies jammed villages and roads, well over two million men, thousands of guns, hundreds of thousands of horses and wagons, ambulances and supply trains—a military concentration never before seen in the world.

The battle could have been won or lost by either side at a dozen different times. Attacks were beaten off by cliff-hanging counterattacks. Casualties mounted with skyrocket speed. Eventually the Germans lost, not because of lesser fighting skills but because of command ineptness and confusion. Lacking effective command from the top, army commanders, particularly Kluck and Bülow, were fighting their own wars with some subordinates attacking, some counterattacking, some holding.

Soon after the battle started, the incipient gap that had formed between Kluck and Bülow's armies began widening as each commander exercised his own will without always informing the OHL of his decisions. Only on the third day of battle did Moltke order reinforcements to march to the right wing—a corps from nearby Maubeuge, a brigade from Antwerp. He then called a meeting of his staff officers, who seem to have been as bewildered as their chief. Eventually someone suggested sending

Lieutenant Colonel Hentsch on a second visit to the front to determine the true situation, and Moltke agreed. Moltke's oral orders to Hentsch were to cause unending controversy, but historians who have made a close study of "the Hentsch case" more or less agree as to the content. If one of the right-wing armies was retreating, Moltke allegedly told him, Hentsch should try to influence the movement so as to close the gap between these armies, that is, Kluck's First Army should withdraw to the line Soissons–Fismes, the Second Army to a line behind the Vesle River.

Hentsch departed from the OHL before noon on September 8. He reached Crown Prince Wilhelm's Fifth Army about noon, was satisfied with what he found, went on to the Fourth Army, where Duke Albrecht briefed him. From here he telephoned the OHL to report favorably to recently promoted Colonel Tappen. He spoke briefly with Hausen at the Third Army, from where he informed the OHL that the "situation and point of view [were] entirely favorable." Clouds began to gather, however, at Second Army headquarters, which he reached in late evening. Instead of the coldly arrogant, supremely self-confident Prussian commander familiar to every officer in the German general staff, Bülow had turned into a tired and very worried old man whose mind had scarcely been relieved by his having spent that day at the front.

Bülow's main concern was his weak right wing, unmasked by Kluck's withdrawal of two corps and now under attack. Severe losses had rendered the Second Army "no longer capable of forcing a decisive victory," he told Hentsch. An enemy attack in strength against either his own right or Kluck's left could lead to catastrophe, since neither commander possessed reserves with which to meet it. A forced retreat "would have to be made through a hostile country and the consequences to this [Second] Army might be incalculable. It should therefore be considered whether it would not be better, viewing the situation as a whole, to avert the danger by a voluntary concentric retreat of the First and Second armies." The meeting was interrupted by news of another setback on his right, which caused him to withdraw it further to the east, thus widening the gap between the two armies. If that gap could not be closed, Bülow thought that he would have to retire behind the Marne, a decision he made early the next day when he learned that enemy columns had crossed the Marne.[17]

Moltke allegedly had instructed Hentsch that if one of the right-wing armies was retreating, he should try to direct the movements so as to close the breach. Hentsch, in line with Moltke's instructions, now believed that he must now try to persuade Kluck to withdraw toward the line Soissons–Fismes.

Hentsch reached Kluck's headquarters shortly before noon. As he was explaining the bleak situation to the chief of staff, von Kuhl, the latter was handed a message from Bülow—"Second Army begins retirement."[18] Hentsch repeated Moltke's instructions for the First Army to withdraw to the line Soissons–Fismes, where its left would join Bülow's right, a move shortly approved by the First Army commander.

Back at the OHL, poor old Moltke was on the point of collapse. His deputy, General Hermann von Stein, was not much help, telling everyone that "one must not lose one's head," yet doing nothing to stem the panic, muttering only, "One can't know how things will turn out."[19] Once Moltke learned that his right-wing armies were withdrawing, he accepted defeat. "How different it was a few weeks ago," he wrote to his wife, "when we so gloriously opened the campaign—the bitter disappointment has now caught up with us. And now we shall have to pay for all that has been destroyed."[20]

Moltke and Tappen visited Third Army headquarters on September 11 to learn that there was a gap in its wide front. If the enemy pushed through here, the Fourth Army and the right wing of the Fifth Army would be forced in part into very difficult terrain toward fortress Verdun and would be in danger of being destroyed, which would mean the end of the war.[21] At Fifth Army headquarters Moltke struck Crown Prince Wilhelm as "a broken man, literally struggling to hold back his tears" as he called for a general retreat.[22]

Back at the OHL he ordered the Third, Fourth, and Fifth armies to retire behind the Vesle and Aisne rivers. "I must suffer what has happened and will stand or fall with my country," he wrote to his wife. "We shall be choked to death in the battle against east and west."[23]

The retirement was orderly. It surprised Joffre, whose armies were in any case too badly hurt to interfere seriously. In four days the German forces had reached prepared defenses. The "race to the sea" would shortly follow, with no one the winner. After that it would be a matter of position warfare, *Stellungskrieg*, a war of trenches that would last until 1918.

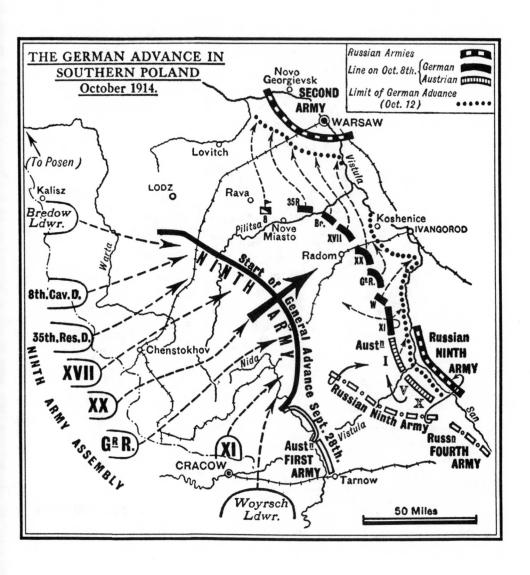

THE GERMAN ADVANCE IN
SOUTHERN POLAND
October 1914.

Russian Armies
Line on Oct. 8th. {German
{Austrian
Limit of German Advance
(Oct. 12) ••••••

(To Posen)
Kalisz
Bredow Ldwr.
Warta
8th.Cav.D.
35th.Res.D.
XVII
XX
NINTH ARMY ASSEMBLY
GꞴR.
Chenstokhov
Nida
XI
CRACOW
Woyrsch Ldwr.

LODZ
Lovitch
Novo Georgievsk
SECOND ARMY
WARSAW
Rava
Pilitsa
Nove Miasto
8
35R
Br.
XVII
Radom
Vistula
Koshenice
IVANGOROD
XX
GꞴR.
W
XI
Austⁿ I
Russian NINTH ARMY
V
X
San
Russian Ninth Army
Russⁿ FOURTH ARMY
Austⁿ FIRST ARMY
Vistula
Tarnow

NINTH ARMY
Start of General Advance Sept. 28th.

50 Miles

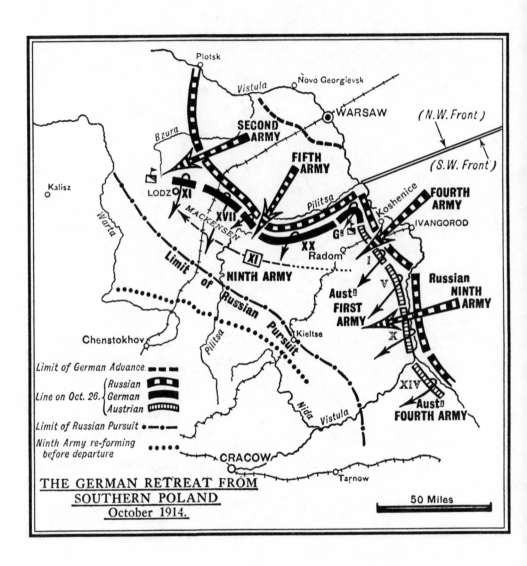

Plotsk

Vistula   Nóvó Georgievsk

WARSAW   (N.W. Front)

SECOND
ARMY

Bzura   FIFTH
ARMY   (S.W. Front)

Kalisz   Pilitsa   Koshenice   FOURTH
ARMY

LODZ XI   IVANGOROD

XVII   Gᵃ

MACKENSEN   XX
Radom   I   Russian
NINTH
ARMY

Warta   XI   V

NINTH ARMY   Ausⁿ
FIRST
ARMY   X

Limit   Kieltse

of   XIV

Chenstokhov   Russian   Ausⁿ
FOURTH ARMY

Pursuit

Pilitsa

Limit of German Advance.
Line on Oct. 26. { Russian
                    German
                    Austrian
Limit of Russian Pursuit   Nida   Vistula
Ninth Army re-forming
before departure

CRACOW

THE GERMAN RETREAT FROM
SOUTHERN POLAND
October 1914.   Tarnow   50 Miles

9

Enter Falkenhayn

Heavy fighting for three days . . . constant flurry and
panic. . . . Ludendorff and I support each other, and and Hindenburg says, "We must trust in God."
—LIEUTENANT COLONEL MAX HOFFMANN,
OCTOBER 12, 1914[1]

Toward the close of the battle of the Marne a prescient member
of the Reichstag noted that "spirits are not so jubilant in Berlin
as they were a week ago. Reports from the battlefields are not so
stimulating to the nerves. The High Command has already pampered
the morale of those at home. At least one victory a day is demanded.
When that fails, general apathy is evident."[2]

Defeat at the Marne was thus a two-fold disaster for German arms.
The defeat could not be admitted, not even to leading members of the
Reichstag, much less to the main body which had so blindly voted its
confidence in the army on August 4. General Friedrich von Bernhardi
in Posen wrote that he and his fellow officers "learned nothing of the
importance of the Marne battle. It was said that a few units had to fall
back to reorganize. We could conclude nothing from the reports and
grew all the more confident as the magnificent achievements in the east
surmounted all our expectations."[3] Incredibly Conrad von Hötzendorf
was not informed of Moltke's dismissal, nor did he learn of the disastrous
results of the battle until late October.[4]

The OHL insisted that it had won a victory on the Marne, and it
brushed away contrary reports as seditious propaganda. Total casualty
figures, which were appalling, were not published. Localized casualty lists

were instead posted in towns and villages to minimize the effect. Wounded filled the hospitals. Dead covered the fields of France. Tons of materiel and guns had been lost. Lieutenant General Erich von Falkenhayn, whom the kaiser had appointed "acting" chief of the general staff a few days after the battle, found his "fighting strength greatly reduced; everywhere a shortage of junior officers, huge gaps in the ranks."[5] To avoid unpleasant rumors, Moltke's relief was to be kept secret until early November.

Moltke was not the only ranking casualty. One of the kaiser's closest advisers later wrote that "defeat at the Marne was the real turning point in Wilhelm's behavior, that he had believed himself capable of conducting (and winning) this battle only to find himself unable to do any such thing."[6] Gone was the dream of emulating his hero, Frederick the Great. Now he must step aside and leave the war to the generals.

Ironically, the kaiser and Moltke's failure only enhanced Hindenburg and Ludendorff's success in East Prussia. Having pronounced the inconclusive outcome of the first battle of the Masurian Lakes as another great victory, their stock could not have been higher—Hindenburg's within army and empire, Ludendorff's within the army. A schism had already developed between the OHL and the Eighth Army by the time of Moltke's relief. Like the gap between Kluck and Bülow's armies on the Marne, it would in time widen with even more serious consequences to Germany.

Erich von Falkenhayn had been molded from the same military dough as Hindenburg and Ludendorff, but without the same results. He was born into an army family on an estate near the Baltic port of Thorn in 1861. In 1914 he was fifty-three, fourteen years younger than Paul von Hindenburg, four years older than Erich Ludendorff. After enduring the traditional cadet school, he was commissioned, served variously in junior command and staff posts, won entrance into the *Kriegsakademie*, and became a member of the general staff. In 1896 he married and was posted to China, where he served as a military instructor. He subsequently served as a staff officer in the German expeditionary corps, fought in the Boxer Rebellion, and remained with the occupation forces until 1903. He returned to Germany militarily and politically wiser, his professional reputation considerably enhanced. In 1906 he was appointed chief of staff to an infantry corps. Seven years later he was promoted to lieutenant general and appointed minister of war.

Falkenhayn was a complete army man. He had alienated numerous liberal members of the Reichstag through his vigorous defense of dueling and of the army in the notorious Zabern affair,[7] but this had also increased his standing with the kaiser and had brought him a general reputation as the "strong man" desired by a great many people. In spring of 1914 he had made his position clear in a speech to the Reichstag: "If cultural progress signifies that we can no longer count upon our army in case of war, culture may go to the deuce for all I care."[8]

Falkenhayn ran the war ministry efficiently enough, considering the bureaucratic procurement jungle and other anomalies of the German military system. In September 1914 he persuaded the kaiser to retain him as minister of war while he simultaneously served as acting chief of staff. His camps were training hundreds of thousands of recruits to replace the dreadful losses in armies east and west. His minions were working overtime to keep supply lines moving while factories throughout the empire produced the necessities of war. Prodded by Walther Rathenau, the brilliant and forceful director of the enormous AEG electrical combine, who foresaw a long war and the need for a war economy, Falkenhayn early established a special department to procure and allocate raw materials.

Tall, with perennial youthful good looks (despite close-cropped gray hair), he was as cool as Hindenburg, as strong-minded, arrogant, and vigorous as Ludendorff, and more intelligent and perceptive than either Ludendorff or Conrad. His adjutant described him as a real war-horse, unlike Moltke, iron-willed and determined, but also having "a high sense of responsibility."[9] His deputy, General Adolf Wild von Hohenborn, described him as "an outstanding personality even if no strategical genius," but he did not deem a genius necessary and he believed that Falkenhayn was the best possible chief of staff.[10] Max Bauer described him as very bright, energetic, and perceptive, but lacking the intensiveness necessary to make valid command decisions and then see them through. Bauer believed that he would have made a better statesman, diplomat, or parliamentarian than a general, and perhaps he was correct.[11] Karl von Treutler, who had known him since student days in the *Kriegsakademie* and who admired him in general, nonetheless found him "overly ambitious," a man who like Admiral von Tirpitz and the former chancellor Prince von Bülow and later Erich Ludendorff was lacking in character, a man who thought of himself first and only then of his country.[12] General Count von Stürgkh, the Austro-Hungarian representative at the OHL, enjoyed his cheerful temperament and stimulating conversation but also noted his flashes of devastating sarcasm, an offshoot of the innate arrogance all too common to general staff officers.[13] Falkenhayn did not suffer fools gladly, be they military or civil, and his biting tongue had made him powerful enemies in both circles.

There was no doubt that Falkenhayn was a loner, and in time it would cost him dearly. A lieutenant colonel named Friedrich von Lossberg joined the OHL in early 1915 and was assigned as assistant operations officer to Colonel Tappen. Lossberg, who had known Falkenhayn well in peacetime, later made an interesting judgment of the man: "I gained the impression in the following months that General von Falkenhayn through the previous erratic management of operations and also through his flexible and self-confident behavior had not won too much respect and trust. Although he gladly listened to intelligent proposals and suggestions, he mostly went his own way. Extremely lively in temperament, very adroit and sure of himself in behavior, he readily ignored the consequences of his command mistakes. General von Falkenhayn, as I soon recognized, had only conditionally gained the unrestricted trust that the men at the front and their leaders must have in the supreme command."[14]

Two schools of basic German strategy were forming in September 1914, the eastern school and the western school. Victory at Tannenberg taken with defeat on the Marne and in Galicia had momentarily thrown strategy out of traditional perspective. Like the poet Keats, Hindenburg had awakened to find himself famous, henceforth a prophet who would preach Ludendorff's messianic strategy to the high command, indeed to the empire. The two men already had begun to question the OHL's wisdom before Moltke's fall. The process would soon become an ugly inquisition that would end in a Teutonic version of an auto-da-fé.

Falkenhayn, concerned with Conrad's precarious position in the south, wanted to form a new army to protect Silesia while supporting Conrad's left wing. Hindenburg and Ludendorff, still insisting that the battle of the Masurian Lakes was a great victory, objected to this plan, arguing that German strategy should be reversed, the eastern front to become the priority theater of war, the western front to take up the defensive until Russia was defeated. Given sufficient reinforcement, Hindenburg's Eighth Army would cross the Narev River to begin encirclement of Ivanov's southern armies. Conrad von Hötzendorf naturally enough supported this demand and coolly asked Falkenhayn to give him an incredible thirty divisions for his part in it.[15]

The new chief of staff refused to endorse either the Eighth Army's or Conrad's excessive demands. The "race to the sea" was still being run in the west, and his right flank was far from secure. The French were receiving reinforcements from the colonies, and British troops were daily arriving in France. An indecisive naval engagement off Heligoland in late August seemed to offer little future threat to British sea communications from Tirpitz's highly vaunted battle cruisers and dreadnoughts, once again lying impotently at anchor in heavily defended ports. To strip the western front of troops would mean a general withdrawal that would abandon immense areas of captured coal mines; in Falkenhayn's mind this would be a virtual admission of failure if not defeat. It was therefore vital to consolidate his lines and reassume the offensive as soon as possible.

As for the eastern front, Falkenhayn agreed that it was necessary, strategically and politically, to bolster the Austro-Hungarians if Turkey and Romania were to be won over as allies. But this was a far cry from the all-out offensive demanded by Hindenburg and Ludendorff. Time and space furnished the most persuasive counterarguments. The rainy season was approaching. Transport was difficult enough on dry roads. Such was the vastness of the territories concerned that a successful offensive would require months and years, not just weeks. An unsuccessful or prolonged action would expose Silesia with its immensely rich minerals and coal mines and important factories to the enemy, as it would Conrad's fragile lines in the south.

Falkenhayn accordingly compromised by stripping the Eighth Army of three of its corps to form a new army, the Ninth, under command of Hindenburg with headquarters at Breslau in southeastern Silesia. Perhaps with malice aforethought Falkenhayn ordered Ludendorff to remain behind as chief of staff to the new Eighth Army commander, an order subsequently rescinded because of Hindenburg's anguished cries to the kaiser. Hindenburg's mission was to fashion a new offensive with Conrad's help in order both to push the Russians away from the Silesian frontier and to force Grand Duke Nicholas to transfer reinforcements from the south, thus easing the pressure on Conrad. In Falkenhayn's mind it was in every sense to be a limited offensive with a further design of giving himself time to repair the critical situation on the western front, but there was also the hope of inflicting a serious defeat on the Russians.

* * *

On September 18 Erich Ludendorff, saddened by news that his stepson, Franz, had been seriously wounded, was driven through miserable weather over bone-jarring roads to Conrad's headquarters at Neusandez. Here he conferred with Conrad and Archduke Frederick, commander in chief of the Austro-Hungarian army. Despite Conrad's recent severe setback he eagerly accepted Ludendorff's plan to attack the area between Ivanov's armies in the south and the northwestern forces, now commanded by Ruzski. The Ninth Army, its right protected by Dankl's Austro-Hungarian First Army, would cross the nine-hundred-meter-wide Vistula River and move northeast toward Warsaw.

The operation began ten days later. On the second day Max Hoffmann exuberantly, if prematurely, noted in his diary: "We are on the point of a brilliant success: from the moment of our advance the Russian army ceased to press the Austrians [to the south] and is now in retreat behind the Vistula. The direction our attack will take cannot yet be foreseen, and depends entirely on the news we get."[16]

That was the end of the good news. Heavy rains dogged movement from the beginning. As Falkenhayn had feared, the roads soon turned to mud, which greatly hindered the transport of heavy guns and supply trains. Ludendorff later wrote that the main road from Cracow to Warsaw was knee-deep in mud which, according to Hindenburg, also covered the wretched inhabitants (along with assorted vermin).[17]

A major problem soon developed from the slow advance of the Austro-Hungarians. Ludendorff's initial abruptness and rudeness had been deeply resented by Conrad and his staff.[18] Hoffmann had written in his diary five days before the advance began: "Yesterday was our first row with the Austrians. They aren't out for business as we are."[19] By October 8 the Ninth Army was strung out along the Vistula River. Hoffmann wrote: "Here everything is in excellent order, except for the Austrians! If only the wretches would move!"[20] While he was writing these words the first of some sixty Russian divisions began closing on the Vistula, while advance elements of another fourteen divisions commenced probing attacks on Mackensen's XVII Corps to the north. German attempts to cross the Vistula before the Russians arrived in strength came to nothing. Heavy casualties could not be replaced. Constant pleas to the OHL for more divisions were rejected.

A successful enemy crossing of the river at Koshenice added to

Ludendorff's worries, as did disturbingly accurate intelligence reports of enemy strength and plans culled from Russian wireless messages and confirmed by orders and a sketch map taken from a dead Russian officer. On October 12 Hoffmann noted: "Heavy fighting for three days . . . constant flurry and panic. . . . Ludendorff and I support each other, and Hindenburg says, 'We must trust in God.' " On October 18: "Very heavy fighting here with more battles to come—how it will end God alone knows. . . . We can't rely on the Austrians in the slightest, otherwise everything would be simple. In any event we have already achieved much more than we could have hoped for. It was the best operation of our campaign to date. . . . I continue to count on victory, Ludendorff no longer."[21]

When on this same day Ludendorff saw that his left was about to be outflanked, he ordered Mackensen to fall back to a line about forty miles west of Warsaw. With Mackensen holding the new line to the north and Dankl's Austro-Hungarian First Army finally in position on the line of the Vistula, Ludendorff intended to attack in the bend of the Vistula. In view of preponderant enemy strength, this was probably a poor idea, but we shall never know. Conrad, tired of playing the poor relation and forever dreaming of a great tactical coup, ordered General Dankl to let the Russians cross the Vistula near Ivangorod, then take them in a flank attack. Hindenburg and Ludendorff advised against the plan, to no avail. Hoffmann noted on October 21: "Ludendorff has become terribly nervous and the whole load lies on me." Three days later he angrily wrote: "The worst here is that Hindenburg cannot understand why we cannot give him another victory like that in East Prussia. The greatest general of all times—yesterday I almost had to be rude to him."[22]

Conrad's daring operation might have worked with a superior army. Dankl's polyglot force, which was on very short rations, virtually promised failure. The Russians soon crossed the Vistula, the Austro-Hungarians attacked without success, the Russians counterattacked, and Dankl, having suffered 40,000 casualties, ordered a general retreat that exposed the German right flank.

Hindenburg later wrote that he decided to abandon the entire operation by a general retreat. We can allow him credit without emphasizing that neither he nor Ludendorff had much choice in the matter. The movement began in late October. It was well organized, having previously been planned by Ludendorff and Hoffmann. Losses were minimal; railroad lines and bridges, vital to enemy supply, were systematically destroyed. In a few days the Ninth Army was back almost to its original lines, the Russians only halfheartedly in pursuit.[23]

Despite the discouraging result—100,000 German casualties, of whom 36,000 were killed—Ludendorff at once began planning a new offensive. "Ludendorff and I get on very well," Hoffmann noted at the end of October, "despite occasional differences of opinion where in the end he always gives in."[24] On one point there was no disagreement: The new operation would require heavy reinforcements from the western front.

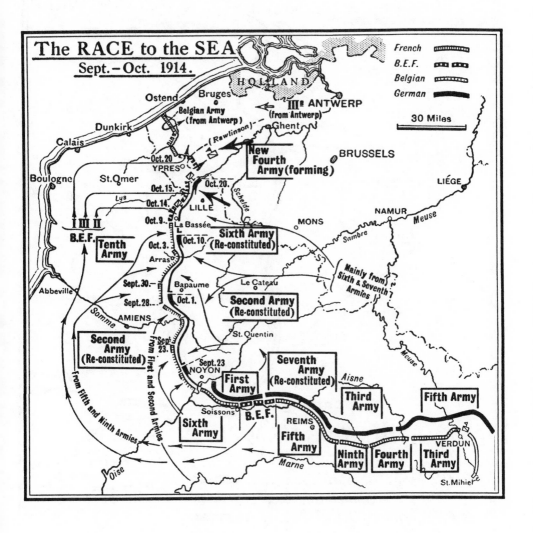

The RACE to the SEA
Sept. – Oct. 1914.

French
B.E.F.
Belgian
German

30 Miles

HOLLAND

Ostend
Bruges
ANTWERP
Belgian Army (from Antwerp)
III⁹ ANTWERP
(from Antwerp)
Dunkirk
Ghent
(Rawlinson)
Calais
New Fourth Army (forming)
BRUSSELS
Oct. 20
YPRES
Boulogne
St.Omer
LIÉGE
Oct. 15.
Oct. 20.
Oct. 14.
LILLE
Lys
NAMUR
Meuse
Oct. 9.
La Bassée
MONS
Sixth Army (Re-constituted)
B.E.F.
Tenth Army
Oct. 3.
Oct. 10.
Sambre
Meuse
Arras
Mainly from Sixth & Seventh Armies
Sept. 30.
Bapaume
Le Cateau
Abbeville
Sept. 28.
Oct. 1.
Second Army (Re-constituted)
Somme
AMIENS
Second Army (Re-constituted)
St. Quentin
Sept. 23.
From First and Second Armies
From Fifth and Ninth Armies
Sept. 23
NOYON
First Army
Seventh Army (Re-constituted)
Aisne
Third Army
Fifth Army
Soissons
B.E.F.
REIMS
Sixth Army
Fifth Army
Ninth Army
Fourth Army
Third Army
VERDUN
Oise
Marne
St.Mihiel

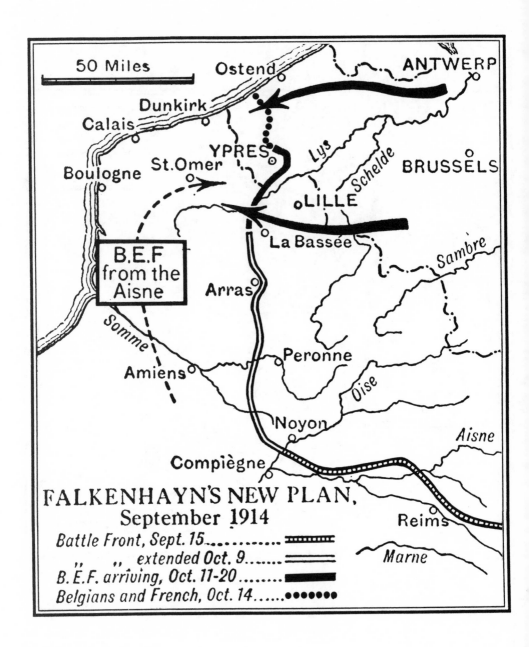

50 Miles

Ostend

ANTWERP

Dunkirk

Calais

YPRES

Lys

Schelde

BRUSSELS

Boulogne

St.Omer

oLILLE

B.E.F
from the
Aisne

La Bassée

Somme

Arras

Sambre

Peronne

Amiens

Oise

Noyon

Aisne

Compiègne

FALKENHAYN'S NEW PLAN,
September 1914

Reims

Battle Front, Sept. 15

Marne

" " extended Oct. 9
B.E.F. arriving, Oct. 11-20
Belgians and French, Oct. 14

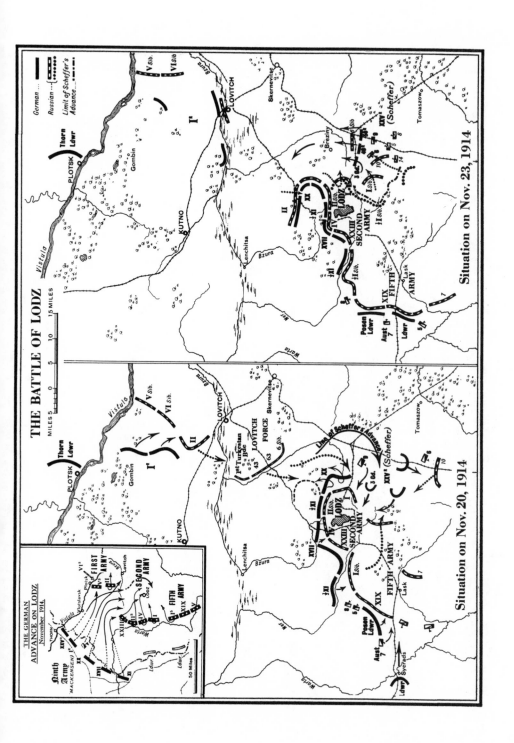

THE BATTLE OF LODZ

Situation on Nov. 20, 1914

Situation on Nov. 23, 1914

German ......
Russian ......
Limit of Scheffer's
Advance ......

MILES 5   10   15 MILES

THE GERMAN
ADVANCE ON LODZ
November 1914

Ninth Army
MACKENSEN)

FIRST
ARMY

SECOND
ARMY

FIFTH
ARMY

50 Miles

10

Continuing Stalemate East and West

The greatest of our battles is in progress; hopefully it will be
a great success. According to human calculation we must win,
but the waiting is nerve-wracking.
—Lieutenant Colonel Max Hoffmann,
November 19, 1914[1]

Erich von Falkenhayn had meanwhile transferred the OHL to
Charleville-Mézières, an important rail center some sixty miles
northwest of Luxembourg, in order to gain better communications
with his armies and better quarters for his staff.

Once again the kaiser tagged along, this time to establish imperial
headquarters in a comfortable villa next to a large park. Each morning
he sawed wood for an hour or two before his aides arrived with the latest
dispatches. Falkenhayn briefed him for about an hour at noon. There
followed a simple lunch, a nap, and usually a drive, "sometimes to the
battlefield of Sedan to relive the 1870 victory," sometimes to what he
liked to call "the front."[2] Admiral Müller recorded that the ritual dinners,
followed by hours of a simple card game called Skat, were as boring as
ever.[3] Falkenhayn saw as little of his master as was possible.

Falkenhayn had inherited a hideous situation. His first attempt to
outflank the Allied left had failed. The "race to the sea" had virtually
halted, as if it were a sack race and each of the enemies had a leg in the
other's sack. A general pessimism gripped the OHL. Admiral von Tirpitz,
the naval minister, was furious because the kaiser would not allow the

High Seas Fleet to leave harbor and challenge the Royal Navy. He was also depressed, writing in early October: "I can hardly imagine how we can come out of this war with honor, after the frightful mistakes made by our generals during August. The one hope is in holding out, and in being able to hold out . . . but for that we want men of iron, and when one sees the men around the Kaiser and Bethmann, hope sinks."[4]

By October 1914 Falkenhayn's right wing occupied a less than comfortable position opposite strong British and French forces north of Menin, about twenty-five miles from the coast. Enemy divisions had reached the Yser River in Flanders and were trying to close with the Belgian army, which King Albert had courageously led from fortress Antwerp shortly before its surrender. Falkenhayn believed that it was vital to gain control of the coast all the way to the Somme River, first to avoid being outflanked, second to deprive Britain of ports, finally to gain bases for future submarine and aerial attacks against Britain in an attempt to break the looming naval blockade. In so doing he intended to turn the enemy flank to bring about the breakthrough so ardently desired by either side.

Toward this end Falkenhayn formed a new army in Belgium, the Fourth, from three divisions that had been freed by the fall of Antwerp and from four corps that had completed accelerated training in Germany. Under the command of Duke Albrecht of Württemberg, the Fourth Army was to attack west while extending its right flank to the coast. Simultaneously Bavarian Crown Prince Rupprecht's Sixth Army, hastily brought up from Lorraine, was to attack on Albrecht's left.

Like Conrad's abortive effort on the Vistula, this would have been a bold plan even with first-class troops. Considering the state of the German divisions and the increasingly serious shortage of artillery shells, it was a desperate attempt to salvage Schlieffen strategy—"an act of despair," in a German historian's apt words. Rupprecht's Bavarians had been fighting for over two months. His regiments had taken appalling casualties, the survivors were tired. Seventy-five percent of the four corps committed to Duke Albrecht's offensive consisted of teenage volunteers, middle- and upper-class students who should have been reserved for officer training to fill already depleted command ranks.

What became known as the first battle of Ypres began on October 12 with a British advance between La Bassée and Armentières. This was quickly checked by the Bavarians, who in turn were fought to a standstill by superior British rifle, machine-gun, and artillery fire. Albrecht broke the subsequent lull on October 20, only to encounter extraordinary resistance from the Belgians who were holding the coastal area around Nieuport. But adrenaline supplied by hatred can only stop so many bullets before superior weight tells. After three days of murderous fighting, the Belgians were about to give way when engineers opened sluice gates to flood the flat battlefield with the waters of the English Channel and halt further German attacks. Albrecht had reached the coast, but he had not achieved the coveted breakthrough.

Continuing British and French attacks east of Ypres were shattered by Rupprecht's Bavarians at enormous cost in lives to both sides. It was hideous terrain for warfare, a flat featureless area marked by numerous farmsteads and villages, small streams, ditches, canals, and hedgerows. Some said that it favored the defender, most agreed that it favored death. Attack was the order of the day—a bugle call that one survivor remembered by the words, "Potato soup, potato soup. The whole year round potato soup, soup, soup, soup."[5] The young German volunteers remained aggressive, cheerful, and confident. One of them watched a friend fall during the unsuccessful attack on Dixmuide and wrote that "there certainly is a no more beautiful, magnificent death."[6] Of 3,600 men of one Bavarian regiment, nearly 3,000 were killed or wounded in four days. One of the survivors was a twenty-five-year-old private, an Austrian volunteer named Adolf Hitler. As a *Meldegänger*, or battalion runner, he was almost constantly exposed to heavy fire. His bravery in this action won him the Iron Cross and promotion to corporal. (He would continue to fight bravely to the end of the war. He would be wounded three times and would be awarded the Iron Cross First Class.)[7]

Falkenhayn, supported by most of his staff and an enthusiastic kaiser, was determined to win the battle. On November 11 he ordered an attack by what was left of the schoolboys against the thin British line defending the Menin–Ypres road. The youngsters did not hesitate. Fanatically devoted to kaiser and fatherland, inadequately trained, poorly led by older reserve officers, and insufficiently supported by artillery, they attacked *à la Russe*, dense waves of them singing "Deutschland über Alles," their voices contesting with the cruel barking of Vickers machine guns to turn the chorale to cacophonous screams. They nearly got through. Nearly, but not quite. Elsewhere along the line vicious fighting continued. "We go slowly forward," one officer wrote, "for each position must be taken singly like a fort."[8] One soldier fighting near Ypres excitedly wrote that his unit had captured two machine guns, for which they were awarded a bonus of 750 marks per gun—the regiment had already earned 2,250 marks.[9]

By mid-November it was apparent that Falkenhayn's offensive had failed. British casualties were officially estimated to be 50,000; French losses were probably higher. So, too, were German losses, which were not published but which probably exceeded 100,000. Some German divisions counted only 2,000 riflemen. Whole units were riddled with typhus and dysentery.[10]

But numbers alone could not explain the cost to the German high command. Falkenhayn was hotly criticized from all sides for what became known as *der Kindermord von Ypern*—the massacre of the innocents at Ypres. Falkenhayn's appointment as chief of the general staff had already drawn Hindenburg's and Ludendorff's resentment. Their complaints against the OHL would henceforth draw support from such powerful voices as those of Crown Prince Wilhelm, Crown Prince Rupprecht of Bavaria, generals Groener and Wild von Hohenborn within the OHL, younger and disloyal members of Falkenhayn's staff such as Max Bauer and Hans von Haeften, members of the kaiser's military cabinet, even the chancellor, Bethmann Hollweg, whom the kaiser insisted would have no voice in military affairs.

The "race to the sea" was over. The fighting line stretched well over 400 miles from the Channel coast to the Swiss frontier. Frontline units were already hunkered down in incipient trenches that soon would grow to vast underground complexes holding millions of wretched men protected by acres of barbed wire and defended by thousands of cannon and machine guns.

The war of maneuver was over in the west. *Stellungskrieg*—position warfare—had begun.

The battle of Ypres had not reached its disappointing end when Erich von Falkenhayn summoned Erich Ludendorff to a meeting in Berlin. We have only Ludendorff's account of the discussion. Falkenhayn, who was "certain" that he would soon break through at Ypres, dismissed out of hand Ludendorff's arguments to make the eastern front the priority theater of war. Falkenhayn did agree to another *limited* offensive in the east, both to protect Silesia and to support Conrad, but he could promise only a limited number of troops from the west. He also agreed to support Hindenburg's appointment as commander in chief of all German forces on the eastern front.

That front had been temporarily quiet. Despite the Duo's claims of victory in their unsuccessful move on Warsaw and Ivangorod, the Russians had gained considerably more than their enemy. But the bitter fighting both in the north and in Galicia had taken a heavy toll. Brusilov later wrote that "after hardly three months of war the greater part of our regular, professional officers and trained men had vanished." Inadequately trained replacements were rushed in to fill the ranks. From this period onward "the army became more and more like a sort of badly trained militia," the bewildered peasant replacements having no idea why Russia was at war and for what purpose they were supposed to die. "The result was that the men were led like sheep to the slaughter, without knowing why—that is, at the whim of the czar."[11] Brusilov's army, fighting in Carpathian cold and snow, had worn through their summer clothing and had not yet been issued winter gear, which included the vital *valenki*, or thick felt snow boots. Captured Russian officers reported marches of thirty-five miles without rest, no rations for five and even nine days—the troops scoured fields for cabbages and potatoes to make a soup without salt.[12]

Nevertheless, had either Sukhomlinov's ministry of war or Grand Duke Nicholas's supreme headquarters, Stavka, been functioning with only minimum efficiency, the Austrian and German retreats could well have been turned into serious tactical defeats.[13] As it was, the Russian army was rapidly running out of small-arms ammunition, artillery shells, and rifles. A hopelessly inefficient supply system frequently deprived troops of proper rations and clothing, which meant hungry, cold men and starving horses. Heavy losses in artillery had not been made up, nor had additional machine guns been provided. In mid-October one army discovered that thirty-two *tons* of mail were filling a rear-area post office because there were no carts to take them forward.[14] The wounded suffered horribly. Doctors at regimental and brigade level were little more than barber-surgeons capable of hacking off limbs and no more. Anesthetics were reserved for officers. Rear-area hospitals were few and were poorly organized. According to a prominent Russian surgeon who was captured, "severely wounded soldiers were left to die, because they were considered to be of no further use and would only prove a burden."[15]

Strategic indecision and tactical inertia, the latter occasioned in large part by incompetent commanders, brought operational delays at a particularly critical time. Brusilov, commanding an entire army, was told nothing "about our general plan of campaign," and it was obvious that Ivanov was equally ignorant. "It is quite possible," Brusilov later wrote, "that no new plan was ever established . . . and that we followed the special policy determined by the needs of any given moment."[16]

Poor intelligence caused General Ruzski, who had replaced Zhilinski in command of the northwest front, to overevaluate the German threat from East Prussia. This in turn caused Stavka to order a needlessly strong buildup of armies in that area without knowing what to do with them, while depriving Ivanov of much-needed strength in his campaign against the Austro-Hungarians. Only after time-wasting deliberation did Stavka order Ruzski to invade East Prussia with General Scheidemann's Second Army and General Plehve's Fifth Army, the offensive to begin on November 11.

Hindenburg's headquarters, now called OberOst by virtue of his appointment as commander in chief of all German forces in the east, was privy not only to Stavka's plan to invade Germany but also to the attendant delay in organizing the offensive, thanks to the continued interception and decoding of Russian wireless messages. Ludendorff and Hoffmann had decided to preempt the plan by attacking Scheidemann's flank, for which purpose Mackensen's Ninth Army was hurriedly shuttled north to Gnesen–Thorn, an altogether remarkable logistics effort completed in five very busy days.

Mackensen attacked on November 11 just as Russian divisions were preparing to move out further to the south. Scheidemann's right was in theory covered by Rennenkampf's First Army, but Ruzski and Stavka's preoccupation with the supposed threat from East Prussia had caused Rennenkampf to shift the bulk of his strength further north.

Mackensen's surprise attack quickly overran an isolated Siberian corps to expose Scheidemann's right to flank and frontal attack while his four other corps were advancing to the west in conjunction with Plehve's Fifth Army. Scheidemann, seeing his right threatened, countermarched his remaining corps eastward to take up a favorable defensive position around Lodz, where they were to be joined by Plehve's Fifth Army. Still not pleased, Scheidemann ordered a general retreat on November 18, a message intercepted by OberOst intelligence which, however, failed to pick up a counterorder from Stavka to stay where he was.

Hindenburg, Ludendorff, and Hoffmann were convinced that a great victory was at hand. Having learned that the Ypres offensive had ended, they demanded from and were promised by the OHL four corps, but with no guaranteed time of arrival. Convinced nonetheless that the Russians were retreating to the Vistula, Ludendorff ordered a frontal attack by Mackensen's remaining corps.

This was a mistake. Lodz was the Russian supply head. Scheidemann and Plehve, already numerically superior, had now strengthened themselves materially. Units such as one Guards division which had had only 180 rounds per rifle left—the troops had fired over two million rounds in three days—took on new life. Contrarily, Mackensen's people had outrun their supply lines and were short of artillery ammunition.

The Russian general, Plehve, had performed remarkably well. Sixtyfive years old, he reminded one observer of "a little, wizened-up rat." He was so infirm that he could not inspect the frontline trenches, but he had a good mind and was quick to recognize Scheidemann's critical situation. As a result, his vanguard corps marched seventy miles in two days to change the shape of battle.[17]

"The greatest of our battles is in progress," Hoffmann informed his wife on November 19; "hopefully it will be a great success. According to human calculation we must win, but the waiting is nerve-wracking."[18]

But now Ludendorff's attempt to encircle the opponent ended in dangerous failure, when three German divisions found themselves isolated east of Lodz. With Rennenkampf's First Army approaching from the north, there seemed to be no way of escape. "Our left wing is beaten," Hoffmann informed his wife on November 22. "How we can put things right and save the situation I still don't know. . . . It stands on the razor's edge."[19]

Stavka had already dispatched a score of special trains to take the anticipated haul of prisoners back to Russia. But for General Scheffer-Boyadel, commanding XXV Reserve Corps, General Karl Litzmann's Third Guards Division and a cavalry corps, the trains would soon have been full. Instead, in one of the more remarkable feats of any war, Scheffer mixed discipline with extreme valor and, playing on enemy confusion and chimerical fears, not only broke out but took 16,000 prisoners with him! OberOst immediately trumpeted this bizarre and extremely lucky action to the world as another great victory. The kaiser, with Falkenhayn in tow, hurried to Posen to reward Hindenburg with promotion to field marshal, Ludendorff to lieutenant general.

Scheffer's escape was the last straw for Ruzski. Food was once again short. There was no *kasha*, the all-important bread, but only *sukhari*, a dried black bread, if even that. The troops lacked winter clothing, and many of them froze to death in the trenches at night. Losses had been enormous. Battle casualties and mass desertions topped 100,000. His plan for the invasion of Germany shattered, Ruzski again urged a retreat to the Vistula before trying to organize a new attack on East Prussia.

This led to intense wrangling with Ivanov and Alekseyev, who wanted to advance in Galicia, a contretemps soon solved by further German attacks on Lodz.

The Duo already had converted a relatively meager tactical gain into a major strategic victory. Strengthened by units arriving from the west, Ludendorff ordered an attack against Ruzski's new lines in early December. The effort failed at a cost of at least 100,000 German casualties—a surprising conclusion to what Hoffmann, confusing technology with result, claimed to be "the finest operation of the whole war."[20]

A few perceptive individuals did not buy it. Falkenhayn's deputy, Wild von Hohenborn, wrote to his wife in late November: "Things are still very shaky in the east. Hindenburg has been made a field marshal too soon."[21] Other voices later criticized Ludendorff for poor judgment in underevaluating the enemy and attacking with inferior forces. A foreign observer faulted OberOst's strategy on the grounds that a Russian offensive would have come to total disaster.[22] Indeed, a study of this campaign suggests that OberOst, by not standing still, missed a splendid opportunity for engineering a local Cannae.

Conrad's offensive on either side of Cracow had meanwhile quickly bogged down, resulting in heavy combat losses and mass desertions of Czechs and Poles (which would reach over a quarter of a million by year's end). Supply failures had been compounded by a cholera epidemic to leave Conrad's two armies in precarious position by the end of the campaign.[23]

What was all this leading to? At the height of the Lodz fighting Max Hoffmann, disgusted with the Austrian performance, had written to his wife: "I told Ludendorff that the day after tomorrow at the latest he *must* go to the kaiser at Messières; we have to know why and for what purpose we are fighting."[24] In short, was the war to be won in the east or the west?

11

Conflict in Command

We stand completely alone and must suffer defeat with dignity.
—KAISER WILHELM II, OCTOBER 28, 1914[1]

First we failed to take Paris, then we failed to take Warsaw.
It will be too much if we fail to take Ypres.
—GENERAL WILD VON HOHENBORN, NOVEMBER 15 1914[2]

Oh blessed Hindenburg, help us soon, we are in need of it.
—GRAND ADMIRAL VON TIRPITZ, CHARLEVILLE,
JANUARY 8, 1915[3]

Falkenhayn's abortive campaign in Flanders caused Chancellor Theobald Bethmann Hollweg to intervene in the traditionally sacrosanct sphere of military operations. He did so through the kaiser's military cabinet, members of which had privately warned him of "the imminent exhaustion of reserves," and he was successful in having the kaiser terminate that offensive.[4]

Bethmann refused, however, to accept Falkenhayn's increasingly pessimistic view of the war. Falkenhayn stressed that defeat at Ypres had destroyed the Schlieffen dream of encirclement. *Vernichtungsstrategie*, the strategy of annihilation so fervently believed in by Frederick the Great, the elder Moltke, and Schlieffen, had given way to *Ermattungsstrategie*, the strategy of attrition. Germany had become a "beleaguered fortress," as First Army chief of staff Hermann von Kuhl put it, and her "battles were the sorties of the garrison to delay the progress of the siege."[5] This did not mean that the war was lost. The dream of a great military victory had to give way to adroit diplomacy. Falkenhayn wanted first to bring about a separate peace with Russia. He would then settle the military issue on the western front in order to achieve peace with France and Britain, a peace with virtually no one the victor: "If we don't lose the war, we have won it."[6]

Falkenhayn's blunt appreciation brought home the inescapable fact that, once the Schlieffen plan had failed, once a quick victory had been denied, the German and Austro-Hungarian empires lacked a cohesive plan for continuing the war. This unpalatable situation has to be looked at from two viewpoints, civil and military, then as now in often self-defeating conflict.

The first problem was the future priority of military operations. Falkenhayn and his supporters, the "Westerners," believed that the war would be won (or lost) in France and that therefore a separate peace with Russia was necessary if maximum strength were to be available on the western front. Bethmann Hollweg was afraid that a diplomatic approach to Russia would be regarded as weakness by the Allied powers. At Falkenhayn and the kaiser's urging, but against his better judgment and the vigorous opposition of the foreign ministry and some politicians, he did accept an offer from King Christian X of Denmark to send an emissary to Petrograd to sound out the Russians regarding peace talks.

This policy collided head-on with that of Hindenburg, Ludendorff, Conrad, and their supporters, the "Easterners," who believed that Russia had to be conquered militarily before a decision could be gained in the west. This strategy was strongly supported by the foreign minister, Gottlieb von Jagow, and by his principal assistant, Arthur Zimmermann, but in a fashion that further complicated matters.

Arthur Zimmermann was a career diplomat, fifty years old, a large man with a heavily jowled square head and thick mustache. He was an East Prussian of middle-class background, and he was an advocate, like Ludendorff, of "total war." Turkey's entrance into the war, Zimmermann informed Falkenhayn in November, made it essential to open a land route to Turkey by completing Austria-Hungary's stalled conquest of Serbia. The stakes were enormous, Zimmermann argued. German logistical support would enable the Turkish army, 700,000 strong, to push the Russians from the Caucasus in the north and, in conjunction with the proclamation of a *jehad*, or holy war, to bring about a revolution in the south to force England from Mesopotamia, Persia, and perhaps even India. Bulgaria meanwhile would join the Central Powers to pit her army of 400,000 against the Russians, and it was likely that Romania would follow with her army of 500,000. In addition, Germany would gain sufficient food and raw materials from Bulgaria and Romania to offset the already telling effects of the British blockade.

Zimmermann was demanding nothing less than a new priority theater of military operations in the Balkans and the Near East. "The outcome of the war is substantially if not entirely dependent upon the immediate solution of the Serbian question. Other military tasks must come after this one."[7] Zimmermann rejected the notion of a separate peace with Russia on grounds that this would drive Turkey into Great Britain's arms. It followed that Russia must be defeated militarily, in accordance with Hindenburg and Ludendorff's wishes.

This would not be the last of Zimmermann's flights of fancy, and it probably would have caused no more than a ripple had so much confusion and uncertainty not existed in government and army. The kaiser favored the plan both on economic and chauvinistic grounds. A Turkish victory would protect Germany's large prewar investment in Turkey and the Baghdad railway, while the expulsion of England from the Near East would forever end British influence in that area. The Duo supported it because it would strengthen their influence on operations at Falkenhayn's expense.

Falkenhayn did not deny the strategic necessity of supporting Turkey by opening a land route to Serbia, but he gave it a low priority. A renewed Serbian campaign could only be undertaken with the help of German troops. Count Berchtold, the Austrian foreign minister who must bear considerable responsibility for the outbreak of war, did not want German troops to fight in the Balkans, which he regarded as an exclusive Austrian preserve. Instead, they would relieve Austro-Hungarian troops in Galicia, who would be transferred to Serbia and thus keep the Balkans clear of German influence. Berchtold's interference in military affairs infuriated Conrad, who had no intention of transferring Austro-Hungarian troops from the fighting in Poland.

Here was a fundamental strategic conflict that should have been solved at once. As supreme warlord, the kaiser was constitutionally responsible for solving it. It would not have been easy. Either Falkenhayn or the Duo would have to go. The kaiser would not relieve Falkenhayn, because he liked and trusted him. He feared and envied Hindenburg's sudden popularity, and he scorned Ludendorff's parvenu ambitions. Lacking the will to act, the kaiser merely retreated further into his fantasy world, dreaming one day of riding a white charger down the Champs Elysée, despairing the next for his empire's salvation.

Bethmann Hollweg was equally irresolute, but more dangerously so, since he was in charge of the government and thus more easily approachable than the kaiser, who found sanctuary behind the screen of his military and civil cabinets. While Falkenhayn resolutely stuck to his guns, Bethmann was being bombarded by doubting voices highly critical of Falkenhayn and the conduct of the war.

A similar discordance existed in the German navy, whose commander in chief was the kaiser. At the beginning of the war Grand Admiral Alfred von Tirpitz, minister of the navy, vociferously called for offensive action by the High Seas Fleet of twenty-one modern battleships, the noisy construction of which had done so much to push England into the Entente.

Tirpitz had not worn well. Count von Stürgkh, who had known him before the war, found him increasingly formal in speech and manner, saying the same things day after day, giving the impression "that 'the Roon of the Germany navy' had outlived his day and was drawing on the capital of his name."* Neither the kaiser nor the admiralty staff nor the commander of the High Seas Fleet, Admiral Friedrich von Ingenohl (soon to be replaced by Admiral Hugo von Pohl), shared his bellicose views, even when in early November Great Britain declared the North Sea a war zone, the opening note in what would become a full-scale naval blockade of Germany. The German fleet refused to pick up the gauntlet and remained impotently in Wilhelmshaven, pursuing its limited mission to protect the coast and reinforce the Baltic fleet when necessary to maintain imports of vital food and raw materials from the Scandinavian countries.

German naval fortunes were otherwise mixed. Rear Admiral Wilhelm Souchon, combining his own professional skill with enemy confusion in the Mediterranean, managed to find sanctuary for his two modern cruisers at Constantinople. A surprise British raid carried out by Vice Admiral Sir David Beatty in the Heligoland Bight in late August sank three German light cruisers and one destroyer. "I am greatly distressed by the affair at Heligoland," Grand Admiral Tirpitz fumed. ". . . Our light forces are not sufficient for such skirmishes. If things go on like this, they'll soon be wiped out."[8] Commander Otto Weddigen became a national hero when his submarine sank three British armored

---

*General Albrecht von Roon was Germany's ambitious and reactionary war minister and army expansionist (1859–1873). Like Tirpitz, he was an enormous figure with penetrating blue eyes glaring from below bushy brows. He called himself "the king's sergeant," but others called him "Ruffian Roon." Walter Görlitz, The German General Staff, 79.

cruisers within an hour in late September. A German mine sank a British battleship. A few German freighters were converted to auxiliary cruisers, lone and dangerous wolves such as Count Dohna's *Möwe* and Count Lucknow's *Seeadler*, whose deeds were added to the exciting and valorous book of sea lore. Admiral Count von Spee's squadron of heavy cruisers steamed from its China station across the Pacific, ran into Vice Admiral Sir Christopher Cradock's cruiser squadron off the coast of Chile, sank two cruisers (with no survivors), and sent the third one running. A month later two hastily dispatched British battle cruisers caught up with Spee near the Falkland Islands and sank all but one of his five cruisers —the *Dresden* escaped to be sunk a few months later. German battle cruisers shelled the east coast of England. An Austrian submarine sank a French battleship in the Mediterranean, but the considerable Austrian surface fleet based at Pola remained bottled up in the Adriatic. By year's end any German threat to Britain's naval supremacy seemed remote.

Most of Germany's merchant fleet—the second largest in the world—was lying idle in neutral ports as the British naval blockade continued. In a move to rescue his and the German navy's waning reputation, Tirpitz, without consulting the chancellor, publicly announced that the empire's salvation lay in a U-boat or submarine blockade of British ports. The concept held instant appeal to a gullible public, who did not know that Germany lacked sufficient submarines to carry it out, this largely the fault of Tirpitz and the kaiser's insistence on a surface-fleet strategy. It was a stunning and deliberate deception that the government could not counter, because to have done so would have revealed a major naval weakness to the world. It was moreover deliberately continued behind the shield of military censorship and in time would grow to a major disruptive issue among kaiser, government, military, Reichstag, and the people, the latter continuing to believe that the submarine was the miracle weapon that alone would bring a satisfactory peace.

This brief survey may raise the question of why, in view of divergent strategies, none of which seemed particularly promising, some consideration was not given at high levels to seeking a peace based on the status quo ante. The answer is somewhat complicated.

The first operative word is greed. It was compounded by fantasy formed from the quaint notion expressed in a score of guises over the years that the Germans were God's chosen people. From top to bottom of this incredulous empire a pervasive belief existed that Germany would win the war or, at the very least, a peace that would bring her Great Power status in the world. Despite the kaiser's frequent change of moods, he believed that German arms would so aggrandize the house of Hohenzollern as to make the name indispensable in history's hall of fame, where his portrait would hang proudly and justly alongside those of the Great Elector and Frederick the Great. German statesmen and politicians, bankers and industrialists, shipping magnates and businessmen saw themselves as lords of a greatly enlarged empire. In early September 1914 Matthias Erzberger—a busybody politician, a leading member of the Center party, and an executive of the powerful Thyssen industrial combine—made his opening appearance on this peculiarly Wagnerian stage by sending a list of what he thought should be Germany's war aims to the chancellor and other influential persons. Germany was to win control of all of Belgium, a strip of the French coast from Dunkirk to Calais, the Channel Islands, the French fortress of Belfort, the Longwy–Briey ore fields in Lorraine, the Baltic provinces, and huge chunks of Russian Poland in league with Austria-Hungary, which would receive the Ukraine. Germany would acquire France and Belgium's enormous holdings in central Africa, while Austria would receive Egypt. Both powers would be paid huge cash reparations. These claims were relatively modest when compared to those of the Pan-Germans, the Army Leaguers and Navy Leaguers, and the great industrialists who foresaw Germany as the ruler of the entire European continent.[9]

A few powerful voices scorned these extreme demands. The chancellor did not share their extravagance. The Prussian minister of the interior, Friedrich von Loebell, warned against large-scale annexations in Poland, which would bring anti-German Slavs into the empire and would ensure Russia's lasting hostility. The colonial minister, Wilhelm Solf, expressed his horror to the foreign ministry "over the annexationist mania that seemed to have suddenly laid hold even of moderates."[10] But Loebell and Solf also agreed with Bethmann Hollweg and Falkenhayn (and the vast majority of German subjects) that Germany's future security must be guaranteed by such measures as postwar control of Belgium in one form or another; by "border rectifications" in Poland, the Baltic provinces, and France; and by gaining uncontestable freedom of the seas.

What of the German people?

The explosion of euphoria in August 1914 had not yet subsided. Rigid censorship carried out by army corps commands inside Germany had enforced the chancellor's decision to forbid public discussion of war aims. There were twenty-four of these commands (not counting those in the Bavarian kingdom), which were a relic of an 1871 state-of-siege law that had been invoked at the beginning of the war to make the army responsible for internal security. Each command resembled a feudal fief-dom controlled by an overlord who was above the law. Their function would eventually be challenged, but for the moment they were accepted by an enthusiastic public only too willing to believe the inflated figures of enemy dead and wounded, the deflated figures of German casualties.

Generated by the basic lie that Germany had been invaded and was fighting a *defensive* war, the national enthusiasm had been expanded by a carefully orchestrated propaganda campaign in which such famous authors, playwrights, and poets as Gerhart Hauptmann and Richard Dehmel "felt themselves obliged, like the bards of the ancient Germani, by songs and runes to inflame the advancing warriors with enthusiasm for death."[11] England more than France or Russia was the focus of their rage. A minor Jewish poet, Ernst Lissauer, enshrined Albion's treachery in a "Hymn of Hate," a hastily scribbled poem that attained instant popularity when published in a Munich newspaper in September. "The Kaiser was enraptured," wrote Stefan Zweig, "and bestowed the Order of the Red Eagle upon Lissauer, the poem was reprinted in all the newspapers, teachers read it out loud to the children in school, officers at the front read it to their soldiers, until everyone knew the litany of hate by heart. As if that were not enough, the little poem was set to music and, arranged for chorus, was sung in the theaters; among Germany's seventy millions there was hardly one person who did not know the 'Hymn of Hate' from the first line to the last."[12] The inflammatory work soon made its way to America, where readers of the *New York Times* were no doubt startled by its martial message, which ended:

> We will never forgo our hate,
> We have all but a single hate,
> We love one, we hate one.
> We have one foe, and one alone—England![13]

Philosophers, professors, doctors, lawyers, clergymen, scientists, and journalists preached Germany's inevitable victory to a still-gullible public daily being deceived by dishonest dispatches from the fronts. Shopkeepers removed French and English signs from their windows, Shakespeare was banned from the stage. People read only of glorious victories by their new god, Hindenburg. Germany was clearly on the march to her manifest destiny. It was no time for peace.

"Only one great value has this war brought with it to us in Germany at least—all that was best and noblest in the nation has risen to the surface; materialism, luxury, and selfishness have slipped from us, and each one of us feels that we are better men and women than before." Thus wrote Dorothy, the Countess von Moltke, cousin by marriage to the chief of the general staff, to President Wilson's confidant, Edward House, in early October. "The spirit among the troops is very sober but most confident. Every one, even the Social Democrats, feels that Germany did not want war, and that therefore they are absolutely right in defending their country, and they all have unbounded confidence in those in command. . . . Our only consolation [for the heavy losses] is that we in Germany are making the best possible use of its lessons and growing morally in an astonishing way. Germany is being new-born, but the travail is heartbreaking."[14]

America was being reviled for selling munitions to France and England and for evident anti-German feeling, as shown in articles and cartoons in its newspapers. "The hate here against England is phenomenal. Actual 'odes of hate' are recited in the music halls," Ambassador Gerard informed House in November. But "life seems perfectly normal here and provisions are only slightly higher. Women send their only sons of fifteen to fight, and no mourning is worn and it is etiquette to congratulate a family who has lost a son on the battlefield." He went on, "The losses to date alone are 4,500 officers and 83,000 men killed— about 280,000 wounded and about 100,000 prisoners. . . . The finances are in perfect order and the country can continue the war indefinitely —a war which is taken quite cooly by the people at large."[15]

A month later the American military attaché reported that "the Swiss Army representative . . . makes the prophecy that the Germans will undoubtedly win in this war in less than a year. This is due to the excellent army and the united people."[16] An American naval lieutenant, S. C. Hooper, reported to naval intelligence in Washington that he had recently visited Belgium: "[German officers and men] are absolutely convinced that Germany is fighting for right and that Germany will win. The feeling is so strong that a stranger visiting the country becomes immediately a party to that spirit, in spite of any previous feeling to the contrary. . . . All hands have great patriotism and love for the Kaiser

. . . each is perfectly willing to die if by so doing the Kaiser will be aided in any way."[17]

Most members of the Reichstag shared the feeling. They still trusted the army and government. "If we want the peace which we need," Prince Max of Baden wrote, "we must now above all things put our trust in the German arms and the German people in the field; but trust also in the desire for peace and the will to peace of the German Kaiser. . . . At the moment we can trust the Kaiser."[18]

The political truce, the *Burgfriede*, was still very much alive. The Reichstag had recently approved another five-billion-mark war appropriation. Its members accepted virtually without question the fact that the war was costing an average of a billion and a half marks per month, a figure that was steadily increasing. They did not seem alarmed that the government was already talking of a *new* appropriation of ten billion marks to carry the war through to the following September.

The figures on food quoted to them by the Prussian food commissioner, Georg Michaelis, were not particularly comforting. Bread ration cards that appeared in January limited each person weekly to four and a half pounds of *Kriegsbrot* (war bread), baked from rye and wheat flour adulterated by potato, barley, oat, and rice flour.[19] Enough potatoes were on hand, hopefully, until the next harvest. There was very little cloth, and luxuries such as chocolate, coffee, and tea were beginning to disappear from store shelves. Food prices except for bread had sharply risen, and there was some grumbling about unfair and inefficient distribution of basic staples. But this was still minimal. "Country optimistic in every respect," Ambassador Gerard reported in late February.[20] Like the people they represented, members of the Reichstag accepted the necessity for *durchhalten*—the carry-on theme that, in view of the empire's limited natural resources, was as full of holes as the German corpses that already littered the fields of Flanders and the plains of Poland.

The only people who questioned this martial insanity were the soldiers doing the fighting. Six weeks after Walter Limmer's "gripping and uplifting" experience of marching to the station, he was dying in agony from tetanus-infected wounds, wanting only to go home, away from "that world of horror."[21]

Letters from soldiers on both fronts spoke of disappointment and disillusionment as the horrors of war engulfed and eventually killed or maimed them. A young student of philosophy, Alfred Buchalski, wrote from the carnage of Flanders in late October: "With what joy, with what enthusiasm I went into the war, which seemed to me a splendid opportunity for working off the natural craving of youth for excitement and experience! In what bitter disappointment I now sit here, with horror in my heart." He died from wounds a few weeks later.[22]

Captain Bloem led his company in the retreat from the Marne. He had marched with 250 men in early August; he was retreating with 85. He himself had experienced "a sudden and complete transformation. . . . Till now I had been an individual entity, fighting, suffering, worrying, hoping: at this moment that individual self ceased to exist, was sacrificed on the altar of patriotism, and from its dead ashes it was resurrected as one small piece of living, struggling, wounded Germany." During the retreat he was wounded. "All my former worldly desires and ambitions, my buried selfishness, had come to life again. Not only was I no longer a piece of a living, struggling, wounded Germany, but I even ceased to be interested in anything unless it concerned my own miserable little scrap of life."[23]

Bloem was scarcely alone. Temporary truces, even of short duration such as that experienced by Fritz Kreisler's unit in Galicia, were more common than generally realized. Sometimes they occurred so that the wounded and dead could be collected, sometimes from boredom and malaise resulting from the unspoken question, "Why am I here trying to kill someone I've never seen in my life?"

Early in the western war "quiet" trench sectors developed which soon led to outright fraternization. It might start by "concerts" in which British or French troops, hunkered down in trenches a few hundred yards from their enemy, would sing favorite songs—"Tipperary" or "The Girl I Left Behind Me." Then the enemy would sing *their* favorite songs—"Die Wacht am Rhein" or "Deutschland über Alles." Once a rapport, however shaky, was established, the enemies met in no-man's-land, and there among the dead bodies of men and horses, in the midst of mud and shell holes and barbed wire, they exchanged handshakes, names, tobacco, newspapers, precious bits of food, and showed each other photographs of girlfriends, wives, children, families.

Reports of these doings horrified senior commanders on either side, who issued strictest orders against such unseemly behavior. The troops paid scant attention. During the first Christmas of war, gifts were exchanged as if everyone were at an Alice in Wonderland house party. A young student wrote from Flanders twelve days before he was killed that on New Year's day "an English officer came across with a white flag and asked for a truce from 11 o'clock until 3 to bury the dead. . . . The truce was moreover extended. The English came out of their trenches into no-man's-land and exchanged cigarettes, tinned meat, and photographs with our men, and said they didn't want to shoot anymore. . . . On New Year's Eve we called across to tell each other the time and agreed to fire a salvo at 12. It was a cold night. We sang songs, and they clapped (we were only 60–70 yards apart); we played the mouth-organ and they sang and we clapped. . . . They produced some bagpipes . . . and they played some of their beautiful elegies on them, and sang, too."[24]

These were strange interludes. They would continue throughout the war, pathetic protests against inhumanity, brief periods of light in a very dark and prolonged and senseless storm. A few months before Alfred Vaeth was killed he complained of "disappointment after disappointment . . . [yet we] know that we have got to win, and that however war-weary we may be, we shall go on doing our duty. We shall not be beaten anyhow, but we may bleed to death."[25]

An officer and gifted writer, Rudolf Binding, sadly observed this phenomenon of alternate hope and resignation prevalent in his sector in Flanders, only to conclude: "Truly there is no longer any sense in this business."[26]

12

Germany's Leaders

[The kaiser] is a child and will always remain one.
—HOFMARSCHALL COUNT VON ZEDLITZ-TRÜTZSCHER,
DECEMBER 1908[1]

All in all his [Bethmann Hollweg] was a Hamlet nature in
which the native hue of resolution was all too often sicklied
over by the pale cast of thought. It was his and Germany's
tragedy that he was called upon to right a disjointed time.
—FRITZ HARTUNG, *DEUTSCHES BIOGRAPHISCHES
JAHRBUCH FÜR 1921*[2]

The leaders who were constitutionally empowered to make "sense
out of this business," that is, to find a way out of a war that had
failed, were not up to the task. They were two: Kaiser Wilhelm
of Germany and his chancellor Theobald Bethmann Hollweg.

Wilhelm was born in 1859 shortly before his grandfather, Crown
Prince Wilhelm, ascended the Prussian throne. His mother was Queen
Victoria's eldest child, "Vicky," the princess royal of England. Wilhelm
was her first of eight children. His breech delivery by forceps required
over ten hours and resulted in nerve damage that irretrievably affected
his left arm. Despite this tragedy he was taught to ride and shoot well
—one can imagine the traumatic discipline involved—and he also
learned to play the piano. He would grow to about five feet nine inches,
but his withered left arm would be about three inches shorter than normal
and not strong enough for him to cut his food.

Tutors taught him Greek, Latin, French, and English. He was glib,
had a good wit and an excellent memory. His mother described him at

age twelve in a letter to Queen Victoria: "He is not possessed of brilliant abilities, but he is a dear boy, and I hope and trust will grow up a useful man."[3] His tutor found him so arrogant that he persuaded the parents to send him to a common school in Cassel for three years, an experience that merely increased Wilhelm's autocratic ways.

Wilhelm was nineteen when he suffered a severe ear inflammation with complications that nearly caused his death. His most recent literary analyst, John Röhl, has suggested that this later led to mental problems, and he may be right—certainly *something* did.[4] Having recovered, he studied jurisprudence and political science at Bonn University, a period in which he became enamored of Prince Bismarck's policies (which his mother and father despised). He then entered the army, and at age twenty-two married Princess Augusta Viktoria ("Dona") of Schleswig-Holstein, a woman whose intellect was as slight as her estate, a pious, intolerant bore as nervous and insecure as her husband. "She is just like a good, quiet, soft cow," wrote a contemporary princess, "that has calves and eats grass slowly and ruminates."[5] Dona would give him six sons and a daughter, but there would be no marital bliss.

Wilhelm enjoyed the army, as well he might considering the homage automatically paid to him as heir to the throne. He was particularly close to Count von Waldersee, the elder Moltke's deputy, a fire-eating conservative who wanted war against Russia and France prior to toppling Britain from her predominant position in the world. He soon came under Bismarck's personal influence, which completed the nascent rupture with his parents. Unfortunately, neither Bismarck's brilliance nor his subtlety rubbed off on his royal ward. A ranking official described Wilhelm in 1884 as "self-willed, devoid of all tenderness, an ardent soldier, anti-democratic, anti-English." "As cold as a block of ice," Bismarck's son noted of him. "Convinced from the start that people only exist to be used—either for work or amusement—and that even then they only do duty for a given period, after which they may be cast aside."[6]

The ninety-two-year-old Emperor Wilhelm died in 1888. Wilhelm's father, terminally ill with throat cancer, held the throne for only a few months. In June 1888 the twenty-nine-year-old Wilhelm became king of Prussia and emperor of Germany.

Filtering through clouds of religious mysticism that surrounded the royal head came the convenient concept familiar to all Hohenzollern rulers, the divine right of kings. Wilhelm's court was strongly autocratic.

One did not speak until spoken to, and did not depart until kissing the royal hand—a medieval frolic that greatly amused the irreverent Austrians. Wilhelm was referred to in reports and dispatches as "the Most High" or "the All Highest." Frederick the Great's grandfather was said to have arisen early "so as to prolong his enjoyment of the kingly state," and so it was with Wilhelm: seventy-six splendid castles, palaces, and hunting lodges; an enormous income exempt from any taxation; five hundred liveried lackeys; elegant carriages; a royal train of twelve luxuriously furnished coaches; a royal yacht; stables full of richly caparisoned horses; an army of coachmen, footmen, grooms; wardrobes full of ornate uniforms including the "imperial hunting costume" that he personally designed, each cut to better hide his withered arm. Jaded Berliners joked "that he would not visit an aquarium without putting on admiral's attire, and had been known to climb into the uniform of a British field marshal to eat a plum pudding."[7] His chest was covered with dozens of decorations, his pudgy white fingers decorated with ostentatious rings, bracelets dangling on his wrists, his arrival by car announced by a bugler's "tadi-tada-ta-ta."[8]

It was all glitter, a constant parade, an unending ego trip. Bismarck once remarked that Wilhelm would like to have a birthday every day. Irreverent Viennese joked that "Wilhelm insisted on being the stag at every hunt, the bride at every wedding and the corpse at every funeral."[9] An elderly friend bluntly told him: "Your Majesty finds life impossible unless Prussia applauds you daily, Germany weekly and Europe once a fortnight."[10] He was a showoff, a spoiled dilettante who played at life instead of trying to govern an empire that he hadn't worked to deserve.[11]

Wilhelm flitted, not only physically but emotionally, and he often did not flit gracefully. At times emperor, warlord, statesman, historian, spiritualist, painter, art critic, ballet choreographer, equestrian, sportsman (shooting and international yachting), archaeologist (he maintained a grand palace in Corfu on which he had spent six million marks up to 1914),[12] he would talk endlessly and often superficially on any subject. With intimates he would brook no argument. Those who acted against his will "betrayed him."[13] His passion for Bismarck turned to envy and hatred when he could not have his way. His respect for Waldersee, his chief of the general staff, turned to contempt when Waldersee argued against his plans for a large navy. He was dismissed after three years in office.

Court cabals and intrigues flourished. Wilhelm had no use for his ministers and saw them as little as possible. They were probably happier for it. He was extremely rude to his diplomats, telling them that they were "so full of shit that the entire Wilhelmstrasse stunk." He addressed his minister of war and the chief of the military cabinet as "you old asses." He told a group of admirals, "You know absolutely nothing. Only I know anything, only I decide."[14]

At a time when England was looking for alliance with Germany, Wilhelm went out of his way to worsen relations. In 1896 he congratulated President Kruger of the Transvaal Republic for disrupting Jameson's invasion—the famous Kruger telegram that infuriated Great Britain. He had already decided to challenge British naval supremacy, a mission given over to Admiral Alfred von Tirpitz, whom he appointed minister of the navy responsible directly to himself. This led to the formation of the chauvinistic and powerful Navy League and the passage of two whopping naval construction bills by the Reichstag that further strained Anglo-German relations.

The new century opened with Wilhelm's disastrous appointment of Prince Bernhard von Bülow as chancellor. Bülow was a sycophant, an arch conservative, able enough but lazy, preferring to bask in power while carrying out the kaiser's mandate to bring Germany to Great Power status. He might have succeeded had he formed the alliance tentatively offered by Great Britain. Instead he listened to the pernicious advice of Baron Holstein and refused to pursue the matter. Subsequent saber-rattling diplomacy further isolated Germany from France, Russia, and Britain, a process encouraged by the kaiser's jingoistic phrases—"the ring around Germany," "the Yellow Peril"—and continued efforts to enlarge the navy.

Despite pretensions to be "the people's ruler," Wilhelm held many of his subjects in contempt and saw as little of them as possible. In 1900 and 1903 he ordered the police to gun down striking workers.[15] When not traveling he preferred the flattering military environment of Potsdam broken by the aesthetic surroundings of a small circle of friends. The "Liebenberg Round Table" had begun in the 1890's, named for Prince Philipp Eulenburg's estate, where the gatherings were held.

Eulenburg was one of Wilhelm's closest friends and advisers—he had been instrumental in having Bülow named chancellor. He was twelve years older than the kaiser, an ultraconservative monarchist, religious spiritualist, soldier, diplomat, and dilettante, an accomplished pianist, composer, and poet. The round table collapsed in 1906 when Baron Holstein, éminence grise of the foreign ministry, was fired. Bismarck had called him "the man with the hyena eyes," not far from the mark in that Holstein devoured some of his former associates by charging the Liebenberg group with homosexual activities. A prolonged investigation resulted in a public trial of three of the group, including Eulenburg, and a scandal of major proportions.

Wilhelm suffered his share of censure—latter-day scholars continue to speculate about his sexual preferences, the consensus seeming to be that he was a "repressed homosexual."[16] Judging by details of some of the all-male parties held at Liebenberg and on the annual royal yacht cruise, this is a mild enough conclusion. The bizarre tastes of the emperor and his friends form a chapter in juvenile vulgarity. One intimate was paraded in a costume "like a clipped poodle" with the "behind shaved, in front long bangs out of black or white wool, in back under a real poodle's tail, a noticeable rectal opening, and, as soon as you stand up on your hind feet, *in front* a fig leaf." In 1908 the forty-nine-year-old kaiser, on a visit to a friend's estate, watched his chief of the military cabinet dance a transvestite ballet—an effort suddenly terminated by a fatal heart attack.[17] Reports of these and other goings-on naturally leaked out and did little to improve the kaiser's waning stature.

Political scandal was added to personal scandal. Such was the trauma of the Eulenburg affair that the kaiser's watchdogs persuaded him to seek relief by a visit to England. There, after making an ass of himself in general, he compounded the damage by granting an interview to an "establishment" colonel. This was published in the influential London newspaper, the *Daily Telegraph*, an honest interview in that it made the flamboyant and egotistical kaiser appear to be the mental lightweight that he was. The reaction at home and abroad was distinctly unfavorable. Wilhelm blamed Bülow, who had authorized publication of the interview, and not without difficulty forced his resignation. In 1909 he appointed Theobald Bethmann Hollweg the fourth chancellor of the German empire.

Theobald Bethmann Hollweg was born at Hohenfinow, a 7,500-acre estate in East Prussia, in 1856. He was a second son of a distinguished haute bourgeoisie family. His mother, Isabella, was French, "elegant and sensitive," according to Konrad Jarausch, whose excellent biography of the imperial chancellor is the basis for the following sketch.[18] His father, Felix, was a gentleman farmer, a conservative but not quite a Junker, a stern man who insisted on the boys arising before dawn to take a cold bath followed by breakfast and long hours of tutored study broken by rigorous riding and hunting.

Theobald was bright. At age twelve he was packed off to an elite school for seven years. He graduated with high honors, enjoyed a grand tour of Italy, served briefly in a distinguished dragoon regiment, studied law at Leipzig, and became a doctor of law at age twenty-four.

After a spell as a junior law clerk he switched to domestic administration and began a bureaucratic career at times aided by his father's friendship with the young Kaiser Wilhelm. He advanced slowly, duly married, inherited his father's estate, and continued to impress his superiors as an excellent administrator. Obviously a marked man, he was appointed Prussian minister of the interior and a year later imperial secretary of the interior and vice chancellor. In 1909 he was made minister-president of Prussia and chancellor of the German empire.

Bethmann was fifty-three, a tall, serious man not in the best of health. Widely traveled, well read, a classicist fluent in French and English, he was cultured, worldly, intelligent. He was also very weak, a man of changing moods and beliefs, very much the cynical loner, a career bureaucrat who in time became not so much a master *of* as a mistress *to* compromise. Unwise compromise dogged his career. It would eventually bring about his ruin.

His office was a strange one. It was created by the imperial constitution of 1871. Bismarck wrote this document, which was intended to keep the twenty-five states that composed the new empire in political and military servitude to the national government, in effect to Prussia and its passion for autocratic government controlled by the aristocracy and the crown.

Even Bismarck could not cloak the new empire against the uncomfortable winds of democracy that were swirling through the Western world. To corral the southern states he agreed to a federal council, the Bundesrat, composed of delegations from each state, and to a federal parliament, the Reichstag, whose members, elected by secret ballot of male voters twenty-five or older, served without pay. Bismarck was also forced to grant additional privileges to the larger kingdoms, such as those of Bavaria, Saxony, and Württemberg, which administered their own armies and enjoyed exclusive tax privileges.

The Bundesrat was the executive body of the empire. It had to approve new legislation and it was supposed to supervise foreign policy. Its fifty-eight members, of which seventeen were Prussian, met in private, the chair being held by either the emperor or the chancellor. Prussian representatives were chosen by the Prussian Landtag, or parliament, whose members were elected by a three-tiered voting system based on wealth to guarantee rule by the privileged propertied classes. Any proposed constitutional reform in the Bundesrat could be blocked by fourteen votes, which virtually guaranteed the survival of Bismarck's autocratic form of government. In practice the Bundesrat was moribund—"in 1914 it was not consulted until after war was declared."[19]

The Reichstag was supposed to symbolize the unity of empire. Although it could not initiate new legislation, it had to approve it and it also had to pass on the military budget. Two factors curtailed even these limited powers. The first was the constitutional right of the kaiser to summon the Reichstag, to postpone its meetings for an indefinite period, or simply to close it in favor of new elections. The other discomfiting factor was the makeup of the elected representatives. Radicals and liberals played only a small role in the Reichstag for several decades, mainly because they could not afford to serve without pay. Elected members, until the rise of the socialist movement, were generally conservatives devoted to the Hegelian concept of individual subservience to the all-powerful state (except when this conflicted with their private interests). Socialist members did not altogether escape this restrictive influence, whose spell enchanted most voting members with their constituencies. A few fiery exceptions aside, the majority approached parliamentary duties with a humble, hat-in-hand attitude, which the chancellor did not hesitate to exploit in favor of his ruling ends. With some justification the communist leader Wilhelm Liebknecht described the Reichstag as "the fig-leaf of absolutism."[20]

Standing giantlike over the Bundesrat and the Reichstag was the federal executive, composed of the kaiser and his chancellor. Bismarck's constitution made the kaiser, who was also king of Prussia, the most powerful ruler in the world. The cornerstone of his authority was the privilege of total command, the *Kommandogewalt*, "a constitutional concept," in Gordon Craig's words, "which jurists found it difficult to explain or define."[21]

The *Kommandogewalt* allowed Wilhelm to appoint and dismiss his chancellor, all federal officials, all army officers except those in the Bavarian, Saxon, and Württemberg contingents, and all navy officers. He held complete control of foreign policy. He could make or break treaties and alliances. He could declare war and make peace. In war he was the supreme commander of all the imperial armies. He did not have to answer, nor did his chancellor, to the Reichstag. Should a constitutional question arise, the kaiser could interpret as he willed.

Wilhelm was advised by a civil and military cabinet that also served as go-between with the chancellery, the foreign ministry, the war and naval ministries, and the very powerful general staff. His chancellor was the second most important man in the empire, responsible for carrying out the imperial will by issuing the executive decrees necessary to running the complex group of states known as Germany.

Bethmann took office at a difficult time. Outwardly Germany was on the climb to major-power status, an industrial juggernaut steadily producing more steel than Britain, exporting more goods, her population expanding as rapidly as the expansionist dreams so fervently preached by the Pan-Germans and Navy Leaguers in their fanatic pursuit of the kaiser's and their own *Weltpolitik* ambitions.

This prosperous picture was marred by increasing internal dissension, growing demands for electoral and financial reforms, and increasingly powerful trade-union demands for industrial and agricultural legislation. Liberal Reichstag members wanted to bring imperial Germany into the modern political world. A ruling aristocracy wanted imperial Germany to remain in the Junker tradition of government by the few for the few. Liberals wanted to cut arms spending. Conservatives demanded a bigger navy and a stronger army.

Bethmann inherited an embittered emperor, a floundering treasury, a Reichstag in partial revolt, the Prussian conservatives unwilling to accept needed reforms, a growing liberal movement supported by a rising but bewildered middle class, and an army general staff stronger than ever.

Germany in 1909 needed a strong chancellor capable of responding to the growing needs and anxieties of the German peoples. Bethmann was not that man. There is some evidence that he did not want the job, partly because he felt himself ill-fitted to accept the enormous responsibility, partly because he realized that it would be exceedingly difficult to save Germany from the morbid acts of her quixotic emperor.

Bethmann's cares were well-founded. A good many responsible people, Germans and foreigners, throughout the 1890's had commented on Wilhelm's refusal to face reality, his unwillingness to be alone, his extreme *Cäsarwahnsinn* with its delusions of either persecution or grandeur, his nervousness and instability, inability to concentrate, constant talking, incessant traveling, charm on the one hand, rudeness, vulgarity and even cruelty on the other, his military posturing exemplified by upturned mustaches waxed into place each morning by a barber who always traveled with him, his utter conceit: "a postcard picture of the Kaiser, signed by his own hand, was, in his own estimation, one of the most priceless gifts he could bestow."[22]

As early as 1888 Britain's prime minister, Lord Salisbury, believed that Wilhelm was "perhaps not in full possession of his senses."[23] Bismarck held that "the Emperor is like a balloon, if one did not hold him fast on a string, he would go no one knows whither."[24] In 1896 his war minister believed that he was "not quite sane," as did some princes of the empire and the Austro-Hungarian military attaché.[25] Philipp Eulenburg noted in 1897 that the "entire Foreign Office now regarded the monarch as insane."[26] Three years later he wrote to a friend of another furious outburst that deeply concerned him because of its violence and fierceness. The kaiser's physician was at a loss, seeing it as a sort of temporary nervous breakdown. Eulenburg felt that he was sitting "on a powder keg."[27]

In 1903 Eulenburg complained that the kaiser had entirely lost self-discipline. Certainly his humor was approaching the macabre. In bidding farewell to King Ferdinand of Bulgaria he suddenly slapped the little man on the bottom, much to the latter's fury. He enjoyed hurting people with his exceptionally strong handshake and he punctuated his incessant conversation by tapping the trapped auditor sharply in the ribs. His entourage dreaded the annual Norwegian fjord cruises, during which young and old alike were summoned to the promenade deck for prolonged and painful calisthenics. He suffered another nervous breakdown during the *Daily Telegraph* affair and recovered only to resume his frequently inane antics.

His blustering performances during the Annexation Crisis and the Moroccan crisis earned him international opprobrium. Britain's prime minister, Herbert Asquith, noted in 1911: "One is almost tempted to discern in some of the things he said . . . the workings of a disordered brain." The foreign minister, Sir Edward Grey, believed that he was "not quite sane, and very superficial."[28] In 1914 a Swiss psychiatrist diagnosed him as having a "manic-depressive psychosis."[29]

But there was always another side to this odd coin. President Woodrow Wilson's confidant, Colonel Edward House, detected none of these traits during a thirty-minute private audience in spring of 1914: "I found that he had all the versatility of [Theodore] Roosevelt with something

more of charm, something less of force. He has what to me is a dis-
agreeable habit of bringing his face very close to one when he talks most
earnestly. His English is clear and well chosen and, though he talks
vehemently, yet he is too much the gentleman to monopolize conversation."[30]

Many biographers have pointed to the *Daily Telegraph* affair as the
decisive turning point in the kaiser's reign in that it broke his self-
confidence. Karl von Treutler, who replaced Philipp Eulenburg as confidant, but with nowhere near the same intimacy, is closer to the mark
in pointing to the kaiser's failure to control the Marne campaign: "From
now on he felt himself only as a supernumerary at OHL and became
treated as such."[31] In turn he withdrew further into his own fantasy
world, thus abrogating his responsibility in a war that almost certainly
he could have prevented.

In early January 1915 Grand Admiral von Tirpitz echoed the complaint of many senior officers and officials: "The wall round the Kaiser
is at the present moment more than ever impenetrable. It is just the
Kaiser's peculiarity that he won't come to any decision, or bear any
responsibility."[32] This was a major defection made the more serious since
executive responsibility was largely shifted to Bethmann Hollweg, who
was not competent to bear the burden, particularly when it came to
controlling the German military machine that had grown stronger as its
imperial master had grown weaker.

13

The War Against Falkenhayn

As a result of the unfortunately widespread catchword "the war must be won in the East," even people in high leading circles inclined to the opinion that it would be possible for the Central Powers actually "to force Russia to her knees" by force of arms, and by this success to induce the Western Powers to change their mind. This argument paid no heed either to the true character of the struggle for existence, in the most exact sense of the word, in which our enemies were engaged no less than we, nor to their strength of will. It was a grave mistake to believe that our Western enemies would give way, if and because Russia was beaten. No decision in the East, even though it were as thorough as was possible to imagine, could spare us from fighting to a conclusion in the West.
—GENERAL ERICH VON FALKENHAYN[1]

At the end of the year [1914], four new Army Corps were formed which were to be ready in February. . . . Naturally I wished the four corps to be under the Eastern command, in order further to maintain our pressure on the Russians and break down their resistance as far as our strength made that possible.
—GENERAL ERICH LUDENDORFF[2]

Chancellor Bethmann Hollweg visited eastern-front headquarters, OberOst, at Posen in early December 1914, the day that Mackensen's army seized Lodz. He found Hindenburg, Ludendorff, and Hoffmann in an ebullient mood, convinced that they could win the "decisive victory" in the east if provided with sufficient troops. All else would follow if Russia were knocked out of the war. Then Austria-Hungary would seize Serbia; Bulgaria and Romania would join the Central Powers; and Turkey's "holy war" would push Britain from the Near East. Their strategical sophistry, at dramatic odds with Falkenhayn's pessimism, so enchanted the uncertain visitor that he violated Falkenhayn's confidence by disclosing the latter's desire for a separate peace with Russia. Absolutely not, cried the trinity, who already had sharply criticized Falkenhayn's military abilities—such a desire was nothing short of heretical.[3]

Confronted with these discordant views, Falkenhayn brushed them aside like so many verbal insects. Hindenburg and Ludendorff were refusing to face reality, he told Bethmann. They were not properly assessing the enemy's determination. A winter offensive against Russia, even if successful, which was highly doubtful, would not end the war, and Bethmann was wrong to press for it. The German army was "a broken instrument." It had suffered 840,000 casualties, including 150,000 dead in just five months of war.[4] Regular officers and noncommissioned officers had suffered particularly heavy casualties. Such had been the losses that new divisions had been formed from Landsturm and Landwehr units and from line-of-communication and depot troops. Each infantry division had been forced to shred one of its four regiments in order that new reserve divisions could be formed.[5] Although this resulted in a total 138 divisions in January 1915, their quality had been reduced to the extent that in Falkenhayn's opinion the army, far from being able to knock Russia from the war, would be fortunate "to maintain itself on all fronts."[6]

Falkenhayn agreed that it would be desirable to remove the Russians from East and West Prussia by a limited offensive. He also accepted Bethmann's arguments for a future offensive against Serbia, where Austria-Hungarian armies had recently suffered another major defeat under the command of General Oskar Potiorek, a man whose "known conceit had degenerated into a morbid megalomania," as Count Stürgkh explained to Falkenhayn.[7] Falkenhayn agreed that a campaign here was necessary, both to open a supply line to Turkey, which had joined the Central Powers in late October and stood in need of weapons and munitions, and to keep Italy, Romania, and Bulgaria in check. But where were the troops to come from? Austria-Hungary was no longer capable of offensive warfare. Germany's own offensive capability dictated a strategic defensive to be carried out by "limited offensives" with the hope of wearing down England and France in the west.

Falkenhayn's realistic appreciation of the situation fell on ears stuffed with wax of ignorance. Temporarily brainwashed by euphoric briefings at Posen, Bethmann decided that the eastern front must now have priority and that Falkenhayn must be replaced by Ludendorff. To this end he approached General Moritz von Lyncker, the doddering old chief of the kaiser's military cabinet, and Colonel General Hans von Plessen, the kaiser's seventy-three-year-old adjutant general. These worthies discouraged the notion. The kaiser, they explained, liked and trusted Falkenhayn, he did not like Ludendorff, and he approved of Falkenhayn's desire for a limited victory.

Bethmann backed off, but only temporarily. Ludendorff, in a remarkable display of insubordination that should have resulted in his immediate court-martial, had recently sent his intelligence officer, Major von Haeften, to the OHL in the guise of liaison officer. In reality Haeften was to lobby for an all-out eastern offensive which would require the support of Falkenhayn's major reserve, four new well-trained and well-equipped infantry corps built on cadres of veteran officers and noncommissioned officers and men.

Sharply rebuffed by Falkenhayn, the forty-five-year-old major's appeal to Bethmann for a change of strategy and in consequence a change of command caused the chancellor to approach the kaiser over the heads of his military keepers—an interesting example of the prestige enjoyed by a general-staff major who, with misdirected loyalty, to put it kindly, informed Bethmann that two of Falkenhayn's subordinates, generals Wilhelm Groener and Adolf Wild von Hohenborn, favored the Duo's eastern strategy.[8]

Bethmann met with the kaiser in early January 1915. Wilhelm agreed to replace Falkenhayn as minister of war with Wild von Hohenborn, his personal friend since student days at Cassel. The kaiser refused to consider dismissing Falkenhayn as acting chief of staff. Ludendorff would never be appointed to this post, because he "is a dubious character devoured by personal ambition."[9] Wilhelm added an exclamation point a few days later by appointing Falkenhayn permanent chief of the general staff. Bethmann did not further press the matter. As usual he had begun doubting his own judgment, defending vacillation by his expressed ignorance of military matters (yet not hesitating to encroach in military affairs when it suited him). He was also beginning to suspect Ludendorff of unhealthy intrigues, and with good cause.[10]

At Ludendorff's instigation Major Haeften extended his lobbying efforts to the western front, or as close as army commanders got to that front. Haeften reported to OberOst a command consensus of opinion that troops could be spared from the west for transfer to the east. He next persuaded Hindenburg to write again to the kaiser, this time to demand Falkenhayn's dismissal, which, if refused, would bring Hindenburg's resignation. He also arranged for the German crown prince, who commanded the Fifth Army, to write to the kaiser in support of the Duo's desires.

Falkenhayn attempted to reassert his authority by meetings with Conrad and Ludendorff at Breslau and with Hindenburg at Posen, which only exacerbated already hard feelings. Haeften had already informed the chancellor of the contents of Hindenburg's unprecedented letter to the kaiser when Falkenhayn arrived in Posen. The meeting was stormy, the old field marshal bluntly stating that the chief of the general staff had lost the confidence of the army and should resign.[11]

Falkenhayn had no intention of either resigning or supporting a full-scale offensive in the east. The Duo now attempted to outmaneuver him by summarily transferring one cavalry and two and a half infantry divisions from the Ninth Army to Conrad's front. Falkenhayn, supported by the kaiser, responded by making this force the cadre of a new German *Südarmee* (South Army) under command of General Alexander von Linsingen, to whom Ludendorff was transferred as chief of staff. An anguished Hindenburg at once appealed to the kaiser for the return of his brain and, just as forcefully, for the transfer of Falkenhayn's precious reserve to OberOst so that he could "inflict on the enemy in East Prussia a decisive and annihilating blow" which would be "decisive for the outcome of the whole war."[12]

The quarrel had now reached the highest level: Kaiser Wilhelm II. Hindenburg, prompted by Ludendorff with Hoffmann and other staff officers in the shadows, was challenging the imperial *Kommandogewalt*. The kaiser's first impulse was to court-martial Hindenburg. This brought an anguished cry from Bethmann Hollweg, who had been born frightened, that he could not accept the responsibility for the political consequences. Such was Hindenburg's immense popularity, in both empire and army, that Wilhelm, who was even weaker than his chancellor, chose to pacify the field marshal by a personal plea to stay at his post while Falkenhayn remained at his post. This abject compromise settled nothing, because successful blackmail never does. Wilhelm had already received and angrily rejected his son's importunate letter. Then came a letter from the former chief of the general staff, Helmuth von Moltke, who in addition to criticizing Falkenhayn pleaded for Ludendorff's eastern strategy. To top this, the emperor received the ubiquitous Major von

Haeften, who delivered a letter from the empress, written at Haeften's persuasion, in strong support of Hindenburg. "The Kaiser was very upset," Müller recorded in late January, "had not slept a wink and read novels all night. He spoke bitterly of the empress and of his friends who had stabbed him in the back."[13]

A weak kaiser struck at the weakest point. Haeften was flicked to a minor post in Cologne (but we shall hear more of him). Not so Hindenburg and Ludendorff, who were to be reunited and given Falkenhayn's four reserve corps.

Falkenhayn had lost the battle but not the war. He accepted the rebuff and remained at his post. He must have been tempted to resign —he is silent on the subject in his memoirs. Perhaps he believed that events would demonstrate the innate fallacy in the Duo's ill-conceived strategy of fighting "decisive" battles and campaigns that could never be won. Perhaps he believed that, so long as he retained the kaiser's trust, he could use the immense power of his office to control future events, if only indirectly. Perhaps he feared for the future of army and empire if the Duo gained control—as the kaiser's adviser, General Baron von Marschall, put it early in the war, "Ludendorff would wage war until the last ounce of strength was pumped from the German people and then the monarchy would have to bear the blame."[14] Or perhaps it was a case of vanity. When he was finally dismissed as chief of the general staff, he was seen off by an adjutant who attempted to console him with the thought of his new command. "Who once has held the laurel wreath in his hand," Falkenhayn told him sadly, "can never be satisfied with another job."[15]

Major Hans von Haeften later wrote of Hindenburg's inner conflict over his quarrel with Falkenhayn and the OHL. Haeften was instructed to tell the German empress "that this quarrel will be the death of me," Haeften adding gratuitously that the field marshal was so distracted "that he was unable to direct operations with his customary vigor."[16] If so, the recovery of Samson Ludendorff seems to have calmed him. To perpetuate his martial deeds he had already summoned a prominent provincial painter, the fifty-nine-year-old professor Hugo Vogel, to Posen.

Vogel arrived in the snow and cold of mid-January. He liked the baroque style of the town, its large *Schloss* full of soldiers and telephone wires, smartly uniformed staff officers peering anxiously at mysterious-looking wall maps and barking orders to waiting messengers. Suddenly the great Hindenburg appeared: "The immense body supported an almost square head. The hair grey with several dark streaks. The mustache in contrast brown, the skin tinged yellow but not unhealthfully so. The whole expression of unbending strength, weatherbeaten; but great kindness in the blue, genuine German eyes. He held out his hand and spoke a few friendly words remarking that he was almost as much a Magdeburger as I."[17]

Hindenburg invited the newcomer to his table of two other guests and twenty-four staff officers. "There was Italian salad, then pork chops with vegetables and apple tart, white wine and red Assmannshäuser, cider, no French claret, later German *Sekt* for the field marshal and his guests." Hindenburg discoursed at length on the amount of mail he received—two clothes basketsful on New Year's day alone. Fortunately an adjutant diligently sifted through the numerous requests, for example "if mustard, sparkling water, hard liquors or an inn could be named after him," otherwise he would have had to neglect the war.[18]

After dinner the field marshal sat in an anteroom in which a corner had been partitioned off by a folding screen. He occupied a giant leather armchair. The centerpiece of the table to his front was a pot holding a small date palm, the *Phönix* which he seemed to be particularly fond of. Vogel's description of the conversation is enlightening. Not once was Ludendorff (temporarily serving in Silesia) mentioned when it came to what Hindenburg had named the battle of Tannenberg. Vogel sketched its victor the next morning and was well praised. The task ahead loomed large. He returned to Berlin to pick up larger canvases and more paints.

Hindenburg posed every morning from nine to ten in a small atelier at the top of the *Schloss*. The field marshal reappeared at four each afternoon to fish horn-rimmed spectacles from a tunic pocket and inspect and often criticize the day's work. Vogel's first portrait, a gargantuan Blücher-like figure standing on some steps, field marshal's baton in one hand, papers in another, sword hilt peeping out from the greatcoat, field glasses hanging rakishly from the bull neck, pleased the subject no end. More followed. While Vogel dabbed away, the field marshal enlightened him on a variety of subjects. He valued Goethe and Wagner as artists, but not as men. Goethe had not been kind enough to his mother and had overrated Napoleon while insufficiently extolling German virtues. He preferred Mozart to Wagner, particularly *Figaro*. But Schiller—ah, there was a true German. Hindenburg always sat through *Wallenstein* enthralled: "I feel uplifted—that is exaltation."[19]

Ludendorff returned to OberOst and was brought to several sittings.

Vogel found him cold and austere, never without his gleaming monocle—it was said that he slept with it. At dinner he usually sat silent, preoccupied, biting his lower lip, frequently leaving the table for hurried conversations with his staff. Hindenburg thought that Vogel should paint them together in a single portrait.

Vogel's next painting, the same giant figure this time posing with hands behind back before the snow-covered glacis of the *Schloss,* brought grotesque admiration: "There in your picture, there I stand as if I would say, 'I shall not halt until I possess all Russians. None can escape me.' "[20] He had already accepted the artist's suggestion for a commemorative canvas of his dramatic arrival in Marienburg and another of the battle of Tannenberg. Vogel's requirement was to find similar terrain near Posen where he would sketch the Duo surrounded by half a dozen staff officers, a map table, folding chairs, stereotelescope and, not least, a background of two hundred Russian prisoners.

Plans were being made for the sitting when the war thoughtlessly interrupted matters. One morning in early February 1915 the old field marshal cryptically announced, "When one goes north one has the sun to his back. Therefore forward."[21] Vogel awakened the next morning to an empty town. OberOst had moved north to Insterburg.

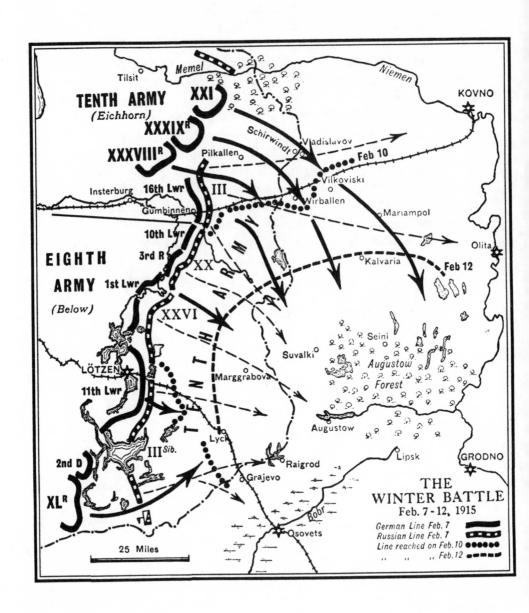

TENTH ARMY
(Eichhorn)

XXI

XXXIX^R

XXXVIII^R

Tilsit

Memel

Niemen

KOVNO

Schirwindt

Vladislavov

Feb 10

Pilkallen

Vilkoviski

Insterburg   16th Lwr   III

Wirballen

Mariampol

Gumbinnen

10th Lwr

Olita

3rd R

EIGHTH

ARMY

(Below)

1st Lwr

XX

Kalvaria

Feb 12

XXVI

Seini

Suvalki

Augustow

Forest

LÖTZEN

11th Lwr

Marggrabova

2nd D

III^Sib.

Lyck

Augustow

Lipsk

GRODNO

XL^R

Raigrod

Grajevo

Osovets

Bobr

25 Miles

THE
WINTER BATTLE
Feb. 7 - 12, 1915

German Line Feb. 7
Russian Line Feb. 7
Line reached on Feb. 10
  "   "   " Feb. 12

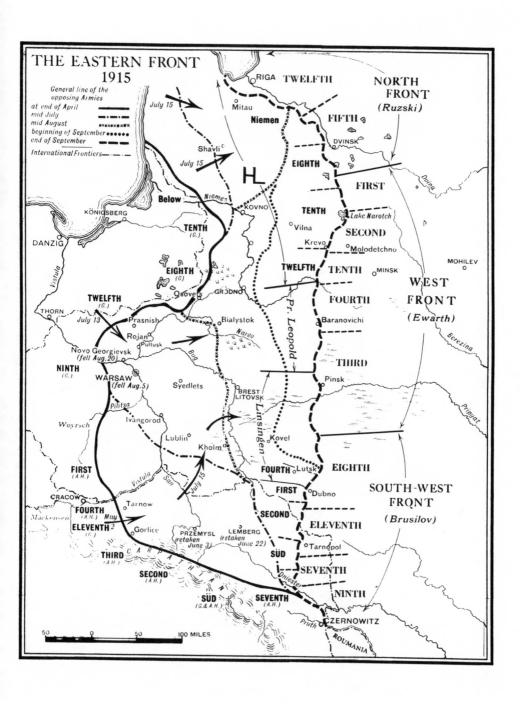

THE EASTERN FRONT
1915

General line of the
opposing Armies
at end of April _____
mid July –·–·–·–
mid August ×ₒ×ₒ×ₒ×ₒ×
beginning of September ●●●●●●
end of September ▬ ▬ ▬ ▬

International Frontiers _____

July 15

RIGA   TWELFTH   NORTH
Mitau   FRONT
Niemen   FIFTH   (Ruzski)

Shavli   DVINSK

Below   EIGHTH

KÖNIGSBERG   Niemen   KOVNO   FIRST

DANZIG   TENTH   TENTH   Lake Narotch
                (G.)   Vilna   SECOND
              EIGHTH   Krevo   Molodetchno
                (G.)   GRODNO   TWELFTH TENTH   Minsk   MOHILEV
         TWELFTH   Osovets   FOURTH   WEST
THORN   (G.)   Bialystok   FRONT
         July 13   Prasnish   Narev   (Ewarth)
              Rojan   Pultusk   Baranovichi
         Novo Georgievsk   THIRD
         (fell Aug.20)   Bug   Pinsk
   NINTH   Berezina
    (G.)   WARSAW   Syedlets   Pripiat
         (fell Aug.5)   BREST
         Pilitsa   LITOVSK
   Woyrsch   Ivangorod   Kovel
                      Lublin   EIGHTH
                            Kholm   Lutsk
   FIRST   Vistula   San   July 15   FOURTH   SOUTH-WEST
   (A.H.)   FIRST Dubno   FRONT
   CRACOW   SECOND   (Brusilov)
         FOURTH   Tarnow   ELEVENTH
Mackensen (A.H.) May   PRZEMYSL LEMBERG
         ELEVENTH   Gorlice   (retaken   (retaken   Tarnopol
           (G.)   June 3)   June 22) SÜD
   THIRD   CARPATHIAN   SEVENTH
    (A.H.)   Dniester   NINTH
         SECOND
          (A.H.)   SÜD   SEVENTH
                  (G.& A.H.)   (A.H.)   Pruth CZERNOWITZ
                                              ROUMANIA

50   0   50   100 MILES

14

Colonel House's Mission

Kill as many of the swine as you can.
—KAISER WILHELM TO THE SECOND PRUSSIAN GRENADIERS,
LYCK, RUSSIAN POLAND, FEBRUARY 14, 1915[1]

You would really have wanted to weep for all the feelings of
mourning, joy, happiness, admiration, longing, but you can't
cry anymore—you just can't do it.
—CORPORAL HERBERT SULZBACH, FLANDERS, MARCH 1915[2]

Conrad von Hötzendorf, chief of the Austro-Hungarian general
staff, opened his new offensive in late January 1915. It was
designed to push several hundred thousand Russian soldiers from
the Carpathians and to relieve the besieged fortress of Przemyśl, which
was considered to be the key to Galicia that would open the gate to
Hungary. It was a massive fortress complex, complete with its own air-
field, the concrete pride of Austria-Hungary.

Falkenhayn had forecast disaster, and it is probable that Ludendorff
at heart agreed. Ludendorff's brief sojourn with Linsingen's *Südarmee* had
opened his eyes to Austro-Hungarian military weakness. "A Jew in Radom," he later wrote, "once said to one of my officers that he could not
understand why so strong and vital a body as Germany should ally itself
with a corpse. He was right."[3]

Snow and extreme cold all but paralyzed the three-pronged operation
from the beginning. Although the Seventh Army on the right struggled
through deep snow to push the Cossacks on the extreme Russian left
some 60 miles back to the Dniester River, Conrad's center and left armies
soon bogged down to bring stalemate along the 150-mile line.

The Duo meanwhile had been frantically preparing for the complementary northern offensive. Thanks to the four corps torn from Falkenhayn's hands, OberOst had three armies at its disposal: Below's Eighth Army, deployed south of the Angerapp line in East Prussia; Mackensen's Ninth Army, deployed to the southwest; and Eichhorn's Tenth Army, which was to be secretly located north of the Angerapp line—altogether some 150,000 troops constituting fifteen infantry and two cavalry divisions.[4]

Ludendorff had good reason to hurry his plans, not alone to assist Conrad's crippled offensive, but because intercepted Russian wireless messages suggested a "gigantic attack" against the Eighth Army's left by Sievers's Tenth Russian Army and confirmed a buildup of Plehve's new Twelfth Army to the south. This was probably confirmed by a military attaché of an unnamed power who obtained a copy of the Russian plan and who also reported on the Russian shortage of artillery shells, information sent to Vienna and presumably to Berlin. More information was allegedly procured from a Russian colonel on Sievers's Tenth Army staff. This man, a protégé of the Russian war minister, was later convicted of treason and hanged.[5]

The Duo obviously held high expectations for the offensive. At the end of January Hindenburg informed the foreign ministry that Italy and Romania must be kept quiet for the next three weeks, "by then, even if everything is still not achieved in the East, the success will be so evident that the world can no longer doubt Germany's final victory in the East."[6]

The offensive kicked off at the end of January with a feint attack by the Ninth Army, an effort made historically remarkable by Germany's introduction of poison gas. This was the work primarily of Fritz Haber and Carl von Duisberg, who not without difficulty had developed a liquid gas, xylylenbromide or chlorine, that savagely burned eyes, nose, and throat and clung to the ground for long periods.[7] Known to the troops as T-Stoff, in this instance it filled 18,000 shells. Max Bauer, who had been involved with its development and who ingeniously claimed that it was not poison gas, witnessed the pioneer attack. Extreme cold and adverse winds nullified effective results on the Russians (except to set a horrible precedent), and the Germans soon broke off the attack. German casualties from the gas blown back at the troops by the shifting wind were so severe that Bauer would never forget them.[8]

The abortive gas shelling was directed against eleven Russian divisions commanded by General Gurko, "a dapper little man" of fifty-three years "who dressed neatly and wore a small imperial [beard]."[9] Unlike most of his peers he was extremely active and frequently inspected frontline trenches. Although known as a strict disciplinarian, he also had a sardonic sense of humor. When some of his men bragged that the enemy would have to pass over their bodies, Gurko told them, "Much better if you pass over theirs."[10] With this in mind he ordered a counterattack à la Russe, lost 40,000 men in three days, but regained the ground that had been lost and inflicted heavy casualties on the Germans before calling it off.[11]

Next came the two-pronged advance from the Masurian Lakes and from the north designed to bring about that elusive Cannae so fervently desired by the Duo.[12] Despite intense blizzards and subzero temperatures that covered the area with over five feet of snow, Ludendorff refused to delay the main attacks. Roads and railroads lay hidden under giant snowbanks. Guns and munition and ration wagons required double and even treble the usual number of horses. The opening attacks nevertheless succeeded remarkably well considering the conditions, and they achieved almost total surprise.

Ruzski and the Grand Duke had misread enemy strength and intentions, believing that their enemy would never dare attack in East Prussia while Plehve's Twelfth Army was forming in the southwest. Stavka was stretching itself at best. Although casualties had been enormous—over five months the general staff put them at nearly 14,000 officers and close to 500,000 men (excluding prisoners and wounded who had returned to duty)—that was not the real problem. There were plenty of bodies but not enough rifles. In some units "unarmed men had to be sent into the trenches to wait till their comrades were killed or wounded and their rifles became available." In Petrograd recruits trained with one rifle to three men. In early 1915 two million replacements could easily have been shipped out had there been rifles to arm them, and had proper facilities existed to train them. The armies were also plagued with a severe ammunition shortage that was far beyond the capacity of Russian factories to repair. While thirty-five thousand artillery shells were being produced *a month*, the armies were firing forty-five thousand *a day*, a consumption that soon exhausted meager prewar reserves. The shortage would continue for some months until the first shipments from foreign suppliers reached Russian ports to begin the long overland journey to the front.[13]

Stavka's concern with the Twelfth Army resulted in neglect of Sievers's Tenth Army, which lacked reserve divisions and was weakened by second-line divisions, poor deployment, confused corps and division commanders, inadequate communications, fragile defensive lines, shell shortages, and ill-armed soldiers depressed by cold and hunger which resulted in lengthy sick lists. Sievers was strategically isolated and was under no illusion as to his combat strength, having notified his superiors in early February that "nothing can prevent the Tenth Army from being exposed to the same fate as [Samsonov's] First Army in September 1914."[14] His was an army destined for a defeat that he wished to avoid. Eichhorn's plodding pressure was sufficient pretext for the Russians to run. Effective pursuit was difficult. "The columns of infantry were straggling, the bulk of the artillery and the vehicles remained sticking in the snow; only a few of the guns, to which twelve or eighteen horses were harnessed, and assisted by the infantry, were able to go on."[15] But for captured supply depots and freight cars full of rations the German attack could not have continued.

Hindenburg and Ludendorff directed the battle from the Hotel Dessauer in Insterburg. In but a few days Below's right had advanced well into Sievers's left, while Eichhorn's divisions were pushing in Sievers's right to threaten his rear. A week after the opening attacks, the Russian Tenth Army was in retreat, its divisions in fearful confusion: "*Ordre, contreordre, désordre,*" as one general put it.[16] Seven days later an entire Russian corps surrendered in Augustów forest, but the Duo's dream of gigantic envelopment dissolved when Sievers's surviving divisions slipped away to the south.

OberOst had gained a substantial tactical victory, though not as grand as that announced to the public. The 100,000 prisoners turned out to be 55,000 and 185 guns along with some unwanted territory soon to be lost to enemy counterattacks.[17] Ludendorff could not safely pursue as long as his southern flank was threatened. In mid-February he turned to the siege of fortress Osovets and to attacking Plehve's Twelfth Army as best he could, an effort hindered by capricious weather, the cold suddenly turning to thaw, with rain and mud taking over.

Conrad meanwhile had suffered still another tragedy. His center and left armies were literally stuck in heavy snow. Supply lines and communications had as usual soon broken down. Starving men froze to death in temperatures that plunged to thirty degrees below zero (Fahrenheit). Conrad and his staff lived in warm villas at Teschen, some with their wives. Linsingen's *Südarmee* took a month to reach its first objective and suffered thousands of casualties from illness and frostbite.

Conrad complained that the German general stuck in the mountains "did nothing but shout for reinforcements."[18]

General Ivanov soon repaired the damage to his left flank and counterattacked on his right. Food ran out for the Austro-Hungarian defenders of fortress Przemyśl, except for garrison officers, who were well fed to the end. Those who did not run away surrendered. One entire garrison, the senior regiment in the army, went over entirely to the Russians.[19] The commandant surrendered the 120,000-man garrison (including over 2,500 officers) in March. This freed three Russian corps and forced Conrad to plead for reinforcements from OberOst simply to hold his weakened lines. Conrad was frantic, complaining that the Germans were "unscrupulous, brutally selfish" while intimating, in order to get his way, that his government should suggest "a separate peace with Russia."[20] A hastily created force of German divisions, the Beskidenkorps commanded by General von der Marwitz, bolstered the wavering line in early April. More to the point, Ivanov, who was plagued by heavy troop losses and supply problems, called off the offensive a few days later. By mid-April Conrad was momentarily safe. His grandiose dream had cost him an estimated 800,000 casualties, three quarters of them from sickness.[21]

In sharp contrast to the miserable failure of their Austrian ally, Hindenburg and Ludendorff had already converted their costly and far from satisfactory *Winterschlacht* into a victory tantamount to that of Tannenberg by claiming to have taken over 100,000 prisoners and nearly 300 guns, a claim false in the extreme.[22] While black-shawled women bawled out the headlines of newspaper extras in German cities, Kaiser Wilhelm hurried to OberOst's headquarters in Insterburg: "I wish to be the liberator of East Prussia," he told his staff, "otherwise it will be merely looked upon as another triumph for Hindenburg."[23] Prompted by political necessity and with great fanfare, he awarded Hindenburg the prestigious medal, the Pour le mérite (normally given for heroic action in frontline combat). A well-known painter, Professor Ludwig Dettmann, was busily recording the carnage of the recent northern fighting. His realistic sketches impressed Hugo Vogel, who had painted Hindenburg in Posen, and who was now summoned to OberOst. Hindenburg put him in a captain's uniform, since he would be touring the battlefields as a war artist. "Now I must try to find a Russian painter whom we have taken prisoner," he laughingly told the apprehensive artist, "so that we can exchange him for you if you are captured."[24]

Dettmann's paintings and Vogel's sketches and letters leave no doubt of the recent vicious fighting. Vogel toured the area in a seventy-horse-power open Mercedes staff car and nearly froze to death in subzero weather and snow so deep that it reminded him of the North Pole. It was a gruesome task. Village after village had been destroyed by shell and rifle fire. He spent the night of his sixtieth birthday in the ruins of Darkehmen, where, after drinking a bottle of champagne thoughtfully placed in his kit by Hindenburg, he watched German troops hovering over a campfire in the market square. Then, "in bluish mist, the ruins under deep snow, a deathly silence. Not a person in the street. Only in the market square the giant fire and the tents of sleeping soldiers. Slowly and silently the sentries marched to and fro."[25]

Farmhouses in the nearby countryside were imprisoned by wire, their battered walls pierced by loopholes. Village dwellings were honeycombed with bullet holes, old and beautiful trees had been felled to open fields of fire. Then came zigzag German trenches protected by small sheets of metal pierced with fire holes and holding dugouts often furnished with stoves, straw mattresses, and furniture taken from nearby houses. The trenches were fronted by a fifty-five-yard belt of electrified wire. Russian trenches, five hundred yards distant, were protected by sandbags in the Japanese fashion and by chevaux-de-frise, rows of sharpened stakes. Open graves were everywhere, as were bodies of men and horses frozen in the snow, their positions made more grotesque by heavy mist. One large grave was marked by a wooden cross with the arm diagonal, a soldier's cap and two empty vodka bottles. In Lyck, Vogel watched Kaiser Wilhelm distribute Iron Crosses to the troops after thanking them for victory, but he did not record the savage end of his speech, "Kill as many of the swine as you can."[26] "All then sang 'Nun Danke Alle Gott.' A powerful scene. As background the still-burning houses and the bullet-riddled church. Russian prisoners by the hundreds were being herded to the rear, mostly amazingly robust men from the best Siberian regiments, all excellently equipped." In still another village: "The activity was beyond words. Generals halted with their staffs; in front of a burning house a young chaplain intoned prayers which the soldiers devoutly heard with bared heads. A sled with wounded lying on the straw was pulled past. . . . Right and left the city burned."[27]

Vogel received virtually a hero's welcome back in Insterburg. Both Hindenburg and Ludendorff praised his stories and sketches. Hindenburg gave him a delayed champagne birthday party, and Ludendorff advised him to paint the kaiser, "as you have seen him in the burning town of Lyck surrounded by troops," adding, perhaps maliciously, "Indeed it was the first time that His Majesty was so close to the firing line. It will remain an historic, glorious occasion."[28] Hindenburg had not forgotten the grand project of the Tannenberg memorial. Vogel was soon painting Russian prisoners plucked from a nearby camp and grouped to his pleasure in the freezing countryside. When he complained of the cold, Hindenburg sternly informed him, "One is always cold in war."[29]

OberOst moved to Lötzen once the fighting shifted to the south. It was a pretty, if battered, little border town already being cleaned up by Russian prisoners. Hindenburg, Ludendorff, and Hoffmann shared a small but comfortable house, staff sections worked in a warehouse, staff officers were housed variously in town. In remarkably short order skilled signalmen had tamed the miles of ganglia into humming performance essential to control of the vast forces spread north and south. Staff cars roared through the tiny streets, uniformed motorcyclists delivered reports from distant commands. Observation balloons kept wary track of enemy movements. Aviators wearing long leather fleece-lined flying coats defied freezing cold to monitor the Russian retreat from single-engine open-cockpit monoplanes.

Vogel saw a great deal of Hindenburg at this time. The field marshal continued to sit for him every morning for at least an hour. He frequently took "his little professor" on a midday walk or a motor trip, and he again visited the atelier in the afternoon to admire and often criticize his work. Hindenburg was a great stickler for gold braid, decorations, and buttons. "A coat without a button is like a flower without scent," he told the artist.[30]

Vogel was now a regular guest at dinner, where the field marshal entertained a stream of important guests, writers, journalists, painters, sculptors, politicians, civil officials, ministers of state, bankers, industrialists, royalty, and such personalities as Wolf Metternich and the famous Swedish explorer Sven Hedin.

Dinner was promptly at eight. Ludendorff usually sat at table saying very little, but those in the know carefully watched him break bread and compress it into small balls. If he rolled the balls slowly with one hand things were all right, but if he did it violently there was a storm approaching. If he did it with two hands, things were very bad and everyone went on his guard.[31]

Ludendorff and the staff officers left the table at nine-fifteen to return to work, normally until after midnight. Hindenburg and his guests retired to a salon. The field marshal always sat in an enormous leather armchair by a round table that held the small date palm, the *Phönix*, familiar to Posen and Insterburg. (Vogel thought that it looked more desolate than immortal.) While guests lighted pungent cigars, a soldier servant offered beer, punch, brandy, and sometimes champagne. Hindenburg directed the conversation, which covered a wide range of topics including that of German annexation of occupied territories. The subject evidently was of considerable interest to Hindenburg, and a letter to his wife at this time is particularly significant in view of later events. "We should not want too much land come peace," he wrote, "otherwise the Slavs and Latin races (French, Belgians, and Italians) will gain the upper hand and we will cease to be Germans. To remove the present inhabitants and then Germanize the entire area all sounds good but in practice it is impossible. 1864–66 and 1870–71 both correspond to [Frederick the Great's] Silesian war [1740–1745] in which territory was won. 1914–15, however, is comparable to the Seven Years War [1756–63] in which the earlier conquests had to be maintained against numerous grudges. . . . Naturally the borders must be adjusted and a few important places taken, but no more than that."[32]

The *Cercle*, as Vogel called it, usually broke up before midnight, when Hindenburg's adjutant delicately squeezed a lemon into a tall crystal glass and filled it with water. Hindenburg then ponderously arose, spooned sugar into the mixture, and, laughing, said, "The secret is in the stirring." The *Cercle* regarded this *Abendtrunk* almost as holy ceremony—and Vogel duly sketched it for posterity.[33]

Hindenburg worshiped posterity. Tannenberg was to be immortal. Vogel must go there and study the hill at Frögenau from where Hindenburg directed the battle. He must go to Marienburg to study the bridge that held the refugees. The field marshal loved to talk about the battle. Vogel was not to believe that he had planned it before the war or that thousands of Russians had been driven into the swamps to drown, as countless journalists, assiduously encouraged by OberOst's publicity machine, had reported. All that was nonsense! On the other hand he did not publicly refute the stories. "Legends are necessary," he told Vogel. He left no doubt who was responsible for the victory. "I am fortunate that His Majesty, at my suggestion, also named my battle Tannenberg."[34]

Promoting Tannenberg was promoting himself, already a living legend to those who visited OberOst. The visitors were rarely disappointed.

They listened to prosaic pronouncements as if they had been taken from the holy tablets. "The war could end next summer." "The conduct of war is also an art." "The one with the best nerves will win the war."[35]

The gifts that arrived by the hundreds delighted him, as did the thousands of letters, testimonials, newspaper articles, even books extolling his virtues and fame. His picture hung in thousands of beer halls in Germany and Austria. He was petitioned for advice and favors. The director of a zoo wanted to name a new hybrid killer beast after him. An association of midwives asked him to end the war as quickly as possible because with the men away, few babies were being born and the midwives were out of work.

Visitors found him gracious, confident of victory, imperturbable. Hoffmann interrupted the Cercle festivities one night to report that 3,000 Russians had just been captured but that German losses were heavy. "Yes," Hindenburg said, "very sad, but unavoidable."[36]

While Hindenburg basked in his own glory, grim reality was slowly overtaking the rest of OberOst. An Allied fleet had been bombarding Turkish forts in the Dardanelles for the last two weeks of February, one result being that Italy had sharply increased her territorial demands to Austria in return for continuing neutrality. At the same time the German army on the western front had been holding against a French offensive in the Champagne with no letup in the ferocious fighting. The Russian Tenth Army that Ludendorff had described as "annihilated" was back in action and it was not alone. On March 1 Hoffmann wrote in his diary, "The position yesterday was very unpleasant. The Russians had collected, on foot and by rail, about twelve army corps, and fell upon our whole line from the south up to this sector."[37] A few days later Vogel remarked on the serious mood of staff officers at dinner. They arrived at table late and left early in order to counter new threats posed by Russian reinforcements.

The imperial chancellor, Bethmann Hollweg, visited OberOst in early March. Contrary to his expectations he learned that a virtual stalemate existed along a large part of OberOst's front, with heavy but nonproductive fighting in the south. Labor battalions were building fixed defenses along the East Prussian border in case the army had to go on the defensive. Max Hoffmann bluntly told the chancellor that there was "no prospect of completely defeating all our enemies," particularly since the Austrians were beaten, and he implied that the time was ripe for a negotiated peace on modest terms favorable to Germany.[38] The Duo, however, in no way despaired of achieving victory in the east, and Hindenburg archly refused Bethmann's suggestion of sending reinforcements to Falkenhayn's hard-pressed front, since that would possibly force him to yield occupied Poland and parts of East Prussia to the enemy.

Bethmann realized that with stalemate on both fronts a negotiated peace seemed the only way out. Never an optimist, he was worried about an incipient war-weariness at home and by growing army command resentment of Falkenhayn, who was becoming ever more difficult. Karl von Treutler had never seen him "so overbearing, ill-bred, almost rude," but he continued to be supported by the kaiser. But Bethmann could not rely on the kaiser, who as usual changed his mind like his uniforms. Favorable reports from OberOst turned Wilhelm into a conquering hero. Unfavorable news from the Austrian front depressed him so much that his confidant, Treutler, dared to suggest that the army should hold what it had and forgo any further useless and costly offensives.[39]

Neither the government nor the public had learned the extent of human losses on both fronts, which would sharply rise before the French offensive in Champagne ended in late March. The armies were demanding 180,000 replacements a month. As yet there was no manpower shortage, but there was already a serious shortage in officers and noncommissioned officers.

The public knew none of this. They believed only that OberOst had won another great victory. German armies everywhere occupied enemy soil. Conservatives and annexationists seemed confirmed in their demands for vast territorial gains, and a great many of their countrymen agreed with them. Even moderates such as Max Hoffmann, who argued for a separate peace with England and who would forsake major land gains in Europe, held for "the return of our colonies, together with a few additional ones, the Congo in particular, a few colonies from France and twenty-five billion in money."[40] Those in the army and government who favored peace negotiations wanted the initiative to come from the enemy so as to avoid a suggestion of weakness. Count Lerchenfeld, the Bavarian minister in Berlin, perceptively noted in his diary in early March that the public would never dream of accepting an unsatisfactory peace. Although there was considerable grumbling about growing shortages, this was still too slight to change the prevailing mood. "Thank God the army is intact and Germany is still far from the end of her resources."[41]

The operative factor remained the army and its leaders. "Germany can declare peace only when the military states that this is necessary and suitable," Bethmann told a colleague in early April.[42]

*   *   *

President Woodrow Wilson was slowly waking up to the fact of an immense war that could not but complicate his administration. He was not in a comfortable position. Ambassador Gerard had informed him from Berlin that "a veritable campaign of hate has been commenced against America and the Americans" for selling munitions to the Entente powers. Arthur Zimmermann of the foreign ministry had told House "that perhaps it was as well to have the whole world against Germany, and that in case of trouble there were 500,000 [militarily] trained Germans in America who would join the Irish [-Americans there] and start a revolution. I thought at first he was joking, but he was actually serious . . . impossible as it seems to us, it would not surprise me to see this maddened nation-in-arms go to lengths however extreme."[43] Then had come a row over Great Britain's unauthorized use of the American flag on her merchant ships followed by Germany's declaration in February of a "war zone" in which all merchant ships would be sunk on sight, a declaration immediately and sharply challenged by the American government.

Entente and Central Powers refusal of Wilson's initial offer of mediation had not discouraged him from wanting to defuse an increasingly vicious war. Once again he called on his confidant, Edward House, to visit European capitals and search for a way out. House was fifty-six years old, a soft-spoken, dapper little man, an honorary Texas colonel and progressive liberal, independently wealthy, politically astute, but with slight knowledge of the Old World cant and hypocrisy. He had met Wilson in 1911 when Wilson was governor of New Jersey and had become his political adviser. Quiet, perceptive, and very intelligent, he would serve the president well for the remainder of the war—his "Dear Governor" letters and reports have to be read along with his diaries to appreciate the importance and accomplishments of his various difficult and often seemingly hopeless diplomatic missions during these war-torn years.

House reached London in early March and soon reported his audience with King George to Wilson: "He is the most bellicose Englishman that I have so far met . . . he evidently wanted to impress me with the fact that this was no time to talk peace. His idea seemed to be that the best way to obtain permanent peace was to knock all the fight out of the Germans, and stamp on them for a while until they wanted peace and more of it than any other nation."[44] Subsequent talks with leading statesmen were pleasant and productive, but the door remained closed to a mediated peace.

Worse was to come in Berlin. Although Zimmermann, whom he had met before the war, was "cordial and delightful," he did not disguise Germany's fury over American munition sales—without actual war, relations "could not be worse. . . . The bitterness of their resentment towards us for this is almost beyond belief."[45] Any notion of peace seemed as far away as the moon. "I am somewhat at a loss as to what to do next," he reported to Wilson on March 20, "for it is plain at the moment that some serious reverse will have to be encountered by one or the other of the belligerents before any Government will dare propose parleys. I can foresee troublous times ahead, and it will be the wonder of the ages if all the Governments come out of it intact."[46]

Only one man favorably impressed House. This was the industrialist Walther Rathenau, who "has such a clear vision of the situation and such a prophetic forecast as to the future that I wonder how many there are in Germany that think like him. It saddened me to hear him say that as far as he knew, he stood alone. He said he had begun to wonder whether all the rest were really mad, or whether the madness lay within himself." House was plainly discouraged: "I found a lack of harmony in governmental circles which augurs ill for the future. The civil Government are divided amongst themselves. . . . The military and civil forces are not working in harmony."[47]

Fighting in the east continued to wind down during March. Hindenburg followed his usual routine, interrupting it with frequent elk hunts and motor journeys to a nearby estate where his wife was spending a few days (not being allowed by army regulations to appear at headquarters). Vogel departed with two gigantic portraits of the national hero to hang in the Berlin Academy and duly reported their enthusiastic reception. Ludendorff motored to Thorn to spend a few hours with his wife. Hindenburg arranged an elegant champagne birthday party for his chief of staff, took the fifty-year-old Ludendorff's hand in both of his, and pronounced him irreplaceable, which brought a storm of applause from the guests.[48]

In early April Hoffmann wrote in his diary, "We are stuck fast on the whole front . . . we have not the strength for an operation of any importance. I am convinced that we shall be able to prevent the Russians from ever invading Germany; but that is all we can promise, unless we are given a new army. . . . From the military point of view our position is undoubtedly good, in so far as all our armies stand on enemy soil and we have obtained control over valuable properties, such as railways and coal mines. But we are nowhere victorious, in the proper meaning of that word."[49]

Peace seemed now a remote dream. At one meal the usually quiet Ludendorff remarked that the war "would now become a prolonged war of position which only exhaustion and bankruptcy could end."[50] A few days later Hoffmann noted in his diary, "There is only one possibility of victory. The center of gravity of the war must be shifted to the east."[51]

Hindenburg meanwhile had concluded that posterity should gaze on his marble bust and sought Vogel's recommendation for a suitable sculptor to come to OberOst. Vogel continued to paint him in a variety of poses. One day he sketched him conferring with Ludendorff, which brought a repeated command to paint a formal double portrait (Vogel had not yet heeded the first one). Ludendorff unenthusiastically appeared for a sitting, but was less than pleased with Vogel's concept, which showed the field marshal ostensibly hurling orders at his subordinate. Ludendorff angrily pointed out that this did not accurately reflect their relationship and would only give posterity the wrong impression.

Vogel solved the contretemps by judicious juggling. The finished work shows Hindenburg seated, one uniformed leg over the other, on one side of a large map-strewn table, a look of rapt concentration on the iron features. Ludendorff is opposite, bent over the table, magnifying glass to monocled eye, intent only on finding the military solution.

A later charcoal sketch of Hindenburg won instant approbation. "I want thus to be represented to posterity," he told Vogel, taking the chalk and signing the work as a personal memento.[52]

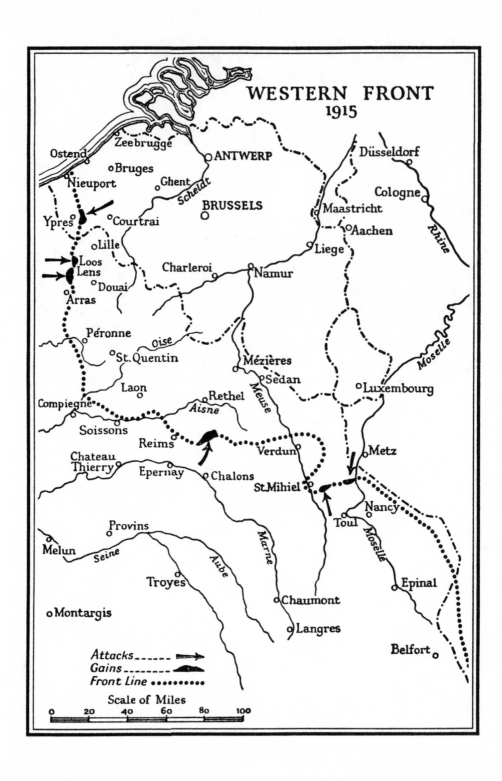

WESTERN FRONT
1915

Ostend
Zeebrugge
Bruges
Nieuport
Ghent
ANTWERP
Düsseldorf
Cologne
Ypres
Courtrai
Scheldt
BRUSSELS
Maastricht
Aachen
Rhine
Lille
Charleroi
Liege
Loos
Lens
Namur
Douai
Arras
Péronne
Oise
St.Quentin
Mézières
Sedan
Luxembourg
Moselle
Laon
Rethel
Meuse
Compiegne
Aisne
Soissons
Reims
Verdun
Metz
Chateau
Thierry
Epernay
Chalons
St.Mihiel
Provins
Nancy
Toul
Melun
Seine
Aube
Marne
Moselle
Troyes
Epinal
Montargis
Chaumont
Langres
Belfort

Attacks ------- ➤
Gains ------- ◣
Front Line ••••••••

Scale of Miles
0   20   40   60   80   100

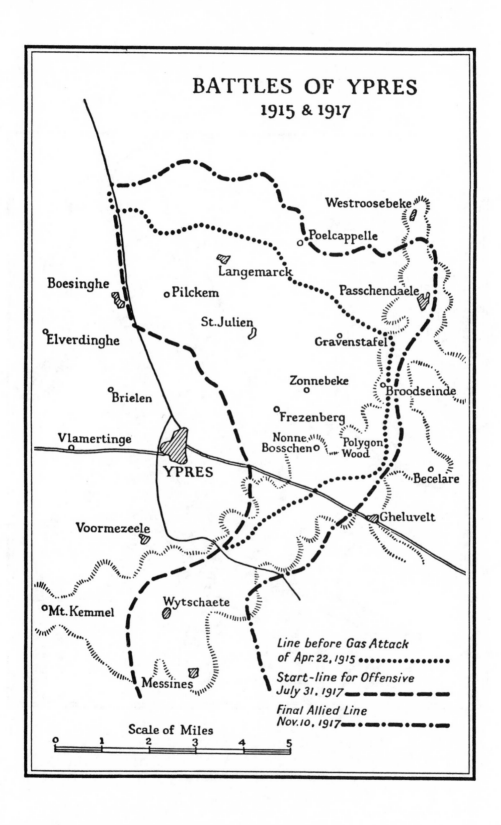

BATTLES OF YPRES
1915 & 1917

Westroosebeke

Poelcappelle

Langemarck

Boesinghe

Pilckem

Passchendaele

St.Julien

Elverdinghe

Gravenstafel

Zonnebeke

Brielen

Broodseinde

Frezenberg

Nonne
Bosschen

Polygon
Wood

Vlamertinge

YPRES

Becelare

Gheluvelt

Voormezeele

Mt.Kemmel

Wytschaete

Messines

Line before Gas Attack
of Apr. 22, 1915 •••••••••••••••

Start-line for Offensive
July 31, 1917 ▬ ▬ ▬ ▬ ▬

Final Allied Line
Nov. 10, 1917 ▬•▬•▬•▬•

Scale of Miles

0   1   2   3   4   5

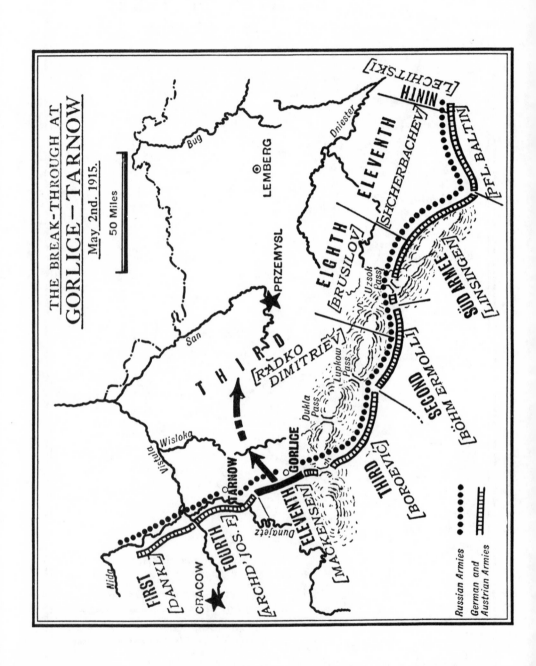

THE BREAK-THROUGH AT
GORLICE—TARNOW
May 2nd. 1915.

50 Miles

Bug

LEMBERG

Dniester

PRZEMYSL

San

THIRD
[RADKO
DIMITRIEV]

Wisloka

TARNOW

GORLICE

Wisula

Dunajetz

Nida

FIRST
[DANKL]

CRACOW

FOURTH
[ARCHD' JOS. F.]

ELEVENTH
[MACKENSEN]

Dukla
Pass

Lupkow
Pass

Uzsok
Pass

EIGHTH
[BRUSILOV]

ELEVENTH
[SHCHERBACHEV]

NINTH
[LECHITSKI]

PFL. BALTIN

SÜD ARMEE
[LINSINGEN]

SECOND
[BÖHM ERMOLLI]

THIRD
[BOROEVIC]

Russian Armies ●●●●●
German and
Austrian Armies ▭▭▭▭

15

Breakthrough at Gorlice-Tarnów

I can only love or hate, and I hate General von Falkenhayn,
with whom it is impossible to work together.
—GENERAL LUDENDORFF TO GENERAL GROENER,
LÖTZEN, MAY 1915[1]

Erich von Falkenhayn had never been impressed with the Duo's claim of a great victory in the Masurian Lakes fighting. OberOst's figure of 90,000 prisoners (later raised to 110,000 by Ludendorff, while the actual number was some 56,000), seemed a poor return for the sacrifice of his four reserve corps that had been shattered in the Augustów Forest battle. What the Duo had won was a tactical victory that could not be exploited. "Victories in the east that are won only at the cost of our position in the west are worthless," he warned the German chancellor.[2]

Falkenhayn did not stand alone in his belief that the war would be won or lost on the western front. General Joffre and Sir John French, commanding French and British forces in France, shared Falkenhayn's faith in a one-front strategy. Other influential voices disagreed. Winston Churchill, first lord of the admiralty, and Lord Kitchener, minister of war, argued that to keep Russia in the war a supply route had to be opened through Turkey: thus the genesis of the ill-fated Gallipoli campaign, the attempt to force the Dardanelles, first by a combined British-French naval attack, second by an amphibious landing on the peninsula itself. The landing was to be carried out by British and Australian troops, including an infantry division from England that had been promised to the BEF. The French contingent, scraped up from rear-area depots, consisted of two divisions. French and Joffre forcefully protested the loss of manpower from their own forces without success.

Although the German armies were by now well entrenched along the entire western front, as were the British and French, their commanders had not yet realized the futility of attacking trenches defended by barbed wire and deadly artillery, machine-gun, mortar, and rifle fire. Costly attacks and counterattacks had filled the winter months with no appreciable gain to either opponent. Despite thousands of casualties, Joffre remained optimistic, determined to drive the hated *Boches* from France and Belgium. His new plan consisted of a two-pronged attack of the Meuse salient, one prong pushing north from Champagne, the other east from the Artois plateau. Once these succeeded, fresh armies from Verdun would march north to cut enemy rail communications and force a general retirement.

The attack in Champagne opened in mid-February 1915 after an artillery barrage so intense that the Germans coined a new word for it —*Trommelfeuer* (drumfire). Just over a month of hard fighting resulted in miniscule gains at horrendous cost, perhaps a total of 90,000 French casualties. Joffre broke off the action in mid-March. By then the British had attacked at Neuve-Chapelle, a surprise move that met with early successes followed by the usual inability to exploit them. Three days of fighting resulted in tiny gains at another immense expenditure of lives. By the end of March the survivors had returned to their trenches.

Falkenhayn had already decided to mount a limited offensive on the eastern front, which required the transfer of ten infantry divisions and a great deal of heavy artillery from the west. To mask the weakening of his western front he ordered a series of local counterattacks. The principal one struck the Allied salient east of Ypres.

The discouraging results of the first gas attack the previous January had brought new techniques now employed by an entire gas regiment that included scientists and meteorologists. The attack opened in late April, with the release of chlorine gas from large cylinders. Max Bauer and his colleagues watched the entire sky turn a sickly yellow as enemy gunfire died away.[3] Allied intelligence had disregarded reports that the enemy was planning to use this new weapon. Sympathetic winds carried the deadly mist to maskless soldiers. Now the troops of a newly arrived Algerian division saw "two curious greenish-yellow clouds . . . [which] spread laterally, joined up, and, moving before a light wind, became a bluish-white mist, such as is seen over water meadows on a frosty night."[4] Algerians and French territorials ran vomiting from their trenches, throwing down rifles and shrugging off packs in trying to escape from silent, formless monster. German infantrymen met no resistance for nearly two miles—the first big breakthrough on the western front—before being stopped by their own gas. (Fritz Haber had not yet developed an effective gas mask but would soon do so). "The effects of the successful gas attack were horrible," Rudolf Binding wrote two days later. "All the dead lie on their backs, with clenched fists; the whole field is yellow."[5]

Their gains were nevertheless spectacular in a war in which progress had been measured by a few hundred yards. The opening attack in what became known as the second battle of Ypres was checked by a Canadian division only with difficulty and with heavy losses: "a sleeping army lies in front of one of our brigades," Binding wrote five days after the offensive opened, "they rest in good order, man by man, and will never wake again—Canadian divisions. The army's losses are enormous."[6]

A series of ill-conceived counterattacks ordered by Sir John French further shredded British divisions without coming close to penetrating the new German lines on the high ground northeast of Ypres. The local British commander, General Sir Horace Smith-Dorrien, who had saved the British Expeditionary Force by his stand at Le Cateau in 1914, wanted to stop the slaughter and very sensibly recommended withdrawal to cover Ypres. To Sir John French and General Ferdinand Foch, commanding French divisions in the north, this was heresy. Smith-Dorrien was relieved and sent home, but Sir John was forced to make the recommended move.

The battle continued into May. Joffre meanwhile had launched the second prong of *his* offensive, an attack east of Arras. Although French troops managed to penetrate two and a half miles on a narrow front, the attack bogged down for the usual reasons—faulty command and supply, reserves held too far in the rear, swift enemy reinforcements—the sum of the parts producing the single result: stalemate. To aid his ally, Sir John French ordered Haig to make another counterattack in early May, an effort best judged by a German regimental diary entry. German gunners waited while the artillery barrage lifted and the smoke cleared: "there could never before in war have been a more perfect target than this solid wall of khaki-men, British and Indian side by side. There was only one possible order to give—'Fire until the barrels burst.' "[7] Failure enraged Haig, who insisted on a second, equally futile afternoon attack, then another attack in the evening which was canceled, still another attack the next morning, also canceled. One day's fighting cost the British 458 officers, 11,161 men.[8]

As Sir John French had earlier concluded that the enemy "could not be very strong or very numerous, as he must have lost heavily and be exhausted,"[9] so now Falkenhayn concluded that the fighting power of both British and French armies had deteriorated. In late May, though weakened by sending divisions to the eastern front, he attacked again after a heavy gas barrage. This time the British were provided with primitive masks, "a nose clip and cotton wool mouth pad which had been soaked in sodium carbonate, sodium thiosulfate and water,"[10] or in some cases only gauze or even socks soaked in urine—but the Canadians in particular suffered high gas casualties. The German attacks were not successful, but when the fighting tapered off in June the Ypres salient had almost been eliminated. The task had cost about 40,000 German casualties and some 60,000 British casualties. The French effort continued until mid-June. For inconsequential gains the French suffered another 100,000 casualties, the Germans perhaps 75,000. Summing up the result, Winston Churchill wrote: "Out of approximately 19,500 square miles of France and Belgium in German hands we have recovered about eight."[11]

By spring of 1915 trench warfare had become a way of life to a generation of Germans, Britons, and French. Observation trenches, forward trenches, communication trenches, night patrols, listening posts, armed raids to capture prisoners, barbed-wire and communication-wire working parties, mess and water details, stretcher parties, foot-deep freezing water, wet uniforms, mud, lice, rats, hunger, diarrhea, constipation, trench feet, fever, wounds, blood poisoning, and death had become as familiar to the men at the front as the backs of their hands. "Our food usually arrived at about three o'clock in the morning," wrote a German survivor, Stephen Westman, "and the menu consisted invariably of a thick soup with noodles and tough meat. In addition, each man received half a loaf of black rye bread, a piece of sausage and some margarine." Part of the fight in Flanders was against nature—flooded trenches in the lowlands. As fast as they were bailed they filled—"I thought of Sisyphus," Westman wrote, "who was condemned in the underworld to push uphill a huge stone which always rolled down again when it reached the top."[12]

Relief came seldom and did not last long. Battalions and regiments were rotated to rest areas where they slept in beds and enjoyed hot meals, at least in theory. Once out of the battle zone the troops were hauled in cattle cars to a delousing station, where everyone stripped to the skin. Filthy clothing was stuffed into numbered net bags and dumped into enormous vats full of boiling water stinking from disinfectant. "We our-selves were treated with quick-working electric clippers which removed every trace of hair from our heads and bodies. Then we had to climb into giant containers, full of evil-smelling disinfectants, and from here we went into another hall to dry and be fed."[13]

Once purified, the troops were supposed to enjoy themselves in camp libraries, canteens, movie houses, and bars, but this idle existence was frequently broken by work details. The army did provide houses of prostitution with a medical orderly on hand to inspect each customer and give him a "preventive injection" upon departure. After a week or two away from the guns the troops said good-bye to the purchased love of whores and the obliterating kindness of wine to return to the nightmare life of the trenches.

Fortunate soldiers who received furloughs were thoughtfully pro-vided with a box that contained three different kinds of antivenereal-disease antiseptic known to the troops as "love parcels." The incidence of syphilis and gonorrhea was still "alarming." Officers so infected were sent to special " 'knights' castles,' where they were treated and kept under a kind of close arrest." A good many officers and men got them-selves reinfected so as to avoid being sent to the front.[14]

Wounded men also escaped—some of them. "Don't ask about the fate of the wounded," Richard Schmieder wrote from the western front in March 1915. "Anyone who was incapable of walking to the doctor had to die a miserable death; some lingered in agony for hours, some for days, and even for a week."[15] The lucky ones were picked up by stretcher-bearers, usually at night having spent the day or days in a filthy, water-filled shell crater fighting off rats attracted by blood and festering flesh. They were carried to primitive dressing stations, where they waited for hours and even for days to be treated by doctors and orderlies who divided them into three categories: those so badly wounded they could not be saved, those who could be saved but who would never fight again, and those who could be saved and would fight again. Priority treatment went to the latter, who were evacuated to rear-area hospitals.

Stephen Westman, who was commissioned a "probationer surgeon" because of prewar medical studies, recalled working in a hospital—a converted textile factory in Le Cateau—that held more than 10,000 German and enemy casualties "brought to us in motor ambulances which pulled behind them up to three two-wheeled trailers, each carrying three more men."[16] They were segregated into wards according to the nature of their wounds. Westman often watched lice "marching out" from underneath the plaster of broken limbs and maggots from flies that had deposited eggs in the open wounds crawling out of a bandage.[17] "Quite often the temperature of a soldier with an innocent-looking wound rose rapidly, and then I found that the dreaded gas-gangrene had set in and that his life depended upon a wide opening of the tissues being made immediately with application of peroxide of hydrogen or amputation."[18] Infected fractures from gunshot and shrapnel were "kept open, and the pus dropped in a constant drip into containers—the smell was almost unbearable and the results were far from satisfactory." Where possible the victim was operated on. Ether was dropped on to a mask "until the patient turned blue, the anaesthetist white, fearing that his victim might die, and the surgeon red in the face with rage, because his patient became restless."[19]

A surprising number of wounded survived these various ordeals before returning to their units to begin the cycle all over again.

Conrad's precarious position on the eastern front meanwhile had greatly worried the OHL. German pressure had caused the new Austro-Hungarian foreign minister, Count Stephan Burián von Rajecz, to offer Italy more territory than she had originally asked for, but because of better Allied offers the Austro-Italian bargaining had come to nothing, and it was supposed that Italy would soon enter the war as an ally of the Entente.

The situation had forced Conrad to send reinforcements from the Carpathians to the Italian border. This was an extremely hazardous move. The Carpathians are not mountains so much as a series of hills some sixty miles wide, each higher than the last. They are full of woods and streams that make for good defensive positions on the hill lines, as do the tight southern passes. But beyond these passes is the Hungarian plain—and, in 1915, a very vulnerable Austria-Hungary.

Falkenhayn feared that a Russian breakthrough could knock Austria-Hungary out of the war. In mid-April he ordered OberOst to try to relieve the pressure on Conrad by forcing Stavka, the Russian supreme command headquarters, to bring reserves north from Galicia. In addition to a gas attack by the Ninth Army and a local attack by the Tenth, OberOst was to make a major incursion into northern Lithuania and Kurland.

Hindenburg welcomed the order. During a morning sitting with Vogel he sang a little song, then tapped out several military marches with his blunt fingers. "Now that I have provided a summer, autumn and winter battle, I must also fight a spring battle," he told the painter. And, as an afterthought, "Tell me what you all had for breakfast when my wife was with you in Berlin."[20]

The subsidiary gas attack ordered by the German Ninth Army was the work of a newly formed gas battalion, which spent considerable time preparing suitable launching sites for the lethal cylinders, a complicated process that required great secrecy to avoid enemy artillery fire. The weapon could only be used with a favorable wind, of course, especially important in this instance because the German troops were not yet equipped with gas masks. The attack was made in early May but was not properly exploited by the infantry, which had expected the enemy to be totally obliterated and gave up the advance when fired upon. A second attempt failed when the wind suddenly shifted to produce "considerable losses" in the German trenches.[21]

Ludendorff was more concerned with the main infantry attack. Recent attempts to punch through enemy lines had failed, despite heavy losses. He finally decided to send a strong cavalry force supported by three reserve divisions into Kurland, which was weakly defended by Russian territorials.

The march began in late April. It did not upset Stavka; the territory was barren and remote, and the Russians did not believe that OberOst possessed sufficient strength to seize Riga with its vital steel mills. The German incursion, however, raised a public outcry in Russia for the safety of Riga and the Baltic coast. In response Alekseyev, who had replaced Ruzski as commander of the northwest front, reinforced the area, and the action soon escalated. By early June entire industrial plants were being transferred from Riga to the east. A force of nine infantry and nine cavalry divisions commanded by the Russian general Plehve was soon defending against five-plus infantry and seven-plus cavalry divisions, which would become the Niemen Army commanded by General Otto von Below. Thousands of Russian soldiers had been captured, along with quantities of precious leather and barbed wire by the time Below took up the defensive. Alekseyev now was forced to build one army to cover Riga, another to cover fortress Kovno, of course at the expense of his other fronts.

OberOst's success in Kurland convinced Hindenburg, Ludendorff, and Hoffmann that a massive drive from East Prussia would destroy the

Russian army and force Russia from the war. Conrad also believed that Russia could be militarily defeated, but only by a southern offensive (for which he wanted ten German divisions) to bring about a collapse in the Carpathians.

This familiar litany was complemented by Falkenhayn's continued insistence that the war would be won or lost in the west, where, only with difficulty and heavy losses, he had recently checked another massive allied offensive. The contretemps was complicated by the voices of Bethmann Hollweg and Zimmermann, who hotly argued for a conquest of Serbia both for the political effect this would have on Bulgaria, Romania, and Greece and for the necessity of opening an overland supply line to Turkey, threatened by an Allied landing in force on Gallipoli in late April. Although Falkenhayn paid lip service to the notion, he wanted nothing to do with what he derisively called the *Balkan Abendteuer*, the Balkan adventure. In mid-May he pointed out to Bethmann that Conrad would not fight in Serbia without Bulgaria, which was still neutral. This meant using only German troops "who neither are used to the terrain nor are equipped to fight a campaign in an area infested with typhus and similar devastating diseases and also defended by a desperate people."[22] He and Conrad were still hoping that Russia would make a separate peace. Further, Turkey's Enver Pasha had informed him that Liman von Sanders, commanding six Turkish divisions on Gallipoli, would continue to hold against Allied attacks. Enver Pasha preferred that the Russians be driven entirely out of Galicia, which would end their influence in the Balkans more than would Serbia's defeat.[23]

Falkenhayn continued to prepare for another offensive in the west, which would strike toward Amiens in the hope of driving a wedge between the British and French armies. Considering the circumstances, including his own relative weakness, this was a daring plan somewhat unwillingly approved by the kaiser. It is doubtful if Falkenhayn really believed in it. He calculated that it would cost him at least 100,000 casualties with no guarantee of success. Judging from eyewitness accounts his doubt was reflected in the pervading pessimism at the OHL brought on by the dangerous situation in the Carpathians. Prompted by his operations officer, Colonel Tappen, and the minister of war, Wild von Hohenborn, Falkenhayn dropped his plan in favor of a watered-down version of an offensive in western Galicia, which he had earlier discussed with Conrad.

This would be a limited offensive, Falkenhayn stressed, which he hoped would cripple Russia's offensive powers for the foreseeable future.

To accomplish this a breakthrough was necessary, and it had to be in the center, not on the flanks as Conrad had suggested.[24] To the Duo's fury, Kaiser Wilhelm agreed with Falkenhayn, who elected to command the operation personally.

In early May the OHL transferred operational headquarters to Pless, a border town in Upper Silesia. The kaiser and his entourage occupied the local palace. The empress frequently visited her husband to the delight of staff officers, who were fed from the palace kitchens, which produced better meals during her visits. Falkenhayn normally ate with the staff, who enjoyed his "dazzling wit, trenchant opinions and quick repartee."[25]

Falkenhayn's contribution to the new offensive was eight divisions hastily sent from the west to form the Eleventh Army under command of General von Mackensen with Hans von Seeckt as his chief of staff. Mackensen would also command the Austro-Hungarian Fourth Army, but Conrad would retain overall command prerogative—at least in theory.

The combined offensive began in early May when heavy artillery opened fire along a twenty-eight-mile front between Gorlice and Tarnów. Surprised and terrified soldiers of the Third and Eighth Russian armies fled from rude trenches to open country to be rounded up by the thousands. Entire units threw down rifles and abandoned cannons as the rout continued. On May 10 Ivanov's chief of staff wrote that "the strategic position is quite hopeless. Our line is very extended, we cannot shuttle troops around it with the required speed, and the very weakness of our armies makes them less mobile; we are losing all capacity to fight."[26] The relentless attacks continued along the line. A British observer with the Russian Third Army, which was retreating to the San River, noted that "their losses have been colossal. They confessed to over 100,000 on the 16th [of May], but I think they have lost more."[27] The Germans captured 140,000 prisoners in six days. "Of 200,000 men and 50,000 replacements, only 40,000 unwounded men reached the San."[28] Nonetheless, the commander of the Russians, Radko Dimitriev, "has fought every yard, pouring in reinforcements like lead into a furnace."[29]

The headlines that daily announced these great victories to the world spelled only sour grapes to OberOst in Lötzen. The Duo deeply resented the eastern limelight passing to their bitter enemy, Erich von Falkenhayn, whose strategy was so obviously inferior to their own. They did not stress that their strategy had undergone a major modification. No longer was Russia to capitulate because of military defeat. Military presence instead was to bring about a separate peace (as Falkenhayn had originally pressed for). The kaiser's presence in Pless could only work to their further disadvantage. He "is entirely under Falkenhayn's influence," Hoffmann noted, "and does not love us. The military situation is such that we are gradually reaching a dead end. Of course we are intentionally thrust into the background."[30]

Their resentment surfaced at a stormy conference called by the kaiser in early June. Ludendorff argued that the Russian retreat was relatively meaningless, since their armies would reform to fight again; thus the strategic necessity was to annihilate the enemy by a gigantic encircling movement. Falkenhayn replied that there could never be sufficient strength for such an operation to succeed. He could not safely transfer further divisions from the western front, already dangerously weak, where the British were about to be reinforced with Lord Kitchener's new divisions. He pointed to Italy's recent declaration of war on Austria-Hungary. Italy's six hundred thousand frontline troops would soon be increased by a third. Conrad would have to remove more troops from the east to meet that threat. The Allied landing in Gallipoli was meanwhile putting the Turkish defenders to a severe test. The Central Powers must now seize Serbia in order to supply the hard-pressed Turks and to keep Romania and Bulgaria at least neutral. Kaiser Wilhelm again supported Falkenhayn (whom he had recently decorated with the prestigious Order of the Black Eagle).

The Duo had no intention of remaining in a secondary role. Back at Lötzen Hoffmann's calipers crawled across maps to fashion a two-pronged offensive that would change the dramatis personae: Otto von Below's Niemen Army would attack southward, Eichhorn's Tenth Army eastward, its target Kovno, which was in Ludendorff's words "the cornerstone of the Russian defense on the Niemen," whose capture would open the road to Vilna behind the Russian armies.[31]

Ludendorff presented this ambitious plan at another stormy conference in early July. Falkenhayn rejected it along with Conrad's desire to push into the northeast to complete the destruction of the Russian armies in Poland. Falkenhayn spoke from a position of strength. His armies had recovered Galicia. They had captured 240,000 prisoners and hundreds of cannon. But losses had been heavy, perhaps 90,000, and would have to be replaced. He had no reserves to support either the Duo's or Conrad's ambitious demands, which were anyway impractical: "The Russians can retreat into the vastness of their country, and we cannot go chasing them for ever and ever."[32] Falkenhayn had been pressing the chancellor to arrange a separate peace with Russia on relatively easy terms. He wanted to end the offensive at this point because it had accomplished his goals and more, but the kaiser refused to hear of it. Compromise resulted. The offensive would continue in the south but, to Ludendorff's fury, OberOst would confine itself to an attack east toward Warsaw while holding on the Kurland front.

Ludendorff returned from the conference "in a savage temper," Hoffmann noted.[33] His fury increased as Falkenhayn's judgment proved valid. Mackensen's army group, over thirty-three infantry and six cavalry divisions, attacked north from Galicia while the Duo's armies attacked east toward the Narev and Vistula rivers. Mackensen handled his forces well, relying as earlier on powerful artillery support against a confused enemy short of reserves. Though progress was slower than at Gorlice because of limited roads, Mackensen continued to employ tactics built around a strong center of heavy guns. Russian defenses were rudimentary, artillery ammunition in short supply. Enemy corps that attempted to hold, as before Lublin, suffered horrendous casualties, while the number of prisoners steadily mounted. By month's end Mackensen's divisions were in Lublin and Cholm, preparing for the final thrust on Brest Litovsk.

Ludendorff meanwhile was preparing to attack. Colonel Gerhard Tappen, Falkenhayn's operations officer who visited Lötzen on July 10, found Ludendorff "hardly obliging, arrogant, makes a nervous impression." Hindenburg on the contrary was "reasonable."[34] A few days later Gallwitz's army group moved out on a seventy-five-mile front, over ten divisions and a thousand guns, the latter sited by a retired artillery genius who had been called to active duty, Colonel Georg von Bruchmüller.

Progress was excellent. Hindenburg drove to the front on the second day to "tremendous enthusiasm, of course, on the part of the troops."[35] The attack surprised two Russian armies, whose commanders were at odds and in addition had neglected the defenses. In four days the Germans advanced five miles and captured 24,000 prisoners. In the north the Niemen Army captured another 30,000 men to send the Russian Fifth Army in confused retreat eastward.

"We are in the midst of the greatest battle that history has ever known," Hoffmann recorded on July 18 with more than normal exaggeration.[36] Ludendorff made another impassioned plea to the OHL for reinforcements so that the offensive could expand toward Kovno and Vilna in accordance with his original grand plan, rejected by Falkenhayn.

The OHL now agreed to release two infantry divisions to OberOst, but no more. In a telephone conversation with Tappen on July 21 Ludendorff was so excited and aggressive as to suggest a nervous breakdown. General Groener was hastily dispatched to Lötzen and reported that Ludendorff had apologized, that his nerves were shot.[37] According to Hoffmann he was overworked: "Hindenburg rarely asks about the military operations. Ludendorff directs everything, Hindenburg learning for the most part much later."[38] He quickly recovered as Grand Duke Nicholas, threatened from north, west, and south, ordered Warsaw evacuated and a general retreat to the east, burning the villages as in 1812.

As the retreat continued, Ludendorff barraged the OHL with demands for an all-out northern offensive. Falkenhayn would not hear of it. It was too late in the year to attempt a campaign in such difficult terrain; in any event "the destruction of an enemy superior in numbers" was impossible when that enemy could retreat at will over vast spaces with no railroads and few roads.[39]

The Duo would not give up. "The quarrel between Falkenhayn and Hindenburg is developing," Hoffmann happily wrote in early August. A week later he noted that "long, argumentative telegrams go back and forth between Pless and here every day, in form very polite, in fact fairly blunt. I regard it as rather useless but Hindenburg and Ludendorff want it for the historical records."[40] Toward the end of August an observer noted that "Ludendorff downright foams. He is utterly beyond himself. He takes everything as a personal insult."[41] Hoffmann wrote on the same day: "Today a lengthy instruction arrived once again from OHL. Lord, how these people think to fight a war! Naturally we won't pay any attention to what they say so no harm is done."[42] Ludendorff's wife wrote that his letters of this time were "nothing but one single elongated accusation against Falkenhayn."[43]

Relations reached a boiling point when the Duo were not invited to attend the kaiser's triumphal entry into fortress Novogeorgievsk, which had yielded 85,000 prisoners, 1,600 guns, and nearly a million shells. They turned up anyway to be coolly received by their supreme warlord. At one point Falkenhayn asked Ludendorff, "Now are you finally convinced that my operation was right?" "On the contrary," Ludendorff coldly replied.[44]

The Russian retreat was never a rout. Towns were evacuated and burned, cattle slaughtered, crops destroyed. "Every day the Russians would retire three miles or so, construct a new line, and wait for the

Germans to stumble up towards it; then a new phase of the retreat would begin."[45] Mackensen's divisions occupied Brest Litovsk in late August.

As the retreat continued, Falkenhayn's expressed worries grew into reality. There were no railroads, and the few roads were poor. Gallwitz by late August had lost 60,000 men, over a third of his strength. Guns were wearing out. Horses were exhausted. Supply carts had to travel seventy-five miles from railheads on roads little better than trails. One corps commander complained that "progress takes ages . . . it is not so much the enemy's strength as the complete impossibility of all observation in terrain of this type."[46]

By early September Mackensen's columns were approaching the Pripyat marshes, beyond which Falkenhayn refused to go. He had wanted to end the offensive in August. The Danish intervention at Petrograd had failed. It was apparent that Czar Nicholas would not conclude a peace independent of his allies, nor did Bethmann want to raise the matter of a separate peace, since it would show German weakness. Although Falkenhayn had strengthened his defensive position in the west by building a second line of trenches two to four miles in the rear of the front, he was in no position to stand against another expected Franco-British onslaught. That threat grew daily until in September he announced the end of the eastern offensive and began moving four divisions to the west.

He reckoned without the Duo, who refused to abandon the forlorn dream of envelopment. Their relations with the OHL had steadily deteriorated, not least when Falkenhayn attempted to eliminate operational insubordination by taping their right claw, Ninth Army and Woyrsch's detachment, which he placed under his own command as the army group of Prince Leopold of Bavaria in order to prevent them from being sent north to the Niemen Army.

Ludendorff and Hoffmann countered by asking Hindenburg to threaten to resign. Hindenburg at first refused but gave in when Ludendorff, who in the manner of Prince Bismarck had probably spent the afternoon in *hating*, said *he* would resign. Hindenburg's threat brought a veiled apology from Falkenhayn along with a promise of a fresh division from the west. But Falkenhayn did not return the sequestered right wing. Instead he slapped OberOst again by persuading the kaiser to appoint General Hans von Beseler as the new governor general of Poland, an independent command of some 60,000 square kilometers and six million people with Beseler directly responsible to the kaiser. Hindenburg sardonically suggested that since he was no longer commanding in the east he be given a new title. Falkenhayn replied that Hindenburg would eventually assume overall command, and conveniently forgot the promise.

Neither the Duo nor Conrad was to be mollified. Under the pretext of misunderstanding Falkenhayn's orders, their separate offensives continued. Ludendorff performed something of an operational miracle by concentrating twenty-eight infantry and five cavalry divisions on the sixty-five-mile front of Eichhorn's Tenth Army. Kovno fell to the Tenth Army, Grodno to the Eighth Army. Vilna was gained in mid-September, but it cost Eichhorn over 50,000 casualties, which Hoffmann blamed on Ludendorff, who had authorized a frontal attack. Attacks further north by a new infantry group under command of General Oskar von Hutier, of whom we shall hear more, failed. As Falkenhayn had foreseen, the enemy retreated and the attackers could not pursue. Many of the German regiments had been on half rations for weeks. Hoffmann recorded the blunt truth on September 24: "Our troops are also exhausted, on top of that not enough railways. Everything broken, no telephone lines, in short, hard times."[47]

A few days later the German troops began moving into long lines of trenches. Hoffmann was disappointed. He had counted on 40,000 to 50,000 prisoners, but only 30,000 were taken: "I now know the reason for our failure. The infantry no longer attacks. Without capable officers, especially able company commanders, the troops are gradually deteriorating."[48] Russian counterattacks along the line were everywhere beaten off to end the year's campaign.

Conrad in the interim had come to grief in eastern Galicia, from where he had hoped to close his end of the pincers. In less than a month his eastern armies suffered perhaps 300,000 casualties. As usual he blamed his failure on the poor quality of his troops.

Falkenhayn was satisfied that his campaign in the east had accomplished what he intended, although at a high cost in German lives. The Russians had been pushed from all Austrian territory except Tarnopol, a small portion of Galicia. Poland, Lithuania, and Kurland, along with parts of Old Russia, were held by the Central Powers. The Russian enemy had lost over two million men, including some 300,000 prisoners, and vast quantities of guns, ammunition, small arms, and supply. In theory it would take Stavka many months to refit and re-form its shattered armies. Bulgaria had formally agreed to join the Central Powers. As a bonus, Czar Nicholas had relieved Grand Duke Nicholas as supreme commander and shunted him off to the Caucasus, a change that created "a most painful" impression in the ranks.* Henceforth the czar would command with disastrous results, which his well-meaning but pedestrian chief of staff, Mikhail Alekseyev, proved powerless to prevent.

Falkenhayn had gained time to cope with more urgent problems on other fronts.

* "The people who failed to prevent Nicholas II, by insistence and even by force, from assuming the supreme command were no better than criminals. His lack of knowledge and ability, his weakness of character, and his vacillating will made him totally unfit for any such post." A. A. Brusilov, A Soldier's Notebook, 1914–1918, 267.

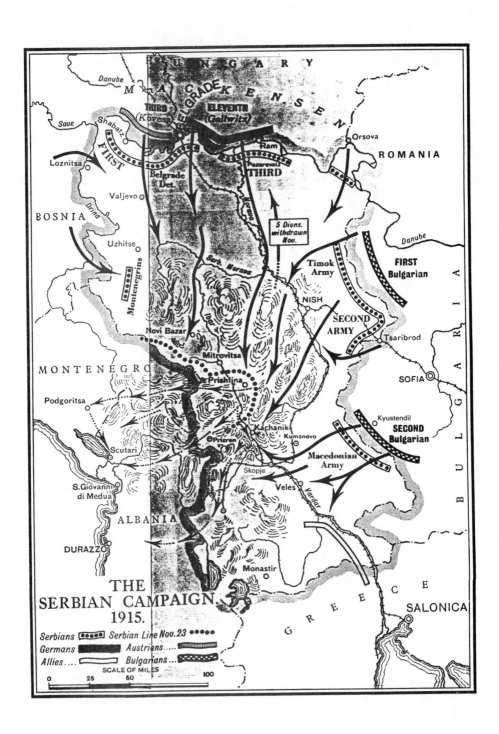

MACKENSEN

Danube

M A C E D O N I A
BELGRADE

Save

THIRD
(Kövess)
ELEVENTH
(Gallwitz)

Shabatz
Loznitsa
FIRST

ROMANIA

Orsova

Ram
Pozarevatz
THIRD

Belgrade
Det.

Valjevo

Danube

5 Divns.
withdrawn
Nov.

BOSNIA

Drina

Uzhitse

Serb. Morava

Timok
Army

FIRST
Bulgarian

NISH

Montenegrins

SECOND
ARMY

Novi Bazar

Mitrovitsa

MONTENEGRO

Prishtina

Tsaribrod

SOFIA

Podgoritsa

Kachanik
Kumanovo

SECOND
Bulgarian

Kyustendil

Scutari

Prizren

S.Giovanni
di Medua

Skopje

Macedonian
Army

Veles

Vardar

ALBANIA

DURAZZO

Monastir

B U L G A R I A

THE
SERBIAN CAMPAIGN.
1915.

G R E E C E

SALONICA

Serbians ○○○○○ Serbian Line Nov.23 ●●●●●
Germans ▬▬▬ Austrians .... ▨▨▨▨
Allies .... Bulgarians ... ▨▨▨▨
SCALE OF MILES
0   25   50   100

16

---◆---

Serbia Falls

Joffre and Sir John [French] told me in November [1914] that
they were going to push the Germans back over the frontier;
they gave me the same assurances in December, March, and
May. What have they done? The attacks are very costly and
end in nothing.
—LORD KITCHENER TO GENERAL SIR WILLIAM ROBERTSON,
JULY 18, 1915[1]

Have the men fix bayonets and throw the wretches out.
—KAISER WILHELM TO GENERAL VON EINEM,
SEPTEMBER 1915[2]

The buildup of German forces in the east had been carefully noted
by Allied intelligence on the western front. By June 1915 French,
British, and Belgian forces outnumbered German forces by more
than half a million men, or something over 600 infantry battalions plus
supporting troops. The number of French artillery batteries had significantly increased, as had the supply of shells. Such was their general
prosperity that Joffre and French decided to launch another major offensive, not only to help their hard-pressed Russian ally but because they
believed that "the moment was a propitious one for an attempt to break
through on this front."[3]

The Allied plan, essentially Joffre's, derived from what he called
the "most important lesson" of the recent offensive in Artois: "That
simultaneous operations carried out by several armies would prevent the
enemy from making full use of his reserves, and would force him to accept
battle with limited means, wherever we elected."[4] Ignoring the unpleas-

ant fact that the enemy, limited means and all, had shattered his previous efforts, Joffre planned to launch his major attack in the Champagne with a secondary attack in the Arras region and a British offensive to the north—an action "which would compel the Germans to retreat beyond the Meuse and possibly end the war."[5]

General Castelnau, commanding three armies, altogether about half a million men, would attack in Champagne on a twenty-two-mile front (later considerably shortened) between Rheims and Verdun. The general idea was to break through the German defenses to cut the vital railway line and force the Germans from French soil. Ferdinand Foch, commanding a smaller but still strong force, would attack in Artois on a twelve-mile front. Sir John French, now a field marshal, wanted to strike in the area of Ypres north of the La Bassée canal but was persuaded by Lord Kitchener to accommodate himself to Joffre's wishes and fight alongside General Viktor d'Urbal's French Tenth Army, the action to be carried out by Sir Douglas Haig's First Army of six divisions, including Territorials, and, for the first time, two divisions of Kitchener's "New Armies." Haig would attack on an eight-mile front, the goal being to seize Loos and Lens north of Arras, spill out on the Douai plain, and, if possible, push on to Lille.

Joffre's new plan encountered considerable opposition from what he termed "the highest circles of the French government." The president of France, Raymond Poincaré, who had the temerity to suggest that prepared defenses were superior to the most carefully planned attacks, believed that a large-scale offensive should be delayed until spring and asked for further details of Joffre's plan. Joffre, sounding like his German high-command opposites, complained that this was "a dangerous interference on the part of the government in the conduct of operations." Poincaré almost at once backed down, saying meekly "that it would be a national danger to interfere with [Joffre] and that . . . he would never allow the Higher Command to be brought into question,"[6] thus ensuring an unimpeded flow of French blood (until the French government regained its senses and clipped the military's wings in 1916). Joffre also rejected a British suggestion to defer the attack until spring because of a serious shortage of men and artillery shells in the British army.

Armed with this patent of supremacy, Joffre continued to prepare an attack daily made more urgent by the general Russian retreat. In mid-August the French ambassador in Petrograd informed his government that "the Russian army has now been retreating for three months. . . . All the officers returning from the front state that it is impossible to picture the horrors of this continual struggle, in which the artillery is without ammunition and the infantry without rifles. Our offensive is, therefore, awaited with the utmost impatience. . . . Apart from the army, there is the nation . . . the terrible sufferings produced by this war are beginning to rouse the masses."[7]

The offensive was twice delayed because of the immense problems of concentrating so many troops and guns. French command optimism ran high. Engineers in some places had tunneled to within a hundred yards of the enemy's forward trenches. In both sectors cavalry stood ready to exploit the breakthrough. Joffre informed his troops that "you will be able to advance to the assault behind a storm of shellfire, along the whole of the front. . . . You will carry all before you."[8] Murderous fire from over two thousand guns directed by aerial observers continued for three days. The American poet Alan Seeger, who had enlisted in the French Foreign Legion and whose days were short, watched the bombardment. "A terrific cannonade has been going on all night. I expect to march right up the Aisne borne on in an irresistible élan. It will be the greatest moment of my life."[9] After a final gas barrage from French guns on September 25, shivering *poilus* clutching rifles and carrying smoke and gas grenades crawled from trenches in heavy rain. They were sent off by regimental bands playing "La Marseillaise."

Erich von Falkenhayn had been fervently juggling tactical balls for what to him must have seemed an eternity. This was the inevitable result of trying to wage a multifront war with increasingly weak and unreliable allies. He had risked a great deal by stripping the western front in order to undertake the successful limited offensive in Galicia. Unlike the Russians, who were always willing to trade space for time, Falkenhayn had no intention of yielding a foot of ground without a fight, partly because of what he regarded as limited space, partly because of the German belief, shared at least in part by the British and French, that loss of ground, any ground, immediately constituted a psychological defeat not only abroad and at home but particularly with one's own troops. The result was that both sides were caught up in a new form of warfare, the "scientific defense," which involved construction of vast complexes of various types of trenches all connected by telephone communications and protected by elaborate barbed-wire defenses, machine-gun nests, and preregistered artillery.

Fortunately the embryonic development of this primitive form of warfare, which soon turned men into lower forms of animals, had held against determined Allied attacks. But meanwhile Italy had declared war on Austria, and the enemy had gained a foothold on Gallipoli, with the concomitant threat to Turkey that was causing the German chancellor and his ministers such agony.

Italy had declared war on Austria in May 1915, but Conrad's defenses had successfully held against General Count Cadorna's offensives on the Isonzo River and in Carinthia and the Tyrol. The Gallipoli landing, however, had changed Falkenhayn's antipathy toward a Serbian campaign. While Max Hoffmann was grumbling to his diary about Falkenhayn's failure to invade Serbia, a team of German general-staff officers under Richard Hentsch (of the Marne disaster) was reconnoitering Austria-Hungary's frontier with Serbia: "Every battery position, every possible bridging point, the billeting of the troops on assembly, and their supplies, were settled, and bridges and other crossing materials, ammunition, and commissariat, were all in readiness."[10] Simultaneously, German diplomats in Sofia were offering the Bulgarians large postwar chunks of Romania and Serbia, which finally induced Bulgaria to ally with the Central Powers.

Germany and Austria-Hungary would each deploy six divisions on the northern border of Serbia within thirty days while Bulgaria deployed four divisions—each double the size of the German division—on her border, with another division to move later into Serbian Macedonia. At Falkenhayn's instigation, the kaiser appointed Field Marshal Mackensen to command the operation, thus further infuriating Hindenburg and Ludendorff, who had expected OberOst to be given this responsibility.

Falkenhayn approached the new offensive with the avidity of any convert to a cause. If successful it would eliminate the threat to the Austro-Hungarian flank, open a land supply line to Turkey, and cause Romania to have second thoughts about joining the Entente. Germany could also count on more food and vital raw materials such as copper from her new ally.

The combined attacks were to begin in early October. A German and Austro-Hungarian force was to strike from the north, the Bulgarians from the east. In mid-September Conrad had to back out because of the crisis in Galicia, an unwelcome development that forced the OHL to divert four more divisions to Mackensen. A more serious check occurred on September 25 when Joffre and French unleashed their massive offensive in the west.

* * *

The Flanders and Artois fronts were defended by sixteen divisions of Crown Prince Rupprecht's Sixth Army, dug in from south of Ypres east to about ten miles from Arras, a thirty-five-mile front backed by a second defensive complex two to four miles in the rear, as strong as if not stronger than the first line.[11]

Three days of incessant artillery fire followed by a gas barrage had taken a heavy toll on the German lines holding the fronts in Flanders, Artois, and Champagne. A German war correspondent described it at first as "a razing, searching fire; now it became a mad drumming, beyond all powers of imagination . . . our strongly built trenches were filled in, and ground to powder; their parapets and fire platforms were razed and turned into dustheaps; and the men in them were buried, crushed, and suffocated."[12]

The French attack in Champagne centered on General von Einem's Third Army of seven-plus divisions, which held a thirty-mile front running from north of Rheims to Massiges, an amazing complex of trenches crisscrossing in a crazy patchwork nearly three miles in depth. The French attack by twenty-seven divisions, nineteen of them in the first wave, was stymied on the first day, not least because of heavy rain that turned the battlefield to mud, but also by a strong and disciplined resistance backed by rapid and accurate counterbattery fire. The attack picked up momentum on the following days, pushing through in places to the second and even third line of trenches, most of which had been destroyed by French shelling. "Devilishly critical," was the German minister of war's trenchant comment, which was about as helpful as Kaiser Wilhelm's semihysterical adjuration, "Have the men fix bayonets and throw the wretches out."[13]

Falkenhayn later wrote that he expected an attack on the western front in September. This would appear to be inaccurate. Von Einem and Rupprecht and their staffs expected an attack, but their reports to the OHL were blithely ignored. Even when the Allies opened *Trommelfeuer* on September 22, which continued for another two days, Falkenhayn refused to believe that a large-scale enemy attack was imminent. Two hours before it occurred he was telling the kaiser that his army commanders "see things too black, that the French were at the end of their strength and no longer in a position to attack."[14]

Upon his arrival at the scene he learned that von Einem's chief of staff was considering a general withdrawal. Falkenhayn quickly replaced him with his own assistant operations officer, a junior but very able colonel named Friedrich von Lossberg, who ordered front-line units to hold every inch of ground until some divisions which were just arriving from the east could stabilize the front. Lossberg's impassioned orders did the job. Artillery reinforcement also arrived and German counterbattery fire increased in fury. Alan Seeger, whose Foreign Legion regiment was still in reserve, wrote that "our role was to lie passive in an open field under a shell fire that every hour grew more terrible, while airplanes and captive balloons, to which we were entirely exposed, regulated the fire." A few days after the initial attacks he wrote that "the regiment had been decimated though many of us have not fired a shot."[15] Massive assaults over a period of weeks failed to break through. Joffre abandoned the attempt in late October.

Foch's attack in Artois followed a similar pattern. D'Urbal's Tenth Army, although opposed by only two divisions, seized the tactically important Vimy Ridge in three days but then abandoned it when bad weather ended the offensive. Paris headlines meanwhile announced great victories with thousands of prisoners and hundreds of guns taken. Joffre did not announce that French casualties counted 190,000.

There remained the British attack on the left. Haig had wanted nothing to do with the operation, an attack over open ground against a well-defended position. He was short of guns and shells. Sir John French was also reluctant, but each fell victim to Kitchener and Joffre's appeals to British "honor" in not letting down their allies. As preparations got underway, Haig became increasingly enthusiastic, even having a tower built from which he would watch the action that was to culminate in a massive cavalry sweep onto the Douai plain.

Haig prefaced the assault with a gas barrage that fell victim to unfavorable wind.[16] The assault along an eight-mile front broke through the first line of defense to reach the small mining village of Loos. Some units reached the second line of defense, but considerable command confusion caused the attack to halt in late afternoon. It was resumed the next morning only to result in massive slaughter of the New Army divisions. As in the Champagne, bad weather and continued stubborn resistance closed down the effort in mid-October at a cost of about 60,000 British casualties.

This was Sir John French's last fling. His failure to release reserve divisions in time to influence the action brought an attack as furious as it was unfair from Haig, who for long had been wanting his job. The ensuing quarrel, which involved the top reaches of government, including the crown, was resolved in Haig's favor, a decision that would ensure future astronomical losses.

So the great autumn offensive. Each side claimed victory. Germany perhaps had the better case, due only to the unarguable power of the defense. Despite weaker numbers her fronts were held by rapid transfer of divisions from quiet sectors combined with an overall remarkably tenacious defense. Although casualties were heavy—somewhere around a quarter of a million—Falkenhayn did not feel himself forced to abandon the attack on Serbia in early October when great battles were still being fought on the western front.

The offensive surprised the Serbian high command. In the north the Austro-Hungarian Third Army and the powerful German Eleventh Army swiftly crossed the Danube–San line to move south against slight resistance. Rugged terrain and lack of improved roads together with fierce storms and heavy rain often slowed movement to a crawl. Bulgarian attacks along the eastern border struck the main Serbian forces, which as usual fought tenaciously and well. In two weeks Mackensen's armies had not yet contacted the Bulgarians. Although the latter had cut the railway connecting Serbia to Salonica, her divisions were beginning to run short of ammunition and supply. By early November, however, the two forces had joined and the Serbs were everywhere retreating toward the Kossovo Plateau. Progress remained slow. Cold weather and disease caused morale to tumble in the German camp. "We shall conquer the beautiful land for somebody else," General Hans von Seeckt, Mackensen's chief of staff, grumbled, meaning the Austrians. A final attack by Serbia against the Bulgarians failed in late November, and by month's end what remained of the Serbian army was in disorganized retreat into the Albanian hills, from where 140,000 survivors reached the Adriatic coast, to be taken by Allied ships to Corfu for re-forming. An Allied force that had landed in Salonica in October had early been repulsed by the Bulgarians but was again moving slowly up the Vardar Valley. Subsequent Bulgarian attacks against this force commanded by the French general Maurice Sarrail sent it stumbling back to its fortified lines at Salonica, where it would continue to be reinforced, mainly from Gallipoli.

Falkenhayn had achieved his objectives. The threat to Austria-Hungary from the south had been eliminated. A supply line was open

to Turkey. In early January 1916 the last enemy soldier departed from
the Dardanelles to end a disastrous campaign that had cost the Allies
some 140,000 casualties and left Russia more isolated than ever.

Against the wishes of Conrad and the Bulgarians, who now argued
for a Balkan war with its promise of territorial aggrandizement, Falkenhayn summarily ended the offensive to return the war to the western
front.

The year had ended very well for German arms despite internal
dissension. Ambassador Gerard reported in early October: "Of course I
may be affected by the surroundings, but it seems to me Germany is
winning the war." Six weeks later he wrote that "the German people
are still absolutely, and probably justifiably confident in the results of
the war."[17]

The march of military events had not escaped President Woodrow
Wilson's notice. He had slowly and with great regret come to accept the
war as a major international crisis, and in the autumn of 1915 he startled
some of his advisers by reversing his earlier somewhat disinterested stand:
"In a series of magnificent speeches he demanded vigorous military preparation and he led through Congress the largest naval bill of our history."[18]

Early in 1916 he sent Edward House abroad once again to assure
the belligerents that the American president "would be willing and glad,
when the opportunity came, to cooperate in a policy seeking to bring
about and maintain permanent peace among civilized nations,"[19] the first
intimation of what would become the ill-fated League of Nations.

House would not have an easy task. America was popular with
neither the Central nor the Entente powers. From Berlin he filed a
memorandum that reported Ambassador Gerard's latest audience with
Kaiser Wilhelm: "The Kaiser talked of peace and how it should be made
and by whom, declaring that 'I and my cousins, George [of England] and
Nicholas [of Russia], will make peace when the time comes.' Gerard says
to hear him talk one would think that the German, English, and Russian
peoples were so many pawns upon a chessboard. He made it clear that
mere democracies like France and the United States could never take
part in such a conference. His whole attitude was that war was a royal
sport, to be indulged in by hereditary monarchs and concluded at their
will. He told Gerard he knew Germany was right, because God was on
their side, and God would not be with them if they were wrong, and it
was because God was with them they had been enabled to win their

victories. I asked Gerard whether he was crazy or whether he was merely posing."[20]

A long talk with Chancellor Bethmann Hollweg brought little hope of conciliation. "The Chancellor drank copiously of beer. . . . The beer did not affect him, for his brain was as befuddled at the beginning as it was at the end."[21] In a meeting with the foreign minister, von Jagow, House condemned submarine attacks, arguing that they were as "brutal and senseless as their Zeppelin raids," which had killed fewer than two hundred people, mostly women and children. He fared better with Zimmermann, who apparently expanded on the controversy over submarine warfare then raging in secret German councils, but Zimmermann insisted that the sinking of the *Lusitania* was not an illegal act. If the United States continued to insist on this interpretation, Zimmermann warned, "a break will be unavoidable which, I am sure, you would regret just as much as I would for the reasons we both recognize as most important for the future policy and the welfare of the white races [by which he meant Germany, Great Britain and America]."[22] The consensus in Berlin seemed to be that war with America would not be as disastrous as the present naval blockade.

The negative attitude toward peace in London, Berlin, and Paris caused House to work out an alternative to America's direct intervention in the submarine issue. This was for Wilson to call a conference of the belligerents to discuss peace terms. These terms, while favoring the Entente powers, would compensate Germany outside Europe. If Germany proved unreasonable, America would probably join the Allied effort. If the Allies proved awkward, America "would probably disinterest themselves [sic] in Europe and look to their own protection in their own way."[23]

It is doubtful if House believed in his own plan. "In each government I have visited [Britain, France, Germany]," he wrote Wilson in February 1916, "I have found stubbornness, determination, selfishness and cant. One continually hears self-glorification and the highest motives attributed to themselves because of their part in the war. But I may tell you that my observation is that incomplete statesmanship and selfishness is at the bottom of it all."[24]

House's well-intentioned but impractical plan was in any case overtaken by events. German submarines sank eight ships in three weeks in March. In April the American president threatened to break diplomatic relations with Germany if submarine warfare continued against "passenger and freight-carrying vessels." In early May House found Wilson "unyielding and belligerent, and not caring as much as he ought to avert war."[25]

House could rest easy, at least for the moment. Although the German reply to the American protest stressed the cruelty of the British naval blockade (without mentioning the Allied offer the previous spring to lift the blockade in return for Germany's abandonment of submarine warfare), it agreed to the American terms. No further merchant ships would be sunk "without warning and without saving human lives, unless these ships attempt to escape or offer resistance."[26] It seemed as if the newest crisis had been surmounted.

17

Germany Occupies the Baltic Countries

Here Ludendorff is more admired if also less venerated than Hindenburg. The admiration is restrained or ardent, the veneration warm from the heart. One places full confidence in Hindenburg, endless hopes in Ludendorff.
—Richard Dehmel, OberOst[1]

I would like to see just once a field marshal who knows something. Here we generally sign the orders 'von Hindenburg' without having shown them to him at all. The most brilliant commander of all times no longer has the slightest interest in military matters; Ludendorff does everything himself.
—Colonel Max Hoffmann, OberOst, September 1, 1915[2]

The Duo continued to play a minor role in the mighty clash of arms that left thousands of soldiers dead on the muddy fields of Champagne, Artois, and Flanders, thousands more in the desolate wastes of Poland, Galicia, and Serbia. The prevailing mood at OberOst is all too clearly revealed in Max Hoffmann's diary entries and letters of this period. In early September he wrote that "von Falkenhayn probably hopes that we shall have bad luck somewhere and suffer a minor defeat." A day later he applauded Ludendorff's refusal to release any troops to the OHL. Then his resentment spilled over concerning Mackensen's appointment to command the Serbian campaign. Mackensen had already received so many honors and decorations that, once he occupied Belgrade, "there would be nothing left but to call him 'Prince Eugen.' "[*][3] On September 10: "There is then to be an attack in the west. I suspect that it will be conducted by Falkenhayn under his own orders and those of the Crown Prince, so as to put himself in an agreeable light in the latter's eyes."[4] On September 18: "Austria's defeat in Serbia means that OHL has to send more troops there and thus postpone its offensive in the west. That is very agreeable to us since it means that we won't have to give up any troops in the immediate future. Now we shall get at least to Minsk and I now see Riga looming in the background." On October 3, when the issue on the western front was still in doubt, he regarded the battle as finished and was relieved that German losses were not as high as he had feared: *The total losses are only about 50,000 while those of the French and English are said to be enormous.* Falkenhayn thus has some breathing space which he uses in insulting us assiduously. But Ludendorff won't take it which has resulted in an exchange of rude telegrams."[5] At the OHL General Groener noted in his diary: "The best thing would be to throw the effusions of OberOst into the wastepaper basket. Hindenburg himself is becoming increasingly a mere stooge."[6]

A few days later the Duo again refused outright to make further troop transfers to the OHL and brought the quarrel to a head with a letter highly critical of Falkenhayn's recent campaign in the east. Falkenhayn sharply reminded Hindenburg that his orders were issued in the kaiser's name and were not therefore to be questioned. After criticizing OberOst's operations he demanded (and gained) the desired troops.

This settled nothing. "Trouble with OHL," Hoffmann wrote to his wife. "Ludendorff had sent a rude telegram and today received an even ruder reply. The quarrel has little point since we get the worst of it." On October 10: "We are building our defensive positions and quarreling with OHL . . . Ludendorff is also getting nervous and flares up unnecessarily."[7]

Hindenburg did not seem to concern himself deeply with the feud. "On the whole Hindenburg no longer bothers himself with military matters," Hoffmann wrote at this time. "He hunts a great deal and otherwise comes [to us] for five minutes in the morning and evening to see how things are going."[8]

The painter Hugo Vogel returned to Lötzen in early September to

---

[*] Field Marshal Prince Eugene of Savoy, 1663–1736, Austria's "noble cavalier," a heavily decorated (and richly rewarded) military and political genius, éminence grise to Emperor Charles VI and builder of Vienna's beautiful baroque Schloss Belvedere.

find the field marshal's routine virtually unchanged. He had imported another painter in Vogel's absence and had continued daily sittings when not interrupted by excursions to visit his wife at Steinort or to hunt on nearby estates. He continued to entertain numerous visitors at prolonged dinners, his own appetite as hearty as ever. He sat daily for Vogel, discoursing as usual on a variety of inconsequential subjects. He was intensely interested in Vogel's description of the gigantic new Hindenburg statue that had been erected in Berlin's Königplatz to raise money for the German Red Cross. No less a person than the empress had unveiled it in the presence of the beaming German chancellor. Thousands of loyal subjects were daily standing in line to buy iron, brass, or gold nails to pound into it "like quills upon the fretful porcupine."[9]

Vogel finished the double portrait of Hindenburg and Ludendorff which, prior to being sent for exhibition in Berlin, was hung in the local high school to raise money for charity. Frau Feldmarschall von Hindenburg arrived to view and admire it, as did numerous walking wounded to whom Vogel gave postcard replicas. Ludendorff was so taken with his portion of the painting that Vogel copied his head as a present for Frau General Ludendorff.

Soldiers digging trenches near Lötzen discovered a third-century burial ground. Hindenburg opened one of the coffins to find spurs and pieces of a spear beside the bones. "This would be the last resting place of a knight," he sententiously remarked as Vogel sketched his bulk hovering over the grave site.[10]

The field marshal shot an enormous bull elk and had to be sketched with it—its hide was converted into memorial ashtrays. He kept pressing Vogel to finish the Marienburg and Tannenberg canvases. In addition there must be a group portrait of the Duo, Hoffmann, and Ludendorff's favorite, Major Alfred von Vollard-Bockelberg, chief of the administrative section.

Hindenburg's sixty-eighth birthday was celebrated in early October with an elaborate meal memorialized by Vogel's hand-drawn menus. Hindenburg and Ludendorff exchanged toasts with many Hochs from lesser mortals who enjoyed caviar and other prewar delicacies almost forgotten. Hindenburg was deluged with over a hundred telegrams, three hundred letters, heaps of gifts. Flags covered the town as locals celebrated the event and dinner guests pledged a large sum of money to local charity. A Hindenburg museum was soon to open in Posen, his birthplace, and another smaller one was planned for Lötzen. The commander of the German navy in the Baltic, Prince Heinrich, the kaiser's indolent brother, paid a visit and at table toasted his host as "the people's favorite hero."[11]

The sittings continued and so did the aesthetic criticism. Vogel's buttons and military decorations were all wrong. "Look at Velázquez, whose portraits show every detail so sharp and clear. The so-called Impressionist school, with its generally vague representations, seems to me not the height of art but perhaps the beginning of decadence."[12]

War occasionally intruded on the scene. On one outing, after Hindenburg had compared the country villages to his memory of the Naples area, he suddenly remarked: "Had I been given another corps recently at Vilna, the rascals would have been trapped. . . . Now they will shortly start all over again. A great pity." At one sitting he mentioned that "successful actions have recently become scarcer but"—he repeated an earlier aphorism—"small animals also make dung."[13]

Vogel at times seemed closer to the war than Hindenburg. He liked to relax by taking solitary walks outside the village, where he frequently paused to watch regiments marching to the front. Sometimes the soldiers sang, "but their faces often looked extremely tired and depressed." One evening he heard a colonel addressing his troops, reminding them of their duty to kaiser and fatherland and assuring them that not all enemy bullets hit their targets. Had they turned, Vogel ironically wrote, they would have seen a forest full of black crosses.[14]

In late October 1915 OberOst moved to Kovno on the Niemen River, over a hundred miles to the northeast. Ludendorff found it "a typical Russian town, with low, mean, wooden houses and comparatively wide streets."[15] Its most noteworthy historical feature was a nearby hill where in 1812 Napoleon had stood to watch the French army cross the Niemen on its ill-fated invasion of Russia.

The Duo and Hoffmann lived in a requisitioned villa, the other staff officers in another. Private houses were stripped of furniture to furnish the villas and offices. Hindenburg no longer enjoyed his sittings with Vogel, whose health had not permitted the move, but his Nimrod existence continued. Although he complained that troops passing through a nearby forest had poached most of the pheasants, he nonetheless shot a bison and four stags during a four-day hunt. The flow of adulatory and important visitors continued, undoubtedly to the Duo's gratification.

Ludendorff's priority task was to consolidate the long front that stretched over three hundred miles from the Baltic to Białystok. The Russians had torn up railroads and demolished bridges, which made it difficult to establish adequate supply lines to the forward divisions still under attack in the Dünaburg (Dvinsk) area to the northeast. Though there was little danger of a breakthrough, the troops needed better rations and warmer clothing to raise their morale and thus their defensive capability.

Morale was not particularly high at OberOst. Max Hoffmann marked the true drift of war, recalling that the German military position was much better than a year ago, "yet at that time it was more interesting. One had everything still before one, one looked to big battles and crushing victories. . . . Things now are more negative. I don't want to do any more than to prevent the enemy from doing something to me." In early November he complained: "Everything here dreary. . . . Although no great tactical actions are in progress, there is still much to do. Ludendorff is bored and keeps everyone moving from morning to night. This drive to activity—work for work's sake—is extremely uncomfortable to all."[16]

Ludendorff had already decided to bring a new order to the vast conquered area which included Kurland, Lithuania, Latvia, and parts of Russian Poland, an area as large as East and West Prussia, Posen, and Silesia combined. "I determined to resume in the occupied territory that work of civilization at which the Germans had labored in those lands for many centuries. The population, made up as it is of such a mixture of races, has never produced a culture of its own and, left to itself, would succumb to Polish domination." Lithuania and Kurland would be ruled by a German prince and colonized by German farmers once the war was over. Poland must become "a more or less independent state under German sovereignty."[17]

To properly Germanize the lands, Ludendorff divided them into six administrative areas, each with its own lines-of-communication responsibility. Each area commandant oversaw a number of district and town commandants, all of whom were subordinate to an intendant general, General Ernst von Eisenhart-Rothe, who was further assisted by three general officer inspectors. This bulky administrative apparatus in time was paralleled by separate financial, judicial, religious, agricultural, and forestry systems which remained independent from more forward army operational areas.

The task of reconstruction was enormous. Most government officials of the occupied areas had fled, which Hoffmann found advantageous, since "there were no officials who could put obstacles in the way of the new administration." But neither could OberOst replace these officials with persons speaking the local languages. The harvest had been abandoned, there was a general shortage of food, factories had been shut down or destroyed. The Balts hated the Letts, the Letts hated the Poles, and all three hated the Germans. "We were governing a country, the conditions of which were absolutely unknown to us," Ludendorff later wrote. "We were among a foreign population, consisting of many different, rival races, a population that did not speak one tongue and was, generally speaking, secretly hostile."[18]

The priority task was the revival of agriculture and industry to exploit the land to the fullest so that food and raw materials could be sent to Germany. OberOst's armies were culled for experts in farming, forestry, and industry. Scores of civilians were hastily recruited in Germany to join area staffs in one specialty or another.

Progress was slow, but in time plants were established for drying potatoes and mushrooms, producing animal fodder from wood and straw, canning vegetables and fruits, processing fish from the lakes and sea. Factories were taken over or built to manufacture barbed wire and to repair locomotives and engines. Hundreds of sawmills supplied the wood necessary for repair of railroads, roads, and bridges. Cellulose wood, essential for the manufacture of gunpowder and paper, was exported to the homeland. A resin factory was built, charcoal burning instituted.

Ludendorff directed this immense undertaking from October 1915 to July 1916. By spring of 1916 he had made concrete plans to settle Kurland and Lithuania with Germans—non-Germans would be forced to leave their own lands. A large corps of publicists vigorously supported his efforts in the German press. "During the winter of 1915–16 virtually the entire cultured and politically engaged German bourgeoisie was dreaming of the 'liberation of the land of the Teutonic Order' and its German-speaking inhabitants, or at least demanding a strengthened border defense for East Prussia."[19]

Hindenburg was still bored with the whole idea. On New Year's Day, 1916, he complained in a letter to his wife of the preposterous demands of such annexationists as "good old" Count Zeppelin, who wanted Germany to seize Brest, Gibraltar, and Malta. Members of the All-German party, who wanted to annex "Ceylon to Brunswick and put the Mona Lisa in the Berlin arsenal," belonged in the insane asylum: "one does not know whether to laugh or cry over such arrant nonsense."[20] Whether these sentiments were mentioned to Ludendorff is a moot question. Political matters bored Hindenburg to the extreme, and he probably would not have taken exception to Ludendorff's later assertion that the occupation "was admirable in every respect and worthy of the German character. It benefited the army and Germany as well as the country and its inhabitants."[21]

The inhabitants would scarcely have agreed. Ludendorff's claims of a humanitarian administration are nonsense. Unemployment was rife. OberOst employed a few local workers only in Kurland, which was Protestant. Balts and Poles lived under strict martial law. Political activity was *verboten*. No meetings were allowed, newspapers were heavily censored. The few schools that remained open were taught by invalid soldiers speaking only German. A Polish request for their own university in Vilna was refused by Ludendorff. OberOst set the price for farm produce and paid in occupation currency. The agrarian effort was a virtual failure. The soil was tired, there was no manure, the fields were not drained, what produce resulted was often left to rot because transport was not available to take it to market. Forests were ravaged to feed rapacious sawmills. Thousands of horses and cattle were swept up and shipped to Germany. Jewish middlemen scoured the provinces buying up skins and hides, copper and brass, rags and scrap iron for export. OberOst collected customs duties at the frontier and exercised monopolies in liquor, salt, matches, and sugar. Direct taxes were levied on each household. The banks were German. Courts were presided over by German judges, and local laws had to be translated into German.

Far from the benevolent overlordship later claimed by Ludendorff, he and his minions were hated in the conquered lands.[22] Humanitarian considerations aside, his failure is of interest mainly because it was his first practical effort to mobilize all elements of society, civil as well as military, in order to carry out his nation-at-war thesis. His later attempt to put this thesis into play produced even more disastrous results.

While Ludendorff was attempting to colonize eastern lands, OberOst's quarrel with the OHL continued. "I often have the feeling," Hindenburg wrote to his wife in late November, "that His Majesty senses how heavily I am exposed to insults and slights from certain quarters and that he tries to compensate for this by awarding me honors since, due to his weakness vis-à-vis Falkenhayn, no other means stand at his disposal. I no longer believe that the final decisive victory will be given to the fatherland through my personal effort."[23]

About the same time that Hindenburg was writing these words, Hoffmann was informing his wife that the field marshal "daily grows older and less important. Ludendorff no longer can bring him to make a move against the kaiser. That something must happen is clear to all of us, but one will not bring Hindenburg to open rebellion."[24]

Such were the dimensions of the quarrel that the minister of war, General Wild von Hohenborn, himself a fence sitter in the tradition of all political generals, adopted a sort of "plague on both your houses" attitude. Falkenhayn was inclined to crow over the capture of twenty Englishmen, he wrote to his wife, "but if Hindenburg took seven thousand prisoners, then he laughed sympathetically over the ignoramuses in the east who should have taken twelve thousand prisoners. On one such occasion he went so far as to say to me: 'Ludendorff must face a court-martial after the war.' " OberOst, which Wild visited in December 1915, was not without fault: "This staff has no comprehension of the West, of Belgium or Serbia, one will fight only his Russian campaign and hopes thereby to bring the war to an end."[25]

Ludendorff was clearly depressed, writing to a Bavarian general at this time: "Twice the chance to hit the Russians decisively has been denied to us. Well, bitter hate brews in me, so I'll have to keep quiet. What has been left undone in this war, missed opportunities, to the detriment of the fatherland, is too much to prevent the perceptive man from being oppressed." Nor was his spleen confined to the OHL: "I am not an embittered critic, Excellency, but a German who sees with sorrow how the country's strength is wasted, how the skill was lacking to fetter the fortunes of war, how so many rule who do not deserve to do so."[26]

Early in 1916 Hoffmann wrote that to celebrate the new year "we have had another active quarrel with the OHL. They want some heavy artillery and we don't want to give it to them. Their tone is always so insolent that I don't understand how Hindenburg is able to accept it." A few days later he noted that "the times when Hindenburg could outmaneuver Falkenhayn are long since past. Time has taken the trumps out of his hand. . . . I do not believe that this will change under the present kaiser."[27]

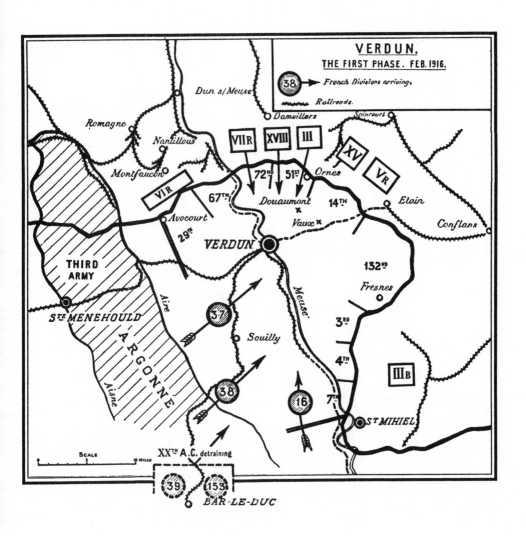

VERDUN.
THE FIRST PHASE. FEB. 1916.

③⑧ → French Divisions arriving.

—— Railroads.

18

Falkenhayn's Gamble at Verdun

In Charleville I have had three long conversations with the
chancellor over the objectives of this war and other matters.
I have left no doubt in his mind that by next summer we shall
have no more replacements . . . whether the French have
sufficient men to carry on until then is indeed the question.
—Minister of War General Wild von Hohenborn
to his wife, November 1, 1915[1]

The German army is now entering into a period of operations
in the west which must bring the decision.
—General Erich von Falkenhayn to
his army commanders, February
11, 1916[2]

Max Hoffmann was correct: Erich von Falkenhayn's position was
secure so long as he retained the kaiser's and, to a lesser degree,
the chancellor's support. His unsuccessful attacks at Ypres in
1914 and his subsequent pessimism seriously eroded Bethmann's support
but did not lead to an open break, and he had continued to enjoy the
kaiser's confidence.

This was due in part to Falkenhayn's reviving the OHL's shattered
morale after Moltke's collapse, to his victorious offensives in the east
and in Serbia, and to his successful defense of the western front against
the great Allied offensives of late 1915. It was also due to his "iron will,
strong nerves and intelligence," wrote one of the kaiser's inner circle.
"His opponents forget that he has a great deal to his credit."[3]

Not least on the credit side was his support of the chancellor and the kaiser on the difficult question of submarine warfare. Germany's defeat in the naval battle of Dogger Bank in early 1915 had greatly weakened Admiral von Tirpitz's campaign to challenge the British fleet to a grand surface action. Tirpitz and Pohl now persuaded the kaiser to authorize a submarine offensive, promising extravagantly that it would soon bring England to her knees. A number of experts, including several admirals, protested that Germany's submarine strength was inadequate for the task, pointing out that there were only twenty-four long-range submarines in the fleet, of which only a third could be on station at one time.[4]

The major dissenting voice was that of the chancellor, who had become increasingly skeptical "of the political value of Germany's military successes."[5] Bethmann still hoped to seduce England from her alliances to bring about a favorable peace, and he correctly foresaw that an underseas campaign would not only destroy the possibility of rapprochement with England but also would greatly complicate relations with neutral nations, in particular the United States. Most diplomats agreed with him, as did Falkenhayn.

Bethmann lost the battle in early February 1915 when the admiralty, without consulting the foreign ministry, announced that in two weeks enemy and neutral vessels in British and Irish waters would be attacked with or without warning. Britain countered by using Q-ships, armed merchant ships that flew neutral flags, to set ambushes for submarines, and by stepping up its formidable naval blockade to prevent neutral vessels from entering German ports. The protests of neutral nations, particularly the United States, went unheeded in Germany, while the British government refused to narrow its definition of contraband and continued to stop, search, and if necessary seize neutral vessels despite the American government's not-so-gentle reminders that it was this sort of arbitrary action that had brought on the War of 1812.

America's burgeoning imbroglio with Britain virtually disappeared in May when the commander of the German submarine U-20 sighted a magnificent target off the southern Irish coast. This was the Cunard liner Lusitania, which sank eighteen minutes after two torpedoes ripped into her sleek hide. Over 1,100 persons drowned, of whom 128 were American citizens, mostly women and children.

This was a terrible blunder. No matter that the liner was carrying munitions, no matter official German apologies or reparation offers. The deed—more than even the rape of Belgium; the execution of Edith Cavell, the British woman who was executed by the Germans for having allegedly helped British soldiers to escape from Belgium; and the introduction of poison gas—awakened America and other neutral countries from general lethargy to recognition of the true nature of this supposedly civilized empire. The German people did not help matters, their jubilation being so general that Arthur Davis, the kaiser's American dentist in Berlin, believed that "America would have declared war immediately had it been known."[6] Equally irresponsible was the government's issue of a gaudy medal commemorating the deed.

Bethmann did his best to pacify the angry American giant, while insisting at home that the underseas campaign be abandoned. Although Falkenhayn supported his stand, it was vigorously opposed by Tirpitz, whose naval press bureau led a public campaign for its continuance to the applause of conservative expansionist groups and indeed the general public.

President Wilson's confidant, Edward House, was in London when the tragedy occurred. Like Wilson, House did not want war (though he pressed continually for preparations *for* war). Foreseeing the implications of the *Lusitania* sinking, he opened a secret diplomatic initiative of his own with Sir Edward Grey, Britain's able foreign minister. House proposed that Germany would "cease submarine warfare on merchant vessels and discontinue the use of asphyxiating or poisonous gases," and in return England would lift her embargo on foodstuffs. Grey agreed to do all he could to push the proposal through his government *providing* that the initiative came from Germany. The issue never came to trial: the German government refused to consider any such move.[7] President Wilson's firm note to Germany in early June drew apologies, but refusal to admit the illegality of the action. The main result of the note was to cause the pacifist American secretary of state, William Jennings Bryan, to resign for fear that the administration was leading America into the war. He was replaced by Robert Lansing, ultimately to Germany's disadvantage.

International furor continued. Ambassador Gerard in Berlin informed House in late July: "The people here are firmly convinced that we can be slapped, insulted and murdered with absolute impunity, and refer to our notes as things worse than waste paper. . . . They feel that our 'New Freedom' is against their ideas and ideals, and they hate President Wilson because he embodies peace and learning rather than caste and war."[8]

Vitriolic arguments filled the summer as the kaiser veered from one side to the other. The sinking in August of a large British freighter with passengers brought renewed protests from Washington. Bethmann's view was still supported by Falkenhayn, mainly because he wanted Bulgaria to join in the invasion of Serbia and Bulgaria was holding off for fear that the submarine offensive would bring America into the war.

Bethmann and Falkenhayn's view prevailed, and in early September the unrestricted attacks were called off. Tirpitz and Admiral Gustav Bachmann responded by angrily offering their resignations. Bachmann was replaced as chief of the naval staff by Admiral Henning von Holtzendorff, who at this time sided with Bethmann, but the kaiser refused to accept Tirpitz's resignation, which would have caused a furor in right-wing circles. The campaign had sunk 850,000 tons of merchant shipping at a cost of fifteen submarines[9]—hardly the overwhelming result promised by Tirpitz and his minions.

Bethmann's victory was short-lived. Alarmed by increasing shortages of food and raw materials and the antiwar mutterings of leftists and trade-union members, worried about insufficiency of manpower, convinced that there would be no revolution in Russia,[10] he suggested that once Serbia was conquered Germany should invite her enemies to the peace table even at the expense of desired large-scale annexations. This suggestion horrified both Wild von Hohenborn and Falkenhayn, who refused to consider any such display of "weakness."[11] Bethmann as usual caved in. In a Reichstag session of early December 1915, he failed to denounce annexations and he rejected a German peace initiative as premature.

A concentrated building program meanwhile had increased the submarine fleet to nearly sixty operational U-boats of all types, a figure said to be steadily increasing by having shipyards work around the clock. Naval hawks vehemently argued that it was vital to starve Britain into submission but neglected to add that two thirds of the operational U-boats were suitable only for limited coastal operations.* Unrestricted U-boat warfare—sink on sight and neutrals be damned—was the only way to do it. It is to Bethmann's credit that he would not accept this. It is to Falkenhayn's discredit that he changed course.

It is also understandable.

Three months after the war had begun, Falkenhayn warned Bethmann Hollweg that it could not be won in the conventional sense. He

---

* At least one admiral insisted on a euphemistic difference: "It was not the purpose of the U-boat war to starve England, as many have erroneously assumed to be the case; the purpose of the [underseas] war was to inflict such losses upon British tonnage that England would be brought to the point of saying: 'It is better for us to make peace now, since time is working against us.' " James B. Scott, *Official German Documents Relating to the World War*, 1, 536, Admiral Koch's testimony, November 7, 1919.

had not since changed his mind. It was now evident that Russia would not make a separate peace. German casualties on the western front in 1915—over 2,500,000, including 630,000 dead and nearly 250,000 missing[12]—far outweighed the importance of victories in the eastern and southern theaters of war. Falkenhayn recognized the war for what it was—a war of attrition.

Unfortunately for the German empire's sake, he was not equipped to fight it. Had he won the race to the sea, had he broken through at Ypres, he might have grown into his job. As it was, failure put him on a defensive course that even his victories in the autumn of 1915 could not adequately correct. He saw enemies everywhere. The insidious campaign waged by Bethmann Hollweg, Hindenburg, Ludendorff, and others to have him replaced drove him to frantic measures to retain his self-esteem and with it his job. Of the German generals he alone had realized early in the war that the Central Powers were in a no-win situation. Instead of raising the kaiser and the government to this eminently sound realization, and commanding the army accordingly, pride and frustration were about to change him into a rampaging bull in the china shop of strategy.

Bulgaria's entrance into the war on the side of the Central Powers and the subsequent victory over Serbia had removed Falkenhayn's main objection to unrestricted submarine warfare. The Bulgarian alliance and the opening of land communications to Turkey seemed to him to have diminished the chances of America entering the war because of a submarine offensive. For reasons to date unknown but possibly buoyed by new political fantasies born of innate geopolitical ignorance, he no longer believed that "war with America was unbearable."[13]

This was sheer heresy in Bethmann's mind, but Falkenhayn was also growing away from the chancellor in other political matters. In autumn of 1915 he, along with many influential Germans, had turned to the notion of a *Mitteleuropabund*—a central European union—under the aegis of Germany. This was the brainchild of Friedrich Naumann, whose book, *Mitteleuropa*, was published in autumn 1915 and rapidly became a best-seller. The appeal to Falkenhayn was strategic, a defensive alliance of Germany, Austria-Hungary, Bulgaria, and Turkey, with later perhaps Sweden, Switzerland, and Greece, which would help counter the British naval blockade. Encouraged by one of his favorites, General Hans von Seeckt, he soon toyed with the notion of establishing German economic and cultural hegemony over this vast area, not altogether dissimilar to Ludendorff's imperialistic notions in Poland and the Baltic lands. Falkenhayn's flight of fancy brought him into conflict with Beth-mann because he was meddling in political affairs and because his ut-terances made little sense.

Further conflict developed between the two when Bethmann in late November sounded Falkenhayn out on the subject of a German peace offer. It was senseless to make a peace offer to the Allied powers, Fal-kenhayn told him. "This is no longer the kind of war with which we are familiar. In a very real sense it has become a struggle for survival for all the belligerents." Germany no longer had any choice but "to continue the war until the enemy's will to victory was broken and with that its desire to carry on the war."[14]

Recognizing this and aware of Germany and Austria's military and economic shortcomings, Falkenhayn might have grasped the importance of subordinating military to political strategy and working with Bethmann to fashion a realistic political goal. This admittedly would not have been an easy task. Although Falkenhayn, along with other moderates, claimed that he was willing to conclude peace on the basis of the status quo ante, he wanted sufficient German hegemony in Belgium and Poland to protect Germany from any future threats from these areas. Bethmann not only agreed with these demands, but shortly after his meeting with Falkenhayn we find him conversing with Ludendorff and Zimmermann in Berlin, apparently receptive to their demands for a hard peace which could only be won by a significant increase in military power.[15]

Falkenhayn enlarged upon his nebulous thinking in an estimate of the situation written for the kaiser on Christmas Day 1915, in which he asserted that Germany must wage a war of attrition designed to cripple one or more of her enemies sufficiently to bring them to the peace table.

How was this to be done?

The villain was England, whose goal was "the permanent elimi-nation of what seems to her the most dangerous rival. . . . Germany can expect no mercy from this enemy, so long as [it] still retains the slightest hope of achieving [its] object."[16] England somehow had to be shown that she could not win a war of attrition.

Falkenhayn had recently met Tirpitz—"Who will come to grief as a result of it is a pleasing speculation," Hoffmann caustically noted.[17] The army chief of staff had been assured by Tirpitz that sufficient sub-marines were on hand to force England to sue for peace within two months of unrestricted submarine warfare, and that this could be done before America could intervene decisively.[18] Holtzendorff was more cautious—it would take four months, a figure shortly changed to six months.[19] Assuming "that the naval authorities are not making a mistake," Falkenhayn wrote, "there can be no justification on military grounds for refusing any further to employ what promises to be our most effective weapon,"[20] and he called for the new campaign to begin in February 1916.[21]

At the same time, Falkenhayn continued, it was necessary to destroy England's allies on the European continent. Italy posed no great problem, since her military achievements were so small and her internal condition so unstable. Conrad von Hötzendorf's desire for a major offensive against Italy was not to be thought of (as Falkenhayn bluntly informed his Austrian opposite). The present line on the Isonzo must be held while time did its work to topple Italy. Russia was also in trouble: "Even if we cannot perhaps expect a revolution in the grand style, we are entitled to believe that Russia's internal troubles will compel her to give in within a relatively short period. In this connection it may be taken for granted that she will not revive her military reputation meanwhile."[22] A fresh offensive against Russia would have to wait until April because of weather and terrain. At that time the target was not to be Petrograd or Moscow, for which Germany lacked sufficient troops and which in any event would solve nothing, but rather the breadbasket of the Ukraine, hopefully in conjunction with Romanian forces.

There remained Germany's real continental enemy, France. Falkenhayn along with other general-staff officers was convinced that "the strain on France had almost reached the breaking point—though it is certainly borne with the most remarkable devotion. If we succeed in opening the eyes of her people to the fact that in a military sense they have nothing more to hope for, that breaking point would be reached and England's best sword knocked out of her hand."[23]

This was not merely Falkenhayn rhetoric. The previous July Max Hoffmann had reckoned that "by February [1916] at the latest the French will have lost so many men that from that date they can no longer keep their army up to its previous strength."[24] In the same month Bethmann Hollweg, on the basis of foreign ministry reports, concluded that "a definite war-weariness in enemy lands" was emerging, "especially in France where the defeat of the Russians and their own failure to break through our lines is depressing."[25] Hoffmann concluded in early August that "France would now be easiest to defeat. Those who know the conditions maintain that a breakthrough at one point would cause France to collapse." Two months later he wrote that "in the west we must wait. French manpower is coming to an end. During the winter France must reach the point where no new recruits will be on hand, for coming losses cannot be replaced. If they become convinced on top of that that we can and will hold on, they will gradually weaken. But this requires time and we must be patient."[26] These words gain weight because Hoffmann was in daily telephone communication with the OHL, where many of his prewar colleagues were on duty. In addition, numerous important officials and officers visited OberOst to offer facts and opinions. But if Hoffmann unknowingly agreed with his archenemy Falkenhayn as to the strategical target, he would soon sharply disagree with the tactics chosen to accomplish the strategy.

In Falkenhayn's opinion a major offensive designed to break through French lines was not necessary, and anyway was beyond German capabilities, an opinion shared by Max Bauer. Instead, a limited offensive against a vital part of the front would allow Germany to claim the initiative and would compel France to "throw in every man they have. If they do so the forces of France will bleed to death—as there can be no question of a voluntary withdrawal—whether we reach our goal or not. If they do not do so, and we reach our objectives, the moral effect on France will be enormous."[27] He seems also to have believed that a successful submarine offensive would force the British into a precipitate attack to gain the U-boat bases on the Flanders coast, an attack that would be shattered by Crown Prince Rupprecht's northern army group to further weaken Britain.[28] The perfect target, Falkenhayn continued, was the bastion of Verdun, defended by a group of outer forts, only twelve miles from a German railhead, thus ensuring the necessary logistical support to continue the operation at the pace desired. The limited offensive in terrain suitable for the use of poison gas was to be carried out by Crown Prince Wilhelm's Fifth Army Group, which would attack on February 12, 1916.

Falkenhayn's plan fell victim to political, strategical, and tactical shortcomings from the beginning. Partly as the result of obsessive secrecy, partly of his lack of trust in Bethmann's government, he did not inform the chancellor of his plans, much less suggest a complementary diplomatic offensive that might have brought realistic peace negotiations. He does not seem to have asked himself what he would do if his military strategy failed and how such a failure would affect Germany's political situation.

A tactical misunderstanding developed because of his obsessive secrecy, which he believed was necessary to gain surprise and probably to avoid further grumbling by Hindenburg and Ludendorff and their adherents at the OHL, as well as by Conrad, who was fighting his own war in Montenegro and Albania. The plan approved by the kaiser was not shown to Crown Prince Wilhelm or to his chief of staff, General Schmidt von Knobelsdorff. Instead an oral directive called for "an offensive in the Meuse area in the direction of Verdun."[29] Wilhelm and Knobelsdorff interpreted this as an order to capture Verdun, and plans were made for an offensive on a wide front that stretched some twenty miles east to west on each side of the Meuse.

Falkenhayn summarily rejected this plan. Instead Wilhelm's assault divisions were to attack the French forts on the eastern bank of the Meuse River after an intensive artillery preparation, and were to continue the offensive on a limited front of five to seven miles. A second attack west of the Meuse would depend on the progress of the first attack. It would appear that Falkenhayn intended to keep his options open in the manner laid down by the elder Moltke in a memorandum dated 1865: "The task of a skillful offensive will consist of forcing our foe to attack a position chosen by us, and only when casualties, demoralization, and exhaustion have drained his strength will we ourselves take up the tactical offensive."[30]

Six fresh assault divisions were transferred to the Fifth Army during January and February to make a total of nine divisions, each to attack on less than a mile and a half of front. Other divisions stood ready to move out on the west bank of the Meuse, still others remained in reserve in anticipation of a French counterattack. Over a thousand guns, howitzers, and heavy mortars were emplaced behind the Meuse ridges, where they would be largely impervious to enemy counterbattery fire. Five hastily built field railroads carried three million shells to camouflaged dumps. Most of this activity was carried out at night. German armies distant from Verdun made a series of local attacks to further disguise German intentions.[31]

Falkenhayn later wrote that the French high command learned of the planned offensive only in late January or early February from remarks overheard in Berlin social circles.[32] According to General Joffre, the first suggestions of German intentions reached him in mid-January in reports from French diplomats in Denmark and Switzerland.[33] Local commanders added spice to the rumor stew by reporting increased activity in the German sector, information confirmed in part by captured soldiers and deserters.

Joffre did not attach much importance to these reports that arrived in his headquarters at Chantilly.[34] So far as he was concerned the area was devoid of strategical importance. Unlike most generals of World War

I, Joffre believed that fortress complexes such as that created by the famous engineer General Séré de Rivières at Verdun were *déclassé*, a view upheld by the rapidity of their destruction in Belgium, Russian Poland, and Galicia.[35]

Joffre had already stripped the outlying forts at Verdun of their guns and a good many of their defenders, leaving the remaining *poilus* to rely on rather primitive trenches. He did, however, send one of his trusted and able subordinates, General Noël de Castelnau, to inspect the area. Castelnau reported an unsatisfactory state of defense in general, but his suggested improvements were being made by the local commander, who had been reinforced with two divisions. A corps commander in late January sharply criticized the state of defenses in what he called "a catastrophic terrain."[36] Convinced that "Verdun is not an enemy target," Joffre remained far more concerned with other sectors of his long front and continued to hold on to his general reserve of twenty-six divisions with the avidity of a military scrooge.[37] "I ask only one thing," he announced shortly before the opening enemy bombardment, "and that is that the Germans will attack me, and if they do attack me, that it will be at Verdun. Quote me."[38] Joffre's error was familiar to many commanders through the ages: He could not fit an attack on Verdun into his own strategical concept and so refused to accept the possibility. Only two days after the enemy's scheduled kickoff he learned the harsh truth.

Had Wilhelm's attack begun on schedule it could possibly have achieved a major success by capturing the entire fortress complex, to make its recapture exceedingly costly for the French—exactly what Falkenhayn hoped to achieve and what Wilhelm later agreed was likely.[39] Snow and heavy rains turned the difficult terrain to mud, which prevented movement of both men and guns and denied the visibility necessary for accurate artillery fire. The attack was postponed for eight days. Assault troops huddled in forward trenches and the underground *Stossen*—specially constructed concrete dugouts—where they ate only cold field rations that brought on acute diarrhea: "Over the top with shit in your pants," the troops told each other while they grimly bailed ice-cold water that filled trenches and dugouts alike.[40]

The weather having somewhat cleared, the big guns opened fire on February 21, a bombardment unprecedented in the history of warfare due to Falkenhayn's determination to replace flesh with steel. Shells big and small, shells holding shrapnel and poison gas, poured from the skies in the German effort to create a rain of death. Every hour 100,000 shells

fell on soldiers huddling in the old defenseless forts, all but stripped of
guns, and in shallow, pathetically inadequate trenches. German observers
stationed in Zeppelins and in the baskets of "captive" balloons (balloons
attached to cables anchored to the ground) directed the awesome fire,
while above them German fighter squadrons formed a protective cordon
against enemy intruders. In all, two million shells were fired before assault
units moved out only to find, incredibly, that groups of *poilus* had survived
the storm of steel and were fighting back. But not for long. Assault teams
carrying machine guns, trench mortars, and flamethrowers pushed steadily forward. Gains of up to two or three miles on a seven-mile front were
made in two days. In another two days Fort Douaumont fell, "the strong
and reputedly impregnable northeastern pillar of the Verdun defense
system," Falkenhayn later wrote, knowing full well that it was nothing
of the sort.[41] To the east other assault divisions pushed through the Orne
Valley to the heights of the Meuse. Here the advance was halted by
costly French counterattacks, which seemed to justify Falkenhayn's overall strategy.

Joffre was still not convinced that this was a major attack, but he
nevertheless reacted calmly and professionally, first by persuading Sir
Douglas Haig to relieve the French Tenth Army with British troops,
thus securing a stronger reserve, second by sending Castelnau back to
Verdun to represent him in the crucial days necessary to bring up the
Second Army and place General Henri Philippe Pétain in overall command, third by requesting the Russian high command to attack as soon
as possible in the east.

Pétain was a good choice, a smoothly competent commander and
outstanding tactician whose excellent battlefield performance had earned
him rapid promotion from the rank of lieutenant colonel at the opening
of the war. The only problem was that he was on leave and could not
be located. A perceptive aide finally found him with a favorite *putain* in
a Paris hotel.

The sixty-year-old Pétain arrived on the sixth day of battle. French
losses in men and guns had been severe; the enemy was only six miles
from Verdun itself. Pétain acted quickly and efficiently, ordering long-
range artillery, the new French 155-mm Schneider, to pommel the enemy
while newly arrived French batteries on the western side of the Meuse
began pounding German assault units on the eastern side to give French
reserve units time to reach the threatened front. An anonymous correspondent watched French preparations for a counterattack on a wood:
"The searchlight threw patch after patch of trees into bright relief, like

the swiftly changing scenes of a cinematograph. . . . Not a yard of ground fails to receive the shock of a projectile. The solid earth bubbles before my eyes. Trees split and spring into the air. It is a surface earthquake with nothing spared, nothing stable."[42]

Rapid French reinforcement surprised German commanders. Assault divisions were rapidly running out of ammunition, men were exhausted and hungry, casualties heavier and heavier in humans and horses, gains meager. The thick, hilly terrain that had helped to hide German preparations became a quagmire, claiming heavy guns that defied extrication even by double and triple teams. A week after the assault, casualties topped 25,000 to shred battalions and regiments. "Falkenhayn is very nervous because of the checks and heavy losses that have occurred," the minister of war, Wild von Hohenborn, ominously noted.[43]

Once the enemy offensive was blunted, Pétain's major problem was the supply line. Bar-le-Duc was the nearest railhead, with only a dilapidated narrow-gauge line and an improved secondary road to serve Verdun thirty-four miles distant. This road, which soon became famous as the Sacred Way, saved Verdun. A herculean effort by thousands of conscripted laborers working around the clock transformed it into what Georges Blond called "the first express highway in history"—a single lane of hope, no passing permitted, disabled vehicles shoved off the road and burned, 6,000 light and heavy trucks a day carrying every conceivable type of weapon and tool of war to the defenders of beleaguered Verdun.

Such was the vigor of the French defense that Castelnau reported to Joffre at the end of February that "Verdun was for the moment safe."[44] German disappointment was evident: the OHL seriously considered transferring the offensive to another sector of the long front. This was rejected and on March 6 a new attack opened on the western side of the Meuse. It made only slow progress because of determined defense in rugged terrain that again prevented bringing up heavy artillery necessary for continued assaults. French pilots were actively challenging German air supremacy and would soon enough wrest it from their enemy, despite the talented and brave efforts of such flyers as the famous ace Oswald Boelcke in shooting down the intruders.

At month's end General Wild von Hohenborn informed his wife: "All goes slowly at Verdun—unfortunately! Knobelsdorff [Crown Prince Wilhelm's chief of staff] is finished and the troops are burning themselves out. To Falkenhayn's deliberations whether one should call a halt, I say no. It has to be carried through, but of course it must not become another Ypres."[45]

Fierce fighting continued throughout March and April, but it did not follow Falkenhayn's planned scenario. German losses were as heavy as those of the enemy. One infantry division suffered 11,000 casualties. Falkenhayn was rapidly running out of both reserve infantry and heavy artillery units. By the end of March Pétain was stronger in numbers and guns than the Germans.

Although exhorted by Joffre to grasp the initiative, the cautious Pétain preferred the defensive, not that the choice made much difference in mounting daily casualty reports. Pétain regarded the battle of Verdun as the be-all and end-all of the war, and kept demanding reinforcements. Joffre regarded Verdun as just another battle, a prelude to the massive Franco-British offensive that was to take place on the Somme in July. Pétain's attitude brought about a quarrel with Joffre, who finally promoted him upstairs to command of the central armies, leaving the Verdun command to General Robert Nivelle.

At this point, the beginning of May, Falkenhayn was a very frustrated general. Verdun had become nothing more than a meat-grinding battle of attack and counterattack, "a battle of madmen in the midst of a volcano," as one correspondent reported. "Whole regiments melt in a few minutes, and others take their places only to perish in the same way."[46]

Crown Prince Wilhelm wanted to call a halt. The German attacks never got far beyond Fort Douaumont on the eastern side and were virtually stymied on the western side. Divisions that should have been relieved were forced to remain in line. Troop morale was rapidly reaching rock bottom—"many men are refusing to leave their trenches" when ordered to attack, Wild von Hohenborn wrote.[47] Falkenhayn later tried to justify the slaughter by claiming that five Frenchmen died for every two and a half Germans, an inaccurate statement that nonetheless adequately sums up the command idiocy of the great war.

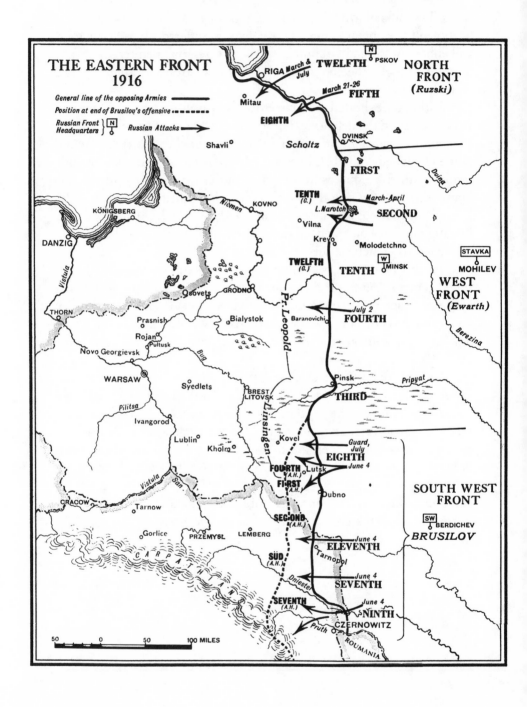

THE EASTERN FRONT
1916

General line of the opposing Armies ——————
Position at end of Brusilov's offensive ·····-------
Russian Front Headquarters } N
Russian Attacks ——————→

RIGA March & July
TWELFTH N PSKOV
March 21-26 FIFTH
Mitau
EIGHTH
Scholtz DVINSK
Shavli
Dvina
FIRST
Niemen KOVNO
TENTH (G.)
March-April
L. Narotch
SECOND
Vilna
Krevo Molodetchno
STAVKA
MOHILEV
TWELFTH (G.)
W MINSK
TENTH
WEST FRONT (Ewarth)
KÖNIGSBERG
DANZIG
Vistula
Osovets GRODNO
Pr. Leopold
Baranovichi
July 2
FOURTH
Berezina
THORN
Prasnish
Bialystok
Pripyat
Pinsk
Rojan
Pultusk
Bug
Novo Georgievsk
WARSAW
Syedlets
BREST LITOVSK
THIRD
Pilitsa
Ivangorod
Linsingen
Kovel
Guard, July
EIGHTH
Lublin
Kholm
FOURTH (A.H.)
Lutsk
June 4
FIRST (A.H.)
SOUTH WEST FRONT
Vistula
San
Dubno
CRACOW
Tarnow
SECOND (A.H.)
SW BERDICHEV
BRUSILOV
Gorlice
PRZEMYSL
LEMBERG
ELEVENTH
June 4
SÜD (A.H.)
Tarnopol
Dniester
June 4
SEVENTH
SEVENTH (A.H.)
June 4
NINTH
CZERNOWITZ
Pruth
ROUMANIA

NORTH FRONT (Ruzski)

50   0   50   100 MILES

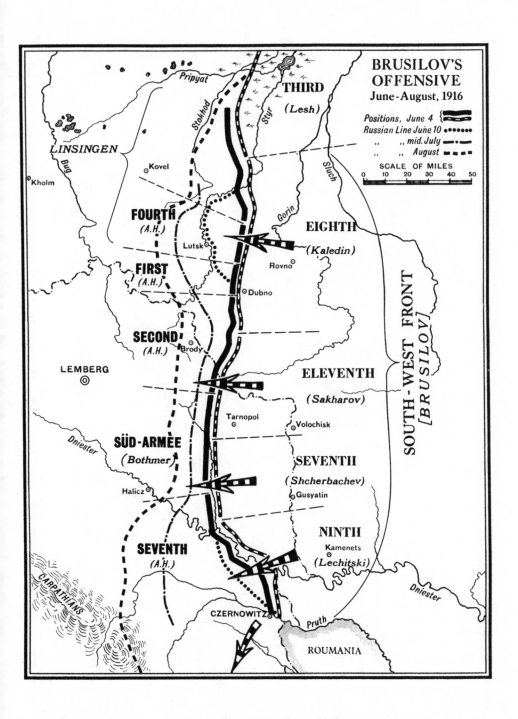

BRUSILOV'S
OFFENSIVE
June - August, 1916

Positions, June 4
Russian Line June 10 •••••••
     ,,   ,, mid. July
     ,,   ,, August

SCALE OF MILES
0 10 20 30 40 50

Pripyat

THIRD
(Lesh)

LINSINGEN

Stokhod   *Styr*   *Sluch*

Kovel

Bug

Kholm

Gorin

FOURTH
(A.H.)

EIGHTH
(Kaledin)

Lutsk

FIRST
(A.H.)

Rovno

Dubno

SECOND
(A.H.)

Brody

LEMBERG

ELEVENTH
(Sakharov)

SOUTH-WEST FRONT
[BRUSILOV]

Tarnopol

Volochisk

Dniester

SÜD-ARMEE
(Bothmer)

SEVENTH
(Shcherbachev)

Halicz

Gusyatin

NINTH
(Lechitski)

Kamenets

SEVENTH
(A.H.)

Dniester

CARPATHIANS

CZERNOWITZ

Pruth

ROUMANIA

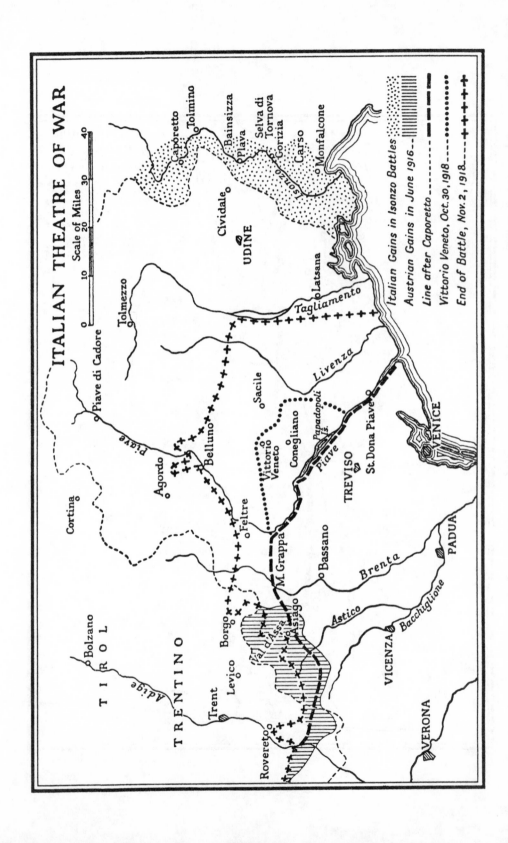

ITALIAN THEATRE OF WAR

Scale of Miles
0   10   20   30   40

Italian Gains in Isonzo Battles ·········
Austrian Gains in June 1916 — — —
Line after Caporetto — · — · —
Vittorio Veneto, Oct. 30, 1918 · · · · · ·
End of Battle, Nov. 2, 1918 + + + +

Bolzano

T I R O L

Adige

Trent

Levico

Rovereto

Borgo

Val d'Assa

Asiago

Cortina

Piave di Cadore

Agordo

Belluno

Feltre

M. Grappa

Bassano

Brenta

Astico

Bacchiglione

VICENZA

VERONA

PADUA

TRENTINO

Tolmezzo

Caporetto

Tolmino

Bainsizza

Plava

Selva di
Tornova

Gorizia

Carso

Monfalcone

Isonzo

Cividale

UDINE

Latsana

Tagliamento

Livenza

Sacile

Papadopoli
Is.

Conegliano

Vittorio
Veneto

Piave

St. Dona Piave

TREVISO

VENICE

19

Brusilov's Offensive Against
Austria-Hungary

The name Hindenburg frightens our enemies, galvanizes our army and people, which have boundless confidence in him. . . . if we were to lose a battle, which God forbid, our people would accept it, and likewise any peace to which he put his name.
—CHANCELLOR BETHMANN HOLLWEG
TO GENERAL VON LYNCKER,
JUNE 23, 1916[1]

The chancellor has made a new attack on Falkenhayn . . . it is rather exciting. Ludendorff [is] naturally very anxious. The only one here who maintains a truly Olympian calm is the Field Marshal. I believe that he just does not think at all . . . never has a man with so little mental and physical effort become so famous.
—COLONEL MAX HOFFMANN TO HIS WIFE, JULY 2, 1916[2]

Stalemate at Verdun was only one facet of Falkenhayn's failing strategy. A few days before the Verdun offensive had begun, Falkenhayn learned that an important part of his overall plan had fallen victim to the German chancellor's persuasive arguments. Bethmann Hollweg was dead against a renewal of unrestricted submarine warfare. He did not believe Tirpitz's optimistic claims, which conflicted with the opinion of other experts. Germany certainly did not have enough U-boats to carry out an absolute blockade of England. Without doubt, enough ships would slip through to prevent her people from starving. He pointed out the likelihood of the enemy developing effective defenses and increasing their shipbuilding potential, he warned that German merchant ships forced to remain in U.S. ports because of the British naval threat would be seized if America broke with Germany, and he condemned it on moral grounds in that it would cause neutral nations to unite against Germany as the "mad dog" among the peoples of the world. Its effect on the United States would be catastrophic unless a favorable agreement with Washington could be previously negotiated. Tirpitz, supported by Falkenhayn, argued that such an agreement was impossible in view of America's anti-German attitude.

The kaiser was of two minds as usual. He had told Holtzendorff and Müller that "the drowning of innocent passengers was an idea that appalled him. He also bore a responsibility before God for the manner of waging a war"—this from one who exhorted the troops to take no prisoners and bayonet as many of the "swine" as possible. "On the other hand . . . could he go against the counsel of his military advisers, and from human consideration prolong the war at the cost of so many brave men who were defending their Fatherland? He was faced with the most difficult decision of his life."[3] He finally overrode Tirpitz and Falkenhayn by postponing the unrestricted submarine campaign, which had been scheduled to begin on February 20.

The issue reemerged at an imperial council in Charleville in early March after Falkenhayn, stymied at Verdun, demanded the immediate opening of the underseas campaign. Hot words filled Belleaire, the kaiser's new villa outside of town, which had been lavishly furnished at the expense of Charleville's citizens—"a luxurious jewel case," Müller disapprovingly called it.[4] Bethmann had used the interval well by furnishing the kaiser a list of impressive arguments agreed to by important voices that a favorable peace could still be gained without risking a single throw of the dice on unrestricted submarine warfare. Members of the Bundesrat and the foreign ministry agreed that the campaign should be postponed until the American government could be prepared to accept it. The present campaign against armed enemy ships could meanwhile be stepped up. Holtzendorff, on the other hand, now favored an all-out campaign, as did the majority of the Reichstag and indeed the German people.[5]

Bethmann's reasoned arguments backed by his threat to resign if the campaign commenced brought another imperial crisis. Only two weeks earlier the kaiser had been celebrating Falkenhayn's victory at Verdun with pink champagne, as he celebrated all victories. That victory was now turning to ashes. "His Majesty's nerves are strained to the breaking point," Müller noted in his diary on March 9. "Today for the first time since the outbreak of war he showed unmistakable defeatism. He said: 'One must never utter it nor shall I admit it to Falkenhayn, but this war will not end with a great victory.' "[6] The imperial decision was again postponed. Tirpitz, who had not been invited to the council, offered his resignation, which this time the kaiser gladly accepted, scribbling on the paper, "He abandons the sinking ship."[7] He was replaced by a moderate, Vice Admiral Eduard von Capelle, a choice that displeased the minister of war "in every respect . . . his interest restricted to material and administrative affairs, slight confidence in the effectiveness of U-boats, extravagant respect for England, languid to the extreme. . . . Falkenhayn as offended as I."[8] Tirpitz subsequently took the submarine issue to the Reichstag in a manner that, to Max Hoffmann, suggested high treason.

Bethmann had won breathing space until April. He badly needed it. One observer described him as "tense, tired and nervous," probably smoking sixty or seventy cigarettes a day. "His hair has become white, his face is lined with deep furrows. He seems the personification of despair."[9] Plainly puzzled by the situation at Verdun, as he wrote Karl von Treutler in late March, he could get no clear answer from Falkenhayn. Falkenhayn was also to be faulted for claiming that the Russians could never again make a full-scale offensive, and here they were doing just that in the Lake Naroch area. Neither was OberOst telling Bethmann the true situation. As for the submarine controversy, he was under heavy pressure from the conservatives, the industrialists, and most leading intellectuals and conservative newspaper publishers to reverse his stand. But a number of clear-thinking naval officers sided with him, Capelle among them, and he was not to be moved from his opposition.

Negotiations with Washington had been complicated by a German submarine's sinking of an unarmed French vessel carrying American passengers (among a host of other sinkings). Washington's threat to break diplomatic relations reinforced Bethmann's demands to limit further the scope of underwater warfare. Probably more telling was the vindication of the chancellor's suspicions of naval integrity. At the end of March the new minister of the navy, Capelle, testified before a select committee of the Reichstag that, as opposed to the inflated numbers earlier presented by Tirpitz, Germany possessed only twenty large U-boats, five of which were committed to the surface fleet. At the moment of his testimony exactly *three* U-boats were lying in ambush off the British coasts, one at each entrance to the Irish Sea, one on the western end of the English

Channel. Unrestricted submarine warfare would "doubtless inflict great damage on England. But that is not enough. Our aim is to bring England to her knees—which I do not believe can be accomplished in this way."[10] This unpalatable testimony, taken with continuing pressure from the American government, caused the kaiser to confirm his earlier decision against expanded submarine warfare.

The kaiser's action only heightened already outraged feelings. Admiral Scheer furiously reacted by calling in the few submarines that were on station, virtually ending undersea warfare for several months. Falkenhayn used it as an excuse for going on the defensive at Verdun, in other words attempting to make Bethmann responsible for the military failure. Falkenhayn's intransigence had turned Bethmann into a dangerous enemy who henceforth would do what he could to have Falkenhayn replaced by Hindenburg (before either of them replaced him).

Falkenhayn suffered an even more serious loss, however. The kaiser had been his loyal supporter, albeit from mixed motivations, the main one being his dislike of Ludendorff and his envy of Hindenburg's popularity. Falkenhayn's performance in the east and his defense of the western front had won the kaiser's praise, and he had enthusiastically endorsed the Verdun offensive (despite complaining to the minister of war that he had learned of its opening only from the newspapers). Falkenhayn's increasingly imperious behavior had frequently gone against the grain, and so had his abrupt reversal on the question of unrestricted submarine warfare. His belligerent attitude in ensuing discussions had further annoyed Germany's ruler, as had the general's blunt response to the kaiser's recent decision—"a misfortune for kaiser and empire."[11]

Wilhelm considered Falkenhayn's reply insolent and joined Bethmann in disapproving the general's undue interference in imperial and government policy. He nonetheless preferred him to Hindenburg, and when Falkenhayn asked to be transferred to the front, the kaiser, for want of finding anyone more suitable or competent, persuaded him to remain at his post.

Falkenhayn received yet another unpleasant surprise in that spring of 1916 when his highly touted claim to have eliminated the Russian threat for the foreseeable future fell victim to events. In response to French pleas, the Russian supreme headquarters, Stavka, ordered the army groups of generals Evert and Kuropatkin to make a major attack, "the one to the southwest against Vilna, the other due west from the line of lakes east of Vilna," the goal being to drive the Germans back behind their frontier.[12]

The Russians had made an amazing comeback in numbers, guns, and ammunition since their armies had been shattered in the 1915 fighting. By March 1916 the Russian Second Army counted about 350,000 men with almost a thousand guns. It was commanded by General Smirnov, sixty-seven years old, described as "a soft old man with no distinction of any kind."[13] Smirnov faced General Hermann von Eichhorn's German Tenth Army, some 75,000 men with 300 guns, but its strength would soon be nearly doubled.

Numbers are generally deceptive in war. Men have to be commanded wisely and well and guns used effectively for numbers to count. Internecine feuds continued to wrack the Russian officer corps, many of whose senior commanders could not have effectively commanded a regiment. A profound and dangerous schism separated infantry and artillery arms. Envy and hatred compounded by fear ruled the Russian command.

What is known as the battle of Lake Naroch opened on March 18 "with a drumfire such as we had never experienced in the east before," wrote Max Hoffmann.[14] Despite Russian optimism, expressed by a large cavalry force waiting in the rear to exploit the breakthrough, the results were predictable. The weather had turned to a thaw, the battle area to mud. There was no surprise. The Germans had known of the plan for at least two weeks and had acted accordingly. Ludendorff had even gone to Berlin to attend a royal wedding. Aerial observers had early spotted long enemy columns marching west in the snow. Despite its intensity, the two-day Russian artillery preparation was poorly planned and executed. One assault group, attacking "with the utmost bravery and determination and with complete disregard for the loss of life," lost 15,000 men in eight hours.[15] Over 9,000 Russian dead littered a single corps front. A German officer watched one attack through narrow passes that forced the living to tread on dead comrades. His interrogation of prisoners revealed that they had had to be driven into battle and were threatened with being shot if they fell back.[16] In the first three days the Russians suffered nearly 40,000 casualties. Sheer mass, however, managed to push back the German Tenth Army, and the situation soon grew critical. "The Field Marshal's spirit has sunk to about his boots," Hoffmann wrote. "Ludendorff and I look at each other without saying a word. If the German people could see their hero, they would be truly amazed."[17]

German reserves were hurried to the area, but the railway ended at Vilna–Dvinsk, which forced the troops to a lengthy march through swamps and on roads turned to quagmires.

Even while German troops were slogging to the front, the Russian offensive was slowing. Mud was one reason, supply problems another, command confusion still another. Russian soldiers often went hungry. Twelve thousand men died from frostbite alone. Hospital trains broke down. The offensive was over by the end of March, a failure that cost the Russians around 100,000 casualties, the Germans perhaps 20,000. In late April a German counterattack recovered the lost territory.

Ludendorff later wrote that aside from one or two anxious moments, there never was a real crisis during the battle. This did not prevent the Duo from using the event to back up persistent demands for more divisions from the western front, this time for Hoffmann's plan of an attack on Riga. In late May a direct appeal to the kaiser was refused, since Falkenhayn was running short of reserves due to the insatiable demands of the Verdun grinding machine—*die Mühle* (the mill), as it had derisively become known.

Also testing Falkenhayn's patience was the chief of the Austro-Hungarian general staff, Conrad von Hötzendorf, whose desire to launch a major offensive on the Italian front he had summarily rejected. Conrad was not to be put off. He had frustrated the Italian offensives on the Isonzo—no less than five major efforts in ten months. He would now launch an offensive southeast from the Tyrol to cut off Cadorna's armies and force Italy from the war, an offensive he proudly announced that would require only Austro-Hungarian divisions. In Falkenhayn's opinion this was like robbing Peter to pay Paul, that is, robbing the eastern front of Austro-Hungarian divisions and heavy artillery necessary for its security. Falkenhayn could do no more than warn Conrad not to weaken his eastern front.

Conrad opened his offensive in mid-May. It went well at first, his center armies pushing forward to the line of Arserio–Asiago to capture 40,000 prisoners and 380 guns. All seemed ready for the final push to the southeast, which would isolate the Italian armies on the Isonzo. The Italian and French governments sent urgent appeals to Petrograd to make diversionary attacks while the British and French high commands frantically prepared to send reinforcements.

But Conrad had made two major errors. He had attacked with insufficient strength and he had failed to complement the offensive with a push on the Isonzo. As a result, his ensuing push to the southeast soon stalled dangerously on right and left. Mountain terrain made it particularly hard going for the heavy artillery, which fell miles behind the center. Cadorna meanwhile was bringing in reserves and soon would launch a series of powerful counterattacks. What appeared to be victory at the end of May would shortly turn to shattering defeat with immense loss in men, munitions—and what remained of Conrad's reputation.

Russian failure at Lake Naroch brought only a temporary lull on the eastern front. The Russian supreme command, Stavka, had been informed of the planned spring offensive in the west, which Alekseyev would have to support. In mid-April he called a meeting of his army commanders to discuss the problem. Pointing to the Russian superiority in men north of the Pripyat marshes—well over 700,000—he proposed an offensive by Evert and Kuropatkin's armies, a plan similar to the abortive March effort. His generals did not like the idea: German defenses were too strong and there was not enough heavy artillery to breach them. Evert finally agreed to attack on a front no wider than twelve miles. Two months would be needed to collect the artillery, nearly a thousand guns in all, from other fronts. Alekseyev and the czar accepted this scarcely original plan. No one paid much attention to a new voice, that of General Aleksey Brusilov, who had replaced General Ivanov in command of the southwestern front and who agreed to attack with "only trivial reinforcements in men and guns."[18]

Brusilov was sixty-three years old, a much more imaginative commander than most of his peers, and he had an excellent combat record. The material conditions of his armies had also considerably improved, despite heavy losses. By early spring every division was up to strength numerically and was being supplied with machine guns, grenades, and ammunition. Brusilov did not believe that a breakthrough could be made on a narrow front. His reasons were several, and they were all backed by bloody experience. As always in warfare, surprise was the handmaiden to successful attack, but surprise could scarcely be achieved when hundreds of thousands of troops had to be deployed in flat terrain behind a narrow front, and when hundreds of large guns had to be brought up under a sky of observant German airmen. If a breakthrough were made on a narrow front, assault columns would soon be taken in enfilade or raking cross fire from enemy flanks, as had happened to the Germans at

Verdun and to the Russians at Lake Naroch. Such resistance slowed or even stopped the assault until heavy artillery could be moved forward, which gave the enemy time to bring up reserves.

Brusilov's answer was to attack along the line with each army threatening a front at least eighteen miles long. Commanders were to achieve surprise by tunneling underground to extend their forward trenches under their own barbed wire, in places only seventy-five yards from enemy outposts. Reserves were placed in deep dugouts close to the front lines, from where they could be quickly committed to the assault. Brusilov used extensive aerial photography to map enemy trenches and artillery emplacements. Assault units trained in models of enemy trenches. Heavy artillery was moved forward and its commanders made to work in close liaison with the infantry. Active night patrols kept the Germans quiet, as did the prevailing opinion that the Russians would need weeks to shift troops from the north in order to attack in the south.

Considering Brusilov's slight numerical superiority, his was a bold plan. Alekseyev strongly objected to it, begging him to attack in the traditional fashion on a single twelve-mile front. His own army commanders also objected to wide-front attacks, but Brusilov refused to budge. Appeals from Italy and France for action on the eastern front caused Alekseyev to yield in late May, and Brusilov's offensive opened in early June.

It succeeded beyond his wildest hopes. In the north, Kaledin's Eighth Army, after a day-long bombardment, smashed through the lines of Archduke Joseph Ferdinand's Austro-Hungarian Fourth Army at Lutsk in only two days. On Kaledin's left, Sakharov's Eleventh Army pushed forward to score more extensive gains. Lechitski's Ninth Army in the extreme south opened its attack with a bombardment by 200 guns firing 100,000 shells. Advance patrols struck only confused resistance. In one sector alone the Russians captured 11,000 prisoners and 14 guns. In two days Austro-Hungarian losses topped 70,000 with dismal prospects of survival for the remainder. In just over two weeks the Russians had captured more than 200,000 enemy including over 4,000 officers and scores of cannon and machine guns. Only one army, Shcherbachev's Seventh, was checked, this because its commander refused Brusilov's tactical doctrine and advertised his attack with a two-day bombardment on a narrow front.

As Brusilov had foreseen, these divergent attacks along most of his front created an enormous problem to enemy commanders as to where they should commit reserves. Baron von Pflanzer-Baltin met Lechitski's attack by shifting the bulk of his strength to south of the Dniester River. A second attack north of this river flung back a protecting corps to open his flank and cause a general retreat. In less than a week Conrad had lost over half his fighting strength. The Seventh Army continued its wild retreat to end in virtual disintegration, having lost 100,000 men. The front was saved only because Brusilov had outrun his supply capability and because he lacked reserves to guard his northern flank and replace his own heavy losses. Kaledin's Eighth Army had suffered 35,000 casualties in four days of fighting.

With his southern offensive temporarily halted, Brusilov concentrated on the northern sector where Kaledin's Eighth Army was being reinforced from Evert's and Kuropatkin's enormous forces. Kaledin, however, was anxious about exposing his right flank, while Evert and Kuropatkin found a hundred excuses not to attack in their sectors, which could have prevented OberOst from bolstering Conrad's shattered lines. By mid-June Brusilov's offensive had stalled.

Erich von Falkenhayn had been taken for a ride. As is often so in such cases, he was partly responsible. He had been far too optimistic concerning the success of his winter offensive against the Russians. He had defended his false prognosis by writing off the Russian attacks in March as virtually suicide efforts to aid her allies. Conrad had told him at a meeting in Berlin in late May that the Russians could not possibly attack in less than four to six weeks from the time of the first indications, the period necessary to concentrate adequate forces. Conrad at the same time, however, asked for and received a promise of support from the north if he needed it in Galicia. "This promise was most willingly given," Falkenhayn later wrote, "on the supposition that some movement of Russian troops from north to south must have taken place."[19] Two weeks later Conrad's cri de coeur for help in the east arrived at the OHL.

Brusilov's offensive thus took the OHL completely by surprise. "We were therefore faced with a situation which had fundamentally changed. A wholesale failure of this kind had certainly not entered into the calculations of the chief of the general staff. He had considered it impossible."[20] Falkenhayn was facing a major defeat and possibly the end of the war.

The priority task was to check Kaledin's advance in the Lutsk area before it rolled up the flank of the First Army on the right. Falkenhayn reinforced General von Linsingen's army group with two divisions from OberOst and four from the west and ordered him to prepare for a counteroffensive.

Falkenhayn met again with Conrad in early June. Conrad received short shrift. Falkenhayn had warned him not to take reliable troops and heavy artillery from the eastern front for what he termed the Italian "excursion," and a quarrel had ensued. Now see what had happened! Very well, von Linsingen's army group would counterattack, but Linsingen would take command of the Fourth and First Austrian armies and would brook no nonsense about Austrian military aspirations in this area. Conrad would at once transfer two and a half divisions from the Italian front to the east as harbinger of a total eight divisions. Further, a German general, Hans von Seeckt, was to become chief of staff of Pflanzer-Baltin's shattered Seventh Army in the south. As a final insult, Conrad had to promise not to engage in further operations without the OHL's approval.

Having turned his ally into a satellite, Falkenhayn unleashed his counteroffensive in mid-June. A force of twelve-plus German and Austro-Hungarian divisions commanded by General von der Marwitz attacked east from Kovel. Resistance was stubborn, progress slow, casualties soon rose to some 40,000. The retreat of the newly constituted Austrian Fourth Army caused Marwitz to shift the offensive to the southern end of Kaledin's sector. It made no difference. The counteroffensive had failed.

Falkenhayn's failure to assess correctly the tactical problem on the eastern front by sending hastily transferred divisions here and there in an almost panic-stricken manner played directly into Brusilov's hands. In conjunction with promised offensives by Evert and Kuropatkin on his right, Brusilov's two northern armies, Lesh's Third and Kaledin's Eighth, attacked west in early July and in a few days captured 30,000 prisoners and 30 guns. The effort petered out on the line of the Stokhod, which was held by two hastily transported German divisions. On Kaledin's left Sakharov's Eleventh Army advanced to take Brody and threaten the left flank of Bothmer's *Südarmee*. Lechitski's Ninth Army met only weak resistance in overrunning most of the Bukovina to threaten Bothmer's right and cause him to retreat to a line only thirty miles east of Lemberg.

Evert's offensive in the Baranovichi area did not fare nearly as well. It opened in early July, a grand affair of over twenty divisions and a thousand guns attacking a salient held by only two Austrian divisions, one of which collapsed on the second day. The arrival of two German divisions caused the Russian commander to stop his attack. The Russians had lost 80,000 men, the Germans 16,000. Evert and Kuropatkin now decided that it would be more prudent to transfer troops to Brusilov than to continue attacking in the north. Brusilov certainly needed help. By early July he had lost 50,000 officers and almost half a million men, of whom 60,000 were dead.

Once reinforced, Brusilov decided on another major offensive northeast from the Stokhod toward Kovel. Instead of using his earlier successful tactics, Brusilov chose the old battering-ram concept, a gigantic effort that involved three armies, all told some 250,000 troops against 115,000.

The offensive began in late July. Kaledin's Eighth Army attacked westward, Lesh's Third Army struck out to the northwest, and Bezobrazov's two corps of Guards crossed the Stokhod River to move on Kovel. The Guards had the worst of it because of marshy terrain on either side of the river. Although the German line was penetrated and 5,000 prisoners taken, the attack cost the Russians 30,000 casualties in but a few days, effectively ending the action in that sector. Kaledin's Eighth Army had easier going against the Austro-Hungarian Fourth Army and early captured 12,000 prisoners. Resistance grew stiffer in August, however, with Kaledin's advance noticeably slowing. Further south, in Galicia, Shcherbachev's Seventh and Sakharov's Eleventh armies forced the *Südarmee* to retreat before reserves, including two Turkish divisions, arrived to stabilize the line. Lechitski's Ninth Army on Brusilov's left made the best progress, early reaching the Carpathian passes and seizing the whole of the Bukovina to threaten Hungary and Romania. The OHL hurried in four divisions and the new Austro-Hungarian Third Army to meet the crisis. But Brusilov had gone as far as he could go. Unsupported in the north, his men exhausted, ammunition in short supply, he was forced to slow and finally halt his troops. Total losses are almost beyond the realm of belief, perhaps 350,000 Germans, one million Russians, one million Austrians.

Brusilov's achievement was still immense. His armies had captured over 400,000 prisoners and nearly 500 guns, and had killed or wounded well over a million enemy. He had forced Conrad to abandon his offensive in Italy and he had shown the world that the Austro-Hungarian army was a paper tiger. No longer would Austro-Hungarian troops fight in the east except under German command. He had graphically exploded the validity of the narrow-front offensive in flat, exposed terrain. He had caused Falkenhayn, close to panic, to transfer divisions from the west without any clear idea of which sector they should support. Perhaps more important, he had proven wrong Falkenhayn's optimistic estimate of Russian weakness, further damaging the German chief of staff's rapidly deteriorating reputation with the army, government, and Reichstag.

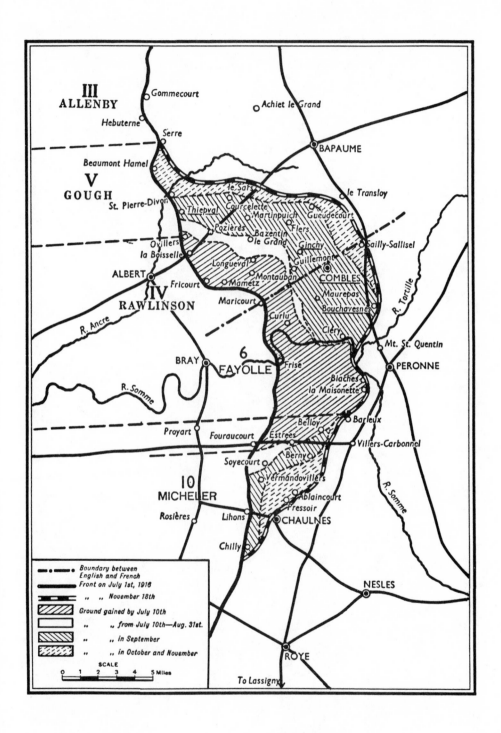

III
ALLENBY

Gommecourt

Achiet le Grand

Hebuterne

Serre

BAPAUME

Beaumont Hamel

V
GOUGH

le Sars

le Transloy

St. Pierre-Divon

Thiepval   Courcelette

Martinpuich   Gueudecourt

Pozières   Flers

Bazentin
le Grand

Sailly-Sallisel

Ovillers
la Boisselle

Ginchy

Longueval   Guillemont

ALBERT

Montauban

COMBLES

R. Tortille

Fricourt   Mametz

IV
RAWLINSON

Maricourt

Maurepas

Bouchavesnes

Curlu

Cléry

R. Ancre

Mt. St. Quentin

BRAY   6
FAYOLLE   Frise

PERONNE

R. Somme

Biaches
la Maisonette

Belloy   Barleux

Proyart   Fouraucourt   Estrées   Villers-Carbonnel

Soyecourt   Berny

10
MICHELER

Vermandovillers

Ablaincourt
Pressoir

Rosières   Lihons   CHAULNES

Chilly

R. Somme

NESLES

Boundary between
English and French
Front on July 1st, 1916
„   „   November 18th
Ground gained by July 10th
„   „   from July 10th—Aug. 31st.
„   „   in September
„   „   in October and November

SCALE
0 1 2 3 4   5 Miles

ROYE

To Lassigny

20

Falkenhayn Loses Command

God help you and our fatherland.
—GENERAL VON FALKENHAYN'S DEPARTING WORDS TO FIELD
MARSHAL VON HINDENBURG, WHO REPLACED HIM AS
CHIEF OF THE GENERAL STAFF ON AUGUST 28, 1919[1]

Neither Czar Nicholas nor the Russian supreme command had contributed significantly to Brusilov's valiant effort to capture the strategic initiative in the east. His major allies in the long and bitter fighting of that spring and summer were the French and British armies on the western front.

Despite the sickening battle that was raging at Verdun, neither Joffre, the French commander in chief, nor Douglas Haig, commanding the British forces in France, had given up the idea of a massive summer offensive. Haig had argued for his effort to take place in Flanders, but Joffre persuaded him to attack in the Somme sector, quiet since the battle of the Marne.

General Foch's army group would attack on Haig's right. Foch commanded three armies, a total of forty-two divisions and about 1,700 heavy guns. The attack would extend along a front of twenty-five miles, which Haig would carry another fifteen miles to the north. The purpose was threefold: to complement Italian and Russian offensives; to relieve pressure on Verdun; to break through enemy lines.

Joffre had miscalculated the cost of the Verdun counteroffensive, for which he would soon be raked over the coals by an angry parliament.[2] In May he perforce shortened Foch's attack front and reduced his strength to 26 divisions and 700 guns, a comedown that showed the price being paid at Verdun. Only one French army, General Fayolle's Sixth, was now to participate in the summer offensive. This meant that the British were to make the main attack, an uncomfortable fact handed to Haig in late May.

Haig wanted to delay the offensive until mid-August, when he would have received more heavy artillery, but Joffre, apparently without too much difficulty, persuaded him to stick to the original plan. By late June Haig's command consisted of fifty-four divisions, twenty-six of which were slated for the offensive that was to open on June 24.

The OHL was expecting an allied offensive, but Falkenhayn believed that it would strike Crown Prince Rupprecht's Sixth Army in the north and thus he failed to strengthen the actual target sector. Crown Prince Wilhelm later stated that he and General Otto von Below, commanding the Second Army, had warned the OHL that, judging by enemy troop movements, the Second Army would be attacked but that the warnings were ignored.

The German Second Army faced the British and French armies in the Somme sector. Five divisions held the area north of the Somme, three divisions the area south of the Somme, with another three divisions in reserve. These troops had been equipped with gas masks and with the new steel helmets that replaced the old leather *Pickelhaube*. This had been a quiet sector, which had allowed for the construction of very strong defensive positions behind rows of barbed wire, with artillery, mortars, and machine guns registered on priority targets. All units were now on the alert, since considerable enemy activity suggested an impending attack.

Below was short of heavy artillery and airplanes because of the demands of Verdun. Falkenhayn, strongly influenced by his chief of operations, Gerhard Tappen, and by Crown Prince Wilhelm's chief of staff, von Knobelsdorff, still refused to admit the bankruptcy of the Verdun operation. This is understandable, if not laudable. By late June 1916 Falkenhayn had many critics and few supporters. If he could break through at Verdun he might just salvage a rapidly waning reputation.

It was the last try. On June 21 German guns opened fire on the left (western) bank of the Meuse. For two days high-explosive shells mutilated already dead ground. Then the troops ripped open cases marked with green crosses. These contained shells filled with a new type of deadly phosgene gas that now saturated the target area. Then 70,000 German soldiers moved out in brilliant sunlight and almost overpowering heat. As was the case with so many past offensives, they pushed forward, slowed, then stopped. On June 24 Allied guns roared a new challenge on the Somme to end Falkenhayn's final fling. What was left of the German Fifth Army would remain on the defensive at Verdun.

In that last week in June Allied guns on the Somme fired over 1,500,000 shells. For seven days and seven nights "the drumfire never ceased," wrote Stephen Westman. "No food or water reached us . . . men became hysterical and their comrades had to knock them out, so as to prevent them from running away and exposing themselves to the deadly shell splinters. Even the rats panicked and sought refuge in our flimsy shelters; they ran up the walls and we had to kill them with our spades."[3] Falkenhayn later wrote that "all obstacles were completely swept away, and the trenches themselves were for the most part flattened out."[4] Allied planes filled the sky, bombing and strafing. German airmen in inferior numbers fought desperately against the tide—the ace Max Immelmann was shot down and killed.

Officer whistles sounded on July 1 and British Tommies and French *poilus* moved from forward trenches in early dawn. Hopes ran high in Haig's headquarters. British cavalry, like the Russian horse at Lake Naroch, stood ready to exploit the breakthrough that Haig was convinced would cut the German army in half. At eight A.M. Haig wrote in his diary that early reports were "most satisfactory. Our troops had everywhere crossed the enemy's front trenches."[5] That was about it. By night all twelve British divisions were shattered. The day's effort had cost 60,000 casualties, of whom 20,000 were dead—"the greatest loss in the history of the British army."[6]

The seven assault divisions of Fayolle's Sixth Army on the right made better progress and in some places penetrated the German second line. Fayolle reached his first objective, the plateau of Flaucourt, on July 10, but this did not greatly influence the fighting on his left, where the British made minuscule gains at a terrible cost in lives. The battle raged throughout July and August, one of the fiercest and most futile in all history. In early August a German officer wrote in his diary the morbid result of enemy artillery fire: "The infantry [of his unit] lost probably half of its men, if not more. Those who survived are at this moment not men, but more or less finished beings, fit neither to defend nor attack. Officers whom I once knew as very vigorous are only sobbing."[7]

Later in August a veteran of the eastern front without many months to live, Friedrich Steinbrecher, wrote that "what I have been through during this time surpassed in horror all my previous experiences during the second year of the war . . . how the English, with the aid of their airmen, who are often 1,500 feet above the position, and their captive (i.e., observation) balloons, have exactly located every one of our batteries and have so smashed them up with long-distance guns of every caliber that the artillery here has had unusually heavy losses both of men and material. Our dugouts, in which we shelter day and night, are not even adequate, for though they are cut out of the chalk they are not so strong but that a 'heavy' was able a few days ago to blow one in and bury the whole lot of men inside."[8]

Still the German lines held. Falkenhayn was fighting for his life and he knew it. He replaced Below's chief of staff, who was "too weak," with Friedrich (Fritz) von Lossberg, a relatively junior colonel who had already made his mark as a "defense specialist" in the Champagne battles, a reputation soon enhanced in this gargantuan clash of forces.

The battles continued for another two months to end with a British gain of some seven miles on a nine-mile front. The offensives had cost nearly 500,000 British and 195,000 French casualties against an estimated German loss of some 465,000.[9] One of the casualties was Erich von Falkenhayn—toppled from his command throne in the midst of crisis.

Hindenburg and Ludendorff in headquarters at Kovno had become increasingly agitated over Falkenhayn's handling of the war. "The year 1916 is being dawdled away in blood," Ludendorff angrily complained to one visitor.[10] Prompted by Ludendorff and Max Hoffmann, Hindenburg broke all precedent by writing to the kaiser that "Falkenhayn did not hold the confidence of the army—and at the same time designated himself as the successor desired by the army," an extraordinary communication greeted by the kaiser with, "These are the airs of a Wallenstein."*[11]

The number of Falkenhayn's enemies had reached formidable proportions by mid-1916. Spearheaded by Ludendorff and Bethmann Hollweg, they included several members of the kaiser's civil and military cabinets, the foreign minister and other senior diplomats, a good many junior and senior staff officers at the OHL, army group and army com-

---

* Albrecht Eusebius Wenzel von Wallenstein (1583–1634) was a wealthy and ruthless conquering general who eventually forced Emperor Ferdinand II of The Holy Roman Empire to grant him dictatorial powers that included absolute control of the army, complete subservience of the emperor, who was to issue no orders without his consent, control of all confiscated territories, and so forth. Defeated by Gustav II Adolphus in 1632, Wallenstein lost control of his army, turned traitor, and was assassinated. This was the hero of Schiller's drama which so captivated Hindenburg. See J. F. C. Fuller, A Military History of the Western World, II, 46–8, 66–8.

manders, Crown Prince Wilhelm and Bavarian Crown Prince Rupprecht, Austro-Hungarian chief of staff Conrad von Hötzendorf and most senior officers on his staff, almost all conservative industrialists and business leaders including Rathenau, Albert Ballin, Duisberg, and Gustav Krupp, such important demagogues as Alfred von Tirpitz and Matthias Erzberger, who had mobilized the support of the German princes and even the Habsburg emperor on behalf of Hindenburg.

The Bulgarians favored a single eastern command under Hindenburg, as did prominent Hungarian politicians who were disgusted with Conrad. Conrad had not helped matters by divorcing his wife and marrying a young divorcée, whom he installed at the Teschen headquarters and stupidly allowed to maintain a social salon that soon became the target of vicious Vienna gossip.[12]

Falkenhayn was still supported at times by the minister of war, General Wild von Hohenborn; by the chief of the kaiser's military cabinet, General von Lyncker; and by the chief of the naval cabinet, Admiral von Müller, each of whom, like the ancient willow, bent to the imperial wind. Only one member of the kaiser's military staff, Colonel Baron von Marschall, remained consistently loyal to Falkenhayn, as did his chief of operations, Colonel Tappen. His position was also buttressed by such indirect forces as the kaiser's increasing fear of the Duo's dominance and by Conrad's dislike of Ludendorff, which was even stronger than his dislike of Falkenhayn.

In late June, at the height of military crises east and west, the kaiser called a conference to settle the command issue in the east. Bethmann Hollweg had been campaigning for some time for Hindenburg to be given command of the entire eastern front as prelude to replacing Falkenhayn as chief of the general staff. In a private conversation with Ludendorff at Pless, Bethmann severely criticized Falkenhayn's conduct of the war, particularly the Verdun operation, which continued to devour large chunks of the German army. Backed by Bethmann and other influential voices that claimed to speak for the German public, Ludendorff made an impassioned plea to the kaiser to appoint Hindenburg commander in chief in the east.

Falkenhayn and Conrad argued against the appointment on the principal ground that the name Hindenburg could not conceivably reinvigorate disaffected Czech and Ruthenian divisions. If anyone could, it was Conrad. Falkenhayn insisted that a war could not be fought by two "supreme commands," and the kaiser agreed. To Ludendorff and Hoffmann's fury, Hindenburg did not seem much interested in the matter.

Possibly he realized that the kaiser could not override Conrad's opposition; possibly as a *kaisertreu* general of the old school, he resented his subordinates' challenge of the sacrosanct *Kommandogewalt*. Though Ludendorff complained that the conference was "fruitless," he was apparently buoyed by Bethmann's criticism of Falkenhayn.

The Duo returned to Kovno to spend an active month countering attacks from Evert and Kuropatkin's armies, which were supposed to complement Brusilov's new offensive in the south. According to Falkenhayn and Hoffmann (who unknowingly agreed with the former, the man he loathed above all), these were merely "demonstrations." Ludendorff contrarily claimed that the situation was highly critical and had been caused by his generous release of divisions to meet the earlier crisis in the south.[13]

Brusilov's renewed offensive, taken with the Allied attack on the Somme, brought further quarrels between the OHL and OberOst, the latter refusing to release any more divisions for transfer to the south. Falkenhayn and Ludendorff met in Berlin on July 20, a fruitless effort that settled nothing, since Ludendorff continued to press for an overall command in the east, while Falkenhayn spoke only of future operations in the west. Ludendorff returned to Kovno "in a pretty savage temper," Hoffmann recorded.[14]

The worsening situation caused the kaiser to call another imperial council at Pless in late July, the same day that Austro-Hungarian defenses of the town of Brody were shattered by Sakharov's Russian Eleventh Army, forcing the *Südarmee* to retreat. Falkenhayn, who appeared to be on the defensive, attempted to defer the command issue, but the kaiser, visibly nervous and impatient, demanded a solution. Bethmann and his clique refused to compromise. Hindenburg was the man of the hour, Bethmann told the kaiser, the only person who could save the Hohenzollern dynasty: "With Hindenburg he [the kaiser] could make [even] an unsatisfactory peace, without him he could not."[15] The kaiser, visibly distraught, finally decided that Hindenburg's command should be extended as far south as Brody, a five-hundred-mile front that stretched from Riga on the Baltic to east of Lemberg. "Falkenhayn's position very shaken," Hoffmann noted approvingly, "ours very strengthened."[16] Indeed it was. On the journey back to Berlin, Brutus in the form of the war minister told Rudolf von Valentini, chief of the kaiser's civil cabinet, that Falkenhayn, whom he was still ostensibly supporting, must be replaced by Hindenburg—"but please don't tell anyone I said so."[17]

Hindenburg's enlarged command sphere meant setting up a new

headquarters, since Kovno was too far to the north. The operations staff lived aboard OberOst's special train while visiting the new command kingdom. The situation everywhere struck Ludendorff as critical, with little time available to train Austro-Hungarian divisions—now under OberOst's command—to his exacting standards. Once again Ludendorff was hurling demands at Falkenhayn for more and still more troops, and when his requests were refused, Hindenburg appealed directly to the kaiser.

The command train halted finally at Brest Litovsk. It was a strange choice for a new headquarters, made probably because it was an important rail junction. The town had been burned to the ground, with only a derelict citadel remaining. The Duo and their staff lived and worked on the train and were daily roasted by a hot August sun beating down on the metal roofs of the carriages. Ludendorff in desperation finally converted the abandoned citadel into a new headquarters, "in truth not very tempting," noted one staff officer, who was upset by the sparsely furnished living cubicles of rock-hewn, damp walls and numerous rats. [18]

OberOst was soon flexing its new command muscles in its vendetta against Falkenhayn. The quarrel escalated when Falkenhayn, having refused to transfer several divisions to the east, directed OberOst to transfer a division to Archduke Charles's Austrian army. Ludendorff and Hoffmann persuaded Hindenburg to telegraph a strong, almost insulting complaint to the kaiser. This was not well received by Wilhelm, who now directed OberOst to pay attention to its own command, not to the western front, and to follow Falkenhayn's recent decision.

Ludendorff and Hoffmann had been pressing Hindenburg to submit his resignation in order to force Falkenhayn's dismissal, but the old man had held off. When his two subordinates threatened to resign, Hindenburg requested an audience with the kaiser so that he and Ludendorff could present their manifold grievances against the OHL. This was refused, which caused Ludendorff and Hoffmann to compose a lengthy letter of grievances that was sent to the chancellor under Hindenburg's signature.

The chancellor had long since fallen victim to Ludendorff's propaganda, which had been complemented by a memorandum from Falkenhayn's staff artillery specialist, Max Bauer, recently promoted to lieutenant colonel. Bauer had been plugging the Ludendorff line for a long time. He was bright, ambitious, and ruthless. He had early insinuated himself with the heavy industrialists and with the chancellor. His virulent memorandum, in part inaccurate and unfair, condemned what

250 ROBERT B. ASPREY

he termed Falkenhayn's "hand-to-mouth" strategy. Germany would be able to hold out only until the end of the year, Bauer warned. "Perhaps a strong-minded man can save us, a man who can inflame the people, by the trust they have in him, and who knows how to make an audacious decision to carry it out."[19]

Bethmann incorporated Ludendorff and Bauer's sentiments in a lengthy paper to the kaiser in which he insisted that "every single man who can be spared [in the west] should be committed at the scene where the final issue of the world struggle now impends," that is, the eastern front.[20] Bethmann's letter reached Pless about the time that Hindenburg's latest epistle arrived. Falkenhayn learned of these communications and instantly struck back, demanding among other things that Hindenburg be denied direct access to the kaiser in military affairs. Wilhelm timidly rejected this demand but did support Falkenhayn in an otherwise friendly reply to Hindenburg.

The field marshal responded with another complaining letter to the supreme warlord, followed by a telegram to the chief of the imperial military cabinet that he would resign unless he and Ludendorff were granted a private audience with the kaiser. Ludendorff followed this with *his* threat to resign. When the kaiser again refused the audience, Hindenburg submitted a third lengthy letter, which concentrated more on petty complaints than on substantive strategical issues.

Bethmann arrived in Pless on August 21 "intent on convincing the kaiser that Falkenhayn no longer enjoyed the confidence of the army."[21] Falkenhayn meanwhile had written to the kaiser concerning Bethmann's indictment. To the latter's assertion that the Verdun operation had failed despite heavy losses, Falkenhayn countered that it was serving its purpose. He had never expected it to win the war. His was a limited goal, "on the one hand to paralyze France for the further course of the war by bleeding it white if it chose to commit its army at Verdun, and by causing internal repercussions if it relinquished that fortified position; and on the other hand to provoke Britain into committing its full resources prematurely. Both of these goals have been attained, although not presently to the degree that had been anticipated—that almost never happens in war—but still to an appreciable degree." Falkenhayn claimed that the French had suffered 250,000 casualties more than the Germans (an exaggeration), then reverted to the "numbers game" by asking what would have happened had that number joined the British offensive on the Somme.[22] He conveniently failed to point out that he would have been proportionately stronger to meet this attack. But this was a minor aberration in an otherwise well-written and forceful document that made it abundantly clear that Falkenhayn would not take the war away from the western front as desired by "amateurs, many of them in field gray and some in the highest ranks of the army."[23]

Bethmann remained in Pless for three days but was unable to erode the kaiser's support of Falkenhayn. Wilhelm did soften his refusal of Hindenburg's request for a private audience by appealing to his sense of duty to carry on, words that put the field marshal in "terrible agitation" and "deepest remorse." Hoffmann sourly noted that the imperial words showed "no grasp of our difficulties . . . We might again have saved ourselves the bother."[24]

Falkenhayn might have emerged the winner in this internecine battle had he not dogmatically formed certain unfortunate conclusions regarding the continued neutrality of Romania. It was no secret that the Bucharest government would sell its alliance to the highest bidder. German and enemy diplomats had been trying to outbid each other for years, and Falkenhayn had long urged the foreign ministry to win the auction. The Romanian army, some 600,000 strong, was not highly valued by military experts, but its psychological value was considerable. More important, Germany continued to need Romanian grain and oil, which she had been importing in large quantities since the war began.

Romania's attitude understandably hinged on the fortunes of war. When the Central Powers were militarily successful, she swayed their way. Falkenhayn was well aware of the delicate political situation and had done his best to hold Romania in check. He had responded to Lechitski's successful offensive in July and August that brought Russian armies uncomfortably close to Romania by transferring weighty forces to the threatened front. At his urging Romania had been notified that if she went to war against Austria-Hungary the latter would receive full military support from Germany. The Turkish and Bulgarian governments concurred with Falkenhayn and made similar representations in Bucharest. The OHL also wrote a contingency plan for the invasion of Romania, if necessary, and participation was promised by Austro-Hungarian, Turkish, and Bulgarian military leaders.

Falkenhayn still did not believe that Romania would declare war, at least not until after the September harvest, nor did the majority of general-staff officers.[25] Kaiser Wilhelm also accepted this view. They had underestimated Allied diplomacy. British and French guarantees of generous postwar land gains, to be taken from Austria-Hungary, combined with the psychological effect of Brusilov's terrifying offensive, finally tipped the scales. Romania signed a military convention with the Allied powers in mid-August and ten days later declared war on Austria-Hungary. (Italy two days earlier had declared war on Germany.)

Bethmann and Falkenhayn were taken completely by surprise. Colonel Bauer had met the kaiser while walking in the park at Pless earlier that day. "He was calm and cheerful and told us that Romania would certainly not declare war."[26] He learned the news that evening while playing cards and immediately plunged into deep melancholy, declaring that the war was lost and that nothing remained except to seek peace.

Falkenhayn's enemies pounced on this development to discredit him further (without mentioning the diplomatic failure of the foreign ministry). Protests civil and military poured into the kaiser's headquarters in Pless. The campaign was well orchestrated to play on the kaiser's worst fears. Assured that Falkenhayn had lost the army's confidence, Wilhelm summoned Hindenburg and Ludendorff to discuss the situation. Falkenhayn refused to attend the meeting, since OberOst held no command responsibility for the Romanian front. The kaiser had called in the Duo without consulting his chief of staff. It followed that Falkenhayn no longer possessed his supreme warlord's confidence and wished to resign.

Wilhelm did not want to lose Falkenhayn. Jealous of Hindenburg's popularity, frightened by Ludendorff's ambition, he spent a sleepless night before bowing to the anti-Falkenhayn cabal. Perhaps he sensed that his meager substance would now be "degraded to the position of a shadow," as Emil Ludwig put it.[27] In tears he accepted Falkenhayn's resignation and as an ironic sop appointed him to command an army on what would soon become the Romanian front.

Hindenburg later wrote that the kaiser awaited his and Ludendorff's arrival in front of the castle at Pless. Bethmann Hollweg had arrived from Berlin. The kaiser informed Hindenburg that he had been appointed chief of the Great General Staff. Ludendorff received the title of second chief, which he haughtily rejected in favor of one of his own composition, first quartermaster general. At his insistence he would share command responsibility with the field marshal "in all decisions and measures that might be taken."[28] Hindenburg was authorized to issue orders in the kaiser's name and to deal directly with the military chiefs of Austria-Hungary, Bulgaria, and Turkey.

The Duo had finally arrived.

BOOK TWO

———◆———

I know whence I arrive
Unsatisfied like the flame.
I glow and writhe.
Everything I embrace becomes light,
Everything that I leave becomes coal.
Flame am I, surely.
—FRIEDRICH WILHELM NIETZSCHE[1]

21

The Duo Takes Charge

I will not hesitate to admit that it was only now that I fully
realized all that the western armies had done hitherto.
—FIELD MARSHAL PAUL VON HINDENBURG,
SEPTEMBER 1916[1]

I began to realize what a task the field marshal and I had
undertaken in our new spheres . . .
—GENERAL ERICH LUDENDORFF, SEPTEMBER 1916[2]

The Duo faced a serious but not yet critical military situation. On
the western front two great battles were being fought, one on
the Somme, the other at Verdun, fighting that consumed men
and munitions almost as rapidly as they reached the German front-line
divisions. By late August 1916, British and French casualties on the
Somme were approaching their final figure of above 400,000 British and
195,000 French troops, against estimated German losses of 650,000.
French losses at Verdun had reached the insane figure of 315,000, German losses 281,000. Eighty percent of the French army had been committed at one time or another in the "hell of Verdun," compared to
about a third of the OHL's available strength. In either sector a few miles
of territory had been won or lost.

General Conrad von Hötzendorf's abortive Austro-Hungarian offensive in Italy was finished. Exhausted, half-starving Austro-Hungarian
soldiers were again defending scraggly lines on the Isonzo. The subsequent
collapse of his Galician front had been repaired only by an infusion of
German troops. Russian armies in the northwestern Carpathians had

been temporarily halted, but Lechitski's Ninth Russian Army continued to attack in the southeastern Carpathians to threaten the Hungarian frontier. The battered Austro-Hungarian divisions on this front needed rest and refitting. Conrad would participate in the offensive against Romania, but little could be expected from his demoralized divisions.

Severe food shortages in Austria had brought the home front to a dangerous apathy manifested by growing indifference to the war and an increasingly vocal desire for peace. Hungary was somewhat better off for food, but her leaders were dissatisfied with Conrad's conduct of the war. Although the government sent limited quantities of food to the army, it refused to supply the Austrian civil population, which increased general hard feelings in Vienna. Bulgaria was also fairly well off for food, but deliveries fell victim to an archaic distribution system that often caused crops to spoil before they reached Bulgarian and foreign markets. The Bulgarian offensive against Sarrail's Allied army in Macedonia had been broken off, its main purpose having been to keep Romania neutral, but Bulgaria would also participate in the offensive against Romania.

Turkey, although delivered from the threat to Gallipoli by a gallant defense immensely aided by Allied confusion and weak senior commanders, was not in a strong position. Her attempt to raise a *jehad*, or holy war, had failed signally, as had the highly touted expedition to seize the Suez Canal. General Judenich's Russians were well ensconced in the Caucasus, having virtually destroyed a Turkish army that was to have evicted them. Enver Pasha was slightly better off in Mesopotamia, where the British surrender of Kut had given him a much-needed psychological victory. But while British forces were building, Turkish forces remained meager, everywhere on the defensive, ill-armed and ill-clad, initiative sapped by scanty supply and too often by cruel and incompetent commanders. Enver Pasha nevertheless had agreed to join in the invasion of Romania and could be counted on to hold elsewhere, so long as Germany continued to send food, money, and arms to Constantinople.

So it would be difficult for the Duo to undertake a large-scale offensive either in the east or west. In that autumn of 1916, six million German soldiers faced ten million Allied soldiers. Germany's most serious military debit was the increasing shortage of infantry reserves, particularly junior- and company-grade officers and trained noncommissioned officers. Adversity in war can only be overcome by outstanding leadership. Too many of the German army's natural leaders, commissioned and noncommissioned, were rotting on the cratered battlefields of Ypres, the Somme, Verdun, East Prussia, Poland, and Galicia. "For the first time,"

Max Hoffmann wrote, "the feeling of absolute superiority of the German soldiers was lost, and signs of war-weariness and despondency began to be observable in certain quarters."[3] Hospitals were jammed with wounded. One doctor put the number of shell-shocked veterans alone at the strength of two army corps.[4] Desertions were increasing, as was malingering. Even the bravest and most highly motivated volunteers were heartily sick of animal life in the rat- and lice-infested trenches that looked onto wire concertinas draped with moldering, half-eaten corpses, of inadequate rations, frequent illness and death never far distant. "In what way have we sinned," demanded Johannes Haas, a former theological student with but seven months to live, "that we should be treated worse than animals? Hunted from place to place, cold, filthy and in rags, we wander about like gypsies, and in the end are destroyed like vermin. Will they *never* make peace?"[5] Soldiers along the line were asking the same question. Not without reason did Crown Prince Wilhelm of Germany and Crown Prince Rupprecht of Bavaria, whose armies were bearing the brunt of the fighting in the west, favor a peace without victory.

The navy, too, had proved disappointing. Its inactivity had early sapped morale of officers and men who had trained for years to fight the British. Vice Admiral Reinhard Scheer, who replaced Pohl in command of the High Seas Fleet in early 1916, finally ordered his battleships to sea in May in an attempt to suck out and trap the British fleet. The result was the battle of the Skagerrak (called the battle of Jutland by the Allies). German naval commanders, enthusiastically supported by every propaganda device in the empire (including such military writers as Hans Delbrück), tried to blow the indecisive action at Skagerrak into a great victory. It was nothing of the sort. Had the Royal Navy lived up to its prewar claims of excellence and had it been more ably commanded, Scheer's ineptly maneuvered fleet would have been blown out of the water (despite Hipper's meritorious performance). In the event, it was the naval version of the land stalemate—a few tons of ships sent to the bottom, a few more tons and several professional reputations badly damaged, some 10,000 dead and wounded brave sailors. The highly vaunted German dreadnoughts—Kaiser Wilhelm and Admiral Tirpitz's costly toys—steamed back to port like frightened turtles. They and their crews would stay there until they fermented into mutinous explosion. Only the submarine would grow.

And so would the airplane. In 1914, the airplane, whether the "tractor" with the engine in front—a flimsy monoplane that evoked the image of Icarus—or the "pusher" with the engine mounted in rear, was used almost solely for reconnaissance. Small bombs weighing a few pounds were sometimes dropped by hand and on occasion pilot fought pilot by trying to get above his target to drop a hand grenade on him or to nail him with pistol or rifle fire—probably no one in the world was safer than the target. But then machine guns were mounted on "pusher" planes to step up the action as better and faster aircraft were produced. Planes equipped with rudimentary wireless transmission and cameras began to report favorable targets for artillery on missions which had to be protected by fighter aircraft overhead. Single-plane combat began to give way to squadron and even larger-formation combats. In October 1915 the Germans gained air superiority with a "tractor" plane designed by a young Dutch engineer, Anton Fokker. Faster and more maneuverable than anything in the air, thanks to Fokker's genius its machine guns were synchronized to fire without striking propeller blades. German air superiority was successfully challenged in mid-1916 during the battle of the Somme by French and British pilots flying the new and superior Nieuport and Spad planes, which almost knocked the Germans out of the sky. They soon struck back with skillful pilots flying the new Halberstadt and Albatross planes, and in early 1918 the versatile Fokker biplane. German "circus" tactics made famous by such aces as Boelcke and von Richtofen regained air supremacy in early 1917 only to yield it soon after the final German offensive opened in March 1918.

As Count Zeppelin informed Hindenburg, the days of the airship were numbered. These gigantic sausages had bombarded English and French cities until they began falling victim to improved fighter aircraft. In 1917 they would be replaced by heavy bombers, the Gothas, which carried up to 1,700 pounds of bombs. The main problem facing the Duo was to increase aircraft production to match the impressive output of French and British factories—a task, as it turned out, impossible to achieve.

Meanwhile the British blockade continued to cause serious shortages in the German homeland. Imports were drastically slowing, while factory and transport appetites were growing. Food imports, mostly essential grains from Denmark, Holland and Romania, were drastically falling short of demand. The 1915 harvest was two and a half million tons short of expectations—the worst harvest in nearly half a century. Fodder was sadly lacking. The country could no longer supply the thousands of horses needed each month by artillery and supply depots, and those supplied were weakened by short, mostly ersatz rations.

Prospects were little better for the 1916 harvest. Bread of increasingly poor quality had been rationed since January 1915, potatoes, butter, eggs, milk, flour, sugar, soap, dry groceries, and meat since early 1916. The American military attaché reported from Berlin that "the problem of an adequate feeding of the civil population is the question of the hour." Meat had disappeared from shops, most butchers had closed their doors. "The fact is that Germany has reached the practical limit of her meat supplies and from now on must subsist her civilian population mainly on a vegetarian diet." In Berlin scores of women, many with children, were bedding down at midnight in front of markets and warehouses to wait for morning openings.[6]

Civilians carried no less than twelve different ration cards. The butter ration was three ounces a week, when available, and was described as "a white, greasy, evil-smelling mass that is certainly not more than half real butter."[7] There was almost no coffee, no cream, few eggs. Public kitchens in the larger cities, manned in part by volunteers, served workers and their children or anyway those who could afford to pay fifteen or twenty cents for a meal of soup, stew and some type of dessert (for all of which individual ration cards were required). Ordinary restaurants served a maximum two- or three-course unappetizing meal—a *Brotkarte* (bread ration card) was required for one piece of "black and sour-tasting bread, done up in sealed paper packages."[8]

The wealthy diner fared better in elegant hotel restaurants that were supplied from the black market. In late 1915 people were "feasting in splendor" in Berlin's Hotel Esplanade, seemingly with no difficulty about ration cards.[9] On "meatless days" the famous Hotel Adlon "served chicken, ducks and other fowl which was not considered meat."[10] In spring of 1916 an American traveler, Ernesta Bullitt, was given "a most royal dinner" in the mansion of the well-known banker, Max Warburg —"roast beef . . . and many courses. We even had nectarines from their hot-house in the country, and the most glorious big strawberries with plenty of sugar."[11]

Black markets flourished throughout Germany, not only among civilians but on army lines of communication, where officers had first crack at food, wines, and liquors siphoned from occupied territories—a misuse of authority so heavily criticized by soldiers and civilians that the OHL would soon issue a secret order calling for increased depot supervision.[12] "Under the stress of the changed food conditions," one observer noted, "the happy German soon replaced the honest German."[13]

Cloth and leather had become almost nonexistent, clothes and shoes had long since been rationed. There was no oil for lamps or heating. Bethmann Hollweg noted that as early as March 1915 the working classes were asking, "Why don't we make peace?"[14] The following November a member of the Reichstag, Hans Hanssen, noted in his diary: "In the train there was talk only about the war. The dread of another winter of war is noted in all classes of society . . . 'We win and win, but we win ourselves to death,' people say." Early in 1916 he wrote: "Spirits are very low in the Reichstag. People are facing the new year with thoughts of tears, blood and misery."[15]

On leave in Berlin in January 1916, Stephen Westman found the snow-covered streets "dimly lit or in darkness, although there was no blackout. There was no coal to heat homes or apartments. Large heated halls had been opened to warm the elderly. There was no sugar, only ersatz bread. No longer were parents congratulated upon losing a son on the battlefield. In the streets the women wore shabby and mended dresses or coats, mostly black because they were mourning for their dead." Westman and his friends found little in common with the civilians. They soon grew bored and were glad to leave the dying city.[16]

Increasing shortages combined with long casualty lists, rigid censorship, and leftist opposition to sweeping annexationist demands by center and right had ended the *Burgfriede* and the feeling of national unity that had survived the first year of war. "In 1916, one grew conscious of an undercurrent of criticism," Prince Max of Baden later wrote.[17]

Military censorship initially had sealed the fighting fronts from the homeland. The seal had begun to warp when soldiers were furloughed home. Their stories did not jibe with the patriotic pap and exaggerated claims of the OHL and OberOst communiqués. It was evident that things were not going as well as the top commands insisted. Civilians did not like what they heard from soldiers, and soldiers did not like what they heard from civilians. By mid-1915 the initial trust of both in army and government began to waver. It had continued to do so. The Social Democrats, who had meekly succumbed to the war despite all their previous antiwar rhetoric, had finally asserted themselves in the Reichstag. In March 1916 the more radical members had splintered to form the minority socialists under Hugo Haase. This group not only renounced the *Burgfriede* but refused to vote for new war credits, instead calling for peace on the basis of the status quo ante. Strikes and demonstrations in favor of peace had broken out in several cities. Some union agitators had been jailed, others remained covertly active. The communist par-

liamentarian Karl Liebknecht had been jailed for demanding peace—
fifty thousand workers had gone on strike during his trial. Repressive
measures by commanding generals of interior army corps districts had
become increasingly unpopular. The Reichstag's effort to curb their ex-
cesses by subordinating corps commands to the ministry of war was only
partially successful.

All was not gloom. Foodstuffs continued to arrive from Denmark,
Holland, Sweden and the conquered eastern territories. New methods
of food preservation, including dehydrated potatoes, were developed.
Horse fodder was prepared from straw, wood and leaf hay. Factories
produced nitrogen for the manufacture of nitric acid and saltpeter, essential ingredients of gunpowder; artificial manure from phosphates
mined in occupied France and Belgium; synthetic rubber and glycerine;
sulfur from plaster of paris. Copper and coal came from mines in Serbia,
the former often replaced by steel and zinc. Sweden and other neutral
countries supplied iron ore, as did the occupied areas of France. Gun-
cotton was manufactured from cellulose. The eastern lands supplied wool,
flax, hemp, wood, wire, some grain and cattle, horses, and hides for
leather. Iron was procured by melting down village church bells and from
razed factories in occupied countries, the timber and rubble going to the
front to be used for trench defenses.

Factories throughout the empire were daily turning out tons of weapons and ammunition. A variety of new and improved armament was
coming off assembly lines. New and more powerful aircraft were appearing
in the skies. Shipyards were building more long-range submarines. Truck
production was increasing, although the finished product had to run on
iron wheels because of the rubber shortage. "Everyone complains about
the scarcity of food supplies," Hans Hanssen wrote in his diary in March
1916, "but all are firmly determined to hold out."[18] Despite the blockade,
it appeared that the Central Powers would be able to carry on the war
long enough to gain a satisfactory peace.

The major difficulty lay in the definition of "satisfactory peace," a
term that meant many things to many people. To the German chancellor,
as he told a colleague in the spring of 1915, it meant a resumption of
the status quo ante, though he hoped to gain some border rectifications
necessary to appease the military, "full indemnity" of German expenditures, and some new colonies in the French and Belgian Congo—in

other words, a profitable, an annexationist peace.[19] In September 1916 Max Hoffmann hoped that a successful defense in the west taken with victory over the Russians would make it possible "to talk about peace. And I can give you my word that if the slightest possibility offers itself of concluding a fairly reasonable peace I shall grasp it with both hands."[20] Crown Prince Rupprecht of Bavaria had long since favored the renunciation of all conquests in order to gain a "peace of understanding."

In contrast to these more moderate attitudes stood the strident demands for a peace that would grant Germany and her allies enormous financial reparations and vast territorial gains both on the European continent and abroad. These had been bruited before the war by the Pan-Germans and the Army Leaguers and Navy Leaguers. Initial victories had caused these expansionists to establish the *Kriegszielbewegung*, or War Aim Movement, that called for territorial gains far beyond "the dreams of avarice," a goal fervently shared by a Reichstag majority, the *Kriegszielmehrheit*, composed of Conservatives, National Liberals, Catholic Centrists and not a few "imperial" socialists. By spring of 1915 the movement had been joined by a number of industrial, agrarian, and middle-class organizations to reinforce its persistent demands to the government for guarantees of hefty territorial aggrandizement. In June 1915 the "petition of the intellectuals," prepared by such prominent nationalist historians as Otto Hintze, Friedrich Meinecke and Hermann Oncken, called for annexations as demanded by the Pan-Germans. This was signed by 1,300 prominent professors, artists, writers, journalists, clergymen, teachers, judges, lawyers, industrialists, senior civil servants, and politicians, and was only feebly challenged by a counterpetition. "I can do nothing about it," Bethmann complained to Valentini. "The mentality of our people has been so poisoned by boasting for the last twenty-five years that they would probably become frightened if this were denied to them. Only accurate daily reports of the OHL could help."[21]

The euphoric greed grew like Topsy. In autumn of 1916 it was not just the few but the many who firmly believed that Germany would win, indeed was *entitled* to win large territories in east and west, the Baltic countries, thousands of square miles of Poland, concessions in Romania and Serbia, large pieces of the Ukraine, the Longwy-Briey coalfields of France, a series of French coastal ports, the vassalage of Belgium, new colonies in Africa and Asia.

The extent of acquisitions was not really very important. The significant fact is that in autumn of 1916 all but a few members of govern-

ment, several military commanders, some radical members of the Reichstag and a few, very few thoughtful German subjects expected the war to
end with Germany richer by far in territory, gold, and prestige.

It was up to Hindenburg and Ludendorff to see that their dreams
were realized—no matter the cost.

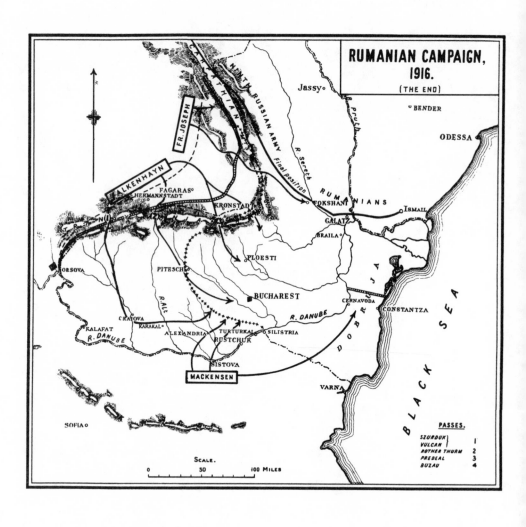

RUMANIAN CAMPAIGN,
1916.
(THE END)

22

The Western Front: The Tactical Problem

One can work extremely well with Ludendorff. The new command is entirely different from the previous one with the Tappen shortsightedness. . . . Hindenburg is extraordinarily versed in military history and has an unusually clear mind. He is also gifted with a very well aimed and appropriate wit and sense of humor. Falkenhayn and Tappen always made him out to be a sort of fool, purely a front man for Ludendorff. That is not the case. I have also changed my opinion of Ludendorff, which was clouded by the atmosphere of the OHL.
—GENERAL WILHELM GROENER, OHL, OCTOBER 11, 1916[1]

Generals von Stein and Ludendorff are both two-faced rogues. Ludendorff's character contains a strong element of intrigue, as proven by his tactics against Falkenhayn and Bethmann.
—GENERAL WILHELM GROENER, DIARY ENTRY,
SEPTEMBER 28, 1917[2]

As a man Hindenburg is certainly to be respected. But he is not a strategist, and as a statesman he does not have the least talent. Hindenburg and Ludendorff are certainly not to be separated. The human dimension, which Ludendorff entirely lacks, is provided by Hindenburg. But neither is Ludendorff a statesman and never will be. And yet peace must be made by Messrs. Hindenburg-Ludendorff.
—GENERAL WILHELM GROENER, DIARY ENTRY,
OCTOBER 6, 1917[3]

The Duo settled into the OHL's headquarters in Pless, a small town in Upper Silesia chosen for its proximity to Teschen, where the chief of the Austro-Hungarian general staff, Conrad von Hötzendorf, maintained his headquarters. Command of OberOst had been turned over to Prince Leopold of Bavaria, with Max Hoffmann remaining as his chief of staff. Hoffmann found him likable and relatively harmless but a bit thick, tucked him away in a distant villa and got on with the war. Ludendorff took only his protégé, the hard-working but dogmatic Major Alfred von Vollard-Bockelberg, whom he made chief of the OHL's administrative section. Falkenhayn's loyal chief of operations, Colonel Gerhard Tappen, was sent east, where he became Mackensen's chief of staff. He was replaced by Major Georg Wetzell, an industrious if pedantic and stubborn officer who was soon quarreling with most of his colleagues. Lieutenant Colonel Max Bauer, heavy weapons specialist when he wasn't politically intriguing on Ludendorff's behalf, remained as head of the second section. Another dangerous intriguer, Walther Nicolai, remained as head of the intelligence section. As in Lötzen, the Duo occupied a private villa, staff officers were quartered variously, staff sections utilized public buildings. Allied and neutral liaison officers further crowded the small town, as did the kaiser and his entourage.

A day after moving to their new headquarters, Hindenburg and Ludendorff attended an imperial conference called to discuss the simmering subject of unrestricted submarine warfare. Most senior naval officers and various expansionist pressure groups had continued lobbying on behalf of the weapon to the extent that the previous April the Reichstag had voted for its usage. More recently, Admiral Henning von Holtzendorff, chief of the admiralty staff, supported now by the formerly cautious naval minister, Eduard von Capelle, assured his colleagues that such a campaign would bring England to her knees by the end of the year. Chancellor Bethmann Hollweg had not changed his views from the last conference on the subject. He again argued against the proposal, citing the danger of bringing not only America into the war but also Denmark and Holland. The Duo, along with most army and navy officers, denigrated any threat from America. The enmity of other neutrals, including their immediate neighbors, was something else, because these borders were undefended. Hindenburg and Ludendorff agreed that the subject should be deferred, at least until the end of the Romanian campaign, when troops would be available for border defense vis-à-vis Holland and Denmark. Ludendorff carefully preserved his options by pointing out that public opinion strongly favored such an offensive, "the only means of bringing the war to a successful conclusion within a reasonable time." According to Ludendorff, Bethmann agreed that the offensive would start "when the field marshal wished it to start."[4]

A more immediate problem concerned the eastern front, where fresh Russian offensives in Galicia and the Carpathians had pushed Bothmer's *Südarmee* considerably to the rear. A recently formed army group, commanded by the Austrian Archduke Charles with German General Hans von Seeckt as chief of staff, had fallen back on the Carpathian passes and on the frontier of the Bukovina, a setback that Hoffmann blamed on Seeckt's "extremely bad generalship." "I am continually taking troops out of the line and sending them south in support," Hoffmann grumbled in early September.[5] No further ground could be lost here if Romania were to be punished. Romanian troops were pressing into Transylvania to threaten Austria-Hungary's virtually undefended right flank. A counterattack could not begin until Falkenhayn's Ninth Army was assembled in the north. Though cursing the inept Austrian command, Ludendorff was compelled to reinforce the concerned armies with three divisions from the western front.

The crisis in the south passed as quickly as it had arisen. The huge Romanian army, meeting but slight resistance from militia and groups of hastily armed miners, perhaps 30,000 in all, inched into southeastern Transylvania like a timid snail, seemingly oblivious to the operations of its flanking Russian ally. Mackensen's Austrians, Bulgarians, Germans, and Turks, on the other hand, moved swiftly into the Dobruja to threaten Bucharest from the south even while Falkenhayn in the north continued to build his new army.

Hindenburg and Ludendorff learned of these successes in early September from messages received on their special command train that was taking them on an inspection of the western front. They had already agreed that the Verdun offensive, which they long had been cursing, had to end. The German position had steadily deteriorated, the morale of the German crown prince was as low as that of his men. Indignant commanders spoke of enormous human wastage, of driblets of soldiers cut from essential supply, huddling in small holes like frightened animals. So much for Falkenhayn's theory of attrition warfare. Prior to leaving Pless, the Duo had persuaded the kaiser to cancel the offensive, which, because of heavy and persistent French counterattacks, had for some time turned into a defensive—and would remain so, "an open, wasting sore," in Ludendorff's bitter words.[6] It would claim half a million German and French dead before it was finished: "at least 150,000 were never buried, but were simply absorbed into the ground."[7]

Their train stopped in Frankfurt to pick up Margarethe Ludendorff, who traveled as far as Metz. "You cannot conceive of the perpetual stir and bustle on the train," she later wrote. Enormous crowds greeted them at each station, while Metz "was like a sea of flags until air-raid alarm sirens sounded to disperse the cheering subjects."[8]

The Duo were met at Charleville, OHL administrative headquarters in the west, by Bavarian Crown Prince Rupprecht, to whom Hindenburg presented a field marshal's baton. Ludendorff was particularly impressed by Rupprecht's honor guard, an assault battalion equipped with steel helmets, which had not yet been issued to the eastern front.* He was not so pleased to learn of Rupprecht's expressed desire for peace.

Two days later the party was at Rupprecht's headquarters in Cambrai, where army commanders and their chiefs of staff had been summoned and where Hindenburg presented another field marshal's baton, this time to Duke Albrecht of Württemberg. The conference took place at a critical time in the Somme fighting. Hindenburg and Ludendorff listened to a series of briefings by various army corps and division chiefs of staff that revealed the immense complexities and problems which had plagued Falkenhayn. The German armies lacked sufficient artillery, shells, aircraft. Attrition was high, the front required a fresh division daily, which did not permit sufficient relief periods for front-line units. Ludendorff was not pleased. The armies were poorly organized, he later wrote; a wholesale shuffle would be necessary once the vicious enemy attacks had been checked. Although no one could fault numerous examples of individual heroism, the army was not fighting well. Loss of ground was not so important as the reason for the loss. Enemy artillery firing millions of shells and accurately directed by countless squadrons of observation planes had outgunned German artillery to prepare the way for massed infantry attacks that frequently succeeded against what Ludendorff called a "flabby" defense. The Germans "fought too doggedly, clinging too resolutely to the mere holding of ground, with the result that the losses were heavy. The deep dugouts and cellars often became fatal mantraps. The use of the rifle was being forgotten, hand grenades had become the chief weapon, and the equipment of the infantry with

---

* The genesis of the German "coal scuttle" steel helmet occurred in 1900 when experimental artillery firing on corpses showed the vulnerability of the leather helmet, the spiked *Pickelhaube* that had been designed to protect the head from saber slashes.

machine guns and similar weapons had fallen far behind that of the enemy."[9]

There was much to be changed. "Enormous errors have been made," Ludendorff told Hoffmann on the phone, "and it is high time to put things right."[10] Communications had to be improved—messages from division headquarters to front-line units often took eight to ten hours to arrive. The artillery required more accurate and rapid information on front-line infantry locations. The armies needed more long-range and flat-trajectory artillery, more shells, aircraft and observation balloons to reach parity with the enemy. Responsibility for improved artillery fire must be transferred to division commanders, working with front-line artillery specialists. Aviators had to be better trained to spot targets for the big guns. Infantrymen had to be weaned from hand grenades to return to the disciplined rifle fire necessary to break up mass attacks before the enemy closed in hand-to-hand fighting. The infantry needed light machine-gun companies, more trench mortars and grenade launchers. Deep underground dugouts in the forward trenches had to be razed in favor of lighter defenses. Ludendorff demanded a fluid, not a fixed defense. Long lines of trenches, snaking coils of barbed wire, forward infantry posts with wide fields of fire were too easily spotted by aircraft and destroyed by artillery. Front-line troops must be moved back, given narrower fields of fire and artillery cover. More troops had to be trained in offensive warfare. Special storm battalions had proved valuable, but they required better organization and more systematic training.

The conference lasted only a day. The battle of the Somme was still raging when the special command train departed—neither Hindenburg nor Ludendorff had been near the battlefields.

Back at Pless, the field marshal and the general resumed a familiar routine. Hindenburg briefly visited Ludendorff's office each morning to discuss the night's reports from the fighting fronts. He then walked for an hour, accompanied by an adjutant, occasionally by an important visitor or one of the allied generals or neutral representatives attached to the OHL for liaison purposes. At midday he and Ludendorff reported the military situation to the kaiser, an audience sometimes attended by senior ministers.

Luncheon followed, a simple affair according to Hindenburg. He devoted most of the afternoon to answering letters which an aide had culled from the hundred and more that daily arrived at the OHL, and he also wrote to his wife virtually every day when she was not in the near vicinity of headquarters. *"Der alte Kerl"*—the old man—was more popular than ever. Postcard pictures of the leonine head—often reproduced from one of Vogel's portraits—sold by the tens of thousands. He was the subject of popular poems and songs. Newspaper after newspaper ran lengthy interviews of the hero who was so surely leading Germany to victory. Streets, parks, theaters, hotels, cafes, and bars all over Germany were named after him. Gifts continued to pour in, anything from hand-knit woolen stockings to precious cigars and brandy to his favorite marinated eels. Regiments in Germany and Austria-Hungary named him honorary commander. When he was rumored to be ill—he suffered from intermittent fever for the rest of the year—nostrums of all sorts were sent to him. Wooden statues similar to the one erected in Berlin sprung up in several German towns and were soon studded with nails pounded home by patriotic subjects. A young lady from Chile asked if he could help her find a lost certificate of baptism. A mayor of a small town asked his advice on the removal of garbage. Advice was freely offered on how best to win the war.

Visitors arrived almost daily. Hindenburg entertained the more important ones at dinner, which began at eight, sometimes with Kaiser Wilhelm in attendance. Ludendorff and his staff officers returned to their desks at nine-thirty. Hindenburg removed his guests to the small drawing room, to the *Cercle* that sometimes carried on until midnight. Despite various "alarums and excursions," it was a satisfactory life. Max Bauer remembered it as "the most agreeable period of the entire war" for the OHL staff.[11] Hugo Vogel, Hindenburg's court painter, rejoined his master in mid-October. "I have already perceived that the situation at the OHL is entirely different from that at Lötzen [OberOst]," he wrote to his wife. "Extreme relaxation is much more evident here than there."[12]

Vogel enjoyed the narrow streets of Pless that were bordered with hundreds of telephone poles supporting myriad wires, and behind them squat thatched houses, no more than three to four yards high. Military police roamed the streets, and sentries guarded the military buildings. Polish peasants hawking wares filled the marketplace, where innumerable fat geese made a terrible din.

The kaiser and his wife together with the imperial civil and military staffs lived in the local prince's palace at the end of the main street. A modest structure of some three hundred bedrooms, its entrance was guarded by two towers that supported a drawbridge surrounded by huge old trees. The palace lay in the center of a lake-studded park, but Vogel found its interior design too florid for his taste. The kaiser's American dentist was awestruck by the beauty of the palace and its life "totally free from any war conditions."[13] Admiral Müller was disgusted with the enormous staff, which "could be safely reduced by half without the remaining half being over-burdened with work."[14]

Pless became very busy on Sunday, when the country peasants attended church, the women in their dress costumes with colorful headscarves and blue aprons. Crowds gathered in front of the palace to greet the kaiser, who appeared promptly at eleven, his iron gray hair meticulously parted, a perfectly tailored uniform covering his 175 pounds, his stance aggressive as if he were about to lead an infantry charge. "His chest was covered with decorations, and in one hand he carried a field marshal's baton," Vogel noted, watching him respond graciously to local greetings.[15]

Vogel had brought the carefully packed large painting of the operations section for which he had made numerous sketches in Lötzen. It was hung in the district administration building where the kaiser viewed it. "Splendid! Hindenburg's head is perhaps a trifle too dipped, and Ludendorff's mouth could be opened more. But otherwise I am very pleased. . . . You have correctly emphasized the field marshal as the decisive one."[16]

The kaiser struck Vogel as fresh and healthy, full of jokes, talking continually. Vogel showed him the sketches for the huge canvas of the Tannenberg scene, which brought critical approval: "Less space makes the figures larger. More important to me than anything is that the field marshal's figure is brought into prominence."[17] The kaiser particularly liked Vogel's sketch of Hindenburg, done in Lötzen—the one Hindenburg declared that posterity would remember him by—and urged him to base a portrait on it in the Blücher fashion.

Hindenburg was delighted with the idea, but brought up a more urgent matter at his first sitting. He had discovered that Vogel's early portrait of him standing in the snow at Posen, which for some time had been hanging in the Dresden gallery, lacked a button on the greatcoat. He did not wish to be known as the "buttonless Hindenburg" and wanted it corrected immediately.

Vogel remained in Pless for nearly three weeks. Despite the increasing tempo of the war, little seemed to have changed. Ludendorff looked fine and at table seemed to be in good humor. The little date palm, the *Phönix*, was shabbier than ever, and the meals were not quite up to the Lötzen standard. Hindenburg still enjoyed coffee, cognac and conversation after meals, complaining now about the many shirkers at home with their alleged heart problems, now chiding Vogel about the missing button. He hunted frequently, mostly stags and wild boar. He often sat for Vogel, urging him to furnish the portrait desired by the kaiser. He carefully examined the painting of the operations section, remarking that Ludendorff should be looking at *him*, a change Vogel was unable to make. He counted all the buttons on the blouses, pointed to a missing Iron Cross on someone's tunic and made other helpful comments. Vogel returned to Berlin, laden with sketches. The field marshal would visit him there, the moment he could get away from his onerous duties in Pless.

Hindenburg's guests varied greatly and it should not be said that they were dull. King Ferdinand of Bulgaria arrived to explain his desire to eliminate Russian influence in his country and to unite all Bulgarians under one flag. Conrad von Hötzendorf was a frequent guest, "a gifted personality, a glowing Austrian patriot, and a whole-hearted adherent of our common cause,"[18] Hindenburg later wrote, a curious appraisal considering that Conrad loathed Hindenburg and Ludendorff, who themselves felt contempt for him and his army. General Enver Pasha briefed the Duo on the Turkish situation. He was not optimistic. He expected to be pushed farther back by the Russians in Armenia and to be attacked by the British in Iraq and Syria. "But, whatever may happen in Asia," he told his concerned hosts, "this war will be decided in Europe, and for that reason I put all my available divisions at your disposal."[19] The Turkish grand vizier, Talaat Pasha, and Count Tisza of Hungary dropped by. Scientists and industrialists from Germany, allied and neutral countries were entertained and listened to. Newspapermen by the score, including American war correspondents, were fêted and flattered. The famed Count Zeppelin, soon to die, surprised Hindenburg by declaring that the warship was obsolete—the airplane had taken over to begin a new era in warfare. A few war heroes appeared, including Captain Manfred von Richtofen, who was in the process of training his famous flying "circus."

While Hindenburg played the front man—and he was a very good front man—his deputy was deeply involved in political and military concerns. Ludendorff's major tactical project was to prepare the western front for a prolonged defensive role. Three weeks after he arrived at the OHL, he approved a new training manual. *Grundsätzen für die Führung in der Abwehrschlacht im Stellungskriege (Principles of Conduct for Defensive Battle in Position Warfare)* discarded the principle of the unconditional holding of the first line, a tactic already objected to by many, but also defended by many as the way to reduce losses including men captured. Future battles would be fought not on a fixed, inflexible line but by a defense organized in depth. Considerable amounts of heavy artillery were to be placed under command of the division artillery officer in order to eliminate costly delays in target selection and counterbattery fire. Special instructions covered the defensive potential of trenches, dugouts (which were to have concrete walls and roofs), and protective wire. A new allied weapon, the tank, which had recently appeared in limited numbers on the Somme front, was causing some problems, but Ludendorff did not wish to overestimate its threat: "The best weapons against the tanks are coolness, discipline, and courage."[20] He would shortly ask the war ministry to study the problem, but judging by results—five German tanks produced by early 1918—he did not press the matter.

Construction of the *Siegfriedsstellung*—known to the Allies as the Hindenburg Line—was started shortly after Ludendorff's return from the Cambrai conference. In the Somme area it would run from Arras to the Chemin des Dames, behind the large sector then being so viciously attacked by the enemy. Similarly, the Michel Line would be constructed south of Verdun behind the Saint-Mihiel salient. If necessary, the armies could fall back to these strong positions of fixed defenses in order to shorten the front and save manpower, while giving the troops proper rest and training periods and the factories time to supply more munitions.

Ludendorff's reforms fell victim to continuing enemy offensives in September and October, which in some sectors pushed German lines back five miles. Plans for systematic relief of front-line divisions soon evaporated in the heat of battle. Trains traveling with frantic urgency rushed reinforcements to threatened areas. Thousands of German dead covered the battlefields, thousands of prisoners were herded into barbed-wire camps, thousands of wounded were evacuated to hundreds of hospitals. "It is obvious that bad mistakes have been made," Hoffmann, who spoke to Ludendorff almost daily and sometimes hourly by telephone, noted on October 14. "In the first place, further strong positions should have been constructed, one behind the other, and more ammunition, etc., should have been available. These are our blunders, but they are now recognized, and Ludendorff is doing what is humanly possible to put matters right."[21]

The military situation was more favorable in the east. In Transylvania, the Romanians waited for the Russians to cross the Carpathians and join them in a wide sweep across the Hungarian plain. Lechitski's Russians, whose attacks on the Carpathian passes had failed with heavy losses, waited for the Romanians to open these passes from the rear.

Falkenhayn used the impasse to assemble his army and attack southward in mid-September while the weak Austrian First Army, commanded by General Arthur Arz von Straussenburg, struck on his left. He was scarcely a free agent. Perhaps avenging the frustrations of two years, Ludendorff attempted to direct the offensive from Pless by streams of telegrams that Falkenhayn found "equally superfluous and annoying."[22] His two-pronged offensive against the Romanian First Army took place on a thirty-mile front spread southwest and northeast from Hermannstadt. While the main force marched on Hermannstadt, General Krafft von Dellmensingen's veteran Alpine Corps on the right moved in behind the enemy to secure Roterturm Pass and block the Romanian exit to the south. Falkenhayn's people broke through after a four-day battle in late September to continue the march eastward against general light resistance. This advance forced a second Romanian army in the north to retreat, thus allowing Arz von Straussenburg's army to reach the frontier mountains of Moldavia. Stiffening enemy resistance coupled with mountainous terrain and snow to slow and then halt the advance.

Mackensen's southern offensive meanwhile continued. In early September a siege force approached the Danube fortress of Turturkai—"our Verdun," as its commandant told visiting journalists.[23] Two of its divisions surrendered their arms the next day. A few days later fortress Silistria surrendered without a fight. By the end of September Mackensen's army stood only twenty-five miles south of the important Black Sea port of Constantza but was forced to pause until more troops arrived.

Ludendorff faced a difficult situation by mid-October. Perhaps for the first time, he and Hindenburg began to appreciate the enormity of Falkenhayn's earlier problems, most particularly where to use a limited number of reserve divisions to the best effect. Romania seemed to be the most propitious theater. If Romania could be knocked out of the war, her rich grain and oil fields could be had for the taking. But more troops were needed for Ludendorff's new plan of attack designed to trap the enemy army in Wallachia.

Where were the necessary divisions to come from? Nothing could be spared from the western front writhing against renewed Allied attacks. The Italian front likewise claimed Conrad's enfeebled Austro-Hungarian divisions, bracing themselves for still another offensive on the Isonzo River. The shaky Macedonian front demanded more, not fewer, divisions. Otto von Below, who commanded Eleventh Army, anticipated a further retreat of his Bulgarians, perhaps to behind Monastir. In late November, Greece would declare war on Germany and Bulgaria to increase Below's problems.

There remained the eastern front. Had Falkenhayn still reigned at the OHL and the Duo at OberOst, the latter undoubtedly would have pointed to renewed Russian attacks and refused to release any troops. The new chief of staff of OberOst, Max Hoffmann, was more pliant when summarily ordered to transfer three infantry and two cavalry divisions to the south.

Mackensen, assisted by his new chief of staff, Gerhard Tappen (recently of the OHL), spent several weeks reorganizing his polyglot army of German, Bulgarian, and Turkish divisions, which held a sixty-mile line stretching from the Danube southeast to the Black Sea. He attacked on October 19, broke through Romanian lines immediately, four days later seized the port of Constantza with its precious oil storage tanks, pushed on twelve miles north of the Bucharest–Constantza railway and halted only on Ludendorff's orders. Mackensen was now to build a defensive line with a weak force and transfer his main strength to the southwest, where he would prepare to cross the Danube south of Bucharest. At the same time Falkenhayn's Ninth Army was to force the mountain passes in the north and press into the flatlands of Wallachia.

Falkenhayn had tested several of these passes at the end of October only to find the enemy strong and alert. From the reports of these actions, Ludendorff ordered the main attack to be made on the Vulcan and Szurduk passes on Falkenhayn's right. This difficult task was given to General Kühne's army group of four infantry and two cavalry divisions, the latter commanded by General Count von Schmettow. The troops were issued special mountain equipment. Narrow roads were widened, supplies and equipment including motor-driven cars for use on Romanian railways, were stockpiled. Kühne attacked on November 11, fought and beat his enemy in six days, continued south to Craiova, as per plans, and wheeled left to reach the Alt River, whose bridges had been destroyed. Schmettow's cavalry poured through the open passes to reach the Alt south of Kühne's infantry and seize the one bridge that was still standing. Romanian forces east of Orsova were now outflanked and forced to retreat south along the banks of the Danube, eventually to surrender.

Mackensen complemented Kühne's success by forcing the Danube at Sistova on November 23, wheeling northeast and in only a week advancing on a thirty-five mile front to within twelve miles of Bucharest. Simultaneously, Krafft von Dellmensingen's Alpine Corps on Kühne's left fought through the Roterturm Pass, reached Piteschi in late November and continued on to north of the Arges River. This in turn cleared the way for the Kronstadt army group, heretofore held up by heavy fighting, to debouch from the mountain passes on Krafft's left. Kühne's group had been held up in trying to cross the Alt, and by month's end his flanks were nearly fifty miles distant from the Alpine Corps on his left and the Danube Army on his right.

The Romanians now made their move, throwing caution to the winds to counterattack the Danube Army southwest of Bucharest and cut off Mackensen's forward units. A Turkish division prevented the intended breakthrough, which would have cut Mackensen from the other armies. Kühne's cavalry pushed through to Mackensen's left, and the infantry quickly followed to launch a counterattack. Kühne's left meanwhile had joined Krafft von Dellmensingen's right to continue the advance into the heart of Wallachia. Bucharest and Ploesti fell early in December. Ludendorff had feared that Bucharest would be defended and was greatly relieved to find it open. He was not so pleased to learn that the Ploesti oil fields had been savaged by the retiring enemy, or that at long last Russian troops were being transferred from north Dobruja to Wallachia to support the wavering Romanians.

Ludendorff reorganized his southern forces to expedite the final phase of the operation. Field Marshal Mackensen—the pictures of his triumphal entry into Bucharest astride a white stallion having claimed the front pages of every German newspaper—was given command of Ninth Army, while General Kosch took command of the Danube Army. Mackensen's mission was to advance to the northeast as quickly as possible to complete a defensive line along the Moldavian border, at the same time inflicting maximum damage on the Romanian and Russian armies.

The campaign henceforth resembled a bloody slugging match. Almost no maneuver was possible against a well-defended enemy line in bitter cold weather. Ammunition had to be laboriously brought up and stockpiled, a barrage opened, a breakthrough made. It was slow, hard, costly work, but it paid off. By early January 1917 the Romanian army was in retreat into Moldavia, beaten but not destroyed. Mackensen's new defensive line protected the treasures of the Wallachia that were so essential to Germany's survival.

23

---◆---

The "Hindenburg Program" for German Victory

Enough of tedious politics with which, as long as I am a soldier,
I concern myself only with profound reluctance.
—General Erich Ludendorff to Alexander Wyneken,
  January 23, 1916[1]

There was scarcely a political question in which he [Ludendorff]
not only requested OHL's participation but also insisted on its
right to make the decision, arguing that otherwise the war
would be lost and that Field Marshal von Hindenburg could
no longer bear the responsibility.
          —Chancellor Theobald Bethmann Hollweg,
          Reflections on the World War[2]

Theobald Bethmann Hollweg was born for disappointment, the inevitable result of a weak leader who must find his strength in others. When Falkenhayn let him down in late 1914 with his realistic appreciation of Germany's difficult if not impossible military situation, he turned to Hindenburg and Ludendorff, in whom he found the strength he had sought from Falkenhayn (and the kaiser). Without perceiving the relationship that existed between the two, that is, Hindenburg's almost total subservience to Ludendorff in military operational matters, he was convinced that Hindenburg's appointment to the supreme command would provide a stabilizing rudder to his own somewhat erratic ship of state. Within a few weeks, undoubtedly to his astonishment, he found his authority being challenged by the two men whose cause he had so heartily and unethically championed.

Admiral Müller wrote that on the day of the Duo's new appointment Bethmann was "dissolved in bliss over Hindenburg's personality."[3] The word *personality* is advisedly used. Hindenburg appeared to be big, strong and safe, secure in his belief of victory, modest in annexationist demands. It is doubtful that Ludendorff would have upset this impression—indeed he maintained a relatively smooth relationship with the German chancellor, whom on occasion he had defended against his many critics. The basis of the relationship between Bethmann and the Duo was, however, negative, based on a common desire to dump Falkenhayn and on Bethmann's pathetic sycophancy displayed at all times to the Duo in military matters. With Falkenhayn's fall, whatever bond there was largely disappeared.

Nor could Bethmann count on other than quixotic support from the kaiser, who was behaving more fatuously than ever. When not sawing wood or rushing off to what he liked to call "the front," Wilhelm had been on a shooting kick. In mid-September, when German soldiers were being wounded and killed by the thousands on the Somme, the kaiser shot two stags, "and appeared this evening wearing his Pour le mérite, two Iron Crosses and the Hunters' Jubilee badge."[4] This stupid, insensible and heartless conduct had for some time tested the patience of his military and civilian advisers, some of whom had the audacity to suggest that he should dispense with his "unncessarily numerous staffs and lackeys" and live in Berlin "to share the lot of the civilians" and thereby raise national morale. The kaiser was not interested. He instead shifted imperial headquarters to the luxurious Neue Palais in Potsdam to distance himself even further from the unpleasant war. In late October, when German lines on the Somme were struggling to hold, Müller sourly noted: "The kaiser has not made the slightest effort to carry out his duties as a reigning monarch. As I feared, his stay at the Neue Palais has turned out to be no more than an unjustified vacation."[5]

Had the Duo confined themselves to purely military concerns, the war might have gone better for Germany, or at the very least an escape might have been found from a no-win situation, if only by means of a no-win peace treaty. Hindenburg in the *kaisertreu* military tradition was basically disinterested in politics but was neither sufficiently strong to bridle his overeager alter ego, Ludendorff, who had lived with intrigue, the kissing cousin of ambition, for as long as he could remember, nor was he sufficiently perceptive to realize where Ludendorff's intrigues were leading. It can be said that he was unaware of some of these intrigues. It can also be said that he should not have been unaware of them, and further that those of which he *was* aware brought his official approbation and support. Hindenburg had soon grown used to basking in his own pretended glory, and as long as Ludendorff allowed the charade to continue, even if passively, the old man was more than content to play along with few if any questions asked.

Falkenhayn's bed at Pless was still warm when a train of important industrialists, bankers, and conservative politicians began streaming to the OHL. This was largely the result of Max Bauer's orchestrated campaign against Falkenhayn and his promises to the industrial complex for a new and better day under the likes of Hindenburg and Ludendorff. The mere presence of such financial potentates as Carl von Duisberg, Gustav Krupp, Albert Ballin, August Thyssen, and Hugo Stinnes, to name only a few, immensely flattered Hindenburg's inflated ego, and while at times he entertained them with food, cigars, champagne, and his limitless fount of rather tiresome stories, at other times they were deep in conference with Ludendorff deciding on Germany's future. Ludendorff's public stance of simple soldier uninterested in "tedious politics" was now simple soldier who must embrace politics if Bethmann's maladroit government and the undisciplined socialist element in the Reichstag were not to lead Germany to ruin.

The first challenge to the quarterdeck of the ship of state came almost immediately in connection with submarine warfare. As we have written, the Duo agreed to defer the question until the land military situation was clarified, but had nevertheless taken upon itself the authority for the final say. Bethmann glossed over this insult, possibly because he believed that it was enough of a military issue to justify the Duo's stand.

But then had come Germany's relations with Austria-Hungary, particularly in connection with the eastern occupied territories, primarily Poland but also Kurland, Lithuania, and Romania.

Ludendorff had long had his eye on Poland as a source for troop replacements. Its future had been discussed at the imperial conference in September, and it was the main item at another conference in late October.

The occupied portions of Poland had neither been consistently administered nor exploited. The German army ran two fiefdoms, one from OberOst in Brest Litovsk, one from General von Beseler's command in Warsaw. The Austro-Hungarians ruled their territory from Lublin. Neither of the victors was popular. Poland's most powerful political party was pro-Russian and did not want postwar domination by either Germany or Austria-Hungary. Józef Piłsudski's minority Socialist party wanted Polish independence, and toward this end he formed a not very eager Polish Legion to fight with the Austrians against the Russians.

Considerable conflict had early developed concerning Poland's future, first between Germany and Austria-Hungary, then between Bethmann's government and the military. Germany and Austria-Hungary each intended to control Poland after the war, but neither wished to admit it. Shortly before the change in command at the OHL, Bethmann and Count Burián, Austria-Hungary's foreign minister, had agreed to establish a Polish state greatly diminished in size and function. It would have no independent foreign policy, and Germany would control its army while sharing the exploitation of material resources with Austria-Hungary. Bethmann privately intended to establish an "autonomous" Poland completely under German control. Burián intended not to let this happen, but for the nonce each pretended to trust the other.[6]

Bethmann's intention at this point coincided with Ludendorff's desires, but they differed on timing. In September 1915 Ludendorff had written to a friend, an influential conservative newspaper publisher named Alexander Wyneken (to whom he subsequently imparted classified information), that he hoped Arthur Zimmermann of the foreign ministry would put the screws on the Austrian government over Poland: "Why do we let all those potential recruits go unused? Hopefully, events have taught the Poles how weak Austria is—thus a union with Germany is safer."[7] The Duo had already proposed a German unified military command of Poland and the raising of a Polish army. Though Burián and Conrad angrily rejected the proposal, it gained weight in German conservative circles and soon led to a demand for outright annexation. Bethmann's attempts to soft-pedal the move got nowhere, indeed General Beseler informed the German chancellor: "Since the whole question of Poland is concerned not with Poland itself but with the security of Germany and her dominant position in the east, it is primarily a military question and must be dealt with by the OHL, with whom I am in contact." This won hearty approval from Ludendorff, who wrote friend Wyneken: "As for Poland, we must take action, there is no ideal solution. It is all a matter of power, and we need soldiers."[8] Ludendorff was referring to Beseler's promise that he could at once raise five divisions of Polish volunteers with another million recruits to follow if Germany would guarantee an independent postwar Poland.[9]

This was the main subject of the October conference, where Bethmann, after much shifting about, deferred to military wishes. Burián and

Conrad, well aware that Austria-Hungary's military future lay in German hands because of massive Austrian losses and the increasing inability to make them good, went along. In early November the Warsaw and Lublin military commands informed the Polish peoples of an imperial edict that Poland would become an independent state with a constitutional monarchy once the war was over.

This was only a makeshift arrangement and did little to repair relations between the two allies. Germany's overbearing attitude, reflected particularly by Ludendorff's dictatorial behavior, had long been resented by the Austro-Hungarian army and government. In early November Count Burián surprised his German ally by announcing an imperial edict that promised Galicia eventual autonomy. This rather clever political move, intended to defuse the nationalist movement, went unchallenged by the German chancellor but not by Kaiser Wilhelm, who, prompted by the infuriated Duo, pronounced it as "scandalous" and proceeded to upbraid his chancellor.

Rudolf von Valentini, chief of the kaiser's civil cabinet, returned to Pless at this time from sick leave to find a noticeable deterioration in relations between supreme headquarters and the foreign ministry. He held this to be largely the fault of the OHL and particularly criticized the "brusque and dogmatic" tone of their letters.[10] He had reason to be concerned, judging from Hindenburg's stinging letter to Bethmann regarding Austria's action: "By not interfering in the internal affairs of Austria-Hungary before and during the war, our conduct of the war has constantly been made more difficult. If we continue to be afraid of such interference in an area where our interests are directly at stake, we will give up all hope of strengthening Austria-Hungary and the question arises then why we are still fighting for Austria at all."[11] Bethmann refused to retrench, angrily pointing out that undue German interference in their ally's affairs might well push Vienna into a separate peace with France or England.

Bethmann's stand was well-taken. Austria was on the verge of starvation. The eighty-six-year-old Emperor Francis Joseph died in November 1916. He was succeeded by his great nephew, twenty-nine-year-old Archduke Charles. Charles had visited the OHL shortly before the emperor's death. Ludendorff, who had met him two years earlier, thought that he had grown "more manly" and that he spoke well on military subjects. Limited praise soon turned to displeasure. In an attempt to repair internal ruptures in his shaky empire, Charles pardoned Czech and Ruthenian political dissidents and made friendly overtures to other minority peoples of the empire. He did not, however, mend relations with Hungary, and his conciliatory political attitude, greatly encouraged by his anti-German wife, Zita, tended to alienate the army. He also challenged the OHL's supreme command role, to Ludendorff's intense annoyance, and in December summarily moved Conrad's headquarters from Teschen, close to Pless, to Baden just outside of Vienna—a considerable distance from the Duo's influence.

Ludendorff did not take the hint and continued to insist on German hegemony in Poland. This naturally made Bethmann's relations with Burián and Count Czernin, who replaced Burián in December, increasingly difficult. It also ensured continued friction between the OHL and Bethmann's government.

By late 1916 most German leaders, including Hindenburg and Ludendorff, had reluctantly concluded that Germany was fighting a war of attrition, as Falkenhayn had been insisting for two years. Ludendorff had long been an advocate of "total war" to be waged by developing "the economic, physical and moral strength of the fatherland to the highest degree."[12] Every man who could serve in the army would serve, every man and woman who could work in a factory would work, every subject of the empire would be infused with the moral resolution vital to survival. The army would continue to do its part, but that would not be enough. The army depended on the home front for support, and it was from the home front that more men, arms, and ammunition must come.

Ludendorff's pronouncements fell on eager ears of German industrialists and other conservatives, who urged the OHL to force draconian labor laws, including wage controls, on the government and to eliminate bureaucratic inefficiency by establishing a Supreme War Office at the OHL, with civilian industrial advisers to control production and distribution. Although Ludendorff blamed Falkenhayn and the minister of war, Wild von Hohenborn, for ammunition and other shortages, he told Hoffmann "that, in general, there had been a complete failure of a united effort of OHL and the civil administration." Bethmann's government was not taking requisite action against war profiteers, and the high prices of commodities and their unfair distribution, especially of foodstuffs, was causing widespread unrest that some officials believed would result in ultimate rebellion. This failure was to be repaired by an all-out mobilization of German human and material resources under the aegis of the

OHL. The German economy was to be turned into what one politician called "a single munitions factory."[13]

The OHL provided the key to the transition with what soon became known as the Hindenburg Program. The minister of war was undoubtedly startled when he read Hindenburg's letter that revealed its goals. The OHL called for a one hundred percent increase in the production of ammunition and trench mortars by spring of 1917, a three hundred percent increase in the production of artillery and machine guns, and very substantial increases in airplanes, antiaircraft weapons, and scores of other items. The OHL was to overhaul the labor force, cull out those suitable for military service, tighten labor and production controls, and dictate priority usage of raw materials, oil, and coal.

These and other demands—including an overhaul of the civil court system to ensure swifter trials and heavier punishments for war profiteers and slackers—that called for a virtual end to civil government raised an immediate storm. Bethmann and his minister of the interior, Karl Helfferich, argued that "one can command an army, but not an economy."[14] Helfferich pointed out that there was already sufficient manpower for the jobs available. Minister of war von Hohenborn held that compulsory labor would only increase discontent. When the Duo remained adamant, Bethmann insisted that the new office created to implement the program, the Kriegsamt, or war office, headed by General Wilhelm Groener, should be under control of the war ministry, not the OHL. The Duo agreed, but only with the proviso that the present minister be replaced by General Hermann von Stein, Moltke's former deputy, an overbearing, tactless, and inept administrator who "could not think, speak or write coherently," according to one who knew him.[15] Stein, who was squarely under Ludendorff's thumb, was to remain at Pless instead of going to Berlin where he belonged.

The Duo proposed to control the labor force by a Hilfsdienstgesetz, or auxiliary labor law, that would make every German subject from sixteen to fifty eligible for involuntary wartime service—in short, forced labor. "There are thousands of childless soldiers' wives who are only a burden on the finances of the state," Hindenburg informed the chancellor. "In addition there are thousands of women and girls at large who are doing nothing or are engaged in quite useless callings. The principle that 'he who does not work shall not eat' is truer than ever in our present situation, even as applied to women." Hindenburg wanted all universities, technical colleges, and other schools closed for the duration except for training in such indispensable professions as medicine. ". . . Students of chemistry and technical colleges will be employed in factories." Action must be taken against radicals and war profiteers. "The whole German nation must live only in the service of the fatherland."[16]

Bethmann's reply pointed out the illogic of closing upper-level schools, since all physically fit students had been called up, and he objected to compulsory labor for women, since there were far more unemployed women than there were jobs. Although the Duo grumped about a mysterious reservoir of "untapped energy," liberal parties in the Reichstag refused to accept their more draconic measures and the debate dragged on. In mid-November Hindenburg notified the chancellor that "the solution of the labor problem becomes more urgent from day to day. Deliveries of war matériel threaten to fall off instead of increasing. I must decline to take further responsibility for the future course of the war if the home land does not support me."[17]

The bill was passed in late November. It bound all males between seventeen and sixty to enforced labor that was judged essential to the war effort. One could be fined or imprisoned for refusing employment. Once employed one could not leave his job without permission. In an attempt to conciliate increasingly militant trade unions, employers of more than fifty persons had to allow the formation of Workers' Councils, which were to "promote a good understanding among the workers and between the workers and their employers."[18]

A modern historian, Martin Kitchen, has concluded that "it is difficult to see the auxiliary service law as anything but a piece of repressive legislation against the working class." This may be true, but it was also a splendid example of what cynical Germans call Zurückversicherung, or back insurance, in this instance the OHL's putting the onus for the war effort onto the public, which would become the scapegoat if, as seemed inevitable, the economy worsened. Bethmann himself marked it as something of a watershed in that the total experience revealed "unbridgeable differences" between him and the Duo.[19]

24

Unrestricted Submarine Warfare

Sooner or later the die will be cast and we will be at war with Germany. It is certain to come. We must nevertheless wait patiently until the Germans do something which will arouse general indignation and make all Americans alive to the peril of German success in this war.
—United States Secretary of State Robert Lansing, January 28, 1917[1]

I do not believe [President] Wilson will go to war unless Germany literally kicks him into it.
—Theodore Roosevelt to Henry Cabot Lodge, February 12, 1917[2]

While Hindenburg and Ludendorff dreamed of mobilizing an empire to fight "total war," Bethmann Hollweg was still looking for a negotiated peace as the only way out of Germany's predicament. His proposal in September 1916 that the American president, Woodrow Wilson, negotiate a peace aroused instant hostility in German conservative circles. Bethmann nevertheless won the kaiser's approval and instructed the German ambassador in Washington, Count von Bernstorff, to approach the American government on the matter. No answer was received, presumably because of the approaching presidential election, nor did a reply at once follow Wilson's reelection, the reason perhaps being the American president's inclination "to handle all matters in a dilatory fashion," as Count Bernstorff put it.[3] Austria-Hungary's foreign minister, Count Burián, now suggested that the Cen-

tral Powers should take the initiative and make their own peace offer to
the enemy.

The Duo, not at all certain that Germany would win the war, did
not object to Bethmann's initiative, although it seemed unreasonable
that the Entente, preponderant in men, money, and matériel, would
want to conclude peace on any but its own terms. President Wilson's
silence enforced this belief, but when Burián's proposal gained weight
in government circles, the Duo went along, providing the offer was
announced after victory in Romania so that the Entente would not
construe it as the result of weakness. Bethmann next learned that Wilson
after all was to make a peace proposal and that he wished it to precede
any proposal by the Central Powers. Not wishing to have the initiative
preempted by Wilson at this critical point, Bethmann announced his
offer to the world in a Reichstag speech of mid-December.

This was premature. Bethmann's peace note may have been occasioned by a sincere desire to end the war, but it was an act more of
desperation than of statesmanship. At home it enjoyed only slight support. The Reichstag had played no part in its preparation. Hindenburg
and Ludendorff objected to it, which led to a quarrel and to the dismissal
of the foreign minister, Gottlieb von Jagow, who was replaced by Arthur
Zimmermann. The chancellor had refused to pledge himself to a specific
statement of war aims, and none was included in the note. It was favorably received by Germany's neutral neighbors, by large segments of
the American public, and by liberal parties in Italy, France, and Britain.
Allied governments were unanimous in rejection, but the rejections had
to be carefully crafted to avoid adverse criticism by the governments'
own peoples and by the neutrals. The Allied reply was still in preparation
when President Wilson's own olive branch reached the belligerent powers
five days before Christmas.

Wilson's note was a curious business that put him at odds with his
confidant, Edward House, his own state department, his ambassadors in
Paris and London, and both the Central and Allied powers. Wilson had
been reelected as a president who did not want to lead his country into
war. America was not ready to fight a war, and Wilson was also suspicious
of Allied war aims that underlay otherwise sanctimonious statements.
He was appealing to belligerents to help him fashion a lasting peace by
forming a concert of powers to replace the old European system of alliances. He did not offer his services as mediator, nor did he make specific
peace proposals. He was placing his government in the role of a "clearing
house for further steps toward peace," seeking a basis for further nego-

(*Above*) Unter den Linden, Berlin, August 1914: "The streets were thronged with crowds, singing and cheering for war."

(*Left*) Berlin, August 1914. Some of Germany's two million reservists headed for mobilization depots. The inscription on the right may be translated: "On to Paris."

East Prussia, August 1914. German cavalry on the march HOOVER INSTITUTION

East Prussian dead, August 1914

Hindenburg (*center*) and Ludendorff (*right*) in the field
NATIONAL ARCHIVES

General Hermann von François, the hero of Tannenberg.
Ludendorff ordered François to attack the Russian left
wing on August 25, 1914. François refused and thereby
saved Hindenburg's army from what he later termed "a
complete disaster."

The Battle of Tannenberg, Hugo Vogel's five-and-a-half-yard-long canvas. (*Hoffmann at the periscope; Hindenburg in the center; Ludendorff with map*)

Hindenburg and Ludendorff. The artist, Hugo Vogel, incurred Ludendorff's wrath and was forced to make some changes. HOOVER INSTITUTION

"A later charcoal sketch of Hindenburg won instant approbation. 'I want thus to be represented to posterity,' he told [the painter] Vogel, taking the chalk and signing the work as a personal memento."
HOOVER INSTITUTION

Arthur Zimmermann, who replaced von Jagow as Germany's foreign minister: "an East Prussian of middle-class background...an advocate, like Ludendorff, of 'total war' "

Hugo Vogel's painting of Hindenburg in front of Posen headquarters, 1915. "There in your picture," Hindenburg told him, "there I stand as if I would say, 'I shall not halt until I possess all Russians. None can escape me.' " HOOVER INSTITUTION

Chancellor of the German Empire, Theobald von Bethmann-Hollweg, "a tall, serious man...cultured, worldly, intelligent. He was also very weak...not so much a master *of* as a mistress *to* compromise."

German Foreign Minister Gottlieb von Jagow, who ran afoul of Hindenburg and Ludendorff and in 1915 was replaced by Arthur Zimmermann

Helmuth von Moltke The Younger, nephew of von Moltke The Elder, who had led Prussia to victory in the Franco-Prussian War. The competent but hardly brilliant younger von Moltke commanded Germany's armies as Chief of Staff of the General Staff in 1914. He was forced to make way for von Falkenhayn when his execution of the Schlieffen Plan did not produce success.

General Erich von Falkenhayn, chief of the German Great General Staff from 1914 to 1916, who "recognized the war for what it was...[but] was not equipped to fight it"

Field Marshal Paul von Hindenburg. General Groener noted: "As a man Hindenburg is certainly to be respected. But he is not a strategist and as a statesman he does not have the least talent."

Field Marshal Conrad von Hötzendorf, chief of staff of the Austro-Hungarian army: "Conrad was a great dreamer, forever coming up with Tannenberg-like envelopment schemes while forgetting the pathetic inadequacy of the forces at his disposal."

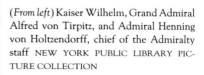

(From left) Kaiser Wilhelm, Grand Admiral Alfred von Tirpitz, and Admiral Henning von Holtzendorff, chief of the Admiralty staff NEW YORK PUBLIC LIBRARY PICTURE COLLECTION

Marshal Joseph Jacques Césaire Joffre. During the French retreat in August 1914, "a good many commanders would have given up. Joffre did not."

Sir John French. Relying on his military experience during the Boer War, Sir John French commanded the BEF that landed in France in 1914. He combined mediocre military talent with a prickly disposition and a pessimistic attitude toward the French Allies that made cooperation with the French high command extremely difficult. He was replaced as British Supreme Commander by his former subordinate Haig in December 1915.

Marshal Ferdinand Foch, who during the March 1918 crisis stormed: "You aren't fighting? I would fight without a break. I would fight in front of Amiens. I would fight in Amiens. I would fight behind Amiens. I would fight all the time."

Field Marshal Lord Haig, commander of the British army in Europe, who noted in March 1918: "I was only afraid that the enemy would find our front so very strong that he will hesitate to commit his army to the attack with the almost certainty of losing very heavily."

Hindenburg and Ludendorff in Brussels market square NATIONAL ARCHIVES

The Alsatian front, 1915. The *Pickelhaube* helmet was replaced with the steel helmet only in late 1916. NEW YORK PUBLIC LIBRARY PICTURE COLLECTION

Field Marshal von Hindenburg inspecting a regiment equipped with the new steel or "coal scuttle" helmets that appeared in 1916

Western Front, April 1915. German gas attack. "The [Allied] troops saw two curious greenish-yellow clouds...[which] spread laterally, joined up, and, moving before a light wind, became a bluish-white mist, such as is seen over water-meadows on a frosty night."

Western front, 1914. Early German (and Allied) bombing technique NATIONAL ARCHIVES

Western front. A protective box against gas for German carrier pigeons NATIONAL ARCHIVES

Czar Nicholas of Russia (*left*) and his field commander, the Grand Duke Nicholas. In 1915 the czar replaced the grand duke in command, a change that brought "a most painful" impression in the ranks.

Russian General Aleksy Brusilov: "a much more imaginative commander than most of his peers"

March 1917. Russian prisoners NATIONAL ARCHIVES

Wilna, Lithuania, September 1917. No amount of German propaganda, exemplified by the rich assortment of vegetables and fruit, could surmount the look on the seated woman's face. NATIONAL ARCHIVES

Brest Litovsk, 1917. The redoubtable diarist, Colonel Max Hoffmann, is on the right; on the left is Major Brinckmann.

Field Marshal von Hindenburg (*center*) and General Otto von Below (*on his right*) at a corps commanders' conference, western front, June 1917. Von Below would command the successful offensive in Italy in late 1917, but would not do well in the crucial fighting in France in March 1918. NATIONAL ARCHIVES

Germany 1918. German civilians waiting for a food market to open: "People were disillusioned and hungry. There was no more meat, no fat, and potatoes were at an end."

Germany 1916–1917. It was called "the turnip winter." The average citizen was subsisting on 1,200 calories a day, "corresponding to the needs of a two- or three-year-old child."

Western front. One of the early Allied tanks. In 1918 Kaiser Wilhelm remarked, "It is very strange that our men cannot get used to [enemy] tanks."

French tanks moving to the attack, August 1918

Western front, April 1918. Tanks destroyed by artillery fire in the Somme valley NATIONAL ARCHIVES

General Georg von der Marwitz, who turned the battle of Cambrai from defeat into victory
NATIONAL ARCHIVES

Principal Allied generals (*left to right*): Marshal Henri Pétain of France; Field Marshal Lord Haig of Great Britain; Marshal Ferdinand Foch of France; General John J. Pershing of the United States

English tank used as German weapon. Driving the tank into the repair shop.

German stormtrooper in full equipment ready to carry out General von Hutier's new tactics: "Surprise was the keynote. After a short but very powerful artillery barrage of gas and high explosive shells, small groups of *Sturmtruppen* armed with automatic rifles, light machine guns, flame throwers and trench mortars would move out under cover of a barrage that crept forward as they advanced." NATIONAL ARCHIVES

Western front, Operation Blücher, May–June 1918. German infantry reserves await orders to the front. The German advance reached, and briefly crossed, the Marne, before it was stopped with the help of U.S. marines and soldiers. NATIONAL ARCHIVES

Western front, 1918. German stormtroopers moving out at dawn LIBRARY OF CONGRESS

Operation Blücher, Western Front, June 1918. A German canal crossing NATIONAL ARCHIVES

Western front, May 1918. German columns march through a devastated village. NATIONAL ARCHIVES

Sturmtruppen capturing a British detachment, Western front, 1918 LIBRARY OF CONGRESS

Western front, 1918. German machine-gun nest
LIBRARY OF CONGRESS

Western front, 1918. German stormtroopers caught in Allied artillery fire LIBRARY OF
CONGRESS

Western front, 1918. German stormtroopers under cover from Allied artillery fire LIBRARY OF
CONGRESS

Western front, June 1918. Wounded being carried to dressing station behind the Montdidier-Noyon sector NATIONAL ARCHIVES

Western front, May 1918. Shelled German aid station and ambulances NATIONAL ARCHIVES

Western front, 1918. German armored tanks NATIONAL ARCHIVES

Western front, 1918. German armored tanks NATIONAL ARCHIVES

Western front, 1918. German armored tanks NATIONAL ARCHIVES

Western Front, June 1918. While hundreds and thousands of German soldiers were being wounded and killed, while civilians were dying by the thousands from malnutrition, the thirtieth anniversary of Kaiser Wilhelm's reign was celebrated at German supreme headquarters. NATIONAL ARCHIVES

General Wilhelm Groener, who replaced Ludendorff as Hindenburg's deputy in October 1918—
when it was too late

Prince Max of Baden, appointed chancellor of the
German empire, October 1918. The brilliant
historian Gerhard Ritter sized up the choice as
"surely one of the strangest phenomenon in the
history of the Wilhelminian Germany."

Marshal Foch's railroad car in the forest of Compiègne, where the armistice was signed on
November 11, 1918. NEW YORK PUBLIC LIBRARY PICTURE COLLECTION

The giant figure of Hindenburg in Berlin's Königplatz. "Thousands of loyal subjects were daily standing in line to buy iron, brass or gold nails to pound into it."

tiation by asking each belligerent to state its terms for ending the war, and he implied that the United States favored a peace with no one the winner.[4] The vital matter was to bring the belligerents to the negotiating table. Only then would it become a question of who would mediate what: "The objects which the statesmen of the belligerents on both sides have in mind in this war," Wilson stated in a plague-on-both-of-your-houses frame of mind, "are virtually the same, as stated in general terms to their own peoples and to the world."[5]

Neutral nations welcomed the initiative, Secretary of State Robert Lansing and the American ambassadors in London and Paris did everything possible to negate its importance, the Allied powers cursed the president's "above-it-all" stance but prepared to respond, the German leadership exploded into a dozen conflicting opinions and for the moment did not know what to do. Bethmann could not state his relatively modest (if still overly ambitious) war aims without bringing down the wrath of the OHL and the conservatives, yet to state the extravagant conservative aims would cost Germany what little world support she still retained and would unleash a row of major proportions in the Reichstag.

Bethmann's reply was delivered the day after Christmas. He declined to furnish America with peace terms, since Germany preferred to deal directly with her enemies, a position subsequently maintained despite assurances from Washington that her declaration would be treated in confidence, and despite Ambassador Bernstorff's insistence that peace could only be gained through the American president's mediation, indeed that there was no other way of avoiding war with America than by accepting this mediation if it was eventually offered, which it undoubtedly would be. *

Bethmann received the Allied reply to *his* note a few days later. Belligerent speeches in Paris, London, and Petrograd had foreshadowed its content. The note condemned Germany as an immoral aggressor seeking to justify her crimes and impose her own form of peace on the civilized world. It left little doubt that the Allied powers were not interested in peace negotiations.[6]

The Allied reply to the American note was released on January 10, 1917. It required considerably more verbal gymnastics, in view of a series

---

* Foreign Minister Zimmermann to Ambassador Bernstorff, Berlin, December 26, 1916: ". . . for your own strictly personal information. We will only consider some place in neutral Europe as the spot for the eventual gathering of the delegates. . . . [We have learned from previous experience] that American indiscreetness and intermeddling makes it impossible adequately to conduct negotiations. The interposition of the President, even in the form of a clearing house, would be detrimental to our interests and is therefore to be avoided. . . ." Scott, II, 1005.

of secret treaties that the Allied powers had drafted in an attempt to satisfy almost insatiable greed. Allied war aims, like those of the Central Powers, were sufficient to fill a book. The Allied tack was to downplay them as no more than suitable indemnity for the saviors of civilization. The Central Powers were international criminals who would have to forfeit illicit territorial gains and tyrannical rule over victim governments. Like the reply to the German note, their words left little doubt that the Allies would enter peace negotiations only on their own terms.[7]

Bethmann's peace initiative was motivated in part by the hope of preventing the employment of unrestricted submarine warfare, which he was certain would bring America into the war on the Allied side. After the Duo's qualified refusal the previous August to endorse such a campaign, the question had continued to be hotly debated by the government and the Reichstag. Among the many influential voices which favored the offensive was that of the chief of the naval staff, Admiral Henning von Holtzendorff, who was circulating a document called the Kalkmann Memorandum, which Ludendorff had read in September. At that time he was still not prepared to press for the offensive but was pleased to see that there were now so many U-boats available "that even he, no expert, was able to believe in success."[8] He regretted that the campaign had become a political issue because he considered it "a purely military matter."[9]

Holtzendorff informed Hindenburg and Ludendorff in October that an unrestricted submarine campaign would bring England to her knees within six months. It was now time for the kill. Bethmann and the kaiser demurred, agreeing only to a vigorous submarine-cruiser action in which ships would be stopped and searched for contraband in accordance with the international law of prize.

Bethmann's position remained equivocal. Although he insisted that the decision to open the submarine offensive was his to make (with the kaiser's approval), since it was a matter of foreign policy, nonetheless "the judgment of the field marshal would naturally have the greatest weight with him."[10] At this delicate juncture, the Center party's peripatetic Matthias Erzberger, in part responsible for the Duo's elevation to the supreme command, won a large majority vote in the Reichstag for a motion that has been described as "momentous in the political life of Germany."[11] "The Imperial Chancellor is solely responsible to the Reichstag for all political decisions in connection with the war. In taking his decisions the Imperial Chancellor must rely upon the view of the Supreme Command. If it is decided to initiate a ruthless submarine campaign, the Imperial Chancellor can be certain of the support of the Reichstag."[12] In other words, the chancellor would subordinate himself to the Duo's wishes, which would automatically be supported by the Reichstag! Chancellor and Reichstag were now subordinate to the wishes of Hindenburg and Ludendorff.

The Duo had already decided to open the underwater offensive, "the only means left," in Ludendorff's words, "to secure a victorious end to the war within a reasonable time."[13] The only question was timing. The matter of peace negotiations had first to be resolved, and the Romanian campaign had to be wound up and reserves built up at home, which could not happen before February 1917. Germany's victory in Romania would keep Holland, Denmark, and other neutrals quiet, but the United States would certainly not tolerate such a campaign and would enter the war against Germany. Ludendorff argued that this would not precipitate a military crisis, since America would need a year to train even five or six divisions. When Karl von Treutler at the kaiser's direction pointed to the danger of America entering the war, Hindenburg in "his quiet jovial way" assured him that German submarines would prevent America from landing any troops in Europe. Ludendorff reacted more succinctly: "I don't care two hoots about America," he told Treutler.[14] Arthur Zimmermann assured military and government that the American people in general did not want to go to war, a comfortable thesis apparently based on Count Bernstorff's less than precise dispatches on this important point. At a time when America's naval tonnage had doubled, Ludendorff repeated the naval argument that America had no ships of her own and would have to rely on British bottoms to transport troops. Neutrals would be intimidated by the offensive and would withhold ships. Holtzendorff's naval experts reckoned that over five million tons of shipping were necessary to transport one million American soldiers across the sea and thereafter supply them. England could not furnish that many ships and still survive economically, therefore the soldiers could not arrive. If by some miracle ships were found submarines would sink them en route to France, just as submarines would stop the flow of ammunition ships from England to France.

Ludendorff had inflated his own figures of enemy casualties and prisoners for so long that he probably did not demand proof of these comfortable statements from his naval colleagues. He later wrote that he discounted naval estimates to a certain degree, but that he hoped the submarine offensive would end the war in a year. He also discounted the current peace initiative, which he happily sabotaged when possible. Acting on OHL instructions, the War Department News Bureau in Berlin held frequent press conferences and released countless dispatches to inform the German public that President Wilson was Germany's enemy and that the war could only be won by unrestricted submarine warfare.

The fall of Bucharest in early December was celebrated by the kaiser and the Duo in a round of champagne luncheons and dinners at Pless. (Kaiser Wilhelm elatedly exclaimed that since Mackensen "already possessed every honor a military man could be awarded, the next battle cruiser should be named after him.")[15] Ludendorff subsequently toured the western front to report to Hindenburg that the army could withstand enemy offensives long enough for the submarine campaign to win the war. Coupled with Prime Minister Lloyd George's hostile speech to the British parliament concerning Bethmann's peace note, this prompted Ludendorff to telegraph Zimmermann that "the U-boat war should now be launched with the greatest vigor." Hindenburg seconded the demand a few days later in a telegram to Bethmann: ". . . at the end of August your Excellency made the decision on the question of launching of an unrestricted U-boat war depend upon my statement of opinion that from the military standpoint the time had come. This moment will be the end of January. . . ." Bethmann reminded him that such a campaign involved neutral states and therefore "constituted an expression of foreign policy for which I have to bear the sole responsibility, a responsibility which is constitutional and can not be delegated, although, in forming my opinion at the proper time, your Excellency's opinion would, needless to say, be entitled to a wholly unusual consideration."[16] Bethmann did not wish to make a decision until his peace offer was "cleared up in America,"[17] and until the necessary security precautions existed on the Holland and Denmark frontiers. "On this condition, and to the extent that I may find myself able to agree with your Excellency that the advantage of an absolute ruthless U-boat war are greater than the disadvantages resulting from the United States joining our enemies, I shall be ready to consider the question even of an unrestricted U-boat warfare."[18] Hindenburg unsympathetically replied that he regarded the campaign as "the only means of carrying the war to a rapid conclusion" and it must not be postponed.[19] Bethmann agreed only to a renewed discussion once the Allied powers replied to his peace note.

The OHL and the navy's demand had been accepted by the kaiser (momentarily a hawk because of the Allied reply) and by his naval advisers, Admirals Müller and Capelle. The arguments were impressive. Capelle testified that a hundred submarines were built in 1916, of which a quarter were lost. Eight submarines were being completed each month. In six months the British fleet would be reduced by half. Britain lacked sailors, her shipyards were short of steel, iron, and labor. The Allied powers were suffering from a poor harvest. France and Italy depended on the British navy for coal deliveries. Hindenburg reported that all fighting fronts were secure. Romania's collapse would keep the neutral nations quiet. America would be stymied by a successful underwater offensive. Capelle was convinced "that almost no American will volunteer for war service."[20]

The negative and exceedingly bellicose reply of the Allied powers brought the submarine issue to full heat and Bethmann to the crossroads of decision. He believed that his peace offensive had failed along with his hope for a revolution in Russia (it began six weeks later). He doubted President Wilson's "good offices" so far as Germany was concerned. This was partly the work of Ludendorff and the admirals, who kept insisting that America hated Germany and would come into the war anyway, a stance that grimly resembled prewar arguments for a preventive war and one that in the present case was totally contrary to facts. Bethmann succumbed further to the numbers game of his opponents, who claimed that 400,000 tons of allied shipping were sunk in November, 416,000 in December, a higher yet prediction for January—what would *unrestricted* submarine warfare produce? Economic experts pointed to poor harvests in America, Canada, and Argentina, a "world famine" that would surely restrict exports to England and France. It was the hour of the experts, and it is a great pity that neither the kaiser nor Bethmann respected Lord Salisbury's dictum: "No lesson seems to be so deeply inculcated by the experience of life, as that you should never trust in experts."

The issue was decided at an imperial council at Pless on January 9, 1917. Although Bethmann had been fortified with strong arguments against the proposed campaign, the transcript of his preliminary meeting with Hindenburg, Ludendorff, Holtzendorff, and Müller shows him at his weakest. Ludendorff emphasized that France and Britain were planning an enormous spring offensive, thus it was vital to break sea and cross-channel shipping lanes. Bethmann apparently did not contest this and other arguments. Instead he replied that "if the military authorities consider the U-boat war essential, I am not in a position to contradict them."[21]

The subsequent meeting with the kaiser seems to have been little more than a formality. Admiral Holtzendorff stated that England would sue for peace within six months: "I give your Majesty my word as an officer that not one American will land on the continent."[22] Hindenburg repeated the OHL's demand for immediate action. After some discussion, Bethmann yielded: "Your Majesty, I can not counsel you to oppose the vote of your military advisers."[23]

Kaiser Wilhelm, who had impatiently listened to Bethmann's halting doubts, was obviously glad to have the matter done with. Bethmann should do his best to keep America out of the war, the kaiser said, but if she declared war "so much the better."[24] The campaign would open on the first day of February. Neutral powers were to be notified on the last day of January that *all* ships traveling to or from Britain and France would be sunk without warning. Rudolf von Valentini, chief of the kaiser's civil cabinet, noted despondently in his diary, *"Finis Germaniae."*[25]

The Duo was not yet satisfied. On the following day Hindenburg informed the kaiser that he and Ludendorff could no longer work with the spineless chancellor, who must be replaced. Visibly shocked, the kaiser told Valentini that he could not consider a change in chancellors at this critical moment, and Valentini so informed Hindenburg. Hindenburg reasonably accepted the decision. Not so Ludendorff, who stated that Bethmann and such as Karl Helfferich and Arthur Zimmermann must go, if not now then as soon as possible. This was an open declaration of war on civil government. From this point on Bethmann would work not beneath the sword of Damocles but beneath the sword of Ludendorff.

25

---◆---

The Zimmermann Telegraph:
The Fatal Error

We intend to begin unrestricted submarine warfare on the first
of February. We shall endeavor in spite of of this to keep the
United States neutral. In the event of this not succeeding, we
make Mexico a proposal of alliance on the following basis. . . .
—ARTHUR ZIMMERMANN TO THE PRESIDENT OF MEXICO,
DELIVERED FEBRUARY 17, 1917[1]

Neither Hindenburg nor Kaiser Wilhelm seemed in the least disturbed by the momentous decision to unleash German submarines in unrestricted undersea warfare. A few days after the
decision was made, Hindenburg, back in Pless, was posing for his painter,
Hugo Vogel, whose mission was to portray him in the uniform of a
Hungarian regiment, "a completely gray and rather cheerless uniform,"
he informed his wife. Vogel found his subject relaxed and in good humor.
When he admired the field marshal's magnificent greatcoat with red
facings, the old man laughed and said that the kaiser wanted to know
which Balkan prince he had lifted it from. Hindenburg examined a newly
completed portrait of himself in the uniform of a Guards regiment and
noted that the sword was wrong. The number of buttons on the tunic,
however, was correct.

Scarcely had Hindenburg left the studio when an adjutant appeared
to inform Vogel that the new portrait and the Tannenberg and Marienburg sketches would be hung for the kaiser's inspection the following
day. The portrait would have to be set off by red velvet, the kaiser's

favorite color. Not without difficulty Vogel hunted down the material, part of a bride's dowry, which the mother, hearing it was for the kaiser's pleasure, happily handed over while shrieking to neighbors, "Such an honor, what good luck!"

The final result reminded one observer of the altar of the Holy Grail. The kaiser complained that the figure was too large. He also objected to the new Tannenberg sketches. Ludendorff was standing too close to Hindenburg: "the chief [Ludendorff] must be more in the background. The field marshal has won the battle."

Vogel also failed to get the decorations right for the new portrait in Hungarian uniform. Hindenburg had grown fatter and did not adjust well to the foreign garment, but the work was finally finished to everyone's satisfaction. Hindenburg hoped that Vogel's printer, Ullstein, would make lots of copies, since he liked the colors.

Prior to Vogel's departure for Berlin, the field marshal gave him a farewell dinner. His final admonition to his "little professor" was to repair the portrait hanging in the Dresden gallery: "Otherwise posterity will believe that I had run around with missing buttons."[2]

The Duo later attempted to disassociate themselves from the contentious diplomacy that followed the decision to unleash the submarine monster. Not so Foreign Minister Zimmermann and Admiral Holtzendorff, who traveled to Vienna to persuade Austria-Hungary to open a similar campaign in the Mediterranean. Zimmermann informed his Austro-Hungarian counterpart that Germany would establish and maintain fifteen U-boat stations to completely cut Britain from her sea-lanes. Holtzendorff told Emperor Charles and his ministers that Germany had 120 U-boats available for the offensive, yet a few days earlier, Württemberg's prime minister had learned that only 18 long-range submarines could go to sea, an unpalatable fact which he indignantly repeated to his court.[3]

President Wilson, oblivious to the momentous decision reached at Pless, meanwhile continued to hope for peace negotiations in one form or another. Count Bernstorff in Washington, who had been informed, warned his government that "war [is] unavoidable if we proceed as contemplated. The danger of a break could be lessened by the setting of a definite period, say, one month, for the purpose of sparing neutral ships and passengers. . . . Wilson believes he will be able to obtain peace on the basis of the principle announced by us of equal rights to all nations."

Bernstorff had earlier reported on the basis of his own and other expert observations that "America's resources, even of a military nature, were inexhaustible." Bethmann and Zimmermann were of course familiar with these reports, and Ludendorff had been shown a private letter expressing a similar expert opinion.[4]

Further messages from Bernstorff that reported Wilson's conciliatory attitude and extreme desire to maintain American neutrality while finding a way to end the war should have caused far more thought in government and military than was the case. Hindenburg and Ludendorff, however, were as one with naval commanders, who considered the argument closed.

Woodrow Wilson suddenly reopened it with a major speech to the United States Senate on January 22, in which he called for a "peace without victory" with all countries large or small choosing their own form of government, their security to be guaranteed by adoption of universal principles of peace. Bernstorff cabled that Wilson believed he could arrange a peace conference if Germany would inform Washington of her war aims, but that a brief delay in commencing the submarine offensive was necessary: "If the U-boat war is commenced forthwith . . . war with the United States will be unavoidable."[5] Great was the shock at the OHL when Bethmann's draft of these aims arrived, to be followed the next day by the chancellor with Zimmermann in tow to advise postponing the offensive just three days before submarine commanders were to begin pushing lethal buttons.

The Duo met with Bethmann, Zimmermann, and the kaiser in a room at the imperial palace with the kaiser's numerous birthday presents still lying about. All agreed that Bethmann's intentionally vague statement of war aims should be sent to Bernstorff, even though the Entente's terms had made them obsolete. Bernstorff was informed by cable that "in spite of best will in the world" there was no question of postponing the offensive, since the U-boats were on their way to target stations and could not be contacted, a dubious statement that puts one in mind of Moltke's unsatisfactory reply to the kaiser in August 1914. The submarine offensive would cease the moment that Wilson's efforts "lead to a peace that would be acceptable to us."[6]

Ludendorff, who was more responsible for the offensive than any other person, later wrote that he had mentioned his resentment to Hindenburg "at the manner in which our cooperation in these tremendously important decisions had been obtained. Although we had no clear knowledge of the situation, we had to bear the moral responsibility."[7] Lacking clear knowledge, it might have been prudent for the warlords to insist on a postponement until a reply had been received from Washington. Such a suggestion from Hindenburg could not have been turned down, and it is doubtful that naval communications were so poor that the submarines could not have been notified.

The thought apparently did not occur to them. Two days later Bethmann stood before the Reichstag to plead the case for unrestricted submarine warfare. Karl Helfferich, the minister of interior who had consistently argued against the offensive, assured Reichstag members that "by fall the Island Kingdom will sprawl like a fish in the reeds and beg for peace."[8] On July 31 Bernstorff delivered the fateful note to the American government of Germany's decision to announce unrestricted submarine warfare. The course of the war would now drastically change—though not in the way conceived of by the Duo.

The German note told heavily on the president of the United States. Vanished was his dream of peace without victory, of a better world free from the feuds of centuries, fashioned by the benevolent overlordship of a neutral America unsparing in her efforts to end war forever.

Wilson did not immediately take the nation into war. He broke diplomatic relations with Germany in the hope that this would cause her to rescind the underseas offensive. He held off arming American merchant ships, the ones that Ludendorff and the admirals claimed did not exist. He drafted a new plan for world peace and almost immediately discarded it in light of hopeless reality. He tried to arrange a separate peace between Austria-Hungary and the Allied powers, still another exercise in futility.[9]

The American president did not stand alone in his reluctance to ask for a declaration of war. A powerful pacifist and isolationist bloc existed in the Senate, indeed in the nation. Had Germany properly exploited this target with a persuasive propaganda campaign, the American government might have remained hobbled to the nation's traditional belief in isolationism.

Germany did no such thing. Her brutal behavior in Belgium and France in 1914 had occasioned the first large swing of American public opinion against her. Then 1915, the sinking of the *Lusitania*, the execution of nurse Edith Cavell, the introduction of poison gas, the naval and air attacks on British and French cities. Subsequent ship sinkings brought additional converts. German attempts to sabotage ships in

American harbors added to the sentiment, as did the very successful anti-German propaganda effort that England carried out in America.

Then came the declaration of unrestricted submarine warfare. Neutral ships, *American* ships, would be sunk on sight. England and France would be starved of food and munitions, the war would end with Germany the victor, the new ruler of Europe. One hundred and eighty-one ships were sunk in January *before* unrestricted submarine warfare, a figure that rose to 259 in February. The president still held off from seeking a declaration of war, even from arming American ships that were clogging American ports, afraid to sail.

There then occurred another supreme stupidity of the wartime German empire. This was the work of Arthur Zimmermann, long an important career diplomat, foreign minister since late 1916, "a very jolly sort of large German," House reported, far more intelligent than either Bethmann or Jagow.[10] His judgment was superficial. It was Zimmermann who in 1914 had wished to focus the war in the Near East by promoting a Turkish-led *jehad* to cleanse Persia and Mesopotamia of the filthy British infidels—which turned out to be an expensive flop. It was Zimmermann who had threatened House with an uprising of German-American citizens should America go to war against Germany. Zimmermann, slavish to his idol Ludendorff (who wanted to get rid of him), doggedly determined to topple Falkenhayn (which was accomplished). Zimmermann, charged by the constitution to serve Bethmann Hollweg, whose policies he constantly sabotaged. Zimmermann, "the *Beamte*—the civil servant—gone to seed," as H. L. Mencken characterized him, "the diplomat all thumbs, the skeleton at all feasts."[11] Zimmermann, proponent of unrestricted submarine warfare, a self-styled expert on America, who told the Reichstag on February 1, 1917, that middle westerners and westerners would not let America declare war on Germany.[12] Zimmermann, a man of unlimited vision and unbelievable stupidity, who now rescued Wilson and the American nation from the terrible dilemma of in or out.

It was all Zimmermann's idea. It was a natural, it could not fail. It was nothing less than a German alliance with Mexico to be followed by one with Japan. Mexico for long had been one of those secret weapons fashioned by German arrogance of ignorance—"Every night fifty million Germans cry themselves to sleep because all Mexico has not risen against us [the United States]," Ambassador Gerard had reported in April 1915. Now, in 1917, if America declared war on Germany, Zimmermann and his cohorts supposed that Mexico would declare war on America, as would Japan, which longed for new territories in the Pacific. Mexico's reward would be to regain her old territories of Texas, New Mexico, and Arizona. With the Duo's blessing Zimmermann informed his ambassador in Mexico City:

We intend to begin unrestricted submarine warfare on the first of February. We shall endeavor in spite of this to keep the United States neutral. In the event of this not succeeding, we make Mexico a proposal of alliance on the following basis: Make war together, generous financial support, and an understanding on our part that Mexico is to reconquer the lost territory in Texas, New Mexico and Arizona. The settlement in detail is left up to you. . . ."[13]

The message was sent in code via the Washington embassy, but British intelligence, which long since had cracked the German code, picked it up. Once Wilson broke relations with Germany, Zimmermann cabled his ambassador to make the offer to the Mexican president.

British intelligence sat on its interception until it could be released without compromising the source. The American public read Zimmermann's words on the first day of March. They created an enormous sensation. It was as if the nation had survived the earthquake of unrestricted submarine warfare only to fall victim to a postearthquake shock that sent remaining neutralist sentiment out the shattered windows. Congress was still agonizing over a bill that authorized merchant ships to arm. When Senate pacifists opened a filibuster to prevent a vote on the bill, Wilson ordered the ships armed by executive order, their guns to be manned by trained naval personnel.

In mid-March German submarines sank American ships.

Wilson's agony was nearly over.

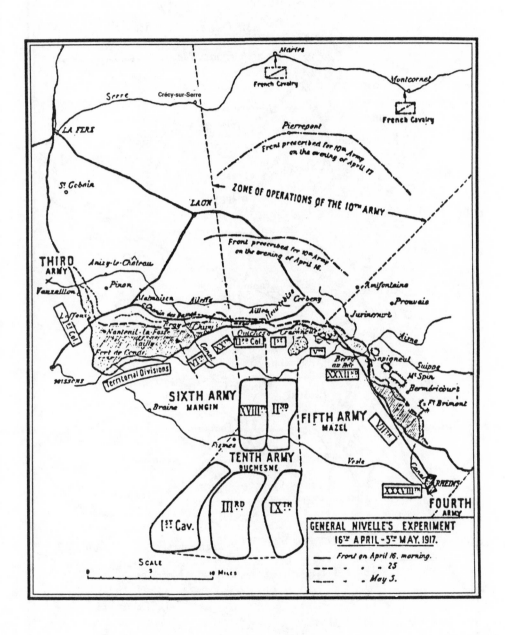

GENERAL NIVELLE'S EXPERIMENT
16TH APRIL – 5TH MAY, 1917.

——————— Front on April 16. morning.
— — — —   „   „   „   25
—·—·—·—   „   „   May 5.

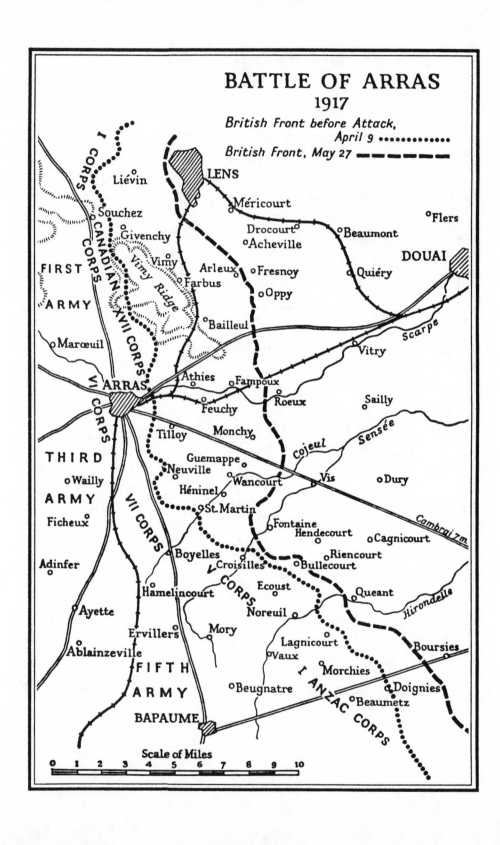

BATTLE OF ARRAS
1917

British Front before Attack,
April 9 •••••••••••••
British Front, May 27 — — —

Liévin

Souchez

Givenchy

FIRST

Vimy

ARMY

Marœuil

CANADIAN XVII CORPS

Vimy Ridge

I CORPS

LENS

Méricourt

Drocourt
Acheville

Arleux
Farbus

Fresnoy

Oppy

Bailleul

Flers

Beaumont

Quiéry

DOUAI

Scarpe

Vitry

ARRAS

Athies

Fampoux

Roeux

Sailly

V CORPS

Feuchy

Tilloy

Monchy

THIRD

Waily

Guemappe

ARMY

Neuville

Wancourt

Héninel

St.Martin

Fontaine
Hendecourt

Cojeul

Sensée

Vis

Dury

Cagnicourt

Ficheux

VII CORPS

Riencourt

Adinfer

Boyelles

Croisilles

Bullecourt

Cambrai 7m.

Hamelincourt

Ecoust

Queant

Ayette

V CORPS

Noreuil

Hirondelle

Ervillers

Mory

Lagnicourt

Boursies

Ablainzeville

Vaux

FIFTH

Morchies

ARMY

Beugnatre

Doignies

BAPAUME

I ANZAC CORPS

Beaumetz

Scale of Miles
0 1 2 3 4 5 6 7 8 9 10

26

General Nivelle's Offensive: The Second Battle of the Aisne

> I insist that the stamp of *violence*, of *brutality* and of *rapidity* must characterize your offensive; and, in particular, that the first step, which is the *rupture*, must in one blow capture the enemy positions and all the zone occupied by his artillery.
> —GENERAL ROBERT NIVELLE TO HIS FRENCH ARMY COMMANDERS, FEBRUARY 1917[1]

Ludendorff's military strategy was clear enough. On land, 1917 would be the year of the defensive for the Central Powers. Germany's allies were all in shaky condition. The Austro-Hungarian army was in desperate straits. Conrad was about to be shunted off to an army command in the Tyrol and replaced by General Arz von Straussenburg. Following Emperor Charles's instructions, Arz would continue to distance the army from German influence even while maintaining an even keel in his own relationship with the Duo.

The German army was tired, reserves were drying up, munitions in short supply. Germany's air force, however, had grown to 2,000 planes, which included long-range aircraft. While the armies of the Central Powers held fronts east, south, and west, U-boats would scourge the seas to cut Britain's vital supply lines, and aircraft would continue to bomb English and French cities. The number of sinkings by submarines rose steadily in those early months of 1917, nearly 800,000 tons in February, which sharply increased in March, and with a forecast that over a million tons would be sunk in April. Admiral Jellicoe at panic-station warned his government that England would run out of food and essential raw materials by July. With England on her knees, an all-out offensive would smash through French lines to give Germany the coveted victory.

The Duo had come full circle in strategic thinking in but a few months of command. Vanished as if it had never existed was the supreme importance of the eastern front. Their inspection of the western front had shown that Falkenhayn was correct in *his* strategic evaluation (but not in his faulty tactics). In early 1917 the enemy counted 190 divisions against 154 (of a total 210) German divisions, many of the latter being in an exhausted and weakened state. Although the eastern front was anything but secure—the Russians were expected to attack the Austro-Hungarian front in April—Ludendorff further thinned his eastern defenses by bringing fresh divisions west and replacing them with worn-out divisions.

Ludendorff looked for a renewed British attack on the Somme, probably late March or early April, in conjunction with a French offensive on the Aisne designed to press in both sides of the German salient while the Russians struck in the east.

The prospect was dismal. He did not want to fight a defensive battle. He needed time for more divisions to arrive from the east, time to rest and reorganize shattered divisions in the west, time to complete the concrete and steel emplacements of the Siegfried Line, time to build up ammunition stores. To forestall what he believed to be the Allied plan, he ordered Crown Prince Rupprecht to carry out a unique operation— nothing less than destruction and voluntary evacuation of a seventy-mile-wide sector between Arras and Vailly-sur-Aisne, the troops to fall back fifteen to twenty-five miles to the new Siegfried Line, once the former area had been thoroughly razed.

This was Plan Alberich, named after the king of the dwarves and leader of the Nibelungs so dear to Richard Wagner's heart. Alberich was cunning and cruel, and so was the operation. Under cover of various deceptive measures and a press blackout, the troops began in early February to strip everything valuable from the area before turning it into a wasteland of destroyed villages, towns, and roads, and ravaged orchards left without a tree standing, booby-trapped buildings, mined roads, water wells fouled with horse manure that the Allies later declared had been poisoned, bridges and rail lines blown up. The bulk of the native population, over one hundred thousand civilians, was transported to Belgium and Germany, others were left behind in the graveyards of rubble. Crown Prince Rupprecht protested strongly against these inhuman measures, but Ludendorff was not to be moved: "On the one hand it was desirable not to make a present to the enemy of too much fresh strength in the form of recruits and laborers," he later wrote, "and on the other we wanted to foist on him as many mouths to feed as possible."[2] The damage was done by mid-March, when the retreat was begun and carried out without interference by early April. "We retired singing . . . ," one participant wrote, "confident that we had established superiority over the enemy by an intellectual operation."[3]

Ludendorff judged the operation to be an enormous success. "The fact that much property belonging to the inhabitants was destroyed was to be deplored, but it could not be helped." He had shortened his front nearly thirty miles to bolster his reserve by some thirteen divisions. It would take the enemy some time to repair the evacuated area in order to attack a strongly defended Siegfried Line.

The OHL had moved from east to west during Plan Alberich, from primitive Pless to comfortable Bad Kreuznach, a fashionable health spa southwest of Frankfurt. The Duo occupied an imperial villa in the center of magnificent gardens. Ample luxury hotels and splendid villas housed various staffs, communications to the armies were excellent, but the nights were dark due to a total blackout against the threat of enemy air attacks.

Ludendorff's reorganization of the western front was far from complete at this time. Army groups were still being reorganized, recalcitrant commanders persuaded to adopt new tactics. "In future our defensive lines were no longer to consist of single lines and strong points," Hindenburg later wrote, "but of a network of lines and groups of strong points. In the deep zones thus formed we did not intend to dispose our troops on a rigid and continuous front but in a complex system of nuclei and distributed in breadth and depth. The defender had to keep his forces mobile to avoid the destructive effects of the enemy fire during the period of artillery preparation, as well as voluntarily to abandon any parts of the line which could no longer be held, and then to recover by a counterattack all the points which were essential to the maintenance of the whole position."[4] This in military parlance is known as a "fluid" as opposed to a "static" defense.

A fluid defense still depends on adequate numbers of well-armed and well-trained men. The OHL was not satisfied with the rate of delivery of arms and equipment. Telegraph wires daily carried harsh ukases to Bethmann and other high officials, such as the war minister, von Stein, and the head of the *Kriegsamt*, Groener. Production of war materiel was slowing, not increasing. In late January Ludendorff was complaining to Groener about inadequate deliveries of munitions and barbed wire. Although he believed transportation problems to be the main cause, he still blamed inefficient distribution offices in part (as did Groener, who was trying desperately to remedy the situation). The homeland still had to be disciplined. The government should not permit strikes. Force must be used to prevent them. One can almost hear Ludendorff's shrill voice dictating these demands that attempted to stand the empire at attention to repair the irreparable at a time when forces far greater than Ludendorff were forming undreamed-of threats.

One force was Russia. As supreme commander, Czar Nicholas had proved a disaster. His armies were broken in morale, tired, hungry, sick. The home front had finally rebelled. Rasputin, the czarina's spiritual adviser, had been murdered. Strikes and demonstrations had broken out in cities and towns and were gaining daily in size and ferocity. On March 10, 1917, troops in Petrograd refused to fire on workers and instead joined the revolt. Nicholas abdicated. Aleksandr Kerensky formed a provisional government, which pledged itself to continuing the war. Dissident communist Bolsheviks formed a soviet and pledged to withdraw Russia from the war.

The Duo received the news with open arms. "I felt as though a weight had been removed from my chest," Ludendorff later wrote.[5] Now more troops, more ammunition could be transferred to the western front. If Russia could only be removed from the war . . .

Russia *could* be removed from the war, a somewhat unusual visitor explained to Ludendorff in mid-March. This was a Russian-turned-German, fifty-year-old plump, balding Alexander Helphand, who in addition to being a Marxist revolutionary had made a fortune during the war by shipping horses and coal from Denmark to Germany. Alexander was also a secret agent code-named Parvus, who had been serving German intelligence as an intermediary with exiled Russian revolutionaries since early in the war. He had been sent by Ludendorff's political ally, Arthur Zimmermann, to explain that if a Bolshevik leader, Vladimir Lenin, living in exile in Switzerland, were allowed to return to Russia, the Bolsheviks would seize control of government and summarily end the war. Ludendorff subsequently arranged for the famous "sealed train" to steam from Switzerland across Germany to deliver its incendiary cargo to Petrograd in mid-April.

Another force was America, a dangerous animal when unduly annoyed. Germany had teased her once too often. Germany's declaration of unrestricted submarine warfare had brought unfriendly growls. The exposé of Arthur Zimmermann's ingenious plan to have Mexico go to war against her northern neighbor caused the cage to shake. Keeper Woodrow Wilson increased rations by arming merchant ships. Then in March German submarines sunk American ships with heavy loss of lives. Angry roars from the cage. Wilson's assistant keepers, his cabinet, unanimously declared for war. Still he held off, courageously ignoring the common din. Only when he realized that he could no longer pacify the animal did he act. On the second day of April, 1917, he opened the doors of the cage, but at the same time laid the groundwork for a cunning psychological and ultimately successful strategy: "We have no quarrel with the German people. We have no feeling towards them but one of sympathy and friendship." Once the German people renounced their "imperial masters," they would enjoy peace.[6] Four days later America declared war on Germany.

Profound changes had meanwhile occurred in the Allied camp. A British cabinet crisis in December 1916 had toppled Asquith's government. Lloyd George had replaced Asquith as prime minister and Grey was replaced by Arthur Balfour as foreign minister. Also in December a political revolt had forced the French government to demand Joffre's resignation, a bitter pill to the old soldier only partially palliated by his promotion to Marshal of France, a rank vacant since 1870. (Sir Douglas Haig was shortly after promoted to field marshal.) Joffre was replaced by General Robert Nivelle, whose shock tactics had scored against the enemy at Verdun where French *poilus*, defying vast belts of barbed wire that protected nests of Maxim machine guns, each firing 300 to 600 rounds per minute, had recently recaptured the tactically meaningless but psychologically important forts of Vaux and Douaumont.

Nivelle seemed to herald a new era far removed from Joffre's more conservative tactics, contemptuously summed up by the term *le vieux grignoteur*—the old nibbler. Like Falkenhayn, Nivelle was a great believer in the destructive power of mass artillery barrages to open the way for small infantry assaults to punch through primary defenses before fanning out to be joined by strong following reserves. In contrast to plump old Joffre, his successor was tall and debonair, younger in appearance than his sixty-one years. Thanks to an English mother he spoke fluent English, which greatly impressed Haig and his staff, and he was maddeningly sure of himself. The "Verdun method" was foolproof. "The experiment has been conclusive," he told his subordinates. ". . . I can assure you that victory is certain. The enemy will learn this to his cost."[7] He was also aware that the French army had wasted away like a sick animal in the Verdun fighting. France desperately needed a "decisive victory," both to restore army and civilian morale and to compensate for a possible Russian collapse.

Allied leaders met at Calais in February. Germany's declaration of unrestricted submarine warfare had brought a new crisis. It was imperative to defeat Germany on land before England was defeated at sea. All present agreed that only the major offensive, decided upon at Chantilly prior to Joffre's relief, could accomplish this.

But the plan submitted by Nivelle bore scant resemblance to the repetition of the Somme performance imagined by Joffre and Haig. Nivelle sounded like Ludendorff and Hoffmann together in his call for a "decisive battle" to destroy the German army. "I insist," he informed his army group commanders, "that the stamp of *violence*, of *brutality* and of *rapidity* must characterize your offensive; and, in particular, that the first step, which is the *rupture*, must in one blow capture the enemy positions and all the zone occupied by his artillery."[8] Nivelle seemed so sure of himself that he agreed to halt the offensive if the *rupture* did not occur within forty-eight hours.

The criminal fact of the Calais conference is that neither Nivelle nor Haig properly assessed the significance of the enemy's withdrawal to the Siegfried Line. In effect this enemy act preempted the purpose of Nivelle's offensive, which should have been canceled along with Haig's supportive attacks. Nivelle acted as if the enemy had not moved, while Haig noted in his diary on February 25: "The enemy has fallen back on a front of 18,000 yards: on the whole, such a withdrawal at the present time seems to have greater disadvantages than advantages for the enemy. . . ."[9]

The Allied plan called for Haig's British army to strike at Arras, primarily to pave the way for Nivelle's offensive by drawing German reserve divisions to the north. Haig would have preferred to attack in Flanders in the ambitious hope of pushing through to seize German submarine bases on the coast, but had soon fallen in with Joffre and Nivelle's desired plan. Nivelle would strike on either side of the Aisne with a subsidiary attack east of Rheims.

The British offensive opened on April 9 with attacks on either side of Arras. The assaulting infantry, led by tanks after a short but intense artillery and gas bombardment, ran into General Baron von Falkenhausen's Sixth Army on either side of the Scarpe River. Some divisions retreated, others held but took heavy losses. The indomitable Canadians pushed through to Vimy Ridge to capture German artillery positions on heights that dominated the terrain to the east. The attacks were not easily checked because, according to Ludendorff, Bavarian Crown Prince Rupprecht had failed to place his reserve divisions close enough to the front to be committed in time for an effective counterattack.

Ludendorff was appalled by the first reports, which "upset all his calculations."[10] What had gone wrong with his brilliant defensive tactics? He spent the day of his fifty-second birthday on the telephone to division general staff officers while waiting for front-line commanders to report in person at the OHL. Hindenburg had arranged a gala birthday dinner but found him glued to his desk suffering a thousand deaths. Hindenburg pointed to the evening report—the offensive already had begun to lose its force. Taking Ludendorff's hand between his own he told him, "We have lived through more critical times than today together."[11] They then joined the birthday celebration, which was carried out "quite harmoniously."[12]

Hindenburg had reasoned correctly. The attacks resumed the following day, but the steam was gone. They had penetrated some four miles on a ten-mile front, but the momentum could not be maintained sufficiently to prevent Falkenhausen from throwing in his own and other hastily dispatched reserves.

The critical situation continued a week later, when the French opened a three-pronged offensive northwest of Rheims. *"Notre heure est arrivée,"* Nivelle assured the long-suffering *poilus* shivering in their trenches from a freak April snowstorm.[13] An artillery bombardment of several days had alerted the German defenders, but the main thrust between Vailly and Brimont broke through at several points to push the defenders back to heights of the Chemin des Dames. A subsidiary tank attack on the right pushed through nearly to Juvincourt before being checked. A third attack east of the Aisne toward Brimont was held by a successful counterattack. While this fighting continued, the French attacked east of Rheims in the Champagne, the goal the Moronvilliers Heights, which were seized. This was a serious loss that allowed the French to observe a large area of the country to the north. Although the French failed to push beyond the heights, German counterattacks did not succeed in recapturing them.

Attack and counterattack claimed the remaining weeks of April, with appalling casualties on each side. The British effort had cost some 84,000 British casualties, 75,000 German casualties. The French suffered 187,000 casualties. When Nivelle ordered fresh attacks in late April mutinies broke out in a number of French divisions. Exhausted, hungry, demoralized men were no longer willing to *graisser ses bottes*—to die. Nivelle's newfound glory perished like the April snow in May sunshine. The French attempted to put as good a face on things as possible by keeping Nivelle in command during the Paris conference in early May, where it was decided that pressure must be kept on the enemy in anticipation of a large-scale British attack in the Ypres sector in late May.

Nivelle, who had been contemptuously dubbed *le beveur de sang*— the drinker of blood—was relieved in mid-May by his more cautious chief of staff, Henri Pétain. The fiery Ferdinand Foch, who had been put out to pasture along with Joffre, was recalled and appointed chief of staff to Pétain, which would ensure enduring conflict in the French supreme command.

The immediate result was a slackening of the offensive while Pétain put his army in order. This was no easy task. Mutiny continued to spread and would shortly infect fifty-nine divisions. The sordid story is well told in Richard Watt's splendid book, *Dare Call It Treason*. Pétain employed a carrot-and-stick approach to put things right. Ringleaders were ferreted out and shot. The French official history admits to fifty-five executions, but there were undoubtedly more; in addition, large numbers were deported to penal colonies. The bulk of the troops were won over by overdue reforms in food and leave and by an unwritten understanding that Pétain would not demand the inhuman sacrifices called for by Nivelle and earlier by Joffre. To his ally's dismay, Pétain pledged himself to carry out only "aggressive defensive" tactics—"the basis is to avoid losses and to await American reinforcements."[14]

Incredibly, the extreme seriousness of the affair was kept entirely secret from the enemy, which does not speak very well for German intelligence operations. It was largely kept secret from the British. Prime Minister Lloyd George was upset by rumors of French problems and repeatedly pressed Haig to confirm that Pétain would carry out the complementary attacks recently agreed on. Several meetings with Pétain convinced Haig of French good intentions. All but one of Haig's seniors accepted this happy fact. The doubting Thomas was Field Marshal Sir Henry Wilson, whose pessimistic warnings of Pétain's double-dealing were drowned in the flood of Haig's optimism.

* * *

Ludendorff was greatly relieved when the Allied offensive slackened. Although his armies were holding along the line, they had suffered tremendous losses in men and munitions which could not easily be re-placed. He had been forced to throw in every available reserve at a time when he expected a Russian attack in the east. In mid-April he had summoned Max Hoffmann to the OHL and was heartened to learn that "there were no signs of a possible Russian advance to be noticed as yet." The revolution had shaken the morale and the fighting power of the Russian army, Hoffmann continued, but it would still "be certain to defend itself" if attacked. Russia's defeat was much to be hoped for, they agreed, for only then could large numbers of German troops be transferred from east to west to force a breakthrough and "bring about the decisive battle of the campaign."[15]

In view of what eventually transpired, Hoffmann's next words are of the greatest interest. "We were both agreed that every means must be employed to attain this object. In answer to my question of when, and how, General Ludendorff proposed to make such an attack, he said that the thrust in the west could not be made as it could in the east. To break through in the west was much more difficult, and it would probably be necessary to try at various points, in order to find out where the enemy was weakest, and at which point an attack should be made with all our strength. I was not of that opinion, and I told him my mind quite freely. My opinion was, and I have not changed it, that there is only one form of tactics possible, however great or small the fighting power of the combatants may be. If you wish to take upon yourself the difficult decision of making an attack, you must concentrate all the forces you possibly can collect at the point you consider the most favorable for that object. This is, of course, a gamble—it is staking everything on a single card."[16]

The Allied attacks slowed but did not stop. After a comparatively calm May the British Second Army, commanded by General Sir Hubert Plumer, launched a massive diversionary attack on the German salient south of Ypres. After a lengthy bombardment he sprung one of the great tactical surprises of the war.

Since 1915 British sappers had been tunneling under the Messines Ridge to load nineteen galleries with almost one million pounds of high

explosives. A German observer watched with horror as nineteen enormous mushrooms "rose up slowly and majestically out of the ground and
then split into pieces with a mighty roar, sending up multicolored columns of flame mixed with a mass of earth and splinters into the sky."[17]

The explosion, felt in England, caused the Germans over twenty
thousand wounded and dead. The ground was still trembling when enemy
trenches were smothered by a barrage from 2,300 guns followed by an
assault of over eighty thousand British infantrymen supported by nearly
350 airplanes. Within a few hours the troops seized the tactically vital
Messines Ridge and soon claimed the entire salient to force the enemy
back to his main defensive line. The fighting continued for several days,
but the ridge was held at a cost of twenty-five thousand British casualties.

With that Plumer's task was finished. Haig could now open the
third battle of Ypres.

27

The Turnip Winter: Toward Military Dictatorship

. . . I'm just thinking back to the mood which I found people in at home: My impression is that they were depressed, but by no means in despair, and the mass of the nation are patiently putting up with everything as though it had never been any different.

> —LIEUTENANT HERBERT SULZBACH UPON RETURNING FROM LEAVE, DIARY ENTRY, JUNE 30, 1917[1]

The internal situation, influenced as it is by the external, I should sum up as follows: a growing war-weariness among all classes. Broad masses of our people have been looking forward to the prospect of peace in the autumn of this year.

> —PRINCE MAX OF BADEN TO COLONEL VON HAEFTEN, JULY 7, 1917[2]

. . . Germany took up arms to maintain her freedom and independence and to defend her territorial possessions. The Reichstag is striving for a peace by understanding and the permanent reconciliation of the nations. Annexations by force and political, economic and financial oppressions are incompatible with such a peace.

> —PEACE RESOLUTION OF THE GERMAN REICHSTAG, JULY 19, 1917[3]

T he Russian revolution so wholeheartedly desired by Hindenburg
and Ludendorff soon proved to be a two-edged weapon that raised
uncertain voices in the German government and Reichstag. If
revolution could break out in Russia, it was asked, why couldn't revolution break out in Germany? The British blockade, taken with a disastrous harvest and implementation of the unpopular auxiliary labor law,
had brought a winter of great discontent.

The "turnip winter" it was called. Heavy rains had badly damaged
the potato harvest. The flour ration had been reduced to seven ounces
a day. Meat and potatoes had been rationed since spring of 1916. An
American war correspondent, H. L. Mencken, may have downed "capital martini cocktails" in the American bar of the Hotel Adlon,[4] but the
average citizen was subsisting on 1,200 calories a day, "corresponding to
the needs of a two or three year old child."[5] Little remained to eat except
the sour *Rübe*. "We are all gaunt and bony now," the English-born Princess
Blücher noted, "and have dark shadows around our eyes, and our thoughts
are chiefly taken up with wondering what our next meal will be."[6]

People were cold and hungry and many died from malnutrition.
Threadbare clothes could not be replaced. There was no coal to heat
homes, no fuel for cook stoves, no oil to light lamps against long winter
nights. Theaters and music halls were cold, newspapers heavily censored,
libraries frequently closed. Restaurants offered the most meager of menus,
and they opened late and closed early. Each harvest had yielded significantly smaller quantities of wheat, oats, rye, sugar beets. Farmers lacked
fodder to feed diminishing herds, manure to invigorate tired soil, seeds
to plant. Government failure to control food prices and distribution had
created a flourishing black market. Some farmers and merchants grew
rich while people went hungry. A few fortunate persons continued to
live well, most did not. People grumbled, not only among themselves
but in letters to their loved ones at the front. "The heroic attitude has
entirely disappeared," Princess Blücher wrote. "Now one sees faces like
masks, blue with cold and drawn by hunger, with the harassed expression
common to all those who are continually speculating about the possibility
of another meal."[7] Hungry mothers and wives pathetically continued to
send *Liebesgaben*, love gifts of bits of their meager rations to their men
at the front, to the extent that in spring of 1917, the OHL directed unit
commanders to dissuade their troops from either asking for or accepting
food from home.[8]

People also wept as casualty lists soared. As of April 1917 over one million German soldiers had been killed, against total casualties of over four million. Although troop morale was still satisfactory, troop diet had become meager. No more was there thick soup with noodles and meat, bread and sausage. Bread was made of dried turnips and sawdust spread with a turnip paste called "Hindenburg fat." Front-line soldiers ate a goulash of horsemeat mixed with "dried vegetables, mostly carrots, cabbage leaves, turnips, peas and even stinging nettles." Troops called the mobile kitchens "goulash guns" and the dried vegetables "barbed-wire entanglements."[9]

Doubts as to the purpose of the war had steadily been growing in front-line trenches. As early as January 1915 the excitement of a crusade had yielded to the cruelty of the battlefield. Kurt Rohrbach, a twenty-two-year-old theological student fighting in Flanders, complained in mid-1915 that "this awful war has actually made an old man out of me. . . . Everybody who looks daily into the cold eye of death, and gazes on so many dead faces bearing the stamp of suffering and renunciation, becomes certainly callous, but also old, very old."[10] A nineteen-year-old law student, Friedrich Oehme, wrote five months before his death: "One does become older and graver out here. . . . So much that I used to look up to is now dragged in the mire; so much that used to seem glorious and splendid is proved to be foul and bad. The veil which, for the young, used to cover all that was evil, and which, in ordinary times, is only gradually raised as a man grows older, has now, with one wrench, been torn violently away from the eyes of us schoolboy War-Volunteers. Abominable things are revealed, and the contrast horrifies us."[11]

Our young artilleryman, Herbert Sulzbach, had found that he could no longer sing. "I can't help it: the gay and easy mood has worn off, even for me," he wrote. Yet, a few months later, in June 1917 and now a lieutenant training officer cadets, he was enthralled with "the lessons learned from the latest defense battles. Every order, every instruction, breathes the spirit of Ludendorff." (Back in combat two months later he wrote in his diary: "Sometimes one has a feeling that one will never be able to laugh again.")[12] Herbert Zschuppe, a nineteen-year-old philosophy student who had been wounded, could not stay away from the war. "I have reported fit for service," he wrote a few days before his death. "I am restless. . . . I should like to push the landscape aside as if it irritated me. I must get to the Front. I must again hear the shells roaring up into the sky and the desolate valley echoing the sound. I must go back to my Company. . . . I must get back into touch with the enemy,

I know far too well what the danger is, but I must live once more in the realm of death."[13]

Poets and writers caught the changing mood. The heroic poems of 1914 had given way to "a poetry of faith and introversion" and were steadily becoming more factual and realistic (before changing to "resignation or even disgust").[14] Walter Flex, twenty-seven years old in 1914, had shared the enthusiasm of a friend, Ernst Wursche, for war. Shortly before his death on the eastern front in autumn of 1915, Wursche had told Flex that "for men of great sensitivity, death is the greatest experience."[15] Crushed by his friend's death, Flex concluded that human sacrifice could only be acceptable if it were for supreme moral values, as opposed to crass annexationist aims—the theme of a slender novel published in 1917 that would sell 250,000 copies in less than two years. Fritz von Unruh, who had found in the war "the beginning of a new zest for life," turned an account of the Verdun fighting commissioned by the OHL into an antiwar novel, Opfergang (The Way of Sacrifice), that was suppressed because "of its revolutionary overtones."[16] Ernst Jünger, on the other hand, remained true to his martial mistress, becoming a company commander who by war's end would carry the scars of fourteen wounds and would wear the prestigious Pour le mérite. Some, perhaps a great many officers and men still shared Jünger's enthusiasm. The American journalist H. L. Mencken reported in early 1917 that "Ludendorff's portrait hangs in every mess room, he is the god of every young lieutenant . . . he is, as it were, the esoteric Ulysses of the war."[17] Others, however, were writing to people at home, not protesting so much the daily sacrifices of life in the trenches as wondering what the ultimate purpose was, when it would be achieved, and in some cases questioning the terrible cost in lives.

The war was expensive in more than lives. During 1917 it was costing 3 billion marks a month. Bank notes in circulation amounted to some 13 billion marks, up over 10 billion since August 1914 and far above treasury credits. The internal public debt of Germany and her allies was creeping toward the astronomical sum of 150 billion marks (about $37 billion).[18] Some newspapers were calling for an end to the war, as were some liberal legislators in the Reichstag. The government was under heavy fire, not least because of Zimmermann's idiocy. "And how can we afford to stand with Mexico in war and peace?" a leading socialist, Eduard David, demanded in the Reichstag. "By thus seeking to engage ourselves, our diplomacy has been made the laughing stock of the world."[19]

The auxiliary labor law had backfired. The scheme might have worked had human beings been pegs to put into round or square holes. This not being the case, it was doomed to fail. Numerous eligible workers evaded its call by one deceit or another. Ensnared workers could do little more than complain to their councils when placed in the wrong jobs. The trade unions and the Social Democrats were soon complaining about harsh employer practices of what they termed the "forced labor law." To their surprise, General Groener, head of the *Kriegsamt*, sympathized with them. Union leaders soon recognized the quiet Württemberger's fair-minded approach and in turn often tried to cooperate with him. Industrialists and the war ministry complained to the OHL that the *Kriegsamt* was exceeding its authority. Groener in turn objected to the OHL's interference in the economic sphere, and he also began to clash frequently with interior district corps commanders, who ruled their areas like feudal fiefdoms.

The shortcomings of the new law, coupled with government's failure to control wages and profits, produced a number of uncomfortable side effects. Unskilled workers in war plants received much higher pay than front-line soldiers, who soon were bitterly complaining. Troops employed in lines-of-communication duties worked alongside more highly paid civilians and naturally enough resented it. Soldier-specialists who were brought home to work in factories and mines for civilian pay and then returned to the front did not easily accept army pay. Ludendorff, who had welcomed the law, soon deemed it "not merely insufficient, but positively harmful in operation."[20]

Belgian and Polish workers had been early recruited to shore up the labor market. Belgium was not only being ruthlessly exploited internally, including a monthly payment of forty million francs to Germany, but from mid-1915 to late 1916 about five hundred Belgian workers per week had been sent to German ammunition plants. Others, including women and teenagers of both sexes, had been forced to work on fortifications and roads behind the fronts in Belgium and France. German industrialists wanted still more bodies. Pressed by the industrialists, Ludendorff notified the military governors of Belgium and Poland that "social and legal considerations should be regarded as secondary" in recruiting workers. The governor general of Belgium, General Baron von Bissing, argued that forced deportation would be counterproductive, but finally agreed to meet Ludendorff's new quota of 200,000 workers, which the *Kriegsamt* would mete out to German war industries. The chancellor, who had opposed the plan all along, as usual caved in, later blaming "the argument of *military necessity*" for his decision.[21] Suitable Belgian males were summarily rounded up and sent in cattle cars to Germany, often to arrive half-starved and frozen to live on meager rations in former prisoner-of-war compounds turned into labor camps.

The result was another Ludendorff failure. Almost a third of the deportees were physically unfit, and those who survived had to be sent back to Belgium. There were not nearly enough jobs for the new bodies, who continued to consume precious rations, however meager. Those employed were reluctant to work, and their constant grumbling because of dreadful living conditions and because they drew military pay while working next to German civilians drawing much higher wages soon told on the morale of the German workers. Sickness and cold exacted a grievous number of deaths. Protests came from the United States and many other countries concerning this blatant violation of the Hague agreement on the laws of land warfare. The Allied powers won an enormous propaganda victory by widely denouncing German use of slave labor—see what will happen if the *Boches* win the war—and it was also privately denounced, at least in part, by the German chancellor and foreign ministry, publicly by liberal elements within Germany to widen further the rifts between military, government, and people. Although Bethmann successfully countered the Duo's determined effort to take direct control of the occupied areas, the mass deportations continued into the new year. Over sixty thousand more persons had been brought to Germany when Ludendorff abruptly terminated the program in February 1917. The survivors were returned to Belgium, but the occupied territories continued to be supplied with forced labor.[22]

Ironically, as Groener had soon realized and as Ludendorff finally agreed, the key to Germany's economic problems was not so much an increased labor force as it was better distribution. Hundreds of factories were hobbled by lack of coal, yet thousands of tons of coal were piled at mineheads, victim of frozen waterways and a shortage of rail transport. German defense plants needed 33,000 carloads of coal daily, and for months had been receiving only 22,000. Poor-quality lubricants that failed to work in cold weather damaged already deteriorating locomotives. Rolling stock was rapidly wearing out and could not be replaced. Shell quality had deteriorated because of copper and steel shortages. There was almost no rubber, and oil could not come from Romania until sabotaged wells and refineries had been repaired.

The result was catastrophic. The Duo soon slashed by half its grandiose demands for shells and weapons. Industrialists were complaining to the OHL, the OHL and the war ministry were blaming Groener and the *Kriegsamt*, and Groener was kicking whatever dog he could find.

The real villain, of course, was the military, which had taken on a task foreign to its skills. Almost everything Ludendorff had touched turned to ashes. His labor program was unmitigated disaster. His construction program resulted in a mass of unneeded factories that only hindered production. The OHL had relied on the army's "traditional popularity" in allowing it to enter into politics, technical affairs, and the national economy, so complained one official. Failure only increased the army's conceit and its unwillingness to relinquish or even modify its extraordinary powers.

Ludendorff and Hindenburg's solution to the crisis was to increase the army's power. But first a scapegoat had to be found. Ludendorff all along had blamed the chancellor for having let the government run out of control. It followed that the chancellor would have to go.

Chancellor Bethmann Hollweg was in part responsible for the chaotic state of affairs. The root of the trouble was the Bismarckian concept of constitutional monarchy, which called for a strong chancellor to compensate for a weak monarch while keeping autocratic government unsullied by democratic interference. A weak chancellor needed either a strong or a popular monarch to ease the task of government by keeping it generally independent of military control.

Adversity had increased neither the German kaiser's strength nor popularity. His wartime performance to date had made a mockery of his longing to be accepted as "the people's ruler." He wanted as little to do with the people as possible. Members of his entourage were exasperated by his luxurious lifestyle, his hypochondria, his childish highs and lows, champagne dinners for victory, gloom for defeat, monologues that grew more tiresome as the kaiser retreated to the unsafe ground of his unsure self.

The empire was veering toward the "turnip winter" when Wilhelm announced after a bountiful dinner that he "intended to reform society in Berlin after the war. The members of the aristocracy are to build palaces for themselves once more. He will forbid parties being given in hotels. He then proceeded to read us an article on the need for encouraging motor-racing in Berlin."[23] Against the wishes of his advisers, he retired to the isolated Neue Palais in Potsdam, where Hindenburg was forced to report to him daily until Ludendorff summarily ended the nonsense by substituting a staff officer for the chief of the general staff.

After dinner one night during the "turnip winter" he commented favorably on a report from one of his East Prussian gamekeepers, who proposed to buy rutabagas "for the better development of the stags' antlers." On another winter's evening he "read out a long thesis . . . on the eagle as heraldic beast." He was finally persuaded to leave Potsdam and join the OHL in its move to Bad Kreuznach. He detested the place, "that pestilential hole," and spent most of his time enjoying the "extravagant food and host of servants" in his court at Bad Homburg, which soon became "a constant source of irritation to the public." Pressed by his military chief, General von Lyncker, to return to Kreuznach, he protested, "What is there for me to do at Kreuznach? I am only Hindenburg's adjutant and I have nothing to say." Little wonder that he was rapidly being left out in the cold by army and government, "not because he abandoned his rights," in Admiral von Müller's harsh judgment, "but because he has failed in his duty."[24]

The kaiser's weakness had greatly enhanced the Duo's strength. The efficient Max Bauer had orchestrated an attack designed to eliminate Bethmann in favor of a military dictatorship under Hindenburg and Ludendorff. The OHL used its invidious censorship weapon by passing articles that censured Bethmann's government while forbidding any that attempted to defend it. In February 1917 representatives of the conservative parties had gathered in the Hotel Adlon in Berlin to hear Matthias Erzberger's arguments for replacing Bethmann with Hindenburg. The Adlon Action Group, composed of leaders of heavy industry and extreme political rightists, henceforth continued to attack the chancellor as, in Bauer's term, "the obedient instrument of the Left,"[25] an effort actively supported by Walther Nicolai's army propaganda machine.

Other segments of society also closed in on the chancellor as conditions worsened in the homeland. Whatever he did was bound to draw criticism. One of the most divisive issues that he faced, electoral reform, had been a contentious subject before the war. The root of the problem was a restricted Prussian franchise, a three-class electoral system based on personal wealth, thus guaranteeing a conservative Landtag. To impose universal suffrage in Prussian elections would threaten and possibly terminate conservative dominance in Prussia and empire to open the way to true parliamentary government. The issue had cropped up from time to time during the war, but it reappeared seriously only with the breakdown of the Burgfriede. Socialist members of the Reichstag were now threatening to bring about a political revolution if the reforms were not made. When the Landtag rebuffed Bethmann's suggestion of voluntary reform, he turned directly to the kaiser, who finally agreed to promise *postwar* electoral reforms in his Easter message of early April.

The speech surprised and enraged Hindenburg and Ludendorff. Middle-line liberals applauded, while conservatives cursed. A war-weary, apathetic public seemed more interested in bread than in votes. A week after the kaiser's somewhat meaningless gesture, the flour ration went from seven to six ounces a day, which brought a strike at the Kiel shipyards. Radical socialists formed a new, much more militant party, the Independent Social Democrats, whose aims were but a stone's throw from those of the communists, who, led by Karl Leibknecht and Rosa Luxemburg, formed a party that would become famous as the Spartacists. *

In mid-April the more radical socialist members of the Reichstag traveled to Stockholm to join their brethren from other countries in embracing Lenin's Bolshevik demand for peace without annexations or reparations. This resulted in publication of a socialist peace manifesto in Germany's leading socialist newspaper at the height of a widespread "hunger strike" of Berlin munition workers. The manifesto called for "peace without annexations and indemnities . . . on the basis of the free national development of all peoples."[26]

While Max Bauer advertised this as the work of socialist and Jewish liberals, Hindenburg demanded that the kaiser dismiss Bethmann on grounds that he had lost control of the Reichstag. Valentini's spirited arguments against a change of chancellors at this time made him another marked man in the clandestine war for control of Germany's destiny. The kaiser as usual veered first one way then the other before finally calling an imperial conference at Kreuznach in late April. This produced little more than a formal statement of the OHL's war aims so exaggerated that Valentini and Müller called it "puerile" while Bethmann regarded it as "pipe dreams" that eventually would have to be punctured.[27]

Imperial indecision had given Bethmann breathing space. The question was: could he hold on long enough to save Germany from a military dictatorship?

---

* Named after a Thracian slave, Spartacus, who led an uprising of gladiators in ancient Rome that resulted in a costly two-year war before he was finally killed in battle.

28

---•---

The Duo Overturns the Chancellor

I feel much calmer with [Chancellor] Michaelis at the helm.
I no longer have to worry about things that should not concern me.
> —FIELD MARSHAL VON HINDENBURG TO HIS WIFE,
> JULY 24, 1917[1]

We separated after our first meeting with the chancellor [Mi-
chaelis] under such a cloud of depression that even Bethmann
Hollweg's friends failed to derive any satisfaction from the
embarrassment of his opponents.
> —VICE CHANCELLOR FRIEDRICH VON PAYER[2]

The OHL's inflated war aims, that is, the aims not only of the general staff but of the bulk of German conservatives and a good many moderates, could only have been realized by a German military victory. Hopes for just that, and no later than the end of July 1917, were running high at the OHL in April. Ship sinkings by submarines had passes the million-ton mark that month and were rising steadily; the western front was holding; the Russians were in disarray. Admiral Capelle told the Reichstag that "I am fully and firmly convinced that the war will end by October."[3] Hindenburg remarked in a private conversation that Germany had become so strong on the western front "as to stand up to any attack."[4]

Euphoria continued into May as intelligence reported increasing concern in Allied capitals.[5] Ludendorff, who had coldly received Count Bernstorff, Germany's recent ambassador to the United States, in early May, informed him that only that morning "he had received very definite information that England could, under no conditions, prosecute the war for more than three months longer, and this, on account of the shortage of foodstuffs."[6]

At a champagne dinner in late May, the kaiser "suddenly rose to his feet and said: 'General Ludendorff has just reported to me that the [Allied] spring offensive at Arras, on the Aisne, and in Champagne has been defeated. We have gained a famous victory.' "[7] Ludendorff haughtily informed the government that since time was on the side of Germany, the OHL wanted nothing to do with "modest" peace terms.[8] Hindenburg told the chancellor that "fortress Germany" must use the forthcoming peace "to prepare as soon as possible for the next defensive war, which must inevitably occur. Food, fodder, and raw materials sufficient for at least three years had to be stockpiled, a necessity that must be considered once peace is established."[9]

The kaiser was so elated that he drew up his own list of war aims to which he daily added new fantasies. Even Bethmann, in a major speech to the Reichstag in mid-May, stated that "Germany's military situation had never been more favorable" and implied that the government was in full agreement with the OHL's war aims.[10] Austria-Hungary's new foreign minister, Count Czernin, was obviously impressed with the ebullient mood at Kreuznach when he matched the OHL's acquisition fantasies with a long list of his own.

The euphoria was short-lived. Austria-Hungary, on verge of internal collapse, was soon demanding peace on a quid pro ante basis, "a peace with honor" as Czernin put it, and was in almost open conflict with Ludendorff's annexationist policy in the Baltic which would turn the entire area into a German colony.[11] Emperor Charles, prompted by Empress Zita, was holding secret peace talks with her brother, the Bourbon Prince Sixtus, regarding a separate peace with Italy. Turkey, also in straitened circumstances, was demanding peace. Despite the happy prognostications of the German admirals, England seemed no closer to collapse than ever, at least judging from the militant statements of her leaders and her continued battlefield performance.

Ship sinkings in May dropped in both the Atlantic and the Mediterranean, thanks to an efficient convoy system, various deceptive measures, improved listening devices, antimine devices such as the paravane, and long-distance aerial bombing. Improved countertactics by British submarines brought an increase in German submarine sinkings, as did improved mines. Not only had the hated British blockade not been broken, but fewer neutral ships were reaching Danish, Dutch, and Swedish ports with vital raw materials and foodstuffs intended for further transit to Germany—an unlooked-for side effect of the submarine offensive. The submarine effort in the Mediterranean, where thirty German U-boats were operating, had been hindered by Ludendorff's insistence on secondary operations such as landing agents and supplies for Turkish supporters in Tripoli and interdicting shipping off the Palestine coast. As a result, sinkings throughout the Mediterranean had proved disappointing, with the monthly figures steadily dropping.[12]

Nor, thanks to primitive railways and local corruptions, was the fecund production of Romania's breadbasket reaching Germany in desired quantities. Polish independence had also backfired. It had aroused resentment in Vienna, where conservative parties had anticipated large postwar land gains. Russian authorities adroitly exploited the German political initiative to raise the hatred of Germany to new heights. Beseler's optimistic promise of five Polish volunteer divisions with a million recruits to follow proved empty, "a sorry failure" in Ludendorff's later words. Russian Poles refused to be recruited. Only a trickle of volunteers joined the weak Polish Legion.[13]

The Duo's solution to internal problems, the Hindenburg Program, was largely a failure by spring of 1917. The Reichstag was rapidly tearing itself into irreparable factions, the workers were in the streets shouting for bread.

In April the OHL had been looking for victory by the end of July. In mid-June it was a different story. The Duo now listened to Lieutenant Colonel Haeften's fanciful proposal for "a political offensive" against England (France being "irreconcilable") that would lead to "a peace of understanding."[14]

Although the OHL was certain that the submarine campaign would ultimately bring victory, Hindenburg warned the chancellor not to expect an early end to the war. The enemy "is counting on the collapse of Germany and her allies before its own. It perhaps hopes for a military victory on land, but above all it expects it from economic and internal political causes, that is, shortages of food and raw materials, dissension, discontent, and the victory of German Radical Socialist Democrats. They base this expectation on the decline of our morale, the growth of international sentiments, our food situation and the desire for peace that is unfortunately loudly proclaimed from many sides."

Having told the chancellor little of value, Hindenburg continued in the OHL's attempt to shift military failure onto civilian shoulders: "A strengthening of our internal spirit would be the most rapid way to convince our enemies that prolonging the war will endanger their way of life to the point of destruction. On the other hand, every complaint of disappointed expectations, every sign of exhaustion and longing for peace on the part of us and our allies, any talk of the alleged impossibility of surviving a further winter campaign, can only ensure the prolonging of the war."[15]

Bethmann agreed with the necessity of maintaining the nation's moral resolution, but also stressed the seriousness of the submarine campaign. A reported increase in sinkings for June, however, brought a change of heart, and he was now convinced of the "ultimate success" of the submarine offensive.[16]

Toward the end of June, Bethmann received the new papal nuncio, Monsignor Pacelli (the future Pope Pius XII), who delivered a letter from Pope Benedict XV to the kaiser. Benedict had early involved himself in the war and had been instrumental in arranging for the exchange of prisoners of war, the repatriation of captured civilians, and improved living conditions in prisoner-of-war camps at home and abroad. He now offered to mediate a peace. What terms, Pacelli asked, would be acceptable to Germany, particularly as regarded Belgium and Alsace-Lorraine?

Bethmann informally assured him that Germany would agree to full restoration of Belgian sovereignty providing France and England were prevented from economically and militarily dominating Belgium at Germany's expense. He also believed that the future of Alsace-Lorraine could be satisfactorily negotiated with France. German war aims in Russia could not be discussed because of the existent political chaos due to the revolution. Bethmann's qualified renunciation of claims on Belgium particularly pleased Pacelli, since it opened the way for the pope's further mediation.

This was Bethmann's last effort to bring about a peace that neither the Central nor the Allied powers wanted. At this point he had clearly transcended his limitations. Old, sick in body and mind, long face drawn, nerves shot, fingers stained brown from chain-smoked cigarettes, his spirit crushed by imperial apathy to the Duo's smear campaign, he resembled little more than a living corpse. By trying to satisfy everyone he had satisfied no one. His peace policy was confused and contradictory, his domestic policy a shambles. His government by compromise, what he called "a policy of the diagonal," had failed. Hindenburg and Ludendorff,

supported by bankers, industrialists, politicians, most of the kaiser's entourage, the empress, the crown prince and their adherents, and most
of the officer corps were against him. The kaiser, once firm in his support,
was visibly nervous as it became increasingly obvious that either the
chancellor or the Duo would have to go.

The one institution that could possibly have saved him, the Reichstag, was largely disillusioned with his vacillating performances. Count
Kuno von Westarp, an extreme conservative, regarded him as "lacking
in efficiency and resolution . . . [and] quite unfitted to conduct the
business of government."[17] Gustav Streseman, a Pan-German and leader
of the National Liberals, held that "he never takes responsibility, has
no ideas and lets everything slide. Everyone has the impression that he
fails in everything, and that we are bound to collapse."[18] A moderate
socialist, Eduard David, described him as a "shilly-shallying bureaucrat
clinging to office for dear life" while trying to stymie the OHL's political
plotting.[19]

The Reichstag was growing increasingly fractious and restive. In
early July Admiral Capelle began to back away from the navy's optimistic
promises. In full uniform with clanking sword he told the parliamentarians that although there were "no grounds for doubting the military results
of submarine warfare," the empire must nevertheless be prepared for "a
lengthy war." An unbelieving socialist, Gustav Hoch, protested that the
submarine campaign had failed. "We have now exhausted our strength.
We are in the midst of revolution. . . . Confidence in the government
has gone, and it cannot be resurrected."[20] His words were soon emphasized by stirrings in the surface fleet, "refusal to obey orders, mass desertions, hunger strikes and acts of sabotage" that would culminate in a
mutiny of five thousand sailors, of whom five would be shot and others
sentenced to long terms of hard labor.[21]

And now the leader of the Social Democrats, Friedrich Ebert, demanded a firm peace offensive from the government, along with more
specific electoral reforms that would give Germany a parliamentary constitution. On July 6 Matthias Erzberger, the peripatetic busybody politician of the Center party, in an extraordinary turnaway from hawkish
behavior, quoted impressive figures to a select committee of the Reichstag
to prove that unrestricted submarine warfare had not and could not
succeed—in short, Germany could not win the war and must seek peace
by yielding her claims on the occupied territories. This startling truism
prompted Social Democrats, Progressives, Centrists and National Liberals to form a "peace resolution majority" that was determined to send

a message to the world. Bethmann's argument that a second peace initiative was not in Germany's best interests—Brusilov's new Russian offensive had opened a week earlier—was overruled. "The Reichstag strives for a peace of understanding and the permanent reconciliation of peoples," so read the motion. "Forced territorial acquisitions and political, economic or financial oppressions are irreconcilable with such a peace . . ."[22]

These momentous events were reported to Hindenburg and Ludendorff by minions such as Max Bauer, Hans von Haeften, and Walther Nicolai, who maintained an army of informants inside government and Reichstag. The minister of war, von Stein, urged the Duo to come to Berlin to discuss the military aspect of the Reichstag's action with the kaiser. Wilhelm, who had just returned from Vienna, was already depressed when Bethmann apprised him of the situation. Annoyed by the Duo's appearance in Berlin without his permission, he received them coldly, refused to discuss politics, gave them dinner and sent them back to Kreuznach to run the war.

Hindenburg and Ludendorff were not to be so easily put off, and their fury increased when Bethmann approved the resolution (which they had not read). At Stein's instigation, Hindenburg telegraphed the kaiser to protest strongly the Reichstag's acceptance of the resolution, "which must be regarded as a peace of renunciation. I must offer the most serious objections to such a declaration, as it would intensify the existing unrest in the army and would be regarded as a sign of internal weakness at the present moment."[23] Bauer meanwhile had called Crown Prince Wilhelm to Berlin to back up the OHL's war on Bethmann. In an unprecedented violation of imperial protocol, the crown prince invited six influential Reichstag members, all but one (Friedrich von Payer) in opposition to the chancellor, to his palace for individual consultation, during which Bauer remained behind a screen taking notes. Thus armed, the crown prince reported to his father that Bethmann must go.

The two were discussing the matter in the Berlin palace when Bethmann joined them. Bethmann presented the draft resolution, which the kaiser immediately telephoned to Hindenburg at Kreuznach. Hindenburg shortly returned the call to propose some alterations, which were accepted. But now Ludendorff persuaded Hindenburg not to suffer this insult—he himself was going to resign. Hindenburg did a smart about-face and that evening informed the kaiser that he and Ludendorff were resigning and that the rest of the OHL would follow suit because they no longer felt that they could work with the chancellor. The kaiser greeted this insubordinate blackmail with the bitter observation that "this kind of behavior on the part of Prussian generals had never been heard of in the history of Prussia."[24] Determined to clear the air, he summoned the Duo to Berlin for a conference with Bethmann.

Bethmann had had enough. He had lost the support of the Reichstag. He realized not only that the Duo's widespread popularity made it impossible to stand against their machinations, but also that the kaiser would continue to give way in debasement of the imperial concept that was handed down in Bismarck's constitution and that had survived even the onslaughts of the military up to now. Bethmann resigned before Hindenburg and Ludendorff reached the capital. Despite Valentini's impassioned arguments, the kaiser accepted it, but without joy. "I am obliged to discharge the man who towers above all the others," he complained to Valentini,[25] without of course realizing that, by forging a new power brokerage between the OHL and the Reichstag, he had signed his own death warrant. Although Bethmann judged the method of his dismissal as "unworthy," he had no desire to contest it: "Indeed, I feel a serenity of soul that I have not known for many years," he informed a friend.[26]

The kaiser personally greeted the Duo with the news. Their own resignations were not further discussed. Wilhelm later told his entourage that he had been very forceful with them—but that is open to doubt.

Who would replace Bethmann?

The list was not long. No one had given much thought to it, least of all the prime destroyer, Ludendorff. Lyncker and Valentini leafed through almanacs and directories with the fervor of Diogenes looking for an honest man and with the same result. Hindenburg, prompted by the conservative Adlon Group, had on several occasions proposed Prince von Bülow to the kaiser, scarcely a judicious notion, since Wilhelm would never forgive his prewar chancellor for his part in the Daily Telegraph affair. Count Hertling, the prime minister of Bavaria, was Bethmann's candidate, but Hertling saw the futility of trying to play liontamer to Hindenburg and Ludendorff and wisely turned down the office on grounds that he was too old and tired. Rudolf von Valentini opted for Bernstorff, the recent German ambassador to the United States, who was anathema to the Duo because of his determined opposition to unrestricted submarine warfare. Grand Admiral von Tirpitz had made too many enemies to be seriously considered, particularly by the Duo, who did not want to contend against a strong man and an admiral at that.

In the event, General von Plessen proposed Georg Michaelis, who was unknown to the kaiser. Old and deaf, "small, slender, insignificant looking, dressed in a tightly fitting diplomatic suit,"[27] an undersecretary charged with food administration in the Prussian ministry of commerce, he was neither experienced nor informed in internal politics or foreign affairs. Ludendorff heartily endorsed the proposal, apparently because "Michaelis once contradicted him with spirit,"[28] as did Hindenburg, who believed that he would bring "clarity and firmness" into play—"he is such a decent, God-fearing man, that I accepted him in God's name."[29] Hindenburg wrote to his wife a few days later that "I feel much calmer with Michaelis at the helm. I no longer have to worry about things that should not concern me."[30]

The appointment surprised Michaelis, who consulted his Moravian prayer book to read the daily message: "Do not fear and be dismayed, for the Lord, your God, will be with you in everything you do."[31] So assured, he accepted the appointment, which he mistakenly believed was a compromise acceptable to both the Reichstag and the OHL. Important Reichstag leaders such as Gustav Streseman and Matthias Erzberger had not even been consulted. Michaelis himself had not read the peace resolution, nor was he apparently aware of the intense quarrel between the Reichstag and the OHL. As for the rest, he told a friend, "I have been so busy that I have really done little more than jog along beside the ship of state."[32] The vice chancellor, Friedrich von Payer, later wrote: "We separated after our first meeting with the chancellor under such a cloud of depression that even Bethmann Hollweg's friends failed to derive any satisfaction from the embarrassment of his opponents."[33]

A day prior to Michaelis's appointment, the Duo had raised the flag of OHL supremacy in political affairs by summoning parliamentary majority leaders to general-staff headquarters in Berlin for what Hindenburg and Ludendorff called a conference, but what Philipp Scheidemann of the Social Democrats termed a "military cross-examination."[34] Some parliamentarians were nevertheless reassured by Ludendorff's positive attitude concerning the war and did not seem to realize that they were participating in a serious humiliation for the German government, the Reichstag, and, indirectly, the people.

Ludendorff reviewed the current military situation, "serious but secure." He spoke of improved ammunition supply, sufficiency of raw materials, and a successful submarine campaign. The main purpose of the conference was to protest against the passage of the peace resolution, "since it was bound to exercise an adverse influence on the spirit of the troops and on the determination of the people, while the enemy would construe it as a confession of weakness."[35]

The unprecedented meeting did not achieve its purpose, nor did Ludendorff's heavy-handed attempt succeed in suppressing publication of the draft resolution in the leading socialist newspaper. The Duo subsequently, if grudgingly, agreed to a final draft in which, at Hindenburg's insistence, the army was praised for its valiant efforts.

Michaelis next took the resolution to the full Reichstag. After making his position clear, "I do not consider a body like the German Reichstag a fit one to decide about peace and war on its own initiative during the war . . . ," he turned to the matter at hand, stressing the need for a peace that was entirely favorable to Germany.[36] The resolution was carried without difficulty, but it was something of a Pyrrhic victory. Michaelis subsequently informed the crown prince: "My interpretation took from it all its dangers. When the time comes the resolution will allow us to conclude any peace we like."[37]

29

Civilian and Military Reactions and the Third Battle of Ypres

The "Hundred Days of Michaelis" are among those epochs of
the war on which one must look back with bitterness.
—Prince Max of Baden, last chancellor of the
Wilhelmine German Empire[1]

The Russian attack so feared by Ludendorff in April began on the
first day of July 1917. Considering Russia's condition, the army
torn with dissension, many soldiers lacking rifles, a collapsing
home front and tottering government, it was remarkable that Kerensky
dared support the offensive so strongly urged by Britain and France—a
massive effort that stretched from Riga on the Baltic to the Carpathian
mountains. It nowhere achieved surprise. OberOst had known of the
plan for weeks. Max Hoffmann had even drawn up plans for a counteroffensive, for which Ludendorff was reluctantly sending him six divisions
from the western front. "I sit and wait as children wait for Father Christmas," Hoffmann noted, "[wondering] if the Russians will ever attack.
But we have no luck."[2]

The major Russian success occurred in East Galicia, where Brusilov,
attacking toward Lemberg, broke through a long front held by tired
and demoralized Austro-Hungarians, who surrendered in droves. "They
are really impossible . . . ," Hoffman wrote angrily in mid-July. "Not
content with running away, they lie and send false reports, and with it
all they are quite unashamed, and make difficulties whenever they can.

I should like to go to war with *them*."[3] Although Brusilov advanced thirty miles, he lacked reserves to exploit the breakthrough, which was quickly contained by reserve divisions sent from OberOst. A Russian attack against Count von Bothmer's *Südarmee* failed to make any progress nor did other attacks in the north. By mid-July the Russian offensive was finished.

Hoffmann meanwhile was moving his newly acquired divisions into the area between Zoboroth and the Sereth River, his intention to attack southeast toward Tarnopol. The troops moved out on July 19, smashed through Russian lines on a twelve-mile front to push forward up to nine miles on the first day. Tarnopol fell six days later, which forced the enemy to begin a retreat that triggered retreats along the line all the way to the Bukovina. By early August the Russians had fallen back beyond Czernowitz on a wide front. Further gains depended on fighting in the south, but neither Archduke Joseph's Austro-Hungarians south of Czernowitz nor Mackensen's army group in Romania was able to make significant progress.

Although Hoffmann was delighted to win a battle "in a style I could scarcely have dreamed of" and was obviously pleased when the kaiser personally awarded him the Pour le mérite,[4] Ludendorff was disappointed with the overall result. Russia and Romania had to be knocked out of the war as soon as possible "in order to enable us to force a decision in the west in 1918 by means of an attack on France combined with the submarine war, in case the latter should not achieve the desired result by itself."[5] A major attack through Moldavia against the Romanians, whose army had been significantly improved by French advisers, was impossible until inadequate railways had been improved.

More feasible was a move against the Russians in the north. During the Galician fighting, Ludendorff had proposed a crossing of the Dvina River above Riga to Max Hoffmann, who enthusiastically endorsed the plan. The offensive could not be opened until German divisions fighting in the south were transferred north, which Ludendorff calculated would be in late August. It was to be a limited operation "merely intended as a means to a wholesale improvement of our position which would enable us to economize troops." Ludendorff nevertheless expected "great results" because of the proximity to Petrograd, whose citizens were already shaken by the revolution. The operation should be completed by mid to late September, which would free the divisions for transfer once again to the south "to commence operations from the Bukovina across the Sereth River into Moldavia" in order to fall on the Romanians.[6]

An uncomfortable lull had followed the British capture of Messines Ridge in early June. Lloyd George's reservations concerning a new Ypres offensive, delay in the arrival of troop replacements, the usual supply problems, French reluctance inspired by inability to honor previous commitments, and, not least, British command confusion let the weeks slip by.

As it turned out, Lloyd George was correct in his fears of another unproductive bloodbath. Douglas Haig did not see it that way. He had long wanted to seize the Flemish ports Ostend and Zeebrugge, which harbored German submarines, a strategic desire persuasively backed by the Royal Navy, which for several months had been fighting for its life. Haig had also learned that a rash of mutinies had left the French army in extremis, a possible even probable target for a major German blow in the south. On the other hand his intelligence chief, Brigadier John Charteris, had persuaded him that the enemy army and home front were rapidly deteriorating. In early June Haig had informed his army commanders: "After careful consideration of all available information I feel justified in stating that the power of endurance of the German people is being strained to such a degree as to make it possible that the breaking point may be reached this year. . . ."[7] Unfortunately for British arms, Charteris never saw the wood for the trees, and he had a peculiar habit, dangerous for one of his profession, of reporting favorable indications while keeping the bad news to himself.

So it was that Haig remained forcefully optimistic to the extent that the government gave in. Haig's plan had not substantially changed since his meeting with Pétain at Amiens. In essence, his armies were to attack northeast, gain the ridges from south of Gheluvelt to north of Passchendaele and continue on to Roulers. Once enemy lines of communication had been broken, his armies would wheel to the west and, in conjunction with coastal and amphibious forces, fall on the Flemish ports, which Haig and the Royal Navy mistakenly assumed were vital to enemy submarine operations.[8]

For unknown reasons Haig shunted Sir Herbert Plumer's Second Army, the victors of Messines Ridge, to his right flank, replacing it with Sir Hubert Gough's Fifth Army with General Anthoine's French First Army on the left. Gough would fight on eight miles of an eighteen-mile front. Gough made the fatal mistake of changing the planned axis of advance from northeast to north, thus away from the all-important Gheluvelt Ridge, a fundamental change either overlooked or tolerated by Haig who nevertheless kept emphasizing that seizure of this ridge on Gough's right was the key to the operation.

Delay followed delay throughout July. Preliminary artillery bombardment finally opened in mid-month to be furiously answered by German guns, but Haig continued to be optimistic. His chief artillery officer assured him of artillery supremacy and Gough's corps commanders seemed confident. The day before the infantry attack Haig's air officer, Major General Hugh Trenchard, reported enemy air driven from the sky. Now the tanks were in position east of Ypres. Colonel J.F.C. Fuller, chief of staff of the tank corps, thought the operation was madness considering the wet ground, but his opinion went unheeded. Charteris, despite private forebodings of severe rains, gave the intelligence go-ahead.

The rains opened on July 30 to turn the flat wasteland into a sea of mud. A twenty-year-old British poet, Edmund Blunden, watched midnight come and go: "the British guns began; a flooded Amazon of steel flowed roaring, immensely fast, over our heads, and the machine-gun bullets made a pattern of sharper purpose and maniac language against that delirious rush. Flaring lights, small ones, great ones, flew up and went spinning sideways in the cloud of night; one's eyes seemed not quick enough; one heard nothing from one's shouting neighbours, and only by the quality of the noise and flame did I know that German shells crashing among the tree-stumps were big ones and practically on top of us."[9] At 3:30 A.M. on July 31, 100,000 British soldiers, supported by 700 aircraft and 140 tanks, clawed their way from forward trenches to begin the third battle of Ypres.

General Sixt von Arnim's Fourth German Army defended the Ypres sector with eight divisions in line and twelve in reserve. Arnim's chief of staff, Colonel Friedrich von Lossberg, had built a fluid defense à la Ludendorff. Behind a lightly held outpost zone, Lossberg constructed a battle zone of six trench lines protected by scores of mutually supporting machine-gun nests built of thick concrete. Further to the rear, batteries of medium and heavy mortars supported by over 1,500 guns waited to fire on selected targets.[10] In effect, Lossberg had created a trap into which any intruder would be taken by flanking fire from the Gheluvelt Ridge, which the British had neglected to capture in June and which Gough had failed to make his priority objective in July.

The result was a tragic, indeed a criminal record that had been played before. Early gains were considerable, particularly on the flanks. The going got much rougher in the center because of flanking artillery fire followed by well-coordinated counterattacks. Though Haig noted in his diary that it was "a fine day's work,"[11] von Arnim wrote in *his* diary "that he felt undisturbed because the Germans had never faced an attack with reserves so strong or who knew their job so thoroughly."[12] By day's end the attack had penetrated up to two miles on the flanks, considerably less in the center, at a cost of over 15,000 British casualties. Heavy rain continued to flood the battle area. In five days the battle of Pilckem Ridge, the first of nine battles that would continue into November, was over.

A new effort began on August 10. A week of vicious fighting forced the Germans to fall back on Langemarck, where German students had so bravely fallen in 1914, then back to Poelcapelle, where the drive was finally checked, a total gain of another four or five miles. The first phase of the third battle of Ypres was over by the end of August.

Smaller French attacks north of Saint-Quentin and on the Chemin des Dames had been fended off, but a major attack at Verdun sent German forces reeling back one to three miles east and west of the Meuse River in less than a week.

Allied gains, though limited, very much upset Ludendorff and his staff. The concrete defenses of the Siegfried Line had been smashed repeatedly by accurate artillery fire directed from observation airplanes. Both British and French troops attacked with élan. Pétain had brought about a fundamental change in offensive tactics, mainly to spare his still uncertain troops. No longer did the *poilus* pursue unlimited objectives to expose themselves to costly counterattacks. They advanced now by phases, careful not to dilute their strength with useless space. Ludendorff also sourly noted that the German divisions in some instances "no longer displayed that firmness which I, in common with the local commanders, had hoped for."[13]

Crisis on the western front had caused Ludendorff to postpone OberOst's attack in the east. He was in an operational dilemma. He desperately needed the six divisions sent to Hoffmann in July, but he still wanted to force Russia from the war. Hoffmann noted in his diary on August 21: "Ludendorff rang up early yesterday morning: 'I'm sorry,

I need troops.' Fine: I sent out necessary orders. In the afternoon he telephoned again: 'Perhaps I can manage.' I canceled the orders. Counter-orders will probably arrive again today. I can't blame Ludendorff."[14]

The delayed attack opened on the first day of September. It was in the hands of General Oskar von Hutier, who commanded Eighth Army. A cousin of Ludendorff's, Hutier was a man of considerable military imagination, who, like the Russian Brusilov, insisted that standard of-fensive tactics had long since lost their validity. Prolonged bombardments and attacks along the line had proved often futile and always costly. Instead he wanted to hit a single target with surprise and speed. Artillery planning was given to Colonel Georg Bruchmüller, an artillery genius who had been brought out of retirement and who recently had used his bag of tricks for the benefit of the Galician counteroffensive.

Artillery and infantry were brought up at night. Bruchmüller opened a gas bombardment before dawn. At first light 170 batteries supported by over 200 medium and heavy mortars opened fire. Three hours later under cover of smoke shells the first pontoons were pushed into the river to carry assault troops, while three bridges, one for each division, were being constructed. The enemy had already withdrawn from the western part of the Riga bridgehead and soon began to evacuate the remainder. "On the whole, the crossing was almost ridiculously easy," Hoffmann noted.[15] Assault groups of fourteen to eighteen men, called *Sturmtruppen* (storm troops), variously armed with light machine guns, automatic rifles or light mortars, followed a rolling barrage to thread their way around enemy strongpoints. Larger units, supported by attack aircraft, followed to neutralize the strongpoints and clear the way for regiments and di-visions to enlarge the penetration while aircraft strafed and bombed where necessary.

The defenders were soon in general retreat eastward. "We changed their retreat into something of a rout," Hoffmann wrote on September 10. ". . . We should of course like to have continued our advance in the direction of Petersburg, but unfortunately we had to stop, as Luden-dorff with the best will in the world, could not let us keep the necessary divisions. He needs them, and Austria needs them, so we must resign ourselves."[16] As Ludendorff had hoped, the successful operation resulted in a much shorter defensive line. It also caused the panic-stricken Ker-ensky government to flee Petrograd for Moscow, leaving the capital in Lenin's hands.

*   *   *

Shortly before von Hutier's attack on the Riga front, General Cadorna launched the eleventh battle of the Isonzo against the Austro-Hungarians. Cadorna could never be criticized for lack of perseverance. Ten battles of the Isonzo had accomplished virtually nothing except to expand casualty lists to new highs in Italy and Austria-Hungary. This time he fared somewhat better. Despite an immense cost in lives, the Italians pressed the cold and hungry defenders back to stop finally on the Carso Plateau a few miles north of the coast. The Austrians, too, had suffered such heavy losses that commanders despaired of holding against another attack. Appeals from Vienna and the Isonzo front for German reinforcements poured into the OHL to present the Duo with still another operational conundrum.

Ludendorff had hoped to remove Romania from the war by an attack through Moldavia once OberOst's Riga front was secured. There was no doubting the strategic importance of a success here, particularly since it would further influence Russia to make peace. It was a far more beneficial goal than merely bolstering the Austro-Hungarians dug in on a forty-mile front east of the Isonzo. But if the attack through Moldavia was abandoned, the OHL could bring enough divisions west to support an offensive in Italy. If this succeeded, it would not only remove pressure against the rapidly disintegrating Austrian government, but it could conceivably cause the fall of the Italian government and even force Italy from the war. Since it was more important to keep Austro-Hungary *in* the war than to force Russia *from* the war, Ludendorff decided to support Conrad's plan for a new thrust from the north.

Major operational decisions are difficult at the best of times. This was far from the Duo's shining hour. The OHL and government were further out of step than ever, as was shown by an imperial council at Kreuznach in August, which marked the debut of Richard von Kühlmann, Zimmermann's replacement as foreign secretary. Kühlmann was forty-four years old, a bright, experienced diplomat, a liberal Anglophile.[17] Hindenburg praised him as "clever and energetic" shortly after his appointment[18]—and soon lived to regret his words.

Kühlmann was one of the few sane men in German official circles, in that he wanted to negotiate a peace as quickly as possible. The Duo at once turned a deaf ear to his and Michaelis's suggestion that Britain might enter into secret peace negotiations providing Germany would yield postwar claims on Belgian territory. Ludendorff responded by reiterating the now-familiar litany of annexationist aims. The struggle with Kühlmann had begun—it would last almost as long as the war. Nor was Michaelis immune. Ludendorff soon demanded from him a revival of the Hindenburg Program along with more rigorous censorship and propaganda measures.

The OHL had already launched its own propaganda campaign to raise civilian morale, which, Ludendorff wrote, "has sunk to a very low level." Ludendorff's lengthy directive, *Vaterländische Unterricht unter den Truppen (Patriotic Instruction for the Troops)*, cited three reasons for sinking morale. Genuine shortages of food, clothing, and fuel played a part, as did "shameless profiteering" and pursuit of frivolous luxuries. The real villain, however, was "the deliberate agitation of certain revolutionary elements who are unscrupulously exploiting these hardships to further their political ends and are endeavouring to provoke discontent [and] anti-war feeling in every possible way."[19]

"Patriotic schooling" was necessary to counter this subversive socialist influence. Ludendorff believed that morale could be raised by emphasizing German strength and Allied weakness and by advertising the territorial and economic fruits of victory. Each of the twenty-four district corps commands inside Germany established a propaganda committee. Libraries were deluged with rightist newspapers, books, and pamphlets designed to persuade the public that only complete victory, a "Hindenburg victory," would save the empire, a theme embroidered on by posters, free public lectures, and films that extolled German greatness and will for victory.

Initial messages were relatively mild. Housewives were to practice greater economy, for example by using wild greens in salads. They were ordered not to hoard food—this at a time when *Hausfrauen* were searching frantically for enough food to provide one meal. They were not to complain about shortages of food, clothing and fuel. Above all, they were not to have sexual intercourse with prisoners of war.[20]

This was merely the beginning. Within a few weeks Hindenburg was signing letters to the chancellor on such subjects as the annual infant mortality rate from hereditary syphilis, the rapidly rising death rate from tuberculosis, and the decreasing birthrate. Every healthy man must marry and procreate. Contraceptives should be forbidden and bachelors should be taxed.[21]

Shortly after the internal campaign opened, Ludendorff signed a secret order calling for troop education. Special "education officers" appeared in each army corps to direct the program. Troops attended compulsory lectures twice a week and were surfeited with printed propaganda. They were told that the war resulted from England's manipulation of "French lust for revenge and Russian greed for land." At Ludendorff's insistence the lecturers denounced the Reichstag peace resolution and criticized weak government policies—only a "Hindenburg victory" would result in massive postwar gains. Germany's military supremacy was emphasized, both on land and sea, where submarines were everywhere sinking Allied ships. Troops were told of Allied atrocities against prisoners of war and were constantly warned that a weak peace would mean Germany's destruction. "Classic works of German militarism" were presented on stage and film in rear areas. Wagner, Kleist, Schiller, and Lessing were favorite choices. Hindenburg was undoubtedly gratified that Schiller's *Wallenstein* was staged, and he may have been responsible for the avoidance of Goethe's works. Troops on leave were to convince civilians that Germany was winning the war.[22]

The program was not altogether successful. It was very difficult to persuade soldiers who, if fortunate, were subsisting on 2,400 calories a day derived mainly from potatoes and bread and who had been fighting defensive battles for as long as they could remember that Germany was winning the war.

General Groener called it "sheer madness to try and overcome social-democratic sympathies with Pan-German leaflets and lectures."[23] Had either Hindenburg or Ludendorff or their staff officers deigned to talk to the front-line soldiers, they would soon have discovered that most of them did not give a damn for postwar gains. Their one interest was to leave the subhuman trench life of mud and shit, of lice and rats and foul food, of death hovering about like the unwanted visit of a hated relative. They wanted decent meals, proper rest areas, their overdue furloughs (Ludendorff sharply reduced furloughs in September because of the coal shortage and thus restricted trains for all sectors and rear areas except Verdun and the Somme).[24] They resented spending months cheek by jowl with front-line officers only to find rank segregation in rear areas, where canteens, barbershops, bars, hotels, and whorehouses were designated "only for officers" or "only for noncommissioned officers."[25] They resented the lack of recreational facilities and of often being forced to join rear-area working parties when they should have been relaxing in perhaps their last few hours of life. Other than trying to stay alive, their major interest was when the war would end and postwar gains be damned. Little wonder that some senior commanders even confiscated the printed propaganda, since, as Groener discerned, "it would simply have destroyed the men's confidence in their officers."[26]

No amount of propaganda could have brought the political unity demanded by the Duo in the autumn of 1917. Socialist members of the Reichstag and increasing numbers of ordinary citizens were clamoring for a peace of reconciliation. Continuing strikes had brought the wrath of the industrialists against government labor policy. In mid-August the *Kriegsamt* was subordinated to the war ministry and Groener was replaced by General Heinrich Scheüch, who scarcely managed to maintain an uneasy peace with the trade unions.

The July peace resolution remained a bone of great contention between liberals and conservatives. The latter had been heartened by the appearance of a new political party, the Vaterlandspartei, in late August. The brainchild of a provincial and dangerous official demagogue, Wolfgang Kapp, its president was Admiral von Tirpitz. It was a party of the extreme right; its platform fulminated against electoral reforms or any hint of parliamentary government. Its major target was the July resolution. It insisted that a compromise peace was out of the question and demanded large-scale annexations. Ludendorff later claimed to have had no connection with the party, which would soon boast well over a million members, but he welcomed its credo and ensured that its inflammatory pronouncements, designed to isolate and destroy the moderate and liberal elements in and out of government, reached the men in the trenches.

Hindenburg and Ludendorff were summoned to a crown council in early September to discuss a reply to the pope's latest peace initiative. It was a difficult time for Ludendorff, whose eldest stepson, a pilot, had been shot down and killed. Nor was he in sympathy with the subject, which he considered a study in futility. Britain, France, and Italy, already suspicious of papal dealings with the Central Powers, had received the pope's words coldly but had withheld rejection while awaiting the German reply. This was preempted by President Woodrow Wilson, who refused any dealing with "the bloody and inhuman tyranny of the kaiser's government," another salvo in his incessant barrage intended to topple Prussian autocracy by internal revolution.[27]

The Duo's position on peace was again made clear at this meeting, which thanks to the kaiser's antics resembled something of a madhouse.

They would consider yielding the Flanders coast to Belgium only if Germany retained control of Liège. This compromise vanished a few days later when Ludendorff in a lengthy paper reverted to his normal annexationist demands. Hindenburg sent this document to Chancellor Michaelis, noting that it was entirely in accordance with his own views.

The Duo were scarcely back at the OHL when the British resumed the Flanders offensive. Ludendorff hurried to the front, an effort interrupted when the command train collided with another and his coach was overturned. Having somehow escaped injury, he completed his inspection of the front. Satisfied that the lines would hold, he returned to Kreuznach to open the Italian offensive.

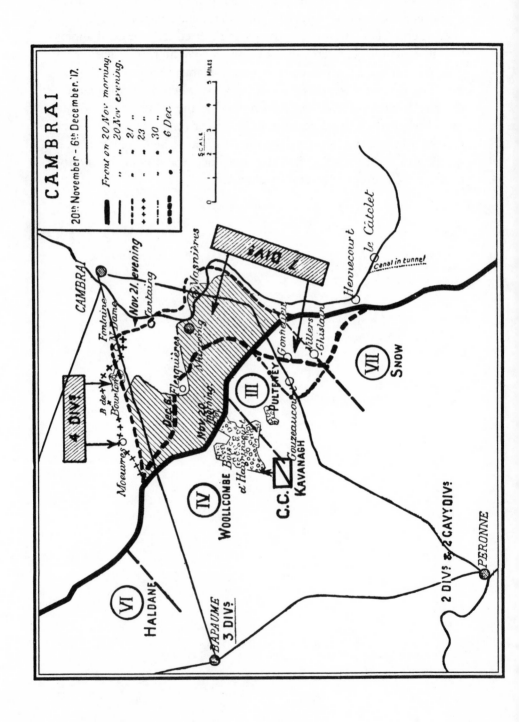

CAMBRAI

20th November – 6th December '17.

Front on 20 Nov. morning.
" " 20 Nov. evening.
" " 21 "
" " 23 "
" " 30 "
" " 6 Dec.

SCALE
0   1   2   3   4   5 Miles

30

---◆---

Cambrai: The Surprise
of Tank Warfare

The consequence is that the war has become a short-range
instead of a long-range war as was expected. . . . The question
to be solved is . . . the actual getting across 100 or 200 yards
of open space and wire entanglements. . . . It would be quite
easy in a short time to fit up a number of steam tractors with
small armoured shelters, in which men and machine-guns
could be placed. . . . The caterpillar system would enable
trenches to be crossed quite easily, and the weight of the
machine would destroy all wire entanglements. . . .
—First Lord of the Admiralty Winston Churchill to
    Prime Minister Herbert Henry Asquith,
    January 1915[1]

Cambrai had become the Valmy of a new epoch in war, the
epoch of the mechanical engineer.
        —J.F.C. Fuller, writing on the tank battle of
            Cambrai, November 1917[2]

Ludendorff could not muster enough divisions to attack from the
Tyrol as he would have preferred. Insufficient strength was one
reason that Conrad's 1916 offensive in Italy had failed, and he
did not wish to fall into the same trap. He instead chose to attack from
the Austro-Hungarian front about twenty miles northeast of Cividale,
an unlikely choice because of difficult mountainous terrain and inadequate communications. But the Italians did not dream that an attack
would come in this area, their lines were only weakly held, and Luden-

dorff counted on surprise to push through them, cross the mountains north of Cividale, and advance on Udine to outflank the Italian right.

The attack would be made by a newly organized Fourteenth Army commanded by General Otto von Below. Ludendorff recalled the Alpine Corps of two mountain-trained divisions from the Bukovina as nucleus, to which he added three infantry divisions and some *Jäger* battalions along with artillery and support troops. After receiving special equipment, this force began training in mountain warfare before being deployed on both sides of Tolmino on the Isonzo River. It was reinforced by two Austro-Hungarian corps and in time by two divisions from the east. The offensive would begin in mid-October and was to be complemented by a force under Conrad attacking from the Tyrol.

A new crisis caused postponement. In late September the third battle of Ypres reopened in Flanders with a major British assault of the Passchendaele–Gheluvelt line. To Ludendorff's fury, German defensive tactics again failed to stop the enemy from gaining ground; the use of phase-line tactics, which helped to prevent dilution of strength, and powerful and accurate artillery fire repeatedly smashed German counterattacks. Ludendorff took the enemy success as a personal insult. After repeated telephone conversations with the local chiefs of staff, General von Kuhl and Colonel von Lossberg, he traveled to the front to discuss the problem with individual commanders.

Ludendorff was told that the army should revert to former tactics by slightly reinforcing front lines and abandoning the use of special counterattack divisions. Each front-line division would instead be backed by a second division to be used for local counterattacks. Improved artillery techniques were necessary to stop enemy attacks. According to Ludendorff, local commanders did not believe that enemy tanks were particularly dangerous, and they refused to be baited by his contemptuous term of troop "tank fright," which they indignantly denied was the case. Although Ludendorff was appalled by the manpower involved in placing a division behind each front-line division, he agreed to the experiment.[3]

After a slight lull, the British offensive continued in early October, being announced by two days of violent artillery bombardment that included final barrages of smoke shells to blind the defenders. Once again British and Canadian troops fought through wire, shell, and bullet to gain a little ground. Once again they were stopped at a heavy cost in German lives. The new German tactics had unquestionably failed. A disgusted Ludendorff recommended that the Fourth Army "form an advanced zone . . . a narrow strip between the enemy's front line and the line which our troops were to hold by mobile defense. The enemy would have to cross this strip in making his attack, and our artillery would have time to get on to him before he could reach our main line of resistance"—not an ideal solution as he himself admitted.[4]

The Fourth Army adopted the new tactics somewhat reluctantly, but in two subsequent attacks the line held, though with enormous losses. The two divisions from the east that were earmarked for Italy were diverted to France. Then in late October the British opened what the Germans called the fifth battle of Ypres while the French attacked a salient southwest of Laon. Heavy fighting lasted in Flanders until November 10, when it wound down to leave the British defending a line northeast of Passchendaele, an anticlimax determined not so much by German resistance as by heavy rains that turned the shell-cratered land into quagmire. The French attack succeeded in forcing the German line to retire behind the Oise–Aisne Canal, again with heavy losses, and this forced an evacuation of the Chemin des Dames.

There was some cheer. OberOst had launched a joint attack with the navy that soon would capture the off-shore Baltic islands to spread further panic in the Russian capital. Below's Italian offensive opened against slight resistance. After a massive barrage of gas shells holding the new and sinister mustard gas, the troops quickly crossed the mountain barrier while one division slipped through the valley on the right toward Caporetto. In only three days the assault troops occupied Cividale and were pushing through the mountains toward the upper Tagliamento. The Italian lines on the Isonzo and on the Carinthian border began to fold. By mid-December Below's vanguard had reached the Piave River, nearly seventy miles from the Isonzo.

But now French and British reinforcements had arrived to bolster the beaten Italians, and so had bad weather to complicate the ever-present supply problem in a mountainous country of poor roads and railroads that had caused Conrad's complementary attack to fail. No matter. The offensive had attained its major goal of relieving pressure on Austria-Hungary. The Italian army had lost some 400,000 men, most of them prisoners, and was saved from ultimate humiliation only by its allies. Italian defeat taken with the Russian collapse breathed new hope into the Austro-Hungarian army and empire. The OHL had benefited from the transfer of enemy divisions from France to Italy. Ludendorff was satisfied. The offensive ended in December.

*　*　*

Victory on the Italian front did not much change the face of war. For every step forward Germany fell two steps backward. Despite Ludendorff's incessant bullying of the new chancellor, Georg Michaelis, the home front had not snapped to as demanded. Strikes had increased and would number over five hundred involving a million defense workers for the year. The army was still not receiving enough men and supplies. Even worse, perhaps, the flow of incendiary propaganda continued despite the OHL's concentrated propaganda campaign and stringent censorship controls. Ludendorff's insistence on press control taken with Michaelis's conservative sympathies and general ineptness had made the chancellor increasingly unpopular in empire, Reichstag, and army. He resigned in late October 1917 and after a great deal of political maneuvering was replaced by the seventy-five-year-old Bavarian premier, Count von Hertling, more philosopher than politician, and more pro- than anti-Ludendorff. Although the Duo promised to no longer "mix in politics," this changed radically. Hertling soon brought the Duo's combined wrath on his old head by calling for a peace of reconciliation while refusing their demand to annex Belgium.[5] Clearly Hertling was not the strong man of Ludendorff's standards. Clearly Hertling would have to be educated by the OHL.

Such had been the decline in influence of the imperial chancellor's office, such the sapping of its authority by Hindenburg and Ludendorff, that Hertling was a relatively minor problem. Chancellor or no chancellor, the war would continue as the Duo wished it to continue.

Their land strategy had largely succeeded, though at a high cost in lives. During 1917 the enemy everywhere had been held or even pushed back while the submarine offensive continued. By November, however, it was obvious to most observers that this offensive had failed to achieve its optimistic goals. The admirals continued to insist that it was a success. The same admirals had promised that not one American would land in France, whereas there were now over 100,000 combat troops—four immense divisions—in training, with more troop ships arriving daily. No troops ships had been sunk, and other sinkings were steadily decreasing, as antisubmarine measures became more and more effective. By November a German submarine could expect to survive only six cruises.

England and France were suffering from numerous shortages at home and from heavy losses on the fighting fronts, but they were alive and well, fighting boldly and tenaciously in Britain's case, with French morale somewhat revived by the arrival of American troops. Germany on the other hand was alive but not well. Recent fighting had left her divisions decimated, survivors exhausted, morale sinking. The army lacked trained junior officers, there were serious equipment shortages, insufficient rations, inadequate rest periods.

Hospitals were jammed with wounded, whose torn bodies were bound with paper bandages. An inferior kind of cellulose paper had replaced cotton wool. A severe shortage of doctors had developed, one result of the Duo's insistence on drafting all eighteen-year-olds instead of sending the qualified ones to university. Doctors lacked proper equipment and medicines. There was no rubber to make surgical gloves and aprons. In stripping mustard gas casualties of their clothing, doctors and orderlies were often themselves burned to produce ghastly ulcers that often penetrated to the bone. There was never enough oxygen or morphia to treat the serious cases.[6]

Socialist propaganda had helped to bring on a serious mutiny in the idle surface fleet and was now reaching the trenches. Conditions in the homeland were appalling. Thousands of people were starving, unable to buy either clothes or blankets against the wintry cold made colder by almost no coal, darker by almost no oil. The paper shortage was so serious that in August 1917 Ludendorff published a special army order: all staffs were to sacrifice appearance in preference to utilization in all future orders, making narrower margins and using both sides of the paper; all reports to be brief and to be made in person or by telephone if possible; copies to be held to a minimum, distribution carefully controlled.[7] Germany was obviously losing the war of attrition.

What was to be done?

Hindenburg and Ludendorff offered only one solution. The war was to be won or lost on the western front, a truism that they had treated with derisive protest when made by Erich von Falkenhayn in 1914, 1915, and 1916.

The war was to be won in 1918 by a gigantic offensive that would split the French and British armies before defeating each in turn. On November 11, 1917, Ludendorff summoned army commanders and their general-staff chiefs to Mons to learn how the war would be won.

Ludendorff pointed to three possible offensive sectors, north, center, and south. Crown Prince Rupprecht's chief of staff, General Hermann von Kuhl, argued for an attack in Flanders toward Hazebrouck. Crown Prince Wilhelm's chief of staff, Count Friedrich von der Schulenburg, countered with a proposal to attack the flanks of the Verdun salient, defeat the French, then go after the British, a plan supported in part by Ludendorff's chief of operations, Major Georg Wetzell.[8]

Ludendorff rejected Schulenburg's plan on two counts. A year of relative inactivity had allowed the French army to recover its strength partially. The British army, on the other hand, had been greatly weakened by the recent Ypres offensives. "The British must be defeated," he told the group, but he did not agree with Kuhl's plan, mainly because the ground would not be dry in the north until April. It was essential to strike earlier before the American divisions were ready for combat. He himself favored an early attack in the Saint-Quentin area, but a decision would not be made until army commanders and staff chiefs had studied all proposals and reported in detail. Crown Prince Rupprecht was disturbed by Ludendorff's insistence on a British defeat, writing in his diary that "Ludendorff underestimates the toughness of the British who would scarcely come forward with a peace offer since they remain in a position to continue the war."[9]

While Ludendorff was holding forth at Mons, his British adversary was putting the finishing touches on another attack plan. Douglas Haig was a very stubborn Scot. Having lost 320,000 men to obtain a little tongue of land north of Passchendaele—"this vast obscene excrescence . . . this abomination of desolation," a survivor called it[10]—in the Ypres fighting, he still refused to abandon his dream of reaching the enemy's submarine pens on the Belgian coast, not knowing that these havens were not vital to continued submarine operations. Stopped by the mud of Passchendaele, he turned to a new and very imaginative operation.

British experts who had pioneered development of what came to be known as the tank had warned that for it to be effective it must be deployed in large numbers. This had been blithely ignored when seven of the new machines, grotesque in their mechanized awkwardness, appeared on the Somme in 1916. It had more recently been ignored in the Ypres fighting. A military Pollyanna could point to the advantage gained by tactical ineptitude in that the inauspicious performance of these machines had decided the German high command, and Ludendorff in particular, that since there was nothing to worry about from the tank, there was no reason to build the tank.

Fortunately for the Allied cause, Colonel J.F.C. Fuller, chief of staff of the tank corps, recognized the true potential of the new weapon—if used correctly. How to convince his seniors? In August 1917 he submitted plans for a surprise tank raid to last no more than twenty-four hours. "The whole operation may be summed up in three words: ' Advance,

Hit, Retire. ' It would take place in a quiet, unsuspecting sector south of Cambrai. Its object was to destroy the enemy's personnel and guns, to demoralize and disorganize his fighting troops and reserves—and not to capture ground or hold trenches."[11]

The Cambrai sector came under operational command of General Sir Julian Byng's Third Army. Byng liked the idea and passed it on to Haig, apparently proposing a much larger operation than that envisaged by Fuller. Haig had never been enthusiastic over the new weapon, and he approved the Cambrai attack only after being stymied at Passchendaele. It was to commence in late November.

During these uncertain weeks General Byng expanded Fuller's relatively modest raid into still another breakthrough offensive, a major attempt to attack the Hindenburg Line, capture Cambrai, cross the Sensée River and cut off the enemy to the south, then drive north of Saint-Quentin, Le Cateau, and Valenciennes. This was the mission of 381 primitive tanks, 1,000 guns and 6 infantry divisions with 4 cavalry divisions supported by fighter and bomber aircraft. Haig was not so ambitious. He designated Bourlon Hill as the main objective and ordered that the operation would cease after forty-eight hours.

General Georg von der Marwitz, who now commanded the Second Army of Crown Prince Rupprecht's army group, was defending the Cambrai sector, a quiet area known as the "Flanders Sanitarium," where tired divisions were sent to recuperate.[12] The recent fighting at Ypres had diluted much of Rupprecht's defensive strength. The Siegfried (Hindenburg) Line, in reality an outpost line backed by two main defensive lines with a third one being constructed, was strong enough, its maze of sector trenches sited on the reverse slopes of the important ridges, thus reasonably immune to artillery barrage, and well protected by enormous complexes of barbed wire and machine-gun nests. It was held in many places by second-class Landwehr divisions, but Marwitz was not especially worried despite considerable enemy activity on parts of his front. In mid-November he reported that "there was no likelihood of an attack," but three days later an intercepted telephone message aroused his suspicions, as did interrogation reports of prisoners captured in a night raid. He at once ordered a troop alert. If there were to be an attack, he told himself, it would be preceded by the usual lengthy artillery bombardment of high explosive and gas shells.[13]

There being no bombardment on the night of November 19–20,

Marwitz and his staff rested easily. But at the front the misty morning stillness was suddenly shattered by the unmistakable noise of heavy engines roaring toward German outposts. Ten minutes later shells from a thousand guns began exploding 200 yards ahead of the tanks. Before the forward troops realized what was happening, the mechanical monsters had torn through protective wire to spew fire from machine guns while caterpillar treads ground men into earth as if they were ants.

Incoherent messages of breakthroughs along the line poured into Second Army headquarters to bring staff officers rushing to subordinate headquarters in an attempt to pinpoint the action. Forward trenches had been easily overrun. Each tank had been equipped with a miniature bridge, a fascine of heavy brushwood that was dropped across the twelve-foot-wide enemy trenches. Following infantry eliminated any defenders that had escaped the armor.

Almost everywhere along a six-mile front the armor-infantry columns continued to smash through Marwitz's lines. Only south of Flesquières had the drive been stopped, the fault of a division commander who kept his troops too far behind the tanks, thus exposing them to hidden enemy machine-gun fire and the tanks to mortar and artillery fire, supplemented by machine guns using armor-piercing ammunition and by cluster grenades placed by very brave men who crawled to the blind side of the tank. Forward units elsewhere advanced five miles inside the enemy line by nightfall. The Hindenburg Line had been breached. The road to Cambrai was open.[14]

There were problems.

Enemy fire and mechanical failure had taken a heavy toll on the tanks. Crews were exhausted, as were the infantry. Intelligence was poor. The official German historian later wrote that one important gap remained open for "many hours, completely unoccupied. It was great luck, as no reinforcements could be expected to reach there before evening."[15] It probably made little difference. There were no reserve tanks, no reserve divisions to exploit the most important breakthrough of the war on the western front to date.

Ludendorff learned of the initial rupture at eight A.M. He at once ordered several divisions from Crown Prince Wilhelm's army group to the threatened sector and asked Crown Prince Rupprecht to move other divisions north of Cambrai. These could not arrive until the following morning at best. Marwitz meanwhile moved up what reserves he could scrape together during the day, his mainstay being a newly arrived division from the east.

The British attacks resumed the next morning but not with yesterday's drive. Attacks on the left gained another mile or two. Bourlon Wood was taken, but on the right the advance faltered, then stopped. By evening three German divisions had arrived, others would follow. "General Ludendorff was very nervous today," Crown Prince Rupprecht noted on November 22. "He telephoned to ask about a thousand details which was very annoying."[16]

Haig had called for the operation to terminate in forty-eight hours. Byng could not leave his left exposed to German fire from Bourlon Hill and argued for the offensive to continue. Haig and Pétain were being pressed to help their Italian ally by keeping the Germans engaged. Haig sent Byng several more divisions and the offensive continued for two more days with no further gains.

The German commander, General von der Marwitz, meanwhile had been reinforced sufficiently to begin a series of local counterattacks on his right. These were intended in part to mask preparations for a major counterattack by his left. This would be complemented in the north by another attack west of Bourlon Wood.

British division commanders in the south suspected something of the sort, since German guns were registering on rear-area targets and German reconnaissance aircraft were unusually active. The storm struck early on November 30 with a brief but effective bombardment by gas and smoke shells. Small German units composed of *Sturmtruppen* or storm troops used von Hutier's new assault tactics to bypass enemy strongpoints and penetrate weaker points in the British line. Larger units followed to neutralize strongpoints while the spearhead advanced over two miles west of the British line to be halted only with difficulty by infantry and tanks. The German attack in the north failed to gain ground, but in the next six days of fighting Marwitz regained more than half the ground lost in the first two days. The action ended a few days later, much to Byng and Haig's relief.

Ludendorff was pleased in general with the final result, which he described "as a complete victory over a considerable part of the British army."[17] His "victory" did not open his eyes to the potential of the tank, which he continued to hold in low esteem—a not very serious challenge, easily met by a flow of elaborate orders and training directives. Not so Lieutenant Sulzbach, who had written the previous July: "I'm now seeing these tank monsters close up for the very first time, and I can understand what a devastating moral effect they have in an attack." In December he wrote that "the theory and practice of anti-tank training is being taken further all the time." Each artillery battery was to receive two machine-gun teams, while "battle-guns" were to be positioned in concrete before each front.[18] A careful inspection of the newest model captured tanks would have shown that they were impervious to armor-piercing machine-gun fire. As for the "battle-guns," they were unbelievably easy targets for enemy artillery fire. The best defense against tanks, direct field-artillery fire (not to mention one's own tanks) was apparently not considered.

So the immensely important lesson of Cambrai washed over Ludendorff and the OHL staff. Ludendorff did note, however, that one of his "good" divisions "instead of pressing on, stopped to go through an enemy supply-depot," a portent, perhaps, of more serious things to come.[19]

31

Brest Litovsk: A Victory of Sorts

> It therefore would appear intolerable that the Field Marshal
> [Hindenburg] and General Ludendorff should make the pros-
> ecution of their indispensable military labors dependent on the
> fulfillment of political demands when the decision as to the
> necessity of such demands has been assigned by the constitution
> exclusively to the Crown and responsible advisers [the imperial
> chancellor]. . . .
> —CHANCELLOR VON HERTLING TO KAISER WILHELM,
> JANUARY 1918[1]

OberOst's capture of the off-shore Baltic islands in mid-October was followed by a period of relative calm on the eastern front. OberOst was soon reporting to the OHL the rapid disintegration of the Russian army. With the end clearly in sight, Ludendorff ordered all units in the east to begin training for warfare in the west. This was followed in November by the first of many divisions being transferred to the western front.

In late November the new Russian commander in chief, Nikolai Krilenko, telegraphed an armistice offer agreed to by the OHL. A few days later Russian delegates arrived in Brest Litovsk to begin negotiations conducted by General Max Hoffmann and Foreign Minister Richard von Kühlmann on Germany's behalf, by Count Ottokar Czernin on Austria-Hungary's behalf. In mid-December the former adversaries agreed on a month-long armistice while peace negotiations continued at Brest Litovsk.

The situation was complicated by the splintered authority of the Russian government and the diverse, often conflicting interests of Germany and Austria-Hungary in the various occupied territories. Hindenburg and Ludendorff had stated their position at a conference held shortly after Hertling had become chancellor. Count Czernin had persuaded Kaiser Wilhelm, Hertling, and Kühlmann to accept his solution of a union of Congress Poland with Galicia under the Habsburg flag. The Duo argued forcefully against this on military grounds but were outvoted and had to be content with the promise of a wide security belt along the Prussian frontier. Ludendorff also stressed the need for Germany to annex Kurland and Lithuania, but the conference ended with no decision reached.

The armistice caused the kaiser to call another council at Kreuznach, where much the same ground was covered. Hindenburg and Ludendorff pressed the need for an extensive protective belt along the Prussian frontier even though this meant the absorption of some two million Slavic people by Germany. Chancellor von Hertling, who respected the Lithuanian desire for independence so long as Germany was given certain military and economic guarantees, agreed with the notion of a personal union of Kurland and Lithuania with Germany. Kaiser Wilhelm wanted the Central Powers to invite Russia to evacuate Estonia and Livonia, whose peoples would then exercise the right of self-determination. The Duo countered with a plea for large-scale annexation of the Baltic lands. "But why do you so particularly want these territories?" Kühlmann asked Hindenburg. "I need them for the maneuvering of my left wing in the next war," was the unexpected reply.[2] Ludendorff hurriedly explained that they were needed for food and manpower. The conference adjourned with almost nothing settled. Another meeting was scheduled for early January 1918.

Ludendorff's major adversary at these councils was the foreign secretary. Kühlmann was not alone in his refusal to consider large-scale annexations in the east, and he did not hesitate to stand up to either Hindenburg or Ludendorff, who eventually would destroy him for his studied integrity. Germany needed peace, Kühlmann argued, not continued strife. Perhaps he recalled, as had Hindenburg in his talks with Vogel, Frederick the Great's momentous decision to end the Seven Years' War with no territorial gains for Prussia. Now, just over a century and a half later, Germany must offer Russia a peace based on the status quo ante and thereby display pacific intentions and innate fairness to the world. Hindenburg had been of the same mind in 1915. His about-face is an unpleasant measure of Ludendorff's domination and the unrelenting influence on the OHL by Germany's political leaders and captains of industry and finance. Hertling and numerous lesser officials remained opposed to large-scale Baltic annexations, as did a good many Social Democrats in the Reichstag. Still another opponent, perhaps unexpectedly, was Max Hoffmann, chief of staff at OberOst and since October a major general.

On New Year's Day, 1918, Kühlmann invited Hoffmann to Berlin for a private talk with Kaiser Wilhelm to discuss peace negotiations with Russia. Hoffmann's acceptance was somewhat daring, since Ludendorff had forbidden any officer to speak to the kaiser without a preliminary interview with himself, even if the kaiser ordered him to do so. Hoffmann nevertheless spoke his mind. He had never favored these annexations but now it had become evident to him that they could not be carried out, since Germany could not win the war. At the kaiser's bidding, Hoffmann embarked on a studied analysis of the Brest Litovsk negotiations. The kaiser then moved on to the Polish problem, hurling question after question at his guest. Hoffmann attempted to back off in order not to incur Ludendorff's wrath but was ordered to give candid answers. Very well: unlike the Duo, he recommended nothing more than a few unimportant "corrections" of the present frontier, a matter involving the absorption of perhaps fifty thousand Poles.[3]

Hoffmann attempted without success to contact Ludendorff prior to the imperial council, which met the following day. When Kühlmann had finished briefing the group on negotiations at Brest Litovsk, the kaiser spoke on the Polish question, stating that he no longer agreed with the Duo's views because of the conversation that he had enjoyed yesterday with Hoffmann. Ludendorff jumped to his feet. His face a violent red, his chins trembling like disturbed jelly, he shouted in his shrill voice that the kaiser had no right to consult with a subordinate officer and that he refused to consider any proposal that was the result of such an action. The awkward silence was broken by Hindenburg, who mumbled that "we must certainly think this matter over carefully." Wilhelm replied coldly: "I shall await your report."[4]

The report never arrived. The reversal of roles had come full circle. Ludendorff had not only challenged imperial authority but had done so in a most insulting fashion. Once again the kaiser should have "braved the slings and arrows of outrageous fortune" by dismissing his recalcitrant first quartermaster general and damn the consequences.

It would not have been easy. Two days after the conference Ludendorff informed General von Lyncker that he was resigning, rumors of which were duly reported in the Pan-German press, causing an instant furor in conservative circles and a flood of telegrams imploring the kaiser not to let their hero go. Crown Prince Wilhelm underhandedly persuaded the empire princes to support Ludendorff and sent Crown Prince Rupprecht a secret memorandum written by Ludendorff's publicist, Colonel Max Bauer, that called for Kühlmann's removal along with the removal of Valentini and Admiral Müller.

The quarrel was intensified by President Woodrow Wilson's announcement on January 8 of his terms for peace—the famous Fourteen Points. Eight of the points echoed the Entente's aims as stated a year earlier. A further clause called for evacuation of occupied territory in Russia. This unwelcome development coincided with a long letter to the kaiser, signed by Hindenburg, that was a direct attack on Kühlmann's vapid policies in Alsace-Lorraine and Brest Litovsk. By lowering morale in the army and at home he was destroying the monarchy—either he or the Duo would have to go. Further, "in the Polish question your Majesty has chosen to place greater reliance upon the judgment of General Hoffmann than upon that of General Ludendorff and myself. General Hoffmann is my subordinate, and bears no responsibility whatsoever in the Polish question. The events of January 2 have been the cause of pain to General Ludendorff and myself, and have shown us that your Majesty disregards our opinion in a matter of vital importance for the existence of the German Fatherland."[5]

Count Hertling urged the kaiser to pick up the gauntlet, but Wilhelm confined himself to a mild warning for the Duo to stay out of political affairs. The OHL meanwhile had orchestrated a press attack against Hoffmann "hinting that his wife came from semitic-liberal circles." Hoffmann's transfer was demanded and refused, as was Kühlmann's dismissal.[6] The Duo further demanded support of OHL policy in the Baltic lands and in Poland and once again threatened to resign if this was not granted.

The Duo's attack continued, fired in part by Philipp Scheidemann's declaration in early January "that the majority of the Reichstag continues to uphold the declaration of July 19, 1917, wherein we stated that we desire a peace of understanding, a peace of conciliation, which precludes annexations as well as political and economic leadership by force."[7] This was a red flag to the bulls at the OHL. "The war does not in any way justify democratization and parliamentarianism," Ludendorff had recently informed a Prussian minister. "A policy of concessions to the spirit of the age is exceedingly dangerous."[8] At an audience in mid-January Hindenburg backed the kaiser to the wall, threatening his and Ludendorff's resignations unless the kaiser's chief of the civil cabinet, von Valentini, "who was entirely to blame for the swing to the Left in the government," was replaced by a candidate of their own choice. This time the kaiser shouted, "I don't need your paternal advice," and waved away the field marshal. Wilhelm later spoke of Ludendorff as a "malefactor with whom he would never shake hands again."[9] Having bravely asserted imperial independence he at once fell victim to the influence of the empress and crown prince, who had all along been working with the Duo, Max Bauer, and Pan-German conservatives for Valentini's removal, and shamefully forced Valentini to resign. He was replaced by the Duo's candidate, an extreme political conservative named Friedrich von Berg, governor of East Prussia and confidant of Crown Prince Wilhelm, a further accession to the Duo's humiliating authority.[10]

Hindenburg and Ludendorff had now taken virtual control of Germany's future. Their authority dominated all battle and domestic fronts. Military press officers continued to feed false information to newspapers, deliberately disguising military defeats, cóoking casualty figures, inventing stories of atrocities against German prisoners of war. Commanders of area military districts within Germany for some time had answered to Ludendorff. The great Berlin munition workers' strike in January 1918, when over half a million men left their jobs, evoked a formal declaration of a state of siege or martial law. Police closed down labor newspapers, broke up meetings, and arrested workers, who were tried by military courts. Fifty thousand munition workers were reportedly drafted into the army. Hindenburg wanted agitators and strikers to be charged with treason and punished accordingly. Civilian reaction to the repressive measures was sufficiently unfavorable that Ludendorff in February recommended to the war minister that future strikes should be settled without force. Nevertheless he was not removing the troops who had been transferred to the troubled areas, and he secretly ordered army commanders to designate two battalions in each army that could be used to quell civilian strife.[11]

Chancellor Hertling's attempts to reassert his constitutional authority in foreign affairs, which Michaelis had abysmally abandoned, drew only an insolent reply from Ludendorff. In certain circumstances, he insisted, not only the chancellor but also the kaiser must yield to military considerations. To Hertling's assertion that he alone was responsible for peace terms, Hindenburg replied: ". . . In our position, as it has developed—without any conscious action on our part—we feel ourselves justly responsible to the German nation, history and our own conscience for the form which the peace takes. No formal declaration can relieve us of that sense of responsibility. . . ."[12] The OHL continued to bombard OberOst with blunt and unsolicited demands to make a rapid peace with Russia that would include vast territorial gains for Germany.

Peace talks had resumed in Brest Litovsk in January with one of Lenin's star players, Leon Trotsky, heading the Bolshevik delegation. The thin, lanky Trotsky was not only a leading Bolshevik intellectual but was also an able negotiator: "clever, versatile, cultivated, possessed of great energy, powers of work, and eloquence, he gave the impression of a man who knew exactly what he wanted," so Hoffmann wrote.[13]

The talks proceeded slowly. Trotsky was negotiating from weakness and was probably playing for time in the hope that a socialist revolution would break out in Germany while he hurled wireless messages to Bolshevik troops everywhere inciting them "to revolt, to disobedience, to the murder of officers."[14] The situation was further complicated by the arrival in Brest Litovsk of a delegation from the Ukraine which opened their own negotiations for independence in return for economic concessions to Germany along with some territorial grants to Austria-Hungary, an effort that resulted in a separate peace despite Trotsky's every effort to halt it.

Ludendorff continued to fire invectives against Trotsky's delaying tactics and the Bolshevik menace, conveniently forgetting that he had played Frankenstein to the monster Lenin. In mid-February the kaiser and the chancellor agreed that military operations against the Bolsheviks could resume. Foreign minister Richard von Kühlmann courageously held out, to no avail—little wonder in view of the kaiser's conclusion that the Bolsheviks formed part of a worldwide Jewish-Freemason conspiracy: "Bolsheviks are tigers, round them up and shoot them."[15]

The German offensive began on February 18. Five days later, with strong German forces advancing against fragmented resistance deep into Russia, the Bolsheviks agreed to a peace on enemy terms. The treaty of Brest Litovsk was signed on March 3, 1918. Its terms, dictated almost entirely by Hindenburg and Ludendorff, were violent in the extreme, and the Allied powers wasted little time in tagging it "the peace of violence." The Bolsheviks lost control of Georgia, the Ukraine, Russian Poland and Russia's Baltic lands—nearly a million and a quarter square miles, fifty-six million people or thirty-two percent of her entire population, a third of the railways, seventy-three percent of iron production, eighty-nine percent of coal production, over five thousand factories, mills, distilleries, and refineries, control of the navy, a reparations payment of six billion marks, "a peace of humiliation . . . without precedent or equal in modern history," in the words of one historian.[16]

It was one of the silliest and most dangerous treaties ever. In direct contrast to the positive goals of Wilson's Fourteen Points and his recently announced "Four Principles," it was a declaration of German and Austrian arrogance and future intentions. Accepted even by the Social Democrats in the Reichstag—to their enduring shame—it flashed the brutality of German greed to the world. This was to be the fate of Belgium, France, Britain, and Italy should Germany win the war. It also set a precedent, fatal to Germany, for harsh terms in case the Allies emerged on top. The terms of the treaty of Brest Litovsk and the later treaty of Bucharest with Romania were more ruthless than the terms of the 1919 treaty of Versailles, which several generations of German historians have used to justify Germany's irresponsible political behavior that led to the takeover of government by Adolf Hitler.

Ludendorff's military leitmotiv since the outbreak of the Russian revolution had been peace in the east in order to gain troops for the west. Yet this "peace of violence" created a gigantic salient that had to be defended. Troops would shortly be sent to Finland to put down a Bolshevik revolt and pave the way for future German control of that country; troops to Batum and Baku in Georgia and Azerbaijan, respectively, to protect oil supplies; troops to Odessa; troops to keep the fragile peace in Romania; troops to support the German-backed hetman in the Ukraine; troops to Lithuania, Kurland, Livonia, Estonia. In all a million German soldiers remained in the eastern theater until October 1918.

That was only the tip of the iceberg. The garrison troops for the most part were older men, between thirty-five and forty-five, who wanted to return home as soon as possible. Service conditions were not the best. They often served in isolated detachments where they were particularly prone to the blandishments of Bolshevik propaganda and the bribes of Jewish traders. Those who were transferred to the western front often carried the social disease of Bolshevism with them.

There was more. Ludendorff insisted on sending troops to the Crimea, which he planned to turn into a German Riviera, and ordered the navy to commandeer the Russian fleet at Sevastopol, most of which he would give to Enver Pasha. This arbitrary move, a treaty violation, infuriated both the German foreign ministry and navy. It soon led to estrangement between Ludendorff and Admiral Holtzendorff, indeed between the OHL and the entire naval staff, a quarrel that would continue to the end of the war.

Nor did the conquered territories live up to their material expectations. Only small quantities of oil were found in Batum and Baku. The discordant political situation in the Ukraine soon forced General Groener to set up what amounted to an army of occupation against the wishes of the foreign ministry. Hostile peasants and insufficient troops resulted in far fewer grain deliveries than predicted. This area in time supplied the German army with 140,000 horses and considerable herds of cattle, but its rich harvest in 1918 could not be transported to Germany because of lack of trains.

Ludendorff's expansionist policy inevitably collided with that of Turkey, not to mention the Bolshevik government, which showed its disapproval by murdering the German ambassador to Russia, Count Mirbach, and shortly thereafter the military commander in Kiev, General Eichhorn. The conflict between the OHL and the foreign ministry as to the proper handling of these territories continued to poison their relations and was never fully resolved by the end of the war.

32

Ludendorff's Bid for a Knockout Victory in the West

> The whole offensive action must not consist of a single great
> attack in one sector. . . . The whole action must rather be
> composed of several attacks, having the strongest reciprocal
> effect, in various sectors, with the object of shaking the whole
> English front.
> —MAJOR GEORG WETZELL, OHL CHIEF OF OPERATIONS,
>   DECEMBER 12, 1917[1]

> If the mind have no fixed aim, it loses itself, for, as they say,
> to be everywhere is to be nowhere.
> —MONTAIGNE, *ESSAYS*[2]

The OHL was gripped by rising optimism as more and more divisions from the east reached the western front for the final great battle. General Arz von Straussenburg on behalf of Kaiser Karl promised to release the German divisions in Italy as soon as he could replace them with Austro-Hungarian divisions from the east; in addition he would supply "heavy artillery" and "as much immediate support as possible."[3] In mid-December the representative of the foreign ministry at the OHL reported: "The generals are talking now very big and are full of the idea of smashing the enemy."[4]

The feeling was not unanimous. Ludendorff was so upset from reports of defeatist remarks by officers on leave that he issued a secret directive on the subject. One officer had told important personages in Berlin that an offensive was out of the question because of a shortage of horses and fodder. Such statements could only damage the vital interests of the Fatherland—regimental commanders were to impress this on officers and men alike.[5]

Wilhelm Groener and Crown Prince Rupprecht of Bavaria were opposed to an immediate offensive in the west, both because of the increasing shortage of troop and horse replacements and because they favored the defense as being less costly. Far better to seize Salonica and push forward in upper Italy. To take the pressure off the weakened Italian army, the Allies would probably attack on the western front where they would further weaken themselves. Rupprecht, though forever patronized by Ludendorff, had long since proven himself to be an able and consci-entious commander,[6] who at this point was far more realistic than the Duo, warning Kaiser Wilhelm that despite the favorable military situation "we still suffered two evils which are beyond remedy, the gradually in-creasing shortage of troop replacements and horses which would only become worse. We are indeed in a position to strike a few powerful blows at the enemy in the west but scarcely to bring on a decisive defeat, thus it is to be expected that the battle within a few months will once again become a tedious war of position. Who will finally win depends above all on who is able to make do the longest with his effective manpower, and in this respect I am convinced that the enemy is better off, thanks to the Americans, who of course can become effective only gradually."[7]

Rupprecht was shocked by the condition of troops that were arriving from the east. One such group had traveled for five days in unheated coaches with broken windows, no blankets, inadequate food. One trans-port included a hundred Westphalians who were over forty-five and who had been promised long-overdue furloughs to see their wives and chil-dren, after which they would be assigned to rear-area duties. They arrived in the west half-starved and frozen, received no furloughs, and were pushed into the trenches.[8]

Colonel Albrecht von Thaer noted in his diary that the generals from the eastern and Italian fronts were more optimistic than those from the western front: "The former underrate the tenacity of the British as well as the potential advantages to be gained from the Americans." Nevertheless, all of the generals were convinced of an enormous initial success. "But how great must this be or how far must it extend," Thaer asked himself, "to bring the enemy to the peace table?"[9]

It was a good question. Almost from the moment of inception Ludendorff's strategy began falling victim to vagueness. Major Wetzell wrote that "the whole offensive action must not consist of a single great attack in one sector. . . . The whole action must rather be composed of several attacks, having the strongest reciprocal effect, in various sectors, with the object of shaking the whole English front. . . ."[10] The task, in Hindenburg's later words, was to shake "the hostile edifice by closely connected partial blows in such a way that sooner or later the whole business would collapse"[11] (what Marshal Foch derisively called "buffalo strategy"). Ludendorff had said much the same thing to Hoffmann the previous spring, and it is possible that Wetzell's tail was wagging Ludendorff's dog. Hoffmann had vigorously opposed the notion, but Ludendorff was not to be moved.

Ludendorff had decided to open his offensive in the center sector: "Here the attack would strike the enemy's weakest point, the ground offered no difficulties, and it was feasible at all seasons." If the major attack were directed toward the area between Arras and Péronne, that is, west toward the coast, "the strategic result might indeed be enormous, as we should separate the bulk of the English army from the French and crowd it up with its back to the sea."[12]

As finally worked out, the action was to open with Plan Michael, an offensive stretching some forty miles on either side of Saint-Quentin. Two weeks after Plan Michael had begun, another offensive would strike between Ypres and Lens toward Hazebrouck, as General von Kuhl had proposed at the November conference. This was code-named Plan St. George. Ludendorff notified the kaiser in early February that the offensive would commence on March 21. "It must not be believed that we will have an offensive such as we had in Galicia or Italy," Ludendorff warned. "It will be a gigantic struggle beginning in one place, continuing in another, and demanding much time, which will be difficult but finally successful."[13]

These cryptic words, which stand at odds with what Ludendorff confidently told government ministers and various politicians, cause one to wonder how he intended to carry out this high-risk offensive. Did he mean that he intended to throw everything he had into the attack between Arras and La Fère before turning on one or another enemy? Or did he mean that if his opening offensive were contained he would revert to offensives in the north and south? Whichever he intended, and it is possible that he did not know *what* he intended, the plan lacked political, strategical, and tactical reality.

France and Britain were bending but were far from broken. Despite the submarine campaign—now visibly waning because of ever more effective countermeasures—Britain was a long way from starvation. A massive German victory might well have altered the national wills to resist, although this was improbable in view of the American colossus rapidly coming to the fore.

But a massive German victory was highly doubtful. German armies had successfully held off much stronger Allied offensives in the last three years. Ludendorff enjoyed only a slight superiority in numbers and would be hard put to find replacements for what certainly would be heavy casualties. Contrary to Ludendorff's later statement that the ground offered no difficulties, two of the three armies involved would be crossing the old Somme battlefield. As Major Wetzell pointed out, this was a quiet sector, so "preparations for the attack will hardly remain undetected and . . . the requisite *surprise* . . . will be very difficult to attain."[14] The troops would have to attack over cratered terrain cut by hundreds of miles of crumbled, rat-filled trenches and holding thousands of unexploded shells, toxic barbed wire, and stinking piles of dead men and horses, obstacles that would benefit the defense.

If the attack reached open country, division commanders lacked the mobility necessary for rapid exploitation. The entire German army possessed only 35,000 trucks (so much for the Hindenburg Program), and most of these had iron wheels, which quickly tore up fragile roads and were not suitable to move troops. The army was very short of horses, and those they had were undernourished and weak, scarcely up to pulling heavy guns long distances over difficult terrain. The enemy was numerically superior in artillery, airplanes, and tanks, the Germans having only a handful of the latter. So it would not be a swift action, and in view of the enemy's excellent road and rail complex, Haig would have time to call in British reinforcements from the north, French reinforcements from the south.

What was Ludendorff after politically? A leading member of the Reichstag, Conrad Hausmann, sent him a warning in February by a respected Swiss military expert that even if Amiens and Rheims were seized, the political result would be a failure: "I have repeatedly pointed out that in this war the strategical threat has a more powerful effect and is easier to turn to political account than the completed operation." Germany stood to lose Austria and Bulgaria, the expert continued, "to say nothing of Turkey by the proposed offensive which should at least be deferred until the Belgian question was cleared up." Hausmann received only a "delphic" reply from Ludendorff.[15] Other voices asked for a political offensive before military action, such to include a renunciation of claims on Belgium and other foreign territories, a move indignantly rejected by Ludendorff. Lieutenant Colonel von Haeften also expressed doubts but insisted that Germany needed one more victory to bring the British to the peace table, adding that "in any case the defensive would cost us more men than the offensive," a fatuous statement, since he had learned and reported to Ludendorff that the British did not plan to make a new offensive.[16]

What was Ludendorff after strategically? By his own admission he disdained firm strategical goals, holding to the German general-staff credo that "strategy is made up of expedients," and that "strategic victory follows tactical success."[17] When Crown Prince Rupprecht wanted to know the operational goal, Ludendorff angrily replied, "We make a hole and the rest will take care of itself."[18]

What about tactical failure? The question was put to Ludendorff by Prince Max of Baden in mid-February. "In that case Germany must go under," Ludendorff replied.[19]

On a January day in Berlin, when the German armies on the western front were feverishly preparing for the big offensive, our old friend Hugo Vogel was splashing away at his Blücher-like canvases when he received a surprise visitor. Field Marshal von Hindenburg had stopped by to inspect the Tannenberg canvas, a monumental work nearly five and a half yards long. Hindenburg carefully examined the assembled figures, pointing out faults in various uniforms. Suddenly he let out an uncharacteristic shriek: on the immortal day of Tannenberg his prewar black trousers had been painted gray! This would have to be changed. Vogel's remonstrance that it would ruin the artistic effect went unheard—the memorial would be historically accurate and that was that. Ludendorff's figure was also wrong—he would send his deputy to the studio soon. He next scrutinized the Marienburg canvas. Suddenly he scooped up Vogel's palette and began to alter his own spurs. "Then he altered the refugees on the opposite river bank. 'They are moving much too rapidly. The Russians are as far from Marienburg as Magdeburg is from Berlin. Would they then already run away?' " With that he departed for luncheon with the chancellor.[20]

Ludendorff showed up for a sitting a few days later. Letters from Hindenburg followed. The argument over the trousers was still going on when the final German offensive opened in March. Shortly thereafter Hindenburg yielded to the advice of an expert, and Vogel was told "to do what you wish with my trousers."[21]

(The canvas was privately purchased and presented to Hindenburg on his seventieth birthday. Four days before the war ended he returned it to the donor because it was too big for his house. The painting went to the kaiser, who ordered it sent to a war museum that was never built.)[22]

Ludendorff's offensive involved two army groups, those of the Bavarian Crown Prince Rupprecht and the German Crown Prince Wilhelm, which had been allotted seventy-one divisions. An immense force of thirty-two assault divisions backed by thirty-nine reserve divisions were to attack on a forty-nine-mile front between Arras and La Fère. The assault would be supported by seven thousand cannon which would share a four-day supply of nine million shells. Rupprecht commanded Otto von Below's Seventeenth Army and Georg von der Marwitz's Second Army. Wilhelm commanded Oskar von Hutier's Eighteenth Army. This less than satisfactory command arrangement was made both to allow Ludendorff to retain maximum control of the action and to permit Crown Prince Wilhelm to share in a decisive victory of German arms.

The axis of attack was to the northwest. The left wing of Below's Seventeenth Army was to attack on the line Croisilles–Moeuvres, assisted on his left by the right wing of Marwitz's Second Army. Once Below and Marwitz broke through to the line Péronne–Bapaume, their attack would shift more to the northwest toward the line Albert–Arras.

Among army commanders summoned by Ludendorff from other fronts was General Oskar von Hutier, whose tactical innovations had proved successful on the eastern front. Ludendorff now attempted to convert his armies to von Hutier's teachings as well as to those of Colonel Georg Bruchmüller, Hutier's acknowledged artillery genius. Surprise was the keynote. After a short but very powerful artillery barrage of gas and high-explosive shells, small groups of *Sturmtruppen* armed with automatic rifles, light machine guns, flamethrowers, and trench mortars would move out under cover of a barrage that crept forward as they advanced to punch channels through enemy defenses to the immediate rear, thus disorganizing the defense before reserves came up. If necessary the assault groups would bypass isolated centers of resistance, leaving them to be neutralized by close-support units of heavy machine guns and mortars, flamethrowers, and mobile artillery, while the advance troops, aided by artillery and tactical aircraft, continued forward. Larger units would follow on to enlarge the channels and consolidate gains against enemy counterattacks.

These were sound enough tactics in theory, although they had been found somewhat deficient in Nivelle's disastrous 1917 offensive. By beefing up the firepower of the battalion with trench mortars, flamethrowers, and close-support artillery, it became the tactical unit of the division, with the assault groups the tactical units of each battalion. Here was a fundamental tactical transition imposed on younger officers and men who had known only defensive warfare, while to the veterans who somehow had survived three years of slaughter, the old offensive concepts seemed a century away. The complete turnabout from defensive to offensive warfare on the western front meant that the German army was caught up in one vast training and reorganization program that was difficult if not impossible to complete in the short time allotted.

The new bible was Ludendorff's *Der Angriff im Stellungskrieg (The Attack in Position Warfare)*, but this was supplemented by numerous training and operation directives (paper shortage and all), most of them signed by Ludendorff, that overflowed the in-baskets of infantry and artillery troop commanders. The documents that have survived emphasize the appalling problem of converting armies that had developed defensive tactics into a way of life to offensive armies employing storm infiltration tactics that called for the closest coordination between assault troops and artillery firing on targets provided by aerial observers. Early directives spell out infantry and artillery tasks in almost childlike simplicity, repeatedly offering tactical maxims more appropriate to a class of junior noncommissioned officers than to division and regimental commanders: artillery cannot be expected to win the battle—that is up to the infantry; commanders must make sure that ample ammunition is on hand and must not wait until the last shot is fired before requisitioning more; a division making good progress in the attack must not be relieved by another division; leadership is all-important—and so on.[23]

Other shortcomings existed. The French and British offensives of 1917, in some cases spearheaded by tanks, had failed against far fewer numbers than Ludendorff would now be attacking—without tanks. The German army possessed five tanks at the beginning of 1918, which during the year would be joined by ten more plus about seventy-five converted enemy tanks. Ludendorff had spurned the new weapon. The infantry would have to carry the whole load.

In the first two months of 1918 the attack divisions were moved to rear areas for training. Commanders from generals to lieutenants attended special schools to learn the new tactics. Troops trained with live ammunition, learning how to live a short distance from a lethal curtain of their own artillery fire. Infantry would eventually outrun the heavy artillery and had to be trained in the use of field guns and light mortars. They were taught how to defend against tanks by building field fortifications, traps, and barricades with mined approaches defended by infantry using multiple-head grenades and heavy machine guns firing armor-piercing bullets. To preserve secrecy, artillerymen were taught to register guns on priority targets without prefiring, a Bruchmüller formula that judiciously blended mathematical calculation with physical reality.[24]

Not all commanders embraced the new doctrines. Otto von Below, who had recently commanded the German-Bulgarian defense in Macedonia and the successful Italian offensive, seemed to scorn Bruchmüller's ingenious formula that helped prevent the enemy from becoming alerted to a possible attack. Neither did all commanders subscribe to von Hutier's innovative tactics, preferring instead "the old way"—not an unusual experience in any army.

The OHL moved from Kreuznach to Spa in early March. Ludendorff was determined to control this offensive, and Kreuznach was too far away. Now it was time for the guns and trench mortars to move into elaborately camouflaged positions close to the front, where millions of shells filled enormous underground caverns.

Three days before the offensive was to begin, the Duo moved to advanced headquarters across the border in Avesnes, a pretty little town surrounded by woods. Hindenburg remembered it from the Franco-Prussian War nearly half a century earlier. "Even our presence added little to its activity . . . ," he later wrote, "the different types I saw in the streets seemed to be so unchanged that I could easily have forgotten that there ever had been such an interval."[25] It was something of a comedown from the splendor of villas and comfortable hotels at Spa and Kreuznach. Kaiser Wilhelm arrived the following day, turned up his imperial nose at the place and remained in his luxurious train.

Time was short now, the days tense. "It is good that one has to work in exciting circumstances," Hindenburg wrote to his wife, "otherwise the stay here would be very tedious. I brought some books along—Goethe's *Faust* and *The History of German Literature in Outline* —for the days will be somewhat long."[26]

After weeks of fine weather the sky had darkened with thunder pealing like distant cannon fire. The wind no longer favored the important opening gas bombardment. In late morning on March 20 the OHL's meteorologist reported a slight improvement in the strength and direction of the wind.

Decision could no longer be postponed. At noon Ludendorff informed Hindenburg that he wanted the attack to begin on schedule. Hindenburg calmly agreed. Ludendorff was visibly nervous. At luncheon he asked a table companion, "Do you know tomorrow's text by the Brethren?" He referred to the little red Moravian Brethren prayer book which he frequently consulted. The officer shook his head. "It is," Ludendorff told him, " 'This is the day of the chosen people.' Can we fail therefore to have confidence?"[27]

33

French and British Countermeasures

I also told Army Commanders [at a conference] that I was very pleased at all I had seen on the fronts of the three Armies which I had recently visited. Plans were sound and thorough, and much work had already been done. I was only afraid that the enemy would find our front so very strong that he will hesitate to commit his Army to the attack with the almost certainty of losing very heavily.
—FIELD MARSHAL LORD HAIG, DIARY ENTRY, MARCH 2, 1918[1]

Although the Germans employed utmost secrecy in preparing for the new offensive, the probability of a large-scale enemy attack was never far from the minds of Allied commanders. From the Channel coast to the Swiss border, a battle line wormed nearly 450 miles, the tired and depleted Allied armies on the defensive. Aware that Germany even then was transferring large numbers of troops from the Russian and other fronts to the western front, the Allied primary hope was to hold until the Americans arrived in sufficient quantity to offset German reinforcements.

The earlier crisis in Italy had led the Allies to form the Inter-Allied Supreme War Council, which began meeting at Versailles in November 1917, its mission being to coordinate the war effort. The civil side of the council exercised very real powers that enabled its members to realistically allot manpower, equipment, supply, and shipping. The officers composing the military side, however, lacked executive powers and functioned primarily in an advisory capacity. Since this function was already performed by respective army chiefs of staff, the additional counsel was not always welcome to the Allied commanders in chief, Douglas Haig, Henri Pétain, and John Pershing.

Despite the best efforts of Colonel House, President Wilson's personal representative in France, and General Tasker Bliss, Wilson's military adviser at Versailles, to effect a more central Allied leadership, the principals spent the winter in acrimonious argument. Pershing detested General Peyton March, the U.S. Army chief of staff in Washington, D.C., who was his junior, and paid his directives scant attention. Haig loathed Henry Wilson, who had replaced Robertson as British chief of staff, and ignored him when he could. Pétain held no more than lukewarm regard for his chief of staff, Ferdinand Foch; he resented Pershing's insistence on keeping his few burgeoning American divisions under his own command; and he regarded Haig's strategical views with considerable suspicion. Neither he nor Haig would agree to commit a few of their divisions to a central reserve, as requested by the War Council.

By mid-March 1918 the Allied front continued to resemble feudal fiefs ruled by separate barons. In the extreme north, King Albert's twelve Belgian divisions held eighteen miles of front. Albert's right flank tied in with Haig's command, four armies that carried the line another 125 miles to the south. The British right nudged Pétain's huge domain: Franchet d'Esperey's Army Group of the North—three armies holding the next 70 miles—and, beginning at Verdun, Castelnau's Army Group of the East, four armies which carried the line south to the Swiss border. Of the 312 miles of front held by the French, Pershing's four American divisions, equal in size to about eight French or British divisions, held 17 miles in "quiet" sectors. In all, 173 Allied divisions faced 194 German divisions, theoretically a satisfactory proportion of defender to attacker, but one particularly prone, in view of the elongated line and lack of well-thought-out defensive systems, to exploitation by concentration of fighting strength.

Pétain believed that *his* front would be the target of enemy attack, specifically east of Rheims in the Champagne country. To guard against this, he kept sixty of his ninety-nine divisions in line, with another fifteen screening the Vosges sector. He held twenty divisions in reserve behind his center and another four in reserve to aid the British, in accordance with a private agreement with Haig.

Haig believed that Ludendorff intended to attack *his* line, which is one reason that he had refused to furnish any divisions to a central reserve. He was correct in his belief but stupid in his stubbornness, nor did he and his staff accurately read enemy intentions. Plan Michael was aimed at Haig's southern, or right, flank, which rested on the Somme River and was held by Julian Byng's Third Army on the left and by Hubert Gough's Fifth Army on Byng's right.

Byng was given sixteen divisions to protect twenty-eight miles of front, Gough fourteen divisions to hold a forty-mile line. Of these forces, most of which had been mutilated in the Passchendaele offensives and had received inadequate replacements, Byng held four divisions in reserve, Gough only one. Haig's army reserve amounted to only eight divisions, five divisions having been sent to Italy during the November crisis, where they remained. Massive numbers of troops were in England, but the British prime minister, Lloyd George, disapproved of Haig's enormous losses in Flanders and insisted on holding them at home to be doled out as a careful father might dole out money to a prodigal son.

In early December 1917 Haig had received an intelligence estimate of German intentions for 1918, which read in part:

In the early spring (not later than the beginning of March) she [Germany] should seek to deliver such a blow on the Western Front as would force a decisive battle which she could fight to a finish before the American forces could take an active part, i.e., before midsummer.

For such a battle it is essential that Germany should choose a battlefield where the Allies are defending some objective of vital importance to them. . . . Numerous objectives of this nature are offered on the Western Front, e.g., Verdun, Nancy, Chalons, Reims, Amiens, Bethune, Hazebrouck and Dunkirk."[2]

Haig had not abandoned his offensive strategy despite disasters at Ypres, Passchendaele, and Cambrai. His plan to continue the offensive in Flanders had been delayed, but only until he could cajole the government into releasing more men. It was obvious that for the winter he must remain on the defensive. The day after receiving Charteris's intelligence report, Haig called in his army commanders, who learned that "we must be prepared to meet a strong and sustained hostile offensive." His generals were "to give their immediate and personal attention to the organization of their Army zones for defensive purposes, and to the training of their troops in defensive tactics . . ."[3]

His orders were timely. A few days after this conference, French intelligence reported large German concentrations in the Mézières area.

Haig told his French liaison officer that such a concentration "threatened Amiens and might foreshadow an advance in force S.W. [southwest] of St. Quentin more than an attack on Chalons. I suggested that he should find out the state of the defences of Amiens."[4] Amiens was an important railroad junction of north-south and Channel traffic, and its loss would effectively separate the British and French armies.

Just how seriously Haig regarded the situation is open to conjecture. After receiving a field marshal's baton from King George in early January 1918, he attended a meeting of the war cabinet in London:

As regards the enemy's action, I stated that I thought that the coming four months would be the critical period of the war. Also that it seemed to me possible that the enemy would attack both the French and ourselves, and that he would hold Reserves in hand ready to exploit wherever he might have gained a success. . . . In my opinion, the best defense would be to continue our offensive in Flanders, because we would then retain the initiative and attract the German Reserves against us. It is doubtful whether the French Army can now withstand for long, a resolute and continued offensive on the part of the enemy.

Having thus spoken, only two days later he told Lloyd George that "Germany having only one million men as Reserves for this year's fighting, I doubted whether they would risk them in an attempt to 'break through.' If the Germans did attack it would be a gambler's throw. All seemed to depend on the struggle now going on in Germany between the Military and Civil parties. If the Military party won, they would certainly attack and try and deliver a knock-out blow against the Western Front. We must be prepared for this."[5]

It is surprising that Haig should speak of a mythical military-civil struggle when even a junior intelligence analyst must have been aware of Hindenburg and Ludendorff's supremacy, and even more surprising that he should do so when hundreds of trains were daily bringing thousands of troops to the western front. Judging from his words and later actions, it seems unlikely that Haig expected a massive German offensive.

No matter which way he stood, he was guilty of professional ineptitude. If he did not expect an offensive, then he and his staff must be faulted for poor evaluation of existing intelligence. If he did expect an offensive, then he must be faulted for not having concentrated on strengthening defenses and ensuring that his troops were intensively trained in defensive tactics. Of a total labor force of over 100,000 men in the army areas, only 1,700 were working on defenses at the turn of the year, a figure that rose to 2,700 by March 1918—obviously Haig attached little importance to strengthening fixed defenses in the threatened area.

One of Haig's biographers, John Terraine, has ingeniously defended this misjudgment by citing his subject's belief that his southern flank had ample room to fall back until *French* reserves arrived to stem the attack. Haig had come to trust General Pétain, with whom he had made a gentleman's agreement that each would reinforce the other when necessary, despite Field Marshal Wilson's warning to Haig that he suspected Pétain of "not playing straight."[6] But it was Haig who told the war cabinet that the French would probably be attacked and would soon be in dire straits. How then could he expect Pétain to rush reserve divisions to his aid?

Haig's ambiguity did not wash well with his Fifth Army commander, General Sir Hubert Gough. Up to late November 1917 this had been a quiet sector, but enemy raids several nights a week during December suggested that it would not remain so. Gough had inherited twenty-eight of his forty miles of front from the French. The trench system had been badly neglected, telephone lines were unburied, French peasants were actually removing barbed wire to clear ground for cultivation.[7] Gough protested to Haig's headquarters in early February that his front was much too weak to hold against an enemy attack. He was informed that he was not expected to maintain a static defense. If attacked, he would make a fighting withdrawal to the Somme. It was his twofold responsibility to construct adequate defenses at Péronne and to build a defensive zone along the Somme—in all, to dig about 300 miles of new trenches and lay protective barbed wire, a task that "no amount of labor—nothing short of a fairy wand" could have accomplished in a few weeks.[8]

If German intentions were problematical in January, they had considerably clarified in mid-February when Haig called another meeting of his army commanders, who were warned "that we must be prepared to meet a very severe attack at any moment now." Tactics were reviewed for all sectors, and Haig noted that "all felt confident on being able to hold their front."[9]

Haig's preoccupation with his northern sectors continued throughout February. Having inspected Lord Horne's First Army, guardian of Vimy Ridge, he wrote in his diary, "I look upon this part of our front as the backbone and center of our defensive system and [it] must be held firmly at all costs."[10]

He inspected Gough's Fifth Army in early March. The Fifth Army had confirmed that the German Eighteenth Army opposite was commanded by General Oskar von Hutier, whose innovative offensive tactics were known to the Allied powers. A thoughtful intelligence officer might have concluded that Hutier's presence, coupled with the known buildup of enemy strength on the western front, 179 divisions in February, 182 in early March, boded no good for the Fifth Army. Haig was somewhat disturbed by the inadequately defended forty-mile front and went so far as to reinforce Gough with *one* division from Fourth Army, noting that "I have no more troops available to send him, without uncovering *vital* points elsewhere,"[11] by which he meant the northern sectors.

Haig also noted that Gough had insufficient labor to build adequate fallback lines, but he did nothing to ameliorate this deficiency. That he was not overly worried is suggested by an entry in his diary on March 2: ". . . I also told Army Commanders [at a conference] that I was very pleased at all I had seen on the fronts of the three Armies which I had recently visited. Plans were sound and thorough, and much work had already been done. I was only afraid that the enemy would find our front so very strong that he will hesitate to commit his Army to the attack with the almost certainty of losing very heavily."[12]

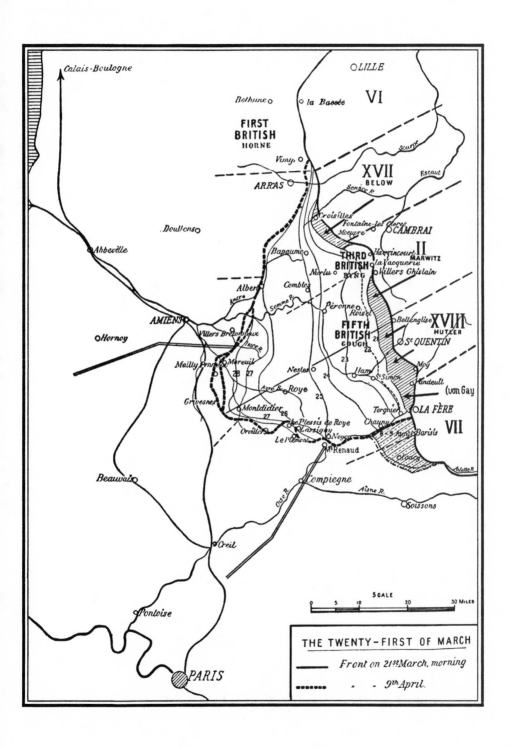

Calais-Boulogne

○LILLE

VI

○Bethune ○la Bassée

FIRST
BRITISH
HORNE

Vimy○ Scarpe

XVII
BELOW

ARRAS○ Sensce R. E.Scaut

○Doullens ○Croisilles Fontaine-les-Cleres ○CAMBRAI
Mceuvre

Abbeville○ Bapaume○ Harincourt II
THIRD la Vacquerie MARWITZ
BRITISH ○Villers Ghislain
BYNG
Nurlu○

Albert○ Combles○ Ancre
Somme R. ○Peronne XVIII
AMIENS○ Roisel ○Bellenglise HUTLER

Hornoy○ Villers Bretonneux○ FIFTH
Avre R. BRITISH ○St QUENTIN
Mereuil○ GOUGH 28

Mailly Renneval○ Nesles○ 23 Moy
28 27 24 Ham○ ○St Simon
Gruesnes○ Avre R. ○Roye 22 Tindeull
Montdidier○ 25 (von Gay)
27 26 Tergnier ○LA FÈRE
Orvillc○ Le Plessis de Roye Chauny Fanis○Barisis VII
Lassigny○ ○Noyon 8-9 Apr.
Le Plémont Foucy
Mt Renaud○ Ailette R.

Beauvais○ Compiegne○ Aisne R. ○Soissons
Oise R.

Creil○

SCALE
0   5   10   20   30 MILES

Pontoise○

┌──┐
│ THE TWENTY-FIRST OF MARCH   │
│   │
│ ———————— Front on 21st March, morning│
│   │
│ ▪▪▪▪▪▪▪▪ · · 9th April.   │
PARIS└──┘

34

March 21, 1918: The Big Push

The object is now to separate the French and British by a rapid advance on both sides of the Somme. The Seventeenth and Sixth armies and later the Fourth Army will conduct the attack against the British north of the Somme, in order to drive them into the sea. They will keep on attacking at new places in order to bring the whole British front to ruin.
    —GENERAL ERICH LUDENDORFF TO HIS ARMY GROUP CHIEFS
        OF STAFF, MARCH 23, 1918[1]

It is serious, very serious, but it is in no sense desperate. You understand, I refuse to speak of a possible retreat. There can be no question of a retreat. The time has come when we must make both armies realize this to the fullest extent. Haig and Pétain have offered a magnificent resistance. The situation can be likened to a double door: each of the generals is behind his half of the door without knowing who should push first in order to close the door. I quite understand their hesitation: the one who pushes first having his right or left wing turned . . .
    —GENERAL FERDINAND FOCH TO THE FRENCH MINISTER OF
        MUNITIONS, MARCH 24, 1918[2]

A t 4:40 A.M. on March 21, 1918, the German army unleashed the most powerful concentration of artillery fire in the history of war. On a forty-mile front between Croisilles and La Fère, nearly seven thousand guns, firing high-explosive and gas shells, shattered the eerie quiet of a fog-filled night to announce Germany's final bid for victory.

For five hours German shells tore into outposts and supply dumps, turned communication wire into heaps of jumbled spaghetti, smashed into trenches, demolished troop dugouts, exploded ammunition dumps, punched large holes in wire defenses—a vast, seemingly omnipresent cannonade that hurled flesh and concrete to the heavens while turning the gas-drenched land into a living hell.

For five hours the big guns remorselessly combed from front to rear and back to front, laying "an iron carpet" as one German commander described it.[3] At 9:35 mortars opened direct fire on forward trenches while engineers blew charges planted beneath barbed-wire defenses. After a final, furious bombardment of the forward zone, the artillery began creeping fire, the signal for the specially trained small units of assault troops, the *Sturmtruppen*, to move out.

These elite units had trained well. Armed with automatic rifles, light machine guns, grenades, and flamethrowers, the troops punched through fog-shrouded peripheral defenses to double-time across forward trenches into battle zones. Larger units followed close on to kill or capture surprised and stunned defenders of isolated strongpoints. German attack aircraft dove over the heads of the *Sturmtruppen*, machine guns spitting lethal fire, while overhead observation planes and captive balloons protected by a blanket of fighter planes called down artillery fire over the vast battlefield.

At Avesnes, Hindenburg as usual remained calm, Ludendorff nervous. Early reports from Hutier and Marwitz showed progress despite fog that impeded rapid movement and precise reportings. Von Below on the right complained that his assault troops were not keeping up with the creeping barrage.

The fog lifted in mid-morning to give the battle some shape. By noon forward zones had been overrun almost everywhere. Hutier and Marwitz pushed through the enemy first line in the afternoon and by evening had penetrated the second line with relatively light casualties. Below's left wing had also pushed through the first line but was then stopped cold despite having sustained horrendous casualties.

This pattern continued the next day. Hutier's Eighteenth Army was the star of the show, advancing without pause, punching through Gough's Fifth Army defenses to cross the Crozat Canal between Saint-Quentin and La Fère, which forced Gough to begin a general retreat behind the Somme and on the following morning to abandon what Haig regarded as the vital bridgehead at Péronne. Gough's retreat exposed the right flank of Byng's Third Army, already hammered by von der Marwitz's

Second Army, the other star of the show, which forced Byng to a hurried retreat to try to close the gap with Fifth Army. Only in the north was there failure. On the third day of fighting, Hutier and Marwitz's vanguards stood fifteen miles inside British lines. Below's Seventeenth Army had advanced less than four miles and in many places far less than that.

March 23 had opened on a bright if meaningless note for German arms. At a camouflaged railway sidetrack seventy-five miles from Paris, German artillerymen made the final adjustments on the complicated aiming mechanism of a secret weapon, a Krupp twenty-one-centimeter (eight-inch) cannon fondly named the Kaiser Wilhelm Geschütz—the Kaiser's Gun. This long-range weapon, which would soon become famous in the Western world as the Paris Gun, early that morning began hurling high-explosive shells, each weighing 264 pounds, on the French capital, an intermittent and very stupid bombardment that would continue until early August to deliver a mere 283 shells on random Paris targets.[4]

Bombing Paris was not going to solve Ludendorff's tactical quandary. For a man who expected to tie tactical knots in the Wellington tradition as the offensive continued, he seemed dangerously inhibited, unwilling to alter his original plan for a breakthrough at Arras despite Below's repeated failure to advance. Rather than allowing the Seventeenth Army to hold in that sector and throw in everything he had to exploit Hutier and Marwitz's remarkable victories, he continued to supply Below with precious reserve divisions. On March 23 Below received three fresh divisions along with orders to attack north in the direction of Arras–Saint-Pol, an attack which would be supported by von Quast's reinforced Sixth Army on Below's right. Marwitz was to continue his advance in the center, but Hutier was to shift more to the south toward Noyon. At Avesnes that afternoon Ludendorff told army group chiefs of staff:

The object is now to separate the French and British by a rapid advance on both sides of the Somme. The Seventeenth and Sixth armies and later the Fourth Army will conduct the attack against the British north of the Somme, in order to drive them into the sea. They will keep on attacking at new places in order to bring the whole British front to ruin.[5]

If Hindenburg remained stoically calm and Ludendorff understandably nervous, their supreme warlord was ecstatic. The bombardment of Paris, all twenty-three shells on the first day, was such a world-shaking event that he would allow no one but himself to announce it. "His Majesty returned from Avesnes bursting with news of our success," Admiral Müller confided to his diary. "He shouted to the guard on the platform as the train pulled in: 'The battle is won! The English have been utterly defeated.' There was champagne for dinner. The communiqué was read telling of our great victory under the personal leadership of His Majesty the Emperor, a well-meaning lie issued by the Hindenburg-Ludendorff firm which the German people will not believe for one moment."[6] Ludendorff's offensive was well on the way to failure when in a fit of euphoria the kaiser ordered flags flown to the accompaniment of cannon salutes throughout the empire.[7] He followed this by awarding Hindenburg the Iron Cross with Golden Rays, a supreme decoration whose last recipient was Field Marshal Blücher for his part in the battle of Waterloo (1815). Ludendorff received the Grand Cross of the Iron Cross. Hindenburg himself seemed unimpressed, writing to his wife: "What is the use of all these decorations? A good and advantageous peace is what I should prefer. It is not my fault in any case if the struggle ends unfavorably for us."[8]

Military historians have variously treated Ludendorff's orders of March 23. He himself glossed over them in his memoirs. It is difficult to explain why he greatly enlarged his original goal without yet having separated the French and British armies, or why he failed to send all of his reserves the previous day to exploit the breakthrough by Hutier and Marwitz instead of continuing to feed divisions into the insatiable maw of the Arras front. If he did intend to separate the British and the French by striking at Amiens, why did he not order subsidiary attacks to the south to hold French reserves in place? The tone of the victory communiqués that streamed from the OHL to electrify the world suggests that Ludendorff and his staff believed that the British Fifth and Third armies were shattered, but if this were the case where were the humbled prisoners, where the captured guns?

While failing to ask himself such uncomfortable questions, Ludendorff apparently envisaged two enormous envelopments in the Schlieffen tradition, the first against the British in the north, followed by the second against the French west of Paris. In view of his limited resources in men and matériel, his lack of mobility and recent enemy control of the air, he was in Napoleon's phrase trying to mount cannons in the sand, and one must seriously wonder at the state of his mental health at this time.

The result of his orders was disastrous. Otto von Below had been the odd man out since preparations had started for Plan Michael. Early in the offensive Ludendorff complained of Below's lack of control of infantry units. Contrary to Hutier's proven *Sturmtruppen* tactics, these units were depending too much on each other, which impeded advancement. Below's lack of progress on March 26 caused Ludendorff to telephone Crown Prince Rupprecht. "He was quite beside himself," Rupprecht wrote, "and very dissatisfied with the chief of staff [Krafft von Dellmensingen], whom he talked of relieving."[9]

On the seventh day of the offensive Below attacked with nine divisions. None of the earlier faults had been rectified. His artillery was ineffective. His infantry attacked *à la Russe*. A British regimental historian later wrote that "the enemy, who was coming on in great numbers, shoulder to shoulder, offered a splendid target to the rifles and Lewis guns."[10] By evening the attack had failed. A dispirited Ludendorff canceled Sixth Army's attack scheduled for the following day and sent nine divisions to Marwitz with orders to advance on Amiens. Hutier would receive four divisions but was not to cross the Avre River without fresh orders.

Ludendorff had waited too long. The German troops were exhausted after a week of hard fighting, not least because enemy air attacks frequently made rest impossible. Hutier's and Marwitz's divisions had advanced over thirty miles in six days, but now two days were needed to push on another few miles. Rear-area supply could not meet the demand. Trucks running on metal wheels tore up rear-area roads. In the battle areas the British had destroyed roads, railroads, bridges, and tunnels. Divisions stood miles ahead of their supply trains, whose wagons, pulled by skinny, underfed horses, lumbered with increasing difficulty over the pockmarked wasteland. Units were running short of ammunition and none was arriving.

The OHL lacked ample reserves behind each front and had to move replacements laterally—a slow task in view of overcrowded rail lines and torn-up roads—then send them forward over the difficult terrain. That terrain frequently prevented mobile artillery from keeping up with assault units. Disciplinary problems also existed: hungry and tired soldiers, existing mainly on nervous energy, thoroughly sick of war, deprived of many basic necessities not to mention luxuries of any sort for two years, fell like scavenging hordes on villages, towns, and enemy supply depots that stood in the way of war. The troops had soon discovered that their British opposites, far from starving as German propaganda insisted, were well-clothed and well-fed. Looting of Lucullan luxuries was much more fun than fighting.

In late March the advance of a division west of Albert suddenly halted. A staff officer, the poet and novelist Rudolf Binding, was sent to discover the reason. He found the streets "running with wine," drunken soldiers by the thousands. Binding watched one staff officer interrupt an urgent mission to pick up a discarded British raincoat from a ditch. "The madness, stupidity and indiscipline of the German troops is shown in other things as well. Any useless toy or trifle they seize and load into their packs, anything useful which they cannot carry they destroy."[11]

Ludendorff's delay in switching the major effort from the north had cost Hutier and Marwitz that invaluable ingredient of offensive war—momentum. Where a day or two earlier the way to Amiens and beyond was open, it was now being challenged by the arrival of two French armies commanded by General Fayolle with orders to support the remnants of Gough's Fifth Army. Lieutenant Sulzbach, commanding an artillery battery in von Hutier's army, wrote on March 30: ". . . I bring the battery up behind, and now we've got so much shrapnel rattling down on us that you can hardly hear or see anything. The machinegun fire, chattering away at us from only a few hundred meters distance, keeps on as heavy as ever. All hell has been let loose. The French seemed to have been transformed, they must have thrown completely fresh, properly rested troops into this sector, and a large number of them too. . . ."[12]

British reinforcements were arriving from the north, British and French planes in increasing numbers were bombing and strafing German columns. By the end of March, Ludendorff's offensive was halted along the line. He ordered another attack by fifteen divisions in early April, and when this failed he "was forced to take the extremely hard decision to abandon the attack on Amiens for good,"[13] his armies having suffered 230,000 casualties, including prisoners.

One could ask why Ludendorff arrived at this decision, and shortly after the war one of his former staff officers did ask this question. Ludendorff replied, "Nothing can be forced in war, one has a feeling how far one can go, and also a feeling if he can go no further."[14] The mystical process is undoubtedly simplified if one attacks in the wrong direction to start with.

The German avalanche had soon produced a crisis in Allied command relationships, which were being sorely tested. Haig had not been unduly upset at first by Hutier's advance in the south. On the second day of battle, when Fifth Army defenses were rapidly crumbling, he noted in his diary: "All reports show that our men are in great spirits. All speak of the wonderful targets they had to fire at yesterday. Enemy came on in great masses." That evening he learned from Gough that his reserve line was broken. "I concurred on his falling back and defending the lines of the Somme and to hold the Péronne bridgehead. I expect a big attack to develop towards Arras."[15] Haig visited Byng and Gough the next morning only to learn that Fifth Army was now *behind* the Somme River, its divisions and regiments shattered and dispersed.

Finally recognizing the situation for what it was, Haig on the same day opened an advanced headquarters at Dury, where Pétain arrived in the afternoon. Haig was greatly relieved to learn that Pétain was putting two armies under General Fayolle to operate on his right in the Somme Valley. But Pétain turned down Haig's request to deploy twenty French divisions around Amiens, his explanation being that he expected to be attacked in the Champagne. Pétain was obviously depressed and mentioned the possibility of the French and British armies being separated with the British being driven into the sea.

The situation grew very critical on the fourth day of fighting. While Haig was stripping his northern front to bring divisions south, the first French units reached Montdidier. Some divisions arrived without artillery, and division commanders appeared to be uncertain and confused and not a little apprehensive as German gains continued through the day.

The final blow fell late that night when Pétain again visited Haig. The prisoner of his own deep pessimism, he struck Haig "as very much upset, almost unbalanced and most anxious." This was understandable. Not only was he worried about being attacked in the Champagne, but on the previous day shells falling on Paris had convinced the citizenry (and politicians) that an attack on their capital was imminent. Pétain had conferred with General Fayolle earlier in the day and had ordered him "in the event of the German advance being pressed still further, to fall back southwestwards to Beauvais in order to cover Paris," a move that would uncover Haig's right flank.[16]

Haig was appalled. He and General Mangin later wrote that only a few enemy cavalry divisions could have wedged between the Allied armies. If the British and French armies were separated, the war would probably be lost. Late that night he reported Pétain's defection to London and asked the chief of the imperial general staff, Henry Wilson, and the minister of war, Lord Darby, to come at once to France "to arrange that General Foch or some other determined general, who would fight, should be given supreme command of the operations in France."[17]

The upshot of this was a top-level conference at Doullens on March 26. When Haig entered the council hall to the sound of enemy guns, Pétain whispered to Clemenceau, "There is a man who will be obliged to capitulate in open field within a fortnight, and very lucky if we are not obliged to do the same." It was clear to the French president, Raymond Poincaré, and to his premier, Georges Clemenceau, that Pétain had lost his nerve. They were debating the situation when a military car roared up to the town hall. In Clemenceau's later words, "There was a bustle, and Foch arrived, surrounded by officers, and dominating everything with his cutting voice. 'You aren't fighting? I would fight without a break. I would fight in front of Amiens. I would fight in Amiens. I would fight behind Amiens. I would fight all the time.' "[18]

The meeting opened and Clemenceau bluntly asked Haig if he intended to fight at Amiens or to continue falling back. Haig replied that he was doing everything he could to prevent the enemy from reaching Amiens—what were French intentions? Pétain explained that he was bringing up twenty-four divisions from the east at a rate of two per day. Foch then entered the discussion, stressing time and again that the war would be won by fighting, not by withdrawing.

With Foch's words ringing in their ears Lord Milner, representing Lloyd George, and Clemenceau conferred privately before announcing a decision that could have been made with profit several years earlier: the Allies must coordinate present and future actions under one commander. The man chosen was Foch, and although his authority was very limited, the appointment brought two immediate results. One concerned General Pershing. Pershing had visited Pétain to offer him those American divisions which were in training sectors. On March 28 he called on Foch to place all of his forces at Foch's disposal—providing they remained American divisions under American command.

The other result was a second high-level conference held at Beauvais a few days later which enlarged Foch's authority. Foch was now charged with "the strategic direction of [all] military operations."[19] Although each commander in chief, including Pershing, would retain "full control of the tactical action of their respective Armies" and "the right of appeal to his Government, if in his opinion his Army is endangered by reason of any order received from General Foch,"[20] the appointment nonetheless gave a new and vital direction to the Allied effort, an interesting example of how the fortunes of war often operate in inexplicable ways.

Foch was an excellent choice. At sixty-seven he breathed more fire than most junior officers. A pipe-smoking Gascon, he was a proud Roman Catholic in a republic of heretics. His religion, along with a rebellious nature—he believed that officers must *think*—had brought him professional martyrdom, first in peacetime when he was dismissed from the faculty of Staff College and put to grass for several years, next as scapegoat for the Somme debacle in 1916.

He could not be kept down. His military talents and above all his aggressive spirit far outshone those of his contemporaries. Foch was eager, brusque, confident, but he did not underrate the task at hand. On the way back to Paris from the Doullens conference, Clemenceau said to him: "Well, you have had your way." Foch replied: "Yes! A nice mess! You give me a lost battle, and tell me to win it."[21]

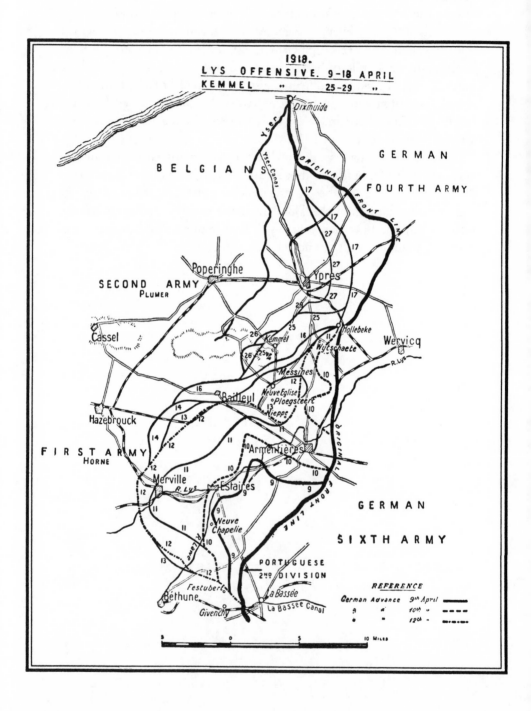

1918.

LYS OFFENSIVE. 9-18 APRIL

KEMMEL   „   25-29   „

BELGIANS

Yser

Yser Canal

ORIGINAL FRONT LINE

GERMAN

FOURTH ARMY

Dixmuide

17

17

27

17

27

SECOND ARMY
PLUMER

Poperinghe

Ypres

27   17

25

Cassel

26

25

Kemmel

26 25

16

Hollebeke

Wytschaete

18

Wervicq

R. Lys

Messines

10

12

FIRST ARMY
HORNE

16

Bailleul

Neuve Eglise

Ploegsteert

14

13

Nieppe

13

10

Hazebrouck

14

13

12

12

11

10

ORIGINAL FRONT LINE

12

11

Armentières

10

Merville

R. Lys

Estaires

10

10

12

11

9

9

9

GERMAN

11

Neuve
Chapelle

9

SIXTH ARMY

11

12

10

9

13

Festubert

12

PORTUGUESE
2ND DIVISION

Bethune

La Bassée

La Bassée Canal

Givenchy

REFERENCE

German Advance 9th April ———
     „   „   10th   „   — — —
     „   „   12th   „   —·—·—

5   0   5   10 MILES

35

Ludendorff Contrives Failure

Thus we drifted into hopeless disaster. Added to this, nobody among the people knew how serious the situation really was. The announcements of victory sent out by G.H.Q. [OHL] after the March attack caused not only the greater part of the nation, but also the greater part of the army, to believe that all was going well. We—the Eastern Command—heard nothing of the heavy losses that the offensive had cost, we did not know that Germany was no longer in a position to make good these losses . . .

—MAJOR GENERAL MAX HOFFMANN,
WRITING OF SPRING 1918[1]

Ludendorff called it "a brilliant feat." The early successes of Plan Michael had undeniably induced near panic in the government and peoples of France, Italy, and Great Britain. The collapse of the British Fifth Army had resulted in Hubert Gough's relief, most unfairly in the judgment of many historians, and would have brought Haig's dismissal had Lloyd George been able to find a suitable replacement. It cost the British 160,000 casualties, including 90,000 prisoners of war, and France over 70,000 casualties. The German territorial gain was immense. Enormous quantities of weapons and matériel had been captured. The new line was only seven miles from Amiens, whose vital railway complex was being shelled daily.

But Plan Michael was expensive. The Germans suffered an estimated loss of 70,000 prisoners and 160,000 casualties (including the death of Ludendorff's youngest stepson, who was shot down over the battlefield), * unacceptable figures in a war of attrition where Allied gaps would eventually be filled by divisions arriving from the colonies, Italy, and Palestine, and by an increasing flow of American soldiers, who were reaching France at the rate of 125,000 a month.

Plan Michael was also a strategical failure of the first degree. Shelling Amiens would end the war no more than the Kaiser's Gun would end the war by desultory firing on Paris. Ludendorff's new and awkwardly located salient extended rather than shortened his lines, to reverse his strategy of the previous year. Extended lines meant more troops com- mitted to position warfare, more resources devoted to defending the salient already being pounded by Allied guns and aircraft.

Plan Michael having failed, Ludendorff turned to Plan St. George, an offensive against fifty miles of British front running north from La Bassée. This plan called for attacks on either side of the Ypres salient to seize the commanding Mont Kemmel–Mont des Chats heights, con- verge on the rail junction of Hazebrouck, and then wheel north to seal off and destroy the British and Belgian armies in that area. This was Crown Prince Rupprecht's and General von Kuhl's preferred plan, which Ludendorff had rejected because of the wet ground in late winter.

It was not an ideal plan. To move men and guns to the north took over a week, time used by the Allies to recover somewhat from the shock of Plan Michael. Time did not permit night movement alone. British airmen were soon reporting road and rail traffic so considerable that one is put in mind of the ancient Florentines who "so far from seeking to gain advantage over their enemies by surprise . . . would warn them, a whole month before placing their army in the field, by the continual ringing of the bell they called Martinilla."[2] Surprise, the handmaiden of victory, having been forfeited, it followed that the enemy would appro- priately strengthen the target area.

On the credit side, a mild spring had dried the ground considerably. Ludendorff also correctly reasoned that Haig had greatly weakened his northern armies to meet the Plan Michael offensive. But Ludendorff's own reduced strength—he was forced to use "trench" divisions to sup- plement "assault" divisions—caused him to compress the original plan to a major strike between La Bassée and Armentières, with comple- mentary attacks to the north—an uncomfortable adjustment that

---

* Ludendorff issued orders for a search to be made for one Lieutenant Pernet's aircraft. Lieutenant Sulzbach stumbled on some wreckage in late April which turned out to be Pernet's plane. His grave was discovered nearby. Ludendorff wrote a personal note to Sulzbach and enclosed his photograph as a sign of gratitude. Herbert Sulzbach, *With the German Guns*, 164, 166, 169.

caused a whimsical staff officer to change the codename "St. George" to "Georgette."

The offensive was given over to General Ferdinand von Quast's Sixth Army, which would attack General Sir Henry Horne's First Army; General Sixt von Arnim's Fourth Army would strike General Sir Herbert Plumer's Second Army.

Quast attacked on the morning of April 9. A Bruchmüller-orchestrated bombardment opened at four A.M. to fling masses of mustard gas and tons of high-explosive shells along Horne's front. The *Sturmtruppen* moved out a few hours later. As planned, the bulk of Quast's nine divisions struck a single Portuguese division that was holding six miles of front and cut through it as if it had been butter.

Continuing favorable reports reached Hindenburg and Ludendorff during the morning. It was Ludendorff's fifty-third birthday. The kaiser, bowing to circumstances, honored the man "with whom he would never shake hands again" with a luncheon, during which he eulogized his first quartermaster general (whom he privately referred to pejoratively as his *Feldwebel*, or sergeant) and thoughtfully gave him a brass statuette of himself.

After-luncheon reports from the battlefield were not so favorable. Progress had slowed due to soft ground, the roads did not favor the attack, poor weather hindered aerial reconnaissance, strong resistance from British defenders on the Givenchy flank was funneling movement from west to northwest, a detachment of German tanks (mostly captured Allied tanks) met early disaster, British machine guns were taking a heavy toll of men attacking across flatlands devoid of cover, and supplies, particularly of ammunition, were not reaching the forward troops. Nevertheless by evening the Germans had advanced six miles to the River Lawe, which they crossed the following day. By evening of April 10 they had pushed across the lower Lys River, while in the north von Arnim's lead divisions had captured Messines and Ploegsteert. Armentières fell to the Sixth Army the next day, which saw good progress all along the front despite the slowness of some divisions that had turned to looting villages and supply dumps. On April 12, Quast's center stood less than five miles from Hazebrouck.

Haig was in trouble. He had convinced himself that Ludendorff's next attack would center on Vimy Ridge north of Arras, despite reports from British aerial observers that indicated a major enemy buildup opposite Horne's First Army. Ludendorff had correctly surmised that both Horne and Plumer had been stripped of their best divisions to meet the Plan Michael onslaught. These had been replaced with divisions shredded in the early fighting there. Horne and Plumer were defending a twenty-four-mile front with six British divisions, of which five were survivors of the southern fighting, and a corps of two second-rate Portuguese divisions. The Portuguese corps had been protecting a six-mile front on either side of Neuve-Chapelle. It was overdue for relief. Horne had relieved one division and the other was to have been relieved on the night of April 9.

Four days before the German attack, Haig noted that "a surprise attack by three or four divisions is also to be expected. The First Army [Horne] is quite alive to these possibilities and is prepared to meet them."[3] Two days later, "air observers reported the main roads immediately opposite the Portuguese to be full of moving transport, and ground observers told of men carrying ammunition into the German support lines. The impression conveyed by the combined air and ground reports was that the tactical concentration was nearing completion."[4]

That Haig's staff paid little attention to what in the trade is known as "hard" intelligence is evident by a staff paper of the same date that warned of "a converging attack on the Vimy Ridge."[5] Horne's intelligence chief sharply disagreed and predicted an imminent attack on First Army. Horne disagreed with this. Contrary to Haig's blasé assumption that Horne was prepared for an attack, he had refused either to expedite the relief of the single Portuguese division or to back it with an available reserve division.

Haig meanwhile had been begging Foch to release some reserve divisions for the British front, but Foch had proved no more cooperative than had Pétain. On April 5 Haig informed Foch that he was expecting an attack by twenty-five to thirty-five divisions on the Bethune–Arras front. He asked Foch either to open a "vigorous" French offensive "on a considerable scale in order to attract the enemy's reserves," or to relieve the British troops south of the Somme (and thus free four divisions), or to deploy four French divisions to the Saint-Pol area "as a reserve to the British front."[6]

Foch was also in a tight spot. As was his wont, he sought the garden of his headquarters to ask himself his favorite question, *"De quoi s'agit-il?"*—What is the problem? He was dealing with three prima donnas, the smoothly manicured British commander, Douglas Haig, the rumpled pessimistic French commander, Henri Pétain, the slim, maddeningly self-assured American commander, John J. Pershing. He could have filled some holes with Pershing's largely untrained divisions, but Pershing would not release them except under American command. Haig quite naturally was looking only at the Channel ports. Just as naturally Pétain was looking at Paris. Foch was still not willing to test the fragile French army, particularly when it was commanded by the pessimistic Pétain. As Haig was transfixed with the danger of an enemy attack between Bethune–Arras, Foch and Henry Wilson were convinced that Amiens remained the danger area. Foch in consequence would meet none of Haig's requests, but he did agree to send four divisions west of Amiens as a reserve. The two commanders were still haggling when Ludendorff struck on April 9.

Haig immediately appealed to Foch to commit his strategic reserve to the threatened front. Foch refused. Hot words passed between them in Haig's headquarters at Montreuil, but Foch was not to be moved. Perhaps he had guessed that Ludendorff had overextended himself. One of his favorite axioms was that "a battle won is a battle in which one will not own oneself defeated."[7] Haig must carry on, but must not be defeated. Only reluctantly, while the British commander was virtually stripping Byng's Third Army, Foch agreed to start five French divisions on their way.

Haig's desperation clearly showed in his famous Order of the Day issued on April 12. After a brief review of the critical situation, it concluded:

There is no other course open to us but fight it out! Every position must be held to the last man: there must be no retirement. With our backs to the wall, and believing in the justice of our cause, each one of us must fight on to the end. The safety of our homes and the freedom of mankind alike depend on the conduct of each one of us at this critical moment.[8]

This somewhat melodramatic order was not really necessary. British soldiers had been fighting hard and well for four nightmarish days. Many had been killed, many more wounded. The survivors continued to fight hard and well. A German witness wrote of their tenacious resistance: to his front lay the dead "as thick as prunes on a prunecake."[9] British and Australian reinforcements supported by heavy air attacks had stopped the enemy drive on Hazebrouck. On April 14 Crown Prince Rupprecht received a personally signed order from Hindenburg and a similar one from the kaiser for the Sixth Army to advance. "But what help are all orders to attack," Rupprecht complained to his diary, "when the troops are no longer able to attack?"[10] On the British left Plumer brought his lines back almost to Ypres, a voluntary evacuation of ground won the previous autumn at a cost of at least 250,000 casualties, but one necessary to gain fresh reserves by shortening the front. Two days later the first French divisions arrived and Foch grandiloquently declared that "the battle of Hazebrouck is over."[11] He was not quite correct. Such were von Arnim's losses that he persuaded Ludendorff to authorize an attack against the northern side of the Ypres salient in an effort to obtain a less costly breakthrough. His attack fell on Plumer's evacuated area, which was too deep to exploit with available strength and was called off by nightfall.

By April 19 Ludendorff's entire offensive stood still. Although von Quast had penetrated seventeen miles into enemy land, he now held a line roughly double his original front and possessing none of its static defenses. German land gains began to resemble the Jurassic dinosaur which became weaker as it grew larger.

The impasse continued for a week, a particularly sad time for German arms. On April 20 Manfred von Richtofen shot down his eightieth enemy aircraft, only to be shot down and killed the next day. While the empire mourned, Ludendorff ordered a fresh attack in the original Plan Michael sector, to be followed by a final effort in the northern sector. On April 24 Marwitz's Second Army, spearheaded by thirteen of the first German A.7.V. tanks, moved out on the Amiens front to bring about the first tank-to-tank battle in history, an inconclusive affair, as was the subsequent infantry battle. On the following day von Arnim's Fourth Army seized Mont Kemmel from its French defenders and in four days of fighting pushed a few miles beyond, having been stopped north of Ypres by the Belgian army. By April 29 Ludendorff's second great offensive had failed.

The dual operations nevertheless accomplished a great deal. Psychologically Ludendorff had reversed the tables of the previous year. Now it was Germany which stood on the offensive, not one that had gained a few hundred blood-soaked yards but one that in just over a month had seized far more territory than had either opponent in three years of war in the west. The British had suffered 236,000 casualties, including 9,500 officers, in forty days of defensive fighting. French casualties numbered over 75,000, plus the loss of 15,000 prisoners. Of fifty-nine British divisions, fifty-three had been engaged, twenty-five of them several times. Ten divisions were judged "exhausted," and five were broken up.

More than anything else, the offensives allowed Ludendorff to retain the tactical initiative. Fear characterized the French headquarters. One of Pétain's staff officers, Jean de Pierrefeu, later described the prevailing mood:

In truth we found ourselves confronted by a new condition. The rapidity of maneuver of the enemy was amazing; not only the speed with which the German command shifted the battle area and the assault against the spots they considered least protected, but also the efficiency of their method, the short and savage artillery preparation which paralyzed the defenders, and the skill of their units in making their way always to the point of junction of French and British corps. The Allied troops seemed ill adapted to these unexpected methods, and had no defensive parry corresponding to the offensive thrust. . . . For the future the brains of the Chiefs must find a method capable of counter-balancing that of our adversaries. Up till now the indomitable will of the joint [sic] command not to give way, transmitted to the troops, was merely a makeshift. Things could no longer remain in this state. The moment when the infantryman would weary of being one against six must be foreseen. . . . All General Pétain's cares were directed to the solution of the problem.[12]

Neither was everything roses at the OHL. Ludendorff's armies had suffered more casualties than England and France combined, an estimated 250,000 or 300,000, although a considerable number of these were lightly wounded and soon returned to duty.[13] The best divisions were rapidly becoming *abgehängt*—unhinged. "We are all utterly exhausted and burned out," Rupprecht wrote on April 15. "I went to Seventeenth Army headquarters. Everywhere I heard complaints of the accommodation of man and horse in the totally ravaged country and the heavy losses from bombs, particularly in horses which could not be hidden from sight."[14]

In late April Colonel von Thaer noted in his diary the breakdown of operational command. No longer were divisional commanders functioning in traditional command roles. "The moral influence on the troops has passed to company commanders and junior officers and NCOs." As one result, it was difficult for army commanders to effectively assign reserve divisions. No longer being in close touch with troop commanders, division staffs could not properly assess tactical needs. As soon as a unit incurred heavy losses, its commander called for relief. Such was the unreliable quality of the troops that the tendency was to relieve units prematurely. The problem essentially was that of troop quality. Most of the brave and able officers and men were dead; many of the survivors suffered either from shattered minds or bodies, very often from both.

The entire army had anticipated an overwhelming victory from the March offensive, and when this did not occur morale sank, particularly when battle-worn divisions were transferred north for the Plan Georgette offensive. This second failure left luckless commanders the problem of filling the holes with insufficient replacements, while those that did arrive were so infused with socialist demands to end the war that they did far more harm than good.[15]

Allied casualties, on the other hand, could be replaced in part by new drafts from the colonies and, in Britain's case, with fresh divisions from Italy, Palestine, and the home islands. Had this been the extent of their manpower, there perhaps would have been justification for the Duo to continue the war long enough in an attempt to win a face-saving peace.

But this was not the extent of Allied manpower. The first American troops had arrived in France in mid-1917. By January 1918 they numbered 225,000 healthy, young men who were being actively trained in both the French and British sectors. By March they were arriving at the rate of 125,000 a month. By May they numbered nearly 670,000, and whereas early contingents had to be equipped from French and British armories in part, they were now bringing their own heavy weapons, though not artillery, motor transport, or aircraft.

The Duo paid them scant heed. They first performed in combat on April 20 at the village of Seicheprey between Saint-Mihiel and the Moselle River, a quiet sector held by the Twenty-Sixth (Yankee) Division. On the morning of April 20 it became a very active sector when raided by 3,200 German shock troops. The fighting continued for two days before the intruders departed, leaving 160 dead but taking 136 prisoners of a total 634 American casualties.[16] Ludendorff smugly noted: "The American fought well; but our success had nevertheless been easy."[17]

Nor was the pervasive fear noted by Pierrefeu shared at either Foch's or Haig's headquarters, where a new offensive was being planned while the dead of Plan Georgette were still being buried.

The unalterable fact in that spring of 1918 was that while the Allies were growing stronger, the Central Powers were weakening. Wiser German heads had come to see the futility of fighting a war without a realistic strategical goal. Total victory was an impossible ambition, not a strategy. A few persons, such as Chancellor Hertling, Crown Prince Rupprecht of Bavaria, Prince Max of Baden and the foreign minister, Richard von

Kühlmann, recognized this. Germany could only be saved by a peace negotiated while she still held large portions of foreign territory.

Although the Duo paid lip service to this thesis, they continued to pursue their military goal of total victory. As with the British and French, the dead were still being buried when Ludendorff began planning for the next offensive.

36

Trouble on the Home Front: The Duo's Myopia

What is Hindenburg? Minna Cauer, who was here a few days ago, rightly said: "A strategical beer vat." If our regime goes under, and if after a few hundred years only the faces of Hindenburg and Ludendorff remain as a reminder of it, the people of that time will certainly say: "God bless us! What a civilization these people must have had!"

—Privy councillor Richard Witting, Berlin, January 10, 1918[1]

Napoleon once told a staff officer: "You can ask me for anything you like, except time." By spring of 1918 Hindenburg and Ludendorff were running out of time and the German people were running out of patience. People were tired of sacrificing husbands and sons. They no longer believed in victory. In January over 400,000 workers went on strike in Berlin to demand the "speedy conclusion of peace without annexations and indemnities, on the basis of self-determination of peoples." In February the respected newspaper, the *Frankfurter Zeitung*, published an open letter to the OHL: "The course of events might be such that considerable sections of the people will prefer any peace, peace at any price, to the continuation of the war."[2] The majority of the Reichstag held to its peace resolution of July 1917. Numerous members no longer believed the "facts" presented to them in "confidential" briefings—and they were right. The OHL and the naval high command were juggling figures with the desperation of a corporate board on the brink of bankruptcy. In late April General von Wrisberg claimed that Germany had 200 tanks "materially better than those of the English" ready to go.[3] He did not add that most of them were captured enemy tanks that had been converted, or that those used in the Georgette offensive were knocked out within a few hours, or that the enemy now possessed several thousand tanks, with more arriving daily.

The winter of 1917–1918 had been as hard as the previous "turnip winter." Rampant inflation had reduced the fixed-income middle class to paupers. Even those with money found little to spend it on. Food shortages were epidemic, black markets the order of the day. There was virtually no coal, no oil. People arose in the dark cold and went to bed in the dark cold. Laborers worked in cold factories. Children played in parks denuded of benches and trees. But for the winter wheat harvest in Romania, there would have been widespread starvation. Widespread emaciation had existed for over two years. Medicines were rare. People grew sick, they filled hospitals and graveyards. Inflation was rampant. In June 1918 Ludendorff pointed out to the chancellor that since 1913 "suits and shirts have increased in price nearly 700 percent, boots nearly 300 percent."[4] Including loans to Turkey, Austria-Hungary, and Bulgaria, the war had cost 111 billion marks and by March 1918 was costing 3 billion to 4 billion marks a month.[5]

In that sordid German spring of 1918 people no longer believed in themselves or in their leaders. "The cessation of the offensive in the West has caused much disturbance and anxiety in the Reichstag," Hans Peter Hanssen noted in early May. "Great expectations are replaced by deep and bitter disappointment; certainty of victory gives way to dark pessimism."[6]

Hindenburg and Ludendorff were no longer the idols of former days. People will sacrifice for only so long without wanting some sort of favorable return. The hollow military communiqués issued with monotonous regularity by the OHL were not a sufficient return. An advance of forty miles here, twenty miles there, the valorous conduct of German soldiers, the telling effects of the submarine offensive—all this now meant little to people thoroughly weary of sacrifice. "We ourselves have little to eat but smoked meat and dried peas and beans," Princess Blücher noted in June on her estate in the country, "but in the towns they are considerably worse off. The potatoes have come to a premature end, and in Berlin the population have now a portion of one pound a week, and even these are bad."[7] A Reichstag member, Conrad Hausmann, informed Colonel von Haeften in May that "the public no longer reads the army communiqués. One is uncertain over the state of the offensive—if it continues or is to start again. Feeling in the villages and cities is very quiet. People are concerned more and more only with food and clothing shortages."[8]

The Duo did not get the message. Justified protest to them was only the stuff of mutiny, the work of deserters, shirkers, war profiteers and socialist-communists who believed the lies of evil conditions at the front spread by disgruntled soldiers invalided home. "In some places wages are so high that there is no longer any inducement to work," Ludendorff complained to the chancellor. "On the contrary, disinclination to work, love of pleasure and high living are on the increase. Workmen often lounge about all day."[9]

The problem, as seen by the Duo, was lack of discipline. In that final spring of empire, the OHL created a *Heimatsheer der Frauen*—a Woman's Home Army—whose members were to report any defeatists or other subversives to the authorities. They were to request bands to play only patriotic tunes and were to prevent people complaining about food shortages—we are not told how.[10]

The Duo believed that such draconic measures could put things right. Denmark and Holland must be made to return the tens of thousands of army deserters to whom they had given sanctuary. Armament plants must pass to military control. Wages should be brought in line with soldiers' pay. Workers must be forbidden to strike. Draft dodgers must be rounded up and sent to the front to serve in labor battalions. War profiteers and black marketers would be jailed, even shot. Army discipline would be intensified. Reforms in military justice passed by the Reichstag in the first half of the war would be nullified. Soldiers sentenced to "close arrest" once again would suffer the painful humiliation of *Anbinden*, what the British called *crucifixion*, the victim being tied to a post or wheel to remain as a warning to others. Military courts were to deal out more severe sentences. Defeatism would not be tolerated. Censorship must be increased along with punishments for those who violated the rules. Only in this way could Germany continue to fight until victory was achieved.

It is a moot question whether Hindenburg or Ludendorff believed that the tide of defeat could be reversed. They probably did, because their knowledge of human behavior, of human hopes and aspirations and fears, was minimal. Had they talked to ordinary people, perhaps they would have gained a more realistic notion of civil and military morale.

They did not talk to ordinary people. They talked to people as pigheaded, blind, and greedy as themselves: industrialists, conservative politicians, bankers and economists who lied about production capabilities and fiscal soundness; to army group and army commanders and their chiefs of staff who lied about ground gained and enemy killed and the state of morale of their men; to navy admirals who had guaranteed that not one American soldier would land in France and who fatuously continued to claim that the crippled submarine offensive would any day force Britain from the war.

Many prominent Germans were no longer blind believers in the military gods, but the Duo did not, would not, listen to them. Anyone who suggested a negotiated peace was a defeatist. Hertling was a defeatist, as Michaelis and Bethmann Hollweg had been defeatists. The Social Democrats and members of other political parties who agreed with them were defeatists. Count Bernstorff, the former German ambassador in Washington, was a defeatist who had had no right to report all those lies about American capabilities. The foreign ministry, indeed the government, was full of defeatists.

"Anyone who was skeptical concerning the enemy's defeat was marked as a weakling," Major Niemann complained. Any army officer or enlisted man who complained about anything was a defeatist. Colonel Albrecht von Thaer, a highly respected general-staff officer who before the war had served under Ludendorff and more recently had participated in the Mont Kemmel offensive, was convinced that neither Hindenburg nor Ludendorff was being told the truth about the conditions on the front. Thaer believed that this was due to the "demigods" of the OHL general staff who either did not pass on his and other reports or in passing them on diluted them to a dangerous degree.[11]

Thaer was so worked up that in early May he most courageously traveled to Avesnes to set Hindenburg and Ludendorff straight. He described the OHL in his diary as a tumultuous scene of "agitated activity." He was well received by Hindenburg, who calmly listened to his calamitous report. "In his deep, soothing voice he said to me: 'My dear Thaer, while it may be true that things recently have not gone so well for you, you must remember that you are talking about a front of twelve miles as opposed to our front that stretches from the [English] Channel to the [Swiss] Alps. I daily receive reports from the entire front, not only over the tactical situation but over troop morale. Morale is in every way very good, almost everywhere even splendid, while according to our reports enemy morale is rather poor. The same situation prevailed in Russia until the colossus collapsed. There we attacked here and there . . . as we will do here. Look, we have, thank God, still five months to go before winter which means we can attack here and there, here and there.' " Hindenburg emphasized this by rhythmically moving his right and left fists forward.

Thaer was partially hypnotized by this man's powerful personality, his serene, almost saintly voice, but nonetheless he insisted that the remaining time before winter was a disadvantage, not an advantage for the army. This brought the incredible response: "You see, my dear Thaer, the last few weeks have affected your nerves. You will soon recover in the optimistic air of OHL . . ." Thaer correctly regarded this as a rather harsh rebuff.

His temper was not improved when a conference with the OHL's operations officer, recently promoted Lieutenant Colonel Georg Wetzell, was interrupted by a telephone call from a division operations officer who complained that his division's average company strength was thirty rifles. "Unbelievable—how is it possible?" Wetzell demanded. Thaer bluntly told him that it was not only possible, it was probable. This particular division had just been in heavy combat and had suffered heavy casualties; men had been taken prisoner, units were dispersed and men were temporarily lost. The trouble with the OHL, Thaer went on, is that it constantly insisted on regarding one division as equal to another division despite one of them having been in major combat.

On to Ludendorff, to whom Thaer repeated what he had told Hindenburg. Ludendorff listened quietly, eyes closed, his expression betraying nothing. He had no bread rolls to crumble, but "the increasing briskness with which his fingers belabored a pencil showed his increasing emotion. When I had finished he suddenly cried in his very high voice: 'What is the real purpose of your prattle? What do you expect me to do? Shall I make peace at any price?' " Thaer explained that this was beyond his ken, he wanted only to emphasize that the quality of replacement troops was worse, not better. Still visibly excited, Ludendorff said: "If the troops are worse, if discipline is deteriorating, then that is your fault, the fault of all the commanders at the front not being tough enough. How could it be otherwise possible that entire divisions ate and drank themselves silly from enemy depots instead of continuing the attack? That is indeed the reason that the March offensive and now Georgette got no further." Ludendorff listened to Thaer's lengthy explanation before closing the audience by denying that a legitimate peace offer had been received by the OHL.

A depressed Thaer wrote off the experience as null: "They are absolutely convinced that they can make the enemy ripe for peace. . . . Thus they will continue to place highest demands on the troops." He only wished that winter would come rapidly to give the exhausted soldiers a breathing spell.[12]

What did Hindenburg or Ludendorff know about civilian and army morale? Their world was light years distant, a world of warm and comfortable villas and offices, of uniforms pressed and boots shined and three healthy meals a day served by soldier servants, a world of good wines, of champagne parties to celebrate birthdays, victories, promotions, anniversaries. Similar conditions, with a few exceptions, prevailed in army group and army headquarters. Neither the OHL nor army and corps staff officers liked to soil crisp uniforms and polished boots to inspect muck-filled trenches and witness the inhuman existence of human beings; to listen to their grievances, to show them that someone cared. When they did so, it was with the patronizing attitude of a feudal lord visiting peasant tenants.

The famous Field Marshal Gebhard von Blücher of Waterloo fame used to sit by the roadside to eat his bread and sausage. The troops saw him, even identified with him. They could not identify with Hindenburg or Ludendorff. If they ever saw either, it was from a distance as a motor cavalcade or a special train sped by. There was once a time when Hindenburg was cheered by the troops. No more. Neither he nor Ludendorff was capable of *seeing* their soldiers. Their world was a sanctuary of chattering telegraph keys, ringing phones, sputtering motorcycles racing in with the dispatches from some battered front. Their sanctuary was papered with maps sprouting colored pins and fouled by lines and arrows that daily sent thousands of human beings to death or mutilation in pursuit of nebulous nothings called "decisive battles" and "total victory."

How could Hindenburg have permitted Ludendorff to go on with his insane offensives in the spring of 1918? Ludendorff had opened the March offensive with divisions that had long since been reduced from 12 to 9 battalions. A battalion originally numbered about 1,000 troops. At the end of 1917 a German battalion counted about 900 men with an average fighting strength of perhaps 640 rifles. By the end of May 1918 the average battalion strength was 692 with a rifle strength of under 500.

These impoverished figures do not present the whole picture. The earlier offensives in France and on the eastern front, the defensive battles on the western front and now the heavy losses of Plan Michael and Plan Georgette had taken an inordinate toll of officers and noncommissioned officers. Von Hutier's *Sturmtruppen* tactics were effective but also expensive, costing the lives of highly trained and motivated men who could no longer be replaced. Such was the problem that lightly wounded veterans were sent back to their units instead of being allowed a well-earned convalescence. In many units boys were commanding boys. Replacements, young or old, were not the spirited volunteers of earlier years. The newcomers had been living on short rations, had seen the misery of families and friends, had watched loved ones sicken and die from malnutrition and lack of medicines, had absorbed what Hindenburg and Ludendorff constantly cursed as defeatist ideas. They came to the army older than their years and they passed unpleasant wisdom on to already disillusioned soldiers in the trenches.

Ludendorff started complaining of lowered troop morale after the battle of Cambrai. He fulminated against any division that gave way before an enemy attack. (One is reminded of Frederick the Great, who furiously reprimanded what he regarded as a cowardly regiment by ordering hat tresses of the soldiers slashed off and the officers relieved of their swords.) He was horrified both during Plan Michael and Plan Georgette to learn that some divisions preferred looting to fighting. He later wrote that the army "as a whole was still orderly and disciplined. . . . I hoped that [its] sense of duty and determination . . . was still strong enough to overcome the numerous adverse influences."[13]

He was hoping for a great deal. "One who wishes to build an army," Homer instructed in the *Iliad*, "should take the stomach for foundation." For over two years the men had rarely received adequate rations. Their uniforms were in tatters, their boots leaked, they lacked blankets, they were hungry and undernourished. An inadequately supplied medical service made it difficult to survive wounds or illness. The joy of an apprentice surgeon was great when he hit on a British medical depot in Flanders full of *real* bandages and rubber gloves: "For months the German doctors had had to use crepe paper bandages, like toilet rolls, to cover wounds, and one can imagine how long these flimsy dressings lasted. Instead of cotton wool, we used a kind of cellulose paper, which in no time got soaked with blood and pus and just dissolved into a wet and stinking mass."[14]

The troops that replaced the losses of March and April would scarcely instill a noble spirit into this ebbing army. Prisoners of war who had been repatriated from harsh Russian and French camps believed that they would not be sent to the front. When rounded up and sent by rail from east to west they frequently mutinied and deserted. They were fleshed out by older men from the eastern armies and from the technical and supply services, scarcely the type of soldiers suitable to win the victory demanded by Ludendorff.

His was increasingly a dream world remote from reality. While admitting to Crown Prince Rupprecht that replacements were insufficient, he insisted that the enemy was up against the same problem. American troops could arrive only gradually because of the shortage of shipping. It was doubtful if America would wholeheartedly enter into the war, which was inimical to her interests and because she feared Japan. Such was the food shortage in England that he doubted if the British could carry on much longer. Rupprecht could not accept his optimism: "He lacks any psychological understanding of foreign or domestic politics."[15]

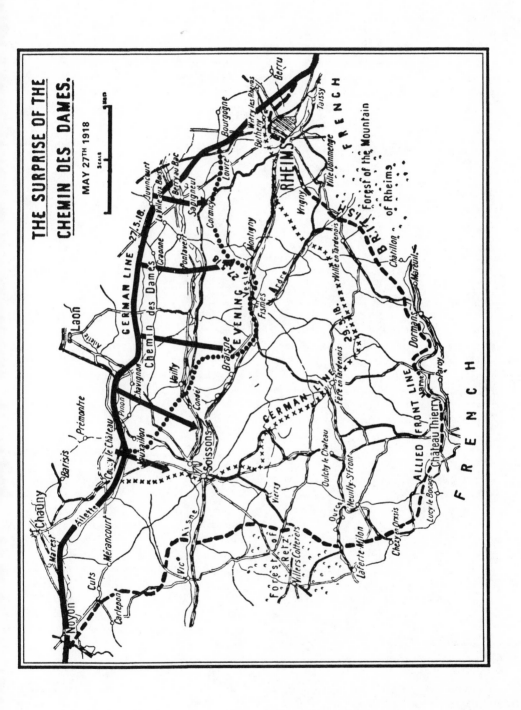

THE SURPRISE OF THE
CHEMIN DES DAMES.
MAY 27TH 1918

37

---•---

Ludendorff Tries Again: Success and Failure on the Marne

I had thought that we should only succeed in reaching the neighborhood of Soissons and Fismes. By the second and third days these objectives had in places been left far behind. We had gained ground, especially beyond Fismes; not so much beyond Soissons.

—GENERAL ERICH LUDENDORFF,
MY WAR MEMORIES 1914–1918[1]

The divisions sent by the Sixth Army melted away as fast as they were flung into battle, and this army, consequently, remained in such a disquieting state of inferiority that General Pétain began to wonder if he would succeed in the object at which he now aimed, namely, to hold the Marne, the Montagne de Rheims and the high ground south of Soissons.

—MARSHAL FERDINAND FOCH,
THE MEMOIRS OF MARSHAL FOCH[2]

Ludendorff would have preferred to continue his offensive against the British and Belgians in the north in a new operation, code-named Hagen,* but abandoned that notion in view of the strong Allied buildup there. Perhaps sensing the consternation that had pervaded the Allied high command and aware that Pétain had weakened his other fronts to support the British, Ludendorff chose Georg Wetzell's new and daring interim plan designed to suck French reserves from the

---

*Gunther and Gutrune's half-brother in Wagner's *Götterdämmerung*.

British front to the southeast and give Crown Prince Rupprecht time to rest and refit his armies before commencing Plan Hagen.

The new plan, Blücher-Yorck, * called for an attack by Crown Prince Wilhelm's army group across the formidable Chemin des Dames. It involved three armies, von Hutier's Eighteenth, von Boehn's Seventh, and von Mudra's First, a total of only forty-one divisions. They were to attack on a twenty-two-mile front running southwest from Anizy to Berry-au-Bac. This was a "quiet" sector believed to be weakly held by seven French and four British divisions, the latter having been sent from the Georgette fighting to rest and recuperate.

The primary objective was the line Soissons–Rheims, south of the Aisne River. Subsequent phases were to extend the line on either flank, from which attacks would be made on Compiègne and Rheims.

Ludendorff approved Plan Blücher toward the end of April, when Plan Georgette was dying down. Plan Blücher would have been better opened in early May, but this was impossible. Replacements had to be trained, divisions and guns transferred, ammunition dumps built up, supplies stockpiled. Ludendorff wanted the tactical lessons of recent offensives driven home to senior commanders. A training division was formed near the OHL's advanced headquarters at Avesnes to demonstrate the correct *Sturmtruppen* tactics, "more extended formations for infantry . . . better cooperation between . . . infantry and artillery." A fifth light machine gun was added to each infantry company, which also received improved rifle grenades. Supply columns and motor transport units were given machine guns for antiaircraft use and were also given improved artillery protection. Antitank rifles appeared, long cumbersome weapons that required a two-man team.[3]

Plan Blücher was to commence on May 27 with an attack by fifteen divisions, with another seven in reserve. The secretly assembled assault divisions began night marches to the line on May 20. All appeared ready for the massive blow. Up to this point Ludendorff regarded Plan Blücher as a limited offensive designed solely to clear his Flanders front of French reserves. But now in a conference with Crown Prince Wilhelm's chiefs of staff a new thought appeared. As later described by Colonel von Unruh, chief of staff of General von Conta's IV Reserve Corps, which would play a major role in the action:

---

* In 1814, The Prussian field marshal von Blücher had crossed the Chemin des Dames from the south, fought a fierce battle against Napoleon at Craonne, then defeated him on the eastern slope of Laon. Count Johann Hans Yorck von Wartenburg was a dour Prussian Junker, opponent of Scharnhorst's reforms and open enemy of Blücher and Gneisenau.

Ludendorff ended [his review of the situation] by asking whether any of us had questions to put. I asked whether, if the attack went according to plan, we could not push on to the Marne. Ludendorff asked when I thought we should have reached the objectives south of the Vesle [River], to which I replied: 'We shall reach the Vesle on the morning of the second day.' Ludendorff reminded me that it was twelve miles to the Vesle, and 'how could I be so optimistic?' I answered that our preparations were so thorough that if the information of their [Allied] weakness was correct, we should overrun the English [divisions sent from Flanders]. Ludendorff's opinion was that his information was absolutely reliable. We were actually up against a single English corps of four divisions, without reserves. He admitted it would be very welcome if my optimism were justified, but in spite of it he did not intend to go beyond the Vesle.[4]

Plan Blücher, then, was to remain a limited offensive. "On all occasions," Ludendorff later wrote, "I emphasized the need of not forgetting the necessary formation for defense, and of recognizing the moment when the attack must be stopped and the defense resumed. This must be felt by the systematic hardening of the enemy's resistance."[5]

The four British divisions referred to by Ludendorff had been sent south to the Aisne, a sector that had been quiet since the horrendous fighting in the spring of 1917 pushed the Germans behind the twenty-three-mile-long barrier formed by the Chemin des Dames. Here the British newcomers joined the French Sixth Army, six divisions commanded by a fifty-six-year-old general, Denis Auguste Duchêne, who assigned General Sir Alexander Hamilton-Gordon's IX Corps to the eastern end of the sector.

Duchêne was a martinet whose position was attributed to his being the brother-in-law of General Anthoine, Pétain's chief of staff at Provins. His first cardinal error consisted not so much in underestimating his enemy as in ignoring him. Jean de Pierrefeu of Pétain's staff later wrote: "The staff of the Sixth Army . . . had not the least idea of the preparations which the enemy had been making for a month on this front."[6]

Other eyes were more observant. A brilliant analysis of enemy intentions had been worked out by one of General Pershing's staff officers, who concluded that Ludendorff would attack the Chemin des Dames between May 25 and May 30. None of the Allied commanders was disposed to pay attention to an American estimate of German intentions, despite French intelligence reports that Ludendorff still had seventy-five to eighty divisions at his disposal. What, after all, did the parvenu

Americans know about war? After some hesitation, however, Pétain's intelligence chief concurred with the estimate and Duchêne was notified. Neither he nor his staff was impressed, nor did they sound the tocsin when German prisoners on two occasions a few days before the attack "declared that an important German offensive was in course of preparation between the Oise and Rheims." Only the day prior to the attack, when two German prisoners offered more detailed information, did Duchêne begin to take the enemy seriously.[7]

By then it was too late. Had Foch, Pétain, Anthoine, or Franchet d'Esperey, Duchêne's immediate superior, inspected the concerned sector, the horrible truth would have emerged. Duchêne had ignored Pétain's orders to organize a defense in depth. He instead stuffed four of the French and three of the British divisions sardine fashion in forward trenches with only one British and two French divisions in reserve. In vain had British commanders pleaded for a fluid defense, at least in their zone.[8] Here was a major tactical error which, along with the intelligence failure, was going to cost thousands of French, British, and American lives—a needless sacrifice that would result in the greatest Allied crisis since the German drive on Paris in 1914.

The German bombardment opened at two A.M. on May 27, another Bruchmüller spectacular that featured the combined violence of nearly 4,000 guns. Preceded by thousands of gas shells, the barrage exploded seven to eight miles deep throughout the battle zone, while mortar fire concentrated on barbed-wire defenses and the densely packed trenches of the immediate front. At four-forty A.M. the guns shifted to a rolling barrage, the *Sturmtruppen* moved out. The guns worked with ghastly efficiency. Corpses filled observation, fire, and communication trenches. Batteries were blown to bits before they could return the fire. Isolated survivors, vomiting in their gas masks, huddled in dugouts to be rounded up like senseless sheep.

By dawn, organized resistance had turned to carnage and confusion as German assault teams plunged forward along the line. In places British and French survivors struggled valiantly, on occasion to the last man, to halt the gray tide. In vain. By noon the *Sturmtruppen* had crossed the Aisne in determined rushes. By night they had pushed through Duchêne's center to approach Fismes on the Vesle, a penetration twelve miles deep. The OHL was ecstatic. Kaiser Wilhelm had left his Spa villa to monitor the action. He returned that night to toast "a great victory, 10,000

prisoners taken, a host of guns captured . . ."⁹ The swift advance continued on the following day. Soissons and Fismes fell, the Vesle was
crossed, the momentum of attack ensured by a flow of reserve divisions.
An OHL communiqué joyfully proclaimed a "complete success . . .
15,000 prisoners," all units advancing.[10]

The spectacular advance in two days, which killed and captured
thousands of French and British soldiers with only light German casualties, surprised everyone but its prognosticator, von Unruh. It was an
enormous achievement celebrated by everyone from the lowest German
private to Kaiser Wilhelm, who now exuberantly moved his headquarters
to the scene. An OHL report on the following day announced progress
everywhere, "25,000 prisoners including one French and one English
general." Forward units were being well supplied through the combined
efforts of pioneer, railroad, and ordnance troops. Doctors, orderlies, and
stretcher-bearers were working around the clock in evacuating and treat-
ing the wounded. Observation planes and observers in captive balloons
were directing artillery fire, while other aircraft bombed and strafed
targets of opportunity.[11]

Hindenburg and Ludendorff were astounded by the advance. When
the Seventh Army continued to push forward toward the Marne against
only splintered resistance, Ludendorff began to wonder if this subsidiary
operation could turn into a decisive victory. Dissatisfied with the progress
on May 28, he began feeding in reserves while ordering "an accelerated
rate of pursuit. . . . The infantry in the firing line were to be accompanied
everywhere by trench mortars and field guns which were to blast away
opposition by directly observed fire."[12]

Corps von Conta moved out early on May 29. The assault divisions
made excellent gains in the morning but met increasing resistance in
the afternoon and visibly slowed by evening. When von Conta, six miles
from the Marne, asked Seventh Army headquarters if he should attempt
the Marne crossing, the answer was no. But the OHL continued to report
impressive gains. Prisoners now numbered 35,000, the official report for
May 30 stated, while immense quantities of weapons, munitions, railroad
trains and cars, medical supplies, airfields with planes intact had been
seized and numerous enemy aircraft shot down. A day later the OHL
claimed 45,000 prisoners, over 400 cannon, and thousands of machine
guns.[13]

All well and good—but Ludendorff was already worried about
lengthening supply lines, particularly in the center where von Conta's
assault corps was rapidly forming a southern bulge. Corps quartermasters

lacked either railroads or motor transport to support forward corps adequately. Communications were stretched beyond the capabilities of wire communication or carrier pigeons. Ludendorff's right wing had captured Soissons but was meeting heavy resistance from the French located on the southern heights. A lag was also developing on his left, where British remnants were still stubbornly holding on.

Ludendorff now faced a critical decision. He could slow the present action, which was increasingly consuming French reserves as planned, and revert to his northern offensive. On the other hand, the present offensive was achieving undreamed-of gains, and it was beginning to look as if thrusts west toward Montdidier–Noyon—Plan Gneisenau*—and then southwest toward Paris might very well bring him the desired grand decision, albeit over the French rather than the British. Still not sure of himself, he called for the first divisions to be transported south from Rupprecht's armies. Crown Prince Wilhelm's Eighteenth and Seventh armies would continue their push, the latter to the Marne.

The broad-front offensive began to approach its climax on May 30. On the German right north of Soissons, hard-fighting French divisions were slowly overwhelmed and pushed back on the Nouvron Plateau. On the left two German corps continued to advance southwest of Soissons toward the Ourcq River. Von Conta's center divisions reached the Marne that evening, but the advance of his left was slowed by the arrival of French reserves. By month's end the Germans had seized Château-Thierry and were preparing to cross the Marne only fifty miles from Paris.

Ludendorff's crushing attack at first confused rather than alarmed the French high command, the result principally of poor communications. Clemenceau upon confronting Foch was told

that such things are inevitable in war, that any one, soldier and civilian alike, may be found at fault, and that it was no good dwelling upon the fact. After this opening Foch changed the conversation. When he saw me insisting with my questions he wanted to know if I intended to court-martial him, to which I replied there could be no question of that.[14]

Pétain's staff officers on May 28 struck General Pershing's representative at French headquarters, Major Paul Clark, as "very calm . . .

---

*Count August Neithardt von Gneisenau, an early nineteenth century Prussian military reformer along with Scharnhorst and others.

angry, peevish, but not frightened or anxious." One reason for this was that this headquarters was running far behind events. At the time the German vanguard was approaching the Vesle River, a ranking officer told Clark that "we hope and expect to hold them on the Aisne."[15] Another reason was Hanson Ely's successful attack at Cantigny, where the 28th Infantry Regiment of the First U.S. Division began consolidating its objectives an hour after the initial attack.

On this same day a frantic General Duchêne was committing his reserves direct from railheads, the battalions according to a French officer evaporating "immediately like drops of rain on a whitehot iron."[16] Pétain had at last gained some notion of German progress and began frantically committing fourteen infantry divisions, supported by four heavy artillery regiments and 75-mm field-artillery regiments, to the threatened area.

The timely arrival of General Micheler's Fifth French Army to bolster the wavering British–French line south of Rheims and the partial stabilization of that front allowed Pétain to concentrate on the western portion of the battle line. Identification of new divisions from Crown Prince Rupprecht's northern sector taken with aerial reports of German divisions marching west indicated that this was the sector requiring urgent countermeasures. That afternoon Major Clark was shown the plan for a two-pronged counterattack to check the supposed German drive: four divisions to attack north toward Soissons, three divisions to strike northeast toward Fismes. The attack that was scheduled for May 31 was the principal subject of conversation at French general headquarters. General de Barescut, Pétain's chief of staff, told Clark that "this is the greatest, most important battle of the war. We will do all in our power to arrest the German advance on Paris." Although Clark found de Barescut in a "jovial mood," Colonel Rozet set a more sobering tone:

He said: 'We will launch our offensive tomorrow morning. We hope it will give good results.' . . . We must stop the drive for Paris [he continued]. If Paris is taken, that probably means the end of war for France. The great trouble is that our reserves are so far away . . . The situation bears much resemblance to the battle of the Marne [1914]. Then as now we were in a very difficult situation, in great strain to get our troops to the point of contact. We succeeded then and let us hope we can do it again. . . .[17]

Rozet's fears were by no means isolated. On May 31 Clark reported to General Pershing that, in response to his question as to what the loss of Paris would mean to the prosecution of the war, three officers at general headquarters answered in such a way that Clark concluded "that they really feel that the loss of Paris . . . probably means the conclusion of the war for France."[18]

Foch confirmed the planned counterattack to Pershing, who dined with him that night. "It would be difficult to imagine a more depressed group of officers," Pershing wrote in his diary. "They sat through the meal scarcely speaking a word as they contemplated what was probably the most serious situation of the war."[19]

The French counterattack could not succeed until the German advance had been stopped on the line of the Marne. At Pétain's urgent request, Foch now ordered the French Tenth Army of four divisions to march from Haig's area around Amiens to the Marne, along with some recently arrived American divisions being trained by the British. To fill the interim gap, Pétain turned to Pershing, who immediately ordered two of his divisions, still in training, to march to the sound of cannon.

38

---•◆•---

Enter the Americans

Though we told ourselves and our men, "On to Paris,' we knew
this was not to be . . . In truth the brilliant offensive had
petered out.

—COLONEL VON UNRUH, CHIEF OF STAFF
GERMAN CORPS CONTA, JUNE 1918[1]

The battle seemed to be shaping well for the Germans. On the first day of June, Plan Blücher had brought Crown Prince Wilhelm's vanguard divisions to within thirty-nine miles of Paris. Over 65,000 prisoners and quantities of weapons and matériel had been taken. Thousands of refugees choked roads south and west of the battle lines. Thousands of French citizens were streaming from Paris with thousands more soon to follow.

But like Ludendorff's earlier victories, this one was scarcely complete. Although German troops stood before Rheims, they still had not taken the ancient town. They had reached the Marne between Dormans and Château-Thierry, but they still had not crossed the river in force. Elsewhere in the center and on the right they were continuing the advance, but now it was perceptibly slowing, as it had earlier slowed on the Somme and the Lys.

And for similar reasons.

One was overextended supply lines in difficult terrain with inadequate roads. Failure to capture Rheims restricted Seventh Army's major supply route to the single Soissons–Fismes railroad. This meant not only limited transport of supply and replacement troops but also a long and difficult march over congested roads from the railhead to forward divisions. Communications had already fallen behind the capability of the carrier pigeons, the messenger dogs, and the motorcycle dispatch riders that had to cope when telephone wire was lacking.

Tied to these problems was that previously encountered during Plan Michael and Plan Georgette: widespread looting and drunkenness. To troops heartily sick of war, the mundane appeal of a few more miles of territory scarcely matched the allure of well-stocked wine cellars and vintage shops strung like convenient oases between Soissons and Fismes and containing "quantities of tinned food and preserves of all description . . . clothing . . . plentiful supplies of alcohol," as one corps commander noted. Nor could hundreds of baton-wielding *Feldpolizei* drive drunken men from instant pleasure to dubious glory.[2]

By month's end these and other difficulties appeared to Ludendorff as more shadow than substance. Failure to capture Rheims was annoying—he later termed it a "strategical disadvantage"—but scarcely decisive. At the time he did not seem so certain of himself as suggested by his later writings. Crown Prince Wilhelm later wrote that after Ludendorff abandoned the attack on Rheims on May 31 he considered ordering the left wing of Seventh Army to cross the Marne and move on Épernay in order to cut off the Rheims resistance. Wilhelm and his chief of staff, von der Schulenburg, persuaded him to drop this idea because of German weakness and increasing Allied resistance.

Judging from Colonel Wetzell's extant planning papers, no one at the OHL seemed certain of what to do next. The strategical requirement had not changed. French divisions in Flanders had to be sucked to the south in order to pave the way for Crown Prince Rupprecht's Hagen offensive. Should Plan Blücher fail—and it was slowing—several possibilities existed. One was Plan Gneisenau, an attack by von Hutier's Eighteenth Army southwest toward the line Montdidier–Noyon, an operation favored by Ludendorff. Wetzell disagreed. He wanted to continue the present offensive, Plan Blücher, by crossing the Marne around Château-Thierry, an advance favored by Crown Prince Wilhelm and his army commanders. Should Plan Blücher fail to bring the French down from the north, Wetzell proposed nothing less than to cancel Plan Gneisenau in favor of an offensive against Verdun: "Even the slightest success at Verdun will strike the French at their most sensitive point (nationalistically also). They must and will bring up forces and they can do so henceforth only by weakening the Flanders front."[3] Apparently disinterested in a revival of von Falkenhayn's strategy, Ludendorff opted for Plan Gneisenau.

German arms might have enjoyed greater success had Ludendorff expanded Plan Blücher in its natural direction, thereby preserving the momentum of the offensive. As it was, his new plan meant that the right of First Army and the left of Seventh Army would assume the defensive with the impetus of attack shifted to the west. To Corps Conta it meant a shift of strength from left to right. Château-Thierry and Jaulgonne would be held, with bridgeheads established across the Marne, while other units reached a line to the west and northwest.

The two American divisions so hastily ordered to the Marne front by Pershing were not ready for combat. The order to move the 3rd U.S. Division (less artillery) reached Major General Joseph Dickman in headquarters almost a hundred miles southeast of Château-Thierry. Dickman swore while his staff drew up marching orders to send Major James Taylor's motorized machine-gun battalion to join a French corps south of Château-Thierry. Infantry brigades would follow by rail to Montmirail, then by foot to the battle area.

Taylor's advance units commanded by Captain Charles Houghton closed on Montmirail about noon on May 31. Exhausted French officers told them to turn back, "that it was useless to try to stop the Germans whose artillery shells were exploding in the town of Condé-en-Brie" about nine miles to the north.[4] The Americans pushed on, a trip slowed by hundreds of refugees clogging the narrow, tree-lined roads. In mid-afternoon they reached Condé to find massive confusion with no one expecting them nor holding any notion of what to do with them, a contretemps finally solved by a French general, who ordered Houghton to join a French colonial division fighting at Château-Thierry. They arrived that evening to find French infantrymen, the *poilus*, desperately trying to hold the battered town on the north bank of the Marne. Houghton deployed behind the main bridge and the railroad bridge and sent two machine-gun teams across the Marne to help the colonials.

The rest of Taylor's battalion arrived that night, and during the next two days fought hard to help prevent the Germans from crossing the river. Dickman's infantry meanwhile was strung along a ten-mile front from Château-Thierry east to Dormans. At Jaulgonne, where the enemy had established a bridgehead, the Americans joined the French in a counterattack that pushed the intruders back across the river.

Major General Omar Bundy's 2nd Division of U.S. Regulars, one army and one marine brigade, was spread out in the pastoral countryside

northwest of Paris, enjoying a day's rest while preparing to relieve the
1st U.S. Division, which was still fending off German counterattacks at
Cantigny. The march in the opposite direction was a nightmare. There
were not enough trains. While the artillery rode, the troops of the heavy
machine-gun battalions and the supply columns walked. Refugees soon
became a way of life, and so did retreating, demoralized French *poilus*,
many without rifles, warning the newcomers that *la guerre est fini*. Certainly *their* war was *fini*. Corps Conta had captured Château-Thierry.
General Degoutte, commanding French XXI Corps, to whom Bundy
reported, had retreated over thirty miles in three days and was nearly at
the end of his strength.

The immediate danger, Degoutte explained, lay in the north and
east, particularly the latter, where the enemy stood only a little over
four miles from his own headquarters. The Americans should join the
French units here and attack at once. Like General von François at
Tannenberg in 1914, Bundy would have none of it. Only one regiment
had closed on the immediate area. The others were strung out west and
south of Montreuil. The men were tired and hungry, they carried only
a hundred rounds of rifle ammunition per man, they lacked artillery and
machine guns, their supply trains were miles away. Surely the best plan
was to form a defensive line behind the French divisions and attempt to
hold until division support arrived. Degoutte disagreed. Bundy's chief of
staff, Preston Brown, held his ground. As worked out, the division deployed on either side of the Paris–Rheims road, army on the right,
marines on the left, a weak line nearly twelve miles long that promised
no more than local defense.

Had Corps Conta broken through the thin French line, the Americans would have been in serious trouble. But two battered French divisions managed to hold until the new arrivals had gained tactical
integrity. When the French center yielded on June 3, the marines and
soldiers, backed by French artillery, were ready.

The adjutant of the U.S. Sixth Marines, Major Francis Evans,
described the first attack:

From one side we had observation of the north, and when the Germans attacked
at 5 p.m. we had a box seat. They were driving at Hill 165 from the north and
northeast, and they came out, on a wonderfully clear day, in two columns across
a wheat-field. . . . The rifle and machine gun fire were incessant and overhead
the shrapnel was bursting. Then the shrapnel came on the target at each
shot. . . . It seemed for all the world that the green field had burst out in patches

of white daisies where those columns were doggedly moving. And it did again and again; no barrage, but with the skill and accuracy of a cat playing with two brown mice that she could reach and mutilate at will and without any hurry. . . . Then, under that deadly fire and the barrage of rifle and machine gun fire, the Boches stopped. It was too much for any men. They burrowed in or broke to the cover of the woods.[5]

So far as the Americans were concerned, the Allied retreat was over. That evening a French major informed a marine captain, whose company was just digging in, of the German breakthrough and ordered him to retreat. "Retreat, hell. We just got here," was the insubordinate reply.[6]

Corps Conta continued to attack, not trying for a breakthrough as the panic-stricken French and the newly arrived Americans believed, but in an effort to establish a strong defensive line. That Conta and his subordinates were not far removed from panic was evident from the abandonment of Hutier tactics. No *Sturmtruppen* tactics here; only sharp, vicious attacks preceded by artillery and supported by machine guns and in turn halted by French artillery and the superbly accurate rifle and machine-gun fire of the American marines.

Neither French nor American high commands recognized what was happening. On June 2 Major Clark described the mood at Pétain's headquarters as "very serious." On the following day Pershing notified his superior in Washington, "Consider military situation very grave." But on this same day senior French officers on the scene began to send favorable reports of the Americans to Pétain's headquarters. French enthusiasm continued to grow until on June 6 Major Clark informed Pershing of specific compliments paid to the American performance: "They are very enthusiastic over the American troops. It is in some instances touching to hear their expressions of praise and gratitude over the rapid arrival of the Americans."[7]

Ludendorff's orders to launch a major attack by von Hutier's Eighteenth Army against the Noyon–Montdidier line had effectively changed Cinderella Plan Blücher into a pumpkin. By building up von Hutier at Seventh Army's expense, Ludendorff had once again forfeited tactical momentum. Blinded by Boehn's initial successes, he was trying to do too much with too little. His error had plunged him into a vicious circle in which hesitation and delay served more to dissipate than to concentrate his strength at a decisive time and place. By June 3 Ludendorff in effect had forced Crown Prince Wilhelm to abandon the offensive, at least until Plan Gneisenau had run a favorable course.

The decision came as no surprise to General von Conta, who had been reading dismal reports from front-line commanders for what must have seemed an eternity. On his left the bridgehead across the Marne had been demolished by French and Americans. His center was stopped by a line of more Americans. On the right, recently arrived French divisions were not only holding but were beginning to counterattack. He lacked essential supply, his divisions were woefully understrength, his request for replacements ignored. General Sydow's Tenth Division, fanned out around Bouresches, was short over 2,700 men. Five rifle companies in one regiment were fighting without officers. Another regiment reported an average company strength of forty men, and these were "not fit for front line service."

Corps Conta's chief of staff, von Unruh, later wrote:

Though we told ourselves and our men, 'On to Paris,' we knew this was not to be. . . . Our casualties were increasingly alarming; ammunition was running short and the problem of supply, in view of the large demands, became more and more difficult. It became all too clear that actions so stubbornly contested and involving us in such formidable losses would never enable us to capture Paris. In truth the brilliant offensive had petered out.[8]

Von Conta's corps order of June 4 began:

Corps Conta . . . is compelled to temporarily assume the defensive, after positions most suitable for this purpose are captured. I insist that all commanders inform their troops, leaving no doubt in their minds, that our attack up to this time has passed far beyond the objectives that were first assigned, and has achieved far greater successes than had been anticipated. The offensive spirit must be maintained even though a temporary lull in the attack seems to exist. In the general picture of the operations, no halt or lull exists. We are the victors and will remain on the offensive. The enemy is defeated and the High Command will utilize this great success to the fullest extent.[9]

Considering the situation, these words must have seemed incongruous to officers and men when they read further that "the infantry must organize itself in depth and dig in."[10]

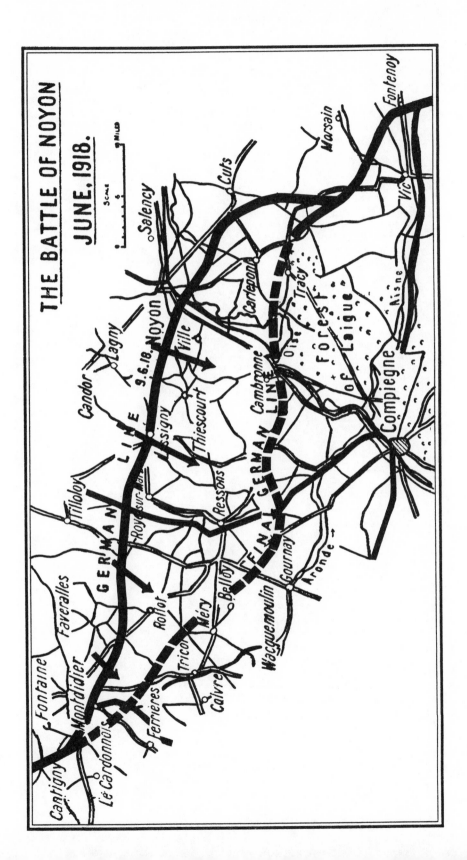

THE BATTLE OF NOYON
JUNE, 1918.

SCALE

Fontaine
Cantigny
Le Cardonnois
Montdidier
Faverolles
Tilloloy
Candor
Lagny
Solency
Cuts
Marsain
Fontenoy
Vic
Ferrieres
Calvre
Trico
Néry
Belloy
Royes-sur-Mar
Assigny
Ville
Noyon 9.6.18.
Ressons
Thiescourt
Carlepont
Oise
Tracy
Forest
of
Laigue
Aisne
GERMAN   LINE
Rollot
Wacquemoulin
Gournay
Arondе
Cambronne
FINAL GERMAN LINE
Compiègne

39

Plan Gneisenau: Ludendorff's Final Failure

In consequence of the great accumulation of enemy troops G.H.Q. [OHL] directed the 18th Army to break off the attack on the 11th [of June], in order to avoid casualties. . . . The action of the 18th Army had not altered the strategical situation brought about by the attack of the 7th Army.

— GENERAL ERICH LUDENDORFF,
MY WAR MEMORIES 1914–1918[1]

The failure of Plan Blücher meant postponing if not abandoning Crown Prince Rupprecht's northern offensive, Plan Hagen. Ludendorff faced a dilemma even before Plan Blücher had stalled. At the beginning of June Rupprecht informed Chancellor Hertling that "General Ludendorff shares my view that in all probability a crushing defeat of the enemy is out of the question; he is now resting his hopes upon the succour of a *deus ex machina* in the shape of an internal collapse in the Western Powers." Rupprecht did not share this hope and stressed to Hertling the need to bring about a negotiated peace and to make a firm declaration that Germany had no postwar designs on Belgium.[2]

This was not acceptable to the Duo, who now reverted to their original strategy of striking a continuous series of tactical blows when and where possible. The choice had grown much more restrictive than in March. Ludendorff was not strong enough to attack in more than one place at one time. Plan Blücher had gained him another enormous salient some forty miles deep and over thirty miles wide, an awkward bulge with inadequate roads and railroads and very vulnerable flanks within easy

range of French aircraft and long-range guns. Already on June 6 the
U.S. marine brigade of Omar Bundy's 2nd Division of U.S. Regulars
had begun the valiant but costly task of pushing von Conta's vanguard
from Belleau Wood, a story the author has told elsewhere.[3] Ludendorff
could not weaken himself here. He abandoned an attack on Rheims as
impractical owing to time and strength factors. He toyed with going on
the defensive but decided against it "because quite apart from the bad
influence it would have on our Allies, I was afraid that the army would
find the defensive battles an even greater strain than an offensive, as
such a policy would make it easy for the enemy to concentrate."[4] This
left Plan Gneisenau, an attack by von Hutier's Eighteenth Army, which
on June 9 would move against Fayolle's hastily organized front. This front
was held by General Debeney's First French Army and General Humbert's
Third French Army between Noyon and Montdidier.

As had happened in the buildup for Plan Georgette, there was not
enough time to conceal troop movements by night marches. French
airmen began reporting the buildup in early June. French intelligence
warned Foch that Ludendorff held

some sixty divisions in reserve and could launch an offensive between the Oise
and the Somme composed of forty-five divisions, a stronger force consequently
than he had used on May 27th against the Chemin des Dames, and in any case
greatly exceeding the total of all we had available.[5]

Foch and Pétain had reason to be nervous. Respite on the Marne
had calmed neither nation nor army. Powerful voices had accused them
of negligence and demanded their dismissal, which Clemenceau refused
out of hand. Another disaster, however, would seal their fate and perhaps
that of Clemenceau's government as well.

They accordingly had strengthened the defended sector, which Fayolle had reorganized into a defense in depth. To meet Pétain's needs,
Foch recalled several French divisions earlier provided to the British,
and he further persuaded Haig and Pershing to release five American
divisions being trained behind the British front. By June 4 these and
other radical measures gave Humbert seven divisions in the first line of
defense and five in the second line, with further support "by seven other
infantry divisions and three cavalry divisions assembled further in rear."[6]

Unlike Duchêne, Fayolle and Humbert believed in elastic defense.
A day prior to the attack, the newly named British minister of munitions,
Winston Churchill, visited Humbert's Third French Army front and its

massive defenses that stretched over 10,000 yards to the rear. "I walked over the center of the French line in front of Compiègne," Churchill later wrote. "The presage of battle was in the air. All the warnings had been given, and everyone was at his post. The day had been quiet, and the sweetness of the summer evening was undisturbed even by a cannon shot. Very calm and gallant, and even gay, were the French soldiers who awaited the new stroke of fate."[7]

French intelligence had credited Ludendorff with strength that he did not possess. Only by considerable effort had he scraped together more replacements, and these amounted only to 23,000 recruits from the eligibles born in 1899 along with 60,000 troops culled from various auxiliary services. By considerable and time-consuming shuffling he had managed to build von Hutier's Eighteenth Army to 11 first-line divisions backed by 7 reserve divisions of varying combat strength. The effort would be supported by 625 artillery batteries, a large number of mortars, and some 500 aircraft. Many of the soldiers were tired, all were hungry, many victims of a vicious flu epidemic that reduced already understrength units as much as 50 percent more.

Nine of these understrength divisions began marching to forward concentration areas shortly after midnight on June 9, their steps cadenced by Bruchmüller's big guns, which hurled high-explosive shells on enemy outposts and strongpoints while saturating the terrain with mustard gas. The first wave of gray-clad *Sturmtruppen* moved out at 3:45 A.M. along fifteen miles of hilly, wooded front. Although thick fog slowed the advance, by 6:00 A.M. the German left had reached the Oise River. Von Hutier had kept his flanks light and concentrated his strength in the center. Here, on a ten-mile front between Rollot and Thiescourt, he pushed through the enemy's first line in just under three hours. Vanguard units continued forward to seize Humbert's second line before noon with some units continuing on to the valley of the Aronde.

But now any hope for a rout ceased. If here and there a French division broke and ran, the bulk of the defenders yielded ground only grudgingly, only in terms of feet and yards, while reserve divisions hurried to the threatened sector. By evening Hutier's forward divisions held a seven-mile front running southeast from Méry, a forward gain of six and a half miles, impressive but scarcely decisive.

Nor did the second day of hard fighting bring Hutier the desired breakthrough. The most important gain occurred on the left. Here a retreating French division allowed Hutier's left to gain the west bank of the Oise, which forced Fayolle's right back to the old 1914 lines east of the river. Hutier could not exploit this development until his center advanced, and he was rapidly running out of time.

Fayolle had already decided to counterattack with five carefully hoarded divisions commanded by General Charles "Butcher" Mangin, an old fire-eating colonial soldier whose star had temporarily eclipsed with General Nivelle's fall. The only question was when. Fayolle remained cautious and wanted everything ready before he moved. Mangin rejected caution. Foch later told an aide that on the afternoon of June 10 only one of Mangin's divisions had arrived, "the second was just detraining, the third was expected during the evening, the fourth at midnight, and the fifth later still. He said to me: 'I shall attack tomorrow.' "[8] Fayolle demurred, but with Foch's assent finally agreed, the importance of his decision emphasized in the final paragraph of his orders:

Tomorrow's operations should be the end of the defensive battle which we have been fighting for more than two months. It should mark the definite check of the Germans and the renewal of the offensive on our part. It must succeed. Let everyone understand this.[9]

It did succeed. In the morning of the third day of battle Hutier's stymied center was attacked from three directions. In but hours the French had cleared the valley of the Aronde. Ludendorff had been surprised at the tenacious resistance, and now he was dismayed by the strength and fury of Mangin's counterattack. Boehn's subsidiary attack southwest of Soissons had also failed. Hutier received orders on the following day to take up defensive positions. The offensive cost the Germans some 25,000 casualties, the French 40,000. The German offensives to date had yielded 212,000 prisoners, 2,800 guns, over 8,000 machine guns. But they had not caused a significant Allied reduction of strength in Flanders—Plan Hagen was as far away as ever.

Ludendorff at this point resembled a trapped animal which to escape would be forced to bite off its own leg—by making peace as soon as possible. He instead continued to struggle. Unable to support a new effort by Rupprecht in Flanders, he reverted to his earlier notion of attacking the Rheims sector, where the enemy's line from Château-Thierry eastward was "only weakly held." His rather flaccid goal was to strengthen the rear communications of Seventh Army and, the same old song, to produce a "very decisive" weakening of the enemy in Flanders by forcing him to release reserves to the south. "Immediately following this operation," Ludendorff later wrote, "we meant to concentrate artillery, trench mortars and flying squadrons on the Flanders Front, and possibly attack that a fortnight later."[10]

The attack on Rheims was to open on July 15.

Ludendorff's strategical and tactical ambitions stood in dreary contrast to his military capabilities. Most of his torn and bleeding army was hungry. Army commanders were informed on June 15 that there could be no more deliveries from the homeland of either corn or potato fodder for horse and only negligible deliveries of potatoes for the troops until the next harvest.[11] The army was suffering from a vicious flu epidemic. Replacements were insufficient in quantity and lacking quality, young recruits hungry and ill-clothed for three years, scarcely inflamed by the patriotic ardor of their predecessors, most of whom had been killed, wounded, or captured; older men from other fronts; and repatriated prisoners who had had enough of war and wanted only to go home. Plans Michael, Georgette, Blücher and Gneisenau had cost the army a half a million casualties, of whom 95,000 were killed and 32,000 taken prisoner.[12]

Replacements from the eastern front were a mixed blessing. Far too many of them had listened to the siren song of Bolshevism and were talking the socialist line of immediate peace without annexations or reparations. Other recruits from the homeland, taken from defense plants and resenting the loss of highly paid jobs, had no desire to lose their lives in what they regarded as a senseless prosecution of the war.

Discipline had also slackened within the army, with entire units turning to looting and drinking during the recent offensives. The appearance of Americans in strength had produced an extraordinary effect that spread through the German armies to lower further already declining morale. "The American soldier showed himself to be bold if inexperienced," General von Kuhl later wrote. "Lively, well nourished and with an unused reservoir of nervous strength he appeared opposite a German army exhausted by unheard-of exertions of four years of war."[13] Soldiers on furlough had startled civilian friends with news that American troops were fighting alongside the French and British, big, healthy men fighting like wildcats. Desertion rates rose so alarmingly in June that Ludendorff published a general order that all deserters would forfeit lives and property.

The Duo long since had declared that defeatism would not be tolerated either in the army or on the home front. Their definition of
defeatism meant that any solution short of a German military victory
was anathema. Yet they did not reject panaceas, no matter how impractical. One such was offered by the OHL liaison officer to the foreign
ministry, Lieutenant Colonel Hans von Haeften, whom we met earlier
as Ludendorff's hatchet man in the vendetta against Falkenhayn. Inspired
by antiwar speeches of General Jan Smuts and Britain's former prime
minister, Herbert Asquith, in London, Haeften dusted off his earlier
suggestion to launch a massive propaganda effort under the guise of a
"peace offensive" designed primarily to bring about a collapse in Britain.
This optimistic scheme, which sought to replace torpedoes with words,
was submitted in January 1918 and was vigorously supported by the Duo,
but with a few changes. Haeften had written that Germany must make
a favorable declaration on "the Belgian question." The Duo in passing
the scheme on to the chancellor made no mention of this point, nor
did the government press the matter. Only after the June military disasters
was Haeften able to revive the plan, which Ludendorff again embraced.

The German foreign minister, Richard von Kühlmann, had also
listened to Smuts and Asquith, whose words caused him to open secret
peace talks with the British at the Hague. In a major foreign policy
speech in the Reichstag in late June, Kühlmann reviewed the overall
situation. After carefully stressing Germany's immense strength on the
battlefield and in the homeland, he called for peace talks, since an end
to this war of titans could "hardly be expected from military decisions
alone," words taken nearly verbatim from Haeften's memorandum that
had been read and approved by Ludendorff.[14] Kühlmann's expressed desire
for peace, although favored by many officials, Reichstag members, and
large portions of the German public, brought an immediate uproar from
the conservatives headed by Count Westarp and seconded by the leader
of the National Liberals, Gustav Stresemann. "The speech has had a
shattering effect upon the army," Hindenburg telegraphed the chancellor.[15] Ludendorff furiously canceled Haeften's proposed peace offensive.

Kühlmann had long been on the Duo's hit list. They despised him
for having defended Count Czernin's Austro-Polish solution against their
own insistence on acquiring a large chunk of Poland for future security
purposes. By sabotaging Kühlmann's every effort to work with Austria-
Hungary, they had brought about a new low in Germany's relations with
its major ally. Incongruous as it may seem, Hindenburg and Ludendorff
were convinced that Germany's *next war* would be fought *against* Austria-

Hungary, which explained in large part their refusal to accept the foreign minister's *Mitteleuropa* policy of seeking an economic confederation of central European states, as opposed to unquestioned German hegemony over the Crimea, the Ukraine, Romania, and the Baltic lands.

Hindenburg and Ludendorff's vigorous pursuit of these goals, none of which was achieved more than briefly with disappointing and very costly material results, is enlightening. To the objection that the acquisition of Polish territory would mean absorbing more than two million Poles, mostly Jews, into Germany, they replied that Germany would take the land and forcibly relocate the people further east in Poland. Kühlmann, who along with Czernin had been in Bucharest negotiating a treaty with the Romanian government, was subjected to a savage smear campaign personally ordered by Ludendorff. In opposition to Czernin and Kühlmann's wishes, Ludendorff had wanted the Dobruja to be taken from Romania and given to Bulgaria, which would be an important ally in any future war against Austria-Hungary. The Duo moreover did not favor negotiation. Force must be used to bring Romania around. Although Kühlmann prevented this, he could not prevent the OHL from forcing an unfair peace on the defeated country, which he bitterly declared made her a colony of Germany and Austria-Hungary.

The Duo closed in on Kühlmann in a meeting with Chancellor Hertling at Spa in early July. Hertling tried to defend his foreign minister against the charge of defection, but they would not listen. There was no place in the government for defeatists. There would be no peace of understanding. The war must continue. England either must be defeated or must offer a peace compatible to German war aims. If Kühlmann remained at his post, they would resign. A weak chancellor and a hopeless kaiser bowed to the imperious demand. Kühlmann was replaced by an archconservative and imperial favorite, Rear Admiral Paul von Hintze, regarded by Ludendorff and his senior associates at the OHL as "a fine German, a good diplomat and soldier."[16] Hindenburg described him as "clever, cunning, cold, ruthless, but still likeable, a thorough Prussian"—just the man to straighten out the foreign ministry.[17]

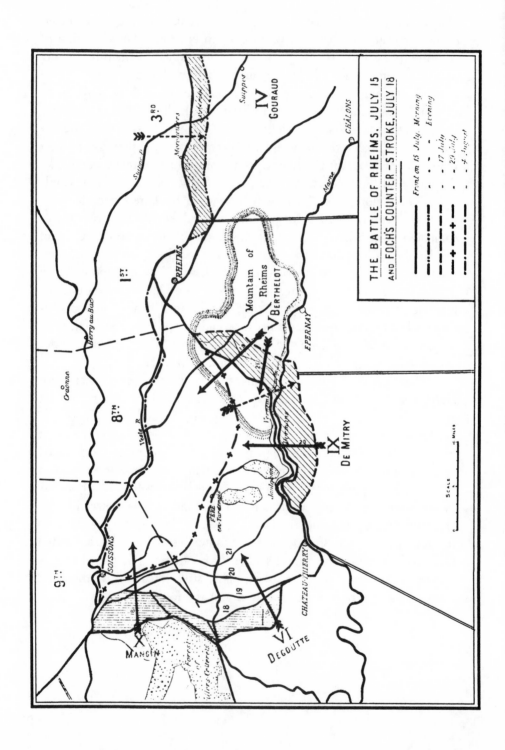

THE BATTLE OF RHEIMS, JULY 15
AND FOCH'S COUNTER-STROKE, JULY 18

Front on 15 July, Morning
"   "   "   "   Evening
"   "   17 July
"   "   20 July
"   "   4 August

SCALE
0   10 MILES

40

The French Attack:
The Battle of Rheims

Never have such demands been made on our men's strength of character, morale and physical endurance as have been made in these last few days: brought in over long distances by continuous forced marches, in hot weather and without rest, and after the failure of their own offensive on which they embarked with great expectations, thrown into a defensive battle of a gigantic scale; they do their duty, they fight, they keep going.
—LIEUTENANT HERBERT SULZBACH, DIARY ENTRY, JULY 21, 1918[1]

. . . [from July 18 on] Ludendorff's leadership of the German army was based on incorrect suppositions, as is shown by my own personal experiences [with him]. Ludendorff undoubtedly was inwardly convinced of the correctness of his decisions at that time, but he had underrated the breakdown of the larger part of the German people at home and very much overrated the remaining strength of the German army. Because of his own cocksureness he continued to insist that he could successfully ward off enemy attacks. This alone accounts for the final complete breakdown of the German army.
—GENERAL FRIEDRICH VON LOSSBERG, MEINE TÄTIGKEIT IM WELTKRIEG 1914–1918[2]

Plan Marneschutz und Rheims called for a two-prong attack by a total forty-nine divisions supported by sixty air groups flying the new Fokker biplanes. Max von Boehn's Seventh Army would cross the Marne near Dormans east of Château-Thierry in order to seize

Fère–Champenois. Bruno von Mudra's First Army and Karl von Einem's Third Army would strike east of Rheims in order to seize Châlons-sur-Marne.

Hindenburg and the kaiser's entourage enthusiastically endorsed the plan, as did the OHL's operations officer, Georg Wetzell. Wetzell's extant working papers for June and July form an interesting study of operational fantasies. Once Plans Rheims and Hagen succeeded, he believed that the way would be clear for a new thrust at Paris, a conclusion written the day after the U.S. Marines had cleared the last living German from Belleau Wood. If this were not feasible he would break the stalemate on the western front by a new German offensive in Italy! An offensive in Alsace-Lorraine was also under consideration, and other plans unknown to us may have existed in Wetzell's fecund mind that failed to differentiate between desire and possibility.

More practical officers at the OHL and most army commanders did not favor Plan Marneschutz und Rheims, arguing that the army should not go on the offensive until it had regained strength. Ludendorff also seems to have held some doubts, principally owing to the exhausted condition of the troops and the lack of ready replacements. Overriding these, however, was his almost fanatical belief that the war had to end in 1918 and that therefore no risk was too great. He also placed great stock in the surprise that he hoped to achieve by Boehn's attack east of Château-Thierry. Colonel Baron von Oldershausen, chief of the OHL's railway section, conferred at length with Ludendorff on July 7 and noted that he was very confident but very serious: "Troop replacement situation is very tense."[3] If Ludendorff entertained doubts, he hid them well. When Admiral von Hintze, the new foreign minister, asked if the coming offensive would "defeat the enemy definitely and decisively," Ludendorff replied, "Yes."[4]

Plan Rheims kicked off on July 15 in the usual brisk fashion and with the usual early success, except that contrary winds largely nullified the effect of the heavy mustard-gas barrage. By nightfall six of Boehn's divisions had established a bridgehead four miles deep across the Marne. Mudra and Einem east of Rheims did not share Boehn's good fortune. "The attack is coming to a halt outside Prosnes," Lieutenant Sulzbach wrote in his diary. "Enemy resistance seems to be insurmountable. . . . We haven't got the same morale that we had on 21 March or 27 May. . . ."[5] "Why is the attack not making ground?" Ludendorff angrily demanded of Lieutenant Colonel von Klewitz, Einem's chief of staff. "It must be carried out at once." Klewitz explained that the enemy had moved its artillery out of range of the German guns and that those guns were insufficient to provide a strong enough creeping barrage for the infantry, which would be slaughtered. Ludendorff somewhat surprisingly agreed.[6] He next telephoned Rupprecht's chief of staff, Hermann von Kuhl, who noted that he was "very sad about the poor result." Kuhl advised him to continue the attack, but Ludendorff declined because "he thought that we would risk heavy losses,"[7] a profound change in one who a few days earlier had been willing to chance everything for victory. Ludendorff's decision was tantamount to defeat, since Seventh Army could not continue its advance without support on the left.

Colonel Mertz von Quirnheim of the OHL's operations section wrote in his diary on the second day of the offensive: "Fairly depressed mood. Difficult question—what is to happen from now on?" The following day he noted ominously: "I am convinced that at the moment neither Ludendorff nor Wetzell knows what further action they must take."[8] There was only one answer and that was for Boehn to withdraw across the Marne as soon as possible. This was not so simple, because French artillery and air strikes had already interdicted the bridges to prevent his retreat.

Ludendorff somewhat desperately drove to Crown Prince Rupprecht's headquarters at Tournai on July 17 to press for the opening of Plan Hagen, Rupprecht's offensive against the British. Discussion continued through the night and into the next morning. Nothing had been decided when Ludendorff was telephoned from Avesnes. The Americans and French had attacked the German Ninth and Seventh Armies from the woods of Villers Cotterêts southwest of Soissons.

Ferdinand Foch to the fore. The fiery little French general had been planning an offensive since early May, only to be frustrated by Ludendorff's continuing attacks. But Ludendorff's failure on the Marne, the increase in the number of American divisions, and Haig's promise to release British reserve divisions had brought new hope. On July 12 General Mangin's Tenth Army was to advance on the rail center of Soissons, which, if seized, would effectively isolate the Germans in the enormous Marne salient and eastward.

Pétain did not favor the plan until French counterattacks on either side of Rheims had first drawn away German reserves from Mangin's front. Pétain managed to postpone the offensive until July 18 and cancel it altogether when the Germans struck on July 15, but Foch furiously countermanded this order.

Mangin disposed of ten divisions in the first line, which included Major General Bullard's 1st U.S. Division and the heroes of Château-Thierry and Belleau Wood, the 2nd Division of U.S. Regulars, commanded now by Major General James Harbord. Mangin's second line consisted of six infantry divisions and a cavalry corps, and he held two British divisions in reserve. General Degoutte, who had replaced Duchêne as commander of Sixth Army, counted seven divisions in his first line, of which two were American, and only one in his second line, but three more American divisions had been earmarked for his support.

Mangin's attack began at dawn with no preliminary bombardment but with a spearhead of 225 light and heavy tanks. Degoutte opened his attack an hour or so later with a brief artillery bombardment. Mangin pushed on about four miles the first day, advanced slightly the second day—and stopped.

The German Seventh Army's first line of defense consisted of five divisions with six in reserve against Mangin's attack. The German Ninth Army's first line of defense against Degoutte consisted of six divisions with only two in reserve. None of the divisions was strong; half or more of them were considered to be of little or no value.

Still at Rupprecht's headquarters, Ludendorff ordered his chief of operations at Avesnes to commit certain reserves to Seventh and Ninth armies. The Flanders offensive would have to wait. "Understandably in a state of the greatest nervous tension," as Ludendorff later wrote, he boarded a special train for Avesnes, where Hindenburg met him at the station.[9] The situation was growing worse, and Mangin's attack appeared to be gathering momentum. Ludendorff had no more reserves at hand —"we could only await further developments."[10]

Hindenburg did not seem to be too upset. On July 18 old General von Plessen noted in his diary: "Hindenburg—in best form—reported the situation clearly and calmly to the Kaiser, that the attack on Rheims would absolutely be continued as soon as this [enemy] attack on the flank had been stopped and repaired. Because of this some weeks would be lost."[11]

Perhaps in an effort to bolster Ludendorff's flagging confidence, Hindenburg at noon dinner the following day made one of his rare incursions into operational affairs. "The field marshal suddenly turned to me and said," Colonel Mertz later wrote, "the simplest and most solid solution of the present crisis would be in his opinion to at once bring all [reserve] troops including those from Flanders here to open an offensive south over the heights northwest of Soissons against the left flank of the enemy attack. Then General Ludendorff suddenly broke into the conversation, saying that this was totally impracticable and must not be thought of, as he believed he had already made clear to the *Generalfeldmarschall* in detail. The *Generalfeldmarschall* arose from the table without a word, and General Ludendorff, face flushed and in obvious anger, left the room."[12]

Hindenburg refused to be intimidated. At the evening conference he spread his immense hand over the appropriate portion of the battle map and repeated the proposal. "Nonsense!" Ludendorff snapped, his expression furious as he stalked to the door. Hindenburg followed him, saying, "I would like a word with you."[13] They retired to Ludendorff's office, where, according to Hindenburg, he told Ludendorff to remember his subordinate position. Neither Hindenburg nor Ludendorff later recorded the incident.

General Friedrich von Lossberg, Fourth Army chief of staff and acknowledged expert in defensive warfare, had meanwhile been summoned to the OHL by Ludendorff. He found his superior "rather nervous and agitated," openly criticizing his chief of operations, Wetzell, and his subordinates for having overrated the German Seventh Army's combat capability. Lossberg soon learned that Ludendorff and his staff, being *frontfremd*—strangers to the front—, held a far too optimistic belief in the fighting capability of the western armies. Morning reports from the Ninth and Seventh German armies that enemy attacks had resumed in strength and had punched severe holes in the front further depressed Ludendorff, who, contrary to custom, constantly interrupted Lossberg "with digressions concerning details for which the serious situation offered no time."[14]

Well aware of the exhausted state of the army in general and the proximity of a large number of enemy reserve divisions in the critical area, Lossberg called for a general withdrawal, not only of the Seventh Army and the left wing of the Ninth Army to the Aisne–Vesle position, but also of the armies on both sides of the Somme to the old Siegfried Line (thus abandoning all the territory won in the Plan Michael offensive). The Plan Hagen offensive in Flanders should be restricted to a tactical success, and if it could not take place, then the armies there must withdraw to prepared positions to put the entire western front on the defensive.

Although Ludendorff seemed to be impressed with Lossberg's proposals, he said that political reasons prevented him from this move—he feared its adverse effect "on the enemy, on our army and on the homeland." Lossberg told him that it was wrong not to carry out the correct military decision for political reasons in time of crisis. This made a painful impression on Ludendorff, who basically agreed and then concluded that under these circumstances he had better resign. Lossberg argued against this for army morale reasons, but repeated his advice to give up any thought of an offensive victory—the problem was to use a methodical defense to prevent a victory by the enemy. (Lossberg later regretted that he had not encouraged Ludendorff to resign: "His behavior from July 19 on showed me that he could not persuade himself to make the urgent decision to withdraw to prepared positions. Only because of this could the misfortune which struck the German army take its catastrophic course.") Ludendorff responded by ordering Lossberg to visit the Ninth and Seventh armies and report their condition to him. Lossberg left the OHL with the belief that his arguments had fallen on fertile ground and that his proposals would soon be carried out. He was wrong.[15]

Lossberg completed a tour of the Seventh Army's divisions before conferring with the army commander, General von Boehn, and his principal staff officers. All agreed that to hold the present position would require heavy reinforcements of both men and artillery, with no guarantee of success. Lossberg explained all this by telephone to Ludendorff, who still refused to order the proposed withdrawal. Lossberg instead was to remain with Seventh Army and report the situation daily to the OHL.

Lossberg's fears grew during the next few days as he witnessed the murderous effect of Allied artillery, tanks, and aircraft and the entirely unsuitable German defensive tactics that, imposed by the OHL, were appropriate to Flanders flatlands but not the rolling lands and overgrown wheatfields of the Marne salient. All this and more was reported to Ludendorff, who responded by sending in reserve divisions that arrived piecemeal and were soon chewed up in the heavy fighting. On July 25, the situation had become so critical that Lossberg felt "a catastrophe could not be ruled out."[16] With Boehn's permission, he returned to the OHL to argue further for a withdrawal.

* * *

Ludendorff's position had improved on the night of July 20, when Boehn's isolated left-wing divisions managed to recross the Marne west of Rheims to escape potential disaster. Mangin's counteroffensive was visibly slowing and by July 22 had halted, but at a heavy cost to the German armies in men killed, wounded, and taken prisoner and in the loss of enormous quantities of weapons and matériel. (Between July 15 and August 2, German casualties would total 110,000, Allied casualties 160,000.) On the afternoon of July 22 Kaiser Wilhelm was driven to Avesnes to hear a report. For the first time he learned that Plan Blücher, despite the flood of victory communiqués, had flopped. Hindenburg himself admitted "total failure." The bewildered kaiser, who had come to cheer, asked what he should now do, and Hindenburg advised him to return to Spa. After dinner that evening he informed his entourage that they must show consideration for "a defeated War Lord."[17]

Ludendorff was still in deep trouble. Although Lossberg did not know it, on July 22 he informed Colonel Mertz that he was going to order a withdrawal from the Marne salient. Visibly distressed, he astonished Mertz by stating that he had had no confidence in the July 15 offensive. With that he removed a ragged prayer book of the Moravian Brethren from his desk and read Mertz the unfavorable passage for July 15!

"Ludendorff much quieter," Oldershausen noted in his diary on July 23.[18] But on the same day, Mertz ominously wrote in his diary: "His Excellency [Ludendorff] seems to feel that it is absolutely necessary for something to be done to revive our prestige. But what?"[19]

Quietude did not last long. On the following day Mertz wrote: "Serious question of Excellency Ludendorff's nervousness and the inconsistency in his work. Decisive for our fate is the answer to the question: 'Can we again regain the initiative or is it to remain lost to us?' Excellency works himself to the breaking point, concerns himself too much with details. This situation is really serious."[20]

Major General Count Schwerin, chief of staff of the German Balkan army, visited the OHL at this time. "Count Schwerin highly concerned over the appearance and nervousness of his Excellency," Mertz confided to his diary. "The real impression is that his Excellency has lost all confidence. The army commanders suffer terribly from this. . . ."[21]

At this point Lossberg returned to the OHL from the Seventh Army, a depressing journey slowed by clogged supply lines with seemingly no one in authority to put matters right. He found a very troubled Ludendorff. Withdrawal from the Marne salient was to begin on this day. Perhaps Ludendorff recalled Frederick the Great's warning against retreat because "the first step backward makes a poor impression in the army, the second one is dangerous, and the third becomes fatal."[22] Certainly he feared the adverse effect of the withdrawal on the home front, which still supposed that the offensive was prospering. In any event he was still reluctant to withdraw the Seventh Army and was arguing with Hindenburg about this when Lossberg arrived to report his litany of woe. Hindenburg at once ordered Ludendorff to send out the withdrawal order and left the room. Ludendorff attempted to postpone the command, but Lossberg insisted and it was sent off.

The delay, taken with Ludendorff's piecemeal tactics, was catastrophic. The reserve divisions that should have occupied and strengthened the Aisne–Vesle line had been wasted in a week of fruitless defense, which meant that the withdrawing divisions would not be able to rest and recuperate. In Lossberg's later words: " . . . July 18, 1918, was the precise turning point in the conduct of the war. The OHL's failure to understand that the combat strength of the German army was already severely shattered in July 1918 and required systematic rebuilding, which would certainly have succeeded if the troops had received their urgently necessary recuperation in proper camps, finally drove us to the position in which we found ourselves at war's end."[23]

Ludendorff seemed relieved once the Seventh Army began to fall back. "Ludendorff's frame of mind seems slowly to improve . . . Reason [is] the comparative quiet at the front," Mertz noted on July 29, adding, "The nervous breakdown has not been altogether glorious. His own admission of nervousness does not improve the situation and does not permit the actual situation to appear in a fairer light. I cannot help it that for me these have been days of great disappointment. *Generalfeldmarschall* Hindenburg unfortunately apparently offers no sort of support." General von Plessen wrote in the same vein: "[General] Marschall from Avesnes tells me that the mood is very depressed, especially Ludendorff, whom Hindenburg must cheer up." Two days later Mertz noted: "Afternoon with Excellency [Ludendorff], who is not fully in form, much shattered, very sad."[24]

Ludendorff was still refusing to face harsh fact. On the second day of August he ordered army group commanders to undertake a strategical defensive: "The situation demands that on the one side we place ourselves on the defensive, that on the other side we go over to the offensive as soon as possible . . ." The purpose of the fresh attacks "will be not so much a matter of winning ground as of smashing the enemy and gaining more favorable positions."[25] To Major Alfred Niemann's question if the front was being shortened, Ludendorff replied that he hoped the attack on Amiens would resume once the troops had recuperated. Mertz wrote on August 4: "Excellency Ludendorff is seemingly still completely at wit's end, is still concerned only with small operations. . . . Wetzell [OHL's operations officer] complains constantly over Excellency Ludendorff's irresolution . . . sees no way out. . . . Major Niemann . . . is shocked by the extent of Excellency Ludendorff's loss of control, says that Excellency has not abandoned the hope of ending the war by the sword. All the more mysterious is the present irresolution. . . ."[26]

Ludendorff was hallucinating, telling the foreign minister, Admiral Paul von Hintze, that he was still capable of decisively beating the enemy. "Five times I have had to move troops back during this world war," he informed Chancellor Hertling, "but in the end I beat the enemy. Why shouldn't this happen a sixth time?"[27] Doubting Thomases at the OHL were warned to mend their ways by a top secret order that read: "To my regret despondent views and rumors have been confirmed, whose origin was traced back to the OHL. The eyes of the homeland and army are turned on the OHL. Rightly or wrongly, each member of the OHL is believed to be particularly well informed and his statements given corresponding value. Therefore each member of the OHL must be aware of his responsibility away from the OHL and be the bearer of the ruling mood at the OHL. The OHL is free of despondency. Supported by the earlier performances of front and homeland, the OHL looks on the coming tasks with a strong will. No member of the OHL may think and act otherwise."[28]

On August 7 Mertz recorded Ludendorff's "completely inert mood" and added: "This spectacle is scarcely impressive. Woe unto us if the Allies should notice our slowdown. We have lost the war if we cannot pull ourselves together."[29]

41

The Black Day of the German Army: The High Command's Dilemmas

> I have a feeling that there is much concern felt by many people over enemy attacks. This is not justified, if our troops are vigilant and perform their duty. . . . As I have already explained, we should be pleased if the enemy *does* attack, since he will expend his strength all the quicker by doing so.
> —GENERAL ERICH LUDENDORFF
>   TO DIVISION COMMANDING GENERALS, AUGUST 1918[1]

The French and American spring offensives in the Champagne had given the British a well-earned respite, broken only by Haig's sending reserve divisions now and again to the south. Replacements had continued to arrive from the colonies and the home country. Tanks appeared in increasing numbers, ammunition stocks were replenished, worn-out guns and other weapons replaced, units rested and retrained, morale improved by the successful counteroffensive that had pushed the enemy from the Marne salient.

Haig had been wanting an offensive to avenge the humiliation to British arms brought on by Plans Michael and Georgette. Like Ludendorff in the previous year, he wondered where it should take place and what it should seek to accomplish. The answer came from one of the more intelligent generals in the British army, Sir Henry Rawlinson, who had replaced the unfortunate Hubert Gough after the March debacle.

Rawlinson's Fourth Army, which included some American troops for training purposes as well as the trusted Canadians and veteran Australian brigades, had made a successful raid against the enemy at Le Hamel, twelve miles east of Amiens, in early July. Rawlinson was pleased with the number of Germans taken prisoner and now proposed a similar but larger operation, which, spearheaded by tanks, would force the enemy back far enough to free the Amiens railway complex from artillery interdiction fire. Haig and Foch enthusiastically endorsed the plan, which was scheduled to begin on August 8.

Rawlinson was looking at what he believed to be a strongly defended ten-mile front. To penetrate it he secretly concentrated fourteen infantry divisions, three cavalry divisions, over 2,000 guns and 450 tanks. Sixty trains of artillery arrived from the north, the big guns moved up at night to begin registration fire on enemy targets in such a way that it seemed to be part of the army's normal interdiction program. Tank movements were partially smothered by a noise barrage invented by nearby air squadrons. Rawlinson counted on 800 aircraft in his army and on 1,100 in General Debeney's First French Army on his right to prevent enemy air from spying out his concentrations.

His was a neatly planned affair that probably would have achieved its limited goal with minimum casualties. Unfortunately, perhaps, Foch fell victim to tactical greed, as Haig had done at Cambrai in late 1917. In late July, Rawlinson was ordered to push the attack toward Roye, some thirteen miles distant. He would be assisted by Debeney's First Army, which Foch placed under Haig's command. At a final conference three days before the attack, Rawlinson learned that once he gained the line Roye–Chaulnes, he was to push on another fifteen miles to Ham. Humbert's Third French Army was meanwhile to advance between Montdidier and Noyon.

What Rawlinson had proposed as an operation with strictly limited objectives had been expanded by Foch and Haig to a major offensive.

Rawlinson's target was General von der Marwitz's Second Army of six understrength divisions only weakly dug in between Albert and the Avre River. The sector seemed to be quiet enough. At Ludendorff's instigation, General von Kuhl inspected it in early August and found nothing amiss. British prisoners seized a few days before the attack offered no valuable information, because they had been given none. Forward posts did report on several occasions that they had heard tanks moving at night, but intelligence officers wrote this off in accordance with Ludendorff's derisive term, "tank panic."

Nothing about the night of August 7 seemed different to the dispirited, hungry, and extremely bored troops of the forward zone. Lookouts tried to peer through heavy fog while their mates slept in rude trenches and crudely constructed dugouts. Their sleep terminated at 4:20 A.M. when 2,000 artillery pieces opened drumfire along a six-mile line, the signal for some 450 tanks to spearhead an assault by determined British, Canadian, and Australian infantrymen.

Total surprise of demoralized men brought rich rewards of 16,000 prisoners and 200 guns within a few hours. Entire divisional staffs were captured without hindrance. While tanks crawled forward, in some instances absurdly accompanied by cavalry, armored cars raced behind the enemy shooting at whatever moved to spread confusion, while hundreds of airplanes bombed and strafed further to the rear. By evening, forward units in the center were reporting gains of up to nine miles. Progress was not as spectacular on Rawlinson's left north of the Somme, where there were fewer tanks and where enemy batteries had fired an effective counterbarrage of gas shells. On the right, Debeney's army was slow off the mark and failed to win its assigned objective, but nevertheless captured 5,000 prisoners and 161 guns on the first day.

The following day Humbert's Third Army on Debeney's right executed a neat flanking maneuver to seize a major supply center at Montdidier, with its rich stores of ammunition and matériel. But progress elsewhere was slow, as the troops began nudging the lunar lands of the old Somme battlefield, pockmarked with enormous shell craters and corpse-filled trenches, the paths blocked by fields of rusted barbed wire. Although casualties the previous day had been relatively light, almost 300 tanks had been knocked out by enemy fire and mechanical failure. And now the advance was running into the strong defenses of von Hutier's Eighteenth Army. Marwitz's own center and left had been strengthened by six divisions, and three more divisions had arrived during the day.

Rawlinson rightly divined that his troops were tiring, and Haig agreed that the operation should end. General Foch sharply disagreed, insisting that it was necessary to seize Ham, force the enemy back across the upper Somme, and recapture Péronne. Haig, who was generally outshouted by French commanders, reluctantly gave in. On August 10, only sixty-seven tanks were in service, no progress was made on the flanks, the center gained less than a mile. After an abortive attack by the Canadians and Australians on the following morning, Rawlinson put his foot down and this time Haig agreed, softening the blow by a promise to Foch that he would soon open fresh offensives in the north.

Considering the slaughter of the years, the casualty scoreboard was mild. The French and British each lost about 22,000 killed and wounded, the Germans an estimated 75,000, of which over 50,000 were taken prisoner, and some 500 guns. It was a satisfactory result, but it would not have rated more than a page or two in an official history of the war, except for one thing: the effect it exercised on the German high command.

August 8, 1918.

Ludendorff called it "the black day of the German army."[2] To Friedrich von Lossberg it was "the worst defeat that a [single] army had suffered in the war."[3] Early reports of the British attack struck the OHL a sledgehammer blow. Gloom deepened as it learned of broken front-line divisions and captured staffs. Marwitz had immediately committed all available reserve divisions. Ludendorff frantically ordered Hutier to send divisions into the fighting southeast and northwest of Roye, and Rupprecht was asked to start reserve divisions south. By evening the hole in the center had been plugged, but six or seven divisions were reported as "completely broken."[4]

The Duo's spirits sank further the following day, when divisional commanders and line officers summoned to the OHL confirmed the overall disaster. "I was told of deeds of glorious valor," Ludendorff later wrote, "but also of behavior which, I openly confess, I should not have thought possible in the German Army; whole bodies of our men had surrendered to single troopers, or isolated squadrons. Retiring troops, meeting a fresh division going bravely into action, had shouted out things like 'Blackleg,' [strikebreaker], and 'You're prolonging the war,' expressions that were to be heard again later. The officers in many places had lost their influence and allowed themselves to be swept along with the rest."[5]

Paranoia is a strange affliction. The victim can sink from a high of hope to a depth of despair within minutes. Vanished was Ludendorff's vision of Rupprecht's offensive, gone the dream of a despondent enemy humbly signing over chunks of France, Belgium, and Poland at the peace table. First the German people, the *gottverdammte* civilians, and now the

German army, *his* army, had let him down. Having gambled recklessly and often ineptly with the fortunes of the German empire for two years, it was suddenly time to leave the game. "Leadership now assumed . . . the character of an irresponsible game of chance, a thing I have always considered fatal. The fate of the German people was for me too high a stake. The war must be ended."[6] Fighting would continue, but only to gain time for the start of peace negotiations.

Having so concluded, the logical course was to retire the army behind a defended Siegfried Line, where it could be rested and refitted —as General von Lossberg had recommended in July. Lossberg, now chief of staff designate to what would soon become General Max von Boehn's group of three armies, again proposed this move on August 10. He urged Ludendorff to occupy, extend, and strengthen the Siegfried Line immediately and defend it with reserves coming up, sending only the most necessary of them to the front. There were no prepared defenses east of this line. The partially built Hermann-Gudrun-Stellung defensive complex existed only between the Oise River and Verdun. Similarly, the Antwerp–Maas-Stellung existed only on paper, although the Maas (Meuse) River could be expected to hold up tanks.[7] Ludendorff refused to consider the move and stuck by his resolution to carry out the defensive in the forward lines, authorizing only the construction of an intermediate defensive line that could not possibly be built in time.[8]

General Kuhl noted in his diary on the same day:

Yesterday afternoon Tschischwitz [chief of staff, Second Army] declared that the [Second] Army could no longer stand on the 10th [of August], it must withdraw behind the Somme [River]. I said that then the entire Eighteenth Army would be outflanked and could no longer withdraw. Marwitz [commanding the Second Army] himself came on the telephone and said the same. The [division] commanding generals had reported to him that the troops could no longer hold on the morning of the 10th. I spoke with Ludendorff, he said that the [Second] Army had lost its nerve, Marwitz and Tschischwitz were finished according to Mertz, whom he has sent there. Tschischwitz is being replaced by Lieutenant Colonel von Klewitz. He must absolutely hold and the situation must be repaired. Everything that can be sent there must be sent. I don't believe that we can completely restore the situation. Thus we are playing *va banque*, we are stripping our fronts too much, wearing ourselves entirely out. We must retire behind the Somme but in segments and not immediately. The Second Army must first hold so that the Eighteenth Army can bend back accordingly, only then should the Second Army retreat to behind the Somme. It was impossible to argue with Ludendorff. I had [Major] Leeb speak with Wetzell [Ludendorff's operations officer], who again repeated Marwitz's report. But Ludendorff interrupted the conversation and declared that [Second Army] would have to hold the line.

Ludendorff finally authorized a partial withdrawal during the night of 9–10 August. "Ludendorff constantly set all details," Kuhl continued,

spoke with all army commanders and chiefs of staff, ordered particulars often entirely different from what he had ordered me to do. When one speaks at this time with the chiefs of staff, one hears that they are doing something quite different from what he had ordered me. That makes everything very difficult. In doing so he is very excited, accepts no objections.[9]

At a meeting with the kaiser in Avesnes on the same day, Ludendorff made it clear "that we have suffered a severe defeat," wrote one participant. "Especially alarming was that the martial spirit of some of the divisions left much to be desired. . . . The failure of Second Army on August 8 could not be blamed on over-fatigue of our divisions. The operational presentations of the First Quartermaster General [Ludendorff] culminated in the resolution, not to yield a foot of earth without tenacious battle. . . ."[10] The kaiser was not in good spirits. At dinner the previous night he remarked that "it is very strange that our men cannot get used to tanks."[11] Now, having heard Ludendorff's dismal words, he merely said, "I see that we must draw up the balance sheet, we are on the brink of solvency. The war must be ended. . . . I therefore expect to see you shortly in Spa!"[12]

The situation improved slightly on August 11 as more divisions arrived from the north. "Yesterday Klewitz replaced Tschischwitz," von Kuhl scribbled in his diary.

Since no big attack came in the morning, he brought Marwitz around and reported that the army could hold. Second Army was withdrawn to the second position. . . . We must now become clear over further aims. . . . I am of the opinion that we cannot fight at length in front of the Somme in order to hold there. We lack the strength. We thereupon come to the most difficult positions, the Somme behind us. If the enemy attacks from north of the Somme around Albert, he can strike our rear. We must therefore retire behind the Somme. . . . By this we save forces. Klewitz is of a different opinion and says: We must and will hold out for morale purposes. The enemy cannot win, he must exhaust his forces. . . . Naturally we want to hold, but only so long until we have organized a new line and a pause sets in. . . . Ludendorff telephoned yesterday evening and was of the opinion that the English can now attack at Lens, Bethune, Kemmel, etc. We cannot allow ourselves to be overrun, we must win time until the exhausted divisions regain strength. He therefore proposed that everywhere where an attack was possible to at once withdraw to the second position, holding the first line solely with battle battalions. [13]

So went the great debate, to retreat and refit or to stand and fight. It was Ludendorff's decision to make. Not being able to bear the thought of retreat, he chose to stand and fight, only to learn that this was not altogether possible. At this point Ludendorff more than ever was refusing to face facts—and that for a commander is the kiss of death.

Colonel von Haeften found Ludendorff "outwardly calm, but very grave" on August 12. "It was not the loss of territory or the superiority of the tank . . . which disturbed him. . . . What depressed the General was that he had lost confidence in the morale of his troops, the indispensable element in victory. Ludendorff said to Haeften that the men could no longer be depended upon and we needed peace quickly. . . . No longer could any hope be placed in an offensive."[14]

Hindenburg and Ludendorff met with Chancellor Hertling and the foreign minister, Paul von Hintze, on August 13 at Spa. "We expressed ourselves clearly and precisely," Ludendorff later wrote, "that we were not in the position to win the war militarily, but that we hoped to maintain ourselves in France. Von Hintze concluded that our earlier intentions must give way to peace negotiations. . . . I again referred to the [troop] replacement situation, as so often previously, and demonstrated the damage of enemy propaganda. . . ."[15]

Hintze later testified under oath: "Before the four of us met . . . General Ludendorff took me aside and told me that he had said to me in July that he was certain that the current offensive would break the enemy's will and force him to make peace. He no longer had this certainty. To my question of how he now intended to continue, he replied that a strategic defensive would enable us to cripple the enemy and so bring him gradually to make peace. . . . General Ludendorff then declared that 'the grand offensive' was no longer possible but that a strategic defensive with occasional offensive strikes had a good chance of crippling the enemy's will. . . . Field Marshal von Hindenburg judges the situation even more favorably."[16]

The contradiction between what Ludendorff was telling such officers as von Haeften and what he was telling Hertling and Hintze is evident. Hintze later testified that "not by one word or by one syllable did Hindenburg or Ludendorff even hint that they concluded from the military situation that diplomatic steps to bring about peace were indicated."[17] This evidence is in part corroborated by Mertz's diary entry a month or so later, when von Lersner, the foreign ministry's representative at the OHL, told him that in mid-August von Hintze had been fed false hopes. To Lersner's protestations that the situation was very serious, Hintze replied: "I am very pleased to be able to tell you that you are far too pessimistic. Field marshal and Ludendorff assured me that they could not only maintain the [military] position at this time but that in a few weeks they could again undertake a big affair." "A puzzling optimism," Mertz wrote. "It completely contradicts what Excellency [Ludendorff] has repeatedly told me."[18]

Hintze reported the result of the talks to the kaiser at a crown council on August 14. Kaiser Wilhelm had been going through a bad patch only partially eased by his military and civil nurses, "who did their best to divert the monarch's thoughts from the grave troubles of the day, and to discuss with him the important problems of art, science or technique. . . . When the emperor took up such a theme, drawing upon the inexhaustible sources of his personal experience, the otherwise dreary hours passed in a flash, and were a perpetual refreshment"[19]—and damn the muted thunder of enemy guns and damn the cries of the wounded and dying men who couldn't get used to tanks.

Now, on August 14, the kaiser reluctantly faced more concrete issues. He learned from Hindenburg that since the army could no longer hope "to break the enemy's will," which would now have to be crippled through a strategic defensive, Germany's diplomacy would have to be altered. The pessimistic effect of Hindenburg's words on the supreme warlord was somewhat lightened by his assertion that he hoped the army could remain on French soil so as to finally "enforce their will on the enemy."[20] Unaware that at this point Hindenburg did not even know the location of the German army corps, much less the divisions, the kaiser took heart. Instead of ordering Hintze to make a direct peace offer to the Allied powers, he directed him to seek the mediation of the Spanish king and the Netherlands queen. Such was the strength of the Duo's fraudulent representation of the military facts that Hertling designated a "suitable time" to be "after the next German success in the west," a decision meekly accepted by the compliant Hintze.[21]

This was a very serious deception. As von Haeften later recorded: "If the generals had been anything like as frank to the statesmen as they were to myself, it would have been plain to the statesmen that not an hour must be lost before initiating political negotiations . . ."[22] According to one colonel at the OHL, Ludendorff openly admitted the deception: "Perfect candor would have led to a catastrophe! If I had told them the truth, they would have completely lost their heads."[23]

The Duo's deception does not excuse von Hintze's obtuse behavior. Baron von Lersner's record was too good for his warnings to have been ignored. At the very least, Hintze should have repeated them to the Duo and demanded categorical replies. Opinion as to Hintze's deception is divided. From what remains of the record, one is inclined to side with Gerhard Ritter, who wrote that Hintze is guilty of a cover-up, that is, that he was aware of Germany's military weakness at this time. On August 21, the day a fresh British offensive opened north of Albert, he told party leaders that according to the OHL "there was no reason to doubt ultimate victory. We shall be vanquished only when we doubt that we will win. We . . . are entitled to anticipate that we shall achieve a military position from which we shall be able to gain a satisfactory peace."[24] Several days later he told the Bundesrat: "We have, it is true, suffered a few minor checks, but not such that we need describe our military situation as bad or desperate."[25]

The OHL continued in its criminal deception of the public. Huge placards signed by Hindenburg were posted in cities and towns: "We have won the war in the East, and we shall win it in the West." In September the public was told by Admiral Scheer: "There can be no doubt that our submarine campaign will compel England to sue for peace."[26]

Coincidentally, the Austrian emperor, Charles, his foreign minister, Count Stephan Burián (who had replaced Count Czernin), and his new chief of staff, General Arz von Straussenburg, were in Spa on the same day that the Duo briefed the kaiser. Ludendorff asked Arz to send more divisions to the western front—he had so far received only two despite earlier Austrian promises of more. It was a forlorn request. The Austrian army, along with the Austro-Hungarian Empire, was rapidly crumbling. Wholesale mutinies and desertions were the order of the day—at least a quarter of a million deserters roamed the country in bands, pillaging and looting at will. Arz still spoke hopefully of launching an offensive in Italy but also stressed that the Austro-Hungarian army could hold out "only until December."[27]

Marshal Ferdinand Foch had been justly criticized for tactical impetuosity unwarranted because of physical limitations (Ludendorff had
been similarly criticized). Yet the pursuance of his personal credo, *l'attaque toujours l'attaque*, is difficult to fault in those exciting days of August
1918 when extraneous factors, be they Haig's stubbornness, be they the
French shortage of ammunition, combined to halt the diverse Allied
attacks.

Foch refused to let the offensive die. On Debeney's right, Humbert's
Third Army continued its push northward until August 16. The next
day Mangin's Tenth Army attacked toward Soissons. Four days later
Byng's Third British Army struck toward Bapaume to be joined a few
days later by Horne's First British Army on the left. Rawlinson's Fourth
Army meanwhile resumed its advance, its irrepressible Australians soon
to seize Mont Saint-Quentin and Péronne to breach the barrier of the
Somme River.

Further to the right, General Pershing, now commanding the recently formed U.S. First Army, was planning his own offensive. Pershing
owned nineteen divisions (each equal in size to two British, French, or
German divisions), which as yet lacked their own artillery, tanks, and
aircraft. Not all of them were immediately available for his use. Five
were with the British. Pershing would soon retrieve three of these to
cause Haig a near fit of apoplexy: "What will History [sic] say regarding
this action of the Americans leaving the British zone of operations when
the decisive battle of the war is at its height, and the decision is still in
doubt!"[28] Two more American divisions were fighting with the French
Sixth Army—they would shortly rejoin Pershing, minus 13,000 casualties. Another division was fighting with Mangin's Tenth French Army
in its struggle forward from the Oise to the Aisne.

Pershing was well on his way to bringing off his long-cherished
dream of an all-American offensive. A plan drawn up in part by a thirty-
eight-year-old colonel, George Catlett Marshall, called for a concentric
attack of the Saint-Mihiel salient, which poked out from northeast of
Verdun running to Pont-à-Mousson.

Foch liked the idea and offered up six French divisions to support
it, providing that Pershing would not go beyond the salient in an attempt
to grab the rich prize of fortress Metz. That was agreeable to the American
general, but Foch's next proviso was not. After the Saint-Mihiel operation, Foch wanted to split Pershing's army, half of it to fight in the

Argonne Forest, half in Champagne. Pershing replied that his army would fight anywhere Foch wished, but only as an American army. Discussion grew acrimonious. "I insist," Foch insisted. "You may insist all you please," Pershing told him, "but I decline absolutely to agree."[29] Foch grudgingly gave in, and in return Pershing committed his new army to what would become the Meuse–Argonne offensive.

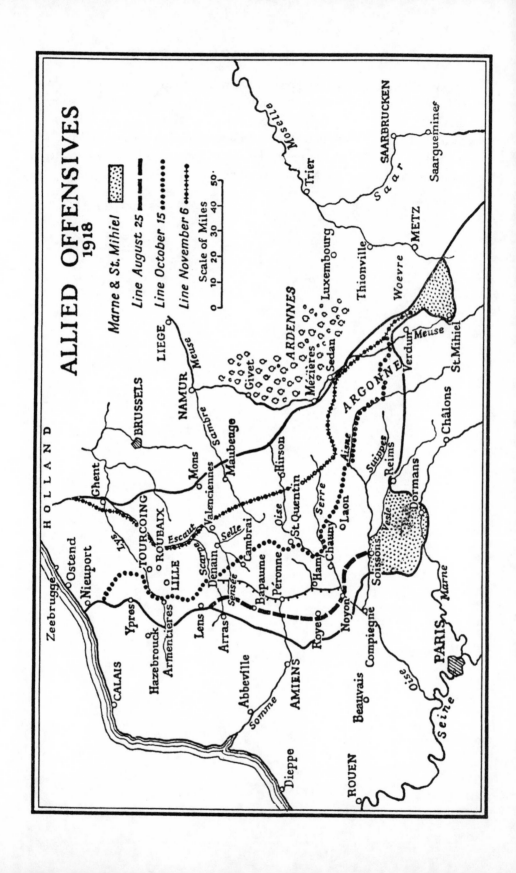

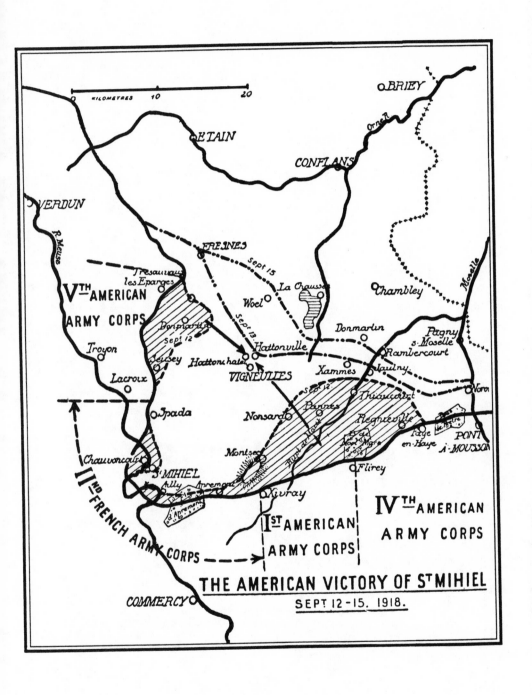

THE AMERICAN VICTORY OF St MIHIEL

SEPT 12-15. 1918.

42

August-September 1918:
The Unavoidable Conclusion

The Americans are multiplying in a way we never dreamt
of. . . . At the present time there are already thirty-one American divisions in France. . . .
  —CROWN PRINCE RUPPRECHT TO PRINCE MAX OF BADEN,
    AUGUST 15, 1918[1]

We cannot fight against the entire world.
  —GENERAL ERICH LUDENDORFF TO GENERAL HERMANN VON
    KUHL, SEPTEMBER 30, 1918[2]

Ludendorff's oscillating emotions continued to fluctuate in tune with
the fortunes of war. A brief lull in the fighting on the western
front brought a noticeable change in his temper. "Ludendorff is
now much more approachable," von Kuhl noted in his diary on August
23. "He frequently asks my opinion." Kuhl's opinion was depressing but
logical: "We can bring about no decision, we are exhausted. The divisions
are not holding properly. . . ."[3]

Kluck again advised, in line with Lossberg's reasoning, that the
army should hold until adequate rear-area positions were prepared and
should then infiltrate back to a new defensive line. This was counter to
Ludendorff's "foot-by-foot" retreat, which he had no intention of relin-
quishing. Neither did he respond favorably to bad news. Colonel Walther
Nicolai, who was reporting to him regularly, wrote on August 24: "I
have the impression that Ludendorff begins to be apprehensive of me as
chief of intelligence in that I come to him carrying in the one hand the

inexorable fact of the undiminished destructive will of the enemy and in the other the warning of the approaching internal revolution against the war. . . . I recognize for the first time that he seems to be at the end of his strength."[4]

As the military action began to pick up with the British capture of Péronne, Ludendorff's lassitude vanished. Daily and sometimes hourly he telephoned Kuhl, complaining now of the Second Army's poor performance, now of army headquarters being too far from the front. "Ludendorff was very cross last night," Kuhl wrote on August 26. "This morning a great crisis, a very exciting morning. Ludendorff frightfully excited. Everyone else is to blame." Kuhl was willing to forgive a great deal because of the pressure on Ludendorff, but was annoyed "that a scapegoat was everywhere looked for, and everywhere the poor leadership is to blame. It is not pleasant to work with him now. He casts everybody aside. There is a great deal of grumbling about him." Kuhl continued to press for an orderly fallback. "If we are to maintain our forward position we risk a total collapse. Then there is nothing more to hold. That is gambling at its best and I fear that Ludendorff's ambition will lead us to it. He will not give up his prestige for anything in the world and will bet the last chip on it."[5]

The gambler was rapidly running out of chips. Too late had the Duo recognized the immense tactical threat from tank attacks. The cavalier attitude adopted by Ludendorff toward the tank was shared by Hindenburg, who upon seeing the first German-made tanks in February 1918 allegedly remarked, "I do not think that tanks are any use, but as they have been made they may as well be tried."[6] The subject was touched on in a six-page critique of Plan Michael's tactical shortcomings. Enemy tanks, it was explained, could be easily killed from behind or above by trench mortars and machine-gun fire or by a stick of grenades placed in the treads."[7]

A cumbersome, slow-firing antitank gun introduced in May proved to be almost worthless. A few days after Mangin's breakthrough on July 18 Ludendorff seemed to see the light: "The utmost attention must be paid to combat tanks—our earlier successes against tanks led to a certain contempt for this weapon of warfare. We must, however, now reckon with more dangerous tanks."[8] Officers were sent to staff levels as low as brigade to teach antitank defense, the message apparently being to keep calm.

The British tank offensive in August brought renewed panic. According to a German division order, the priority mission of artillery to fire protective barrages against enemy infantry attacks and to neutralize enemy batteries was changed to fire on enemy tanks. The swing from scorn to fear was more pernicious than Ludendorff realized. In J.F.C. Fuller's words, "Since the German Higher Command could explain away failure in the event of tank attack the German regimental officer very naturally came to consider that the presence of tanks was a sufficient reason for the loss of any position entrusted to his care. His men came to consider that in the presence of tanks they could not be expected to hold out. . . . From this time onwards explanations [by captured German officers] generally became very simple: 'The tanks had arrived, there was nothing to be done.' The failure of the Higher Command to produce tanks to combat those used by the Allies began to undermine the faith of troops in their generals."[9]

On August 28 Lieutenant Sulzbach, whose field artillery regiment had been fighting for weeks without a break, studied "a recent paper by Ludendorff. . . . The reason for our defeat is regarded, in the main, as being quite undoubtedly the unbelievable effect produced by tanks. New techniques of anti-tank warfare are therefore being brought out, and the Field Artillery is to become even more mobile than hitherto." A few days later he wrote, "New regulations about anti-tank warfare are coming every day."[10]

In early September the British smashed through the Wotan Line that defended the Arras–Cambrai road, a serious development that forced most of the Seventeenth Army, all of the Second and Eighteenth armies and the right wing of the Ninth Army to fall back on the Siegfried Line (which to Lossberg's disgust had not been strengthened). This in turn forced the right wing of the Seventh Army to abandon the line of the Vesle River and withdraw to the Aisne. Ludendorff simultaneously ordered evacuation of the hard-won Lys salient by the Fourth and Sixth armies and the transfer of the OHL from Avesnes to Spa.

Gloom was not confined to the western front. Dispatches from Syria and Palestine, from Macedonia and Italy, all brought disquieting news. Allied forces were pressing in everywhere—the end was near. Nor was there cheer from the home front, where a vicious flu epidemic was daily claiming thousands of lives. "Berlin is indeed a gloomy place," Princess Blücher recorded in September. "The news from the front is more and more depressing, there is nothing to eat, and the methods employed to prevent the depression from gaining ground goad the people to fury. Hindenburg has forbidden anyone, whatever his personal feelings may be, to speak of the present position as being anything else than hopeful."[11]

People were indeed starving. The meat ration had been reduced to four and a half ounces a week, households were allowed two or three ounces of dubious fat a week, and there was another cut in the bread allowance. Nearly every civilian was hungry, illness was rampant from years of undernourishment, child mortality rate was fifty percent above the 1913 figure, civil deaths from hunger well over half a million. There was almost no soap, cloth, shoes; no housing construction, few horses, no cars, almost no manure, increasing slaughter of hogs with no way of replenishing the stock. Farm machinery could not be repaired for want of parts, railroad engines stood idle, there was no rubber, no leather, no coal, no oil. The empire was close to revolution. Liberal members of the Reichstag were demanding sweeping constitutional reforms and a change-over to democratic government. Hertling had done practically nothing to strengthen morale in the homeland, and there was probably nothing left for him to do. Nicolai continued to warn Ludendorff of imminent revolution. The government learned that Austria-Hungary was seeking peace independent of German wishes.

The confused and critical situation was increased by Ludendorff's ambivalent, dangerous, and dishonest attitude toward his own government. Both he and Hindenburg consistently refused to give Chancellor Hertling, Vice Chancellor Payer, or Foreign Minister Hintze an honest appreciation of the deteriorating military position. Colonel Mertz returned from leave on the first day of September and was briefed by Ludendorff on various military setbacks. "Hereupon I asked the general if he had informed State Secretary von Hintze of this serious situation. He answered in the negative, adding that it was difficult to inform the foreign ministry of the actual state of affairs without making it too anxious. (I content myself with this wording of my war diary, in reality his statements against the foreign office were *much* sharper.)"[12] Mertz met with Georg Wetzell and Alfred von Vollard-Bockelberg, chief of OHL administration, that evening: "Chief question, how is one to divert Excellency Ludendorff from his destructive influences on the armies? . . . Wetzell and Bockelberg believe that only the field marshal can do this."

Another general-staff officer, Major Erich Baron von der Bussche-Ippenburg, returned from leave and was privately received by Ludendorff. When Bussche underlined the seriousness of the military situation and pressed for an opening of peace negotiations, Ludendorff replied: "That is entirely my opinion. I have left the state secretary of the foreign ministry during his short visit to the OHL in no doubt over the military situation and asked him to commence peace negotiations immediately."[13]

General Oldershausen returned from Berlin to inform Ludendorff "that people in Berlin, indeed in the leading positions, judged the situation in general as much too favorable,"[14]—that they had no idea of the actual military situation. Ludendorff at once telephoned Colonel Winterfeldt, his liaison officer in the chancellor's office in Berlin, and told him that he had ordered the Seventeenth and Second armies to withdraw to the Siegfried Line. Winterfeldt should immediately brief Hintze and skim over nothing! "The state secretary must draw the consequences from this," were his last words on the telephone.[15]

Winterfeldt's briefing brought an urgent request from Hertling for more information. Hindenburg replied that the military situation was without doubt very tense, the consumption of German forces very high, above all from Allied tank attacks, and would not be covered through arriving replacements. He then continued: "Despite this, I hope nevertheless to maintain the situation, since the enemy must also suffer heavy losses, but I shall scarcely be able to assume any large offensives in this year through which alone a final decisive sudden change were to be quickly obtained."[16]

On September 6 Ludendorff summoned army group chiefs of staff to Avesnes. Hindenburg opened the meeting with an unnecessary reference to the "extreme seriousness" of the days. Ludendorff took over to deliver a tirade against the troops and their officers, whom he held responsible for the recent defeats, "without himself admitting," as Lossberg later wrote, "that the real fault lay in his own defective generalship."[17] With that he announced that battalions would be reduced from four to three companies due to personnel and equipment shortages. Finally came his new defense notions, the major one being to construct three new defensive lines anywhere from five to twenty miles behind the now fragile Siegfried Line and the primitive Antwerp–Maas Line in the north. Asked for an opinion, General von Lossberg (never a shrinking violet) bluntly stated that he and General von Boehn did not believe that the Siegfried defenses could hold out much longer and certainly not long enough to build new lines from scratch. Instead the Antwerp–Maas Line should be completed and equipment and stores moved there in anticipation of the Siegfried Line giving way. The troops would then employ scorched-earth tactics in their retreat to the new line, where they would gain time to rest and refit. Ludendorff refused the suggestion.

Ludendorff's capricious behavior in these crisis-ridden days was due in part to the nature of the man, in part to an obvious deterioration in his mental and physical health. Hindenburg's military physician had for some time been concerned with Ludendorff's erratic ways marked by vicious outbursts of temper, restless nights broken by angry telephone calls to individual commanding generals, on occasion too much drinking, and crying spells possibly evoked by frequent visits to his stepson's temporary grave at Avesnes, possibly by thoughts of the millions of wounded men on whose behalf he had established a voluntary charity, the Ludendorff Fund, the previous February. Having exhausted every medical approach, he consulted an old friend, Dr. Hochheimer, a retired military physician who was practicing psychiatry in Berlin.

Hochheimer turned up at the OHL in early September to meet with Ludendorff. He did not beat about the bush, as he informed his wife: ". . . I now spoke to him seriously, urgently, and with affection, what I had noted with worry: he had for years no longer thought about one thing, about his *soul*. He had only worked, worried, body and mind tensed, no relaxation, no fun, hastily eaten meals, he had not breathed correctly, had not laughed, had seen nothing of nature and art, heard nothing of the rustle of the forest and the ripple of brooks, and thereby had all the longer, all the more hurt his force of energy and creative power and thus himself. . . ." Instead of the outburst expected by the doctor, Ludendorff quietly agreed and asked for help.[18]

Hochheimer prescribed a regimen of rest at Spa: "And there a totally different daily routine, with rest periods, walks, more sleep (at present one to five hours a night), more pleasure, breathing, use of the mind and distraction, massage to relax the body, learn to speak in a different tone (now a strained high command tone), rest of eyes (from continuous map reading with a magnifying glass): look at the mountains and enjoy the wind and clouds, read. . . ." In one of the least likely scenarios of all time, Ludendorff was "to sing German folksongs upon awakening" and was "to contemplate the beauty of the roses in the villa garden."[19] Breathing exercises commenced immediately. Treatment was to last for four weeks.

Ludendorff's admission of illness allegedly exercised an immediate therapeutic effect. Within a day or two Hochheimer was being congratulated by OHL officers, particularly Hindenburg, on Ludendorff's cheerfulness and good humor. Within a week Hochheimer informed his wife that "the man has really become an entirely different, fresher, more liberated, more happy person. The stiffness gives way . . . he became agreeable and personal, asked me about my background and family."

Neither deep breathing, singing folk songs, nor contemplating roses could dissipate the looming military catastrophe of what Ludendorff later termed "the worst days of my life."[20] On September 12, thirteen divisions of Pershing's First American Army, supported by four French colonial divisions—a total 665,000 men—and 3,200 guns, mostly French, 1,500 French and British airplanes, and about 250 light French tanks eliminated the Saint-Mihiel salient to capture 15,000 enemy (about seventy-five percent of German losses) and several hundred guns at a cost of just over 7,000 casualties. The news shocked Ludendorff. The attack had been expected, orders had been given to evacuate the salient. "Why did you allow two divisions to be beaten to pieces yesterday?" he furiously asked General von Gallwitz.[21]

Ludendorff's recuperation nonetheless continued. Colonel Wilhelm Heye, who had been brought into the OHL to relieve him of some of the burden, found him warmer and more tolerant, a welcome relief from Ludendorff's customary crying on his shoulder. Hochheimer reported that Ludendorff was sleeping more soundly, an uninterrupted six hours "for the first time in years." Von Kuhl noted that he was less excited and was warmer on the telephone.

He was also much less communicative. Austria's peace note, published in mid-September, had thrown the Reichstag into uproar, with socialist demands for immediate peace hurled at Hertling and Hintze, neither of whom was prepared for the onslaught. Rumors spread more rapidly than falling autumn leaves. "The tension in September could hardly be borne . . . ," Prince Max of Baden later wrote. "One awoke every morning with the anxious question: What has happened?—and breathed again in the evening to find that [the] front and alliances had held."[22] Hintze had made but slight progress in peace negotiations through Holland's mediation. On September 20 his representative at the OHL, Kurt von Lersner, attempted unsuccessfully to pin down Ludendorff as to the military situation. Ludendorff was obviously worried. On September 21 Lersner telegraphed von Hintze: "General Ludendorff has asked me whether your Excellency intended to approach America on the subject of peace negotiations through Prince Hohenlohe-Langenburg at Berne."[23]

General Wilhelm Groener, who had come to Spa from the Ukraine for discussions with Ludendorff, found him "in a very serious mood but obviously in sound condition." Ludendorff described his military state as " 'extraordinarily serious, but not immediately threatening' . . . and said he will be able to hold out for a few months. . . . 'Peace must be made by Christmas.' " Groener later wrote, "While his staff described the situation to me as much more critical than he had, Hindenburg remained silent and the kaiser had no idea of the seriousness of the situation." Groener nonetheless left the OHL with the impression that an imminent military catastrophe was not at hand. [24]

Ludendorff's false optimism worried Colonel Heye, who attempted to persuade him to report the unvarnished truth to Hintze and to the kaiser in Berlin. Ludendorff refused, saying that "Hintze is instructed well enough, he is doing everything in order to achieve peace." [25] Heye later opined that Ludendorff suffered from a mental block on the subject. "Ludendorff, who dreamed only of victory and fame for his Germany and for this had worked over four years without any rest or quiet, is unable to get used to the thought that from him must come the move to peace and preferred to believe that this initiative will be brought about through the imperial chancellor in the sense of Wilson's proposals without the OHL's particular inducement." [26]

Major Joachim von Stülpnagel, who had replaced Wetzell at the OHL, later wrote that it seemed to him and his general-staff colleagues "that on understandable human grounds General Ludendorff still had an aversion to present the situation correctly and candidly to the imperial chancellor and the foreign minister—" despite daily adjurations by his staff. [27]

Ludendorff was deliberately dissembling while fantasizing that a miracle would save Germany as it had saved Frederick the Great's Prussia in 1763. Then it was the death of Catherine the Great. Now it was a deadly flu epidemic that Ludendorff insisted would decimate the French army. Although this was denied by his own surgeon general, he clung to the hope "as a drowning man clings to a straw," and when his belief was repeated by the chancellor to the kaiser it momentarily eased Wilhelm's "very depressed state." [28]

Most of Ludendorff's close staff were heartily tired of the meaningless and dangerous ambiguity—Colonel Heye wrote that he spent more time listening to their complaints than he did in running the OHL. Colonel Mertz wrote in his diary on September 26: "Excellency [Ludendorff] despairs of fighting but does not have the courage to bring it to an end. He will not take the jump if he is not forced to do so." [29] Heye, Mertz, and their fellow staffers now took the extreme measure of inviting Foreign Minister Hintze to Spa for a detailed briefing, a fait accompli accepted by Ludendorff without comment.

Before Hintze arrived, the final Allied offensive opened, with Pershing's First Army and Gouraud's Fourth French Army attacking from

Verdun toward the major rail junction of Mézières. A day later, September 27, the day that President Wilson drew the noose tighter by adding his "Five Particulars" to the earlier "Fourteen Points" and "Four Principles," three British armies and one French army attacked the Siegfried Line in the area Cambrai–Saint-Quentin. The following day British and Belgian divisions moved out from the Ypres area to begin the liberation of Belgium.

Foreign Minister Hintze reached Spa on the fateful day of September 28. Heye and his colleagues spared him nothing. Germany was facing total defeat, he was told. It was doubtful if the army could hold out in time for peace negotiations. Battalions stood at fifty percent of strength. Over twenty divisions had been broken up in order to reinforce other divisions. Deserters and malingerers by the hundreds of thousands roamed wild behind the front and in the homeland.[30] It was doubtful whether more than 750,000 troops remained at the front.[31] Apprised for the first time of the appalling situation, a greatly alarmed Hintze returned to Berlin to consult with Hertling.

That evening Ludendorff learned that Bulgaria would seek a separate armistice. There is some evidence that at this point Ludendorff suffered a genuine fit, foaming at the mouth and collapsing on his office floor. "Ludendorff is pressed from all sides," Hochheimer cryptically noted. Though Hochheimer and some general-staff officers later denied the severity of Ludendorff's illness, it could not be denied that on the night of September 28, 1918, Erich Friedrich Wilhelm Ludendorff lost his nerve. That night the man who would shoot striking workers and jail political defeatists called on Hindenburg to demand an immediate armistice before the German army suffered total defeat. Hindenburg, who later claimed that he had been thinking along the same lines, at once agreed.

Hindenburg and Ludendorff joined Hintze at an imperial audience the following day. Ludendorff now revealed the gory details of Germany's military decline to the kaiser who had allowed himself to be kept in the dark for so long. The confession and demand for an immediate armistice was softened by Ludendorff's insistence that this would allow his armies to fall back on the border, where, rested and reorganized, they could hold on sufficiently to avoid a "shameful peace." This conception, somewhat optimistic in view of the collapse of Germany's allies and the continuing offensives by Allied armies of preponderant strength, lent itself to a further fantasy of the German people rising in a levée en masse to fight to the finish. Almost incredibly, Hindenburg told Hintze that any peace treaty should respect Germany's claim to the rich areas of Longwy and Briey in France.[32]

Paul von Hintze quietly asserted that the torn and bleeding German empire was neither in mood nor condition to form a *furor teutonicus*. There was one possible way to peace. This was by creating a "revolution from above" in the empire. He had brought with him a document for the kaiser's signature. Chancellor Hertling was to be replaced and a parliamentary government formed that would satisfy the Reichstag by including Social Democrats. Hindenburg and Ludendorff would no longer share joint political responsibility with the government but would be under the chancellor's control. The new government would ask President Wilson to arrange an armistice and to directly preside over peace negotiations on the basis of his Fourteen Points. Only in this way, Hintze argued, could a "revolution from below" be prevented. The kaiser, intent on saving his throne, accepted the plan. Hindenburg and Ludendorff, who had been looking for a scapegoat for months, jumped at the opportunity to shift responsibility to government and Reichstag. Hertling, who arrived in Spa that afternoon, vigorously argued against the decision, but the kaiser had already signed the decree.

Hertling was finished. What was to come?

43

Germany's New Government and Ludendorff's Lies

> What I foresaw has come, not only in the last weeks but much much earlier. Germany must now pay for the sins of three decades. It was politically paralyzed through blind trust and slavish insubordination to the will of a conceited and arrogant fool.
>
> —ADMIRAL ALBERT HOPMAN, DIARY ENTRY, OCTOBER 6, 1918[1]

On the first day of October 1918 Erich Ludendorff summoned senior staff officers at the OHL to a special meeting. Colonel von Thaer recorded Ludendorff's entrance, "his grief-stricken face, pale, but with head held high. Truly a beautiful Germanic heroic figure! I perforce thought of Siegfried with the mortal wound in the back from Hagen's spear."[2]

Siegfried's message was a shocker. "OHL and the German army were finished, the war no longer to be won, unavoidable and final defeat was close at hand."[3] Yesterday he had ordered withdrawal to a temporary defensive line along with a reconnaissance of the Antwerp–Maas Line, construction of which had not seriously begun. Considering the state of these defensive lines, Ludendorff's orders were but prelude to further withdrawal all the way to the German border.

Bulgaria had given in, Ludendorff went on, Austria-Hungary and Turkey were at the end of their strength, the German army was infested with the poison of communist-socialist anarchy, and "the troops could no longer be relied upon." In short order the enemy would break through our lines to send us back over the Rhine while revolution swept Germany. The only way to prevent this tragedy was to negotiate an immediate armistice based on Wilson's Fourteen Points. Ludendorff of course blamed the civil government, which now had to open negotiations.[4]

"The effect of his words was indescribable," Thaer wrote. "While Ludendorff spoke one heard faint groans and sobs, tears ran involuntarily down the cheeks of those present."[5]

Hindenburg did not share Ludendorff's panic. It was his seventy-first birthday. "The time is serious but also momentous," he told assembled officers. "I am totally convinced that Germany with God's help will come through this difficult period."[6] At this point few officers really cared what Hindenburg thought (although the kaiser sent him a bronze statuette of himself as a birthday present). Ludendorff, acting "like a cat on hot bricks,"[7] bombarded the chancellor and the foreign ministry with telegrams that demanded immediate armistice. "I can hold the troops today, but I cannot foretell what will happen tomorrow."[8] "The army cannot wait another forty-eight hours, a breakthrough with disastrous consequences is possible at any moment."[9]

Kaiser Wilhelm and Chancellor Hertling were still trying to agree on a successor when Ludendorff entered unannounced and in a very excited voice demanded, "Is the new government still not formed?" The kaiser curtly replied, "I cannot work miracles!" Undeterred, Ludendorff said, "The government however must be formed immediately—the peace offer has to go out today." "You should have told me that two weeks ago," was the reply.[10]

A parliamentary government, in this case a coalition government, is never easy to form even in a democracy. In autocratic Germany's case it called for something of a miracle, but through the excellent work of Hintze and Vice Chancellor Payer it was accomplished in a remarkably short time. On October 1 Prince Max of Baden, the kaiser's cousin, was asked to become chancellor of the German empire. The brilliant historian Gerhard Ritter sized up the choice as "surely one of the strangest [phenomena] in the history of the Wilhelminian Germany."[11] Old and ill, a Bavarian aristocrat, a conservative with fuzzy but humanitarian notions, inexperienced in internal or external politics, half in respect half in awe of Hindenburg and Ludendorff, a neither-nor man, strong over nonessentials, weak over essentials, scarcely the man to salvage anything from a rapidly sinking ship of state. "An arrogant ignoramus," the kaiser's new chief of the military cabinet, General Ulrich Baron von Marschall, called him "incapable of any work at all, and hampered by being the heir to a federal throne."[12]

Hintze had already opposed Ludendorff's demand for immediate surrender as precipitate, and Prince Max agreed. Far better to hold on until he could form a coalition government and push vital reforms, particularly the electoral reform, through the Reichstag in time to prevent a "revolution from below." A request for an immediate armistice, he argued, could only be interpreted by the enemy as capitulation.

Ludendorff meanwhile had sent his emissaries to Berlin to carry out his demands: Field Marshal von Hindenburg to handle the kaiser, Major von der Bussche to brief party leaders. The issue was aired on October 2 at an imperial council. In response to Prince Max's questions, Hindenburg stated that the army could protect German borders until early 1919, but he repeated demands for an immediate armistice, since the OHL could not guarantee holding its present lines against a fresh enemy offensive. When Max nonetheless argued for a delay, the kaiser told him that the OHL "considers it necessary, and you have not been brought here to make difficulties for the Supreme Command."[13] Undeterred Max asked why, if this were the case, the Duo did not raise the white flag of surrender? Hindenburg offered no immediate reply but on the following day sent the chancellor a letter that confirmed his statements and concluded: "It is desirable in the circumstances to break off the battle in order to spare the German people and its allies useless sacrifices. Every day wasted costs thousands of brave soldiers their lives."[14]

Major von der Bussche had startled party leaders with similar statements. Since a victory was no longer possible, he told his audience— who for two years had been assured by Hindenburg and Ludendorff that Germany *was* winning the war—"the Supreme Command had seen fit to propose to his Majesty that an attempt be made to break off the battle. . . . Every twenty-four hours might make matters worse and lead the enemy to discover our real weakness."[15] The effect of these shattering words—"We have been lied to and cheated," protested one auditor[16]— was to put the government up for grabs by strengthening left-wing demands for peace at any price and absolution of the monarchy! The chancellor's new government, which included two Social Democrats, now faced an irreparable political schism.

Prince Max was sworn in as chancellor on October 3. Did the Duo realize, he asked, what acceptance of Wilson's Fourteen Points implied? Incredibly, neither Hindenburg nor Ludendorff had read the Fourteen

Points, but neither seemed to care what they implied. The only important matter was an armistice to save the army from a humiliating defeat. Against the chancellor's best judgment, a note was sent that night to the United States government asking its president to arrange an immediate armistice to be followed by peace negotiations on the basis of his Fourteen Points. No one, including the new chancellor, seemed to realize that in a speech the previous July the American president had suggested an addendum to the Fourteen Points which called for the destruction or neutralization of any "arbitrary power" that could "disturb the peace of the world"—by which he meant the German monarchy.[17]

The request for intervention drew a mixed reception inside Germany. Such had been the pervasive power of the OHL propaganda, the constant assurances that German armies were winning the war, that only a month earlier "the general public believed in a favorable outcome of the war,"[18] be it outright military victory, be it a peace on Germany's terms. Some conservative politicians were incensed. A leading newspaper published a lengthy and impassioned article by Walther Rathenau that sharply criticized the decision, objecting to peace on the proposed basis and calling for a levée en masse: "The people must be prepared to rise in the defense of the nation." The Duo's hysteria, on the other hand, largely united the socialists in their demand to end the war.[19]

President Wilson's reply arrived in Berlin on October 9, one day after the Siegfried Line had given way. Prince Max and his new cabinet met with the Duo to consider it. Ludendorff had been doing his breathing exercises, or perhaps he had found a favorable passage in his Moravian prayer book. In response to the chancellor's written questions, he opened the session with a military reassessment considerably less gloomy than that which had brought down the government. He confirmed Hindenburg's earlier statement to the new chancellor that the army could protect German borders until early 1919. Here was a confusing and very curious about-face. He and Hindenburg were now inclined to continue fighting if Wilson's conditions were too harsh!

Wilson's conditions were preliminary and discouraging. "My heart bleeds," Hindenburg wrote to his wife.[20] The American president asked if the present German government spoke for the empire. If so, was the government prepared to accept *without conditions* the Fourteen Points? If so, would the government show its bona fides by evacuating all occupied territories in the west?

The German government was not yet prepared to humble itself. Most of those present agreed with the Duo that an armistice need not mean the end of the war. The army could withdraw to the German border and fight on if necessary. But few if any participants shared Walther Rathenau's desire to break off negotiations with Wilson and call the nation to arms, which, in Ludendorff's words, "would cause more disturbance than we can stand."[21] "The armistice is militarily necessary to us," Hindenburg explained to his wife. "We shall soon be at the end of our strength. If the peace does not follow, then we have at least disengaged ourselves from the enemy, rested ourselves and won time. Then we shall be more fit to fight than now, if that is necessary. But I don't believe that after two–three months any country will still have the desire to begin war again."[22]

Prince Max returned a noncommittal but conciliatory reply to Washington on October 12, implying that his new government was stable and intent on democratic reforms. Unfortunately on this same day a German submarine sank the steamer *Leinster* in the Irish Sea, with a loss of nearly 200 American and British men, women, and children. "Since the days of the *Lusitania*," Prince Max wrote, "the sorrow and fury in England and America had never reached such heights."[23] This understandably influenced Wilson's second note, dated October 14, as did France and England's stated belief that the rapidly deteriorating German position could bring surrender rather than negotiation. Clemenceau had already directed Foch to draw up a detailed and very harsh demand for unconditional surrender, which the British not only accepted but expanded. Washington may have had an inkling of this because Wilson's new note insisted on immediate evacuation of occupied lands, an end of the "inhuman" U-boat warfare, and guarantees of constitutional reforms essential to transform Germany into a democracy, the latter being an indirect demand for the kaiser's abdication.

Wilson's new note brought an indignant outburst from the kaiser: "a piece of unmitigated frivolous nonsense," he wrote to Prince Max. "You must use it to arouse the entire people to rally round their emperor in defense of their sacred heritage, just as the government must stand shoulder to shoulder behind him. This impudent intervention in our political affairs must be properly exposed to all."[24] Wilhelm's scatter-brained indignation was not sympathetically received. Max at this point was fending off imminent disaster. "I could have recoiled in horror when I saw that there was no military force to back my policy," he wrote to a friend, "that we had already gone bankrupt on the battlefield. . . . I believed that I had been summoned at five minutes to twelve, and find out that it is already five minutes past."[25]

Another long and stormy cabinet meeting followed in Berlin. Prior to the formal assembly, Ludendorff informed Prince Max that despite the collapsing Flanders front and the imminent fall of Lille, the army could carry out an orderly withdrawal. Prompted by the kaiser, Prince Max suggested that the government would like the opinions of other army commanders. Ludendorff refused to hear of this and threatened that he and Hindenburg would resign. With the kaiser's concurrence, the chancellor postponed the matter until hearing Ludendorff's testimony the following day.

Ludendorff had obviously done more breathing exercises. His lengthy testimony at the formal council is an interesting array of half-truths, irrelevancies, evasions, distractions, distortions, and outright lies. He opened by neatly covering the OHL's recent failures with a homily on the uncertain fortunes of war—perhaps fortune once again would favor German arms. The responsibilities that he had borne for "four long, hard years" would be greatly eased if the war minister would immediately supply him with the 600,000 replacements that he had offered, and if the government would properly inspire the home front to supply 100,000 more replacements per month. Enemy attacks had recently slackened, an Allied breakthrough was now "possible but not probable. . . . I do not fear it," he told his audience. A reinforcement of 600,000 men would repair waning morale, particularly if the home front would do its part, and it would bring battalions up to strength.

Questions from the floor received a variety of replies, often contradictory but generally revealing. The war minister was worried about American strength. Ludendorff replied: "We should not exaggerate the value of the Americans. . . . We have beaten them up to now, even where we were in a great numerical inferiority." Yet he was forced to admit that 350,000 American troops had arrived in France *monthly* in April, May, and June. The new socialist cabinet member, Adolf Gröber, complained about poor food for the men while officers were eating well. Ludendorff denied this, but added that "in the trenches, as is well known, officers and men eat from the same field kitchen. It is only natural that Staff [officers] should have its food prepared better; no one will suggest that we ought to eat out of the field kitchen." The other new socialist minister, Philipp Scheidemann, objected that a reinforcement of several hundred thousand men would not "bring a better spirit into the army." The home front had been deceived by the military and the government once too often. Ludendorff's suggestion that Scheidemann should improve the "morale of the masses" brought an angry reply: People were disillusioned and hungry. There was no more meat, no fat, and potatoes were at an end because "we are 4,000 [rail] wagons a day short." Unless the food situation improved, the home front could not conceivably be inspired. "The workmen are more and more inclined to say: "Better a horrible end than an endless horror!" The chancellor raised the question of tanks. "I hope, when our infantry has recovered again," Ludendorff replied, "that the *tank panic*, too, which had already been overcome and had come again, will be overcome once more. . . . When once the morale of the troops recovers, some formations, such as the *Jäger* battalions and the Rifle Guards, treat tank-shooting as a regular sport. It is attractive too for material reasons, since the tanks are always well provisioned."

There remained the navy's voice. Admiral Scheer testified that it would be a great error to abandon the submarine offensive (as Wilson demanded)—"I think we all have a general impression that the submarine war is making itself very distinctly felt, especially in Italy. Soon its efforts, particularly in America, will be still more marked." The navy had enough oil for eight months of operations, Scheer went on. This statement came as a great surprise to the army, which had only enough for one and a half months, and to the government, which was desperately trying to scrape together a few million tons for dark cities and houses. Perhaps oil supplies should be pooled, someone suggested . . . and the issue trailed off.

As for the impertinent Wilson note, Ludendorff believed that "we ought to tell the enemy that they will have to fight for such conditions."

THE CHANCELLOR: "And when they have been fought for, shall we not have to face even worse?"

LUDENDORFF: "There can be no worse."

THE CHANCELLOR: "Oh yes, there can—the invasion and devastation of Germany."

LUDENDORFF: "We have not yet come to that."[26]

The meeting ended on an inconclusive and disappointing note, as expressed by the new foreign minister, Wilhelm Solf: "I have to give the Chancellor responsible advice upon the tone and contents of the note which we shall have to draft for Wilson. For this task I am not really any better prepared after hearing General Ludendorff than I was before."[27]

Prince Max reacted more positively. Matters could only get worse.

Negotiations with Wilson must continue, "but if dishonorable conditions were made for the armistice, then the people must be called out to make a last stand." Ludendorff, he decided, "was not the man to lead such a desperate struggle. In the course of this meeting I had lost confidence in Ludendorff as a man."[28]

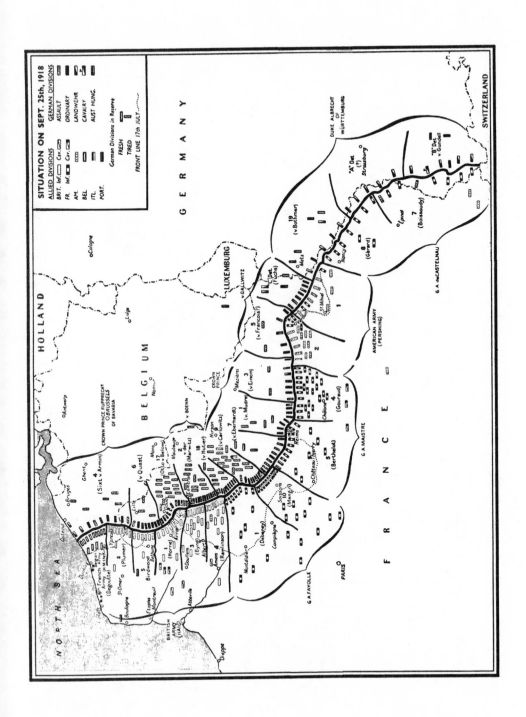

44

Germany's Final Collapse

The army will retire rapidly and orderly to the homeland under
its leaders and commanding generals, but not under the command of Your Majesty, whom it no longer supports.
—General Wilhelm Groener to Kaiser Wilhelm,
November 9, 1918[1]

F aced with increasing political and social chaos reflected in the
differing opinions of ministers and advisers, the German chancellor
drafted a conciliatory reply to Wilson's harsh note of October 14.
Although he protested the accusation of inhuman warfare—with some
justification in view of the British blockade, not to mention the daily
slaughter on the western front—he was aware that popular feeling within
Germany had turned overwhelmingly against the submarine offensive,
and he promised to prevent future submarine attacks against passenger
ships. He also stressed that Germany had introduced parliamentary government, which enjoyed the trust of the empire, and he hoped that this
would open the way to a "just peace."[2]

His draft satisfied almost none of his ministers, that is until Hindenburg shifted ground and, together with Ludendorff and the admiralty,
insisted that the submarine offensive must continue. If this resulted in
breaking off negotiations with President Wilson, Hindenburg informed
the chancellor on October 20, the government "must make up its mind
to fight out the struggle for our honor to the very last man."[3] Thus spake
the military leaders who a few weeks earlier had demanded an instant
armistice and had forced the civil government to open peace negotiations
against its desire.

How to explain this? The most logical answer appears to be that once the Duo had forced the government to open negotiations with Wilson, they wished to distance themselves from the negotiations in an effort to save what they called the "honor" of the army (the same process can be seen with the naval leaders). This convoluted thinking, for which Ludendorff was no more responsible than Hindenburg and a score of senior generals, was nothing short of criminal. Ludendorff had known since July that the army was crumbling and yet had refused to withdraw it to defensive sanctuaries that would have allowed exhausted divisions to rest and refit. His insane refusal to heed the advice of experienced and intelligent front-line commanders and staff officers can only be explained by an overwhelming egocentricity that constantly poisoned rational behavior.

That the German army did its best to carry out Ludendorff's "foot-by-foot" withdrawal is a credit to its professional leadership and the almost incredible loyalty of the combat troops. It is difficult to read the records today and not weep for the victims of yesterday. Allied artillery bombardments defied description. To move outside the trenches, even to a nearby crater-latrine, meant instant death. Stephen Westman furnished one company commander opium to halt bowel movements for ten days—"others relieved themselves in the dugouts on spades covered with earth, and threw the stuff over the parapets."[4] In late September the German crown prince visited his brother, Prince Eitel Friedrich, who commanded a Guards regiment. He found Eitel and his men fighting "with the courage of despair. . . . [The] *entire division* consisted of 500 rifles in the fighting zone. The staff with their dispatch carriers were fighting in the front line, rifle in hand. The artillerymen were extremely fatigued, the guns were worn out."[5] While Ludendorff was telling the chancellor and his ministers that the troops would soon recover from "tank panic," enemy tanks were piercing the Argonne defenses, a line held by one German soldier to every twenty yards of front, to fire from behind. While Ludendorff derided American strength and fighting ability, Prince Eitel described the preliminary artillery bombardment as greatly exceeding "in intensity and heaviness anything we had known at Verdun or on the Somme." Wilhelm reported this and more in writing to the kaiser, who so informed Ludendorff—and there the matter rested.[6] Then there were the defenders of the Siegfried Line. As Lossberg and Kuhl had repeatedly warned, it was breached, its occupants fighting desperate rearguard actions as they retreated, not to Ludendorff's new intermediate defensive line, which existed only on paper, but to the

Antwerp–Maas Line, which also existed only on paper. The retreat would cost some 400,000 men and 6,000 guns.[7]

Now, in late October, at the same time Hindenburg and Ludendorff were burbling on about organizing a "stubborn resistance" and waking up the homeland, Crown Prince Rupprecht was writing the chancellor the true state of affairs on his front: "Our troops are exhausted. . . . In general the infantry of a division can be treated as equivalent to one or two battalions, and in certain cases as only equivalent to two or three companies." A large number of guns and machine guns were lost—"in certain armies fifty percent of the guns are without horses." Shells for the heavy guns were in short supply. "The morale of the troops has suffered seriously and their power of resistance diminishes daily. They surrender in hordes, whenever the enemy attacks, and thousands of plunderers infest the districts around the bases. We have no more prepared lines, and no more can be dug. There is a shortage of fuel for the lorries, and when the Austrians desert us, and we get no more petrol from Rumania, two months will put a stop to our aviation."[8]

This and other confidential messages from army and homeland caused not only a ministerial rejection of the Duo's recent bellicose stand but general indignation at their patent attempt to make the civil government "responsible for losing the already lost war," as the vice chancellor put it.[9] Backed by his ministers, at least on the submarine issue, Prince Max by threat of resignation forced the kaiser to agree to the controversial clause that promised the American government to prevent future German submarine attacks against passenger ships. The Duo withheld formal agreement of the final draft of the chancellor's reply to Wilson's note on grounds that the OHL no longer shared political responsibility with the government, but the reply was nonetheless sent off.[10]

Wilson's third note arrived on October 23. It stated that the Allied governments would agree to an armistice, but only with the proviso that hostilities would not be resumed. Moreover "the nations of the world do not, and cannot trust the word of those who have hitherto been the masters of German policy. . . . The Government of the United States cannot deal with any but veritable representatives of the German people, who have been assured of a genuine constitutional standing as the real rulers of Germany. If it must deal with the military masters and the monarchical autocrats of Germany now . . . it must demand not peace negotiations but surrender."[11] Thus peace negotiations would depend on the kaiser's abdication and the army's renunciation of power in favor of Germany's civil government.

Colonel Haeften, the OHL representative at the foreign ministry in Berlin, telephoned Wilson's message to Spa. The response was predictable. Wilson's note, Ludendorff told Haeften, was an "intolerable humiliation. There was only one solution: break off negotiations with Wilson and fight to the end."[12] Hindenburg telegraphed Prince Max to condemn talks "only of reconciliation and not of fighting the enemies which threaten the very existence of our country."[13]

The chancellor was not greatly impressed with the Duo's outburst. A few days earlier he had been told by Crown Prince Rupprecht that "Ludendorff doesn't accept the seriousness of the situation. We must at all costs secure peace before the enemy forces his way into Germany." Baron von Lersner had also reported from Spa that the military situation was "at least as hopeless as it had been three weeks before" and that "the greater part of the army would now welcome Ludendorff's dismissal."[14] The chancellor, however, failed to prevent the Duo from coming to Berlin to lay their demands before the kaiser.

Colonel Haeften meanwhile repeated Ludendorff's aggressive sentiments to the press section of the foreign ministry in such a way that a member of the military press office interpreted them as the official government view and telephoned them to the OHL. A staff officer there converted them into an official army order to "all troops in the field." Hindenburg and Ludendorff immediately signed it without having received either the government's confirmation of the content or its approval. The fateful telegram, sent on the night of October 24, was an outright violation of the new constitution, as evidenced by its demagogic conclusion:

Wilson's answer is a demand for unconditional surrender. It is thus unacceptable to us soldiers. It proves that our enemy's desire for our destruction, which let loose the war in 1914, still exists undiminished. It proves, further, that our enemies use the phrase 'a just peace' merely to deceive us and break our resistance. Wilson's answer can thus be nothing for us soldiers but a challenge to continue our resistance with all our strength. When our enemies know that no sacrifice will achieve the rupture of the German front, they will be ready for a peace which will make the future of our country safe for the great masses of our people.[15]

Hindenburg and Ludendorff were in Berlin the next day for an audience with the kaiser also attended by generals von Plessen and Marschall and by the new chief of the kaiser's civil cabinet, Clemens von Delbrück. No doubt breathing more heavily than usual, Ludendorff stridently demanded that Wilson's most recent note be rejected and that the war continue. If the homeland would support the army, "the war can be maintained for some months. A fortress that surrenders without having defended itself to the last is dishonored."[16] Ludendorff rudely dismissed Delbrück's attempt to explain the government's position—"nothing is to be accomplished with this government"—until Delbrück interrupted, "Excuse me, but I am not the government, I am only here to inform you of the position in Berlin."[17] The kaiser, frightened to death as usual, referred them to Prince Max, who, seriously ill with flu that was daily claiming over a thousand lives in Berlin alone, shunted them off to his colleagues.

That night the Duo conferred with the vice chancellor, Friedrich von Payer; the new minister of war, General Heinrich Scheüch; the chief of the admiralty staff, Admiral Reinhard Scheer; and his chief of staff, Magnus von Levetzow. Ludendorff delivered still another of his impassioned, inaccurate, and inflammatory lectures about the army's honor, failure of the home front, weakening of the enemy's offensive power, France about ready to give in, before demanding the rejection of Wilson's terms.

The reception was mixed. Hindenburg, Scheer, and Levetzow fervently supported him. This is not surprising, since Scheer and Levetzow, in conjunction with Admiral Trotha, chief of staff of the High Seas Fleet, had worked out a fitting naval Götterdämmerung—at the end of October the High Seas Fleet would leave port to tackle the British navy, a secret plan known only to Ludendorff. General Scheüch passively accepted Ludendorff's sentiments, which he had frequently been subjected to in even his short term of office. Von Payer did not. The vice chancellor was undoubtedly aware of the uproar in the Reichstag, which that afternoon had learned of the Duo's general order to the army, and he was probably aware of the chancellor's intention to resign unless Ludendorff was dismissed. Payer was not a Prussian and did not pay automatic deference to the military. He was a thinking Swabian who objected to Ludendorff's litany of "soldier's honor." "I know nothing of soldier's honor, I am an ordinary, plain citizen and civilian. I see only hungry people."[18] Moreover he was in no mood to believe anything promised by the Duo; he had been warned by von Lersner to have no faith "in any promise which the High Command might make." The greater part of the army would welcome a change, since "confidence in the High Command has gone."[19] His refusal to accept Ludendorff's dogma without hearing reports from the army commanders brought a sudden end to the meeting. "There is no point in speaking further with you, Herr von Payer," Ludendorff told him, "we don't understand each other and we never will understand each other, we shall never agree, we live in different worlds. . . ."[20]

Ludendorff later wrote that early the next morning he submitted his resignation but was persuaded to stay on by Hindenburg. The matter was academic, since they soon were summoned to the kaiser's palace, where Wilhelm angrily took Ludendorff into a private chamber to rake him over the coals for insubordination. Judging from Ludendorff's report to a colleague and from Hindenburg's later testimony, the interview was almost violent. The kaiser vigorously objected to the Duo's insubordinate and unauthorized telegram to the troops and to their frequent changes of mind regarding the military situation. Ludendorff apparently accused the government of attacking rather than defending the OHL, then reminded the kaiser of what he owed the general staff and demanded to be relieved of his post. Hindenburg wrote that at one point the kaiser shouted, "Excellency, I must remind you that you are in the presence of your Emperor." With that the kaiser accepted Ludendorff's resignation. Hindenburg halfheartedly attempted to resign, but was peremptorily told to remain. Hindenburg made no attempt to defend Ludendorff, if the latter is to be believed, or to accept responsibility for the disputatious army order. Their "happy marriage" dissolved outside the palace when Ludendorff accused Hindenburg of "treachery" before storming back to general-staff headquarters.[21]

After submitting a formal resignation, Ludendorff returned to Spa, said good-bye to his staff officers and traveled to Berlin, where his wife was living in a few cheerless rooms. That night the announcement of his dismissal in Berlin movie houses brought prolonged cheering from the viewers.

At Hindenburg's instigation the kaiser replaced Ludendorff with his long-time rival, General Wilhelm Groener, hastily summoned from the thankless task of trying to bring economic order to the politically chaotic Ukraine. He faced an equally thankless task at Spa. The OHL was in a mess, with all the younger officers "blowing their own trumpets" of strategical and tactical brilliance.[22] A tour of the front convinced him that total defeat was very close. Many divisions had battalion strengths of only two or three hundred men or less; numerous units had no officers. The enemy was advancing in almost all sectors and would probably break through before the army could withdraw to the Antwerp–Maas Line (nothing more "than a line on the map," Colonel Heye noted in disgust).[23] Bulgaria had already laid down her arms, Vienna and Constantinople had requested armistices. Sailors at Kiel, ordered to take the ships of the High Seas Fleet to sea in what could only have been a suicide action, mutinied to spark riots throughout the land. A "worker's republic" was proclaimed in Munich. Army commanders reported mass desertions, troops booed films of the kaiser and Hindenburg, some units mutinied. Berlin was on the verge of civil war, the streets filled with troops and civilians carrying red flags and singing revolutionary songs. "The revolution is marching in seven-league boots," a socialist member of the Reichstag told a colleague. "The socialist republic will soon be proclaimed. There is no other way out."[24] Groener hastened to Berlin to present an alarming report on the military position to the chancellor and his ministers. An armistice had to be arranged immediately, he insisted. Prince Max proposed a week's delay. Even that was too long, Groener replied. At Groener's suggestion, the chancellor appointed an armistice commission, which, led by Matthias Erzberger, departed for the vital meeting with Marshal Foch. Groener meanwhile had conferred with trade-union leaders and returned to Spa convinced that civil war was imminent if the kaiser did not abdicate.

Kaiser Wilhelm meanwhile had fled Berlin to take sanctuary in Spa, under the thin excuse that he must be with his army but in reality to escape the growing public clamor for his abdication. Momentarily elated because he believed that Ludendorff's dismissal would bring a reasonable peace, he was soon disillusioned by renewed demands from government and Reichstag that he abdicate in favor of a regency under the crown prince's eldest son, who was twelve. Wilhelm refused to consider it. "A successor of Frederick the Great does not abdicate," he had recently informed Count Lerchenfeld.[25]

Neither did the army want him. Hindenburg and Groener did not favor abdication, which, they feared, would break the army into pieces and which would coalesce into disastrous anarchy. On the other hand they were not sure that he could be physically protected at Spa, where even a Guards regiment could no longer be trusted. Groener thought that the kaiser should go to the front, "not to review troops or to confer decorations, but to look for death. . . . If he were killed it would be the finest death possible. If he were wounded the feelings of the German

people would completely change towards him."[26] Hindenburg, once he
had reluctantly accepted the necessity for abdication, preferred the milder
fate of exile in Holland for his supreme warlord. The kaiser, however,
refused either to abdicate or to leave Spa except, sword in hand, to lead
a force to Berlin to put down the spreading revolution.

Reichstag leaders in Berlin continued to warn the chancellor that
his government would fall if the kaiser did not go. The situation in Berlin
was rapidly running out of control. The mainstay of the government,
three *Jäger* battalions and some artillery units, were gradually going over
to the opposition. The chancellor's frantic calls to Spa urging, even
demanding this move continued to fall on deaf ears.

In Spa a number of division and regimental commanders had been
summoned to report on the attitude of their troops. Hindenburg, emotionally *in extremis,* informed Groener that he now believed the kaiser
must go. On the morning of November 9 the two went to the imperial
château. In addition to the kaiser, Baron von Marschall, General von
Plessen, Admiral von Hintze and Count von der Schulenburg (the crown
prince's chief of staff) were present. Kaiser Wilhelm asked for Hindenburg's report. The old man choked up. Finally, with tears running down
his cheeks, he asked permission to resign—he could not say what had
to be said. Groener was left to pronounce sentence: the kaiser must
depart.

Plessen and Schulenburg angrily challenged Groener's arguments,
but he held firm. Groener apparently was getting the best of his opponents, for someone, probably Hintze, telephoned Prince Max to report
that the kaiser's decision to abdicate was imminent. When it was not
forthcoming, socialist leaders warned that civil war would break out at
any moment.

Prince Max's urgent appeals to Spa during the morning brought no
further information for the good reason that the vitriolic discussion,
intensified by the crown prince's arrival, was still going on. Kaiser Wilhelm insisted that, if necessary, he would abdicate as emperor but would
remain king of Prussia, an ingenious compromise except that it was
impossible under the imperial constitution. Groener's stand strengthened
when Colonel Heye reported that the majority of assembled commanders
stated that their troops would not fire on their own people. Kaiser Wilhelm still stood fast when a telephone call from Berlin took the matter
out of his hands. Prince Max had settled the issue by arbitrarily announcing the abdication of the kaiser and crown prince shortly before

handing the government over to the leader of the Social Democrats, Friedrich Ebert.

Kaiser Wilhelm refused to accept what he furiously called a coup d'état, but at this point he was talking to the wind. The immediate problem was to bury the corpse. At Groener and Hindenburg's insistence, the fallen ruler boarded his special silver train and departed for Holland. There he would spend the rest of his life in exile, never forgiving Hindenburg for what he termed "disloyalty."

On November 11, 1918, Matthias Erzberger and his colleagues climbed aboard a train in the forest of Compiègne to meet with Marshal Foch and Allied representatives. There the armistice was signed that ended the first world war—and the existence of the Wilhelmine empire.

Epilogue

Hindenburg remained as chief of the republican army while Groener organized the evacuation of German forces in France and Belgium and their march back to the homeland, a monumental task finished by the new year, 1919. Meanwhile the two cooperated with Friedrich Ebert's socialist government in suppressing the communist-led revolution, a difficult and dangerous period which saw the rise of voluntary *Freikorps*. These units of former officers and enlisted men, freebooters and hoodlums, were armed and supplied by the army, and were given carte blanche to strike against the communists wherever necessary. Among the victims of what is known as the White Terror were the murdered Spartacist leaders, Karl Liebknecht and Rosa Luxemburg.

Early in 1919 the OHL was transferred to Kolberg on the Baltic, where Hindenburg concerned himself in reorganizing army and *Freikorps* defenses against Soviet forces that were threatening the eastern German provinces. The torn and tottering German government received still another blow that spring in the form of severe Allied peace conditions, most of which, after acrimonious argument, were accepted. Hindenburg neatly sidestepped the issue by turning responsibility for the army's acceptance over to Wilhelm Groener (a repeat performance of the previous November).

In June 1919 Hindenburg returned to Hanover and a second retirement. The legend was still intact. He was greeted by crowds of cheering civilians and soldiers as he moved into an elegant villa, gift of the citizens of Hanover. Aided by General Mertz von Quirnheim and a journalist, he now wrote his not very helpful memoirs, in which he blamed the home front for the army's collapse—what would become the stab-in-the-back legend.

Still the hero of many, a benevolent monarchist content to enjoy the adulation of his followers, he remained generally aloof from partisan politics during the next six furious years of republican government, although he was on occasion involved in Groener's efforts to protect the army's integrity from the violent dictates of the Versailles treaty.

After Ebert's death, Hindenburg was drafted to run for president of Germany in 1925 and was elected by a narrow margin. Despite his advanced age and general ignorance of domestic and foreign affairs, he managed to hold onto the reins of government until Germany was overtaken by events in 1929 and 1930. He had come increasingly under the influence of generals Kurt Schleicher and Groener, who wanted a more authoritarian government with fewer Reichstag controls. Hindenburg did not totally go along with this, but neither did he offer the firm leadership that possibly could have saved the Weimar Republic from dissolution while bringing his country back into a community of nations.

The government began to run away from him with the onset of worldwide depression, which brought almost total economic chaos marked by massive unemployment to Germany. Upset by one cabinet crisis after another, he was persuaded by Schleicher and Groener to appoint the leader of the Catholic Center party, Heinrich Brüning, chancellor. Brüning's austerity program soon put the government at odds with Reichstag and nation. In July 1930 Hindenburg did not interfere with Brüning's decision to dissolve the Reichstag and rule by emergency decrees. September elections brought Hitler's Nazi party a big gain in Reichstag representation along with the Communist party.

Hindenburg was now eighty-three and semisenile, rapidly becoming a pawn of Schleicher and other military rightists in the internecine and vicious war with moderates, Nazis, and communists. This was reaching a crucial stage when his presidential term expired in 1932. Despite his age and failing powers, he ran for a second term to defeat his major opponent, Adolf Hitler, largely with the support of Brüning's Catholic Center party and the Social Democrats, who were violently anti-Nazi.

Persuaded by Schleicher and others that he could come to terms with Hitler, Hindenburg dismissed Brüning and formed a new government under the inept Franz von Papen, whose government by fantasy gave way to the brief Schleicher chancellorship, both governments being constantly harassed by Hitler's obstructionist and divisive tactics.

In January 1933 Hindenburg against his better judgment appointed Hitler chancellor with von Papen vice chancellor. Hitler almost immediately began to take over the German government by illegal and violent methods. Hindenburg sank rapidly and died in August 1934, a willing accomplice in the murder of the Weimar Republic and the promotion of Adolf Hitler to dictator of Germany.

Erich Ludendorff did not remain long in Berlin after being abruptly dismissed from his post by Kaiser Wilhelm. To escape possible danger to his life from Berlin revolutionaries, he disguised himself with wig and colored glasses, and with the aid of false papers fled to Sweden. In a villa furnished by a sympathizer, he wrote his two-volume memoirs, in which he defended his sacrificial role—a victim of evil forces, like Siegfried in the old German sagas—as well as furthering the stab-in-the-back thesis.

Once the revolutionaries had been brought under partial control by the army and by quasi-military *Freikorps* groups, Ludendorff returned to Berlin to be lionized by extreme nationalists. In 1920, along with the sinister Karl Bauer, he participated in an unsuccessful coup attempt by Wolfgang Kapp, the provincial demagogue who had risen to prominence during the war as an all-out annexationist. In 1923 Ludendorff supported another unsuccessful coup attempt, this one by Adolf Hitler in Munich, and only with difficulty escaped trial and possible imprisonment. Elected a National Socialist member of parliament in 1924, he ran for president of the republic the following year. He was easily defeated by his former superior and enemy, Paul von Hindenburg.

Ludendorff divorced Margarethe in 1926 to marry a neurologist and amateur philosopher, Mathilde von Kemnitz, who led him into a never-never land of mysticism. His villains now became the Jews and Freemasons, whose alleged plots were preventing Germany from realizing its divine mission in the world. He published a series of polemical writings under his own imprimatur, his bias sweeping into his otherwise interesting military writings of this period. When not consorting with such Germanic gods as Thor and Odin, whose statues filled the garden of his Munich estate, he continued to write and to support Hitler and the National Socialists. His absurdly prophetic stance soon cost him the support of friends in the officer corps and even of Hitler, whose tyrannical methods he criticized in the early 1930s. He died in 1937.

As for the stab-in-the-back thesis, General Wilhelm Groener left this statement, dated May 17, 1922, in his papers:

It would be the greatest injustice to defame the German people for their collapse at the end of the lost world war. They had sacrificed their youth on the battlefields. They had proven themselves by magnificent feats of arms in the field, in unrelenting work, in privations and sufferings in the homeland. They had been led to the mountain peaks of an illusionary world in which they were held by hope after hope of certain victory. For four long years they lived in illusion. Who can be astonished at their disenchantment, as if they had fallen into a deep abyss upon learning that victory was not to be won?

The military commander in chief Hindenburg hoped by his 1918 offensive to burst as with a hammer blow the iron ring in the west at its strongest point, long since hardened to steel, instead of steadily and tenaciously moving against the line of least resistance to keep opening the surrounding circle of enemies, to support our allies, and to remove every threat in the east, southeast and in upper Italy, to attack finally the enemy in the west at the point of his strongest resistance. Hand in hand with such a military operation designed to open the ring that surrounded the Central Powers, political action had to strive assiduously and fervently to make peace without making too much of an outward fuss.

While we held it as axiomatic that a breakthrough was impossible on the western front, as was demonstrated in 1917, we expected the Franco-English front, despite its superior armament, to yield to a German breakthrough in 1918. Even after the first two attempts failed, one held fast to the belief in the pounding of the steel front and, when the enemy answered with counterblows, deceived oneself until the final hour with the illusion that the enemy would finally exhaust himself, despite his being strengthened from week to week.

In the end the blame for the continued self-deception and the mistaken employment of defensive tactics rests on the military. The victories proclaimed to the people had been those of magnificent deeds by heroes, but they were not victories in the strategic and political sense which had been won by the talents of generals and statesmen.

Notes

Book One

1. Armeson, 2.

Chapter One

1. House, II, 55.
2. Zweig, 167.
3. Fischer, *Germany's Aims* . . . , 50, 90–2.
4. Scott, James B., I, 12.

Chapter Two

1. House, I, 249.
2. Breucker, 17.
3. Asprey, *Frederick the Great*, 11–12, 572–3.
4. Kennedy, *The War Plans of the Great Powers*, 185–8.
5. Ludendorff, Erich, *Das Marne Drama* . . . , 3.
6. Regele, 100.
7. Stein, 52.
8. Moltke, 356–63.
9. Breucker, 17. Ludendorff later tried to distance himself from the Schlieffen plan, which he criticized as too binding to army commanders after the initial deployment. See also, Tschuppik, 25–8, who defends Ludendorff as a victim of general-staff protocol, which prevented him from influencing Moltke and Stein, a defense that does not hold up in view of Ludendorff's close relations with them and, indeed, with Ludendorff's later writings.
10. Kuhl, *Der deutsche Generalstab* . . . , 81. See also, German *Reichsarchiv*, II, 4–14; Craig, "The World War I Alliance . . ."; Freytag-Loringhoven, 232, who sharply criticizes Ludendorff's failure as general-staff section chief of mobilization and deployment for failing to evaluate the Austro-Hungarian army; Stone, "Moltke-Conrad . . . ," 33–5.
11. Ritter, *The Schlieffen Plan*, 51.

12. Kennedy, *The Rise and Fall of the Great Powers*, 203, 210–11. See also, Fischer, *Germany's Aims . . .* , 11–20.

13. Delbrück, *Krieg und Politik . . .* , I, Foreword.

14. German *Reichsarchiv*, I, 41–6.

15. Max, II, 285.

16. Röhl, *Kaiser, Hof und Staat . . .* , 10.

Chapter Three

1. Churchill, VI, 57.

2. Falls, *The Great War . . .* , 35.

3. Stone, *The Eastern Front . . .* , 37.

4. Grey, I, 298–9.

5. Stone, "Moltke-Conrad . . . ," 235–6. See also, Regele, 245 ff., 264–70; Kennedy, *The Rise and Fall of the Great Powers*, 218.

6. Regele, 259. Conrad complained throughout the war of his ally's perfidy, yet he was as much to blame for the lack of planning as Moltke. In 1909 Conrad wrote in an official study of the discussions with Moltke, "still binding commitments could not at the time follow, since everything was dependent on the enemy's deployment and behavior."

7. Stone, "Moltke-Conrad . . . ."

8. Asprey, *The Panther's Feast*, 235–40.

9. Joffre, I, 23.

10. Kennedy, *The War Plans of the Great Powers . . .* , (Williamson essay), 144.

11. Horne, Alistair, 15.

12. Brusilov, 10–11.

13. Brusilov, 29.

14. Stone, *The Eastern Front . . .* , 33–5.

15. Brusilov, 98.

16. Kennedy, *The War Plans of the Great Powers . . .* , (Turner essay), 257.

17. Ironside, 18–24. See also, Knox, *With the Russian Army*, I, XVIII-XXXIII; Stone, *The Eastern Front . . .* , 17–36.

18. Knox, *With the Russian Army*, I, 32–3.

19. Kennedy, *The Rise and Fall of the Great Powers*, 240.

20. Kennedy, *The War Plans of the Great Powers . . .* , (McDermott essay), 109.

21. Asprey, *The First Battle of the Marne*, 25, (quoting Huguet).

22. Kennedy, *The War Plans of the Great Powers . . .* , (Haggie essay), 126–7.

23. Kennedy, *The Rise and Fall of the Great Powers*, 226.

Chapter Four

1. Hanssen, 30.

2. U.S. Naval War College Archives, RG 8, Series II, S 8.3, Number 191, August 3, 1914. The officer is identified only as "Z."

3. U.S. National Archives, Diplomatic Branch, RG 59, 763.72/830, August 18, 1914.

4. U.S. National Archives, U.S. Military Attaché reports, RG 165, 3072, 8584.2, November 4, 1914.

5. Hubatsch, *Germany and the Central Powers in World War I* . . . , 25. See also, Ritter, III, 45.

6. German *Bundesarchiv* (Militärarchiv), Nachlass Müller, N 159/4, 263–4.

7. Hanssen, 26.

8. Evelyn, 8–9.

9. Janssen, *Die Graue Exzellenz*, 162.

10. Hanssen, 29.

11. Armeson, 6.

12. Mendelssohn-Bartholdy, 108–9.

13. Ritter, III, 456.

14. Görlitz, *The Kaiser and his Court* . . . , 17–18.

15. Jarausch, 176–7.

16. U.S. Naval War College Archives, RG 8, Series II, S 8.18, Number 198,* August 8, 1914.

17. U.S. National Archives, Diplomatic Branch, RG 59, 763. 72/830, August 4, 1914.

18. U.S. Naval War College Archives, RG 8, Series II, S 8.18, Number 198, August 8, 1914.

19. Wohl, 55.

20. Wohl, 52–3.

21. Sulzbach, 22.

22. Wedd, 3.

23. Evelyn, diary entry, September 6, 1914, 24.

24. Hanssen, 35.

25. Westman, *A Surgeon's Story*, 37.

26. Kielmansegg, 34.

27. Bloem, 20.

28. Moltke, 20.

29. German *Bundesarchiv (Militärarchiv), Nachlass* Haeften, N 35/1, 32–8.

30. Janssen, *Die Graue Exzellenz*, 163, 165.

31. Görlitz, *The Kaiser and his Court* . . . , 22–3.

32. Edmonds, *History of the Great War*. . . . *1914*, I, 60.

33. Tappen, *Bis zur Marne 1914*, 33.

34. Zweig, 173.

35. Kreisler, 10–11.

36. *Das Kleine Blatt*, 9.

37. Stein, 219.

38. Stone, *The Eastern Front* . . . , 48, 61–2.

39. German *Bundesarchiv (Militärarchiv), Nachlass* Hoffmann, N 37/2, 262.

40. Ironside, 112.

Chapter Five

1. Ludendorff, Margarethe, 70.
2. Hindenburg, Paul von, 81.
3. Wheeler-Bennett, *Hindenburg* . . . , 4.
4. Hubatsch, *Hindenburg* . . . , 10.
5. Ludendorff, Margarethe, 25–6, 31.
6. Görlitz, *The German General Staff* . . . , 94.
7. German *Bundesarchiv (Militärarchiv)*, *Nachlass* Groener, N 46/63, unpublished manuscript, *"Persönlichkeit und Strategie Ludendorffs,"* 105–6. See also, Groener-Geyer, 372–4.
8. Craig, *Germany 1866–1945*, 24–5.
9. Asprey, *Frederick the Great* . . . , 425.
10. Ludendorff, Erich, *The General Staff* . . . , I, 25–6.
11. Balfour, 338.
12. Ludendorff, Erich, *Urkunden* . . . , I, 13–16.
13. Ludendorff, Margarethe, 18.
14. Ludendorff, Erich, *The General Staff* . . . , I, 18.
15. Schäfer, *Ludendorff* . . . , 4–12.
16. Görlitz, *The German General Staff* . . . , 149.
17. Ludendorff, Erich, *Urkunden der obersten Heeresleitung* . . . , I, 60.
18. Schäfer, *Ludendorff* . . . , 4, 7.
19. Ludendorff, Margarethe, 70.
20. Schäfer, *Ludendorff* . . . , 22.
21. Hindenburg, Paul von, 84.
22. Ibid., 83.
23. Ludendorff, Margarethe, 84.
24. Hoffmann, Max, *Diaries and Other Papers*, I, Introduction, 10–11, and II, 33–4.

Chapter Six

1. German *Bundesarchiv (Militärarchiv)*, *Nachlass* Hoffmann, N 37/2, 264.
2. Hoffmann, *Diaries and Other Papers*, II, 313–14.
3. Ibid., 281–2.
4. Asprey, *Frederick the Great* . . . , 528.
5. Knox, *With the Russian Army*, I, 60, 69.
6. Pares, 10.
7. Paléologue, I, 51–2, 74.
8. Ironside, 126, 128–9.
9. Knox, *With the Russian Army* . . . , I, 62.
10. Ironside, 134.
11. Knox, *With the Russian Army* . . . , I, 64–5.
12. Ludendorff, Erich, *My War Memories* . . . , I, 49.
13. Hoffmann, *Diaries and Other Papers*, I, 282.
14. Hindenburg, Paul von, 95.

15. Hoffmann, *Diaries and Other Papers*, I, Karl Novak's introduction citing a letter from François to Hoffmann, 1925.

16. Ibid., II, 274–5, for a revealing example of German general-staff mentality: "The High Command [Eighth Army headquarters] would have done better to listen to General von François's repeated representations and on their own account postponed the attack until all the troops of the I Army Corps had arrived. But the method adopted by General von François to secure the postponement of the attack cannot be approved. And yet the conclusion cannot be avoided that the postponement that actually took place became of capital importance for the progress of the whole battle. If he had followed the letter of his orders . . . the attack would very likely have met with disaster."

17. Ironside, 176.

18. Paléologue, I, 104.

19. Tappen, *Bis zur Marne* . . . , 17–19.

20. Hoffmann, *Diaries and Other Papers*, II, 305.

21. Knox, *With the Russian Army* . . . , I, 74.

22. Ibid., 82, 87–8.

23. Hindenburg, Paul von, 99.

24. German *Reichsarchiv*, II, 230.

25. Hoffmann, *Diaries and Other Papers*, I, Karl Novak's introduction, 19.

26. Ibid., 41.

Chapter Seven

1. Hoffmann, *Diaries and Other Papers*, I, 41.

2. Ludendorff, Erich, *My War Memories* . . . , I, 57.

3. Hindenburg, Paul von, 100.

4. Stone, *The Eastern Front* . . . , 67.

5. Brusilov, 29.

6. Knox, *With the Russian Army* . . . , I, 49–50; II, 403.

7. Brusilov, 29.

8. *Das Kleine Blatt*, 8–9.

9. Hoffmann, *Diaries and Other Papers*, II, 26. See also, Conrad, IV, 516.

10. Kreisler, 64–5, 72–3.

11. Stone, *The Eastern Front* . . . , 67–9.

12. Ludendorff, Erich, *My War Memories* . . . , I, 62.

13. Hoffmann, *Diaries and Other Papers*, II, 44–5.

14. Ironside, 244–5.

15. Stone, *The Eastern Front* . . . , 69.

16. Ludendorff, Erich, *My War Memories* . . . , I, 66.

17. Conrad, IV, 625, 703, 731, 798 ff.

18. Evelyn, diary entry, September 4, 1914.

19. Beaufort, 157.

20. Wheeler-Bennett, *Hindenburg* . . . , 33.

21. Ludwig, *Hindenburg*, 72.

22. Hubatsch, *Hindenburg* . . . , 152.

23. Ludwig, *Hindenburg*, 69.

24. Olden, 132–3.

25. Groener-Geyer, 373.

Chapter Eight

1. Moltke, 385.

2. Tappen, *Bis zur Marne* . . . , 17–19. See also, German *Reichsarchiv*, I, 438–40.

3. Spears, *Liaison 1914*, 195.

4. Bauer, *Der grosse Krieg* . . . , 34.

5. Görlitz, *The Kaiser and his Court* . . . , 25–6.

6. Moltke, 382.

7. Asprey, *The First Battle of the Marne*, 83–4.

8. Bloem, 51.

9. Ibid., 100, 109, 141.

10. Crefeld, *Supplying War* . . . , 96–138, for a well-documented analysis of Moltke's supply problems.

11. Kluck, 94.

12. Asprey, *The First Battle of the Marne*, 94.

13. Crefeld, *Supplying War* . . . , 96–138.

14. Asprey, *The First Battle of the Marne*, 95.

15. Janssen, *Der Kanzler und der General* . . . , 15.

16. Bauer, *Der grosse Krieg* . . . , 36.

17. Asprey, *The First Battle of the Marne*, 135, 139–140. See also, Tyng, *The Campaign of the Marne 1914*; Blond, *The Marne*.

18. Ibid., 146.

19. Bauer, *Der grosse Krieg* . . . , 57.

20. Moltke, 385.

21. Tappen, *Bis zur Marne* . . . , 26–8.

22. Rosner, 196–7.

23. Moltke, 385.

Chapter Nine

1. German *Bundesarchiv* (*Militärachiv*), *Nachlass* Hoffmann, N 37/2, 268.

2. Hanssen, 64.

3. Bernhardi, *Denkwürdigkeiten* . . . , 396–7.

4. Regele, 290, and Conrad, V, 78.

5. Falkenhayn, 11.

6. Janssen, *Die Graue Exzellenz*, 31.

7. In 1913 a German lieutenant stationed in Zabern in the Alsace publicly insulted the Alsatian people, who responded with antiarmy demonstrations. The commanding general defended the lieutenant and to protect the prestige of the army declared an emergency "state of siege" and arrested scores of civilians. The message was clear: the army was the supreme power in Wilhelmine Germany—and would

remain so. It is significant that the chancellor, Bethmann Hollweg, at first opposed the army's stand but then in February 1913 suddenly reversed himself to defend the army in the Reichstag, for which liberal members never forgave him.

8. Ludwig, *Hindenburg*, 43.

9. German *Bundesarchiv (Militärarchiv)*, *Nachlass* Tieschowitz, N 37, M Sg 1/2511.

10. Janssen, *Der Kanzler und der General* . . . , 69.

11. Bauer, *Der grosse Krieg* . . . , 58.

12. Janssen, *Die Graue Exzellenz*, 169.

13. Stürgkh, 25–6.

14. Lossberg, 126–7.

15. Buat, *Hindenburg et Ludendorff Stratèges*, 10. See also, German *Reichsarchiv*, V, 555 ff.

16. Hoffmann, *Diaries and Other Papers*, I, 43.

17. Ludendorff, Erich, *My War Memories* . . . , I, 82, and Hindenburg, Paul von, 116.

18. Janssen, *Der Kanzler und der General* . . . , 266.

19. Hoffmann, *Diaries and Other Papers*, I, 43.

20. Ibid.

21. German *Bundesarchiv (Militärarchiv)*, *Nachlass* Hoffmann, N 37/2, 269.

22. Ibid., 271.

23. Hoffmann, *Diaries and Other Papers*, II, 62, 72. German general-staff doctrine held that the advance of a German army must stop about sixty miles from its railhead. Hoffmann allowed the Russian advance another twelve miles because of "their exceedingly modest [supply] requirements and . . . their great want of consideration for their horses." In the event the Russians were seventy-two miles from their railhead when their corps wireless announced that they were unable to continue their pursuit.

24. Ibid., I, 48.

Chapter Ten

1. German *Bundesarchiv (Militärarchiv)*, *Nachlass* Hoffmann, N 37/2, 272.

2. Stürgkh, 73–6. See also, Dommelier, 16–21, 52–3.

3. Görlitz, *The Kaiser and his Court* . . . , 37.

4. Tirpitz, *My Memoirs*, I, 475.

5. Westman, *A Surgeon's Story*, 31.

6. Dillinger, I, 4–5.

7. Keegan, 236 ff. See also, Schneider, 75, for Hitler's performance in an attack on the Bayerwald, November 15, 1914, and Ibid., 437, for Hitler's own account of the October 1918 fighting.

8. Dillinger, I, 16.

9. Ibid.

10. Kielmansegg, 68.

11. Brusilov, 37.

12. Conrad, V, 132–3.

13. Stone, *The Eastern Front* . . . , 100–1.
14. Knox, I, 149.
15. Westman, *Surgeon with the Kaiser's Army*, 77.
16. Brusilov, 98.
17. Knox, I, 229, 214.
18. German *Bundesarchiv (Militärarchiv)*, *Nachlass* Hoffman, N 37/2, 272.
19. Ibid., 272–3.
20. Hoffmann, *Diaries and Other Papers*, II, 82.
21. Janssen, *Der Kanzler und der General* . . . , 37.
22. Knox, *With the Russian Army*, I, 213–14.
23. Kielmansegg, 60.
24. German *Bundesarchiv (Militärarchiv)*, *Nachlass* Hoffman, N 37/2, 273.

Chapter Eleven

1. Görlitz, *The Kaiser and his Court* . . . , 41.
2. Janssen, *Der Kanzler und der General* . . . , 13.
3. Tirpitz, *My Memoirs*, II, 495.
4. Craig, *Germany* . . . , 347.
5. Goldsmith, 104.
6. Janssen, *Der Kanzler und der General* . . . , 50.
7. Ibid., 42.
8. Tirpitz, *My Memoirs*, II, 456.
9. Ritter, III, 25–6.
10. Ibid., 28.
11. Zweig, 178.
12. Ibid., 180.
13. Doyle, 89. See also, Dehn, 42–3. Hindenburg emphasized this sentiment in a conversation with an American senator, Albert Beveridge, in March 1915, in which he held England entirely responsible for not preventing the war: "We hold nothing against France or Russia . . . But England! We hate England."
14. House, I, 336.
15. Ibid., 336–7.
16. U.S. National Archives, U. S. Military Attaché reports, RG 165, 3096, 8690–92, December 6, 1914.
17. U.S. Naval War College Archives, RG 8, Series 2, 1.19(1), January 19, 1915.
18. Max, *The Memoirs* . . . , I, 18.
19. U.S. National Archives, U.S. Military Attaché reports, RG 165, 3409, 8584.3, March 9, 1916.
20. Ibid., Diplomatic Branch, RG 59, 763.72/1489, February 19, 1915.
21. Wedd, 1.
22. Ibid., 13.
23. Bloem, 157, 204.
24. Wedd, 34–6.
25. Ibid., 167–8.
26. Binding, *A Fatalist at War*, 35.

Chapter Twelve

1. Röhl, *Kaiser, Hof und Staat* . . . , 19.
2. Jarausch, 4.
3. Cowles, 41–2.
4. Röhl, *Kaiser, Hof und Staat* . . . , 29–30. See also, Balfour, 74.
5. Balfour, 86–7.
6. Cowles, 57, 84.
7. Ibid., 281.
8. Davis, 176.
9. Röhl and Sombart, *Kaiser Wilhelm II* . . . , 30.
10. Balfour, 303.
11. Röhl, *Kaiser, Hof und Staat* . . . , for the most recent scholarship on his inadequacies.
12. Hull, 35.
13. Röhl, *Kaiser, Hof und Staat* . . . , 21.
14. Ibid., 20.
15. Röhl and Sombart, *Kaiser Wilhelm II* . . . , 31.
16. Ibid., 47–8. See also, Hull, 64 ff.
17. Hull, 69.
18. Jarausch, opening chapters. See also, Vietsch for an excellent critical study.
19. Balfour, 21.
20. Ibid., 23. See also Jarausch, 70–5; Fischer, *Germany's Aims* . . . , 4–6.
21. Craig, *Germany* . . . , 40.
22. Davis, 48.
23. Röhl and Sombart, *Kaiser Wilhelm II* . . . , 101–2 (Lamar Cecil essay).
24. Ibid., 63 (Kohut essay).
25. Hull, 16.
26. Röhl and Sombart, *Kaiser Wilhelm II* . . . , 38 (Röhl essay).
27. Röhl, *Kaiser, Hof und Staat* . . . , 31. See also, Hull, 112–17.
28. Ibid., 30.
29. Ibid., 32.
30. House, I, 254.
31. Janssen, *Die Graue Exzellenz*, 31.
32. Tirpitz, *My Memoirs*, II, 494.

Chapter Thirteen

1. Falkenhayn, 56.
2. Ludendorff, Erich, *My War Memories* . . . , I, 113.
3. Ritter, *The Sword and the Sceptre* . . . , III, 46 ff. See also, Craig, *Germany* . . . , 348.
4. Hubatsch, *Germany* . . . , 40.
5. Hoffman, *Diaries and Other Papers*, II, 99.
6. Janssen, *Der Kanzler und der General* . . . , 61.
7. Stürgkh, 110.
8. Ritter, *The Sword and the Sceptre* . . . , III, 49.

9. Ibid., 50.

10. Ibid., 50–1.

11. Ibid., 53.

12. Wheeler-Bennett, *Hindenburg* . . . , 50.

13. Görlitz, *The Kaiser and his Court* . . . , 57.

14. Groener-Geyer, 373.

15. Janssen, *Der Kanzler und der General* . . . , 252.

16. Ritter, *The Sword and the Sceptre* . . . , III, 54.

17. Vogel, 8.

18. Ibid., 9.

19. Ibid., 17.

20. Ibid., 24.

21. Ibid., 29.

Chapter Fourteen

1. Görlitz, *The Kaiser and his Court* . . . , 64.

2. Sulzbach, 53.

3. Ludendorff, Erich, *My War Memories* . . . , I, 117.

4. Stone, *The Eastern Front* . . . , 116.

5. Knox, *With the Russian Army* . . . , I, 278.

6. Janssen, *Der Kanzler und der General* . . . , 86.

7. Haber, 24 ff.

8. Bauer, *Der grosse Krieg* . . . , 68. See also, Haber, 80, 83 ff. Bauer was technically correct. This was an asphyxiating gas which produced acute bronchitis with gradual suffocation. Those who initially survived a considerable dose generally died from pneumonia. A more effective gas was soon produced by adding phosgene to chlorine. "The severity of the illness," Haber writes, "depended on the amount of the gas breathed in and its concentration. Most people recovered quickly, but those badly gassed went down within a few hours with severe inflammation of the lungs. The patient coughed, retched, vomited, and these violent spasms aggravated the strain on the heart, which was being deprived of oxygen because of the inflammation of the bronchi and air sacs. People seldom died as the clouds passed over, but after three or four hours the sick reached a critical stage from which they recovered after sleeping, or deteriorated further. In the latter event death within twenty-four hours followed invariably and was due to heart failure caused by pulmonary oedema, a drowning of the lungs in fluid released within them. The inhalation of phosgene did not cause spasms and so was more insidious than chlorine. Its inflammatory action was more localized and took a little longer to develop; in all other respects it was more dangerous."

9. Knox, *With the Russian Army* . . . , II, 400.

10. Pares, 247.

11. Knox, *With the Russian Army* . . . , I, 62, 236. See also, Stone, *The Eastern Front* . . . , 112.

12. Falls, *The Great War* . . . , 118, who correctly points out "that the original Cannae had been won, not in an offensive, but by taking advantage of the enemy's impetuosity, and that this method was the easier to work."

13. Knox, *With the Russian Army* . . . , I, 217–20.

14. Stone, *The Eastern Front* . . . , 116–17.

15. Hoffmann, *Diaries and Other Papers*, II, 80.

16. Knox, *With the Russian Army* . . . , I, 248.

17. Stone, *The Eastern Front* . . . , 118–19.

18. Regele, 343.

19. Hubatsch, *Germany* . . . , 47.

20. Stone, *The Eastern Front* . . . , 128.

21. Ibid., 114.

22. Hoffmann, *Diaries and Other Papers*, II, 92.

23. Görlitz, *The Kaiser and his Court* . . . , 65.

24. Vogel, 38.

25. Ibid., 44.

26. Görlitz, *The Kaiser and his Court* . . . , 64.

27. Vogel, 52.

28. Ibid., 56.

29. Ibid., 57. See also, Dehn, 13, Hindenburg in conversation, September 1916: "When I am told in the field that the going is tough, the rain is holding us up, I always say: 'My boys, the enemy is in the same boat.' "

30. Vogel, 116.

31. Ibid, 63.

32. Hubatsch, *Hindenburg* . . . , 20.

33. Vogel, 66.

34. Ibid., 72.

35. Ibid., 92.

36. Ibid., 81.

37. Hoffmann, *Diaries and Other Papers*, I, 52.

38. Ibid., 53.

39. Janssen, *Die graue Exzellenz*, 226–8.

40. Hoffmann, *Diaries and Other Papers*, I, 59.

41. Janssen, *Der Kanzler und der General* . . . , 92.

42. Ibid., 93

43. House, I, 355.

44. Ibid., 385.

45. Ibid., 404.

46. Ibid., 402.

47. Ibid., 403, 413.

48. Vogel, 48.

49. Hoffmann, *Diaries and Other Papers*, I, 55–6.

50. Vogel, 83.

51. Hoffmann, *Diaries and Other Papers*, I, 57.

52. Vogel, 91.

Chapter Fifteen

1. Groener-Geyer, 372–3.

2. Ritter, *The Sword and the Sceptre* . . . , III, 46.

3. Bauer, *Der grosse Krieg* . . . , 69. See also, Haber, 32 ff.

4. Chapman, 136.

5. Ibid., 147.

6. Ibid.

7. Clark, Alan, 110.

8. Ibid., 125–6.

9. Edmonds, *History of the Great War,* . . . 1914: I, 258.

10. Mollo, 5.

11. Guinn, 88–9.

12. Westman, *Surgeon with the Kaiser's Army,* 57.

13. Ibid., *A Surgeon's Story,* 50.

14. Ibid., *Surgeon with the Kaiser's Army,* 80.

15. Wedd, 208.

16. Westman, *Surgeon with the Kaiser's Army,* 71.

17. Ibid., *A Surgeon's Story,* 57–8.

18. Ibid., 72.

19. Ibid., 55.

20. Vogel, 93.

21. Hoffmann, *Diaries and Other Papers,* II, 104–5.

22. Janssen, *Der Kanzler und der General* . . . , 120, 273.

23. Ibid., 120–1.

24. Falkenhayn, 80–1, 128.

25. Bauer, *Der grosse Krieg* . . . , 73.

26. Stone, *The Eastern Front* . . . , 139.

27. Knox, *With the Russian Army* . . . , I, 284.

28. Stone, *The Eastern Front* . . . , 139.

29. Knox, *With the Russian Army* . . . , I, 284.

30. Hoffmann, *Diaries and Other Papers,* I, 60.

31. Ibid., I, 60–1; II, 107–9. See also, Ludendorff, *My War Memories* . . . , I, 148.

32. Stone, *The Eastern Front* . . . , 176.

33. Hoffmann, *Diaries and Other Papers,* I, 62. See also, Seeckt, *Aus meinem Leben* . . . , 160–1.

34. Janssen, *Der Kanzler und der General* . . . , 265.

35. German *Bundesarchiv (Militärarchiv), Nachlass* Hoffmann, N 37/2, 284.

36. Ibid., 285.

37. Janssen, *Der Kanzler und der General* . . . , 265.

38. German *Bundesarchiv (Militärarchiv), Nachlass* Hoffmann, N 37/2, 285.

39. Kielmansegg, 86.

40. German *Bundesarchiv (Militärarchiv), Nachlass* Hoffmann, N 37/2, 291.

41. Janssen, *Der Kanzler und der General* . . . , 155.

42. Hoffman, *Diaries and Other Papers,* I, 77.

43. Ludendorff, Margarethe, 140.

44. Hoffmann, *Diaries and Other Papers,* I, 76.

45. Stone, *The Eastern Front* . . . , 182.

46. Ibid., 183.

47. Hoffmann, *Diaries and Other Papers*, I, 85.
48. Ibid., 86.

Chapter Sixteen

1. Clark, Alan, 138.
2. German *Bundesarchiv (Militärarchiv)*, *Nachlass* Wild von Hohenborn, N 44/2, 5.
3. Joffre, II, 354.
4. Ibid., 355.
5. Edmonds, *History of the Great War*, . . . *1914*: II, 113.
6. Joffre, II, 358–9.
7. Ibid., 357–8.
8. Ibid., 359–60.
9. Seeger, 162–3.
10. Falkenhayn, 165.
11. Edmonds, *History of the Great War*, . . . *1914*: II, 119–20.
12. Howard-Smith, 167.
13. German *Bundesarchiv (Militärarchiv)*, *Nachlass* Wild von Hohenborn, N 44/2, 5.
14. Rupprecht, I, 398.
15. Seeger, 167–8.
16. Haber, 55 ff.
17. House, II, 81.
18. Ibid, I, 295–6.
19. Ibid., II, 117.
20. Ibid., II, 188–9.
21. Ibid., II, 140–3.
22. Ibid., II, 207.
23. Ibid., II, 201.
24. Ibid., II, 165.
25. Ibid, II, 238–9.
26. Ibid., II, 241.

Chapter Seventeen

1. Hubatsch, *Hindenburg . . .* , 16.
2. German *Bundesarchiv (Militärarchiv)*, *Nachlass* Hoffmann, N 37/2, 296–7.
3. Ibid., 298.
4. Hoffmann, *Diaries and Other Papers*, I, 81.
5. Ibid., 78. My italics.
6. Hubatsch, *Hindenburg . . .* , 15.
7. German *Bundesarchiv (Militärarchiv)*, *Nachlass* Hoffmann, N 37/2, 307.
8. *Frankfurter Allgemeine Zeitung*, January 10, 1955, "Ein armer alter Mann . . ."
9. Wheeler-Bennett, 77, quoting Shakespeare, *Hamlet*, Act I, Scene 4.

10. Vogel, 178.

11. Ibid., 183.

12. Ibid.

13. Ibid., 183–4.

14. Ibid., 182.

15. Ludendorff, *My War Memories*, I, 178.

16. German *Bundesarchiv (Militärarchiv)*, *Nachlass* Hoffmann, N 37/2, 309–10.

17. Ludendorff, *My War Memories*, I, 178–9. See also, Basler, 132.

18. Ibid., 191.

19. Ritter, *The Sword and the Sceptre. . .* , III, 115. See also, Knesebeck, 153–4; Basler, 244.

20. Hubatsch, *Hindenburg . . .* , 20.

21. Ludendorff, Erich, *My War Memories*, I, 189.

22. Hoffmann, *Diaries and Other Papers*, I, 171.

23. Hubatsch, Hindenburg . . . , 15.

24. *Frankfurter Allgemeine Zeitung*, January 10, 1955, "Ein armer alter Mann . . ."

25. German *Bundesarchiv (Militärarchiv)*, *Nachlass* Wild von Hohenborn, N 44/2, 71.

26. Schäfer, *Ludendorff*, 54.

27. German *Bundesarchiv (Militärarchiv)*, *Nachlass* Hoffmann, N 37/2, 316.

Chapter Eighteen

1. German *Bundesarchiv (Militärarchiv)*, *Nachlass* Wild von Hohenborn, N 44/2, 3.

2. Janssen, *Der Kanzler und der General . . .* , 183.

3. Janssen, *Die graue Exzellenz*, 232.

4. Hanssen, 138–41.

5. Ritter, *The Sword and the Sceptre . . .* , III, 91.

6. Davis, 254.

7. House, I, 447, 450.

8. Ibid., II, 23.

9. Hubatsch, *Germany . . .* , 63.

10. Janssen, *Die graue Exzellenz, 232.*

11. Ritter, *The Sword and the Sceptre . . .* , III, 92.

12. Hubatsch, *Hindenburg . . .* , 60.

13. German *Bundesarchiv (Militärarchiv)*, *Nachlass* Mertz, N 242/5, 43.

14. Ibid., 42.

15. Knesebeck, 151–2, 152–3. In his letter of January 6, 1916, Ludendorff expressed his hopes for victory at Salonica, Gallipoli and in Egypt.

16. Ritter, *The Sword and the Sceptre . . .* , III, 92.

17. Hoffmann, *Diaries and Other Papers*, I, 107.

18. Ibid., 110.

19. Scott, II, 1116–21.

20. Falkenhayn, 215.

21. Ritter, *The Sword and the Sceptre* . . . , III, 159–60. See also, Tirpitz, *My Memoirs*, II, 417 ff.

22. Falkenhayn, 216.

23. Ibid., 217.

24. German *Bundesarchiv (Militärarchiv)*, *Nachlass* Hoffmann, N 37/2, 288.

25. Janssen, *Der Kanzler und der General* . . . , 282.

26. German *Bundesarchiv (Militärarchiv)*, *Nachlass* Hoffmann, N 37/2, 290.

27. Falkenhayn, 217.

28. Janssen, *Der Kanzler und der General* . . . , 184.

29. Horne, Alistair, 39. See also, Falls, *The Great War* . . . , 186–94, for an excellent brief study; Liddell Hart, *A History of the World War*, 285–97, for a less objective view. The two classic works in English are Alistair Horne's *The Price of Glory* and Georges Blond's *Verdun* (translation).

30. Dupuy, *A Genius for War* . . . , 91.

31. Blond, *Verdun*, 15–22.

32. Falkenhayn, 223.

33. Joffre, II, 440.

34. King, *Generals and Politicians*, 90–1, 96.

35. Horne, Alistair, 5. See also, Blond, *Verdun*, 24.

36. Blond, *Verdun*, 33.

37. Ibid., 32.

38. King, *Generals and Politicians*, 89.

39. William, 174–5.

40. Blond, *Verdun*, 54.

41. Falkenhayn, 233. See also, Blond, *Verdun*, 85–8. The fort was held by fifty-seven elderly territorials, no officers, two 75-mm and one 155-mm guns with no ammunition; Horne, Alistair, 107–9, 112–19.

42. Howard-Smith, 86.

43. Janssen, *Der Kanzler und der General* . . . , 181.

44. Joffre, II, 448.

45. German *Bundesarchiv (Militärarchiv)*, *Nachlass* Wild von Hohenborn, N 44/2, 121.

46. Howard-Smith, 93.

47. German *Bundesarchiv (Militärarchiv)*, *Nachlass* Wild von Hohenborn, N 44/2, 133.

Chapter Nineteen

1. Janssen, *Die graue Exzellenz*, 242–3.

2. German *Bundesarchiv (Militärarchiv)*, *Nachlass* Hoffmann, N 37/2, 242.

3. Görlitz, *The Kaiser and his Court* . . . , 126–7.

4. Ibid., 114.

5. Kielmansegg, 133, 138–9.

6. Görlitz, *The Kaiser and his Court* . . . , 144.

7. Janssen, *Der Kanzler und der General* . . . , 194.

8. German *Bundesarchiv (Militärarchiv)*, *Nachlass* Wild von Hohenborn, N 44/2, 119.

9. Hanssen, 141.

10. Ibid., 135.

11. Janssen, *Der Kanzler und der General* . . . , 196.

12. Stone, *The Eastern Front* . . . , 228.

13. Ibid.

14. Hoffman, *Diaries and Other Papers*, II, 132.

15. German *Bundesarchiv (Militärarchiv)*, *Nachlass* Hoffmann, N 37/2, 328.

16. Bauermeister, 48–50.

17. *Frankfurter Allgemeine Zeitung*, January 10, 1955, "Ein armer alter Mann . . ."

18. Stone, *The Eastern Front* . . . , 235, 263. See also, Brusilov, 199–200, 213–34, 260.

19. Falkenhayn, 245.

20. Ibid., 247.

Chapter Twenty

1. German *Bundesarchiv (Militärarchiv)*, *Nachlass* Groener, N 46/63, 220.

2. King, *Generals and Politicians*, 115.

3. Westman, *Surgeon with the Kaiser's Army*, 94.

4. Falkenhayn, 263.

5. Blake, *The Private Papers of Douglas Haig* . . . , 153. Lord Beaverbrook noted that with the publication of these private papers Haig "committed suicide twenty-five years after his death."

6. Guinn, 142.

7. Kielmansegg, 320.

8. Wedd, 315.

9. Guinn, 185–6.

10. Max, *The Memoirs* . . . , I, 71.

11. Janssen, *Der Kanzler und der General* . . . , 292.

12. Ritter, *The Sword and the Sceptre* . . . , III, 189.

13. Falkenhayn, 269; Ludendorff, Erich, *My War Memories* . . . , I, 226.

14. Hoffmann, *Diaries and Other Papers*, I, 135.

15. Görlitz, *The Kaiser and his Court* . . . , 187.

16. German *Bundesarchiv (Militärarchiv)*, *Nachlass* Hoffmann, N 37/2, 348.

17. Valentini, 133.

18. Bauermeister, 61.

19. Kitchen, *The Silent Dictatorship*, 38.

20. Ritter, *The Sword and the Sceptre* . . . , III, 202.

21. Ibid., 203.

22. Ibid., 183.

23. Kielmansegg, 335.

24. Hoffman, *Diaries and Other Papers*, I, 144.

25. Ibid., 145.

26. Wheeler-Bennett, *Hindenburg* . . . , 71

27. Ludwig, *Hindenburg*, 99.

28. Ludendorff, Erich, *My War Memories* . . . , I, 239.

Book Two

1. Morton, 155.

Chapter Twenty-one

1. Hindenburg, Paul von, 217.
2. Ludendorff, Erich, My War Memories . . . , I, 267.
3. Hoffmann, Diaries and Other Papers, II, 156.
4. Stein, 122.
5. Wedd, 205.
6. U.S. National Archives, World War I, Germany, U.S. Military Attaché reports, RG 165, 3409–8584–3 of March 9, 1916, and 3487–8584–4 of May 24, 1916.
7. Therese, 99.
8. Doty, 29–30.
9. Evelyn, 95.
10. Doty, 115–16.
11. Bullitt, 87.
12. U. S. National Archives, World War I, Germany, RG 165, OHL Ia. Nr. 2093 secret, 26 December 1916.
13. Davis, 274.
14. Valentini, 226.
15. Hanssen, 114, 122.
16. Westman, Surgeon with the Kaiser's Army, 89–90.
17. Max, The Memoirs . . . I, 18
18. Hanssen, 131.
19. Ritter, The Sword and the Sceptre . . . , III, 91–2.
20. Hoffmann, Diaries and Other Papers, II, 159.
21. Valentini, 226–7.

Chapter Twenty-two

1. Groener, Lebenserinnerungen, 554.
2. Ibid., 558.
3. Ibid., 559.
4. Ludendorff, Erich, My War Memories . . . , I. 312. See also, Bethmann, Reflections on the World War, 127; Birnbaum, 133–7.
5. Hoffmann, Diaries and Other Papers, I, 148.
6. Ludendorff, Erich, My War Memories . . . , I, 267.
7. Blond, Verdun, 206.
8. Ludendorff, Margarethe, 134–6.
9. Ludendorff, Erich, My War Memories . . . , I, 271–2.
10. German Bundesarchiv (Militärarchiv), Nachlass Hoffmann, N 37/2, 357.
11. Bauer, Der grosse Krieg . . . , 130.
12. Vogel, 193.
13. Davis, 219–21.

14. Görlitz, *The Kaiser and his Court* . . . , 220.
15. Vogel, 196.
16. Ibid.
17. Ibid.
18. Hindenburg, Paul von, 181.
19. Ibid., 182.
20. Schäfer, *Ludendorff*, 73 ff.
21. Hoffmann, *Diaries and Other Papers*, I, 155–6.
22. Tschuppik, 65.
23. Stone, *The Eastern Front* . . . , 276.

Chapter Twenty-three

1. Knesebeck, 153–4.
2. Bethmann, *Reflections on the World War*, 47.
3. Ritter, *The Sword and the Sceptre* . . . , III, 209.
4. Görlitz, *The Kaiser and his Court* . . . , 198–9.
5. Ibid., 214.
6. Bethmann, *Reflections* . . . , 93–7.
7. Knesebeck, 150.
8. Conze, 203.
9. Hubatsch, *Hindenburg* . . . , 154.
10. Valentini, 140.
11. Kitchen, *The Silent Dictatorship*, 94.
12. Ludendorff, Erich, *My War Memories* . . . , I, 242.
13. Armeson, vi.
14. Kitchen, *The Silent Dictatorship*, 70.
15. German *Bundesarchiv (Militärarchiv)*, *Nachlass* Groener, N 46/63, 175–6.
16. Ludendorff, Erich, *My War Memories* . . . , I, 76–81.
17. Ibid., 101–2.
18. Kitchen, *The Silent Dictatorship*, 79. See also, Armeson, 137–40, for the entire law.
19. Helfferich, 286.

Chapter Twenty-four

1. Lansing, 208.
2. Lodge, II, 494–5.
3. Scott, I, 128 ff.
4. Ibid., II, 1003–05.
5. House, II, 404.
6. Scott, II, 1006–09, for the full text of the reply. See also, House, II, 404–15.
7. Ritter, *The Sword and the Sceptre* . . . , III, 297–8. Scott, II, 1014–16, for the full text.
8. Ludendorff, Erich, *The General Staff* . . . , I, 279.

9. Ibid., 276. See also, Scott, II, 1163–6.

10. Scott, II, 1179–80.

11. Wheeler-Bennett, *Hindenburg*, 88.

12. Ibid. See also, Eyck, "The Generals . . . ," 49; Gatzke, 83.

13. Ludendorff, Erich, *My War Memories* . . . , I, 312.

14. Janssen, *Die graue Exzellenz*, 209–10.

15. Görlitz, *The Kaiser and his Court* . . . , 222–3.

16. Scott, II, 1202.

17. Ludendorff, Erich, *The General Staff* . . . , I, 296 ff.

18. Scott, I, 466.

19. Ludendorff, Erich, *The General Staff* . . . , I, 298. See also, Scott, II, 1199–1205.

20. Hanssen, 169.

21. Bethmann, *Reflections* . . . , 131–5. See also, Scott, II, 1320–1.

22. Wheeler-Bennett, *Hindenburg*, 90.

23. Scott, I, 450. See also, Valentini, 144–6.

24. Görlitz, *The Kaiser and his Court* . . . , 230.

25. Valentini, 146.

Chapter Twenty-five

1. Tuchman, *The Zimmerman Telegram*, 142.

2. Vogel, 210, 211–13, 218.

3. Ritter, *The Sword and the Sceptre* . . . , III, 326–7. See also, Czernin, 115–18, who criticizes Bethmann for yielding to military dominance in the submarine debate. The OHL's exaggerated arguments and false promises are clearly stated in reports from the Austrian ambassador in Berlin and from one of Czernin's special envoys.

4. Scott, II, 1021.

5. Ibid.,1047–8.

6. Ludendorff, Erich, *The General Staff* . . . , I, 334–6.

7. Ludendorff, Erich, *My War Memories* . . . , I, 322.

8. Hanssen, 157.

9. Ritter, *The Sword and the Sceptre* . . . , III, 336–40.

10. House, I, 186.

11. Mencken, "Ludendorff." *The Atlantic Monthly*, June, 1917.

12. Hanssen, 168.

13. Tuchman, *The Zimmermann Telegram*, 142.

Chapter Twenty-six

1. Watt, 135.

2. Ludendorff, Erich, *My War Memories* . . . , II, 407. See also, Rupprecht, II, 95–8; Kuhl, *Der deutsche Generalstab* . . . , 197–8, who not only defends the operation as historically justified by the Napoleonic and Boer wars, but claims that his army headquarters received numerous unsolicited letters of thanks from displaced persons for the gentle and thoughtful evacuation procedures.

3. Tschuppik, 232.

4. Hindenburg, Paul von, 261.

5. Ludendorff, Erich, *My War Memories* . . . , II, 413.

6. House, III, 127.

7. Spears, *Prelude to Victory*, 32.

8. Watt, 135. See also, King, *Generals and Politicians*, 140–69.

9. Blake, 196.

10. Buat, *Hindenburg et Ludendorff Stratèges*, 183.

11. Hindenburg, Paul von, 265.

12. Bauer, *Der grosse Krieg* . . . , 133.

13. Wheeler-Bennett, *Hindenburg* . . . , 99.

14. Terraine, *Douglas Haig* . . . , 294.

15. Hoffmann, *Diaries and Other Papers*, 172–3.

16. Ibid.

17. Terraine, *Douglas Haig* . . . , 314.

Chapter Twenty-seven

1. Sulzbach, 117.

2. Max, *The Memoirs* . . . , I, 113.

3. Ludendorff, Erich, *The General Staff* . . . , II, 475.

4. Mencken, "Ludendorff," *The Atlantic Monthly*, June 1917.

5. Kielmansegg, 181.

6. Evelyn, 158.

7. Ibid., 162.

8. U.S. National Archives, World War I, Germany, RG 165, OHL General-quartiermeister Ia. Nr. 11875, 1 April 1917.

9. Westman, *Surgeon with the Kaiser's Army*, 114.

10. Wedd, 269.

11. Ibid., 287.

12. Sulzbach, 117.

13. Wedd, 368.

14. Hubatsch, *Germany* . . . , 69–70.

15. Wohl, 48–51.

16. Ibid., 51.

17. Mencken, "Ludendorff," *The Atlantic Monthly*, June 1917.

18. Mendelssohn-Bartholdy, 53.

19. Hanssen, 176.

20. Ludendorff, Erich, *My War Memories* . . . , I, 333.

21. Ritter, *The Sword and the Sceptre* . . . , III, 364–72.

22. Armeson, 28–32, 38–41. See also, Dommelier, 250–3; Kitchen, *The Silent Dictatorship*, 98; Holborn, 454, who puts the figure of Belgian deportations into Germany at 400,000.

23. Görlitz, *The Kaiser and his Court* . . . , 189.

24. Ibid., 215–16, 237, 250, 263, 271, 292.

25. Eyck, "The Generals . . . ," 53.

26. Ritter, *The Sword and the Sceptre* . . . , III, 418.

27. Ibid., 418–21. See also, Görlitz, *The Kaiser and his Court* . . . , 260–1; Jarausch, 222–9.

Chapter Twenty-eight

1. Hubatsch, *Hindenburg* . . . , 27.
2. Wheeler-Bennett, *Hindenburg* . . . , 108
3. Hanssen, 187.
4. Dehn, 16.
5. Sims, 5–7. Sims was an American admiral sent to London in spring of 1917, where Admiral Jellicoe gave him secret figures of sinkings: 436,000 tons in February; 603,000 tons in March and a predicted loss of over 900,000 tons in April. Jellicoe feared that Britain could not hold out much longer against such losses. See also, Scott, I, 544. According to figures presented at the postwar official German Committee of Inquiry, Jellicoe's figures were far too low. Losses topped the million-ton mark in April and June and ran over 800,000 tons monthly through October at a cost of forty-nine U-boats from February to October, 1917. It is possible that both Jellicoe's and German admiralty figures were inaccurate, but it seems more likely that British figures did not include ships that had been hit and were either saved or later salvaged.
6. Scott, I, 312.
7. Görlitz, *The Kaiser and his Court* . . . , 271–2.
8. Ritter, *The Sword and the Sceptre* . . . , III, 434.
9. Kielmansegg, 503.
10. Ritter, *The Sword and the Sceptre* . . . , III, 436.
11. Ibid., 431.
12. Halpern, 312–13.
13. Ludendorff, Erich, *My War Memories* . . . , I, 398. See also, Hubatsch, *Hindenburg* . . . , 154.
14. Max, *The Memoirs* . . . , I, 115–16.
15. Ludendorff, Erich, *Urkunden* . . . , 395–7.
16. Ludendorff, Erich, *The General Staff* . . . , II, 452–3.
17. Ibid., 463.
18. Ibid., 464.
19. Ritter, *The Sword and the Sceptre* . . . , III, 464.
20. Hanssen, 200.
21. Görlitz, *The Kaiser and his Court* . . . , 292.
22. Gatzke, 199.
23. Ludendorff, Erich, *The General Staff* . . . , II, 462.
24. Görlitz, *The Kaiser and his Court* . . . , 285.
25. Valentini, 162.
26. Janssen, *Die graue Exzellenz*, 249.
27. Hanssen, 232.
28. Max, *The Memoirs* . . . , I, 146.
29. Kühlmann, 501–2.
30. Hubatsch, *Hindenburg* . . . , 27.
31. Gatzke, 196.

32. Ritter, *The Sword and the Sceptre* . . . , III, 483.
33. Wheeler-Bennett, *Hindenburg* . . . , 108. See also, Tschuppik, 114.
34. Ritter, *The Sword and the Sceptre* . . . , III, 484.
35. Ludendorff, Erich, *The General Staff* . . . , II, 455–6.
36. Wheeler-Bennett, *Hindenburg* . . . , 107.
37. Tschuppik, 117.

Chapter Twenty-nine

1. Max, *The Memoirs* . . . , I, 134–5.
2. German *Bundesarchiv (Militärarchiv)*, *Nachlass* Hoffmann, N 37/2, 392.
3. Hoffmann, *Diaries and Other Papers*, I, 188.
4. Ibid., 190.
5. Ludendorff, Erich, *My War Memories* . . . , II, 476.
6. Ibid., 478, 482.
7. Terraine, *Douglas Haig* . . . , 313.
8. Bauer, *Der grosse Krieg* . . . , 246.
9. Blunden, 213–14.
10. Marshall, 304.
11. Cooper, II, 141.
12. Falls, *The Great War* . . . , 301.
13. Ludendorff, Erich, *My War Memories* . . . , II, 480.
14. Hoffmann, *Diaries and Other Papers*, I, 195; II, 184.
15. Ibid., II, 185.
16. Ibid., 186.
17. Gatzke, 222–3.
18. Hubatsch, *Hindenburg* . . . , 27.
19. Ludendorff, Erich, *The General Staff* . . . , II, 385–400.
20. Kitchen, *The Silent Dictatorship*, 59–61.
21. Ibid.
22. Ibid.
23. Demeter, 173.
24. U.S. National Archives, World War I, Germany, RG 165, OHL Lu II, Nr. 65615 7./1741 E., 23 September 1917.
25. Ibid., OHL Generalquartiermeister Ic Nr. 8708, 12 March 1917.
26. Demeter, 173.
27. Ritter, *The Sword and the Sceptre* . . . , IV, 52–4.

Chapter Thirty

1. Fuller, *Tanks*, 18.
2. Ibid., 153.
3. Ludendorff, Erich, *My War Memories* . . . , II, 490.
4. Ibid.
5. Hertling, 14, 49.
6. Westman, *A Surgeon's Story*, 62; *Surgeon with the Kaiser's Army*, 120–2.

7. U.S. National Archives, World War I, Germany, RG 165, OHL M.J. Nr. 59237, 28 August 1917.

8. Ibid., RG 165, Box 11, Folders 1 and 2, Report of Major Wetzell to Chief of the General Staff, October 23, 1917 and December 12, 1917; Box 12, Folder 8, Colonel Count Schulenburg to Crown Prince Wilhelm, November 12, 1917.

9. Rupprecht, II, 303.

10. Essame, 8.

11. Fuller, *Tanks*, 144.

12. Edmonds, *History of the Great War, 1917*: III, 47.

13. Liddell Hart, *A History of World War One*, 443.

14. Fuller, *Tanks*, 148–9.

15. Liddell Hart, *A History of World War One*, 445.

16. Rupprecht, II, 294.

17. Ludendorff, Erich, *My War Memories . . .* , II, 497.

18. Sulzbach, 137.

19. Ludendorff, Erich, *My War Memories . . .* , II, 497.

Chapter Thirty-one

1. Ludendorff, Erich, *The General Staff . . .* , II, 534.

2. Wheeler-Bennett, *Hindenburg . . .* , 126.

3. Hoffman, *Diaries and Other Papers*, II, 204–6.

4. Wheeler-Bennett, *Hindenburg . . .* , 129. See also, Ritter, *The Sword and the Sceptre . . .* , IV, 94–5; Balfour, 385–6.

5. Wheeler-Bennett, *Hindenburg . . .* , 129–30.

6. Kitchen, *The Silent Dictatorship*, 168. See also, Hoffmann, *Diaries and Other Papers*, II, 208: "I felt the resentment of OHL personally in a series of orders and questions that were sent to me in a form which showed me that great men can also be very small sometimes" (Hoffmann, I, Introduction). Ludendorff thenceforth refused to deal with Hoffmann directly. For the rest of the war, as Karl Novak put it, "they were not against each other, they worked without each other." But see Baumgart, *Von Brest-Litovsk . . .* , 335–6, Groener to his wife, 3 April 1918, in which he complains of Hoffmann sabotaging Ludendorff's eastern policy and also criticizes his Jewish-Christian wife and her silly liberal statements and acquaintances.

7. Hanssen, 252.

8. Eyck, "*The Generals . . .* ," 51.

9. Görlitz, *The Kaiser and his Court . . .* , 324–5.

10. Ritter, *The Sword and the Sceptre . . .* , IV, 101.

11. Rupprecht, II, 324.

12. Ludendorff, Erich, *The General Staff . . .* , II, 530.

13. Hoffmann, *Diaries and Other Papers*, II, 209.

14. Kitchen, *The Silent Dictatorship*, 179.

15. Wheeler-Bennett, *Hindenburg . . .* , 132.

16. Ibid, 131.

Chapter Thirty-two

1. U.S. National Archives, World War I, Germany, RG 165, Box 11, Folder 2, 17.

2. Montaigne, *The Essays of Montaigne*.

3. Arz, 206–7.

4. Eyck, "The Generals . . . ," 58–9.

5. U.S. National Archives, World War I, Germany, OHL Ia Nr. 6326, geh. op., 2 February 1918.

6. Kuhl, *Der deutsche Generalstab* . . . , 185–6.

7. Hertling, 139–40. See also, Rupprecht, II, 326.

8. Rupprecht, II, 288.

9. Kaehler, 10.

10. U.S. National Archives, World War I, Germany, RG 165, Wetzell, "The Offensives in the West and their prospects of success," December 12, 1917; "The Attacks against the English," December 12, 1917.

11. Hindenburg, Paul von, 356–7.

12. Ludendorff, Erich, *My War Memories* . . . , II, 590.

13. Lutz, 81.

14. U.S. National Archives, World War I, Germany, RG 165, Box 11, Folder 2, 12–17, Wetzell to Ludendorff, December 12, 1917.

15. Max, *The Memoirs* . . . , I, 248. See also, Haussmann, 176 ff.

16. Ibid., 246.

17. Regele, 259.

18. Rupprecht, II, 372.

19. Eyck, "The Generals . . . ," 59.

20. Vogel, 223–31.

21. Ibid.

22. Ibid.

23. U.S. National Archives, Germany, RG 165, OHL II, Nr. 74285 op. geheim, 1 January 1918; OHL II, Nr. 6405 geh. op., 8 February 1918; OHL Ia/II Nr. 6608, 16 February 1918.

24. Schäufer, *Ludendorff*, 73–4.

25. Hindenburg, Paul von, 342.

26. Hubatsch, *Hindenburg* . . . , 34.

27. Foerster, *Der Feldherr Ludendorff* . . . , 132–3.

Chapter Thirty-three

1. Blake, 291.

2. Terraine, *Douglas Haig* . . . , 395.

3. Ibid., 395–6.

4. Ibid., 396.

5. Blake, 277–8.

6. Cooper, Duff, II, 219.

7. Gough, 221–2.

8. Ibid., 225.
9. Blake, 285.
10. Terraine, *Douglas Haig . . .* , 401.
11. Cooper, Duff, II, 227. My italics.
12. Blake, 291.

Chapter Thirty-four

1. Edmonds, *History of the Great War, 1918*: I, 396–7.
2. Bugnet, 220.
3. Hanssen, 280.
4. Hogg, 134–5. See also, Banks, 184–5, 187.
5. Edmonds, *History of the Great War, 1918*: I, 396–7.
6. Görlitz, *The Kaiser and His Court . . .* , 344.
7. Goldsmith, 166.
8. Wheeler-Bennett, *Hindenburg . . .* , 148–9.
9. Rupprecht, II, 357.
10. Terraine, *Douglas Haig . . .* , 435.
11. Binding, *A Fatalist at War*, 210.
12. Sulzbach, 157–8.
13. Ludendorff, Erich, *My War Memories . . .* , II, 600.
14. Breucker, 52.
15. Blake, 296.
16. Ibid., 297.
17. Ibid., 298.
18. Clemenceau, 39.
19. Ibid., 43.
20. Cooper, II, 264.
21. Bugnet, 224.

Chapter Thirty-five

1. Hoffmann, *Diaries and Other Papers*, II, 233–4.
2. Montaigne, *The Essays of Montaigne*.
3. Terraine, *Douglas Haig . . .* , 429.
4. Liddell Hart, *A History of the World War . . .* , 517.
5. Ibid., 517.
6. Terraine, *Douglas Haig . . .* , 429.
7. Bugnet, 194.
8. Edmonds, *History of the Great War, 1918*: II, 512.
9. Hanssen, 276.
10. Rupprecht, II, 382.
11. Terraine, *Douglas Haig . . .* , 434.
12. Pierrefeu, 247.
13. Rupprecht, II, 394.
14. Ibid., 383.

15. Kaehler, 11–12.
16. Marshall, 372.
17. Ludendorff, Erich, *My War Memories* . . . , II, 609–10.

Chapter Thirty-six

1. Hanssen, 225–6.
2. Gatzke, 254.
3. Hanssen, 277.
4. Ludendorff, Erich, *The General Staff* . . . , I, 130–1.
5. Hanssen, 267.
6. Ibid., 280.
7. Evelyn, 231.
8. Haussmann, 197.
9. Ludendorff, Erich, *The General Staff* . . . , I, 130.
10. Hanssen, 274–5.
11. Kaehler, 13.
12. Ibid., 13–15.
13. Ludendorff, Erich, *My War Memories* . . . , II, 6
14. Westman, *Surgeon with the Kaiser's Army*, 159.
15. Rupprecht, II, 399.

Chapter Thirty-seven

1. Ludendorff, Erich, *My War Memories* . . . , II, 629.
2. Foch, 364.
3. Ludendorff, Erich, *My War Memories* . . . , II, 617.
4. Rogerson, 130.
5. Ludendorff, Erich, *My War Memories* . . . , II, 614.
6. Pierrefeu, 262.
7. Foch, 355–6.
8. Edmonds, *History of the Great War, 1918*: III, 30–46. See also, Asprey, *At Belleau Wood*, 64–5.
9. Görlitz, *The Kaiser and His Court* . . . , 358.
10. U.S. National Archives, World War I, Germany, RG 165, German Documents captured by U.S. Forces, 1917–18, OHL *Amtlicher Heeresbericht*, 30 May 1918, and 31 May 1918.
11. Ibid., 29 May 1918.
12. Rogerson, 140.
13. U.S. National Archives, World War I, Germany, RG 165, German Documents captured by U.S. Forces, 1917–18, OHL *Amtlicher Heeresbericht*, 30 May 1918.
14. Clemenceau, 48.
15. Asprey, *At Belleau Wood*, 66.
16. Pierrefeu, 269.
17. Asprey, *At Belleau Wood*, 69–70.

18. Ibid., 71.
19. Ibid., 70.

Chapter Thirty-eight

1. Rogerson, 146.
2. Ibid., 138.
3. U.S. National Archives, World War I, Germany, RG 165, Box 11, 29–30, Georg Wetzell, "The 'Blücher' and 'Hagen' Attacks," May 21, 1918.
4. Asprey, At Belleau Wood, 73.
5. Ibid., 130–1.
6. Ibid., 122.
7. Ibid., 137.
8. Rogerson, 146.
9 Asprey, At Belleau Wood, 140.
10. Ibid.

Chapter Thirty-nine

1. Ludendorff, Erich, My War Memories . . . , II, 634.
2. Hertling, 140.
3. Asprey, At Belleau Wood.
4. Ludendorff, Erich, My War Memories . . . , II, 279–280.
5. Foch, 371.
6. Ibid.
7. Churchill, IV, 457.
8. Bugnet, 233.
9. Foch, 378.
10. Ludendorff, Erich, My War Memories . . . , II, 639.
11. Rupprecht, II, 410.
12. Hanssen, 296.
13. Kuhl, Der Weltkrieg . . . , II, 403.
14. Wheeler-Bennett, Hindenburg . . . , 153. See also, Ritter, The Sword and the Sceptre . . . , IV, 311; Gatzke, 278; Max, The Memoirs . . . , I, 307; Eyck, "The Generals . . . ," 60; Hertling, 116–17; Fischer, Germany's Aims . . . , 618–24.
15. Ludwig, Hindenburg, 162. See also, Max, The Memoirs . . . , I, 308.
16. Kitchen, The Silent Dictatorship, 206.
17. Hubatsch, Hindenburg . . . , 26. See also, Tirpitz, My Memoirs, II, 464. Shortly after the war began, Hintze visited imperial headquarters: "Hintze's view was," wrote Tirpitz at the time, "that the lack of leadership in the ruling classes, either in victory or defeat, must forfeit them their position, and that immediate big conversions (such as Social Democrats being appointed to high posts, and reform of the franchise in Prussia) were the only means by which the gigantic upheaval in the nation could be guided into some sort of favorable channel. . . . He is very clever. . . ."

Chapter Forty

1. Sulzbach, 207.
2. Lossberg, 359.
3. Foerster, *Der Feldherr Ludendorff* . . . , 15.
4. Eyck, "The Generals . . . ," 61.
5. Sulzbach, 202.
6. Einem, *Ein Armeeführer* . . . , 417–19. See also, Foerster, *Der Feldherr Ludendorff* . . . , 16.
7. Parkinson, 166.
8. Foerster, *Der Feldherr Ludendorff* . . . , 17.
9. Ludendorff, Erich, *My War Memories* . . . , II, 668.
10. Ibid., 670.
11. Foerster, *Der Feldherr Ludendorff* . . . , 132.
12. Ibid., 18.
13. Ibid., 19.
14. Lossberg, 344–5.
15. Ibid., 347.
16. Ibid., 349.
17. Görlitz, *The Kaiser and his Court* . . . , 373–4.
18. Foerster, *Der Feldherr Ludendorff* . . . , 34.
19. Ibid., 28.
20. Ibid.
21. Ibid.
22. Asprey, *Frederick the Great* . . . , 513.
23. Lossberg, 351.
24. Foerster, *Der Feldherr Ludendorff* . . . , 29.
25. Ibid., 37.
26. German *Bundesarchiv (Militärarchiv)*, *Nachlass* Groener, N 46/63, 212.
27. Hertling, 146.
28. Foerster, *Der Feldherr Ludendorff* . . . , 39–40.
29. Ibid., 38.

Chapter Forty-one

1. Foerster, *Der Feldherr Ludendorff* . . . , 37.
2. Ludendorff, Erich, *My War Memories* . . . , II, 679.
3. Lossberg, 354.
4. Ludendorff, Erich, *My War Memories* . . . , II, 680–1.
5. Ibid., 683.
6. Ibid., 684.
7. Kielmansegg, 660.
8. Lossberg, 352.
9. Foerster, *Der Feldherr Ludendorff* . . . , 44–5.
10. Niemann, *Kaiser und Revolution*, 44–5.
11. Görlitz, *The Kaiser and his Court* . . . , 377.

12. Niemann, 44–5. See also, Ritter, *The Sword and the Sceptre* . . . , IV, 322–3.

13. Foerster, *Der Feldherr Ludendorff* . . . , 44–5.

14. Max, *The Memoirs* . . . , I, 315–16.

15. Foerster, *Der Feldherr Ludendorff* . . . , 48–9.

16. Ibid., 49.

17. Eyck, "The Generals . . . ," 61.

18. German *Bundesarchiv (Militärarchiv)*, *Nachlass* Groener, N 46/31, 214.

19. Ludwig, *Hindenburg*, 172.

20. Foerster, *Der Feldherr Ludendorff* . . . , 49–50.

21. Ritter, *The Sword and the Sceptre* . . . , IV, 324. See also, Fischer, *Germany's Aims* . . . , 624–30.

22. Ludwig, *Hindenburg*, 168.

23. Ibid., 169.

24. Ritter, *The Sword and the Sceptre* . . . , IV, 331. See also, Fischer, *Germany's Aims* . . . , 628–30.

25. Max, *The Memoirs* . . . , I, 318–19.

26. Ludwig, *Hindenburg*, 171.

27. Arz, 283–4. See also, Ludendorff, Erich, *My War Memories* . . . , II, 688.

28. Blake, 325.

29. Marshall, 425.

Chapter Forty-two

1. Max, *The Memoirs* . . . , I, 318–9.

2. Foerster, *Der Feldherr Ludendorff* . . . , 94.

3. Ibid., 53–4.

4. Ibid., 63.

5. Ibid., 55.

6. Fuller, *Tanks* . . . , 241.

7. U.S. National Archives, World War I, Germany, RG 165, OHL Ia/II Nr. 7745, geh.op., 17 April 1918.

8. Fuller, *Tanks* . . . , 263.

9. Ibid., 240.

10. Sulzbach, 226.

11. Evelyn, 245.

12. Foerster, *Der Feldherr Ludendorff* . . . , 59.

13. Ibid., 60.

14. Ibid., 60–1.

15. Ibid.

16. Ibid.

17. Lossberg, 357.

18. Foerster, *Der Feldherr Ludendorff* . . . , 73–9.

19. German *Bundesarchiv (Militärarchiv)*, *Nachlass* Heye, N 18/5, "Mein Lebenslauf," 72.

20. Foerster, *Der Feldherr Ludendorff* . . . , 138.

21. Ibid., 82.

22. Max, *The Memoirs* . . . , I, 353. See also, Hertling, 165–8.

23. House, IV, 73.

24. Groener-Geyer, 373.

25. Foerster, *Der Feldherr Ludendorff* . . . , 85.

26. Ibid.

27. Ibid.

28. Görlitz, *The Kaiser and his Court* . . . , 399–400.

29. Foerster, *Der Feldherr Ludendorff* . . . , 87.

30. Kielmansegg, 660.

31. Bauer, *Der grosse Krieg* . . . , 31.

32. Eyck, "The Generals . . . ," 63.

Chapter Forty-three

1. Paquet, 615.

2. Kaehler, 27.

3. Ibid.

4. German *Bundesarchiv (Militärarchiv)*, *Nachlass* Heye, N 18/5, "Mein Lebenslauf," 89. See also, Groener, N 46/63, 213–14.

5. Kaehler, 27.

6. German *Bundesarchiv (Militärarchiv)*, *Nachlass* Heye, N 18/5, "Mein Lebenslauf," 99.

7. Görlitz, *The Kaiser and His Court* . . . , 399–400.

8. Tschuppik, 254.

9. Kielmansegg, 668. See also, House, IV, 73.

10. Hertling, 183.

11. Ritter, *The Sword and the Sceptre* . . . , IV, 345.

12. Görlitz, *The Kaiser and His Court* . . . , 399.

13. Max, *The Memoirs* . . . , II, 16.

14. Ibid., 19.

15. Ibid., 11.

16. Ludwig, *Hindenburg*, 175.

17. Wheeler-Bennett, *Hindenburg* . . . , 171.

18. Kielmansegg, 671.

19. Max, *The Memoirs* . . . , II, 56.

20. Hubatsch, *Hindenburg* . . . , 35.

21. Max, *The Memoirs* . . . , II, 68.

22. Hubatsch, *Hindenburg* . . . , 35.

23. Max, *The Memoirs* . . . , II, 84.

24. Ritter, *The Sword and the Sceptre* . . . , IV, 361. See also, Fischer, *Germany's Aims* . . . , 634–8.

25. Max, *The Memoirs* . . . , II, 85.

26. Ibid., 98–100, 117–34, 110, 112–13, 113–14, 125, 129. See also, Ludendorff, Erich, *The General Staff* . . . , II, 660–92; Ludendorff, Erich, *Urkunden* . . . , 557–67, 666, 567.

27. Max, *The Memoirs* . . . , II, 130.
28. Ibid., 136.

Chapter Forty-four

1. Groener, *Lebenserinnerungen*, 460.
2. Max, *The Memoirs* . . . , II, 146–8.
3. Ibid., 151–2.
4. Westman, *A Surgeon's Story*, 70.
5. Wilhelm, 206. My italics.
6. Ibid.
7. Lossberg, 358.
8. Max, *The Memoirs* . . . , II, 157.
9. Ibid., 154.
10. Ibid., 161–2.
11. Ibid., 187–8.
12. Foerster, *Der Feldherr Ludendorff* . . . , 115.
13. Wheeler-Bennett, *Hindenburg* . . . , 174.
14. Ritter, *The Sword and the Sceptre* . . . , IV, 365–6.
15. Ludendorff, Erich, *My War Memories* . . . , II, 761.
16. Tschuppik, 266.
17. Görlitz, *The Kaiser and his Court* . . . , 412–13.
18. Foerster, *Der Feldherr Ludendorff* . . . , 118.
19. Wheeler-Bennett, *Hindenburg* . . . , 176.
20. Foerster, *Der Feldherr Ludendorff* . . . , 118–19.
21. Ibid., 122 ff.
22. Lossberg, 359–60.
23. German *Bundesarchiv (Militärarchiv)*, *Nachlass* Heye, N 18/5, 48.
24. Hanssen, 344.
25. Max, *The Memoirs* . . . , II, 159.
26. Wheeler-Bennett, *Hindenburg*, 186.

Epilogue

1. German *Bundesarchiv (Militärarchiv)*, *Nachlass* Groener, N 46/31, 209.

Selected Bibliography

Abbot, Willis J. *The Nations at War*. New York, 1917.

Albertini, Luigi. *The Origins of the War 1914*. Three volumes. London/New York, 1952–1957.

Andrew, C. *Théophile Delcassé and the Making of the Entente Cordiale*. London, 1968.

Armeson, R.B. *Total Warfare and Compulsory Labor. A Study of the Military-Industrial Complex in Germany during World War I*. The Hague, 1964.

Arminius. *Feldherrnköpfe 1914–1918*. Leipzig, 1932.

Arz, Generaloberst von Straussenburg. *Zur Geschichte des Grossen Krieges, 1914–18*. Vienna, 1924.

Asprey, Robert B. *The Panther's Feast*. New York, 1959.

———. *The First Battle of the Marne*. New York, 1962.

———. *At Belleau Wood*. New York, 1965.

———. *Frederick the Great—The Magnificent Enigma*. New York, 1986.

Aston, George. *The Biography of the Late Marshal Foch*. New York, 1929.

———. *The Great War of 1914–18*. London, 1930.

Baden, Prince Max von. *See* Max, Prince of Baden.

Baldwin, Hanson W. *World War I*. New York, 1962.

Balfour, M. *The Kaiser and His Times*. London, 1964.

Banks, Arthur. *A Military Atlas of the First World War*. London, 1975.

Barnes, Harry E. *The Genesis of the World War*. New York, 1926.

Barnett, Correlli. *The Swordbearers*. London, 1963.

Basler, Werner. *Deutschlands Annexionspolitik in Polen und in Baltikum 1914–1918*. Berlin, 1962.

Bauer, Max. *Österrich-Ungarn im Weltkriege*. Berlin, 1915.

———. *Der grosse Krieg im Feld und Heimat*. Tübingen, 1921.

Bauermeister, A. *Als Ich im Stabe Hindenburgs War*. Lübeck, 1934.

Baumgart, Winfried. *Deutsche Ostpolitik 1918*. Vienna/Munich, 1966.

———. ed. *Von Brest-Litovsk zur Deutschen Novemberrevolution*. Göttingen, 1971.

Beaufort, J. M. de. *Behind the German Veil*. London, 1917.

Behr, Major von. *Die 5. Reserve Division im Weltkrieg*. Munich, 1918.

Bernhardi, Friedrich von. *Vom heutigem Krieg*. Berlin, 1912.

———. *Denkwürdigkeiten aus meinem Leben*. Leipzig, 1927.

Bernstorff, J. H. *Deutschland und Amerika.* Berlin, 1920.

———. *The Memoirs of Count Bernstorff.* Translated by Eric Sutton. London, 1936.

Bethmann Hollweg, Th. von. *Betrachtungen zum Weltkriege.* Two volumes. Berlin, 1919.

———. *Reflections on the World War.* Translated by George Young. London, 1920.

Bewer, Max. *Beim Kaiser und Hindenburg im Grossen Hauptquartier.* Dresden, 1917.

Binding, Rudolf G. *Aus dem Kriege.* Frankfurt a. M., 1925.

———. *A Fatalist at War.* Translated by I.F.D. Morrow. London, 1928.

Birnbaum, K. E. *Peace Moves and U-Boat Warfare: A Study of Imperial Germany's Policy Towards The United States, April 18, 1916–January 9, 1917.* Stockholm, 1958.

Blake, Robert. *The Private Papers of Douglas Haig. 1914–1918.* London, 1952.

Bloem, Walter. *The Advance from Mons 1914.* London, 1923.

Blond, Georges. *Verdun.* London, 1961.

———. *The Marne.* London, 1965.

Blood, W. P. "A Strategical Retrospect." *The Quarterly Review.* Volumes 233–234. London/New York, 1920.

Blücher, Princess Evelyn. *An English Wife in Berlin.* London, 1920.

Blunden, Edmund. *Undertones of War.* London, 1928.

Boehn, General Max von—see German *Bundesarchiv (Militärarchiv).*

Breither, Erhart. *Kriegsbilder.* Berlin, 1914.

Breucker, W. *Die Tragik Ludendorffs.* Oldenburg, 1953.

Brown, Malcolm, and Seaton, Shirley. *Christmas Truce.* London, 1984.

Brusilov, A. A. *A Soldier's Notebook, 1914–1918.* London, 1930.

Buat, Général. *Hindenburg.* Paris, 1921.

———. *Hindenburg et Ludendorff Stratèges.* Paris, 1923.

Bugnet, Charles. *Foch Speaks.* New York, 1930.

Bullard, R. L. *Personalities and Reminiscences of the War.* New York, 1925.

Bullitt, Ernesta Drinker. *The Uncensored Diary from the Central Empire.* New York, 1917.

Bülow, Prince Bernhard von. *Memoirs.* Three volumes. London, 1932.

Bundesarchiv (Militärarchiv)—see German *Bundesarchiv (Militärarchiv)*

Cameron, James. *1914.* New York, 1959.

Canfield, H. S. *The World War. A Pictorial History.* New York, 1919.

Carnegie Endowment for International Peace—see Scott, James B.

Carr, William. *A History of Germany 1815–1945.* London, 1965.

Cecilie, Princess. *Memoirs.* London, 1931.

Chapman, Guy. *Vain Glory.* London, 1937.

Churchill, Winston S. *The World Crisis.* Six volumes. New York, 1920 ff.

Clark, Alan. *The Donkeys.* London, 1961.

Clark, Paul H. *Letters and Messages to John J. Pershing, 1918–1919.* Washington, Library of Congress, unpublished.

Clemenceau, Georges. *Grandeur and Misery of Victory.* New York, 1930.

Conrad, Feldmarschall von Hötzendorf. *Aus Meiner Dienstzeit 1906–1918.* Five volumes. Vienna, 1925.

Conrad, Pierre. *Trois figures de chefs Falkenhayn-Hindenburg-Ludendorff.* Paris, 1923.

Conze, Werner. *Polnische Nation und deutsche Politik im Ersten Weltkrieg*. Cologne, 1958.

Cooper, Bryan. *The Ironclads of Cambrai*. London, 1967.

Cooper, Courtney Riley—*see* Cowing, Kemper F.

Cooper, Duff. *Haig*. Two volumes. New York, 1936.

Corday, Michel. *The Paris Front: An Unpublished Diary, 1914–1918*. London, 1933.

Coulton, G. G. *Four Score Years*. Cambridge, 1945.

Cowing, Kemper F., and Cooper, Courtney Riley. *Dear Folks at Home*. New York, 1919.

Cowles, Virginia. *The Kaiser*. London, 1963.

Craig, Gordon. *The Politics of the Prussian Army 1640–1945*. Oxford, 1955.

———. *From Bismarck to Adenauer*. Baltimore, 1958.

———. "The World War I Alliance of the Central Powers in Retrospect: The Military Cohesion of the Alliance." *Journal of Modern History*, 1965.

———. *Germany 1866–1945*. Oxford, 1978.

Crefeld, Martin—*see* Van Crefeld.

Cron, H. *Die Organisation des deutschen Heeres im Weltkrieg*. Berlin, 1923.

Cruttwell, C.R.M.F. *A History of the Great War*.

———. *The Role of British Strategy in the Great War*. Cambridge, 1936.

Czernin, Ottokar. *In the World War*. London, 1919.

Daisy, Princess of Pless. *From my Private Diary*. London, 1931.

Dallin, Alexander. *Russian Diplomacy and Eastern Europe, 1914–17*. New York, 1963.

Danilov, Jurij. *Russland im Weltkriege 1914–1915*. Jena, 1925.

Das Kleine Blatt. "Ein Volk klagt an!" Vienna, 1931.

Davis, Arthur N. *The Kaiser as I Knew Him*. New York, 1918.

Dehio, Ludwig. *Germany and World Politics in the Twentieth Century*. Translated by Dieter Persner. London, 1959.

Dehn, Paul. *Hindenburg als Erzieher*. Leipzig, 1918.

Deist, Wilhelm. "Die Armee in Staat und Gesellschaft, 1890–1914." Stürmer, Michael (editor). *Das Kaiserliche Deutschland*. Düsseldorf, 1970.

———. *Militär und Innenpolitik im Weltkrieg, 1914–1918*. Düsseldorf, 1970.

Delbrück, Hans. *Krieg und Politik 1914–1916*. Three volumes. Berlin, 1918 ff.

———. *Ludendorff, Tirpitz, Falkenhayn*. Berlin, 1920.

———. *Ludendorffs Selbstporträt*. Berlin, 1922.

Demeter, Karl. *The German Officer-Corps in Society and State 1650–1945*. London, 1965.

Deuerlein, Ernst. *Briefwechsel Hertling-Lerchenfeld, 1912–1917*. Two volumes. Boppard am Rhein, 1973.

Deutschen Bücherei. *Hindenburg—Bibliographie*. Leipzig, 1938.

De Weerd, H. A. *Great Soldiers of Two World Wars*. New York, 1941.

Dillinger, L.E. *Briefe aus dem Felde 1914–1918*. Five volumes. Oldenburg, 1915.

Dobrorolski, S. *Die Mobilmachung der Russischen Armee 1914*. Berlin, 1922.

Dollinger, Hans. *Der Erste Weltkrieg in Bildern und Dokumente*. Munich, 1965.

Domelier, Henri. *Behind the Scenes at German Headquarters*. London, 1920.

Dorpalen, Andreas. "Empress Auguste Victoria and the Fall of the German Empire." *American Historical Review*, 1952.

Doty, Madeleine Z. *Short Rations—Experiences of an American Woman in Germany.* New York, 1917.

Doyle, Arthur Conan. *The German War.* London, 1914.

Dreher, William C. "Von Hindenburg, General and Man." *The Atlantic Monthly,* August, 1915.

Dreyse, Wilhelm. *Langemarck 1914.* Minden in Westfalen, 1934.

Dupuy, Trevor N. *The Military Lives of Hindenburg and Ludendorff of Imperial Germany.* New York, 1970.

———. *A Genius for War. The German Army and General Staff, 1807–1945.* London, 1977.

Edmonds, James E. *History of the Great War. Military Operations France and Belgium, 1914.* Two volumes. London, 1933.

———. *History of the Great War. Military Operations France and Belgium, 1917.* Two volumes. London, 1940.

———. *History of the Great War. Military Operations France and Belgium, 1917. Vol. III: The Battle of Cambrai,* London 1948.

———. *History of the Great War. Military Operations France and Belgium, 1918.* Three volumes. London, 1950 ff.

———. *A Short History of World War I.* London, 1951.

Edwards, Marvin. *Stresemann and the Greater Germany.* New York, 1963.

Eicke, H. *Weltgeschichte in Anekdoten.* Heidelberg, 1961.

Einem, Karl von. *Erinnerungen eines Soldaten 1853–1933.* Leipzig, 1933.

———. *Ein Armeeführer erlebt den Weltkrieg.* Leipzig, 1938.

Eisenhart-Rothe, Ernst von. *Im Banne der Persönlichkeit.* Berlin, 1931.

Eisenmenger, Anna. *Blockade: The Diary of an Austrian Middleclass Woman, 1914–1924.* London, 1932.

Endres, Fritz. *Hindenburg. Briefe—Reden—Berichte.* Munich, 1934.

Engelhardt-Kyffhäuser, Otto. *Meinen taten und lebenden Kameraden.* Görlitz, 1935.

Epstein, Klaus. "The Development of German-Austrian War Aims in the Spring of 1917." *Journal of Central European Affairs.* Volume XVII, April, 1957.

———. *Matthias Erzberger and the Dilemma of German Democracy.* Princeton, 1959.

Erzberger, Matthias. *Erlebnisse im Weltkrieg.* Stuttgart, 1920.

Essame, H. *The Battle for Europe, 1918.* London, 1972.

Evans, Richard J. *Society and Politics in Wilhelmine Germany.* London, 1978.

Evelyn, Princess Blücher. See Blücher.

Everett, S. *The Great War.* Greenwich, 1980.

Evers, Edwin. *Feldpostbriefe aus dem Osten.* Berlin, 1916.

Eyck, Erich. *Das persönliche Regiment Wilhelms II.* Zürich, 1948.

———. "The Generals and the Downfall of the German Monarchy 1917–1918." *Transactions of the Royal Historical Society.* Fifth Series, Volume 2. London, 1952.

Falkenhayn, Erich von. *General Headquarters and Its Critical Decisions 1914–1916.* London, c. 1921.

Falls, Cyril. *History of the Great War. Military Operations France and Belgium 1917.* Volume I. London, 1940.

———. *The Great War. 1914–1918.* New York, 1959.

Farrar-Hockley, A. *The Somme.* London, 1964.

Fay, Sidney. *The Origins of the World War*. Two volumes. New York, 1928.

Feldman, G.D. *Army, Industry and Labor in Germany, 1914–1918*. Princeton, 1966.

Ferro, Marc. *The Great War 1914–1918*. Translated by Nicole Stone. London, 1973.

Fischer, Fritz. *Germany's Aims in the First World War*. New York, 1967.

———. *War of Illusions. German Policies from 1911 to 1914*. Düsseldorf, 1969.

Foch, Ferdinand. *The Memoirs of Marshal Foch*. Translated by T.B. Mott. New York, 1931.

Foerster, Wolfgang. *Aus den Gedankenwerkstatt des deutschen Generalstabes*. Berlin, 1931.

———. *Hindenburg als Feldherr*. Berlin, 1934.

———. *Der Feldherr Ludendorff in Ungluck . . .* Wiesbaden, 1952.

———. *see* Mackensen, August von.

Forster, K. *The Failures of Peace*. Washington, 1941.

Fox, E. L. *Behind the Scenes in Warring Germany*. New York, 1918.

François, Hermann von. *Marneschlacht und Tannenberg*. Berlin, 1920.

———. *Hindenburgs Sieg bei Tannenberg: Das Cannae des Weltkriegs in Wort und Bild*. Leipzig, n.d.

Frankfurter Allgemeine Zeitung. "Ein armer alter Mann . . ." January 10, 1955.

Frauenholz, Eugen—*see* Rupprecht, Crown Prince of Bavaria.

Frentz, Hans. *Der unbekannte Ludendorff. Der Feldherr in seiner Umwelt und Epoche*. Wiesbaden, 1952.

Freytag-Loringhoven, Baron von. *Menschen und Dinge, wie ich sie in meinem Leben sah*. Berlin, 1923.

Frost, Martin. *Von der 9. Reserve Division und ihrer Sturmkompagnie waehrend ihrer Kaempfe im Bereich der 1. Armee*. Düsseldorf, 1917.

Führ, Christoph. *Das K.u.K. Armeeoberkommando und die Innenpolitik in Oesterrich. 1914–1917*. Vienna, 1968.

Fuller, J.F.C. *Tanks in the Great War 1914–1918*. London, 1920.

———. *A Military History of the Western World*. Three volumes. New York, 1955.

Fussell, Paul. *The Great War and Modern Memory*. Oxford, 1976.

Gallwitz, Max von. *Meine Führertätigkeit im Weltkriege, 1914–1916*. Berlin, 1929.

Gamelin, Général. *Manoeuvre et Victoire de la Marne*. Paris, 1954.

Gatzke, H. W. *Germany's Drive to the West*. Baltimore, 1950.

Geiss, I. *July 1914*. London, 1969.

Gerard, James W. *My Four Years in Germany*. New York, 1917.

German *Bundesarchiv (Militärarchiv)*.

    Nachlässe: Boehn, Max von
               Groener, Wilhelm
               Haeften, Hans von
               Heye, Wilhelm
               Hoffmann, Max
               Mertz, Hermann Ritter von Quirnheim
               Müller, Georg Alexander von
               Tappen, Gerhard
               Tieschowitz, Hans von Tieschowa
               Wetzell, Georg
               Wild, Adolf von Hohenborn

German Reichsarchiv. Der Weltkrieg 1914–1918. Fourteen volumes. 1925–1956.

Gersdorff, Ursula von. Frauen im Kriegsdienst 1914–1915. Stuttgart, 1969.

Gibson, R. H., and Prendergast, Maurice. The German Submarine War, 1914–1918. London, 1931.

Gieben, Joseph. Aus Champagne und Vogesen—Kriegsberichte und Aufsätze eines Frontoffiziers. Gladbach, 1916.

Goldsmith, Margaret, and Voigt, F. A. Hindenburg: The Man and the Legend. London, 1930.

Golovin, Nicholas N. The Russian Army in the World War. New Haven, 1931.

Gooch, G. P. Studies in Diplomacy and Statecraft. London, 1942.

Goodspeed, D. J. Ludendorff—Soldier: Dictator: Revolutionary. London, 1966.

Görlitz, Walter. The German General Staff—Its History and Structure 1657–1945. Translated by B. Battershaw. London, 1953.

————. Hindenburg. Bonn, 1953.

————. The Kaiser and his Court. The Diaries, Note Books and Letters of Admiral Georg Alexander von Müller Chief of the Naval Cabinet, 1914–1918. New York, 1964.

Gough, Sir Hubert. Fifth Army. London, 1931.

Gourko, Basil. Memories and Impressions. London, 1918.

Graves, Robert. Goodbye to All That. New York, 1930.

Grew, J. C. Turbulent Era: A Diplomatic Record of Forty Years 1904–1945. Boston, 1952.

Grey, Viscount of Fallendon. Twenty-Five Years. Two volumes. London, 1926.

Groener, Wilhelm. Lebenserinnerungen. Göttingen, 1957

————. see German Bundesarchiv.

Groener-Geyer, Dorothea. General Groener—Soldat und Staatsmann. Frankfurt a. M., 1955.

Guérard, Major von. Von Reims bis zu den Argonnen. Leipzig, no date.

Guinn, Paul. British Strategy and Politics 1914–18. London, 1965.

Haacke, Ulrich—see Schneider, Benno

Haber, L. F. The Poisonous Cloud. Oxford, 1986.

Haeften, Hans von—see German Bundesarchiv.

————. Hindenburg und Ludendorff als Feldherren. Berlin, 1937.

Haig, Douglas—see Blake, Robert; Cooper, Duff; Terraine, John

Halpern, Paul G. The Naval War in the Mediterranean 1914–1918. Annapolis, 1987.

Hankey, Lord. The Supreme Command, 1914–1918. Two volumes. London, 1961.

Hanssen, Hans Peter. Diary of a Dying Empire. Translated by O.O. Winther. Bloomington, Ind., 1955.

Harbord, James G. The American Army in France 1917–1919. Boston, 1936.

Hardach, G. The First World War 1914–1918. London, 1977.

Harden, Maximilian. I Meet My Contemporaries. New York, 1925.

Harnach, Agnes von. Der Krieg und die Frauen. Berlin, 1915.

Hausmann, Conrad. Schlaglichter—Reichstagsbriefe und Aufzeichnungen von Conrad Hausmann. Frankfurt, 1924.

Helfferich, Karl. Der Weltkrieg. Three volumes. Karlsruhe, 1919.

Helmot, Hans J. *Der Weltkrieg in Bildern und Dokumenten nebst einem Kriegstagebuch.* Three volumes. Leipzig, 1925.

Hertling, K. Graf von. *Ein Jahr in der Reichskanzlei. Erinnerungen an die Kanzlerschaft meines Vaters.* Freiburg i. Breisgau, 1919.

Heye, Wilhelm—*see* German *Bundesarchiv.*

Hillgruber, Andreas. *Germany and the Two World Wars.* Cambridge, Mass., 1981.

Hindenburg, Bernhard. *Paul von Hindenburg—Ein Lebensbild.* Berlin, 1915.

Hindenburg, Gert von. *Hindenburg.* Translated by G. Griffin. London, 1935.

Hindenburg, Helene Nostitz von. *Hindenburg at Home—An Intimate Biography.* New York, 1931.

Hindenburg, Paul von. *Aus Meinem Leben.* Leipzig, 1927.

Hoffmann, Hans. *Das Deutscher Offizierkorps 1860–1960.* Boppard am Rhein, 1980.

Hoffmann, Heinrich. *Adolph Hitler.* Berlin, 1935.

Hoffmann, Max. *Diaries and Other Papers.* Two volumes. Edited by Karl Novak. Translated by Eric Sutton. London, 1929.

—————*see Frankfurter Zeitung;* German *Bundesarchiv.*

Hogg, Ian. *The Guns 1914–18.* New York, 1971.

Holborn, H. *A History of Modern Germany 1840–1945.* London, 1969.

Horne, Alistair. *The Price of Glory, Verdun 1916.* London, 1962.

Horne, Charles. *Source Records of the Great War.* Five volumes. U.S., 1923.

Hötzendorf, Conrad von—*see* Conrad.

House, Edward. *The Intimate Papers of Colonel House.* Four volumes. Edited by Charles Seymour. Boston, 1926 ff.

Howard-Smith, Logan. *Earl Kitchener and the Great War.* Toronto, 1916.

Hubatsch, Walter. "Grosses Hauptquartier 1914–1918: *Fur Geschichte einer deutschen Führungeinrichtung.*" *Ostdeutsche Wissenschaft.* Band 5. Munich, 1959.

—————. *Germany and the Central Powers in World War I 1914–1918.* Lawrence, Kans., 1963.

—————. *Hindenburg und der Staat.* Berlin, 1966.

Hubbard, S.T. *Memoirs of a Staff Officer 1917–1919.* New York, 1959.

Huguet, General. *Britain and the War.* London, 1928.

Hull, Isabel W. *The Entourage of Kaiser Wilhelm II, 1888–1918.* London, 1982.

Immanuel, Oberst. *Siege und Niederlagen im Weltkriege.* No place, 1919.

Ironside, Sir Edmond. *Tannenberg: The First Thirty Days in East Prussia.* Edinburgh, 1925.

Janssen, Karl-Heinz. "Der Wechsel in der OHL 1916." *Vierteljahreshefte für Zeitgeschichte.* Number 7. 1959.

—————. *Der Kanzler und der General. Die Führungskrise um Bethmann Hollweg und Falkenhayn.* Göttingen, 1966.

—————. *Die graue Exzellenz.* Frankfurt, 1971.

Jarausch, Konrad H. *The Enigmatic Chancellor: Bethmann Hollweg and the Hubris of Imperial Germany.* New Haven, 1973.

Jephson, Lady. *A War-Time Journal Germany 1914.* London, 1915.

Jochim, Theodor. *Die Vorbereitung des deutschen Heeres für die Grosse Schlacht in Frankreich im Frühjahr 1918.* Berlin, 1927–30.

Joffre, Joseph J.C. *The Memoirs of Marshal Joffre.* Translated by T. Bentley Mott. Two volumes. London, 1932.

Johnson, Paul. *Modern Times*. New York, 1983.

Jonas, Klaus W. *The Life of Crown Prince William*. London, 1961.

Jünger, Ernst. *The Storm of Steel*. London, 1929.

———. *Das Antlitz des Weltkrieges—Fronterlebnisse deutscher Soldaten*. Berlin, 1930.

Junior, Richard. *Das Antlitz des Weltkrieges—Hier spricht der Feind*. Berlin, no date.

Kabisch, Ernst. *Streitfragen des Weltkrieges 1914–18*. Stuttgart, 1924.

———. *Das Volksbuch vom Weltkrieg*. Berlin, 1931.

Kaehler, S.A. "Zur Beurteilung Ludendorffs im Sommer 1918." *Nachrichten der Akademie der Wissenschaften*. Göttingen, 1953.

Keegan, John. *The Mask of Command*. London, 1987.

Keller, Countess Mathilde. *Vierzig Jahre im Dienst der Kaiserin*. Leipzig, 1935.

Kennan, George F. *Soviet-American Relations 1917–1920. Russia Leaves the War*. Princeton, 1956.

———. *The Fateful Alliance: France, Russia, and the Coming of the First World War*. New York, 1984.

Kennedy, Paul. *The War Plans of the Great Powers 1880–1914*. London, 1979.

———. *The Rise and Fall of the Great Powers*. London, 1988.

Kessler, Harry. *Walter Rathenau*. London, 1929.

Kielmansegg, Peter Graf. *Deutschland und der Erste Weltkrieg*. Frankfurt a.M., 1968.

King, J.C. *Generals and Politicians*. Berkeley, 1951.

———. *The First World War*. New York, 1972.

Kitchen, Martin. *The German Officer Corps 1890–1914*. Oxford, 1968.

———. *The Silent Dictatorship*. London, 1976.

Klein, Fritz, ed. *Politik im Krieg 1914–1918*. Berlin, 1964.

———. *Deutschland im Ersten Weltkrieg*. Three volumes. Berlin, 1968–9.

Kluck, Alexander von. *The March on Paris and the Battle of the Marne, 1914*. London, 1923.

Knesebeck, Ludwig von. *Die Wahrheit über die Propagandafeldzug und Deutschlands Zusammenbruch*. Munich, 1927.

Knox, Alfred. "Hindenburg's Second Offensive in Poland: The Operation of Lodz, November 1914." *The Army Quarterly*. Volume II. April–July, 1921.

———. *With the Russian Army 1914–1917*. Two volumes. London, 1921.

Kocka, J. *Facing Total War: German Society 1914–1918*. Leamington Spa, 1984.

Krauss, Alfred. *Die Ursachen unserer Niederlage*. Munich, 1921.

Krieger, L. *The Responsibility of Power*. New York, 1967.

Kreisler, Fritz. *Four Weeks in the Trenches*. Boston, 1915.

Kuhl, Hermann von. *Der deutsche Generalstab in Vorbereitung und Durchführung des Weltkrieges*. Berlin, 1920.

———. *Der Weltkrieg 1914–1918*. Two volumes. Berlin, 1933/5.

Kühlmann, Richard von. *Erinnerungen*. Heidelberg, 1948.

Lansing, Robert. *War Memoirs of Robert Lansing*. London, 1935.

Lasswell, Harold D. *Propaganda Technique in the World War*. New York, 1927.

Launay, Jacques de, and Schutter, Jacques de. *Adolf Hitler*. No place, 1976.

Lee, Sydney. *King Edward VII, A Biography*. London, 1925.

Liddell Hart, Basil. *Reputations Ten Years After*. London, 1928.

———. *The Real War*. London, 1930.

_____. *A History of the World War*. London, 1934.

_____. *Through the Fog of War*. London, 1938.

_____. *Strategy*. London, 1954.

Lincoln, W.B. *Passage through Armageddon: The Russians in the War and Revolution 1914–1918*. New York, 1986.

Link, Arthur S. *Woodrow Wilson and the Progressive Era, 1910–1917*. Oxford, 1954.

Lloyd, Alan. *The War in the Trenches*. London, 1976.

Lloyd George, David. *War Memoirs*. Two volumes. London, 1936.

Lodge, Henry C. *Selections from the Correspondence of Theodore Roosevelt and Henry Cabot Lodge 1884–1918*. Two volumes. New York, 1925.

Lossberg, F. von. *Meine Tätigkeit im Weltkrieg 1914–1918*. Berlin, 1939.

Louise, Sophie, Princess of Prussia. *Behind the Scenes at the Prussian Court*. London, 1939.

Ludendorff, Erich. *Meine Kriegserinnerungen*. Berlin, 1919.

_____. *My War Memories 1914–1918*. Two volumes. London, no date.

_____. *The General Staff and its Problems*. Two volumes. Translated by F.A. Holt. London, 1920.

_____. *Urkunden der obersten Heeresleitung über ihre Tätigkeit 1916/18*. Berlin, 1920.

_____. *Kriegsführung und Politik*. Berlin, 1922.

_____. *Die überstaatlichen Mächte in letzten Jahre des Weltkrieges*. Leipzig, 1927.

_____. *Das Marne Drama. Der Fall Moltke-Hentsch*. Munich, 1934.

_____. *Der Totale Krieg*. Berlin, 1935.

_____. *The Nation at War*. Translated by A. S. Rappaport. London, 1936.

Ludendorff, Margarethe. *My Married Life with Ludendorff*. Translated by R. Somerset. London, 1930.

Ludendorff, Mathilde. *Erich Ludendorff: Sein Wesen und Schaffen*. Munich, 1940.

Ludwig, Emil. *Kaiser Wilhelm II*. Translated by E.C. Mayne. London, 1926.

_____. *Hindenburg*. Translated by E. and C. Paul. Philadelphia, 1935.

Lutz, Ralph H. *Fall of the German Empire, Documents, 1914–1918*. Two volumes. Stanford, 1932.

_____. *The Causes of the German Collapse in 1918*. Stanford, 1934.

Macdonald, Lynne. *Somme*. London, 1983.

Mackensen, August von. *Mackensens Briefe und Aufzeichnungen aus Krieg und Frieden*. Edited by W. Foerster. Leipzig, 1938.

Manchester, William. *The House of Krupp 1587–1960*. Boston, 1964.

Marder, Arthur J. *From the Dreadnought to Scapa Flow: The Road to War 1904–1914*. London, 1961.

Marwick, Arthur. *The Deluge. British Society in the First World War*. London, 1965.

Maser, Werner. *Hindenburg—Eine politische Biographie*. Rastatt, 1989.

Matthias, E., and Morsey, R. *Die Regierung des Prinzen Max von Baden*. Düsseldorf, 1962.

_____, and Miller, Susanne. *Das Kriegstagebuch des Reichstagsabgeordneten Eduard David. 1914 bis 1918*. Düsseldorf, 1966.

Maurice, Frederick. *The Last Four Months*. New York, 1919.

Max, Prince of Baden. *The Memoirs of Prince Max of Baden*. Two volumes. Translated by W.M. Calder and C.W.H. Sutton. New York, 1928.

May, A.J. *The Passing of the Habsburg Monarchy, 1914–1918*. Philadelphia, 1966.

May, E.R. *The World War and American Isolation 1914–17.* Cambridge, Mass., 1959.

———. *Knowing One's Enemies: Intelligence Assessment Before the Two World Wars.* Princeton, 1984.

Meinecke, Friedrich. *Strassburg, Freiburg, Berlin. 1901–1919, Erinnerungen.* Stuttgart, 1949.

Mencken, H.L. "Ludendorff." *The Atlantic Monthly,* June, 1917.

Mendelssohn-Bartholdy, Albrecht. *The War and German Society.* New Haven, 1937.

Merton, Richard. *Erinnernswertes aus meinem Leben.* Frankfurt, 1955.

Mertz, Hermann Ritter von Quirnheim—see German *Bundesarchiv*

Michaelis, Georg. *Für Staat und Volk.* Berlin, 1922.

Michelson, Andreas. *Der U-Bootkrieg 1914–1918.* Leipzig, 1925.

Middlebrook, M. *The Kaiser's Battle 21 March 1918.* London, 1978.

Miller, Henry W. *The Paris Gun.* London, 1930.

Miller, Susanne—see Matthias.

Mollo, Andrew. *Army Uniforms of World War I.* New York, 1977.

Moltke, Helmut von. *Erinnerungen, Briefe, Dokumente 1877–1916.* Stuttgart, 1922.

Mommsen, Wolfgang. *Die schriftliche Nachlässe in den zentralen und preussischen Archiven.* Koblenz, 1955.

Moorehead, Alan. *The Russian Revolution.* New York, 1958.

Morsey, R.—see Matthias.

Morton, Frederic. *Thunder at Twilight Vienna 1913/1914.* New York, 1989.

Moser, Otto von. *Kurzer strategischer Überblick über den Weltkrieg, 1914–1918.* Berlin, 1921.

———. *Ernsthafter Plaudereien über den Weltkrieg.* Berlin, 1925.

———. *Das militärisch und politisch Wichtigste vom Weltkriege.* Stuttgart, 1931.

Müller, Georg Alexander von—see Görlitz; German *Bundesarchiv*

Naumann, Friedrich. *Central Europe.* London, 1917.

Naumann, Victor. *Profile.* Munich, 1925.

———. *Dokumente und Argumente.* Berlin, 1928.

Nicolai, Walther. *Nachrichtendienst, Presse und Volksstimmung im Weltkrieg.* Berlin, 1920.

———. *The German Secret Service.* Translated by George Renwick. London, 1924.

Niemann, Alfred, *Kaiser und Revolution.* Berlin, 1922.

———. *Hindenburg.* Berlin/Leipzig, 1926.

———. *Kaiser und Heer.* Berlin, 1929.

Northedge, F.S. *The Troubled Giant: Britain Among the Great Powers 1916–1939.* London, 1966.

Novak, Karl—see Hoffmann.

Oesterrich Kriegsarchiv. *Oesterreich-Ungarns letzter Krieg.* Seven volumes. Vienna, 1934–1938.

Olden, Rudolf. *Hindenburg.* Paris, 1935.

Paléologue, Maurice. *An Ambassador's Memoirs 1914–1917.* London, 1973.

Palmer, Frederick. *Bliss, Peacemaker: The Life and Letters of General Tasker Howard Bliss.* New York, 1934.

Pankhurst, Sylvia. *The Home Front.* London, 1932.

Pape, Wilhelm. *Unser Kronprinz im Felde.* Berlin, 1917.

Pares, Bernard. *Day by Day with the Russian Army.* London, 1915.

Parkinson, Roger. *Tormented Warrior—Ludendorff and the Supreme Command.* London, 1978.

Passant, E.G. *A Short History of Germany 1815–1945.* Cambridge, 1962.

Payer, Friedrich von. *Von Bethmann Hollweg bis Ebert. Erinnerungen und Bilder.* Frankfurt, 1923.

Peel, C.S. *How We Lived Then.* Oxford, 1929.

Pershing, John J. *Final Report of General John J. Pershing.* Washington, 1920.

————. *My Experiences in the World War.* Two volumes. New York, 1931.

Pétain, Henri. *Verdun.* New York, 1930.

Pierrefeu, Jean de. *French Headquarters, 1915–1918.* Translated by C.J.C. Street. London, 1924.

Pitt, Barrie. *1918 The Last Act.* New York, 1963.

Plenz, Paul G. *Kriegsbriefe eines Feldarztes der Armee Hindenburg.* Gotha, 1916.

Poll, B. *Das deutsche Schicksal 1914–1918.* Berlin, 1937.

Porch, D. *The March to the Marne: The French Army 1871–1914.* Cambridge, 1981.

Potts, J. "The Loss of Bulgaria." Dallin, Alexander. *Russian Diplomacy and Eastern Europe 1914–17.* New York, 1963.

Prendergast, Maurice—*see* Gibson, R.H.

Radziwill, Princess Marie. *Briefe vom deutschen Kaiserhof.* Berlin, 1936.

Rathenau, Walther. *Politische Briefe.* Dresden, 1929.

Redlich, Josef. *Schicksalsjahre Oesterreichs 1908–1919.* Graz, 1953.

Regele, Oskar. *Feldmarschall Conrad. Auftrag und Erfüllung 1906–1918.* Munich, 1955.

Reichsarchiv—see German Reichsarchiv. *der Weltkrieg 1914–1918.*

Reiners, Ludwig. *The Lamps Went Out in Europe.* New York, 1955.

Remarque, Erich. *All Quiet on the Western Front.* London, 1952.

Resheter, John S. *The Ukrainian Revolution 1917–1920.* Princeton, 1952.

Ringer, Fritz K. *The German Mandarins: The German Academic Community, 1890–1933.* Cambridge, 1969.

Ritter, Gerhard. *The Schlieffen Plan.* Translated by A. and E. Wilson. London, 1958.

————. *The Sword and the Sceptre: The Problem of Militarism in Germany.* Four volumes. Coral Gables, Fla., 1969–73.

Robertson, W. *Soldiers and Statesmen 1914–1918.* Two volumes. London, 1926.

Rogerson, Sydney. *The Last of the Ebb.* London, 1937.

Röhl, John C.G. *Germany Without Bismarck: The Crisis of Government in the Second Reich.* London, 1967.

————, and Sombart, Nicolaus (eds). *Kaiser Wilhelm II: New Interpretations.* Cambridge, 1982.

————. "The Emperor's New Clothes: A Character Sketch of Kaiser Wilhelm II." *Kaiser Wilhelm II—see* above.

————. *Kaiser, Hof und Staat—Wilhelm II und die Deutsche Politik.* Munich, 1987.

Rupprecht, Crown Prince of Bavaria. *Mein Kriegestagebuch.* Edited by Eugene Frauenholz. Three volumes. Berlin, 1929.

Schäfer, Theodor von. *Generalstab und Admiralstab.* Berlin, 1931.

————. *Ludendorff: Der Feldherr der Deutschen im Weltkrieg.* Berlin, 1935.

Scheidemann, Philipp. *Der Zusammenbruch*. Berlin, 1921.

Schellenberg, Johanna. "Die Herausbildung der Militärdiktatur in den ersten Jahren des Krieges." Fritz Klein, (ed.). *Politik im Krieg 1914–18*. Berlin, 1964.

Scherer, André, and Grunewald, Jacques. *L'Allemagne et les problèmes de la paix pendant la première guerre mondiale*. Two volumes. Paris, 1962, 1966.

Schmidt, B.E., and Vedeler, H.C. *The World in a Crucible 1914–1919*. New York, 1984.

Schmidt-Bückeberg, Rudolf. *Das Militärkabinett der preussischen Könige und Deutschen Kaiser* . . . Berlin, 1933.

Schneider, Benno, and Haacke, Ulrich. *Das Buch vom Kriege 1914–1918*. Munich, 1933.

Schule, B-F. *Die deutsche Armee 1900–1914* . . . Düsseldorf, 1977.

Schultze-Pfaelzer, Gerhard. *Hindenburg: Peace, War, Aftermath*. Translated by C.R. Turner. London, 1931.

Schutter, Jacques de—*see* Launay.

Schwertfeger, Bernhard—*see* Valentini.

Scott, James B. *Official German Documents Relating to the World War*. Two volumes. New York, 1923. (Carnegie Endowment for International Peace.)

Scott, J.D. *Vickers: A History*. London, 1962.

Seaton, Shirley—*see* Brown, Malcolm.

Seeckt, Hans von. *Thoughts of a Soldier*. Translated by G. Waterhouse. London, 1930.

———. *Aus meinem Leben 1866–1917*. Leipzig, 1938.

Seeger, Alan. *Letters and Diary*. New York, 1917.

Seymour, Charles—*see* House, Edward.

Shanin, Teodor. *The Awkward Class*. Oxford, 1972.

Silberstein, Gerard E. *The Troubled Alliance: German-Austrian Relations 1914–1917*. Lexington, Ky., 1970.

Simonds, Frank H. *They Won the War*. New York, 1931.

Sims, William S. *Victory at Sea*. New York, 1920.

Smith, Daniel M. *The Great Departure: The United States and World War I*. New York, 1965.

Snyder, Jack L. *The Ideology of the Offensive: Military Decision Making and the Disasters of 1914*. Ithaca, N.Y., 1984.

Societäts-Verlag. *Kamerad im Westen*. Frankfurt, 1930.

———. *Wehrlos hinter der Front*. Frankfurt, 1931.

Sombart, Nicolaus—*see* Röhl.

Spears, E.L. *Liaison 1914*. London, 1930.

———. *Prelude to Victory*. London, 1939.

Spindler, A. *Der Handelskrieg mit U-Booten*. Berlin, 1932–4.

Stamps, T.D. *A Short Military History of World War I*. West Point, N.Y., 1950.

Steed, Henry Wickham. *Through Thirty Years, 1892–1922*. Two volumes. London, 1924.

Steel, Johannes. *Escape to the Present*. New York, 1937.

Stein, Hermann von. *A War Minister and his Work*. London, 1920.

Steinberg, J. *Yesterday's Deterrent: Tirpitz and the Birth of the German Battle Fleet*. London, 1968.

Steiner, Zara S. *The Foreign Office and Foreign Policy, 1898–1914.* Cambridge, 1969.
———. *Britain and the Origins of the First World War.* London, 1977.
Stern, Fritz. *The Failure of Liberalism.* London, 1972.
Stone, Norman. "Moltke-Conrad: Relations between the Austro-Hungarian and German General Staffs, 1909–1914." *Historical Journal* 9, 1966.
———. *The Eastern Front 1914–1917.* London, 1975.
———. *Europe Transformed 1878–1919.* London, 1983.
Stürgkh, Josef Graf. *Im Deutschen Grossen Hauptquartier.* Leipzig, 1921.
Sulzbach, Herbert. *With the German Guns. Four Years on the Western Front. 1914–1918.* Translated by Richard Thonger. London, 1973.
Swinton, Ernest D. *Eyewitness . . .* London, 1932.
Swope, H.B. *Inside the German Empire in the Third Year of the War, 1917.* New York, 1917.
Tannenbaum, J.K. "French Estimates of Germany's Operational War Plans"; in May, E.R. *Knowing One's Enemies: Intelligence Assessment Before the Two World Wars.* Princeton, 1984.
Tappen, Gerhard—*see* German *Bundesarchiv.*
———. *Bis zur Marne 1914.* Berlin, 1920.
Taylor, A.J.P. *The Habsburg Monarchy 1809–1918.* London, 1948.
———. "The War Aims of the Allies in the First World War." *Essays presented to Sir Lewis Namier.* London, 1956.
———. *The Course of German History.* London, 1961.
———. *A History of the First World War.* New York, 1963.
Terraine, John. *Douglas Haig—the educated soldier.* London, 1963.
———. *White Heat. The New Warfare 1914–1918.* London, 1982.
Thaer, Albrecht von. *Generalstabsdienst an der Front und in der OHL. Aus Briefen und Tagebuchaufzeichnungen 1915–1919.* Edited by Siegfried A. Kaehler. Göttingen, 1958.
———*see* Kaehler.
Therese, Josephine. *With Old Glory in Berlin.* Boston, 1918.
Tieschowitz, Hans von Tieschowa—*see* German *Bundesarchiv.*
Tirpitz, Alfred von. *My Memoirs.* Two volumes, London, 1919.
———. *Politische Dokumente.* Two volumes. Hamburg, 1924–26.
Toland, J. *No Man's Land: The Story of 1918.* London, 1980.
Trumpener, Ulrich. *Germany and the Ottoman Empire, 1914–1918.* Princeton, 1966.
Tschuppik, Karl. *Ludendorff—The Tragedy of a Military Mind.* New York, 1932.
Tuchmann, Barbara W. *The Zimmermann Telegram.* New York, 1958.
———. *The Guns of August.* New York, 1962.
Turner, L.C.F. *Origins of the First World War.* London, 1970.
Tyng, Sewell. *The Campaign of the Marne 1914.* New York, 1935.
United States Army. *Histories of 251 Divisions of the German Army which Participated in the War (1914–1918).* Washington, 1920.
———. *The Aisne and Montdidier-Noyon Operations.* Washington, 1922.
———. *The German Offensive of July 15, 1918.* Fort Leavenworth, Kans., 1923.
———. *Records of the Second Division (Regular).* Nine volumes. Washington, 1927.
———. *Translations of War Diaries of German Units Opposed to the Second Division (Regular), 1918. Château-Thierry.* Four volumes. Washington, 1930–32.

United States Marine Corps. *History of Second Battalion, 5th Regiment, U.S. Marines.* No place, no date.

———. *History of the First Battalion, 5th Regiment, U.S. Marines.* No place, no date.

———. *History of the Third Battalion, Sixth Regiment, U.S. Marines.* Hillsdale, Mich., 1919.

———. *History of the Sixth Machine Gun Battalion.* Neuwied, Germany, 1919.

———. *History of Second Battalion, Fifth Marines.* Quantico, Va., 1938.

United States National Archives.

    American Expeditionary Forces (Historical Division, Special Staff). *(a)* RG 165. German Files. OHL official war reports; Chief of General Staff directives; OHL staff studies; Translations of German documents. *(b)* RG 120. German Documents Captured by U.S. Forces 1917–1918.

    Diplomatic Branch. RG 59, 1910–29. Series 7632.72. Ambassadorial reports.

    War College Division. RG 165. Military attaché and special observer reports.

Unruh, Fritz von. *Opfergang.* Frankfurt, 1966.

Urbanski, August von. *Conrad von Hötzendorf.* Vienna, 1938.

Valentini, Rudolf von. *Kaiser und Kabinettschef.* Oldenburg, 1931.

Van Crefeld, Martin. *Supplying War—Logistics from Wallenstein to Patton.* London, 1977.

———. *Command in War.* Cambridge, Mass., 1985.

Vedeler, H.C.—*see* Schmidt, B.E.

Venohr, Wolfgang. "Erich Ludendorff." Haffner, Sebastian, and Venohr, Wolfgang. *Preussische Profile.* Athenäum, London, 1980.

Viereck, G.S. *As They Saw Us.* New York, 1929.

Vietsch, Eberhard von. *Bethmann Hollweg—Staatsmann Zwischen Macht und Ethos.* Boppard am Rhein, 1969

Vogel, Hugo. *Als ich Hindenburg malte.* Berlin, 1927.

Vogt, Alfred. *Oberst Max Bauer, 1869–1929.* Osnabrück, 1974.

Voigt, F.A.—*see* Goldsmith, Margaret.

Volkmann, E.O. *Die unsterbliche Landschaft, die Fronten des Weltkrieges.* Two volumes. Leipzig, 1934.

Wagner, Rudolph. *Hinter den Kulissen des Grossen Hauptquartiers.* Berlin, 1931.

Waldersee, Alfred Graf von. *Denkwürdigkeiten des Generalfeldmarschalls.* Three volumes. Edited by Otto Meisner. Stuttgart/Berlin, 1922–23.

Warner, Oliver. *The Sea and the Sword—The Baltic 1630–1945.* New York, 1965.

Watson, A.M.K. *The Biography of President von Hindenburg.* London, 1930.

Watt, Richard M. *Dare Call It Treason.* London, 1963.

Weber, Frank G. *Eagles on the Crescent.* Ithaca, N.Y., 1970.

Wedd, A.F. *German Students' War Letters.* New York/London.

Wehler, Hans-Ulrich. *Das Deutsche Kaiserreich 1871–1918.* Göttingen, 1973.

Weigley, Russell F. *History of the United States Army.* New York, 1967.

Wendt, Hermann. *Verdun 1916,* Berlin, 1931.

Wertheimer, M.S. *The Pan-German League 1890–1914.* New York, 1924.

Westarp, Kuno Graf von. *Konservative Politik im Letzten Jahrzehnt des Kaiserreiches.* Volume Two. Berlin, 1935.

Westman, Stephen K. *A Surgeon's Story.* London, 1962.

————. *Surgeon with the Kaiser's Army*. London, 1968.

Wetzell, Georg–*see* German *Bundesarchiv*.

————. *Der Bündniskrieg*. Berlin, 1937.

Wheeler-Bennett, J. *Hindenburg, The Wooden Titan*. London, 1936.

————. *Brest-Litovsk, The Forgotten Peace, March 1918*. London, 1938.

————. "Ludendorff, The Soldier and the Politician." *The Virginia Quarterly*. Spring, 1938.

Wild, Adolf von Hohenborn—*see* German *Bundesarchiv*.

William, Crown Prince. *Memoirs*. New York, 1922.

William II, Emperor of Germany. *The Kaiser's Memoirs*. Translated by T.R. Ybarra. New York, 1922.

Williams, J. *The Home Fronts: Britain, France and Germany, 1914–1918*. London, 1965.

Wohl, Robert. *The Generation of 1914*. London, 1980.

Wolff, Leonard. *In Flanders Field*. New York, 1958.

Wrisberg, Ernst von. *Erinnerungen an die Kriegsjahre im Königlich Preussischen Kriegsministerium*. Three volumes. Leipzig, 1921–22.

Ybarra, T.R. *Hindenburg—The Man with Three Lives*. New York, 1932.

Zedlitz-Trützschler, Robert von. *Twelve Years at the Imperial German Court*. Translated by A. Kalisch. London, 1924.

Zeller, Ulrich—*see* Haussmann.

Zeman, Z.A. *Germany and the Revolution in Russia 1915–1918*. London, 1950.

————. *The Break-Up of the Habsburg Empire 1914–1918*. London, 1961.

————, and Scharlau, W.B. *Parvus Helphand. Freibeuter der Revolution*. Cologne, 1965.

————. *A Diplomatic History of the First World War*. London, 1971.

Zwehl, Hans von. *Erich von Falkenhayn, General der Infanterie*. Berlin, 1926.

Zweig, Stefan. *The World of Yesterday*. London, 1943.

Index

A Note About the Author

Robert Asprey is a former U.S. Marine Corps officer who served in World War II (he was wounded on Iwo Jima) and in the Korean War. A Fulbright Scholar (New College, Oxford), he also studied at the universities of Vienna and Nice. He is a veteran writer of military history whose articles and books are highly respected in the United States and abroad. His two-volume *War in the Shadows*, an in-depth study of guerrilla warfare through the ages, was a major selection and subsequent best-seller of the Military Book Club and is required reading today in American and foreign military staff colleges. His other books include *The Panther's Feast* (the story of the famous traitor/spy Alfred Redl), *At Belleau Wood*, *The First Battle of the Marne*, and *Frederick the Great* (a major selection of the History Book Club). When not writing, Mr. Asprey indulges his passion for frequent travel, musty archives, golf, duplicate bridge, good books, foreign languages, close friends, cooking, and vintage wines. He also loves dogs.